BLAME WELFARE, IGNORE POVERTY AND INEQUALITY

With the passage of the 1996 welfare reform, not only welfare but also poverty
and inequality have disappeared from the political discourse. The decline in the
welfare rolls has been hailed as a success. This book challenges that assumption.
It argues that although many single mothers left welfare, they have joined the
working poor and fail to make a decent living. The book examines the persistent
demonization of poor single-mother families, the impact of the low-wage market
on perpetuating poverty and inequality, and the role of the welfare bureaucracy
in defining deserving and undeserving poor. It argues that the emphasis on family
values – marriage promotion, sex education, and abstinence – is misguided and
diverts attention from the economic hardships low-income families face. The
book proposes an alternative approach to reducing poverty and inequality that
centers on a children's allowance as basic income support coupled with jobs and
universal child care.

Joel F. Handler is a professor of Law, at University of California, Los Angeles,
specializing in social welfare law and policy, poverty, welfare bureaucracies, and
comparative welfare states. He has published several books and articles, has won
the American Political Science Association Prize for the best book on U.S. national
policy (1997), and is a member of the American Academy of Arts and Sciences.
He has lectured in Europe, Israel, South America, and Asia.

Yeheskel Hasenfeld is a professor of Social Welfare at University of California, Los
Angeles. His research focuses on the dynamic relations between social welfare
policies, the organizations that implement these policies, and the people who
use their services. He has written extensively on human service organizations,
the implementation of welfare reform, and the nonprofit sector. With Benjamin
Gidron and Stanley N. Katz he edited the book *Mobilizing for Peace*, which won
the 2003 Virginia Hodgkinson Research Prize. He has been a visiting scholar at
several universities in Israel, Japan, and Singapore.

BLAME WELFARE, IGNORE POVERTY AND INEQUALITY

Joel F. Handler

University of California, Los Angeles, School of Law

Yeheskel Hasenfeld

University of California, Los Angeles, School of Public Affairs

CAMBRIDGE
UNIVERSITY PRESS

CAMBRIDGE UNIVERSITY PRESS
Cambridge, New York, Melbourne, Madrid, Cape Town, Singapore,
São Paulo, Delhi, Dubai, Tokyo, Mexico City

Cambridge University Press
32 Avenue of the Americas, New York, NY 10013-2473, USA

www.cambridge.org
Information on this title: www.cambridge.org/9780521690454

First published 2007
Reprinted 2009

A catalog record for this publication is available from the British Library.

Library of Congress Cataloging in Publication Data

Handler, Joel F.
Blame welfare, ignore poverty and inequality / Joel F. Handler, Yeheskel Hasenfeld.
    p.   cm.
Includes bibliographical references and index.
ISBN-13: 978-0-521-87035-1 (hardback)
ISBN-10: 0-521-87035-6 (hardback)
ISBN-13: 978-0-521-69045-4 (pbk.)
ISBN-10: 0-521-69045-5 (pbk.)
1. Public welfare – United States. 2. Family policy – United States. 3. Welfare recipients –
Government policy – United States. 4. Poor single mothers – Government policy – United
States. 5. Poor families – Government policy – United States. 6. Poverty – United States.
7. Equality – United States. I. Hasenfeld, Yeheskel. II. Title.
HV95.H257   2007
362.5'560973 – dc22   2006018202

ISBN 978-0-521-87035-1 Hardback
ISBN 978-0-521-69045-4 Paperback

Contents

Acknowledgments

For the past 20 years, we have followed jointly the contours of poverty, inequality, and welfare reform in the United States. We are driven by the passion to understand the social forces and policies that affect the lives of poor people, especially single mothers and their children, and how we can change them to improve their life conditions and, indirectly, ours. This is our third book together in this quest. We have challenged each other, debated, and occasionally strongly disagreed as we pursued and tried to make sense of the empirical evidence. Still, our friendship not only survived but has deepened immeasurably.

We could not have written this book without the support, guidance, and suggestions of many colleagues. Among them are Tom Brock, Evelyn Brodkin, Sandy and Sheldon Danziger, Irwin Garfinkel, Mark Greenberg, Julie Henly, and Marcia Meyers. They and scores of others have directed our attention to important research findings that have been indispensable to our project. Still, we take sole responsibility for whatever errors or misinterpretations might have cropped up in reviewing and analyzing this vast literature.

We were also fortunate to have very dedicated research assistants – Amada Babcock and Cheryl Kelly. We are ever so thankful to Kevin Gerson, Jennifer Lentz, and the research staff of the UCLA Law Library. We also thank Omar Fadel and Edward Tran, faculty assistants to Joel, for their excellent work. Barbara Walthall deserves our special gratitude for her outstanding work in preparing the manuscript for publication.

We dedicate the book to our respective wives, Betsy and Helen, and to our wonderful grandchildren Kate, Jeffrey, Lane, and Samantha Handler; Lydia Igna; Catherine and Alexandra White; and Summer Faith Garland; We hope that they will grow up in a more equal and caring society. Lastly, we acknowledge Rachel and Neil Marcus as they begin their life together.

Acronyms

ADC	Aid to Dependent Children
ADHD	attention deficit hyperactivity disorder
AFDC	Aid to Families with Dependent Children
AFLA	Adolescent Family Life Act
AFL-CIO	American Federation of Labor and Congress of Industrial Organizations
AFQT	Armed Forces Qualification Test
AGI	adjusted gross income
BIG	basic income guarantee
CAA	certified application assistant
CCDBG	Child Care Development Block Grant
CCDF	Child Care and Development Fund
CDC	community development corporation
CDU	career development unit
CETA	Comprehensive Employment and Training Act
CHIP	Children's Health Insurance Program
CLASP	Center for Law and Social Policy
COBRA	Consolidated Omnibus Budget Reconciliation Act
COLA	cost of living adjustment
CPC	child-parent center
CPS	Current Population Surveys
CSE	Child Support Enforcement Program
CSJ	community service jobs
CTC	Child Tax Credit
CWEP	Community Work Experience Program
CWI	Child Well-Being Index
DCF	Department of Children and Families
DHHS	United States Department of Health and Human Services
DI	disability insurance
EBT	electronic benefits transfers

EITC	Earned Income Tax Credit
EPSDT	early and periodic screening, diagnosis, and treatment
ERA	Employment Retention and Advancement
ERISA	Employee Retirement Income Security Act
ESEA	Elementary and Secondary Education Act
ESL	English as a second language
ETP	eligible training provider
FAP	family assistance plan
FCR	Federal Case Registry
FEP	Family Employment Program
FIP	Family Independence Program
FSAs	flexible spending accounts
FSA	Family Support Act
FSP	Food Stamp Program
FUP	Family Unification Program
FVO	family violence option
GA	general assistance
GAIN	Greater Avenues for Independence
GAO	General Accounting Office (pre–July 7, 2004)
GAO	Government Accountability Office (effective July 7, 2004)
GDP	gross domestic product
GED	General Educational Development Test
GPK	Georgia voluntary pre-K
HEW	United States Department of Health, Education, and Welfare
HMO	health maintenance organization
HSS	Department of Health and Human Services
HUD	U.S. Department of Housing and Urban Development
IDEA	Individual with Disabilities Education Act
IHDP	Infant Health and Development Program
IRS	Internal Revenue Service
ITA	Individual Training Account
JTPA	Job Training Partnership Act
LEHD	Longitudinal Employer-Household Dynamics
MCCA	Medicare Catastrophic Care Act
MDRC	Manpower Development Research Corporation
MDTA	Manpower Development and Training Act
MFIP	Minnesota Family Investment Program
MFY	Mobilization for Youth
MOE	maintenance of effort
MTO	moving to opportunity
NAS	National Academy of Science
NGO	nongovernmental organization
NICHD	National Institute of Child Health and Human Development

NIT	negative income tax
NLSY	National Longitudinal Surveys of Youth
NOLEO	notice to law enforcement officials
NLRB	National Labor Relations Board
NSAF	National Survey of America's Families
OASDI	Old Age, Survivors and Disability Insurance Program
OECD	Organisation for Economic Co-operation and Development
OEO	Office of Economic Opportunity
OIC	Opportunities Industrialization Center
OMB	Office of Management and Budget
PFS	Parents' Fair Share
PREP	Prevention and Relationship Enhancement Program
PRWORA	Personal Responsibility and Work Opportunity Reconciliation Act
PSID	Panel Study of Income Dynamic
SCHIP	State Children's Health Insurance Program
SIPP	Survey of Income and Program Participation
SPRANS	special projects of regional and national significance
SRO	single hotel room
SSA	Social Security Administration
SSDI	Social Security Disability Insurance
SSI	Supplementary Security Income
SSP	State Supplementary Payment Program
STD	sexually transmitted disease
TANF	Temporary Assistance for Needy Families
UI	unemployment insurance
UMOS	United Migrant Opportunity Services
USDA	United States Department of Agriculture
USDOL	United States Department of Labor
VISTA	Volunteers in Service to America
W-2	Wisconsin Works
W-2T	W-2 Transition
WES	Women's Employment Study
WIA	Workforce Investment Act
WIB	Workforce Investment Board
WIC	Special Supplemental Nutrition Program for Women, Infants, and Children
WIN	Work Incentive Program

1　Introduction

In 1996, Congress passed and President Clinton signed the Personal Responsibility and Work Opportunity Reconciliation Act (PRWORA). The president claimed, "We have ended welfare as we know it." The centerpiece of the new legislation was Temporary Assistance for Needy Families (TANF), which replaced Aid to Families with Dependent Children (AFDC), commonly referred to as "welfare," the existing cash assistance program for single mothers and their children. Among other things, welfare would no longer be an entitlement: stiff, new work requirements were to be imposed on the mothers, and the work requirements were to be enforced by time limits – states must require recipients to work after a maximum of 24 month on aid or less, and there is a cumulative lifetime limit of five years on receipt of aid. Various "family values" provisions were specified, such as marriage promotion, child-support enforcement, and programs to combat teen pregnancy. State control was increased substantially. Before the 1996 reform, welfare rolls had been declining sharply, and this decline increased substantially in subsequent years. It seemed as if President Clinton's statement was true. Welfare as we know it had finally been ended. Everyone claimed "victory." "Welfare" has dropped out of the political discourse and is virtually forgotten. Unfortunately, discussion of poverty and inequality has nearly disappeared as well – even though significant poverty remains, especially child poverty, and inequality has been increasing over the past few decades.

From colonial times, cash assistance for the able-bodied was always miserly, conditioned, and brief.[1] Single mothers were helped but not much. Starting in the late nineteenth century, concern was raised about the well-being of the children in these families. Children were placed in foster homes and sent to farms in the Midwest. Then, Aid to Dependent Children (ADC), commonly known as Mothers' Pensions (and subsequently, AFDC), was established by

---

[1] G. Nash (2004). "Poverty and Politics in Early American History." In B. G. Smith (Ed.), *Down and Out in Early America*. University Park.: Pennsylvania State University Press.

the states during the early twentieth century. It became a federal grant-in-aid program under the New Deal but remained a relatively small, restricted program for white widows – "deserving" families. Mothers who were divorced, deserted, never married, or nonwhite were mostly excluded. The program was generally of low political visibility until the late 1950s and early 1960s when it grew rapidly and the characteristics of the families changed to include disproportionately unwed single mothers of color. This was the start of the welfare "crisis," which continued until the 1996 reform. "By the 1990s, [welfare] was the most disliked public program in America."[2]

The thesis of this book is that the country has demonized poor, single mothers. "Welfare" has become the code word for the "welfare queen" – the inner-city, young African American mother who has children in order to stay on welfare and produces multiple generations of welfare recipients. These families are characterized by neglect, substance abuse, crime, and delinquency. Poverty is the fault of the individual – in this case, the single mothers – rather than the structural forces of society, and welfare has been construed as a major cause of lack of work effort, unwed motherhood, promiscuity, teenage child bearing, school failure, substance abuse, and other forms of deviant behavior.[3] It is used to define ethnic and gender status. By stigmatizing the "other," it validates the righteousness of the majority.

In United States, the rhetoric of blaming the poor and discrediting income support policies represents what Albert Hirschman terms "the perversity thesis."[4] It argues that policies to alleviate poverty and improve the economic well-being of the poor actually have the opposite effect. These policies increase welfare dependency, erode the work ethic, and reinforce the social pathologies associated with poverty.[5] Hirschman says that the perverse-effect doctrine is closely tied to the idea of self-regulating market, where any social policy that tries to change market outcomes, such as income assistance or the minimum wage, is assumed to be counterproductive.[6] Using the perversity thesis to attack the legitimacy of income assistance has a long history. In the eighteenth century, the English Poor Laws, particularly the Speenhamland system (1795), which supplemented low wages, were attacked by Malthus as being the very cause of poverty. The same argument was made in Charles Murray's attack on AFDC in his book *Losing Ground* (1988): "We tried to provide more for

[2] M. B. Katz (2001). *The Price of Citizenship: Redefining America's Welfare State* (1st ed.). New York: Metropolitan Books, p. 1.

[3] M. R. Rank (2004). *One Nation, Underprivileged: Why American Poverty Affects Us All*. Oxford; New York: Oxford University Press.

[4] A. O. Hirschman (1991). *The Rhetoric of Reaction: Perversity, Futility, Jeopardy*. Cambridge, Mass.: Belknap Press of Harvard University Press.

[5] M. R. Somers & F. Block (2005). "From Poverty to Perversity: Ideas, Markets, and Institutions over 200 Years of Welfare Debate." *American Sociological Review* 70: 260–87.

[6] Hirschman (1991), p. 27.

the poor and produced more poor instead. We tried to remove the barriers to escape poverty and inadvertently built a trap."[7] Lawrence Mead (1986) in his influential book *Beyond Entitlement* has made a similar argument.[8] Embracing the idea of the self-regulating market, the perversity thesis assumes that a social order free of government intervention optimizes the well-being of all through the choices and actions of individuals. Therefore, the perversity thesis reverses the causation of poverty by shifting the focus from poverty as a structural condition to poverty as a behavioral and moral deficiency.[9] It thus provides the ideological justification to distinguish between the "deserving" and "undeserving" poor.

Demonizing welfare allows the country to ignore the economic and social conditions that produce poverty and inequality – class, race, gender, the economy, and the inadequacies of the low-wage labor market. From time to time, proposals are made to address the structural causes of poverty and inequality but they are quickly abandoned because they undermine American "values." The War on Poverty, in the 1960s, fit this pattern. Although this was a liberal period, and poverty did become a national issue, poverty was defined in terms of individual behaviors rather than structural conditions. As part of the civil rights era, welfare was declared an "entitlement" with due process guarantees. Although this may have facilitated access to welfare, it did not by itself address the fundamental issues of income support and equal opportunities. Poverty and welfare continued to grow, and the War on Poverty was declared a failure.

The 1970s ushered in three decades of reaction to what was considered to be the permissive welfare system, which culminated in 1996 with PRWORA. The major policy thrust throughout the three decades has been to transform welfare from a program considered to corrupt individuals and families into a program enforcing work requirements and "family values" – which, we point out, is the contemporary version of the age-old themes of deterrence and reformation. The current "work first" strategy assumes that there are sufficient jobs in the economy for current and potential welfare recipients, that any job is better than no job, that by taking a job and sticking with it the exrecipient will move up the economic ladder and escape poverty, and that there is sufficient child care support. It assumes that the problem with welfare recipients is their poor work ethic. By working instead of receiving welfare, the mother will be a proper role model for her children. The children will learn the values of responsibility, education, and family life. The children will not become welfare recipients. The other sure route out of poverty and into proper

---

[7] Quoted in Hirschman (1991), p. 29.
[8] L. Mead (1986). *Beyond Entitlement: The Social Obligations of Citizenship*. New York: Free Press.
[9] Somers & Block (2005), p. 276.

family life is marriage. In addition to marriage promotion programs, welfare mothers have to cooperate in establishing the paternity of their children, children born to mothers on welfare will not be supported, teenage mothers have to live with their parents, and sanctions are imposed for unsatisfactory school performance.

This book will show that just about every one of these policies is based on *myth*.[10] Although welfare recipients increasingly included more persons of color, the program was never "black." African Americans were always in the minority. Although there were increasing proportions of teenage mothers, they were always a very small percentage of the recipient population. Although there were some large families, the average size of the welfare family is not that different from the nonwelfare family. Rather than long-term dependency, most families are on welfare a short time; the most common form of exit is through a job, but because of the instability of the low-wage labor market and a multitude of family and personal problems, welfare mothers are in and out of the paid labor force. Still, long-term dependency, including generational dependency, applies only to a small proportion of the caseload. School failure is a serious problem, but teen welfare mothers are no different from their peers. The failure of child support is not unique to fathers of children on welfare, although poverty and lack of stable earnings increase the problems of fathers of poor children.

This is not to say that no cases fit the myth. However, this is the *ceremony* that validates the myth. The press and politicians dwell on the extreme examples. The public buys into the story because the message serves to validate its beliefs and attitudes: "They are playing by the rules." Thus, welfare rhetoric and policy are less concerned with reforming the recipients than with reinforcing majoritarian feelings of moral superiority. This not only makes majoritarian society feel better but also allows the country to avoid confronting the difficult structural questions of inequality, poverty, and the suffering of children. It is more comfortable to blame the victim.

Myth and ceremony allow politicians and the public to paper over the massive contradictions of welfare policy. Welfare policy purports to address poverty and inequality but refuses to deal with the structural causes of poverty and inequality or the reality of welfare recipients. Welfare policy requires recipients to enter the paid labor market and improve their well-being but most remain in poverty. Welfare supposedly supports and protects children but deterrence and reformation punish parents and, hence, the children. Work is required because, among other things, an employed parent provides a positive role model for the child, but the child suffers from inadequate child care. Welfare programs have huge numbers of guidelines and detailed rules, yet rely on the

---

[10] J. Meyer & B. Rowan (1977). "Institutional Organizations: Formal Structure as Myth and Ceremony." *American Journal of Sociology* 83: 340–63.

discretion of field-level caseworkers to interpret these rules and guidelines. They are applied in terms of the individual families' circumstances, as long as the caseworkers conform to bureaucratic imperatives, not necessarily in accordance with the goals of the laws and policies. New programs, such as work requirements, are enacted by the legislature and thrust on local welfare offices without adequate resources and implementation. If programs become too harsh, and families break up, then local governments are forced to pay for expensive foster care, group homes, and other forms of child protection, often to the detriment of the children.

Rather than resolve the contradictions, the typical legislative response is *delegation* or *devolution* to lower units of government – from the federal government to the states, from the states to the counties, and from the public to the private sector. We have a new faith that private enterprise can solve the problems of welfare administration. Instead of the cumbersome public bureaucracy, for-profit or not-for-profit agencies will handle welfare cases accurately and efficiently. These private agencies will deal with ground-level conflicts through low-visibility discretionary decisions. The goal is to assure the conflicts will remain at the local level. From time to time, however, conflicts boil over and reappear on the political agenda. The legislative level purports to resolve the problem through general provisions, but, in effect, re-delegates the issue. By concentrating on the "evils" of the welfare system and delegating low-visibility decisions to the state and local level, politicians, policy makers, and the general public can ignore the serious, corrosive problems of poverty and inequality.

Since the 1990s (and before the 1996 welfare reform), welfare rolls have declined dramatically. Political leaders, the media, and the public have claimed victory. Since 1996, welfare has ceased to become a political issue. The contrast between this post-1996 lack of welfare discourse and the anti-welfare political rhetoric of the previous decades is startling. Now that these families are no longer on welfare and are in the paid labor force, the near-universal assumptions are that welfare and poverty are no longer an issue. The absence of welfare means the conquest of poverty, and all is well.

The Argument

This book takes a different approach. The issue is poverty and inequality, not welfare. "Poverty" is generally not discussed, but when it is considered (e.g., "X% are no longer in 'poverty'"), it is grossly misleading because the poverty line is far too minimal. It is assumed that once a family exceeds the official poverty threshold, then everything is okay. We are constantly told about the percentage of families and children that are in "poverty" or are above "poverty." We are still using the official federal poverty threshold. Although the threshold is adjusted for changes in the cost of living, its composition is deeply flawed.

On the one hand, it fails to account for certain items that should be included – for example, food stamps, the Earned Income Tax Credit (EITC), and the value of Medicaid – but on the other hand, it fails to account for changes in family budgets. Two principal problems are the increasing percentage of income that families have to pay for housing and the inadequacy of health care. As is discussed, many families, with incomes substantially above the official poverty threshold, cannot afford minimum, adequate housing, and an illness or a job loss sends them into poverty.

We point out that considerable material deprivation exists well above the poverty line (e.g., at least 200%). Budget studies of various cities show that purchasing only the necessities requires an income substantially higher than the official poverty line. In addition, "necessities" mean just that – no restaurant meals (including fast food), limited clothing, and minimal housing. Millions of people who are not officially "poor" are just above the poverty line. One medical bill, a disappearing job, one extra expense for necessities sends a family below the poverty line. Therefore, people who are near poor often have frequent spells of poverty. The poor and the near poor experience hunger, missed or late utility payments and shutoffs, and a lack of proper health care. When we describe these necessity budgets, it is obvious that none of the readers of this book would want to live this way.

Poverty and near poverty are widespread and diverse. Poverty is not just a problem of the "other." It affects different people (race, ethnicity, immigrant status) in different ways. Most of the people who are poor and near poor are working. They are "playing by the rules," but because of the characteristics of the low-wage labor market, they cannot make it. Jobs pay little, usually lack benefits, and are uncertain. Hours often change, if not disappear, and wages usually remain low.

The instability of the low-wage labor market plays havoc with child care. The adverse consequences to the millions of children living in poverty cannot be exaggerated. They are affected from before birth to adulthood by poor child care, poor health, poor education, poor nutrition, food insecurity, overcrowded housing, and unsafe neighborhoods. For example, one- and two-year-old children from professional families are exposed to approximately one hundred fifty thousand more words *per week* than children in families on welfare, and the inequalities for learning and development persist when these children enter school.[11] Poor children are ill-prepared for adult life, and, as is

---

[11] A. Pallas & Y. Nonoyama (2003). "K–12 Education in New York City." Paper presented at a conference on New York City and the Welfare State, Russell Sage Foundation, New York, citing B. Hart & T. R. Risley (1995). *Meaningful Differences in the Everyday Experience of Young American Children*. Baltimore: Paul H. Brookes Publishing Company, Inc., and U. Bronfenbrenner (1977). "Nobody Home: The Erosion of The American Family." *Psychology Today* 10: 40–47.

discussed, most do not rise above their social class. Social consequences for the children are not only unjust but also contrary to our national interest. We are not producing an educated, trained, competent workforce.

We are not "growing our way out of it." Despite the booming economy of the 1990s, wages in the low-wage labor market have stagnated. There was a small drop in the official poverty line, but millions remain poor and near poor. The rising tide did not lift all boats.

Although the U.S. welfare state – public, private, and not-for-profit – is extensive, most benefits go to the better off and do not reach the poor and near poor. With the exception of Medicaid and the EITC, the targeted programs are relatively small and do little to relieve poverty and near poverty. Rather than redistribution, the U.S. welfare state reinforces social stratification.[12]

Instead of addressing poverty and inequality, we have demonized welfare, the program for poor single mothers and their families, and we continue our incredibly long history of blaming the victim. Now, with the sharp decline in the welfare rolls, we believe that we have solved the problem and that we can ignore the serious, widespread adverse effects of poverty. However, practically all other developed countries do a far better job than the United States in helping the poor.

The Plan of the Book

Chapter 2 discusses the state of poverty and inequality. We start with the measurement of poverty – how the official poverty threshold fails to capture the state of poverty – and the various dimensions of poverty. We then turn to the causes of poverty. We look at poverty over the past fifty years, concentrating on the changes in the economy and the labor market. Most adults rely on earned income. Most of the poor and near poor are in the low-wage labor market, and this chapter discusses the changing market and its increasing inequality and precariousness. The other big change affecting poverty is family composition, principally the rise of the female-headed household. These families are much more likely to be poor.

We then turn to the state of poverty. Here, we show that contrary to common assumptions, many people experience poverty. Even if they rise above the official poverty line, very often they have spells of poverty. This is because the near poor are on the margins, and the bumps in life send them back into poverty. The risks of poverty are widespread; thus, many experience poverty over the course of their lives, even though particular spells of poverty may be short term. Because the risks are widespread, different subgroups experience

---

[12] G. Esping-Andersen (2002). *Why We Need a New Welfare State*. New York: Oxford University Press.

poverty at least some time during the life course – non-Hispanic white men, women, African American men and women, immigrants, Hispanic men and women, Asian Pacific men and women, and, of course, the children. The chapter then turns to a profile of TANF recipients. This section counters a number of prevalent myths about TANF recipients. Although not a trivial number, TANF recipients are a small segment of the total number of poor and near poor. They are not primarily African American; they are primarily adults with small families, on welfare for short spells, and usually employed in the low-wage labor market. In short, TANF families are not a breed apart but are part of the working poor. The chapter ends with a discussion about those who have left welfare, or "welfare leavers." Most are employed in low-wage jobs without benefits and with uncertain hours and duration. Most welfare leavers, although working, remain in poverty.

Chapter 3 addresses the response to poverty and inequality. First, the U.S. welfare state is organized around the distinction between the "deserving" and "undeserving" poor. The former are those who have participated in the paid labor market, have paid into Social Security, and have reached retirement age. They are now excused from paid labor. This includes the widows and children of insured workers. Benefits are reasonably generous (at least by comparative standards) and free of conditions. Other deserving poor are disabled who cannot work. The undeserving are those who should be supporting themselves and their families through the paid labor market. Then, there are the ambiguous. Is the claimant really disabled or malingering? Did the claimant become unemployed through his or her own misconduct or was it truly involuntary? From its earliest inception, a fundamental purpose of the welfare state was to ensure that there were no disincentives to engage in paid labor. Those considered undeserving were stigmatized and paid meager benefits, if they received any benefits at all. The classic case is the working-age childless adult. Benefits for them, if available at all, are low and short term and have work requirements. With rare exceptions, the poor single mother was always considered undeserving. Why was she single? Moreover, if she is a widow, is she engaging in promiscuous behavior? Would supporting this woman encourage irresponsibility on the part of the father? Chapter 4 discusses the demonization of the single mother, which is a uniquely American characteristic.

When considering the public welfare state – Social Security and Medicare as well as TANF and Medicaid – many people benefit from the public welfare state. However, the major public expenditures are universal and go to the nonpoor (e.g., Social Security and Medicare). A much smaller amount is targeted. Thus, the public welfare state has small antipoverty effects. Increasingly, governments are contracting out public welfare services for the poor to the for-profit and not-for-profit private sector.

The private welfare state – primarily employment-related pensions and health care – is extensive and truly American exceptionalism (i.e., in contrast to western European countries, which have very small private welfare states).[13] Here, two points are made. First, the private welfare state benefits primarily the better-off workers. Second, for the less well-off workers, the private welfare state is weakening. Both pensions and health care are riskier, less comprehensive, and more expensive. Thus, as the labor market changes, more workers and their families will be looking to the weakening public welfare state. Then, there is the "third" sector, which also is very extensive in the United States. Charities play an important role in trying to fill the gaps in the public welfare state. They provide food and shelter to the most destitute and also contract with public agencies to administer parts of welfare. Although a great deal of private charity dollars goes to help the poor, significant amounts go to the arts and medical research.

Chapter 4 discusses how the United States demonizes the single-mother family instead of addressing poverty and inequality. Before the twentieth century, single mothers were considered undeserving poor. The model mother was a married woman who stayed home to care for her husband and children. The single mother was morally suspicious. This was especially true for "the others" – Catholics, Jews, and southern European families. A single mother was required to work in the paid labor market but condemned for doing so. By the late nineteenth and early twentieth centuries, welfare reformers realized that they were also harming innocent children. This created a dilemma: How to support the children when the mother was suspect? The "solution," until post–World War II, was to give aid only to "worthy widows," under Aid to Dependent Children, popularly known as Mothers' Pensions. Mostly excluded were divorced, deserted, and never-married mothers and women of color.

During and immediately after World War II, large numbers of African Americans migrated out of the South to northern and western cities. For many reasons, barriers to ADC were breached, and previously excluded single-mother families streamed into the system. This was the start of the welfare "crisis." The rolls and costs skyrocketed, and most significantly, the program came to be identified as primarily African American. The stereotype was that of an unwed, sexually promiscuous mother having children to stay on welfare, fathers shirking their responsibility and living off the welfare checks, substance abuse, delinquency, and generational welfare. Shortly thereafter, the term "welfare queen" was coined, an explosive combination of race and gender discrimination.

The welfare crisis continued until the reform of 1996, which "ended welfare as we know it." The chapter concludes with a discussion of the provisions of PRWORA and TANF and the reasons for the rapid decline in the welfare rolls. Although the booming economy helped, an important part of the decline was

[13] J. Hacker (2002). *The Divided Welfare State: The Battle over Public and Private Social Benefits in the United States.* New York: Cambridge University Press.

state actions terminating welfare or denying entry into welfare. As the economy entered into a recession, the decline in the rolls stopped, and some states have had an increase in the rolls.

Chapter 5 addresses a much-neglected issue – the day-to-day administration of welfare at the field level. The common response handling the "undeserving" is to delegate the controversies to the lower levels of government, such as the county departments of welfare and its field offices. It is here that the sorting out takes place – who gets help and under what conditions and who is turned away. For the most part, these are low-visibility discretionary decisions. There are volumes of rules and regulations, but the most important, crucial decisions are judgments made by the individual caseworkers. This chapter discusses how these decisions are made – bureaucratic ideologies and strategies, local staff ideologies, the working conditions, the pressures, the conflicts, and the incentives in these offices. Most important are the *moral* judgments that the workers make about the applicant or recipient. Is the person honest and really trying to do better, or is she just "gaming" the system?

When the welfare rolls exploded, charges of waste, fraud, and abuse were made. The local offices were too lax in administering welfare; they are letting in too many cheats and unworthy applicants and not applying the account-ability rules to those already on the rolls. Errors had to be reduced, and fraud had to be stopped. Control over the field-level offices was strengthened by tightening the eligibility and payment rules and strictly applying the rules. Field-level case workers were converted into technicians to make sure that eligibility rules were observed, that all the necessary forms were filed, that payments were accurate, and that other rules were complied with. The principal control mechanism was strict supervision over a deprofessionalized staff.

The rolls continued to grow and the "crisis" continued. The next response was to offer social services to welfare families, but these were quickly replaced by a series of mandatory work programs. A problem arose. Helping recipients become employed requires a people-changing technology, involving more or less interpersonal relations between the worker and the client. It is a professional model that calls for an assessment of the skills and problems of individual clients. But the deprofessionalized eligibility workers did not have the skills, let alone the inclination, to engage in these activities. Accurate eligibility and payment administration remained the principal task. The work programs were viewed as unwelcome add-ons to an already overworked, underpaid, undertrained staff. The initial response was to deflect the recipients; a small number were referred to state employment services, but most were put on "administrative hold."

Under TANF, the ideology, the incentives, and perhaps most important, the available enforcement tools have changed. The goal is to move welfare recipients as quickly as possible into entry-level jobs. As noted, the heart of the TANF work requirements, as well as most of the state demonstration projects, is the "work-first" strategy. The work-first strategy is modeled after a program in Riverside, California. Under a charismatic leader, the staff was organized around finding entry-level jobs for welfare recipients and applicants. The staff engaged in job development throughout the area and offered backup services, such as child care, transportation, and social services. Despite great publicity, the results were mixed at best. At the end of the three-year demonstration program, half of the control group was not working and of those who were employed, most remained in poverty. Nevertheless, there was a positive cost-benefit ratio – welfare savings were larger than program costs. Riverside was hailed as great success and became the model for the TANF welfare-to-work programs.

There is very little, if any, concern about support services. Instead, there are strong incentives to reduce the rolls, through either paid employment or sanctions or diversion (not accepting applications). Under the prior welfare regime, the state lost federal cost sharing for every recipient who left the rolls, approximately 50 percent of the grant for each person. Under the TANF block grant system, where the states receive a fixed amount of money based on welfare enrollments in a given year (e.g., 1992, 1993), the states keep all the money for every recipient who leaves the rolls – whether through work, sanctions, or diversion. In addition, many states have contracted out significant parts of administration (primarily the work requirements) to private for-profit or not-for-profit agencies. Under various kinds of performance standards, the private agencies, too, have strong incentives to reduce the caseloads, through either employment or sanctions.

The chapter describes in detail how both public and private agencies apply mandatory work requirements and sanctions. The use of sanctions is extensive. As might be expected, those who are sanctioned lack general information and understanding and are usually more disadvantaged in the paid labor market. In addition to sanctions, agencies engage in *diversion*. The federal requirement that applications have to be acted on within thirty days no longer exists. Several agencies will not accept applications until the applicant completes a certain number of job searches; many applicants become discouraged during the process. Many applicants would qualify for other programs (e.g., food stamps, Medicaid, child care, and housing subsidies) but have to go to several offices to apply. Food stamp and Medicaid enrollment have dropped (although recent state efforts to increase the latter have started to take effect). Applicants must meet more requirements such as appointments, filing forms, and verifying job searches. If an applicant fails to file the proper form or the agency computer system fails to record the filing accurately, then an automatic penalty can result. Recipients often do not know why they are being sanctioned and often drop out of the process because of the hassle.

The relationships between the state agencies and the private contractors are particularly problematic. Private agencies claim to meet performance goals, with little regard for the substance or quality of service. Contractors have excess money because of the rapid drop in caseloads, but instead of using that money to improve the quality of administration and services, they spend it on organizational maintenance, public relations, and staff benefits. There are serious problems of accountability; yet, it is difficult for the state agencies to change contractors.

The chapter shows that at the end of the day, little has changed in the relationship between the public or private agency and the recipient. Despite the rhetoric and ideology, the workers remain unprofessional, undertrained, and overworked. Their main task remains to ensure accuracy in eligibility and payments and to detect fraud. Their goal is to get through the large caseloads as quickly as possible without making any mistakes. Although the application process has become more complicated, especially with the addition of work programs (as well as other programs now in different offices), workers sort and fit the clients into their organizational needs, always with the threat of sanctions. They push the clients into entry-level jobs under the threat of time limits and sanctions. Clients are powerless and have little or no choice. Many drop out or have been deterred from applying.

Chapter 6 brings together two issues that are central to the lives of poor single mothers – how they deal with the low-wage labor market *and* cope with the enormous challenges of managing child care. The chapter examines the assumptions behind the work-first strategy. What kinds of jobs are available for low-skilled, undereducated women? Here, we discuss the rise of nonstandard, low-wage, erratic work. Not only do these jobs pay an insufficient wage, but also often they lack benefits, and the hours are uncertain. Nevertheless, most employees have to be on call, which wrecks havoc with child care arrangements and makes it difficult to have second jobs. The pay is so low that very few welfare leavers who are working are able to escape poverty – and this is the official poverty threshold. Mobility is also a myth. Most of the jobs do not lead to promotions; they are not "starter" jobs.

How job ready are welfare recipients? Again, contrary to myth, most welfare recipients prefer work to welfare and are connected to the paid labor market. Welfare spells are usually short (five consecutive years is relatively rare). Nevertheless, jobs disappear, or family demands change, and, because they are usually not eligible for Unemployment Insurance, they return to welfare until they can find another job. Many welfare recipients have significant employment barriers. Most lack a high school degree and skilled training. Disability is prevalent, especially depression. Children or other family matters have to be cared for.

Child care is a major issue. Quality care is in short supply and is expensive. Most welfare leavers have to rely on family or other forms of informal care. Nonstandard work and on-call scheduling make reliable child care increasingly problematic. The mothers are constantly trying to balance the demands of the low-wage labor market and managing child care. The result is that millions of children, from infants to adolescents, are subject to poor or mediocre care or are left unsupervised. The risks of adverse consequences are apparent. Health programs for poor children have been expanded, and, lately, enrollments have increased. Still, considerable unmet needs remain, such as the lack of facilities, transportation, and inflexible work schedules. In the lack of support for children, the United States stands in sharp contrast with other developed countries. Chapter 8 discusses a series of proposals to increase the income of the parents and to improve child care.

In addition to the work requirements, a second, major part of PRWORA deals with "family values" and the prevention of teen pregnancies discussed in Chapter 7. It shows that although marriage reduces poverty, it does not eliminate it. A major reason for single motherhood is poverty, as shown by the findings from the Fragile Families and Child Well-Being Study,[14] This is a major longitudinal study of a national sample of unwed women and fathers starting with the birth of their first child. A central finding is that, at least at birth, and even for sometime afterward, there are strong bonds between the mother and the noncustodial father. Many cohabit or are in romantic relationships; few fit the classic myth of the absent, indifferent father. At least early on, they would like to stay together and have high hopes of getting married. However, very few actually do because of lack of decent jobs for the fathers and income insecurity.

Similarly, starting well before the 1996 welfare reform, there were continuing efforts to improve paternity establishment and child support. Paternity establishment has reached 72 percent in 2002. However, only 31 percent of poor mothers receive any child-support payment. One reason is that the noncustodial fathers are low skilled, have low earnings, and are often unemployed. There are also financial disincentives for both parents for assigning child support to the state; in most instances the mothers might be better off financially if they can work out an informal support arrangement with the fathers. The fathers also prefer such an arrangement because they can avoid court orders and the penalties for failure to comply.

The chapter examines the several federal and state "marriage-promotion" initiatives that include premarital counseling, marriage education, preseparation counseling, and developing communication and conflict resolution skills. The results so far are inconclusive. There is some evidence, however, that programs such as New Hope, which increase the amount of income available to single parent families, seem to increase their rate of marriage.

Another change in the 1996 reform, which had considerable publicity, is the "family cap," which provides that welfare will not pay for children conceived

[14] M. Carlson, S. McLanahan, & P. England (2004). "Union Formation in Fragile Families." *Demography* 41: 37–61.

while the mother is on welfare. The idea is to reduce the incentives for having children out of wedlock. Several recent studies on the effect of the family cap reach the same conclusion: There is no evidence that it has reduced birth rates or increased the rate of abortion. However, it has created a category of undeserving children known as "cap children." Both these children and their mothers experience undue hardship.

The Family Violence Option (FVO), an amendment to PRWORA, tries to respond to the high rate of domestic violence experienced by welfare recipients, which could be a significant barrier to employment. Nonetheless, several studies suggest that both welfare workers and recipients are reluctant to discuss family violence, in part because the workers expect women to volunteer the information, whereas the women are concerned that such information might lead to unfavorable consequences.

Although marriage or continuing relationships can have positive effects on parents and children, the basic, underlying issue is poverty and the lack of decent jobs that pay decent wages with benefits. This ties together Chapter 7 on marriage promotion with Chapters 6 and 8 on improving the low-wage labor market. Both the mothers and the fathers need to get good jobs. The danger is that the various marriage initiatives are used as a substitute for addressing the structural issues of poverty, inequality, and the problems of the low-wage labor market. It is true that marriage does reduce poverty somewhat, but most of these couples remain either poor or near poor, and poverty increases the likelihood of separation. There also has to be reform in child-support enforcement to take account of the low-wage working father; excessive and unrealistic obligations increase the risk of conflict and withdrawal.

Chapter 7 also addresses how PRWORA frames and responds to teen pregnancy and parenthood. Despite the alarming tone of the legislation, teen non-marital births and the number of teen parents on welfare have been declining. Still, these are important issues. Research indicates that the risk of becoming a single teen parent is associated with sociodemographic factors, such as being African American or Hispanic, living in a high-poverty neighborhood, paternal poverty, being raised by a single mother, and low maternal education. Individual conditions such as early sexual activity, antisocial behavior, poor performance in school, and affiliation with peers with similar characteristics also increase the risk. Moreover, marriage is quite risky for these women because the fathers may have very low education, poor employment, and low earnings. The children of teen mothers also face greater risks of death and illness as well as poorer performance in school.

Teen mothers are required to live with their parents or with other suitable adults. Again, the myth here is that teens are having babies to go on welfare to move into their own apartments. In fact, most teen mothers do live with their parents. However, this is not always a good arrangement. There are reports of more friction and discord with three-generation families. As soon as an infant is twelve weeks or older, teen mothers must participate in school or approved training. Most state TANF officials believe that the school completion and activities requirements have positive effects, but these programs lack necessary supportive services for teens with learning disabilities or mental health and substance abuse problems. Evaluations of school attendance programs before TANF showed moderate, if any, effects.

Teen mothers appear to be sanctioned at fairly high rates. Possibly, living with their parents makes loss of their welfare grant (as distinguished from the children who would most likely continue their grants) less important and not worth the hassles. The more vulnerable families are sanctioned. Overall, the evidence suggests that PRWORA might have increased teen school attendance but had no effect on reducing teen pregnancies or their living arrangements.

Finally, the chapter looks at the effects of abstinence-only-until-marriage programs in reducing teen pregnancies. The existing research suggests that these programs are likely to be ineffective. In contrast, programs that offer sex and HIV education and include information about use of contraceptives tend to delay the onset of sex, reduce the frequency of sex, or reduce the number of sexual partners.

Chapter 8 proposes an alternative approach to reducing poverty and inequality. Our proposals logically and morally apply to all poor people, childless adults, married families, and single-mother families. However, one book cannot cover everything. Because the book is primarily about welfare, we confine our proposals to single-mother families.

The topics in the book and the recommendations have to be presented separately, but it must be emphasized that the issues of poverty and well-being are interrelated. A poor mother is a low-wage worker and a mother of young children; they have health and housing needs and issues with child care, preschool, education, transportation, and neighborhoods. All are connected. Providing a job to a single mother will not work if there is no child care, if there are health problems or transportation is lacking, or if the family faces an eviction. Although this book cannot cover all the issues, we concentrate on income support, employment, child care, and services. We, however, cannot adequately discuss health care, education, transportation, and several other important issues that affect the well-being of these families.

We first address the issue of income support. Both unconditional basic income support and earned income are needed. We emphasize that sanctions and conditionality, such as work requirements, are, in most cases, a proven failure. They cannot be administered fairly, and they result in discrimination and hardship. Both work requirements and sanctions distort agency practices and harm clients. It is time to stop obsessing over the malingerer or shirker and to address the needs of the majority of the poor.

The proposals that would provide families with a basic income merely approach the poverty threshold. This is important – and we do support a universal children's allowance – but as we have argued, the poverty threshold is not an adequate standard. Therefore, improvements in the low-wage labor market are needed, such as raising the minimum wage, providing benefits, improving the EITC, changing labor law, and improving the safety net (e.g., unemployment insurance). We also argue that there should be guaranteed decent jobs for all who want earned income because most people want to work.

The income base for all families should be an adequate children's allowance based on the number of children. Various proposals focus on the level of benefits, methods of financing, and tax rates. The children's allowance would at least get families to the poverty threshold. As to the kind of income assistance system, there could be a means-tested program, but it should be universal, not restricted to single-mother families. Another alternative is a basic income guarantee that would be paid to all individuals but subject to the income tax. Again, logically and morally, a condition-free children's allowance would be the same as a basic income guarantee covering childless adults. Our only reason for proposing the children's allowance is that now there seems to be more of a willingness to support children.

We present a series of recommendations dealing with children, including the provision of adequate child care. The children's allowance, combined with earned income, should allow mothers to purchase better child care. There has to be improved health care for children, including prenatal, and we also propose universal preschool.

Despite a strong work ethic and a full-employment economy, there will be people who will not be in the paid labor force for many reasons: insufficient human capital, family needs, and health problems. Thus, there still will be a need for community-based employment/social services. Some people will need help getting ready for the job market; others will need help improving their human capital; others may have disabilities and need support. Social service departments should be independent, separate agencies. They should not be connected to any income assistance programs. Because clients have an exit option – the children's allowance – they will come to the agency as long as they feel they can benefit from the services. The agencies would get clients only if they offer something of value. The agencies would offer a range of services, including employment services and should be encouraged to deal with the more difficult cases. This raises important issues of evaluation as well as accountability.

2   The State of Poverty

TANF Recipients

The Myth and Reality of Poverty in America

The United States has the astonishing distinction of having one of the highest rates of poverty in the industrialized world, despite having one of the highest average incomes.[1] The latest figures show an increase in the number of people in poverty from 32.9 million in 2001, to 35.9 million in 2003, to 37 million in 2004. The poverty rate rose from 11.7 percent (2001) to 12.7 percent in 2004.[2] More ominously, the United States also has the highest child poverty compared with thirteen western European countries and Canada.[3] How did we earn such a distinction? The United States believes in the central importance of personal independence through earnings in the paid labor force. Other policies are viewed in terms of whether they create incentives or disincentives to achieving this goal. Thus, with the exception of the aged, only mixed, if not suspicious, support is reserved for those considered outside of the labor force (unemployed, disabled). There is begrudging support for those who are considered poor but able bodied. There has never been public support to combat poverty by reducing income inequality, even though increasing inequality is a major reason poverty is so high in the United States. An exception is the Earned Income Tax Credit (EITC) for the working poor, which is discussed in Chapter 3.

These principles shape the ways we conceptualize, measure, and understand poverty, which reflect *moral* assumptions about who is poor and why and justify the antipoverty policies we enact. Poverty is generally measured

[1] T. Smeeding, L. Rainwater, & G. Burtless (2001). U.S. Poverty in a Cross-national Comparison. In S. H. Danziger & R. H. Haveman (Eds.), *Understanding Poverty*. New York: Russell Sage Foundation, pp. 162–35.
[2] Center on Budget and Policy Priorities (2005). *Economic Recovery Failed to Benefit Much of the Population in 2004 (August 30)*. Washington, D.C.: The Center, p. 2.
[3] L. Rainwater & T. M. Smeeding (2003). *Poor Kids in a Rich Country: America's Children in Comparative Perspective*. New York: Russell Sage Foundation.

as lacking the income to obtain daily essentials for basic subsistence. Poverty is viewed as a consequence of individual deficiencies, dependency, and an underclass culture rather than the result of structural conditions, such as lack of jobs, the nature of work, lack of human capital, poor health and education, and environmental conditions.[4]

Public attention and commitment to alleviate poverty has always been marginal. With the exception of the elderly, antipoverty policies, including the War on Poverty in the 1960s, have reinforced the "traditional norms of advancing individual opportunity and self-help."[5] Indeed, since the 1970s, "poverty" has disappeared as a major public issue, receiving little attention from policy makers.[6] Rather than focusing on poverty, policy makers have paid almost exclusive attention to welfare (i.e., AFDC). They did so even though poverty in the United States remains high and affects a broader and more diverse segment of the population. The preoccupation with welfare not only diverts attention from the more pervasive issue of poverty, thus making it invisible, but it also reinforces entrenched myths about poverty.

The first myth is that poverty is a problem afflicting only a small percentage of the population when, in fact, it is quite pervasive. The second myth is that poverty is relatively permanent and intergenerational. In fact, much of poverty is transitory, and people move in and out of relatively short poverty spells. The third myth is that the poor are an "underclass"; that is, African American or Latino single parents and unattached adults who reside in urban ghettos, leading lives marked by lawlessness and personal chaos. In fact, the poor are a diverse population, and many of them are two-parent families. The fourth myth is that poverty is a moral fault; that is, the causes of poverty are personal, such as lack of work effort, lack of human capital, single parenthood, and other personal deficiencies, when in fact many of the poor are hard working and "play by the rules." In fact, we show that a major cause of poverty is structural, having to do with the characteristics of the labor market and with the rise of income inequality. A fifth myth is that the poor are responsible for their predicament; however, innocent children bear most of the brunt of poverty. A sixth myth is that poverty can be alleviated through "trickle down" economic growth, although such growth leaves many behind. A final myth suggests that income support policies to alleviate poverty only exacerbate it by fostering dependency, when such policies can effectively reduce the incidence of poverty.

In this chapter, we address each myth and show how studies and available data on poverty portray a different picture. A major point of this book is that

[4] A. O'Connor (2001). *Poverty Knowledge: Social Science, Social Policy, and the Poor in Twentieth-Century U.S. History*. Princeton, N.J.: Princeton University Press.

[5] H. Heclo (1994). Poverty Politics. In S. H. Danziger, G. D. Sandefur, & D. H. Wineberg (Eds.), *Confronting Poverty* (pp. 396–437). New York: Russell Sage Foundation, p. 409.

[6] S. Danziger & P. Gottschalk (2004). *Diverging Fortunes: Trends in Poverty and Inequality*. New York: Russell Sage Foundation, pp. 1–25.

poverty results from conditions in the low-wage labor market. People have difficulty earning a decent living for many reasons. People have different human capital, skill development, access to education, transportation, and other resources. Many women and people of color suffer discrimination. Large waves of immigrants may lack English and other skills. Understanding poverty means knowing how different groups are affected and how well they cope with the paid labor market. We also show that welfare recipients are victims of similar myths. In reality, they are not appreciably different from the working poor.

Measuring Poverty

What do we mean when we say that someone is poor? This is a crucial question. How we define and measure poverty reflects politically dominant social norms about an acceptable minimum standard of living below which physical and social well-being are endangered. It also underlies how public policy responds to those classified as poor. Indeed, both the official poverty thresholds and the federal poverty guidelines, which are based on them, determine eligibility for many assistance programs and the allocation of federal funds to states. No matter how poverty is defined and measured, it is clearly a normative rather than an objective "yardstick."

Following Rainwater and Smeeding,[7] two different approaches conceptualize poverty. An economic approach narrowly focuses on identifying the income needed to purchase a basket of goods and services that provides a minimum level of material subsistence. This is the approach taken in the United States. In contrast, a social approach considers not only material subsistence but also the ability to participate as full members of society. This is a standard based on a moral imperative that all people should have sufficient resources to develop their capacities and to lead a satisfactory and productive life.[8] This generally is the approach adopted by the European Union, which defines poverty as, "the poor shall be taken to mean persons, families, and groups of persons whose resources (material, cultural, and societal) are so limited as to exclude them from the minimum acceptable way of life in the member state in which they live."[9] Following this broader definition, poverty in the United States would be considerably higher than the official measure.

The official poverty measure in United States, originally developed by Mollie Orshansky in 1963,[10] attempts to define an "absolute" poverty threshold, which is the income needed to purchase a basic basket of goods and services to

---

[7] Rainwater & Smeeding (2003), pp. 4–11.

[8] A. Sen (1999). *Development as Freedom*. New York: Alfred A. Knopf.

[9] Quoted in Rainwater & Smeeding (2003), pp. 5–6.

[10] G. Fisher (1992). "The Development and History of the Poverty Thresholds." *Social Security Bulletin* 55(4): 3–14.

maintain a minimally acceptable standard of living. Orshansky used a formula based on the cost of an economy food plan, the lowest of four food plans, for "temporary or emergency use when funds are low"[11] for a family of three or more persons. The plan was based on a Household Food Consumption Survey by the Agriculture Department in 1955. The survey also showed that, on average, a family of three or more members spent about a third of its income after taxes on food. Therefore, she multiplied the cost of the economy food plan by three to arrive at a poverty threshold. As noted by Glennerster,[12] Orshansky selected the least generous measure to make it politically palatable. This has been the leitmotif of defining and measuring poverty ever since. What most Americans may fail to realize is that this measure has become harsher over time.[13] In the 1960s, the poverty threshold stood for about half of the median income for a family of four. By 2000, it had fallen to 28 percent of the median income.[14] In contrast, the European Union has adopted a relative poverty threshold based on 60 percent of the median income.[15]

The poverty threshold was institutionalized as the official poverty measure in the United States when the Bureau of the Budget (now the Office of Management and Budget, or OMB) adopted it in 1969. It cannot be changed without OMB's approval. And because it is used to allocate federal resources, there are entrenched political forces that resist any changes, especially if they result in a higher estimation of poverty.[16] Yet, it is clear that the official poverty threshold, even with its narrow economic emphasis, and as conceptualized in 1965, is outdated and inadequate in light of economic and social changes in recent years.[17] Some of these include (1) changes in consumption patterns, especially the increase in expenditures on nonfood items such as housing; (2) changes in family composition, particularly the rise of single-parent households; (3) increased participation of women in the labor force and the added expenditures of their employment such as child care; (4) increase in the tax burden on low-income persons; (5) the rise of out-of-pocket medical expenses; (6) geographic differences in cost of living; (7) provision of in-kind benefits such as food stamps; and (8) the expansion of the EITC to low-income families.

The National Academy of Science (NAS) has proposed a revised measure that sets the poverty thresholds to the actual consumer expenditures for food, clothing, and shelter for a family of two adults and two children. The

---

[11] C. F. Citro & R. T. Michael, Eds. (1995). *Measuring Poverty: A New Approach*. Washington, D.C.: National Academy Press, p. 24.

[12] H. Glennerster (2002). "United States Poverty Studies and Poverty Measurement: The Past Twenty-five Years." *Social Service Review* 79: 83–107.

[13] Ibid.

[14] M. R. Rank (2004). *One Nation, Underprivileged: Why American Poverty Affects Us All*. Oxford; New York: Oxford University Press, p. 24.

[15] Glennerster (2002), p. 87. This measure has the disadvantage of underestimating the number of poor people at times of sustained economic recessions when the median income falls.

[16] Ibid., p. 87.   [17] Citro & Michael (1995).

threshold would be increased by a modest amount for other necessities.[18] The budget would be updated annually on the basis of the Consumer Expenditure Survey and would also consider geographic differences in housing costs. Family resources would include disposable and near-disposable income, that is, the value of food stamps, subsidized housing, and school lunches. Some expenses would be subtracted from the resources such as out-of-pocket medical expenditures, taxes (including refundable taxes such as EITC), child care, work-related expenses, and child-support payments from the payer.[19] This new measure generally increases the overall estimates of poverty (from 11.8 percent to 13.8 percent in 1999), lowers the poverty rate for female-headed families (from 54.7% to 31.4% in 1999),[20] but more important, it shows that the rate of poverty for the full-time working family is 40 percent higher than the official rate.[21] This modest proposal is yet to be adopted by the OMB.

The official measure of poverty does not provide a good estimate of how many people are poor, nor does it accurately portray who is at greater risk of poverty. Most people agree that the poverty line is unrealistic. In 2000, more than two-thirds of those polled thought that at least $35,000 was necessary to meet the basic needs of a family of four. In 2001, 60 percent said that a family of four was poor with an income of $20,000, when the official poverty line was $17,029. In a 2002 poll, half of the respondent believed that an income of $45,000 was needed for a family of four to meet basic needs.[22]

In particular, the current poverty thresholds fail to recognize the *minimum* budget people need to have decent housing, food, health, education, and work and to raise their children in safe and healthy neighborhoods. Therefore, even if people's incomes are somewhat above the poverty line and they are not officially poor, their incomes are so low that they cannot manage on a basic budget and are at serious risk of falling below the official poverty line. This is why so many people are in and out of poverty; their lives are so precarious that unforeseen events such as illness, car breakdown, rent hike, or reduced work hours sends them below the official line.

Jared Bernstein and his colleagues constructed a budget just to meet "basic needs and achieve a safe and decent standard of living."[23] The budget is closer in spirit to a social conception of poverty by calculating what a working family needs, while not excluding the family from social activities and participation.

[18] Ibid., pp. 4–7.   [19] Ibid., pp. 9–11.

[20] J. Iceland (2003c). "Why Poverty Remains High: The Role of Income Growth, Economic Inequality, and Changes in Family Structure, 1949–1999." *Demography* 40(3): 499–519.

[21] J. Iceland & J. Kim (2001). "Poverty among Working Families: New Insights from an Improved Poverty Measure." *Social Science Quarterly* 82(2): 260.

[22] W. P. Quigley (2003). *Ending Poverty as We Know It: Guaranteeing a Right to a Job at a Living Wage.* Philadelphia, Pa.: Temple University Press, p. 38.

[23] J. Bernstein, C. Brocht, & M. Spade-Aguilar (2000). *How Much Is Enough? Basic Family Budgets for Working Families.* Washington, D.C.: Economic Policy Institute.

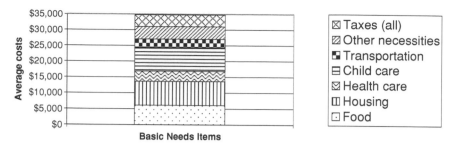

Figure 2–1. Comparison of a Basic Needs Budget for Two Adults/Two Children and the Poverty Thresholds. *Source:* Jared Bernstein, Chauna Brocht, & Maggie Spade-Aguilar (2000). *How Much Is Enough? Basic Family Budgets for Working Families.* Washington, D.C.: Economic Policy Institute, Figure 1.

The basic family budget includes food, housing, health care, transportation, child care, and "other necessary expenses" (e.g., telephone, clothing, personal care, household items, school supplies, television). It does not include *any* restaurant meals (including fast food), vacations, movies, and saving for education, retirement, and emergencies. The study is based on family budgets in nineteen different localities. Budgets for a four-person family vary by geographical area, ranging from $20,000 to $40,000 in 1996, well above the official poverty line of $12,636 (1996).[24]

For a Baltimore family of four, the monthly estimates per item were as follows:

Food: $500 (based on the U.S. Department of Agriculture's (USDA's) Low-Cost Food Plan)

Housing: $628 (a two-bedroom apartment that costs no more than 40% of safe and decent housing in the area)

Health care: $267 (weighted average of the employer's share and the costs of nongroup plans), plus out-of-pocket expenses

Transportation: $222 (for work and other necessary trips, based on the IRS's cost-per-mile estimates)

Child care: $626 (center-based child care or family child care centers)

Other necessary expenses: $338 (telephones, clothing, personal care, school supplies, television)

Taxes: $313 (federal payroll taxes and federal, state, and local income taxes)

EITC funds that are actually received are taken into account. A family of four in Baltimore would have to earn an annual income of $34,732, just for the basic needs. This is twice the poverty threshold (see Figure 2–1).

---

[24] Bernstein, Brocht, & Spade-Aguilar (2000), pp. 2–3. Data were based on the Consumer Expenditure Survey, as well as other surveys (e.g., National Personal Transportation Survey) and then adjusted for selected areas of the country.

A single-parent family with one parent working full time, a seven-year old, and a three-year-old would need an annual income of $30,108, which is 2.3 times the poverty threshold, at an hourly wage of $14.48.[25] They would spend the following percentages on the basic needs items: food, 14 percent; transportation, 6 percent; health care, 10 percent; housing, 25 percent; child car, 25 percent; other necessities, 12 percent.[26]

Not surprisingly, in all of the areas studied, all the estimates were considerably greater than the poverty line. For a single-parent family, the range was from $20,000 to $40,000 (1996 dollars). The authors conclude that few low-wage jobs would provide this annual income. With most of the jobs held by these workers, working full time, the income would be between one-half and two-thirds to meet basic needs.[27]

Experiencing Poverty

The official poverty rate masks the extent of hardship experienced by many low-income groups. In general, the overall poverty rate is higher when using the NAS measure and is considerably higher when a relative measure is used. For 2000, the official poverty rate was 11.3 percent, the NAS rate was 13.8 percent, and the relative measure (one-half of the median family income) was 21.1 percent.[28] Indeed, one of the myths about poor Americans is that they have a higher standard of living than the poor in other affluent countries. However, this is not the case. Christopher Jencks,[29] citing calculations made by Smeeding and Rainwater on the purchasing power of those in the lowest tenth percentile, notes that although poor Americans are better off than the poor in Britain and Australia, they are considerably worse off than the poor in western Europe and somewhat worse off than the poor in Sweden, Canada, and Finland.[30]

No matter how poverty is measured, families and individuals who experience poverty face considerable risks and hardships. Indeed, even when families "escape" poverty by having income above the poverty threshold, they are still effectively poor, even at twice the poverty threshold, because they still experience considerable economic hardships. As a result of low earnings, poor families are more likely to miss utility payments, be victimized by crime, have poor health and inadequate child care, be evicted, and suffer food deprivation.[31] A study of family hardship reported that 29 percent of families below the official poverty line experienced "critical hardships," defined as not enough

[25] Ibid., p. 61.   [26] Ibid., p. 64.
[27] Ibid., p. 64.
[28] J. Iceland (2003b). *Poverty in America: A Handbook*. Berkeley: University of California Press, p. 43.
[29] C. Jencks (2002). "Does Inequality Matter?" *Daedalus* (Winter): 49–65.
[30] Ibid., p. 55.
[31] Bernstein, Brocht, & Spade-Aguilar (2000), pp. 18, 47.

food to eat, missed meals, postponement of needed medical care, eviction, disconnected utilities, or doubling up with families or friends.[32] This was also true for a quarter of families with incomes between 100 percent and 200 percent of the poverty line. Of families with incomes below 200 percent of the poverty line, 18 percent reported they had missed meals often or sometimes, and 12.5 percent said they did not have enough food often or sometimes. The same percentage said that a family member did not receive medical care or postponed necessary medical care in the past year; 25 percent reported that during the past year, they could not pay their mortgage, rent, or utility bill.[33] The effects of poverty are particularly noticeable when it comes to food insecurity and meeting basic needs.[34] Longer spells of poverty and severity of poverty have pronounced effect on material hardship.[35]

A recent study by the National Low Income Housing Coalition found "there is no state where a low-income worker can reasonably afford a modest one- or two-bedroom rental unit."[36] An "affordable" rent was defined by the U.S. Department of Housing and Urban Development (HUD) as no more than 30 percent of household income. A fair-market rent is the HUD standard, typically the fortieth percentile of a given housing market or fiftieth percentile in the markets that are the tightest and most expensive. The national median housing wage necessary to afford a standard two-bedroom house is $15.21 per hour. The national median hourly wage last year was approximately $12 per hour. "In 40 states, the study found, renters need to earn more than two times the prevailing minimum wage to afford basic housing." In Massachusetts, California, New Jersey, New York, Maryland, and Connecticut, they must earn more than three times the minimum wage. Even in West Virginia, the "most affordable state," a low-wage worker would have to earn $8.78, more than $3 more than the state's hourly minimum wage of $5.15. The gap between what low-wage workers can afford and affordable housing has been widening.[37]

Poverty entails significant compromises in the daily necessities of living and of developing one's potential.[38] Rank describes the daily struggle poor people face in deciding on how to spend their meager resources. Often, it is a choice between foregoing food to pay heating bills in the winter.[39] The USDA estimates that 11 percent of all households experienced food insecurity in 2002. The rate is considerably higher for African American (22%) and Hispanic

---

[32] H. Boushey et al. (2001). *Hardship in America: The Real Story of Working Families*. Washington, D.C.: Economic Policy Institute, pp. 29–38.

[33] Ibid., p. 31.

[34] J. Iceland & K. Baum (2004). "Income Poverty and Material Hardship: How Strong Is the Association?" (National Poverty Center Working Paper Series No. 04-17). Ann Arbor, Michi.

[35] Ibid.

[36] L. Clemetson (2003b). "Poor Workers Finding Modest Housing Unaffordable, Study Says." *New York Times* (Sept. 9), p. 18.

[37] Ibid.   [38] Rank (2004), pp. 36–37.

[39] Ibid., p. 43.

(21.7%) families.[40] For households under the poverty threshold, the rate was 38 percent, and 45.5 percent of poor children experienced food insecurity. Despite the economic boom of the 1990s, Freeman says that there was little improvement in either homelessness or hunger. Approximately 10 million households, or 4 percent of the population, reported outright hunger (more severe). Freeman reports that there was no overall change in food insecurity between 1995 and 1998, despite full employment and economic growth.[41] The rate remained the same to 2002. America's Second Harvest (the largest provider of emergency food) served 23.3 million meals in 2001, and the median income of those receiving food aid was 71 percent of the poverty threshold.[42] During the colder winter months, the poor spend even less money on food.[43] Food insecurity has been exacerbated with the decline in food stamps, which is discussed in Chapter 3.

The poor lack good health care. Those in the top 5 percent of the income distribution can expect to live, on average, nine years longer than those in the bottom 10 percent. Medicaid and Medicare have helped, but the poor still have the lowest rates of health care services. In 2002, approximately a third of the poor had no insurance for the entire year, and among poor Hispanics, the rate was 43 percent.[44]

Poverty increases stress and stunts growth. The risk of separation and divorce is increased. The stress is even greater for single-parent families. The lack of a proper diet, shelter, and education compromises individual development, with negative effects on children's cognitive development, verbal ability, early school achievement, and mental health. When combined with inferior schools, poor neighborhoods, a less stimulating home environment, and unmet health needs, children enter adulthood with lower productivity and increased susceptibility to substance abuse.[45]

The Risk of Poverty and Poverty Spells

Poverty slices through many sectors of American society. It is not randomly distributed. As Rank points out, the risks of poverty are correlated with race, ethnicity, gender, children, female-headed families, education, disability, and

---

[40] M. Nord, M. Andrews, & S. Carlson (2002). "Household Food Security in the United States, 2002" (Food Assistance and Nutrition Research Report No. 35). Washington D.C.: Food and Rural Economics Division, Economic Research Service, U.S. Department of Agriculture, pp. 1–51.

[41] R. Freeman (2001). "The Rising Tide Lifts . . . ?" In S. Danziger & R. Haveman (Eds.), *Understanding Poverty.* New York: Russell Sage Foundation; Cambridge, Mass.: Harvard University Press, p. 121.

[42] Rank (2004), p. 28.   [43] Ibid., p. 42.

[44] U.S. Department of Health and Human Services (2004). *Indicators of Welfare Dependence: Annual Report to Congress 2004.* Washington D.C.: U.S. Department of Health and Human Services, p. 19.

[45] Rank (2004), pp. 44–45.

geographical location.[46] These correlates increase economic vulnerability
either because of discrimination, barriers for participation in the labor market, or the characteristics of the low-wage labor market itself (discussed in
Chapter 6). At the same time, social policy fails to protect adequately the economically vulnerable, making them highly susceptible to bouts of poverty.

The overall poverty rate for 2003 was 12.5 percent. Compared with a poverty
rate of 10.2 percent for whites, the poverty rate for African Americans was 24.1
percent and for Hispanics 21.8 percent. Women experience a higher rate of
poverty (12.3%) than men (8.7%). Children (under the age of eighteen) have
the highest poverty rate of any other age group (17.6%). Thirty-five percent
of all female-headed households with children under the age of eighteen are
poor. The poverty rate for adults (twenty-five and older) with less than twelve
years of education is 23.3 percent compared with 10.3 percent for those with
twelve years of education. Persons with disabilities have a poverty rate of 21.4
percent compared with 8.3 percent of those with no disability. Finally, the
South has the highest poverty rate at 13.8 percent.[47] Using the NAS poverty
measure, the rates are somewhat higher for most groups, except for African
Americans and female-headed households, because it considers their greater
dependence on near-cash transfers and lower work-related expenses.[48]

The overall poverty rates do not tell us the "depth of poverty," which com-
pares a family's income with its poverty threshold and expresses that comparison as a fraction. An income-to-poverty ratio that is less than 0.5 would
be considered dire or extreme poverty. In 2002, 4.9 percent of the total population lived in dire poverty. Moreover, the proportion of the poor in dire
poverty increased over time from a low of 26 percent of all the poor people
to 41 percent in 2002.[49] Using the same measure, Short and Iceland[50] show
that in 1998, the rate for African Americans was 11.2 percent, for Hispanics
9.8 percent, and for whites 4.0 percent. Eight percent of all children experienced dire poverty (6.9%, or 5 million, children in 2002). The rate for female
heads of households was 13.3 percent compared with 2 percent for married
couples. And for households with no workers, the rate was 18.4 percent as
compared with 3 percent for those with workers.

Rank points out that most Americans view poverty as chronic, affecting
only a relatively small number of people (e.g., the "underclass"). In fact,
poverty is widespread, and although spells might be short for most, it affects
many people.[51] He bases his analysis on the Panel Study of Income Dynamics

[46] Ibid., pp. 30–32.   [47] Ibid., p. 31.
[48] Iceland (2003b), p. 42.
[49] U.S. Department of Health and Human Services (2004), Chapter 3, p. 6.
[50] K. Short & J. Iceland (2000). "Who Is Better Off Than We Thought?" (paper presented at the
    annual meeting of the American Economic Association, Boston, Mass.), pp. 1–35.
[51] Rank (2004).

(PSID), a study of individuals and households specifically designed to chart income changes over time.[52]

Rank constructs four categories of poverty: (1) dire poverty: those with income below 0.5 of the poverty line; (2) poverty: those with income below the poverty line; (3) near poverty: those with income below 1.25 of the poverty line and (4) those with income below 1.5 of the poverty line. Taking a life course perspective, that is, calculating the cumulative risk of being poor during one's lifetime, Rank finds that a clear majority of Americans experience at least one year of poverty at some point during their lives.[53] By age 40, 18 percent would experience dire poverty, 36 percent poverty, and 52 percent near poverty (1.5 below the poverty line). By age 75, 33 percent would have experienced dire poverty, 58 percent poverty, and 76 percent near poverty (1.5 below the poverty line). Similarly, by age 75, 58 percent would experience at least one year of poverty, 46 percent at least two years of poverty, and 39 percent at least three years of poverty. These risks are not evenly distributed in the population. By age 75, 91 percent of African Americans would experience poverty as compared with 53 percent of whites, 59 percent of women will have experienced poverty as compared with 55 percent of men, and 75 percent of those with fewer than twelve years of education as compared with 48 percent of those with twelve years of education.[54]

The experience of poverty is highly dynamic. Using the Survey of Income and Program Participation (SIPP) from 1996 to 1999, Iceland shows that 3.5 percent of those who were not poor in 1996 became poor in 1999. The percentage increases to 7.4 percent for African Americans and to 6.8 percent for single-parent families.[55] Of those who were poor in 1996, 35 percent were not poor in 1997, 44.5 percent were not poor in 1998, and 49.5 percent were not poor in 1999 (based on annual poverty).[56] This suggests that poverty spells are fairly short (see Figure 2–2). Indeed, a majority of poverty spells[57] are from two to four months. In other words, only a small proportion of the population experiences long-term poverty. Measuring chronic poverty as being poor for

---

[52] Starting in 1968, it is the longest, continuous panel data set in the world. The initial interviews (1968) were 4,800 households of approximately 18,000 individuals. They were tracked annually, including their children and adults who eventually moved out and formed their own households. Those who dropped out of the study were replaced by individuals with similar characteristics. At any given point, the PSID was representative of the entire U.S. population. Between 1968 and 1997, there were thirty waves of interviews. Rank (2004), pp. 91–92.

[53] Rank (2004), p. 92.

[54] Ibid., p. 96.

[55] J. Iceland (2003a). *Dynamics of Economic Well-Being: Poverty 1996–1999.* Washington D.C.: U.S. Census Bureau, pp. 1–9.

[56] Ibid., p. 4.

[57] Measured as being poor for at least two months. A spell ends when the individual is not poor for two consecutive months.

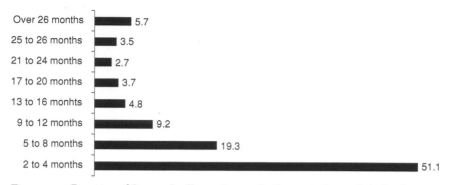

Figure 2–2. Duration of Poverty Spells: 1996–1999 (in Percent). *Source*: J. Iceland (2003). *Dynamics of Economic Well-Being: Poverty 1996–1999.* Washington D.C.: U.S. Census Bureau.

all forty-eight months from 1996 to 1999, only 2 percent were chronically poor. But as shown in Figure 2–3, the risk increases considerably for nonwhite and for female-headed households.

Using the PSID longitudinal data set from 1975 to 1997, Signe-Mary Mc-Kernan and Caroline Ratcliffe calculated the likelihood of entering and exiting poverty, controlling for other events and characteristics.[58] They show that "the likelihood of entering poverty is highest, all else equal, for persons living in households with a head who loses employment, 16.7 percent. The likelihood of entering poverty if one shifts from two-adult to female-headed household is slightly lower at 15.3 percent."[59] The likelihood of entering poverty because of loss of employment by spouse is 8.9 percent, loss of employment by another household member is 7.2 percent, disability of head of household is 5.8 percent, and entry of a child under the age of six into the household is 5.8 percent. Elimination of the same factors increases the likelihood of exit from poverty. For example, the likelihood of exiting poverty if the spouse gains employment is 65.2 percent and 43.1 percent if the head gains employment. The likelihood of exit from poverty is 48.2 percent when a female-headed household shifts to a two-adult household.[60]

Although the movement in and out of poverty is fluid, many of those who exit remain economically vulnerable because they are most likely to be near poor rather than see a major increase in their income. This also explains why poor people experience several poverty spells during their life course. Escaping poverty signifies mobility to a higher income bracket. According to Corcoran, depending on the study, 25–40 percent of individuals changed

[58] S.-M. McKernan & C. Ratcliffe (2002). *Transition Events in the Dynamics of Poverty.* Washington D.C.: Urban Institute, pp. 1–83.
[59] Ibid., p. xxii.   [60] Ibid., p. xxvi.

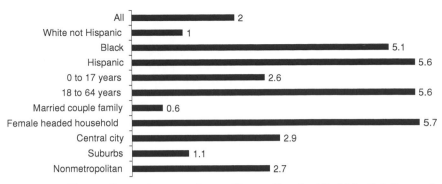

Figure 2–3. Chronic Poverty Rates: 1996–1999 (Percent Poor for All 48 Months). *Source*: J. Iceland (2003). *Dynamics of Economic Well-Being: Poverty 1996–1999*. Washington D.C.: U.S. Census Bureau.

quintiles over a two-year period, 40–50 percent over a five-year period, and 60 percent over a nine-year period. However, in a national sample of individuals aged 22 to 39 between 1968 and 1970, more than half were still in the bottom quintile twenty years later. Upward mobility rates were lower for nonwhites and single mothers who receive welfare.[61]

Thus, although there is a certain amount of mobility, on the whole, social class tends to reproduce itself.[62] Children of working-class or lower-class families are likely to remain in the same condition. This is because class status has a large influence on the resources and opportunities available to the children, especially education, which, in turn, affects their life chances. According to Rank, a sizeable correlation exists between fathers' and sons' incomes. If the father is in the bottom 5 percent of the income distribution, 42 percent of the sons will end up in the bottom quintile, and only 5 percent will be in the top. Conversely, if the father is in the top 5 percent, then 42 percent of the sons will be in the top quintile and only 5 percent in the bottom.[63] Of those who experienced poverty as an adult, half also experienced poverty as a child, and an additional 38 percent grew up in homes that were near poor.[64] Mary Corcoran concludes that "parental economic resources consistently predict children's adult attainments. They predict all outcomes and have large impacts on men's labor supply and earnings. . . . Being poor matters a lot."[65] Individuals do move up and down across adulthood; however, mobility is usually not

[61] M. Corcoran (2001). "Mobility, Persistence, and the Consequences of Poverty for Children: Child and Adult Outcomes." In S. Danziger & R. H. Haveman (Eds.), *Understanding Poverty*. New York: Russell Sage Foundation; Cambridge, Mass.: Harvard University Press, p. 135.

[62] Rank (2004), p. 69, citing Beeghly (2000); Fischer et al. (1996).

[63] Rank (2004), pp. 69–71.   [64] Ibid., p. 72.

[65] M. Corcoran (1995). "Rags to Rags: Poverty and Mobility in the United States." *Annual Review of Sociology* 21: 237–267, p. 261; quoted in Rank (2004), p. 72.

far from their economic origins. In fact, says Rank, "contrary to popular myth, there is somewhat less intergenerational mobility than in a number of developed countries"[66] because children with working-class families do not have the opportunities that children from middle- and upper-class backgrounds have. Lack of access to quality schools is particularly important.[67] McMurrer and Sawhill state: "Family background has a significant and increasing effect on who goes to college, where, and for how long. With the rewards for going to college greater than ever, and family background now a stronger influence over who reaps those rewards, the United States is at risk of becoming more class stratified in coming decades."[68]

Who Are the Poor?

The Working Poor

Contrary to the prevailing myth, a majority of the poor live in households in which one member worked part time or full time during the year. Indeed, at the bottom fifth of the income distribution, 80 percent of family income comes from employment.[69] In 2003, about 56 percent of poor families with children had a household member who worked during the previous year, and 20 percent of all poor families with children had a household member who worked full time.[70] Yet, these figures underestimate the true number of working families in America because of the way the official poverty threshold is calculated. Iceland and Kim show that when using the NAS poverty threshold, which takes into account work-related expenses as well as near-money benefits, "the proportion of people in full-time working families who are poor increases substantially, from 37% when the official poverty measure is used, to 48%, according to the experimental measure."[71] In addition, they show that the poverty rates for full-time working families are particularly high for Hispanic, female-headed families, and the less educated.[72] In other words, these families are "playing by the rules" and yet are poor. To put it in a broader perspective, poor Americans (those at the bottom income deciles) work more hours, on average, than their counterparts in Canada, France, Germany, Sweden, and the U.K.[73] Moreover, in the United States, 25 percent of all workers are

---

[66] Rank (2004), p. 72, citing O. Kangas (2000). "Distributive Justice and Social Policy: Some Reflections on Rawls and Income Distribution." *Social Policy and Administration* 34(5): 510–528.

[67] Rank (2004), p. 73.

[68] D. P. McMurrer & I. V. Sawhill (1998). *Getting Ahead: Economic and Social Mobility in America.* Washington, D.C.: The Urban Institute Press, p. 69, quoted in Rank (2004), pp. 73–74.

[69] Freeman (2001), p. 107.

[70] U.S. Census Bureau (2004). *Current Population Survey, 2004 Annual Social and Economic Supplement.* Retrieved from http://www.census.gov/apsd/techdoc/cps/cpsmar04.pdf.

[71] Iceland & Kim (2001), p. 262.   [72] Ibid., p. 263.

[73] L. Osberg (2003). "Time, Money and Inequality in International Perspective." Halifax, Nova Scotia: Dalhousie University, pp. 1–26.

low-wage workers, as compared with only 12.9 percent, the average of all other industrialized countries.[74]

A primary reason those who work remain poor is change in the labor market, especially the deterioration of working conditions in the low-wage sector, discussed more fully in Chapter 6. Low-wage work is defined as less than 65 percent of the median for full-time jobs. At present, there are simply not enough decent-paying jobs.[75] An increasing number of jobs are part time and lack benefits. In 2000, the Census Bureau reported that the median hourly wage was $9.91. Approximately 3 million people work part time because of the lack of full-time jobs. Because employers do not provide this benefit, 43.6 million people lack health insurance.[76] According to Richard Freeman, how much work one does is the most important determinant of poverty. "For all individuals, regardless of gender, ethnicity, or age, there is a massive difference in the poverty rates of those who work *full-time year round* and those who work less." For full-time workers, the poverty rate is 2.6 percent; for part-time or part-year workers, the rate is 13.1 percent; and for those who do not work at all, the rate is 19.9 percent.[77] There are no differences in terms of gender. The poverty rates of African Americans and Hispanics decline sharply with full-time work, although they still have higher poverty rates than whites.[78]

Full-time work at low wages barely lifts the workers and their families above the official poverty line and is not sufficient to meet the basic family budget. Starting in the 1980s, low-wage earnings declined in real terms, making earnings alone insufficient.[79] In 1990, 45 percent of parents of low-income children worked full-time, year-round. By 2001, the percentage rose to 57 percent. A full-time, minimum wage ($5.15) pays less than $11,000 per year. It would take a full-time, year-round job at $9.00 per hour for a family to meet basic needs.[80] In 1999, for heads of families, 12.1 percent earned $6 per hour; 21.1 percent earned less than $6; 21.2 percent earned less than $8; and 31.7 percent less than $10. To raise a family of three above the poverty line, working full time (thirty-five hours per week for fifty-two weeks), the wage would have

[74] Rank (2004), p. 54. "In all parts of the country, low-wage work alone is not enough to make ends meet. The study found: Across 10 communities, our sample family needs $27,660 per year (or $13.10 per hour) in the lowest-cost location (New Orleans) and $59,544 (or $28.19 per hour) in the highest-cost location (Boston) just to meet its basic needs." A "sample family" is a single working parent with an infant and a preschool age child. Wider Opportunities for Women (WOW) (2004). "Coming Up Short: A Comparison of Wages and Work Supports in 10 American Communities." Retrieved from http://wowonline.org/docs/dynamic-CTTA-43.pdf. (Summer/Fall).

[75] Rank (2004), p. 53.   [76] Ibid., p. 54.
[77] Freeman (2001), p. 114.   [78] Ibid., p. 115.
[79] Ibid., pp. 107–109.
[80] N. Cauthen & H.-H. Lu (2003). *Employment Alone Is Not Enough for America's Low-Income Children and Families, Living at the Edge.* Research Brief No. 1, National Center for Children in Poverty. New York: Mailman School of Public Health. Columbia University.

Table 2–1. *Share of families with income less than family budgets and less than the poverty line*

	Family budget	Poverty line
All	28.90%	10.10%
Race/ethnicity		
White	20.3	6.2
African American	52.1	22.3
Hispanic	56.3	21.5
Other	28.5	10.4
Education		
Less than high school degree	68.6	34.1
High school degree only	38.1	13.3
Some college	27.6	7.5
College degree	7.7	1.6
Age		
18–30	46.8	19.4
31–45	20.1	5.6
46+	21.6	6.8
Work status		
Full time, full year	20.9	3.9
Less than full time, full year	46.8	46.8
Family type		
One adult with one child	60.3	22.5
One adult with two children	75.3	34.5
One adult with three children	87.8	60.6
Two adults with one child	16.9	4.1
Two adults with two children	18.5	5.2
Two adults with three children	35.2	11.9

Source: H. Boushey et al. (2001). *Hardship in America: The Real Story of Working Families.* Washington, D.C.: Economic Policy Institute, Table 3.

to be $7.30 per hour, and for a family of four, $9.36. Yet, nearly one-third of family heads earn less than $10 and face a significant risk of poverty.[81]

The economic hardship of working families is extensive. Using the measure of family budget previously discussed, Boushey and colleagues[82] show that 29 percent of working families have incomes less than the basic family budget (roughly twice the poverty line). As shown in Table 2–1, 21 percent of families with a full-time, full-year worker have income below the family budget, and 47 percent of families with a less than full-time, full-year worker fall below the family budget. As expected, the rates are particularly high for African American and Hispanic families, those with less education, in younger age groups, and single-parent households.

[81] Rank (2004), pp. 58–59.　　　　[82] Boushey et al. (2001), pp. 1–70.

Table 2–2. *Proportion of persons in families with income below 200 percent of poverty and experiencing hardship by work status of family*

	Working part time	Working full time
Critical hardships		
Food insecurity		
Not enough food to eat[a]	14.30%	10.10%
Missed meals	18.8	14.6
Insufficient health care		
Did not receive necessary medical care	14.1	11.3
Housing problems		
Evicted[a]	1.1	0.9
Utilities disconnected[a]	4.6	3.9
Doubling up with friends or family	2.9	1.9
Serious hardships		
Food insecurity		
Kind of food[a]	29.8%	27.8%
Worried about having enough food	44.1	36
Insufficient health care		
Emergency room is main source of care	8.3	6.8
No health insurance coverage	43.4	35.4
Housing problems		
Unable to make housing or utility payments	29.1	23
Telephone disconnected	12.9	8.5
Inadequate child care		
Child care for self	4.7	5.5
Child not in after-school or enrichment activity	21.6	20.3
Inadequate adult-to-child ratio in child care facility	6.4	

[a] Data on these variables from Survey of Income and Program Participation. For the other variables, data from National Survey of Americas Families.
Source: H. Boushey et al. (2001). *Hardship in America: The Real Story of Working Families.* Washington D.C.: Economic Policy Institute, Table 11.

These families also experience critical and serious hardships even at 200 percent of the poverty threshold. As shown in Table 2–2, 14 percent of families with a part-time worker and 10 percent of families with a full-time worker experience critical food hardship. More commonly, despite working, a significant proportion of these families experience serious hardships such as worries about having enough food, lack of health insurance, and inability to make housing or utility payments.

Poverty, Race, and Ethnicity
Poverty has been persistently high for African American and Hispanics as compared with whites. Whereas the poverty rate for African Americans declined rapidly from 1959 to 1972, it remained fairly stable from 1972 to 1995, at about

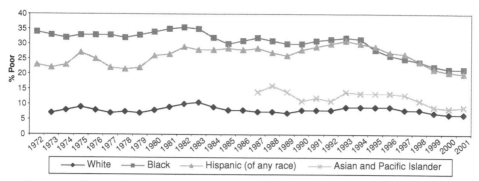

Figure 2–4. Poverty Rates by Ethnicity: 1972–2001. *Source*: U.S. Census Bureau, Historical Poverty Tables.

30 percent compared with 9 percent for whites and then declined somewhat from 1995 to 2001. It remains more than double that of whites (see Figure 2–4). Similarly, the poverty rate for Hispanics hovered between 20 percent and 30 percent from 1972 to 2001. Only Asian and Pacific Islanders have shown a persistent decline in poverty, catching up with that of whites, although as is shown, pockets of high poverty are evident among specific groups.

Different dynamics explain levels of poverty for African Americans and Hispanics. The former, especially males, experience poverty largely because of exclusion from the labor market, the latter mostly because of low wages. In general, the employment situation for less-educated young men (aged 18–24) who are not in school is particularly dire. Approximately 20 percent were not employed, even during the peak years of the past three business cycles (1979, 1989, and 1999). In 1999, at the height of one of the longest economic expansions, 22 percent were not employed, which was higher than the unemployment rate in 1979. Real average wages (adjusted for inflation) have declined 17 percent over the past two decades, from $10.47 per hour to $8.68.[83]

From the 1970s on, as shown in Figure 2–5, adult male unemployment for whites has hovered between 3 percent and 8 percent. In contrast, the unemployment rate for African American males has been at least twice as high, fluctuating from a low of 6 percent to a high of 18 percent. The unemployment rate for Hispanic males has been somewhat in between, and the gap between them and white males has been reduced in recent years.

Another way to appreciate the risk of unemployment and hence poverty for ethnic minorities is to look at the length of their unemployment spells.[84]

[83] E. Richer et al. (2003). *Boom Times a Bust: Declining Employment among Less-Educated Young Men.* Washington, D.C.: Center for Law and Social Policy, p. 3.

[84] A. O. Gottschalck (2003). *Dynamics of Economic Well-Being: Spells of Unemployment, 1996–1999.* Current Population Reports, P70–93. Washington D.C.: U.S. Census Bureau, pp. 1–5.

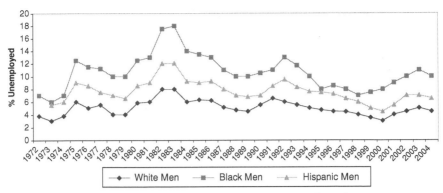

Figure 2–5. Male (20 Years Old and Older) Unemployment by Ethnicity: 1972–2004. *Source*: U.S. Bureau of Labor Statistics.

The median unemployment spell for white workers is 1.6 months. For African Americans it is 2.7 months, and for Hispanics it is 2.0 months. However, for African American males it is 3.1 months.

African American men, overall, made substantial gains through the 1970s; since then, gains have been uneven with some declines.[85] Less than half of African American men had high school diplomas. Only 12 percent had white-collar jobs, as compared with a third of white men. For a time, discrimination eased, affirmative action expanded opportunities, and the education gap narrowed, but most progress stopped in 1973 when the labor market softened. Older manufacturing plants closed, jobs in central cities declined, and the less educated left the job market. The movement of jobs to the suburbs has disproportionately affected African American men, because they are more concentrated in the urban centers than other less-educated workers.[86]

Since the early 1970s, black-white male inequality has increased. In the early 1970s, African American male college graduates had about the same percentages of managers, administrators, and earnings as white college graduates. Then, the gap widened. A thirty-year-old African American male college graduate earns 17 percent less than a comparable white male. In 1996, with unemployment at 5.6 percent, more than a fifth (22%) of African American men had no earned income, and two-thirds of this group (with no income) had dropped out of the labor market. Frank Levy calls these "startling statistics."[87]

For less-educated African American males, the decline in employment and earnings and an increase in incarceration and criminal records has been steady since the mid-1970s. In 2002, more than 190,000 African American men

[85] F. Levy (1998). *The New Dollars and Dreams: American Incomes and Economic Change*. New York: Russell Sage Foundation, p. 93.
[86] Richer et al. (2003), pp. 6–7.   [87] Levy (1998), p. 99.

(aged 18 to 24) were in prison, as compared with 120,000 non-Hispanic white men and 90,000 Hispanics of the same age. In the 1990s, about 3 million African American men were under some form of correctional supervision, with millions more currently or recently on probation, all of which limits their ability get jobs.[88] In a recent survey of employers, more than 60 percent said that they would probably not hire a person with a criminal record and would be more willing to hire any other stigmatized group (e.g., welfare recipients, GEDs, long-term unemployed) than ex-offenders. The negative effects of an ex-offender status reinforce assumptions about African American men. The same study argues that the increase of the incarceration rate for African American men of 5 percent over the past twenty years accounts for a 7 percent drop in labor-market participation.[89]

The decline in the employment rates of young, less-educated African American men (16–24) has continued. Even though the wages of this group did rise during the economic boom of the 1990s, it was not sufficient to offset the long decline.[90] According to Harry Holzer and his colleagues, during the 1990s, the employment rates among white and Hispanic young men stabilized, whereas the declines experienced by young African American men were greater and continued during the 1990s. They attribute much of the gap to both the incarceration rate among young African American men and child-support orders rather than the usual explanations, such as decline of industrial jobs and immigrant labor. Both incarceration and child-support enforcement not only grew dramatically in the 1980s and 1990s but were disproportionately concentrated among this group. Among young African American men, the incarceration rate was 12 percent, and among those who are not currently incarcerated, they estimate that "22 percent of all black men have been previously incarcerated – which suggests that, among the younger cohorts, the rates might reach 30 percent or more."[91] In addition, the growing enforcement of child-support orders "constitute a large tax on the earnings of low-income fathers,"[92] discussed more fully in Chapter 7. Currently, they range from 20 percent to 35 percent of the income for low-income noncustodial fathers. "When combined with payroll taxes and phase-out ranges for food stamp benefits, the marginal tax rates on these men are often as high as 60–80 percent." In addition, if payments are lagging, the state will garnish up to 65 percent of the take-home pay.[93] They argue that past incarceration and child support "can account for most of the declines over time in the labor force activity for this age group."[94]

---

[88] Richer et al. (2003), p. 8.   [89] Ibid., p. 9.
[90] H. Holzer, P. Offner, & E. Sorensen (2004). "Declining Employment among Young Black Less-Educated Men: The Role of Incarceration and Child Support. Institute for Research on Poverty" (discussion paper no. 1281-04, University of Wisconsin, Madison, May, p. 1.
[91] Ibid., p. 7.   [92] Ibid., p. 9.
[93] Ibid., p. 9.   [94] Ibid., p. 29.

In contrast to the experience of lower-skilled African Americans, the risk of poverty for Hispanic men is due to a large extent to very low wages. Hispanics have little difficulty in getting low-wage employment, primarily through networks and ethnic niches.[95] Whereas African American men with a high school degree are less likely than their white counterparts to find employment, immigrant Mexican men with a high school degree find jobs similar to, if not better than, their white counterparts, and Mexican immigrant men who are the least skilled find employment at rates comparable to college-educated African American men. However, Mexican immigrant men cannot find good jobs. Those without a high school degree are severely disadvantaged in the labor market in terms of earnings. More time in the United States does improve earnings somewhat but not significantly.[96] For both Mexican-origin men and women born in the United States, wages are about 20 percent higher than for those born in Mexico, but after the second generation, progress seems to stop. Immigrant earnings are still considerably below the earnings of natives, even after living in the United States for two or three decades. Undocumented Mexicans are a significant factor in lowering the wages of the Mexican born, but even the earnings of native-born Mexican men with a high school education are not on a par with non-Hispanic white men.[97] Less-educated Hispanic men have great difficulty moving up into higher paying jobs.[98]

The downward pressure on wages has affected all of the less-educated workers. Two-thirds of Hispanic men work in blue-collar and service jobs (vs. 47% of white men), and 45 percent of Hispanic women are similarly employed. On average, the hourly wages of Mexican-born men was about 40 percent lower than non-Hispanic white men, which is wider than the gap with African American men (25.9% of non-Hispanic white men's earnings).[99] Native-born Mexicans earn more but still at substantially lower wages than their white counterparts.[100]

Being an immigrant increases the risk of poverty. In 1970, immigrants earned about 17 percent less than natives; by 1990, more recent immigrants (arrived within the previous five years) earned almost a third less. By 1990, a quarter of immigrant households lived in poverty, up from 18.8 percent in 1970.[101] Almost all immigrant groups have difficulties in obtaining decent employment – Dominicans, West Indians, Puerto Ricans, Salvadorans,

[95] R. Waldinger (2001b). "Up from Poverty? 'Race,' Immigration, and the Fate of Low-Skilled Workers." In R. Waldinger (Ed.), Strangers at the Gates: New Immigrants in Urban America (Chap. 3). Berkeley: University of California Press, p. 85.
[96] Waldinger (2001b), pp. 92–97.
[97] F. D. Bean & G. Stevens (2003). America's Newcomers and the Dynamics of Diversity. New York: Russell Sage Foundation, p. 141.
[98] Ibid., p. 117; Waldinger (2001b), pp. 80–116, 84–85.
[99] Bean & Stevens (2003), p. 133.   [100] Ibid., p. 121.
[101] W. Clark (2001). "The Geography of Immigrant Poverty: Selective Evidence of an Immigrant Underclass." In R. Waldinger (Ed.), Strangers at the Gates: New Immigrants in Urban America (Chap. 5). Berkeley: University of California Press, pp. 159–85, 160.

Filipinos, and Cubans (contrary to myth).[102] As a group, immigrants have diverse skills and many are professionals. However, a disproportionate number have the lowest level of education and extensive poverty.[103] From the 1980s, the decline in the relative earnings of immigrants has been attributable to large numbers of low-educated immigrants, especially from Mexico and Central America. At present, the foreign born account for an overwhelming number of the least-skilled urban workers.[104]

Today, much of the increase in poverty in inner-city and metropolitan areas is due to an influx of low-skilled immigrants – for example, immigrants make up about a fifth of the growth in poverty in Los Angeles. The poor are increasingly concentrated and isolated, especially in entry-point cities – Hispanics in Los Angeles, Houston, New York, Phoenix, Sacramento, but also in Denver, Kansas City, and Minneapolis; the Hmong in Milwaukee and the Twin Cities; and the Somalis in Minneapolis. The poverty population in most coastal entry-point cities is 25 percent or more foreign born, reflecting primarily the recent, large influx of very low-skilled Mexican and Central American immigrants.[105] The significant influx of very low-skilled immigrants with high fertility rates can potentially create a dependent, economically segregated path for their children, which contrasts to the experience of earlier immigrants.[106] There is substantial evidence that low family income affects school achievement and other outcomes in child development. The serious effects will increase with the changes in welfare – for example, restricting food stamps is bound to increase hunger and food insecurity and consequent poor school performance and health outcomes.[107] Thus, not only has poverty increased for recent immigrants but concentrated poverty and social exclusion can have serious, dramatic effects on their children. Therefore, the prior experience of immigrant children converging with natives may no longer be applicable with the more recent, low-skilled immigrants.[108]

As reported by Ong and Miller, despite the myth of Asian and Pacific Island immigrants as the "model minority," their poverty rate is still higher than whites – 10.2 percent, as compared with 7.8 percent of non-Hispanic whites.[109] Although there is a sizeable group of highly educated professionals, large groups of mostly recent immigrants are concentrated in linguistically isolated neighborhoods, with low-skill work, overcrowded housing, and low

---

[102] Bean & Stevens (2003), p. 130; Waldinger (2001b).

[103] Clark (2001), pp. 159–60.   [104] Waldinger (2001b), p. 81.

[105] Clark (2001), p. 166.   [106] Ibid., p. 161.

[107] Ibid., p. 183.   [108] Ibid., p. 163.

[109] U.S. Census Bureau (2002). "Poverty in the United States." Retrieved from http://www.census.gov/prod/2003pubs/p60-222.pdf, Table 1, p. 3; P. M. Ong & D. Miller (2002). *Economic Needs of Asian Americans and Pacific Islanders in Distressed Areas: Establishing Baseline Information*. Los Angeles: Lewis Center for Regional Policy Studies, University of California Los Angeles.

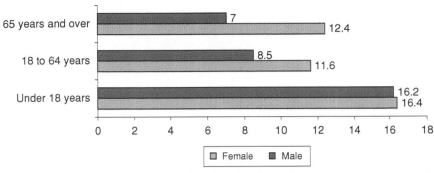

Figure 2–6. Poverty Rates of the Population by Gender and Age (Percentage in Poverty).
Source: U.S. Census Bureau, Current Population Survey (2002).

incomes.[110] A recent study of seventeen poor Asian and Pacific Island neigh-borhoods across the United States ranging in size, degrees of concentration, and employment opportunities found that most neighborhoods were primar-ily immigrant and linguistically isolated, had low educational attainment, low skills, language deficits, low earnings, underemployment rather than jobless-ness, lack of affordable housing, overcrowding, and lack of adequate health care.[111] In only one area out of seventeen did the high school graduation rate match the national average; in all others, the number of those who did not complete high school was two to three times the national average.[112]

Asian entrepreneurship is higher than in other groups, but most are marginal businesses offering low-wage jobs.[113] Only two neighborhoods had a number of private jobs equal to the national average (excluding possible infor-mal jobs); in most neighborhoods, the available jobs were considerably below the national average. The jobs were basically at the low end, in restaurants, small retail, or the garment industry.[114] Most commute out of their immediate neighborhood to find work; nevertheless, the average neighborhood wage was considerably lower than the regional average wage. All Asian neighborhoods had poverty rates significantly higher than the national average, and in six neighborhoods, the poverty rate was at least three times higher.[115]

Poverty, Gender, and Single Parenthood
Women are more likely to be poor than men. As shown in Figure 2–6 for 2001, in each age group, but especially adulthood, the rate of poverty is higher for females. Several factors are cited for this gap. First, caregiving and parenthood lower women's earnings. Having children penalizes women's wages by about

---

[110] Ong & Miller (2002).
[112] Ibid., p. 11.
[114] Ibid., p. 17.

[111] Ibid., p. 1.
[113] Ibid., p. 4.
[115] Ibid., pp. 13, 18.

7 percent per child.[116] Although some of the penalty is due to previous part-time employment and fewer years of experience, much of it remains after controlling for such factors.

Second, and related, gender discrimination continues to play a large role in the difference in earnings between men and women. According to the U.S. General Accounting Office, for the period 1983–2000, approximately 45 percent of the earnings gap between men and women could be accounted for by differences in human capital, occupation, unionization, and hours of work, which suggests that the remainder is due to discrimination.[117] According to the Institute for Women's Policy Research, although women have made significant progress in earnings vis-à-vis men, "at the rate of progress achieved between 1989 and 2002, women would not achieve wage parity for more than 50 years."[118] Gender is also coupled with ethnic discrimination. The median annual earnings of women in 2002 was $30,100 (for full-time, year-round employment), which was only 76.2 percent of the median annual earnings of men.[119] The earnings ratio between Asian American women and men (1999) was 75 percent, white women 70 percent, African American women 62.5 percent, and Hispanic women 52.5 percent.[120] Women are more likely to be concentrated in caregiving occupations (e.g., teaching, health services) that pay lower wages than other occupations even after controlling for education and experience.[121]

Although African American women have made considerable progress in educational attainment (more quickly than white women) and in increasingly diverse and higher-earning jobs, they still earn less than white women and are much more likely to be poor.[122] The poverty rate of African American women, especially single mothers, is among the highest. They are targets of discrimination and residential and occupational segregation, and they lack access to higher education (despite recent gains) and health care.[123]

Hispanic women experience a high rate of unemployment, especially women with children. The employment rate for non-Hispanic white women is 78 percent, for African American women 75 percent, and for Mexican-origin women 61.6 percent.[124] Hispanic women earn less than women in any other racial and ethnic group, are less likely to be employed in white-collar jobs, and more likely to be poor.[125] There are differences among Hispanic women.

[116] M. J. Budig & P. England (2001). "The Wage Penalty for Motherhood." *American Sociological Review* 66(2): 204–225.
[117] A. Caiazza, A. Shaw, & M. Werschkul (2004). *Women's Economic Status in the States: Wide Disparities by Race, Ethnicity, and Region.* Washington, D.C.: Institute for Women's Policy Research, p. 10.
[118] Ibid., p. 4.   [119] Ibid., p. 1.
[120] Ibid., p. 2.
[121] P. England, M. J. Budig, & N. Folbre (2002). "Wages of Virtue: The Relative Pay of Care Work." *Social Problems* 49(4): 455–473.
[122] Caiazza, Shaw, & Werschkul (2004), p. 20.   [123] Ibid., p. 21.
[124] Bean & Stevens (2003), p. 138.   [125] Caiazza, Shaw, & Werschkul (2004), p. 29.

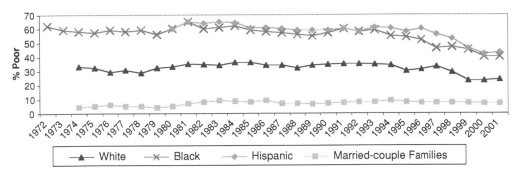

Figure 2–7. Poverty Rates for Female Householders by Ethnicity: 1972–2001. *Source*: U.S. Census Bureau, Historical Poverty Tables.

Cuban women are most likely not to be poor. In 1999, they earned $28,700 (full-time, year-round work), as compared with $22,100 for Mexican women and $19,900 for Central American women. Puerto Rican women had the highest poverty rate – 26.4 percent, as compared with 15.5 percent for Cuban women.[126]

Unemployment for Hispanic women is caused by labor-market gender discrimination, community and cultural expectations of gender roles, and, because of the low wages, disincentives to pay for child care. In addition to discrimination, Hispanic women, in general, have significantly lower levels of education. In 2002, 26.3 percent of Hispanic women had less than a ninth-grade education as compared with 3.8 percent of white women. Only 11.2 percent of Hispanic women have a college degree, as compared with 27.3 percent of white women.[127] Also immigration status varies. Most Hispanics are immigrants. Hispanic women born outside of the United States have earnings of $19,900, as compared with $26,500 for those born in the United States.[128] Because of the combination of low female employment rates and the low level of male wages, for the less-skilled Hispanic immigrants, even two-parent families have great difficulty escaping poverty through two earners.[129]

Third, and most important, single motherhood is a major cause of poverty for women. As shown in Figure 2–7, from 1972 to 2001, although the poverty rate for all married-couple families hovered between 6 and 10 percent, the poverty rate for single-mother families was considerably higher and varied by ethnicity. For white single mothers, the poverty rate ranged from a high of 35 percent in the 1970s and 1980s to a low of 25 percent in recent years. For African Americans, the respective rates were 63 percent and 41 percent and for Hispanic single mothers, they were 64 percent and 43 percent.

In other words, the feminization of poverty has occurred in part because of changes in family composition. The changes have been dramatic. In 1970, 42 percent of all families were headed by two parents; by 1990 that was down

[126] Ibid., p. 29.   [127] Ibid., p. 30.
[128] Ibid., p. 30.   [129] Waldinger (2001b), pp. 83, 101–4.

to 16 percent.[130] At present, only about a quarter of the households consist of a married couple with children.[131] There was a significant increase in cohabitation, which Cancian and Reed think perhaps accounts for a greater part of marriage decline among younger people.[132]

Poor single-parent households face considerable material hardship. Twenty-five percent are likely to experience food insecurity, and 28 percent lost their utilities for failure to pay their bills. They were also more likely to live in unsafe housing. Twenty percent of such families had pest problems.[133] Children who live in single-mother households are at high risk of experiencing poverty. In 2003, 53 percent of all children under age 6 living in single-mother households were poor, as compared to 10 percent of children in married-couple families.[134] The rate of extreme poverty (less than one-third of median family income) of such families is higher than the overall poverty rate for such families in other affluent countries.[135] And yet, the major reason for high poverty among single-mother families in the United States as compared with these countries is its income support policy, not demographics or labor supply variations.[136] In other words, if these single-mother families, with the same demographic characteristics, were living in Sweden, for example, their relative poverty would decline from 50 percent to less than 10 percent, mostly because of Sweden's income transfer policy.[137]

Child Poverty

Among the affluent countries, the United States has the dubious distinction of having the highest child poverty rate. Measuring poverty as half the median,

---

[130] M. Cancian & D. Reed (2001). "Changes in Family Structure: Implications for Poverty and Related Policy." In S. Danziger & R. H. Haveman (Eds.), *Understanding Poverty*. New York: Russell Sage Foundation; Cambridge, Mass.: Harvard University Press, p. 72. Although there were declines in marriage among all subgroups, there were differences: between 1970 and 1999, the white percentage declined from 85 percent to 72 percent, the African American from 61 percent to 44 percent, and Hispanics from 78 percent to 67 percent, American Indians from 76 percent to 58 percent. There were no changes with Asian Pacific Americans (80%).

[131] M. B. Katz (2001). *The Price of Citizenship: Redefining America's Welfare State* (1st ed.). New York: Metropolitan Books, p. 43.

[132] Cancian & Reed (2001), pp. 72–74. Federal, state, and local income taxes, as well as 7.65 percent for payroll taxes, were calculated in the basic family budget (p. 39).

[133] T. Ouellette et al. (2004). *Measures of Material Hardship: Final Report*. Washington, D.C.: U.S. Department of Health and Human Services, Office of the Assistant Secretary for Planning and Evaluation.

[134] C. DeNavas-Walt, B. D. Proctor, & R. J. Mills (2004). *Income, Poverty, and Health Insurance Coverage in the United States: 2003*. Current Population Reports P60–226. Washington, D.C.: U.S. Census Bureau, p. 11.

[135] Rainwater & Smeeding (2003), p. 112.

[136] Ibid., pp. 115–17. See also L. M. Casper, S. S. McLanahan, & I. Garfinkel (1994). "The Gender-Poverty Gap: What We Can Learn from Other Countries." *American Sociological Review* 59(4): 594–605.

[137] Rainwater & Smeeding (2003), p. 116.

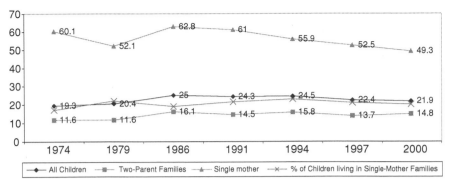

Figure 2–8. Relative Poverty of Children by Family Type: 1974–2000. *Source*: 2000 Luxenbourg Income Study.

Rainwater and Smeeding show that the United States has the highest rate (20.3%) followed by Italy (19.5%), whereas Sweden has the lowest rate (2.4%).[138] Moreover, the probability that children in marginal income families (two-thirds of the median) will experience extreme poverty is 9.4 percent in the United States compared with 0.7 percent in Sweden.[139]

Indeed, the relative poverty of children (50% of the median family income) in the United States has remained exceptionally high for the past three decades, particularly if they live in single-parent households. As shown in Figure 2–8, the relative poverty for all children, starting at 19.3 percent in 1974, increased between 1979 and 1986, reaching a peak of 25 percent and then slowly decreasing to 22 percent in 2000. For children in two-parent families, the rate was 11.6 percent in 1974, reached a high of 16% in 1986, and then remained stable at 14.8 percent in 2000. For children in single-mother families, the rate was 60 percent in 1974. It declined to a low of 52 percent in 1979, despite the increase in the percentage of children living in such families, and then declined gradually to 49 percent in 2000, whereas the percentage of children living in such families increased slightly in the 1990s.

Echoing the same pattern we have seen with relative poverty, the overall child poverty, based on the official poverty thresholds, declined from a high of 26.5 percent in 1960 to a low of 13.5 percent in 1969. It then gradually increased to 21 percent in 1984 and then began to decline slowly to 17.6 percent (12.9 million) in 2003, but up from 16.7 percent (12.1 million) in 2002.[140] Although the poverty rate for white children hovers around 10 percent, for African American children the poverty rate ranged from a high of 46 percent in 1992 to a low of 30 percent in 2001. For Hispanic children, the pattern

[138] Rainwater & Smeeding (2003), p. 21.   [139] Ibid., p. 35.
[140] U.S. Census Bureau (2004). "Income, Poverty, and Health Insurance Coverage in the United States: 2003."U.S. Department of Commerce. Retrieved from http://www.census.gov/prod/2004pubs/p60–226.pdf, p. 11.

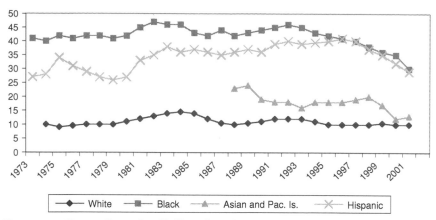

Figure 2–9. Poverty Rates for Children by Ethnicity: 1973–2001. *Source*: U.S. Census
Bureau, Historical Poverty Data.

generally parallels that of African American children, whereas for Asian and
Pacific Island children the poverty rate started at a high of 23 percent in 1988
and declined to 11 percent in 2001 (see Figure 2–9).

According to the National Center for Children in Poverty,[141] in 2003, 38 percent of all children (27 million) lived in low-income (below twice the poverty
threshold) families, and 17 percent (more than 11 million) lived in families
below the poverty threshold. Moreover, 62 percent of all Hispanic children
and 60 percent of all African American children live in low-income families,
as compared with 26 percent of white children. Fifty percent of low-income
children live in two-parent households. Very young children (from birth to
age 2) have the highest risk of living in impoverished families (43% in low-
income families and 21% in poor families). Low-income families experience
considerable hardships. The Early Childhood Longitudinal Study (kindergarten cohort) shows that 12 percent of children living in such families do
not have health insurance, 17 percent did not receive dental care, 13 percent
moved three or more times in the child's life, and 10 percent did not have sufficient food in the last year. These hardships are obviously worse for families
below the official poverty threshold.[142]

The Children's Defense Fund[143] estimates that the majority of poor children fall into extreme poverty (50% below the poverty threshold). Indeed, the

[141] National Center for Children in Poverty (NCCP) (2005). "Basic Facts on Low-Income Children
in the United States" (February).

[142] E. Gershoff (2003). *Low Income and Hardship among America's Kindergartners*. New York: National
Center for Children in Poverty.

[143] Children's Defense Fund (n.d.). *Census 2000: Child Poverty Data for States, Counties,
and Large Cities*. Retrieved from http://www.childrensdefense.org/familyincome/childpoverty/
census2000/childpovertydata.asp.

number of children in extreme poverty is rising almost twice as fast as the overall rate. Moreover, 70 percent of all poor children live in families where someone works full or part time. Although the NAS measure of poverty shows a somewhat lower level of poverty, when counting near-money benefits, it still remains high compared with other age groups.[144]

Although child poverty is widespread, it is mostly temporary. Corcoran looked at a sample of children, aged 1–4, in 1968, and followed them for fifteen years.[145] A third were poor for about one year; two-thirds for less than five years. However, 5 percent of all the children and 15 percent of poor children were poor for ten years or more. Less than 1 percent of white children were poor for ten or more years as compared with almost a third (29%) of African American children. Almost 90 percent of the long-term poor children were African American. Other characteristics of children who were poor for longer than the average lived in single-parent families for their entire childhood, had parents who were disabled, and lived in the South.[146]

According to Corcoran, the situation is particularly alarming for African American children. Almost 30 percent of African American children will be poor ten of their first fifteen years versus less than 1 in 100 white children. About a third of African American poor children will still be poor when they are in their mid-twenties compared with 1 in 14 white children. And almost 3 out of 4 African Americans, aged 22 to 38, in the bottom quintile in 1968, were still in that quintile twenty years later as compared with 1 out of 2 whites.[147]

One of the major factors leading to the rise in child poverty is the increase in single-parent households. The rate of children born outside of marriage rose from 5 percent in 1960 to 33 percent in 1997.[148] By 1990, a quarter of all families were single mothers. Almost 40 percent had never been married. This included 21 percent of white mothers, 37 percent Hispanics, and 56 percent African Americans. In extreme poverty areas, nearly three-quarters of single mothers had not married (although only a third of these families were on welfare).[149] However, the increase in the percentage of out-of-wedlock children was not due to the increase in fertility of unmarried women but rather the sharp decline in the fertility of married women.[150] Now, the mothers of one-third of all children are unmarried, and one-half of all children will spend at least some time growing up with one parent.[151] African American and Hispanic children are much more likely to be in single-mother families than Asian American or white children – almost half (49.7%) of African American children and 21.7 percent of Hispanic children as compared with 15.5 percent

[144] J. Iceland et al. (2001). "Are Children Worse Off? Evaluating Well-Being Using a New (and Improved) Measure of Poverty." *Journal of Human Resources* 36(2): 398–412.
[145] Corcoran (2001), p. 130–31.   [146] Ibid.
[147] Ibid., p. 156.   [148] Cancian & Reed (2001), p. 74.
[149] Katz (2001), pp. 42–43.   [150] Cancian & Reed (2001), pp. 74–77.
[151] Ibid., p. 71.

of white children and 10.1 percent of Asian American children.[152] According to the Institute for Women's Policy Research, the high poverty rates are due to lower wages, racial discrimination, occupation and education segregation, lack of adequate social supports, and higher unemployment. They are less likely to be married, and if married, the husbands are low-income earners.

What is the impact of poverty on children's futures? According to Arloc Sherman, "America's poor children walk a gauntlet of troubles that start at birth and whose consequences often follow them throughout their adult lives."[153] Even at income twice the poverty threshold, children experience cognitive and developmental difficulties compared with children with higher income. They score considerably lower in reading, math, and general knowledge test scores, and they are more likely to be overweight.[154]

Poor children achieve 1.4 fewer years of schooling than nonpoor children; they are more than three times more likely not to graduate high school, more than twice as likely to be a teen mother, and 2.6 times more likely to have an out-of-wedlock birth. Poor boys work less at lower hourly wages, have lower annual earnings, and are out of work more than nonpoor boys. Poor children as adults have higher poverty rates (24% vs. 4%) and lower incomes ($21,514 vs. $36,603) than nonpoor children.[155] Corcoran found that "poor children are twice as likely to be in fair or poor health, to die in infancy, to be hospitalized in the past year, to have a learning disability or cognitive deficit, to have repeated a grade or expelled from school."[156] Even after controlling for family and neighborhood background disadvantages, Corcoran showed that children raised in long-term poverty have lower wages, working hours, earnings, and family incomes. Conversely, increasing parental incomes from $15,000 to $30,000 increases men's annual incomes 26 percent and women's 21 percent.[157] When parental education, family structure, and race and ethnicity are controlled, growing up poor has only modest effects on cognitive deficits, years of schooling, teen births, and nonmarital births.[158]

Children from welfare families have fewer years of schooling, are more likely to drop out, more likely to have teen births, and more likely to receive welfare themselves, but again, the effects are modest when adjusting for family background and neighborhood characteristics.[159] Controlling for income significantly reduces but does not eliminate the negative effects of growing up in a single-parent household; these children have less access to parental resources, both economic and noneconomic, as well as neighborhood resources.[160]

[152] Caiazza, Shaw, & Werschkul (2004), p. 27, citing Urban Institute (2004b) data.
[153] A. Sherman, (1997). *Poverty Matters: The Cost of Child Poverty in America*. Washington, D.C.: Children's Defense Fund, p. 5.
[154] Gershoff (2003).   [155] Corcoran (2001), pp. 140–43.
[156] Ibid., pp. 142–44.   [157] Ibid., p. 144.
[158] Ibid., p. 146.   [159] Ibid., p. 146.
[160] Ibid., p. 154.

Being a teen parent does not affect earnings by the time the mothers are in their late twenties.[161] However, a nonmarital birth for women age 20 and older substantially reduced the mother's future income.[162] Children of mothers under age 18 are at a higher risk of dropping out, having a child before age 18, and being without work as a young adult (boys) than children born to mothers between ages 20 and 21.[163]

Finally, Sherman points to the societal costs of child poverty. "Schools pay for remedial education for poor children, businesses pay for poorly educated and trained workers, consumers pay for lower product and service quality, hospitals and social services pay for the added mental and physical disabilities; citizens pay when poor children grow up to become violent, and ultimately everyone pays for all these losses."[164] Sherman estimates that for every year that children continue to live in poverty, society loses $130 billion in future economic output over the lifetime of the children. Ending a year of poverty will save society $26 billion.[165]

Why Is Poverty Persistently High?

As noted by Sheldon Danziger and Peter Gottschalk, "in the 40 years since the War on Poverty, progress against poverty has been very slow. The poverty rate remains high for many segments of the population – in particular, children (especially those who do not live with both parents); racial and ethnic minorities; and workers who have completed no more than high school education."[166] The authors note that the elderly are the only exception. Their poverty declined dramatically because of improvements in Social Security benefits.

Several major factors have been suggested for the persistence of high poverty: (1) patterns of economic growth and decline; (2) the changing labor market; (3) social inequality; (4) changing demographics, especially the rise of single-parent household; and (5) social policy.[167]

Looking at the historical trend in poverty from the end of World War II (see Figure 2–10) three major periods can be identified: 1949–1969, 1969–1990, and 1990–1999.

During the 1950s and 1960s, real income grew rapidly, especially for the families at the bottom fifth of the income distribution. Median family income grew from $19,500 to $26,800, and the poverty rate dropped from 32 percent to 22 percent.[168] There was a rapid growth in productivity. Between 1947 and 1966, output per worker increased by nearly 3.5 percent, which Frank Levy calls

---

[161] Ibid., p. 155.   [162] Ibid., p. 156.
[163] Ibid., p. 155.   [164] Sherman (1997), p. 14.
[165] Ibid., p. 15.   [166] Danziger & Gottschalk (2004), p. 3.
[167] See, for example, S. Danziger & P. Gottschalk (1995). *America Unequal*. Cambridge, Mass.: Harvard University Press; and Iceland (2003c).
[168] Levy (1998), p. 26.

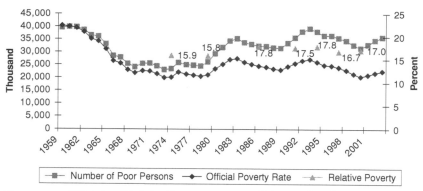

Figure 2–10. Official and Relative Poverty: 1959–2003 (Thousands and Percentage). *Source:* U.S. Census Bureau, Historical Poverty Data, LIS Relative Poverty Rates.

"remarkable." Farm labor declined, and manufacturing jobs increased. Jobs were lost in the central cities, but people could find new jobs. Levy calls this period "skill neutral." Average wages and living standards improved.[169] The entire income distribution moved up, and inequality declined somewhat.[170] During this period, economic growth benefitted almost everyone.[171] During and after the War on Poverty, government spending on social welfare (e.g., Medicare, Medicaid, Social Security, and AFDC) expanded considerably, from "11.0% to 18.2% of the gross domestic product (GDP) between 1965 and 1972."[172] Even though the number of female-headed families increased, their rate of poverty decreased. The poverty rate declined from 22.4 percent in 1959 to 11.1 percent in 1972.

The economy changed after 1972, triggered by the oil shock of 1973. Productivity slowed, both in manufacturing and services, falling to 1 percent, as compared with 2.3 percent in the 1950s and 3.3 percent in the 1960s.[173] Inflation increased to 12 percent and unemployment to 5.6 percent. Real family income fell from a postwar high of $40,400 in 1973 to $38,600 by 1975, which was only slightly above the 1969 level. The poverty rate began to inch upward. By the 1976 recovery, real wages had stagnated. Unemployment began to decline, but so did the wages for the semiskilled.[174] With the second oil shock (1979–80), inflation exceeded 11 percent and unemployment 7.5 percent.[175] As a consequence of Reagan's tight money policy, a deep recession ensued with unemployment above 9 percent. Large tax cuts produced large deficits. From 1978 to 1983, the poverty rate climbed by 3.8 percent. By 1982,

[169] Ibid., pp. 27–29.   [170] Ibid., p. 38.
[171] C. Jencks (2004). "The Low-Wage Puzzle: Why Is America Generating So Many Bad Jobs – And How Can We Create More Good Jobs? *The American Prospect* (January): 35–37.
[172] Danziger & Gottschalk (2004), p. 6.   [173] Levy (1998), p. 38.
[174] Ibid., pp. 180–81.   [175] Ibid., p. 46.

inflation declined to 3.8 percent, but interest rates remained high. Manufacturing jobs were cut and reorganized, eliminating blue-collar jobs and increasing the demand for highly skilled workers. The economy began to pick up in 1982, and unemployment declined. Yet, there was a blue-collar recession, and the poverty rate for families increased to 12.3 percent in 1983. By 1989, median family income rose slightly to $43,600, only $1,400 higher than a decade ago.[176] Productivity increased in the 1980s but not in the large service sector. Wage growth remained weak, and wage inequality increased. By 1985, the gap between college and high school earnings widened dramatically.[177] Yet, the median male earnings remained essentially stagnant throughout the period.[178] Moreover, in the 1980s, income inequality increased rapidly. The ratio between the ninetieth percentile and the tenth percentile increased by 21 percent to 9.1.[179] As noted by Danziger and Gottschalk, "the 1980s stand out as the beginning of an era of increased inequality in the United States that continues to the present."[180] This is also reflected in the rise of relative poverty, which increased from 15.8 percent in 1979 to 17.8 percent in 1986.

Unemployment began to decline in 1994. Wages grew slowly, productivity was weak, and inflation and unemployment were very low. In 1996, median family income was $43,200, about the same as in 1986 and below 1989.[181] The EITC was expanded to become a major antipoverty program, reaching more than $23 billion per year. The trends of the previous two decades were reversed. The bottom wages began to rise more rapidly than the average wage gains. By 1998, unemployment was 4.3%, the lowest since the 1960s, and with no sign of inflation. But inequality continued to widen. The top 5 percent accounted for 15.6 percent of income in 1969, 17.9 percent in 1989, and 20.3 percent in 1996.[182] As a result, the relative poverty rate remained high despite the decline in the official rate.

Summarizing the trends, the U.S. Commerce Department reported that although the output of consumer goods per week rose 58 percent between 1973 and 2001, the mean weekly earnings of nonsupervisory workers rose only 3 percent. According to the Economic Policy Institute, the median worker's real hourly wages rose only 7 percent during this period. For men without a college degree, real wages have actually fallen since 1973.[183]

According to the Congressional Budget Office, mean household income (including capital gains and noncash benefits, e.g., food stamps, and subtracting taxes) rose 40 percent between 1979 and 2000. A third of the gain went to 1 percent of the income distribution, and another third went to the next 19 percent. The median household income of the bottom fifth rose only 9 percent,

[176] Ibid., p. 48.   [177] Ibid., p. 49.
[178] Danziger & Gottschalk (2004), p. 8.   [179] Ibid.
[180] Ibid.   [181] Levy (1998), p. 55.
[182] Ibid., p. 3.   [183] Jencks (2004), p. 35.

and almost all of this gain occurred between 1994 and 2000. Thus, Christopher Jencks concludes, "growth alone is no longer sufficient for improving those in the bottom half."[184]

The economic boom in the second half of the 1990s did have a substantial effect on poverty. With unemployment between 4 and 5 percent, the real wages of the bottom decile rose by about 10 percent. The median earnings of men aged 16–24 increased by 8 percent, reversing the steady decline since the 1980s. The wages of African Americans rose even more; however, their wages were still below the level in the 1970s and only stopped the increase in inequality.[185] There was a significant drop in poverty rates: for individuals, 3 percent; for families, 2.6 percent; for African American individuals, 9.2 percent; for African American families, 8.6 percent; for Hispanic individuals, 8.6 percent; and for Hispanic families, 6.5 percent. The drop in poverty was especially significant for female-headed families, 11.4 percent. According to Richard Freeman, declines of this magnitude were not seen since the 1960s. He concluded that only when an economic boom results in an increase in real wages, a "rising tide can substantially cut into poverty, especially among groups with the highest poverty rates."[186]

With the onset of the recession in 2001, the poverty rate began to rise again, reaching 12.5 percent in 2003. The increase was again a reflection of a weak low-wage labor market and the continued increase in inequality.[187] Although productivity continued to rise, it did not affect the unemployment rate, as earnings in the twentieth percentile hardly grew.[188] African Americans experienced the greatest increase in poverty (1.9% from 2000 to 2002) as compared with whites (1.0%) or Hispanics (1.0%). Yet, it was not due to a rise in the percent of single-parent households.[189] At the same time, dire poverty increased sharply. The percentage of the poor below half the poverty line increased by 2 percent in 2003.[190] Changes in social policy created counteracting effects on the safety net. Although the EITC is an effective antipoverty measure, its effectiveness is diminished as unemployment rises and people work fewer hours. At the same time, the decline in cash aid, especially for single mothers, further eroded the safety net.[191]

Although income growth was effective in reducing poverty from 1949 to 1969, this was no longer the case in subsequent periods,[192] primarily because of

---

[184] Ibid., p. 36.   [185] Freeman (2001), pp. 115–17.

[186] Ibid., pp. 117–18.

[187] L. Mishel, J. Bernstein, & S. Allegretto (2005). *The State of Working America 2004/2005*. Ithaca, N.Y.: ILR Press.

[188] Ibid., p. 312.

[189] According to the Census Bureau, the proportion of single-parent households has stabilized since 1995.

[190] Ibid., p. 323.   [191] Ibid., p. 340.

[192] J. Iceland (2003c). See also Danziger & Gottschalk (1995), *America Unequal*.

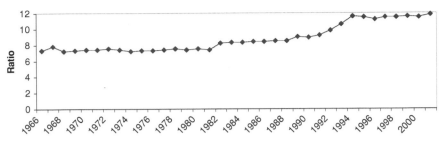

Figure 2–11. Q75/Q25 Ratio of Mean Family Income (2001 Dollars): 1966–2001. *Source:* U.S. Census Bureau, Historical Income Tables – Families.

the rise in income inequality. Indeed, from 1969 to 1990, the rise in inequality pushed the poverty rate up. It had little effect on the poverty rate from 1990 to 1999.[193] This can be seen in Figure 2–11.

The ratio of mean family income of the top income quartile to the bottom income quartile (in 2001 dollars) remained fairly stable at about 7.0 until the 1980s. From then on, it has been increasing almost every year, reaching 11.8 in 2001. As noted earlier, a chief reason for the rise in income inequality is the growing wage disparities between skilled and college-educated workers and the unskilled and less-educated workers. This trend is particularly profound among male workers. For white males, the wage premium of a college degree over a high school degree increased from about 30 percent in the 1970s to 60 percent in the 1990s. During that time, educational intensive industries dramatically increased, coupled with a steep decline in semiskilled jobs in manufacturing. As union membership declined, unions could no longer protect the semiskilled.[194] In addition, the lower end of the service sector emphasizes "soft skills," which favors women rather than less-educated men.[195] Consequently, the real wage inequality between the tenth percentile and the ninetieth percentile rose by 40 percent from 1970 to 1990.[196] Indeed, from 1975 to 1990, the real wages of male workers in the tenth percentile declined by about 30 percent and for female workers by 25 percent.[197] With the economic recovery of the mid 1990s, income inequality declined slightly, and it no longer had an effect on the poverty rate.[198]

The increase in single-parent households during the 1970s and 1980s also affected the poverty rate, but its effect has been exaggerated. To quote Iceland,

[193] Iceland (2003c), p. 510.   [194] Levy (1998), pp. 73–75.

[195] Ibid., p. 60.

[196] K. M. Murphy & F. Welch (2000). "Industrial Change and the Demand for Skill." In F. Welch (Ed.), *The Causes and Consequences of Increasing Inequality* (pp. 263–284). Chicago: University of Chicago Press.

[197] Danziger & Gottschalk (2004), p. 22.

[198] J. Iceland (2003c).

"between 1969 and 1990, the effect of changes in family structure, while moderate, was nonetheless double the effect in the 1949–69 period. Notably, from 1990 to 1999 the relationship between changes in family structure and poverty disappeared. . . . Over all the periods, the association between trends in poverty and changes in family structure tended to be the same or smaller than the association between poverty and income growth and income inequality."[199] Freeman also agrees that the changes in family composition had little effect in explaining changes in poverty. The increasing level of education of female heads over time reduces poverty as much as the increase in family heads raises it.[200] Danziger and Gottschalk arrive at a similar conclusion. The actual reduction in poverty from 1975 to 2002 was 2.3 percent. Holding all other factors constant, economic growth would have reduced it by 4.3 percent, but income inequality would have increased it by 1.8 percent. Changes in racial/ethnic composition raise the rate by 1.0 percent, while changes in family structure increase it by 1.2 percent.[201] Thus, economic factors are key determinants of the high level of poverty.

Many of the poor would not benefit from a full-employment economy because they experience major barriers to employment – disability, family care responsibilities, age, and very limited education and skills.[202] In 1999, less than half (42%) of poor individuals worked at all. Of those who did not work, 24 percent were disabled, 27 percent were retired, 23 percent had family care responsibilities, 15 percent were older than 64, 17.5 percent had only a grade-school education or less, and 23 percent were immigrants with limited skills. Thus, concludes Freeman, "close to 60 percent of all poor adults and over 50 percent of those below retirement or not students are unlikely to benefit from a booming labor market."[203]

The lack of human capital makes individuals vulnerable to poverty. Diminished human capital derives, in large part, from the structural failings of society – the shortage of good jobs, inner cities and rural communities, the lack of decent and affordable child care, the holes in the safety net, the lack of affordable housing, and so forth. Those with diminished human capital cannot compete.[204]

As we have stressed throughout, social policy also plays a role in keeping poverty high in the United States. This is quite evident from the effect of Social Security and Medicare in dramatically reducing the poverty rate among the elderly compared with children. Child poverty remains exceedingly high in the United States, not because of changes in family structure but rather because of the failure to enact social policies that provide income protection to children and their mothers.

[199] Ibid., p. 511.
[201] Danziger & Gottschalk (2004), p. 23.
[203] Ibid., p. 120.
[200] Freeman (2001), p. 103.
[202] Freeman (2001), p. 99.
[204] Rank (2004), pp. 75–76.

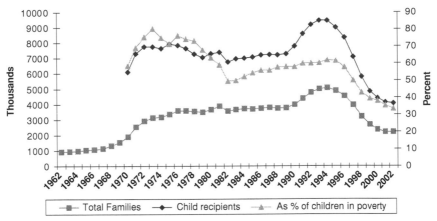

Figure 2–12. Families and Children on AFDC/TANF: 1962–2002. *Source:* U.S. Department of Health and Human Services, *Annual Report to Congress, Indicators of Welfare
Dependence* (2004).

Welfare Recipients

The pervasive misconceptions about the poor are only magnified when
applied to welfare recipients. Arguably, they are the most stigmatized among
the poor and have come to be associated with the pejorative "welfare." The
myths about welfare recipients, mostly poor single mothers and their children,
stereotype them as "welfare dependent," when in fact most stay on welfare
for a short time. They are perceived as promiscuous young women who use
welfare to have more children, when in fact their fertility rates are lower than
for all women in the same age categories. They are vilified for using welfare
to avoid work, when in fact many are working while on aid and most leave
welfare because they become employed. Still, many face many barriers to
employment. Welfare "generosity" is blamed for attracting and keeping single mothers on welfare. In fact, cash aid has declined in real dollars. Most
important, the image of welfare recipients is of mostly young, uneducated
African American women, when in fact there are considerable demographic
variations among welfare recipients.

Historical Trends
Historically, trends in the number of families on welfare reflect the combined
changes in family structure, conditions of the economy, and welfare policy.
As shown in Figure 2–12, there was a rapid expansion of welfare in the 1960s. It
reflected the combination of urban disorders, growing liberalism (e.g., the passage of the Civil Rights Act), grassroots mobilization and legal advocacy, and
the removal of several welfare exclusionary practices.[205] Welfare continued to

[205] J. F. Handler & Y. Hasenfeld (1991). *The Moral Construction of Poverty.* Newbury Park, Calif.:
Sage Publications, pp. 115–19.

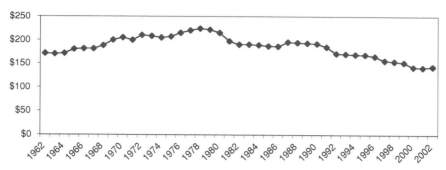

Figure 2–13. Monthly Grant per Recipient (2002 Dollars). *Source*: U.S. Department of Health and Human Services, Annual Report to Congress, *Indicators of Welfare Dependence* (2004), Table TANF 6.

expand because of the recessions of the 1970s coupled with the rapid rise in single-parent households. The rolls remained fairly stable during the 1980s, despite two recessions, in part because the eligibility rules were tightened both at the federal and state levels.

Welfare rolls increased sharply in the 1990s in response to the recession and the rise in unemployment, especially in the low-wage labor market. As the economy improved, the rolls began to decline, and from 1996, the passage of TANF has pushed the rolls dramatically down. The number of families on welfare declined from a peak of 5.04 million in 1994 to 2.19 million in 2002. In 1996, the year of welfare reform, 2.8 million families were on welfare. By 2000, the number had declined to 2.3 million, with almost one-fourth of this decline occurring before the 1996 reform. The rate of decline slowed in 2001 and virtually stopped in 2002.[206] Food stamp enrollment, which peaked in 1994 at 28 million persons, declined by more than 10 million over the next seven years. Since May 2001, food stamp enrollments have increased and in May 2003 reached 21.3 million.[207]

The pattern for children on AFDC/TANF parallels families. However, what is particularly noteworthy is that the percentage of poor children receiving welfare climbed initially to 80 percent in 1973 and then began to decline. By 1983, it stood at 50 percent. It then climbed slowly, reaching 61 percent in

---

[206] Some of the continuing decline in TANF represents families moving onto separate state programs (SSPs). U.S. Department of Health and Human Services (HHS) reports that in fiscal year 2001, there were about eighty-five thousand families in SSPs in twenty-five states. In several of these states, SSP recipients are married families and legal aliens.

[207] U.S. House of Representatives, The Green Book (2004). *Background Material and Data on Programs within the Jurisdiction of the Committee on Ways and Means, March 2004* (2004), pp. 7–27, 31–32. Sixty-four percent of all SSP families were in California (FY 2001). Alabama, California, and Utah reported that more than 80 percent of their SSP adult recipients were married. In Washington and Utah, almost two-thirds of the SSP adult recipients were legal aliens; in California, 46 percent. In New York, the estimated monthly number of maintenance of effort (MOE) safety net program rose from 28,000 to 46,000. Most of these recipients were transferred from TANF after they exhausted the sixty-month limit on federal funds.

Table 2–3. *Percentage of total income from various sources by poverty level: selected years*

	<50% and Poverty	<100% of Poverty	<200% of Poverty
1995			
TANF, SSI, and Food Stamps	65.9	41.3	14.2
Earnings	22.5	40.4	64.8
Other Income	11.6	18.3	21.0
1999			
TANF, SSI, and Food Stamps	53.1	29.8	9.7
Earnings	30.2	49.3	69.1
Other Income	16.6	20.8	21.2
2000			
TANF, SSI, and Food Stamps	54.3	30.3	9.8
Earnings	30.5	49.5	68.7
Other Income	15.2	20.3	21.5
2001			
TANF, SSI, and Food Stamps	53.0	28.6	9.1
Earnings	31.6	49.9	69.3
Other Income	15.4	21.5	21.6

Source: U.S. Department of Health and Human Services, Annual Report to Congress, *Indicators of Welfare Dependence* (2004), Table IND 1d.

1994. With the passage of TANF, the percentage of poor children receiving welfare declined dramatically to 33 percent in 2002.

The benefit level in constant dollars has also declined over the years. As shown in Figure 2–13, the average grant per month in constant dollars was $171 in 1962. It climbed to a high of $224 in 1978 and then declined almost continually to $143 in 2002. Moreover, as shown in Table 2–3, the proportion of total income from mean-tested programs such as TANF, SSI, and Food Stamps for families below the poverty line has declined. For families in dire poverty (below 50% of the poverty line) in 1995, TANF, Supplemental Security Income (SSI), and Food Stamps provided 65.9 percent of their total income. In 2001, it declined to 53 percent of their income.

Welfare Use

Contrary to prevailing beliefs, many people come to rely on mean-tested programs such as welfare during their life course. Mark Rank shows that by age 20, 8.3 percent of the population receive cash assistance (i.e., welfare, SSI, or General Assistance), and 12.6 percent participate in an in-kind program, such as Food Stamps and Medicaid. By age 65, the respective percentages are 37.6 percent and 64.2 percent.[208] In other words, reliance on mean-tested programs is widespread.

[208] Rank (2004), pp. 102–6.

Table 2–4. *Percentage of AFDC/TANF spells of individuals in families with no labor force participants for individuals entering programs during the 1993 and 1996 SIPP panels*

Spells months	≤4 Spells months	5–12 Spells months	13–20 Spells months	>20
Entered AFDC between 1993 and 1996	27.2	16.2	6.9	49.7
Entered TANF between 1996 and 1999	40.5	27.5	13.3	18.7

Source: U.S. Department of Health and Human Services, Annual Report to Congress, *Indicators of Welfare Dependence* (2004), Table ECON 5b.

At the same time, reliance on welfare is episodic and generally for short periods of time. As shown in Table 2–4, of the families without labor-force participation who entered AFDC between 1993 and 1996, 27 percent had a spell of four months or less, 16.2 percent had a spell lasting between five and twelve months, 6.9 percent had a spell lasting between thirteen and twenty months, and 49.7 percent had a spell lasting over twenty months. For those entering TANF between 1996 and 1999, the length of the time spent on welfare declined dramatically. About 40 percent of the spells lasted four months or less, and only 18.7 of the spells lasted more than twenty months.

Individuals may have several spells in any given year. Taking a longer perspective through yearly data from PSID, recipients were tracked over three ten-year periods (1971–1980, 1981–1990, 1991–2000).[209] As shown in Table 2–5, a majority of the recipients stay on aid for two years or less. Only a small proportion receive aid for more than five years. From 1991 to 2000, the percentage of long-term recipients noticeably declined.

According to Bane and Ellwood, the length of the first spell increases when the recipient is African American, has a low level of education, has never married, lacks work experience, and has a disability.[210] These factors also increase the rate of return to welfare. As indicators of economic vulnerability, Sandefur and Cook found that the probability of leaving welfare permanently declined for recipients who were African American or Hispanic, and the longer they were on aid.[211] Furthermore, those with low education, fewer job skills, and little work experience were also less likely to exit permanently. The probability of leaving welfare also declined if they were never married and had two or more children.

---

[209] The base for the percentages consists of individuals receiving at least $1 of AFDC/TANF in any year in the ten-year period.

[210] M. J. Bane & D. T. Ellwood (1994). *Welfare Realities: From Rhetoric to Reform.* Cambridge, Mass.: Harvard University Press, pp. 42–48.

[211] G. D. Sandefur & S. T. Cook (1998). "Permanent Exit from Public Assistance: The Impact of Duration, Family, and Work." *Social Forces* 77(2): 763–87.

Table 2–5. *Percentage of AFDC/TANF recipients across three ten-year time periods by years of receipt, and age*

Years received: AFDC/TANF	All recipients			Child recipients 0–5		
	1971–1980	1981–1990	1991–2000	1971–1980	1981–1990	1991–2000
1–2 Years	44.0	44.8	50.9	36.3	36.1	37.9
3–5 Years	30.1	26.5	30.9	28.1	24.1	33.9
6–8 Years	12.5	16.4	14.5	17.9	20.5	23.3
9–10 Years	13.3	12.2	3.8	17.7	19.4	4.9

Note: The base for the percentages consists of individuals receiving at least $1 of AFDC/TANF in any year in the ten-year period. Child recipients are defined by age in the first year of the ten-year period. This indicator measures years of recipiency over the specified ten-year time periods and does not take into account years of recipiency that may have occurred before or after each ten-year period.
Source: U.S. Department of Health and Human Services, Annual Report to Congress, *Indicators of Welfare Dependence* (2004), Table IND 9.

Characteristics of Families

The average size of welfare families has declined from 3.9 persons in 1970 to 2.5 in 2002.[212] The proportion of children on welfare fell from 14 percent in 1993–1994 to 5.3 percent in 2002.[213] The average number of people per welfare family is 2.6, and the average number of children per family is 2. The average age of the adult members is 31.3, 7.4 percent are under age 20, and 19 percent are over age 39. The average age of the TANF adults is the same as in the previous year. The average age of the adults on welfare gradually increased during the 1990s, from 29.9 years to 31.3. The proportion of older adults over age 39 was the most dramatic increase – from 14 percent to 19 percent.[214] Ninety-three percent of the adults were heads of household. One hundred twenty-two thousand teen parents were also members of a TANF family. The share of AFDC/TANF recipients who are teenage persons dropped from 2.4 percent in 1994 to 1.6 percent in 1998 but rose to 2.3 percent in 2001.[215]

In 2001, 66.9 percent of TANF recipient adults had never married, 11.7 percent were married and living together, 12.5 percent were married but separated, 8.2 percent were divorced, and 0.8 percent were widowed.[216] The 2002 *TANF Annual Report to Congress* states that "the proportion of married adult recipients decreased because many States recently moved two-parent families to SSP-MOE programs."[217] In 2002, there were about 2.3 million adults living

---

[212] U.S. House of Representatives, The Green Book (2004), pp. 7–27.
[213] Ibid.
[214] Temporary Assistance for Needy Families Program (TANF) (2002). *2002 TANF Annual Report to Congress*. Retrieved from http://www.acf.hhs.gov/programs/ofa/annualreports/index.htm, p. X-191.
[215] U.S. House of Representatives, The Green Book (2004), pp. 7–87.
[216] Ibid., pp. 7–88.   [217] 2002 TANF Annual Report, p. X-186.

in TANF households.[218] Sixty-one percent of the adults were TANF recipients. Of the nonrecipient adults (39%) who may be ineligible, 22 percent were parents, 13 percent were caretakers, and 4 percent were other persons whose income was considered in determining eligibility. Of the TANF adults, only 10 percent are men. Only 8 percent (113,000) of TANF adult recipients were noncitizens residing legally in the United States.

The average age of the children is about 7.8 years. Thirteen percent are under two, 38 percent are preschool (under six), and only 8 percent were sixteen years or older. The age distribution is about the same as the previous year. Between 1992 and 2001, the proportion of families with the youngest child between age 1 and 2 declined significantly from 30 percent to 20 percent. At the same time, the proportion of families whose youngest child was age 6 or older increased significantly from 36 percent to 45 percent.[219]

The share of TANF children who live with a grandparent climbed from 6.2 percent in 1998 to 8.4 percent in 2001, and the share living with their parents declined from 90.3 percent to 85.7 percent. The share living with another relative or with a stepparent increased. Family living arrangements were different in no-adult families – 62.8 percent were in the parent's household, 21.8 percent were with a grandparent, 10.4 percent were with another relative, and 2.7 percent were with a stepparent or an unrelated household head.[220]

Most recipient children were children of the head of the household. Only 8 percent were grandchildren of the head. Of all TANF children in child-only cases, 63 percent lived with parents and 22 percent with grandparents who themselves were not recipients. The share of TANF children who live with a grandparent climbed from 6.2 percent in 1998 to 8.4 percent in 2001, and the share living in their parent's household declined from 90.3 percent to 85.7 percent. The share living with another relative or with a stepparent increased. Family/living relationships were different in no-adult families. Among these children, 62.8 percent were in their parent's household, 21.8 percent with a grandparent, 10.4 percent in a household with another relative, and 2.7 percent with a stepparent or an unrelated household head.[221] Almost all (98%) of the TANF children were U.S. citizens; 2 percent were qualified aliens.[222]

Since 1969, the proportion of child-only welfare families more than tripled – to 37.2 percent in 2001, and there was a further increase since 2002.[223]

Race/Ethnicity

The racial composition changed substantially during the past decade. The principal change was from white to Hispanic, which followed population

[218] 2002 TANF Annual Report to Congress, p. X-185.
[219] 2002 TANF Annual Report, p. X-192.
[220] U.S. House of Representatives, The Green Book (2004), pp. 7–91.
[221] Ibid.   [222] 2002 TANF Annual Report, p. X-186.
[223] Ibid., p. X-191.

trends. In 1992, AFDC/TANF was 39 percent white, 37 percent African American, and 18 percent Hispanic. In 2001, it was 30 percent white, 39 percent African American, and 26 percent Hispanic. The shift has accelerated since 1996, driven by the changes in California, New York, and Texas. In 2001, 70 percent of all Hispanic welfare families were in these three states. The proportion of African American families has increased since 1996, following a decline before 1996. The result is that the proportion of minority welfare families increased from three-fifths to just more than two-thirds, primarily as a result of the growth in Hispanic families.[224] Other groups account for 5.2 percent in 2001: Asian/ Pacific Islander, 2.5 percent; Native American, 1.3 percent; and unclassified other, 1.4 percent.[225]

Whites make up a relatively high proportion of the families enrolled in separate state MOE programs in 2001. Out of 84,087 families in these twenty-five programs, whites are 39.1 percent, Asians 22.9 percent, Hispanics 19.9 percent, and African Americans 10.4 percent. American Natives, Hawaiian, multiracial families, and unknowns make up the remaining 8 percent.[226]

Education Level

TANF adults tend to have below-average schooling. In 1998, 47 percent of TANF adults did not have at least twelve years of school or an educational credential, as compared with 15.8 percent of the total U.S. population aged 25 and older without a high school degree in 2000.[227] In 2001, 49 percent of TANF adults had received high school diplomas or a GED, and 3.1 percent attained more than twelve years of education.[228]

Welfare and Work

Before the 1996 welfare reform, significant numbers of mothers on welfare also worked. Harris, relying on monthly data from PSID for the years 1984–86, found that almost half of the women on welfare had worked while receiving aid and that the major reason for exiting welfare was employment.[229] Finding a new job hastened the exit compared with working off welfare. Harris also found that mothers with more education and fewer children were more likely to exit welfare faster. In contrast to other studies, she did not find race to be a factor.[230] Edin and Lein, in their ethnographic study, also found considerable work participation by welfare recipients, albeit in the informal economy and in a

[224] Ibid.
[225] U.S. House of Representatives, The Green Book (2004), pp. 7–89.
[226] Ibid.
[227] U.S. Census, Statistical Abstract (2002), Table 210.
[228] U.S. House of Representatives, The Green Book (2004), pp. 7–91.
[229] K. M. Harris (1993). "Work and Welfare among Single Mothers in Poverty." American Journal of Sociology 99(2): 317–52.
[230] Ibid., pp. 341–43.

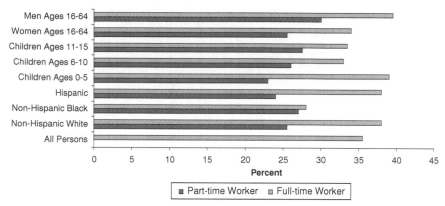

Figure 2–14. Percent AFDC/TANF Recipients with Part-Time or Full-Time Worker, 2001.
Source: U.S. Department of Health and Human Services, Annual Report to Congress,
Indicators of Welfare Dependence (2004), Table IND 2a.

sporadic manner.[231] In the four cities they studied, the percentage of recipients
engaging in supplemental work to augment their welfare grants ranged from
a high of 60 percent in Chicago to a low of 36 percent in Charleston, South
Carolina.

Undoubtedly, TANF has further increased the mixing of welfare and work.
From 1993 to 2001, the percentage of recipients in families with a part-time
or full-time worker increased from 43 percent to 61 percent. As shown in
Figure 2–14 for 2001, there is considerable participation in the labor force,
especially part time, in families of various groups of recipients. The relatively
high participation in full-time work in families with children under the age of
5 is particularly noteworthy. There are also some ethnic differences – Hispanic
and white families have a higher participation rate than African Americans.

The considerable participation of welfare recipients in the labor force is
more remarkable considering the numerous barriers to employment they are
likely to face. These barriers add to the instability of their labor-market participation. Several studies have shown welfare recipients are more likely to
encounter barriers to employment such as lack of human capital and mental
and physical health problems.[232] On the basis of the National Survey of American Families in 1997, Zedlewski[233] reports that athough most welfare recipients
were either working, going to school, or looking for work, about 40 percent
of the recipients reported having two or more significant barriers to

---

[231] K. Edin & L. Lein (1997). *Making Ends Meet: How Single Mothers Survive Welfare and Low-Wage
Work*. New York: Russell Sage Foundation.

[232] For a review, see S. K. Danziger et al. (2000). "Human Capital, Physical Health, and Mental
Health of Welfare Recipients: Co-occurrences and Correlates." *Journal of Social Issues* 56(4):
635–54.

[233] S. Zedlewski (1999). "Work-Related Activities and Limitations of Current Welfare Recipients"
(The Urban Institute Discussion Papers, Washington D.C.), pp. 1–26.

employment. These included low education, lack of work experience, report-ing poor physical or mental health, and caring for an infant child.[234] Work activity declined as increasing barriers increased. For example, although 52 percent of recipients without any barrier worked, only 22 percent with one barrier worked and 6 percent with two barriers worked. Zedlewski also found that women who "recycled" back to welfare were more likely to have employ-ment barriers. In their longitudinal study, Sandra Danziger and her colleagues found a similar pattern.[235] About half of the recipients in their study had at least one employment barrier. The most common barriers were related to mental health, physical health, and human capital. Most women with barriers had multiple barriers. Again, having one or more barrier significantly reduced work activity. In wave two of the survey, 74 percent of the women without any barrier worked twenty hours or more per week. Only 41 percent of the women with human capital as the only barrier worked, 59 percent of the women with mental health as the only barrier worked, and 62 percent of the women with a physical health barrier worked. Having two barriers further reduced work activity. Fifty percent of the women with human capital and physical barriers worked, and 41 percent of women with human capital and mental health barriers worked. Only 38 percent of the women with three barriers worked.[236]

Finally, there has always been a fixation that being on welfare will have deleterious consequences to future employment and self-sufficiency. In fact, there is little evidence for that. Susanna Loeb and Mary Corcoran, compared the work experience and wage growth of welfare recipients to those of nonre-cipients for a period of fourteen years.[237] Although recipients had considerably less work experience, once they returned to work, their wage growth was no different than that of nonrecipients. In other words, the penalty for time out from work was not substantially different for recipients and nonrecipients. There was also little evidence that the length of time on aid reduced the wage gain for work experience.[238]

Monthly Income

In 2001, the average monthly amount of cash assistance per family was $351. More than a fifth (22.8%) of families had non-TANF income, in a monthly amount of $592.87. The monthly average was $288 for one child, $362 for two children, $423 for three, and $519 for four children or more.[239]

---

[234] R. Blank & H. Shierholz (2005). "Explaining Employment and Wage Trends among Less-Skilled Women" (Paper, Working and Poor Conference, Gerald R. Ford School of Public Policy, University of Michigan, June 2005) report there are declining returns to education among less-skilled women (p. 27).

[235] Danziger et al. (2000).   [236] Ibid., p. 646.

[237] S. Loeb & M. Corcoran (2001). "Welfare, Work Experience and Economic Self-Sufficiency." *Journal of Policy Analysis and Management* 20(1): 1–20.

[238] Ibid., p. 17.   [239] 2002 TANF Annual Report, p. X-186.

In most states, the average monthly TANF benefit in 2002 was below the corresponding 1994 AFDC level. And in the sixteen states where benefits were increased, they were generally too small to offset inflation. Only in Louisiana, Mississippi, and West Virginia was there a rise in the real value of average benefits. The employment rates of AFDC/TANF recipients tripled during this period, and some of the decline in average welfare payments was due to an increase in earnings.[240]

Ten percent of TANF families received child support, about the same as in 2000. The average monthly amount was $179. Twelve percent of TANF families had some cash resources (e.g., cash, bank accounts), with an average of $244, which was a determining factor in considering eligibility.[241] Sixteen percent of the families had earned income, with an average amount of $693. Eight percent had unearned income, with an average of $299. Of the newly approved families, 22 percent had non-TANF income, with an average of $489. Of the closed cases, 40 percent had an average of $893 in non-TANF income.

Employment

Temporary Assistance for Needy Families, of course, forces welfare recipients to return to the labor market, and the proportion of welfare recipients who are working has risen sharply. In 1979, before Congress limited the financial work incentive, about 1 in 7 recipients reported work activities. Thereafter, employment rates declined. From the 1980s through 1995, fewer than 1 in 10 adults worked. In 1996, when several states began their own reforms under waivers, the proportion increased to 11.3 percent. In 1998, the first full year when states could disregard earnings and open up welfare to fathers with full-time jobs, the employment rate increased sharply. That year, 22.8 percent of all TANF adults reported working in unsubsidized jobs at least one hour per week. In 1999, the rate climbed to 27.7 percent. In 2001, the rate dropped to 25.8 percent.[242] Almost a fifth (18.8%) of adults were employed in newly approved cases. More than a third (35.8%) of adults were employed in closed cases, regardless of the reason listed for the closure.[243]

In 1982, when Congress sharply curtailed the income gains that AFDC recipients could achieve through work, average monthly earnings of AFDC families fell sharply from $421 in 1981 to $267 in 1982. There was a further decline in 1983 to $247. Under TANF, most states encourage work by relatively generous disregards of earnings. Earnings rose to almost $300 by 1998 and continued to rise to more than $500 by 1998 and above $500 in 1997, the

[240] U.S. House of Representatives, The Green Book (2004), pp. 7–37.

[241] 2002 TANF Annual Report, p. X-187.

[242] U.S. House of Representatives, The Green Book (2004), pp. 7–84.

[243] 2002 TANF Annual Report, p. X-186.

year of transition to TANF. From 1999 to 2001, earnings continued to climb, averaging $598 in 1999, $668 in 2000, and $686 in 2001.[244]

Summarizing the profile of welfare families, most mothers are adults and have small families; many are working, have worked, or will try to work when they leave welfare. However, they are ill-equipped to be successful in the paid labor market and will most likely remain in poverty. In short, most are indistinguishable from the majority of the working poor.

Welfare Leavers: Stuck in Poverty

Reports are starting to come in about the employment of leavers – who finds jobs, what kinds of jobs, and how much they earn.[245] Between one-half and two-thirds find jobs shortly after leaving welfare. Most of the jobs are in sales, food preparation, clerical support, and other service jobs. Moreover, despite the relatively high number of weekly hours of work, there are substantial periods of unemployment. The pay is between $5.67 and $8.42 per hour, and the average reported annual earnings range is from $8,000 to $15,144, thus leaving many families in poverty. Increases in earnings were largely a result of working longer hours rather than a growth in wages. Most do not receive employer-provided health insurance or paid sick or vacation leave. Employment loss was a significant problem.[246] In addition, there were sharp declines in Medicaid and food stamps. Most do not receive child care subsidies.[247]

Families who are no longer eligible for or are deterred from cash assistance may also think that they are no longer eligible for other programs or are not informed of these programs. The poorest 20 percent of families who left welfare lost an average of $577 a year primarily because wages did not make up for lost benefits. The next-to-the-poorest fifth of single-parent families (incomes between 75 percent and 112 percent of the poverty line) had an average increase in earnings of $900 and an average EITC of $400 from 1995 to 1997, but these gains were offset by the loss of means-tested benefits (the average loss was $1,460 per family). The decline in means-tested assistance was particularly severe for poor children. The reduction in means-tested programs is why poverty has not declined as fast as welfare caseloads. Only 40 percent of working poor families eligible for food stamps actually get them, and only one-third of the children eligible for Medicaid actually receive it.[248]

[244] U.S. House of Representatives, The Green Book (2004), p. 7–83.

[245] P. Loprest (1999). "Families Who Left Welfare: Who Are They and How Are They Doing?" (Urban Institute Discussion Paper, Washington, D.C.), p. 10.

[246] J. Strawn, M. Greenberg, & S. Savner (2001). "Improving Employment Outcomes under TANF." Center for Law and Social Policy (CLASP), February 2001, pp. 6–7.

[247] G. Acs, P. Loprest, & T. Roberts, "Final Synthesis Report from ASPE 'Leaver' Grants" (Report to the Office of the Assistant Secretary for Planning and Evaluation, Health Human Services, from the Urban Institute, November 2001).

[248] M. Greenberg & M. C. Laracy (2000). "Welfare Reform: Next Steps Offer New Opportunities" (Public Policy Paper No. 4, Neighborhood Funders Group, Washington, D.C.).

The decline in the use of benefits – primarily welfare and food stamps – usually leaves ex-recipients no better, or even worse off, than when on welfare, but it saves the government money. In a survey of twenty welfare-to-work programs, Manpower Development Research Corporation (MDRC) found that for most of the experimentals, there were higher earnings and lower welfare payments than for the controls, but the totals were very small – about $500 per year. Because welfare payments and food stamps were reduced by about the same amount, these programs seemed to result in savings for the government.[249] Evaluations of eleven state TANF programs show that employment is increased and welfare use is reduced, but net income is either largely unchanged or reduced. Increases in wages are offset by declines in benefits. Few programs have generated substantial gains in incomes or declines in poverty.[250]

Similar results seem to be true even for the programs that emphasize education and training. A national evaluation of welfare-to-work strategies in eleven locations where education and employment-based programs targeted employment and earning potentials, over the study's two-year follow-up period, 81 percent of the participants showed a marked increase in employment and earning rates that equaled or exceeded the results of work-first programs. A recent analysis of the effect of vocational training and education compared with job readiness and job search in Missouri and North Carolina does show that although training leads to the largest initial earning loss, it has the largest earning gains in the long run.[251] Intensive training results in an average increase of about $300 per quarter over quarters 11–15 following entry into the program.[252]

Still, these programs are not able to lift the participants out of poverty. Even though most of the programs helped families rely on their own earnings rather than welfare checks, reductions in welfare, food stamps, and other benefits outweighed this positive finding. In other words, the family net incomes were roughly the same as before. The researchers find that the education-focused program does not produce added economic benefits relative to the job search–focused program. Moreover, the job search–focused approach is cheaper to operate and moves welfare recipients into jobs more quickly than the education-focused approach.[253] However, neither job search–focused nor adult education–focused programs has succeeded in helping welfare

[249] C. Michalopoulos et al. (2000), pp. 4, 7–8. The analysis excluded the EITC as well as work-related expenses such as payroll and income taxes, child care costs, and transportation costs (p. 8)
[250] R. M. Blank & L. Schmidt (2000). "Work and Wages" (Paper presented at the New World of Welfare: Shaping a Post-TANF Agenda for Policy), p. 24.
[251] A. Dyke et al. (2005). "The Effects of Welfare-to-Work Program Activities on Labor Market Outcomes" (Discussion Paper No. 1295-05, Institute on Research on Poverty, Madison, Wis.), pp. 1–32.
[252] Ibid., Table 6.
[253] G. Hamilton et al. (2001), "National Evaluation of Welfare-to-Work Strategies" (Executive Summary, Manpower Development Research Corporation, November), p. 2.

recipients and other low-income parents work steadily and have access to higher-paying jobs.[254]

Another study by Sarah Brauner and Pamela Loprest showed that, in general, leaver families have less post-welfare income. Out of nine states, only South Carolina found that a majority (66%) of leavers had more money after leaving welfare, probably because benefits in South Carolina are lower than other states. In Wisconsin, among families with one child, 51 percent of leavers had less cash income after they left welfare. For families with three or more dependent children, 62 percent had less cash income after leaving.[255] Thus, despite the political claims for success, the gains for welfare-to-work recipients are very modest and often fail to account for the costs of working – transportation, reciprocity in child care, missed days, and so forth.[256]

More than a third of the leavers are not working. Fourteen percent of this group rely on the earnings of a spouse or partner. Of the remaining 25 percent, more than a quarter say that they are disabled or sick or otherwise unable to work. Others report lack of access or lack of work supports, family responsibilities, transitions, and so on. Of those not disabled, 69 percent say that they are looking for work. As for sources of support for nonworkers, only a small percentage received unemployment benefits. Less than half were using food stamps and Medicaid. Almost three-quarters of all former recipients report receiving no private help in the first three months after leaving welfare. As reported by Loprest, former recipients report more economic struggles than low-income mothers – cutting down or skipping meals because of lack of money (33%); worrying about the lack of money for food (57%); running out of food at the end of the month (about 50%); skipping rent, mortgage, or utility payments (39%); or having to move in with others because of lack of money (7%).[257] A rise in no-parent families was recently reported, mostly because very poor inner-city mothers could no longer cope with the low-wage labor market and children-rearing. Rather than leave them with an abusive father or stepfather, the children were placed with a grandmother or other relative.[258] Summarizing all the studies thus far on leavers, Haskins reports that at any one point in time, about 40 percent of leavers are not employed.[259]

[254] Strawn et al. (2001), p. 8.
[255] S. Brauner & P. J. Loprest (1999). "Where Are They Now? What States' Studies of People Who Left Welfare Tell Us" (Series A, No. A-32, May 1999, Urban Institute, Washington, D.C.), p. 6.
[256] L. Pavetti (1995). "And Employment for All: Lessons from Utah's Single Parent Employment Demonstration Project" (paper presented at the Seventeenth Annual Research Conference of the Association for Public Policy and Management, Washington, D.C.), pp. 48–49.
[257] Loprest (1999).
[258] N. Bernstein (2002). "Side Effect of Welfare Law: The No-Parent Family," New York Times, July 29, p. 1.
[259] R. Haskins (2000). "The Second Most Important Issue: Effects of Welfare Reform on Family Income and Poverty" (Unpublished manuscript prepared for the New World of Welfare, Brookings Conference), p. 11.

Robert Haveman comes to similar conclusions. "For some welfare 'leavers,' the increase in earnings has been more than offset by the reduction in cash benefits, while for others the benefit offset has led to only small gains in net income."[260] This result, he says, might seem surprising since there has been an enormous increase in federal assistance for low-income working families. During the decade of the 1990s, federal assistance rose from about $13 billion (2000 dollars) to more than $70 billion. Most of this was the EITC, child care assistance, and health insurance coverage. There are several reasons for the low earnings. The most significant is lack of full-time work – the difficulties of balancing work with child care (discussed in Chapter 6), a significant number of barriers to employment (health, mental health), and low skills. With few exceptions, the wage rates for jobs these women receive average about $8 per hour. Working an average of 30 hours per week for the full year grosses only $12,000. What is generally not considered are the effects of income and payroll taxes. Haveman reports that the Minnesota State Office of the Legislative Analyst finds that "federal and state income and payroll taxes offset about $1,400 of the $4,300 state and working family tax credit for a single mother with two children in Minnesota who works full time at $8 per hour."[261]

Most recipients and leavers are in and out of the labor market. But why do they cycle back and forth with welfare? Because in most states, they do not qualify for unemployment insurance. Some do not satisfy the minimum hours and earnings requirements given the instability of many of their jobs, including the instability within the job itself. Most fail to satisfy the "nonmonetary" requirements.[262] "Nonmonetary eligibility" conditions mean that the work separation was through no fault of the worker, excluding separations for misconduct or a voluntary quit, and the worker must seek and be willing to accept available work. In many states, "available work" means full-time work regardless of how many weekly hours the applicant worked in the last job. Most job separations are not because of job loss (which accounts for only about 25–40 percent of unemployment), and women, especially married women, are much more likely than men to have involuntary reasons for leaving a job;

[260] R. Haveman (2002–3). "When Work Alone Is Not Enough" (La Follette Policy Report, Robert M. La Folette School of Public Affairs, University of Wisconsin–Madison), Vol. 13, No. 2 (Fall–Winter), p. 1.

[261] Ibid., p. 2.

[262] C. K. Gustafson & P. B. Levine (1998). "Less-Skilled Workers, Welfare Reform, and the Unemployment Insurance System" (NBER Working Paper No. W6489, National Bureau of Economic Research, Cambridge, Massa., March 1998); D. Maranville (2003). "Workplace Mythologies and Unemployment Insurance: Exit, Voice, and Exhausting All Reasonable Alternatives to Quitting" 31 Hofstra L. Rev. 456.; G. Lester (2001). "Unemployment Insurance and Wealth Redistribution." 49 UCLA L. Rev. 335; G. Lester (2005). "A Defense of Paid Leave" 28 Harv. J. L. & Gender 1.; L. Williams (1999) "Unemployment Insurance and Low-Wage Work." In J. F. Handler & L. White (Eds.), Hard Labor: Women and Work in the Post-Welfare Era. Armonk, N.Y.: M. E. Sharpe, chap. 8.

that is, quitting a job because of child care and other family responsibilities and transportation difficulties.[263] In other words, for these women, welfare is the equivalent of unemployment compensation. In the past, when jobs disappeared or child care broke down, former recipients would return to welfare. Now, with the time limits, this option will no longer be available.

Conclusions

This review of the extent and nature of poverty – both official and those in need – and the structure, coverage, and gaps of the various parts of the American welfare state, leads to the following conclusions:

1. For many people, the labor market has failed and shows little sign of improvement. People with lower skills work hard and follow the rules, but have great difficulty supporting themselves and their families adequately. Jobs continue to be low pay, with minimum or no benefits, and are becoming increasingly contingent and part time. Many of the lower-income employees do not work full time year-round. Many families require two parents working as much as they can, but they lack affordable child care and cannot meet basic necessities. With the economy continually changing, these low-income workers are increasingly vulnerable.

2. Poverty continues to be widespread and multifaceted. The number of "official" poor has begun to creep up, now that the prosperous 1990s are over. But the official poverty line is out of date and inadequate. People need far more income than a minimum wage to meet basic necessities – housing, food, health care, transportation, and child care.

   We have the image of families in poverty as the female-headed household or the single person begging in the street, both people of color. Many of the poor are in female-headed households. In 2002, 7.2 million families were in poverty. Of these, 3.6 million were in female-headed households. The risk of poverty as well as the income or poverty gap is much higher for female-headed households. But poverty and near poverty is spread across many racial and ethnic groups – non-Hispanic whites, African Americans, Hispanics, and Asian Pacific Americans. Most of the poor are in two-parent families with at least one employed adult and often with two earners. A large group of poor are recent immigrants, most of them working, but who cannot earn an adequate wage. Child poverty is extensive, and, because it is becoming increasingly concentrated, threatens to produce and perpetuate a socially excluded class.

---

[263] Gustafson & Levine (1998), p. 3. In 1995, an individual working half-time for 26 weeks at $6 per hour meets the eligibility requirements in 47 states (p. 6).

The extent of U.S. poverty is highlighted by comparing the United States with other developed countries. In a survey of ten developed countries, Smeeding and his colleagues report that the United States has the third highest poverty rate among the developed countries – Australia and the U.K. are higher – even though the U.S. per capita income is more than 30 percent higher than the ten other countries.[264] When the U.S. poverty rate was 13.6 percent, it was 5.5 percent higher than the other countries, which averaged 8.1 percent.[265] In the majority of other countries, the poverty threshold is half the national median income; the U.S. poverty line is about 42 percent of the median household income. The reason for the lower poverty rates varies. In Scandinavia and northern Europe, there are higher levels of government spending. In Canada, it is careful targeting. A more egalitarian wage structure reduces child poverty. In most rich countries, the child poverty rate is 8 percent or less; in the United States, it was 18.1 percent in 2004.[266] In the United States, the tenth percentile of income is between 34 percent and 38 percent of the U.S. median income, which is five to seven points lower than in any other countries. The United States has the highest proportion of relatively poorly paid full-time jobs and thus the highest poverty rate.[267]

3. Chapter 3 describes more fully that the ideology of the U.S. welfare state is to support work effort, rather than relieve poverty. Programs are generous for those not considered to be in the labor force (e.g., the aged) or to encourage work (the EITC) and not provide disincentives to work. As Richard Freeman puts it, Americans have more faith in schooling and the labor market to accomplish the goals of equality of opportunity than the safety nets of the welfare state. As is discussed in the next chapter, even during the most liberal period – the War on Poverty – the emphasis was on education and training – a "hand up, not a hand out" – rather than redistribution.[268]

For those who are considered outside of the labor market, the U.S. welfare system is relatively generous. These are the "deserving" poor – primarily the aged who have contributed to Social Security and (sometimes) the disabled. They have health benefits – Medicare. For those who are considered to be part of the labor market, whether they can work, can find work, or can find adequately paying work, welfare programs are far less generous. These are the "undeserving" poor, and society worries about work ethic disincentives. For some groups, single adults, childless families, those with work barriers that

[264] Smeeding, Rainwater, & Burtless (2001).   [265] Ibid., p. 163.

[266] U.S. Census Bureau (2004). *Percent of Related Children under 18 Years below Poverty Level in the Past 12 Months: 2004.*

[267] Smeeding, Rainwater, & Burtless (2001), pp. 179–81.

[268] Freeman (2001), pp. 97–98, 100.

are not sufficiently serious to qualify for disability, those who have failed to qualify for unemployment Insurance or have exhausted their benefits (twenty-six weeks, about 70% of the unemployed), there is nothing except the meager, locally administered general relief – about a couple of hundred dollars a month – for a short period of time, or, in some states, nothing at all. There are in-kind programs, primarily Medicaid and Food Stamps, but not cash. And for children, there is "welfare" – formerly AFDC and now TANF, which is the subject of this book. Although children are not considered to be in the paid labor market, their mothers are – hence, the family is part of the "undeserving poor." Here, there is deep concern about the work ethic as well as all sorts of deviant behavior.

There is an extensive private welfare state, which is discussed in Chapter 3. On the one hand, there are religious, secular, and for-profit organizations contracting for traditional welfare functions (e.g., work programs, social services, emergency services, health care). There is, in addition, the extensive employment-based welfare system, primarily health insurance and retirement. The for-profit and not-for-profit sector, although extensive, does not cover many needs, and the employment-based system is unraveling for those workers who are increasingly vulnerable to the changes in the labor market.

Despite the extent of poverty and near poverty, many types of people, both adults and children, suffer from poverty and insecurity, and the country remains fixated on "welfare" – the program for single mothers and their children. Instead of viewing this group as part of the more general working poor, it isolates them in a punitive, harsh program, makes them suffer, and in so doing, masks the more general, pervasive issues of poverty in large segments of our society. The demonization of the single mother is the subject of Chapter 4.

3 The Response to Poverty and Inequality
The Welfare State

Introduction

This chapter is divided into two parts. The first part provides an overview of the U.S. welfare state. In view of the nature and extent of poverty as discussed in Chapter 2, what has been the response? How has the U.S. welfare state addressed these problems? Who receives assistance and in what form? How secure is the safety net? As discussed, with very few exceptions, the basic approach of U.S. antipoverty policy is to focus on individual behavior rather than the structural conditions that cause poverty. Individual behavior, in turn, is primarily an issue of the work ethic. The work ethic has both objective (e.g., earnings) and moral components. Those who earn a living in the paid labor market fulfill social expectations – they "play by the rules." Those who fail to earn a living through paid work and become needy are morally suspect. Why are they not working and supporting themselves and their families?

The distinction is cast in terms of the "deserving" and the "undeserving." In general, the deserving are those who have worked in the paid labor market and are now excused from the paid labor market. The clearest example is the retired elderly who have worked a sufficient period of time in covered employment and made their contributions to Social Security. Today, most regular ("on the books") paid employment is covered by Social Security. Cash assistance does not threaten the work ethic. Widows, widowers, and their children are included. Social Security is called a "pension." It is considered an "entitlement," not aid.

The clearest example of the undeserving are the able-bodied nonaged single adults or childless couples. This group is *expected* to work. The overriding concern is that aid will discourage work effort. Aid is only given as a last resort; it is minimal, short term, and usually with rigorous, mandatory work requirements.

But many of the needy are in ambiguous situations. The disabled are excused from work, but is the person really disabled or malingering? It is hard to qualify for Social Security Disability Insurance (SSDI) or workers' compensation. There are periodic re-evaluations to determine whether the recipient can return to the labor market. The same is true with the unemployed. People lose their jobs but receive benefits only if they are deserving. The dismissal has to be involuntary rather than for cause or a labor dispute. If they quit, it has to be for a specified "cause." It is expected that they will actively seek work and become re-employed in a relatively short period. Consequently, unemployment insurance (UI) has a work requirement – the recipient has to seek work actively and accept a suitable job offer. Unemployment insurance pays a small benefit, considerably below the employed wage, for a short time (usually twenty-six weeks).

Single-mother families, historically, have presented the most morally ambiguous dilemmas. Throughout most of welfare history (in fact, until the latter half of the twentieth century), the model mother was married, stayed at home, and tended to the needs of the family. Single women who worked in the paid labor force were morally suspect, especially those in low-wage factory and service work. Poor single mothers have always been tainted with suspicion of sexual promiscuity, child neglect, and improper role models.[1] Even widows who took in boarders to help make ends meet were viewed with suspicion. For most of welfare history, poor single mothers and their families were treated no differently than the undeserving poor. They had to work to survive but were condemned for working. If they came to the attention of the child protection authorities, their children risked being taken away.[2]

However, there were the children. They were innocent. If the mothers were treated too harshly, the children would be harmed. Needy two-parent families also had children, but aid here would compromise both the husband's work ethic as well as his obligation to support the family. Poor single mothers were especially vulnerable. Consequently, as we see, although poor single-mother families were separated from the general mass of undeserving poor and given assistance, the concern persisted that helping these families would encourage immoral behavior on the part of mothers and lack of family responsibility on the part of fathers.[3] This contradiction – the desire not to harm innocent children but not to encourage dependency, out-of-wedlock births, irresponsible fathers, and improper role models and socialization (at first directed at Catholics, the Irish, Southern European, Jews, and then later combined with African Americans and gender discrimination) – has continually stoked the fires of political controversy surrounding welfare.

[1] L. Gordon (1988). *Heroes of Their Own Lives: The Politics and History of Family Violence, Boston 1880–1960.* New York: Penguin.
[2] Ibid.
[3] W. Bell (1965). *Aid to Dependent Children.* New York: Columbia University Press.

The U.S. welfare state also made another major distinction between cash assistance and in-kind assistance. Cash assistance maximizes the autonomy of the recipient, which makes it potentially corrupting – "beer instead of bread." In-kind assistance maximizes the control of the donor – the aid can only be used for particular purposes. In-kind programs for the poor are generally more popular and better funded than cash assistance – health care (Medicare, Medicaid), special health and nutrition programs for pregnant women and for children, food stamps, Head Start, housing, and child care subsidies, and so forth.

The private welfare state is very extensive in the United States. In fact, as Jacob Hacker argues, it is the extensive private welfare state that is truly American exceptionalism. No other industrialized country spends close to the amount the United States expends on social benefits administered through the private sector.[4] Whereas about 80 million Americans are covered by public health insurance, more than 170 million (about two-thirds of the population) have health insurance coverage through their employment. Although fewer than half of workers have employment-based pensions, the amount of private pension benefits in 2000 was more than $460 billion as compared with $353 billion in benefits under the Social Security system. As Hacker states, "In no other country do citizens rely so heavily on private funds for the protection of the fundamental risk of modern life."[5] When it is compared with other industrialized states, the U.S. welfare state is at the bottom but only when public benefits are counted. When the private welfare state is included, the net public and private spending in the United States is 24.5 percent of the gross domestic product (GDP), which is above the average for the eleven other industrial countries. Thus, Hacker argues, the United States is "exceptional not because of its low social spending but because so much of that spending comes from the private sector."[6]

We divide the private welfare state into two parts. The first part consists of benefits that are employment related, primarily pensions and health insurance. Although these benefits constitute a major portion of the total U.S. welfare state, because they are employment based, they favor the better-off workers, both in terms of benefits as well as tax subsidies. Now, with the transformation of labor, the long-term decline of unions, and the rise of low-wage,

[4] J. Hacker (2002). *The Divided Welfare State: The Battle over Public and Private Social Benefits in the United States.* New York: Cambridge University Press, p. xiii.
[5] Ibid., p. 6.
[6] Ibid., p. 13. Hacker refers to the Office of Economic Opportunity calculations, which uses comparative tax burdens, tax expenditures, private social benefits regulations, or government subsidies. The same applies to children when education and health care is included. See I. Garfinkel, L. Rainwater, & T. Smeeding (2005). "Equal Opportunities for Children: Social Welfare Expenditures in the English-Speaking Countries and Western Europe." *Focus* 23(3): 16–23. Institute for Research on Poverty, University of Wisconsin–Madison.

"flexible" work, there has been a decline of employer-based benefits. Especially health insurance, but also pensions are now threatened.[7] The adequacy of the public welfare state safety net is thus becoming even more important. The second part of the private welfare state is the nonprofit sector. This sector, too, is enormous and very diverse, ranging from the local shelter or soup kitchen to huge national and international charities. About 38 percent of its revenues come from dues, fees, and other charges; 31 percent from government; about 20 percent from charitable giving; and 11 percent from other sources.[8] Most of the private giving in the United States goes to religious organizations (45%), followed by human services (27%), youth development (21%), and health (21%).[9]

Although the three parts of the U.S. welfare state are important, most attention will be paid to the public welfare state. The people that are the subject of this book – the poor, the near poor, and the working poor – rely primarily on the public welfare state, which is very complex, detailed, and uneven. Holes are also appearing in the private welfare state for workers and their families at the low end of the labor market as the labor market changes and health care costs rise. The U.S. welfare state, both public and private, is uneven; many of the most in need do not receive help and many others are in danger of losing support.

In Chapter 4, we return to the main subject – the program for single-mother families. As compared with the rest of the developed world, the American treatment of this group is truly exceptional. Although they may not be the worst off of the poor – compared with single adults and childless couples, they at least have had some more-or-less consistent benefits in most states – why have they been so stigmatized? Why have they been so demonized? We trace the ideological developments and argue that the unique combination of the children *and* gender, sex and race discrimination, the work ethic, and political visibility are to blame. Many of the single adults and childless couples suffer from severe discrimination, but this group of needy is dealt with at the local level, largely hidden from view in shelters and slum-condition single hotel rooms. The stereotype for this group is the "bag lady" or the African American male begging on the street. Sometimes people drop a coin in a cup; most often, people avert their eyes and hurry past. Single-mother families, *because* of the children, are dealt with at the state and federal level. The program

[7] See K. Stone (2004). *From Widgets to Digets: Employment Regulation for the Changing Workplace.* Cambridge, New York: Cambridge University Press, for a discussion of the changes in employment-based pensions. See J. Peck & N. Theodore (2005). "Temporary Downturn? Temporary Staffing in the Recession and the Jobless Recovery." *Focus* 23 (3, Spring) (Institute for Research on Poverty, University of Wisconsin) for the increasing importance of the temporary staffing industry.

[8] Independent Sector (2001). *The Nonprofit Almanac in Brief.* Washington, D.C.: Independent Sector.

[9] Ibid.

Table 3–1. *Expenditures for the public welfare state*

	Costs (billions)	Recipients (millions)
Old-Age, and Survivors, and Disability Insurance (2004)	$493.3	47.7
Old Age and Survivors Insurance	415.0	39.7
Disability	78.2	8.0
Supplemental Security Income (2004)	37.0	7.1
Medicare (2004)	303	41.6
Medicaid (2002)	213.5	49.8
Unemployment Insurance (2004)	36.8	8.7
Workers Compensation (2003)	54.9	1.3
Temporary Assistance for Needy Families (2004)	9.4	4.7
Food Stamp Program (2004)	24.6	23.9
Women, Infants, and Children (FY 2004)	4.8	7.9
Child Care and Development Fund (FY 2004)	8.2	1.7
Federal Child Care and Development Fund	4.8	
State Matching and MOE	2.1	
TANF Direct	1.3	
Housing (FY 2004)	22.4	3.4 (units)
Earned Income Tax Credit (FY 2002)	32	19

Source: The numbers are from the current U.S. government Web sites. See, e.g., http://www.ssa.gov/policy/docs/chartbooks/fast_facts/2004/ff2004.pdf. The data on workers' compensation (2003) is from http://www.bis.gov/news.release/osh2.101.hm.

for this group is more visible, hence more subject to political attack, racial and gender politics, and demagoguery. The country remains torn between punishing the mothers and trying not to harm the children.

The Public Welfare State

The U.S. welfare state is an enormous complex structure, spreading through all levels of government – federal, state, local – both public and private.[10] It includes employment-related benefits, social insurance, public assistance, taxation (incentives, credits, deductions), public funding of private organizations (both for profit and not for profit), and extensive regulation at all levels of government (Table 3–1).

The public social insurance state includes Social Security, Old Age and Survivors Insurance $415 billion; Social Security Disability Insurance, $78 billion; Medicare, $303 billion; Medicaid, $213 billion; the Food Stamp Program (FSP), $24.6 billion, and so on. The Earned Income Tax Credit (EITC), which subsidizes low-wage work through refundable taxes but is

[10] Hacker (2002); M. Katz (2001). *The Price of Citizenship: Redefining America's Welfare State* (1st ed.). New York: Metropolitan Books, p. 9.

not considered "welfare," pays out $32 billion to 19 million workers (tax year 2002). In addition, there are many special federal grants.

Adding to the complexity of the U.S. welfare state is extensive decentralization.[11] Several major programs are entirely federal – Social Security, Medicare, food stamps, and EITC. Others are mixed. There are combinations of federal and state financing and regulations. There are direct federal cash payments and tax credits. Some federal payments are administered by the states, whereas other federal programs are grants to the states. States play a very significant role in determining both eligibility and benefits in workers' compensation and UI. Medicaid is jointly financed by federal and state governments, but state discretion determines benefits and reimbursement rates. With AFDC, states have always controlled financial eligibility. Under TANF block grants, state control has increased, but there are still federal regulations. Then, there is a further devolution at the state level to the county agencies welfare, social services, child protection, and employment – as well as to private agencies.[12] Public agencies are increasingly contracting with for-profit and not-for-profit firms. In sum, thousands of agencies and their employees exercise a great deal of discretion.

In considering the American welfare state, consider the vast changes in the risks now facing Americans. When the welfare state was developed in the 1930s, the accepted scenario was of a two-parent family, with the husband as principal breadwinner working a full-time job throughout his adult working life; relatively rare and short-term unemployment, with a return, usually, to the same employer; retirement at age 65; and the possibility of illness and disability. The breadwinning husband would be responsible for retraining, if necessary. The family would be responsible for family care and child care. At first, there was workers' compensation, Social Security retirement (later expanded), UI, and subsequently Social Security Disability Insurance (SSDI). Eventually, health insurance was provided through employment. Today, the risks have changed significantly.[13] The nature of work has changed from the steady, full-time job to growing instability in employment, long-term unemployment, low wages, and rising levels of income inequality. Cyclical layoffs have been replaced with permanent job losses or temporary employment, which has become increasingly important as the economy emerged from the 2001 recession.[14] Hacker reports that in the 1990s, income instability was five times as great as it was in the 1970s.[15]

[11] Katz (2001), p. 14.   [12] Ibid.
[13] Hacker (2002), p. 249; G. Esping-Andersen (1999). *Social Foundations of Postindustrial Economies.* New York: Oxford University Press; Katz (2001); T. Skocpol (2000). *The Missing Middle: Working Families and the Future of American Social Policy* (1st ed.). New York: W. W. Norton.
[14] Peck & Theodore (2005), pp. 35–41.
[15] J. Hacker (2004). "Privatizing Risk without Privatizing the Welfare State: The Hidden Politics of Social Policy Retrenchment in the United States." *American Political Science Review* 98: 243–60, p. 250, based on PSID data.

Single-mother families have significantly increased because of divorce, separation, and out-of-wedlock births. Fertility has declined. Female paid labor
employment – both married and unmarried mothers, and single women – has
risen dramatically. With the stagnation of low-work wages and rising income
inequality, the two-earner family is now necessary to stay in the middle class.
Divorce and separation raise the risk of poverty. Parents of young children,
especially single parents, are a growing proportion of the poverty population.[16]

Significant developments have occurred in some parts of the American
welfare state but not in others. From the 1950s to 1973, a period of prosperity
and rising incomes, large increases in government transfers took place. Since
the 1970s, the only significant government transfer has been the EITC.

Cash Assistance

Social Security pensions grew significantly, in real terms, between 1959 and
1999, frequently exceeding the cost of living, with almost a two-thirds increase
in real benefits per recipient. Today, the total cost is $421.5 billion.[17] Although
a universal program, Social Security has had a significant antipoverty effect
among the elderly. The pretax, pretransfer poor receive about half the benefits.
In 2004, the average benefit for a single elderly person was $10,740, whereas
the poverty threshold was $9,310; for an elderly couple, the average benefit
was $21,480 and the poverty threshold, $12,490.[18] At present, the concern is
that Social Security will have to be reformed to account for rising numbers of
potential pensioners and shrinking numbers of contributing workers. So far
proposals range from modestly raising the maximum level of earned income
subject to the Social Security payroll tax, raising somewhat the retirement
age, or reducing benefits on the middle- and upper-income brackets, to more
structural, far-reaching reforms such as diverting some portion of the payroll
tax to individual, private retirement accounts.

Other insurance programs are far less generous and do not have significant
antipoverty effects. Unemployment Insurance has always been restrictive. The
system was designed for the steady, full-time worker who temporarily loses his
or her job. States operate their separate programs under federal guidelines.[19]

[16] Ibid.

[17] K. Levine & J. K. Scholz (2002). "The Evolution of Income Support Policy in Recent Decades." In
S. Danziger & R. H. Haveman (Eds.), *Understanding Poverty*. New York: Russell Sage Foundation;
Cambridge, Mass.: Harvard University Press, pp. 193–228, p. 197.

[18] U.S. Department of Health and Human Services (2004). "The 2004 HHS Poverty Guidelines:
One Version of the [U.S.] Federal Poverty Measure." Retrieved from http://aspe.hhs.gov/poverty/
04poverty.shtml; Economic Policy Institute (2005). "Social Security Facts at a Glance: Facts
about Social Security Benefits." Retrieved from http://www.epinet.org/content.cfm/issueguide_
socialsecurityfacts.

[19] G. Lester (2005). "A Defense of Paid Leave" 28 *Harv. J. L. & Gender* 1.; G. Lester (2001). "Unemployment Insurance and Wealth Redistribution." 49 *UCLA L. Rev.* 335.

The state programs are financed by a tax on employers on each employee's earnings up to $7,000 per year, with the money placed in a trust fund. According to Gillian Lester, this is a low tax base, much lower than that of other major social insurance programs and, therefore, is regressive.[20] Benefits are about half of the average wage and last only twenty-six weeks, but whether an employee can receive benefits for the maximum period depends on his or her work history.[21] Although today most workers are potentially covered, they still have to meet the eligibility rules. Basically, UI is for the relatively stable worker, who may experience temporary, short-term unemployment before being re-employed. Unemployment must be involuntary, and the claimant must be actively seeking re-employment. A worker must have worked a minimum number of hours or earned a minimum of earnings within the previous year. The work must be spread out somewhat during the year, rather than in one quarter. These requirements are designed to exclude low-wage, part-time, temporary workers, which, of course, are now a very significant part of the labor force.[22] In addition to earnings requirements, claimants are not eligible if they quit work, are discharged for "cause," or are unemployed because of a labor dispute, and have to be available for "suitable" work. Workers are often disqualified if they have to leave a job for family reasons because they are not considered "able and available" for work.[23] Because UI assumes steady work and is based on earnings rather than time worked, it disadvantages women, African Americans, and other part-time, low-wage workers.[24]

State unemployment programs must be "experience rated." This means that the employer's tax varies with the costs on the trust fund; the purpose is to encourage employers to self-regulate the claims. Although the program was intended to discourage employers from laying off workers, it has also encouraged them to contest claims, which they are doing with increasing success.[25] In 2002, the states paid $43.3 billion to 10.3 million claimants.[26] In that year, on average, 44 percent of all unemployed were qualified for UI, and that percentage has been declining steadily from a high of 75 percent

---

[20] Several states have raised the taxable base, but many have not. The taxable wage base for Social Security is $87,000, or twelve times the UI base. Thus, lower-income employees pay a higher proportion of their income to the UI fund than higher-income employees; Lester (2004), p. 59.

[21] Lester (2005), p. 59. [22] Ibid., p. 60; Peck & Theodore (2005).

[23] Lester (2005), p. 60; D. Maranville (2002). "Workplace Mythologies and Unemployment Insurance: Exit, Voice, and Exhausting All Reasonable Alternatives to Quitting" (unpublished manuscript); P. Levine (2005). "Unemployment Insurance over the Business Cycle: Does It Meet Workers' Needs?" (report, Wellesley College, Department of Economics, April).

[24] Lester (2005), p. 60; Katz (2002), pp. 222–32; Maranville (2003).

[25] Ibid.

[26] U.S. House of Representatives, The Green Book (2004). *Background Material and Data on Programs within the Jurisdiction of the Committee on Ways and Means.* Washington, D.C.: U.S. Government Printing Office, pp. 4-3–4-4.

in 1975.[27] Only about one-third of the less-skilled men and 16 percent of less-skilled women qualified for UI.[28] Five states (plus Puerto Rico) have temporary disability insurance, also funded through a payroll tax.[29] As with UI, benefits vary according to employment history, with limits on the amount of wage replacement and the duration. Lester estimates that the average weekly benefit is about $240 and the average duration is about eight weeks.[30]

Workers' compensation programs are state programs for workers who are injured on the job. Workers' compensation grew rapidly, reaching approximately $43 billion in 1993. Employers protested the rising costs; in most states, reforms were extensive and benefits were reduced. By 1998, both employer costs and benefits had declined by more than a third. Limits were placed on attorneys' fees, and managed care was required.[31] Workers' compensation benefits vary greatly by state; although data on antipoverty effects are sparse, the effects are probably small.

Social Security Disability Insurance (SSDI) was created for workers who are covered by Social Security but who become disabled before retirement age. The SSDI "crisis" started in the 1970s. With unemployment rising, rolls and costs escalated, and loose standards may have encouraged fraud and malingering. Both the Carter and Reagan administrations tightened eligibility and increased control over administrative law judges who were considered to be too lenient. The cutbacks, in turn, provoked widespread opposition from families as well as state governments, and there were some modifications. Still, SSDI remains strict and benefits low. The 1996 welfare reforms excluded drug and alcohol addition.[32] At present time, not even half the claimants are successful. There are approximately 4.5 awards per 1,000 covered workers. About 7.9 million people receive SSDI; most are poor.[33] The cost in fiscal 2004 was $78.8 billion.[34]

Most of the aged poor are covered by Social Security. For those not covered by Social Security, Supplemental Security Income (SSI) is for the poor aged, blind, and disabled, with the latter consisting of almost 80 percent of the rolls. SSI pays less than $600 per month per individual, which, by itself, will not lift people who are elderly or disabled above the poverty line. These amounts can be supplemented by the states. However, a substantial number of SSI recipients do rise above the poverty line by using other sources of income

---

[27] Ibid., pp. 4-6–4-7

[28] Lester (2005), p. 60; Katz (2002), pp. 222–32; Maranville (2002).

[29] The five states are California, Hawaii, New Jersey, New York, and Rhode Island; Lester (2005), p. 61.

[30] Ibid, p. 62.   [31] Katz (2001), pp. 197–203.

[32] Ibid., pp. 209–16.   [33] Levine & Scholz (2002), pp. 199–200.

[34] Social Security Administration (2004). "Fast Facts & Figures about Social Security, 2004" (SSA Publication No. 13–11785, Office of Policy, Office of Research, Evaluation, and Statistics August).

(e.g., food stamps, modest earnings, and earnings from other family members). More than a third of SSI recipients receive small Social Security benefits.[35] Between 1974 and 1990, SSI grew slowly; between 1990 and 1994, the program expanded by more than 50 percent. Then, the Supreme Court expanded the definition of children with mental health impairments, for example, poor school performance, misbehavior in school, and other "individual functional assessments."[36]

Almost all of the SSI recipients (90%) are adults with mental impairments, children, and noncitizens. Here, too, there were reforms to reduce what was considered fraud. Since the mid-1990s, there have been efforts to reduce the number of children and immigrants. The 1996 welfare reform tightened the definition of child disability, for example, individual functional assessments were eliminated as well as behavior problems.[37] The following year, more than half of the children (52.6%) were declared no longer eligible by the Social Security Administration. With a median income of $14,000, of which a third is from SSI benefits, all of the SSI families are below the poverty line. More than half of the single mothers with a disabled child are working. They have a median income of $14,000, of which a third is from SSI benefits. The SSI grant is about $484 per child and, at least in most states, children are automatically eligible for Medicaid.[38] Because of widespread objections, the Clinton Administration modified the restrictions somewhat.[39] In 2002, SSI paid about $18.6 billion in benefits to about 3.8 million working age (18–64) disabled recipients.[40]

There are significant holes in the disability safety net. As reported in the 2000 census, almost 33.2 million people, aged 16 to 64, reported having a disability, which was defined as "'a long-lasting physical, mental, or emotional condition [that] can make it difficult for a person to do activities' or 'may impede a person from being able to go outside the home alone or to work at a job or business.'"[41] More than half (17.8 million) claim an employment disability, but, in 2002, only about 3.7 million people of working age received SSI.[42]

---

[35] E. Sweeney & S. Fremstad (2005). "Supplemental Security Income: Supporting People with Disabilities and the Elderly Poor" (Center on Budget and Policy Priorities, July 19), pp. 1–2.

[36] Katz (2001), pp. 216–18; *Sullivan v. Zebley*, 493 U.S. 521 (1990); Levine & Scholz (2002), p. 203.

[37] Katz (2001), pp. 218–19.   [38] Ibid., pp. 219–21.

[39] Ibid., pp. 219–21.

[40] GAO (2004). "TANF and SSI. Opportunities Exist to Help People with Impairments Become More Self-Sufficient." Report to the Chairman, Subcommittee on Human Resources, Committee on Ways and Means, House of Representatives. GAO-04-878 (September), p. 1.

[41] W. Wilen & R. Nayak (2004). "Relocated Public Housing Residents Face Little Hope to Return: Work Requirements for Mixed-Income Public Housing Developments." Clearinghouse REVIEW, *Journal of Poverty Law and Policy* (November–December): 515–31, 526, n. 61, citing Census 2000 Summary File 3, Table P42.

[42] Wilen & Nayak (2004), citing U.S. Social Security Administration (SSA) (2003), "Annual Statistical Report of the Social Security Disability Insurance Program 2002," Table 7.A9.

At the same time, approximately 5.5 million persons under age 64 received SSDI.[43] Wilen and Nayak argue that assuming a "little overlap and a fairly steady population of people with disabilities between 2000 and 2002, we can roughly estimate that only half (9.2 million) of the 17.8 million people with employment-related disabilities collected SSI or SSDI in 2002. A sizeable number of persons with employment-related disabilities appear not to receive SSI or SSDI. Presumably some portion of these simply do not qualify under the strict standard."[44]

The Government Accountability Office (GAO) conducted a study of the extent to which local TANF offices referred and/or offered services to applicants who had impairments to apply for SSI or had SSI applications pending.[45] The GAO noted that the SSI application process can be lengthy, sometimes extending over two years if there are administrative appeals, and nearly 59 percent of all SSI applicants are denied. There is a considerable overlap between the two programs. Approximately a quarter of the SSI caseload did receive cash assistance before SSI eligibility. The GAO was concerned whether local TANF offices offer employment-related services while the SSI applications are pending. Most TANF offices say that they advise recipients with impairments to apply for SSI; 74 percent say they follow-up to make sure that the application is complete, and 61 percent say that they help recipients with the SSI application. Because of Social Security Administration (SSA) data limitations, how much these referrals affect the SSI caseload cannot be determined. Most (86%) TANF offices say that they either sometimes or always exempt adult TANF recipients with impairments from the work requirements. Although TANF can offer employment-related services, the GAO found many of the recipients do not use these services. One reason, as reported by TANF officials, is that the SSI applicants are afraid that participation will jeopardize their SSI applications. Another reason is the shortage of services. Contact between TANF offices and SSA offices regarding the rehabilitation and employment potential of recipients who had been on TANF is minimal. The GAO report recommends increased coordination to identify individuals with impairments who, although eligible for SSI, could become self-sufficient; they recommend a coordination of services.[46]

At present, with the state fiscal crisis, state supplementation of SSI is threatened. For example, in California, the governor proposed to suspend the state Cost of Living Adjustment (COLA) and withhold the federal COLA for SSI/SSP grants.[47] The governor's proposal would result in a general fund savings of $258.9 million in 2005–6 and $517.8 million annually thereafter

---

[43] Ibid., citing SSA report (2002), Table 5.A1.2.   [44] Ibid., p. 61, n. 61.

[45] U.S. Goverment Accountability Office (2004). "TANF and SSI: Opprtunities Exist to Help People with Impairments Become More Self Sufficient." GAO-04-878. Washington, D.C.

[46] Ibid., pp. 4–5.

[47] California Budget Project (2005a). "Governor Proposes to Suspend State COLA and Withhold Federal COLA for SSI/SSP Grants" (budget brief, February).

but would result in a loss of purchasing power for 1.2 million recipients who are elderly, blind, or disabled. Individual SSI/SSP recipients currently receive $805/month, and couples receive $1,422. By April 2005, it had increased to $812 for individuals and $1,437 for couples. The governor's proposal would equal a 4.6 percent reduction. Because SSI/SSP recipients are not eligible for food stamps in California, food stamps would not help to offset proposed grant reduction.

The Earned Income Tax Credit (EITC)

The largest cash assistance for the nondisabled is EITC, which supplements the earnings of the working poor. This "pro-work" program enjoys bipartisan support. It is not considered "welfare" by either politicians or the general public even though, unlike most tax credits, it is refundable. Whereas other cash assistance for the poor – "welfare" (AFDC, then TANF) – declined by about 2 percent over the past decade, the EITC increased 232 percent and is now almost three times the federal spending on TANF and more than the spending on Food Stamps.[48] The participation rate is high – almost 90 percent for families with children.[49]

In 1996, a family head, working full time at the minimum wage year-round, would earn 70 percent of the poverty line for a family of three and 55 percent for a family of four. The poverty rate increased 42 percent for families with children between 1978 and 1994. The percentage of workers who remained poor increased from 5.9 percent in 1977 to 7.4 percent in 1993. Most of these workers were prime age – between ages 25 and 64.[50] With the EITC, the income of a minimum-wage worker with two children was raised 27 percent, which put them above the poverty line. A worker with two or more children (who qualify) can receive a credit that can exceed $4,000.[51] In 1998, as a result of the EITC, 4.3 million people moved above the poverty line, and half of these were children. As Katz points out, the EITC not only is the most effective antipoverty measure of the U.S. welfare state but also attaches benefits more closely to the labor market. It was a crucial part of "make work pay."[52]

---

[48] Levine & Scholz (2002), pp. 203–4.
[49] L. A. Zelenak (2004). "Redesigning the Earned Income Tax Credit as a Family-Size Adjustment to the Minimum Wage." *Tax Law Review* 57: 301–53. According to the GAO, the participation rate is 96 percent among eligible families with one child, 93 percent with two children, and 62.5 percent with three or more children. The rate is about 45 percent for families with no children eligible for a small no-child EITC. See U.S. Accounting Office, *Earned Income Tax Credit Eligibility and Participation GAO-02-290R.* Washington, D.C., p. 2, Table 1.
[50] Katz (2001), p. 294.   [51] Zelenak (2004), p. 1.
[52] Katz (2001), p. 294; V. J. Hotz & J. K. Scholz (2003). "The Earned Income Tax Credit." In R. Moffit (Ed.), *Means-Tested Transfer Programs in the United States.* Chicago: University of Chicago Press and NEBR, pp. 141–97. "The EITC's popularity relative to means-tested cash transfers . . . stems, at least in part, from the perception that the EITC rewards work" (p. 141).

The EITC has increased substantially over the years. It is administered by the Internal Revenue Service (IRS) rather than welfare, and, as stated, it enjoys relatively strong bipartisan support. What accounts for this unique position in the American welfare state? The answer partly lies in its origins. During the 1960s and 1970s, proposals were made to establish a negative income tax (NIT). The idea originated with Milton Friedman, a University of Chicago economist, who argued, among other things, that the NIT would much more efficiently reduce poverty by direct cash assistance, according to need, and avoid the cumbersome, costly welfare bureaucracies. It would be universal, and hence, replace the grant-in-aid programs. In 1966, the NIT was the principal antipoverty recommendation of President Lyndon B. Johnson's Council of Economic Advisors, but Johnson rejected the recommendation on the grounds that it would undermine work effort.[53] In 1969, President Nixon proposed an NIT called the Family Assistance Plan (FAP). Liberals attacked FAP because of its low benefits and strict work requirements, and conservatives attacked it because it was expensive. It was defeated in 1972. Senator Russell Long, chairman of the Senate Finance Committee, then introduced a proposal to help those who worked. At first, it was in the form of a "work bonus" equal to 10 percent of wages subject to the Social Security tax. In the meantime, over the next three years, the payroll tax increased from 3 percent (on both employers and employees) to 5.8 percent (1973). The following year, a recession started.[54] As part of an effort to stimulate demand (refunding and cutting taxes), Long was able to get enacted, on an 18-month trial period, a variation of the work bonus called the EITC. It would supplement wages by 10 percent up to $4,000 for taxpayers with children and a phase-out range from $4,000 to $8,000. The 10 percent rate included both the employee and the employer contribution, on the theory that the employer contribution lowered wages.[55] Considered an offset to the payroll tax, it was placed in the IRS, and made permanent in 1978. An advance payment option was offered if workers wanted partial payments of the credit during the year. Both liberals and conservatives continued to support the EITC on the grounds that it both encouraged work and reduced the tax burdens of low-earning families.[56]

At first, there was an erosion of the real value of the EITC (it was not indexed for inflation), but starting in the late 1980s, it began to increase. In 1991, the credit was increased for families with two children. A major changed occurred in 1993 – President Clinton announced that the EITC would eliminate poverty for a minimum-wage working taxpayer with a child (plus food stamps, if eligible). There was a significant increase for families with

---

[53] This historical account relies on Hotz & Scholz (2003), p. 144.
[54] Hotz & Scholz (2003), pp. 144–45.   [55] Zelenak (2004).
[56] Hotz & Scholz (2003), pp. 144–45.

two or more children.[57] However, the 1993 changes were supported primarily by Democrats and opposed by Republicans. Hotz and Scholz note that the EITC became partisan for the first time.[58]

Taxpayers must file a regular tax return to claim the EITC, even if there is no federal tax liability. In 2001, a taxpayer with two or more children could receive up to $4,000 (40%) on earnings between $10,020 and $13,090. This was the maximum credit. Thereafter, the phase out would begin – 21.06 percent between $13,090 and $32,121. In 1994, a small credit (7.65%) was added for childless taxpayers aged 24–65.[59] In addition, fourteen states and the District of Columbia added an EITC to their state income tax. According to Hotz and Scholz, most follow the federal EITC and just add a percentage.[60]

Before 1984, states could deduct the EITC payment, whether it was actually received, in calculating AFDC and food stamps. This has been reversed, and states can now only deduct EITC benefits if they were received. With TANF, the situation is not clear. States have the authority to count EITC as income in determining eligibility but cannot count income from "community service" or "work experience" funded by TANF.[61] Temporary Assistance for Needy Families payments are not considered income for the purposes of EITC. Congress has explicitly provided that "work experience" and "community-service" jobs do not qualify for the EITC. However, if the mother on TANF works and receives a TANF grant for child care, she can consider the income for the EITC. But most of the rules regarding the relationship of TANF and the EITC are not clear.[62]

At least as of 1990, it appears that a high percentage (80%–86%) of eligible taxpayers did receive an EITC. During this period, there were extensive outreach efforts.[63] Since 1990, according to Hotz and Scholz, participation rates may have slipped, partly because of the significant increase in the labor-market participation of single mothers, and "new workers in this group presumably have lower filing propensities than typical workers in the population." One estimate (1999) of single mothers in California who had been on AFDC concludes that the participation rate was between 42 percent and 54 percent in 1993 and 1994.[64] The IRS used to automatically send an EITC refund on the basis of the filed return when the taxpayer appeared eligible. This is no longer

[57] Ibid., p. 146.
[58] Ibid., p. 147. It could be that this was a reflection of the anti-Clinton politics, rather than specifically directed at the EITC.
[59] Ibid., p. 147.
[60] Ibid., p. 150. E.g., in New York, the state EITC is 30 percent of the federal credit (2003). In ten states, including the District of Columbia, the tax is refundable. Most states do not require qualifying children.
[61] Ibid., p. 152.　　　　　　　　　　　　　[62] Ibid., p. 190.
[63] Ibid., p. 156, citing the work of J. K. Scholz (1994).
[64] Ibid., p. 156, citing Hill et al. (1999).

the practice; now the IRS sends a letter encouraging the taxpayer to file an amended return.[65]

Still, knowledge about the EITC is uneven.[66] On the basis of a 2001 survey, only 58.1 percent of low-income (below 200% of the poverty line) parents had heard about the EITC. There are disparities based on race, ethnicity, and education. Only 27.1 percent of Hispanics have heard of it, as compared with 68 percent of African Americans (non-Hispanics) and 73.5 percent of "others." Only 39.8 percent of parents with less than a high school education know about the EITC, as compared with 65 percent of high school graduates, and 71.4 percent of parents with some college education. Moreover, these results are similar to those reported in 1998.[67]

The EITC advance payment option is rarely used – about 1 percent in 1998.[68] Policy makers provided for the advance payment option on the grounds that it would provide a periodic pro-work incentive and would be most useful on a monthly basis if families experienced an unusual expense. There continues to be concern about its lack of use. Hotz and Scholz, however, disagree that this is a matter of concern. In the low-wage labor market, there are frequent job changes, and an advance payment would require a lot more paperwork. Besides, low-wage workers worry about owing taxes if they receive too high an amount.[69]

There are proposals to add a third tier to the EITC for families with three or more children, which have much higher poverty rates, adjusting the phase-out range, integrating the EITC, the dependent exemption, and child credit into a "unified universal child credit" that would rise for an initial income range, flatten out, and then phase down but have a minimum benefit of $1,270 per child. The cost of the credit would be more than $30 billion per year.[70] Other proposals are considered shortly.

The most significant question concerning the EITC is its effect on labor market participation.[71] As the EITC was expanding from $9.6 billion (in 1999 dollars) in 1990 to $31.9 billion in 1999, the employment rates for single

---

[65] Ibid., p. 156.

[66] E. Maag (2005). "Disparities in Knowledge of the EITC" (Tax Notes, Tax Policy Center, Urban Institute and Brookings Institution, March 14).

[67] Ibid., p. 1. Data from the 2001 National Survey of America's Families.

[68] Hotz & Scholz (2003), p. 191.

[69] Ibid., p. 191. They point out that the U.K. designed its EITC-like program, the Working Families Tax Credit (WFTC), with incremental payments during the year. It is paid through the employer and based on past hours, earnings, and family income. There still are problems of manipulation – the WFTC is based on the previous six months; thus someone leaving the job before the six-month period ends could still receive benefits for the remaining six-month period. There are rules to cover this, but their effectiveness has not yet been demonstrated. However, Hotz & Scholz think that the British are less concerned with overpayments or underpayments than the Americans (p. 191).

[70] Ibid., p. 190, citing Cherry & Sawicky (2000) and Ellwood & Liebman (2000).

[71] Ibid., p. 183.

mothers with children rose from 55.2 percent to 73.9, percent and the welfare caseloads dropped from a peak of 5 million families (1994) to 2.3 million families.[72] Most studies conclude that the EITC has had a significant and large effect on the labor force participation of these women.[73] One study (2001) estimates that as much as 62 percent of the increase in participation between 1984 and 1996 could be attributed to the EITC and more than a third between 1992 and 1996.[74] However, there was a modest decline of the labor force participation of secondary workers in two-earner families. Hotz and Scholz say that this is to be expected.[75] However, in a recent article, Hotz and his colleagues are skeptical of the positive effect on the employment of single mothers. Looking at TANF recipients in four California counties, their study differs from others in that they examine tax returns. They find that although employment rates increased for families with two or more children (which is consistent with the prior studies), there is no similar increase in tax filing or EITC claims among families with two or more children relative to families with one child.[76] Furthermore, the employment patterns are the same as families who do not claim the EITC. From this they conclude that the "EITC is not causing the observed patterns" (of employment).[77]

Does the EITC have any effect on marriage and family formation? There can be large marriage penalties, depending on the relative income of the two earners. The studies so far show very little, if any, effect on the decision of whether to marry or fertility, which, as Hotz and Scholz point out, is consistent with the evidence on marriage and fertility from other transfer programs.[78] Other issues are the effect of the EITC on human capital formation and consumption, but thus far there is little data.[79] There are proposals to do something about the marriage penalties, but Hotz and Scholz are skeptical – there are important trade-offs and, as noted, the effects of antipoverty programs on marriage and fertility are relatively small.[80]

As noted, the EITC is administered by the IRS. Individuals file income tax returns and, based on income and deductions, exclusions, and credits, determine the amount of the EITC; they then receive either a reduction in tax liability or a refund.[81] The EITC, compared with other transfer programs, is relatively inexpensive to administer. Hotz and Scholz say that most EITC recipients would be filing a return anyway. Scholz (1997) claims that

[72] V. J. Hotz, C. Mullin, & J. K. Scholz (2004). "The Effects of the Earned Income Tax Credit on the Employment of Low-Wage Populations: Are the Apparent Effects for Real?" (paper presented at the Tax Policy and Public Finance Workshop, UCLA School of Law, April 15).

[73] Ibid., pp. 1–2.

[74] Hotz & Scholz (2003), p. 183, citing Meyer & Rosenbaum (2001).

[75] Ibid., p. 183.

[76] Hotz, Mullin, & Scholz (2004), p. 26.

[77] Ibid., p. 27.

[78] Hotz & Scholz (2003), p. 185.

[79] Ibid., pp. 185–87.

[80] Ibid., pp. 187–88.

[81] Zelenak (2004), p. 2.

approximately 95 percent of EITC claimants are either legally required to file
a tax return or would be filing one to claim a refund; thus, most EITC eligible claimants would be in the system without an EITC. In addition, in 1996,
more than half (56.6%) used paid tax preparers, who would know about the
system.[82] The incremental costs to the IRS to administer the EITC, too, are
small.[83]

There are some compliance problems with the EITC. One troublesome
requirement concerning enforcement is what "qualifying child" means. The
child must be younger than nineteen years old, or twenty-four if a full-time
student, or any age if disabled. The claimant has to be the parent, grandparent,
or a foster child (if placed by an authorized agency). The child has to have
lived with the taxpayer for at least six months during the year.[84] An IRS study
in 1999 estimated that between 27 percent and 31.7 percent of EITC claims
(between $8.4 and $9 billion) were in error and should not have been paid.
Almost a quarter of these "overclaims" were "qualifying child errors," primarily
from single fathers not filing joint returns.[85]

Some of these errors are innocent mistakes, say Hotz and Schulz. For example, a divorce agreement gives the dependency exemption to the noncustodial
father who regularly pays child support; because he receives the dependency
exemption, he could easily assume that he can also claim the child for the
purposes of the EITC, but he cannot claim the child for the purposes of the
EITC unless the child actually lives with him for at least six months.[86] It
is difficult for the IRS to monitor the qualifying child rule because they do
not have this information in the tax system. Congress has directed the IRS to
use the Federal Case Registry (FCR) which typically identifies the child, the
custodial, and noncustodial parent. This should reduce errors.[87]

Errors also arise from the complications of other rules, for example, the
adjusted gross income (AGI) tiebreaker and relationship rules.[88] The AGI
rules accounted for 17.2 percent of all errors in 1999. The AGI rules have been
simplified (2002), which should reduce errors. Hotz and Schulz say that the
IRS found that 21.4 percent of overclaims were from reporting errors, ranging
from innocent to intentional.[89] Hotz and Scholz argue that overstating EITC
claims would not likely be systematic and ongoing because the IRS has access

[82] Hotz & Scholz (2003), p. 167.   [83] Ibid., p. 152.

[84] Ibid., p. 147.

[85] Zelenak (2004), pp. 2–3; Hotz & Scholz say that about half the errors involve the qualifying child
(2003), p. 153.

[86] Hotz & Scholz (2003), p. 153.   [87] Ibid., p. 154.

[88] Hotz & Scholz (2003). The adjusted gross income rule is that if a child lives with two filers – e.g.,
the mother and the grandmother – the one with the higher income could claim the EITC refund.
The relationship problem arises when the filer is not the child's parent or grandparent (p. 153).

[89] Ibid., p. 154. Another example they give is whether the custodial parent who separates but does not
divorce should file a joint or married-filing-separate return, rather than file as a head of household.
"Only the savviest taxpayers would likely understand these rules."

to employer returns, and only a small fraction of EITC noncompliance (1994) involved self-employment income.[90]

In any event, whether the EITC noncompliance rate is higher or lower than the errors in the income tax system, it is a concern. The EITC is the only significant transfer program that does not require precertification to establish eligibility; the taxpayer establishes eligibility by filing the return. Congressional critics and the IRS proposed a precertification program for 45,000 single fathers as an experiment. In response to numerous protests, the program was scaled back to only 25,000 claimants, who would have to file residency documentation with their tax returns. Preliminary results, in May 2004, showed that 20 percent of the selected taxpayers did not file EITC claims in 2003. It was not clear from the study whether they were deterred because they were ineligible or eligible. The IRS announced another study, but it is unclear whether it will take place, again because of protests.[91] Larry Zelenak points out that the controversy over precertification illustrates the unique position of the EITC. Millions of dollars are distributed by the IRS based solely on the claims made by the taxpayer, but precertification is required of all other transfer programs – even those to the middle class (e.g., Social Security, Medicare).[92]

Zelenak says that the EITC enforcement, which is stricter than tax enforcement but less strict than food stamps or TANF, is closer to ordinary tax enforcement.[93] The same with administrative costs. Zelenak estimates that the costs of administering food stamps is around 20 percent, TANF about 10 percent, and the EITC no more than 1 percent; although it is hard to estimate the IRS costs of administering deductions, exclusions, and credits, as compared with income, he estimates the costs as probably between 0 percent and 1.87 percent.[94] The same is true with audits. Although more auditing effort is spent on EITC than the income tax, the EITC auditing is much closer to the income tax than to welfare.[95] The same is true with the ratio of underpayments to overpayments. Welfare programs have a high ratio; income tax has a low ratio, and

---

[90] Ibid., pp. 167–68. Only 17.6% of all EITC claimants report any self-employment income.

[91] Zelenak (2004), pp. 3–10.   [92] Zelenak (2004), p. 11.

[93] Zelenak (2004), p. 12. All tax filings, including EITC claims, are subject to a "math scan" to catch mathematical or clerical errors. This is a minimal review. About 6% (1.1 million) EITC filings had math or clerical errors. However, for a minority of EITC claims, there is a further review. If the claim is denied in whole or in part, the taxpayer is not entitled to any EITC refund for any subsequent year unless the taxpayer files detailed information establishing eligibility to an auditor's satisfaction. This requirement applies to several hundred thousand EITC claimants annually. In addition, there are approximately 400,000 EITC audits annually. Again, the payment is not made until the audit is satisfactorily resolved. Combined, less than 1 million EITC returns out of 19 million are subject to some form of precertification (pp. 16–19).

[94] Zelenak (2004), pp. 28–30. The IRS does not keep separate figures on the different administrative aspects.

[95] Ibid., pp. 30–33. Although the EITC audit rate appears to be higher than IRS audits, the vast majority of EITC audits are through correspondence, whereas most of regular IRS audits for taxpayers reporting income of greater than $100,000 are face-to-face audits.

EITC is in between but closer to the income tax.[96] There are very few EITC criminal prosecutions and convictions, compared wither either the income tax or welfare.[97] Civil sanctions are different. A taxpayer who has made a fraudulent EITC claim is ineligible for an EITC claim for ten years, which could amount to a loss of $40,000. A fraudulent underpayment in the income tax system results in only 75 percent of the underpayment. Welfare sanctions vary but are closer to EITC. [98]

Zelenak's conclusion is that there are large concerns about overpayments to welfare recipients and relatively small concerns about underpayments for the wealthy, with EITC in between. The difference is due to the location of the EITC in the tax system.[99] No one has a right to welfare payments.[100] With food stamps, most benefits go to the very poorest; it is a pure antipoverty program, but if there are no earnings, there is no EITC payment. The EITC is a wage subsidy rather than a pure antipoverty program. Both have a phase-out, but the food stamp cutoff is far below the poverty line, whereas the EITC cutoff is much higher. These differences would indicate more concern about the hardships associated with food stamps, hence more tolerance of overpayments than of EITC overpayments.[101] Instead, welfare, not EITC, is strictly enforced. The difference is the perception that the EITC is more in the nature of tax reduction than welfare.[102] In most respects, EITC enforcement is closer to the income tax. Here, form (or the perception of form) – the placement of the EITC in the IRS – disguises function, at least partially.[103]

Zelenak attributes the uniqueness of the EITC as historically accidental but worries about its future. As noted, it was originally proposed (1975) as an offset to the payroll tax burden on low-wage workers. Thus, it was natural for Congress to provide for the credit on the basis of a self-declaration of eligibility, as is true with other income tax credits. Until 1990, the EITC rate was no higher than the payroll tax rate (combining both the employer and employee contribution) and thus could be considered a refundable tax credit. In 1990, the EITC rate was raised above the payroll tax rate (again, combined) but only

---

[96] Ibid., p. 37. Zelenak estimates that errors in favor of taxpayers exceed errors in favor of the government by a ratio of more than 5:1, which is exactly the opposite of food stamps, wherein errors in favor of the government exceed errors in favor of individuals by about 5:1 (this includes eligibles who fail to apply for food stamps). The ratio of overpayments of EITC to underpayments is between 2:1 and 3:1. The EITC ratio of errors is in favor of individuals but lower for nonrefundable tax benefits (pp. 40–43). Then, there is the Improper Payments Information Act of 2002, under which the OMB requires every federal agency to identify programs where there may be "significant improper payments" and to report on steps taken to reduce such payments. The EITC is the only IRS program of which OMB has requested improper payment information, and thus, according to the OMB, is comparable to food stamps and TANF (pp. 55–57).

[97] Ibid., pp. 44–46.   [98] Ibid., pp. 47–52.
[99] Ibid., pp. 59–61.   [100] Ibid., pp. 61–64.
[101] Ibid., pp. 66–69.   [102] Ibid., p. 72.
[103] Ibid., pp. 65–66.

modestly.[104] But in 1993, the EITC was raised substantially higher than the payroll tax – more than twice the total payroll tax. Still, despite the change from a refundable tax credit for the combined payroll tax to a multibillion-dollar transfer program, Congress did not discuss whether self-declared eligibility was still appropriate. Zelenak argues that if the 1993 program was started from scratch, it never would have self-declared eligibility. Congress was simply accustomed to the historical development of the EITC.[105] Although the tax-based administration of the EITC is sound in terms of direct administrative costs, overpayment rates, and participation rates, Zelenak worries that one day Congress might decide that the level of noncompliance is no longer acceptable.[106] Continued strong objections to even a small precertification program might result in the transfer of the EITC to welfare administration or even jeopardize the program itself.[107]

Other programs are designed to assist workers, namely, the Work Investment Act (WIA), which is discussed under the section on services.

In-Kind Programs

Food and Nutrition

There are several federal in-kind food programs – food stamps; school meals; supplemental nutrition for women, infants, and children (WIC); nutrition for the elderly; emergency food assistance; and surplus food. In fiscal year 2004, more than 75 million people received benefits from at least one of these programs, at a cost of more than $45 billion.[108] The largest program is the FSP. It provides benefits to more than 25 million people.[109] It is means tested and has a work requirement. Not only are all public assistance recipients eligible but so are the working poor – with incomes up to 130 percent of the poverty line. Food stamps are uniform throughout the country and indexed for inflation.

[104] Ibid., pp. 77–79. The 1990 legislation also changed the rates for qualifying children: 16.7% for one child, 17.3% for two children.
[105] Ibid., pp. 80–82. However, there are some other refundable tax credits that resemble the EITC (i.e., self-declared eligibility) – the Child Tax Credit (CTC) (partially), the Fuels Tax Credit (FTC), and the Health Coverage Tax Credit (HCTC). The CTC, enacted in 1997, was originally tied to the payroll tax, but it, too, was significantly expanded in 2001. The CTC, however, is tied to the EITC, and is thought of as an enlargement of the EITC.
[106] Ibid., p. 91.   [107] Ibid., pp. 90–92.
[108] Food stamps – 25,858,000, $27.2 million; National School Lunch – 28,957,569, $7.6 million; National School Breakfast – 8,894,448, $1.8 million; Child and Adult Care Food Program – 3,005,010, $2 million; WIC – 7,904,000, $4.9 million; Indian Reservation Food Distribution Program – 104,400, $78 million; Commodity Supplemental Food Program – 521,700, $146 million; Summer Food Service Program – 1,999,096, $263 million; Special Milk Program – $14 million; NISP Elderly Feeding – $4 million. In addition, there are TEFAP Emergency Food Assistance – $417 million and Disaster Feeding – $1.9 million. See USDA Web sites.
[109] I. Shapiro, S. Parrott, & J. Springer (2005). "Selected Research Findings on Accomplishments of the Safety Net" (Center on Budget and Policy Priorities, July 27), p. 2.

There are, however, some exclusions – strikers, undocumented immigrants, legal immigrants (since modified), most students in postsecondary education, and people who are institutionalized. Certain items cannot be purchased with food stamps, such as alcohol, tobacco, ready-to-eat foods, vitamins, and medicines.[110] Just before the 1996 reform, the average assistance was $170 a month per household, which was about a quarter of the average AFDC family's budget and about half in low-benefit states.[111]

In general, in-kind programs are viewed more favorably than cash assistance.[112] There is less concern about "beer versus bread." Although means tested, the FSP enjoy a measure of political support. Both the working poor and the grocery stores they shop in benefit from food stamps. Originally enacted as a commodity program to reduce farm surpluses during the Depression, it is administered by the Food and Nutrition Services of the U.S. Department of Agriculture (USDA) and is supported by agricultural interests. From time to time, it is argued that food stamps should be "cashed out," but the Food and Nutrition Service and its political allies think support will decline if it becomes a cash assistance program.[113] There is continuing concern about fraud – both selling stamps and counterfeit stamps. A plastic card (called electronic benefits transfers, or EBT) is now available and is supposed to reduce fraud as well as stigma.[114]

The use of food stamps is widespread. Nearly half of all children will have used food stamps at least once between ages 1 and 20. About a third will have used food stamps for two or more years, 28.1 percent for three or more years, and 22.8 percent for five or more years. Two-thirds will have used food stamps more than once.[115] Race, education, and marital status increase the likelihood of use of food stamps by children. By age 20, 89.9 percent of African American children will have used food stamps as compared with 37.3 percent of white children, 62 percent of children where the head has not graduated from high school as compared with 30.9 percent where the head is a high school graduate; and 91.2 percent of children in single-parent households compared with 37.3 percent of children in married households.[116] With adults (aged 20–65), the percentages that will have used food stamps at least once are by age 20, 9.6 percent; by age 35, 34.2 percent; by age 50, 44.4 percent; and by age 65, 50.8 percent.[117] Although race and education are strongly correlated

[110] Katz (2001), p. 300.   [111] Ibid., pp. 299, 301.
[112] Ibid., p. 299.   [113] Ibid., p. 299.
[114] Ibid., p. 302.
[115] M. R. Rank & T. A. Hirschl (2003). "Estimating the Probabilities and Patterns of Food Stamp Use across the Life Course" (report prepared for the Food Assistance and Nutrition Research Small Grants Program, U.S. Department of Agriculture, Economic Research Service, Washington, D.C., and the Joint Center for Poverty Research, University of Chicago and Northwestern University), p. 12.
[116] Ibid., pp. 13–15.   [117] Ibid., p. 16.

with food stamp use, gender is not. The use of food stamps among female-headed households is high, but the differences between men and women are relatively small.[118] As with children, adults use food stamps over relatively short periods of time (only 9.9% use food stamps for five consecutive years) but often return. Of those who use food stamps at least once, approximately three quarters (74%) will use food stamps at least once more, and by age 65, 23.8 percent will have used food stamps five or more years.[119]

The Personal Responsibility and Work Opportunity Reconciliation Act (PRWORA) changed food stamps. Benefits were reduced, and legal immigrants were no longer eligible unless they had worked in the United States for ten years or had been in the military. By 1997, about 770,000 immigrants lost their benefits. Able-bodied childless adults (aged 18–50) were restricted to only three months in any three-year period unless they were employed at least twenty hours per week or in a suitable employment or training program.[120] Since the mid-1990s, participation has fallen 27 percent to 18.2 million people, the percentage of poor children declined 13 percent, and expenditures declined 38.3 percent.[121] In 1998, in response to complaints from state governors, advocates, and local stores, eligibility was restored for some of the immigrants.[122] The decline in the FSP caseload that continued through the late 1990s came to a halt in 2000, when enrollments once again began to rise, sharply increasing after 2002.[123] Still, large numbers of immigrants and nonelderly adults are not receiving food stamps, including more than 12 million people who were eligible.[124]

The USDA estimates that only 54 percent of those who are eligible for food stamps receive them. Seniors, working families, and families with members who are legal immigrants who have resided in the United States for five years have lower rates.[125] Recent studies by Abt Associates looked at people who were eligible for food stamps but did not enroll.[126] The study focused on the policies

---

[118] Ibid., pp. 17–18. This is because most women are not in female-headed households.

[119] Ibid., p. 17.   [120] Katz (2001), p. 303.

[121] Levine & Scholz, p. 205.

[122] Katz (2001), p. 304. Some states have established centers providing a number of services for immigrants and other Limited English Proficient (LEP) individuals – e.g., job search, translation, referrals, support services, transportation assistance, and assistance in applying for benefits. Welfare Information Network (2004). "Addressing Linguistic and Cultural Barriers to Access for Welfare Services." *Resources for Welfare Decisions* 8(5, October): 2–3.

[123] C. Danielson & J. A. Klerman (March 2006). "Why Did the Food Stamp Caseload Decline (and Rise)? Effects of Policies and the Economy"(Institute for Research on Poverty Discussion Paper No. 1316–06). Available at http://www.irp.wisc.edu.

[124] Katz (2001), p. 305.

[125] D. Rosenbaum & Z. Neuberger (2005). "Food and Nutrition Programs: Reducing Hunger, Bolstering Nutrition" (Center on Budget and Policy Priorities, July 19), p. 7.

[126] S. Bartlett & N. Burstein (2004). "Food Stamp Program Access Study: Eligible Nonparticipants" (Abt Associates, May); S. Bartlett, N. Burstein, & W. Hamilton, with R. King (2004a). "Food Stamp Program Access Study" (final report, Abt Associates, November); V. Gabor, B. L. Hardison,

and practices in local food stamp offices, the characteristics of participants and nonparticipants, and the reasons for nonparticipation. Eligible applicants differed from the general population – younger, more likely to be single-parent families, and poorer.[127] Eligible nonparticipants were predominately female headed (74%), mostly non-Hispanic white (53%). About half were headed by a person between 20 and 49, children were in a third of the households, and a little more than a third (37%) had an elderly person.[128] Half of the households had some earnings – an average of about $14,400 per year. Almost none received TANF, but almost a third (31%) were on Social Security and 23 percent received SSI. As compared with the active food stamp participants, the eligible nonparticipants had higher average incomes and were more likely to have Social Security income. The study notes that this is consistent with prior research – food stamp participants are more likely to be on TANF or General Assistance than nonparticipants.[129]

Almost half (45%) of the eligible nonparticipants experienced food insecurity during 2000, the year before the survey, and 25 percent experienced hunger at some point. The proportion of eligible nonparticipants who experienced food insecurity in 2000 was higher than the proportion in a previous survey – 1996 – and higher than the proportion of low-income households in the 1999 Current Population Survey (CPS). Thus, say the researchers, eligible nonparticipation cannot be taken as a decline in need.[130]

Practically, all eligible nonparticipants (96%) were aware of the FSP, two-thirds knew where to apply, and almost a third (30%) knew someone who was on food stamps. However, only 43 percent thought that they were eligible – which was also true in prior surveys. Between 6 percent and 8 percent thought that they were ineligible because of the changes in the welfare rules; for example, they had received a TANF lump sum, had reached the TANF time limit, or had unclear citizenship status.[131] Most (69%) said

C. Botsko (Health Systems Research, Inc.), & S. Bartlett (Abt) (2003). "Food Stamp Program Access Study: Local Office Policies and Practices" (Abt Associates, December). The studies were based on data collected in a nationally representative sample of 109 local food stamp offices in June 2000. Telephone interviews were conducted with supervisors and caseworkers, and sampled offices were observed. Samples of food stamp applicants and recipients were drawn from local offices; data were collected from administrative records, telephone, and in-person surveys. Data for eligible nonparticipants were based on a random-digit-dial telephone survey of households that were apparently eligible but not participating. Some states have established centers providing a number of services for immigrants and other LEP individuals – e.g., job search, translation, referrals, support services, transportation assistance, and assistance in applying for benefits. Welfare Information Network (2004); see also S. Cody et al. "Food Stamp Program Entry and Exit: An Analysis of Participation Trends in the 1990s" (final report, Mathematica Policy Research, Inc., February); K. Cunnyngham (2005). "Food Stamp Program Participation Rates: 2003" (Mathematica Policy Research, Inc., May).

[127] Bartlett et al. (2004a), p. E-3.   [128] Bartlett & Burstein (2004), p. iv.
[129] Ibid., p. v.   [130] Ibid., p. v.
[131] Ibid., p. vi.

that they would apply if they knew they were eligible; 27 percent said that they would not. Those who would apply were more likely to be food insecure.[132] Of those who would not apply, practically all (91%) gave as the reason personal independence; 61 percent mentioned some aspect of the application process or the participation requirements. Nearly three-quarters of those who said that they would not apply reported at least one reason related to office policies – 64 percent, the perceived costs of applying; 24 percent, a previous bad experience with the food stamp office or another government program; 17 percent, the costs of food stamp participation; and 12 percent, confusion about how to apply.[133] Forty-four percent mentioned "stigma" as one factor that kept them from applying. The report said that, surprisingly, the debates over welfare reform did not increase the feelings of stigma; in fact, the rates of stigma of those who would not apply were higher in 2000 than in 1996.[134]

A small "but not trivial" number of eligible nonparticipants (4.6% estimated nationwide) approached an office within six months of the survey but did not proceed with an application. About half saw a caseworker, but only half said that they learned what to do. "These data suggest that some eligible nonparticipants – perhaps people with limited knowledge, motivation, or confidence – approach the Food Stamp Program but do not get enough information or support to become participants."[135]

An extensive amount of information was available at the food stamp offices – flyers, brochures, information about TANF, and immigrants – including at least one language other than English. Offices that routinely served non-English speakers had bilingual caseworkers or interpreters available.[136] "Outreach activities were quite prevalent," including community presentations, flyers, posters, toll-free numbers, as well as coordinated outreach with Medicaid and SCHIP outreach activities.[137] In general, smaller offices were somewhat more likely than larger offices to conduct outreach. Most often outreach was general, not targeted to specific groups.[138] Information clarifying eligibility rules for TANF recipients and immigrants was generally less available. Only 10 percent of the offices required a caseworker interview before receiving an application.[139]

How accessible are the offices? Generally offices offered only very limited extended office hours.[140] About 40 percent conducted some eligibility interviews in nonstandard times, but most of these were before 8 a.m., and only a few were after 5 p.m. Practically all offices were physically accessible and

---

[132] Bartlett et al. (2004a), p. E-3.   [133] Ibid., p. E-3.

[134] Bartlett & Burstein (2004), p. vi. See, generally, J. Currie (2004). "The Take Up of Social Benefits" (NBER Working Paper Series No. 10488, National Bureau of Economic Research, May).

[135] Bartlett & Burstein (2004), p. vii.   [136] Gabor et al. (2003), p. vi.

[137] Bartlett et al. (2004a), p. E-5.   [138] Gabor et al. (2003), p. v.

[139] Ibid., p. vi.   [140] Ibid., p. vi.

could be reached by public transportation.[141] In response to the survey, more than 80 percent of the supervisors were considered to have a "pro-participation" attitude; almost all (90%) of the offices always had enough seats in the reception area; about a third were observed to have no waiting lines at any time, and half sometimes had lines.[142]

Despite the uniformity of basic eligibility requirements, the report noted considerable variation among the offices in the application process. Offices serving 55 percent of the national caseload scheduled interviews in advance. In about half the offices, applicants had to have more than one interview. Most offices (80%) required some form of diversion for TANF applicants – lump-sum payments (55%), job-search requirements (38%), a requirement to seek alternative sources of assistance (9%). Non-TANF applicants were required to engage in job search activities prior to receiving benefits in 14 percent of the offices.[143] There was variation in the verification requirements. Third-party verification was used frequently – 66 percent of offices required verification of income of TANF applicants, somewhat less frequently (57%) for non-TANF applicants, 53 percent for household circumstances, and 43 percent for shelter costs. Offices that served half the national caseload routinely conducted unannounced home visits to detect fraud; 13 percent conducted these visits for at least a quarter of all applicants. About a quarter of the offices required fingerprinting or finger imaging.[144]

The TANF applicants had to engage in job-search activities in offices serving approximately 40 percent of the national caseload. The report found that "job search programs that were likely to reduce food stamp access included discussing the requirement before the food stamp application is signed, not mentioning food stamps, requiring clients to go to another office to meet with employment counselors." Offices with about 20 percent of the national caseload engaged in these practices.[145] Job search was required for non-TANF applicants in offices serving about 15 percent of the national caseload.[146]

Of the approximately 440,000 apparently eligible households (June 2000), 83 percent completed the application process and received benefits. Those who did not complete the process were less likely to be poor or receiving cash assistance.[147] Of those who did not complete the application process, about half thought that they were financially ineligible and about a quarter said that because of a change in their situation they no longer needed benefits. A quarter (about 21,000 households) said that they did not complete the application because of some aspect of the process – for example, "acquiring verification

[141] Bartlett et al. (2004a), p. E-6.   [142] Ibid., p. E-6.
[143] Ibid., pp. E-6–7.   [144] Ibid., p. E-7.
[145] Gabor et al. (2003), p. vii.   [146] Ibid., p. vii.
[147] Bartlett et al. (2004a), p. E-3.

documents, the length of time before benefits would be received, long waits at the office, missing work, paying for family care, or general confusion."[148]

Recertification basically involved the same procedures as the initial certification – a completed application, an interview, and verification. States have discretion as to the timing of recertification. With TANF cases without earnings, 58 percent required food stamp recertification between four and six months, 11 percent shorter, and 31 percent longer. About half the offices required short (one to three months) recertification for non-TANF cases with earnings; a third had longer periods. Telephone or at-home recertification interviews were offered for recipients who were elderly or who were disabled. A third of the offices automatically closed cases if the appointment was missed; most other offices rescheduled.[149] For households with earnings, about half the offices required monthly or quarterly reporting; 12 percent of the offices automatically closed the cases if the required report was not filed. Fifty-eight percent of the offices reported sanctioning TANF/food stamp households. Offices with approximately 60 percent of the national caseload imposed sanctions for noncompliance with TANF rules. The full-family TANF sanction was used in a fifth of these offices. Violating the food stamp education and training requirements were less often sanctioned.[150] About a quarter of the offices required an office visit to continue food stamps for households where TANF benefits ended because of sanctions, time limits, or employment.[151]

Office recertification visits were required – from one to three months – for non-TANF cases in offices serving one-third of the national caseload, a fifth in offices with TANF earners.[152] About 5 percent left the rolls (in June 2000). About half left as a result of recertification – 35 percent were no longer financially eligible. Although the data are imprecise, the researchers conclude that "it seems that many households who left without an official finding of ineligibility were in fact still eligible."[153] About a third said that they did not complete the recertification because they thought that they were no longer eligible.[154] Thirty-eight percent mentioned a difficulty with the process. Temporary Assistance for Needy Families did not seem to be a major issue in failing to complete the recertification process. The report finds these results surprising – that people who already had completed the application process reported these difficulties with the recertification; they suspect that there were other reasons at work.[155] Among the recommendations of the report are lengthening the time required for recertification and establishing transitional benefits for those who leave TANF.[156]

---

[148] Ibid., p. E-4.
[150] Gabor et al. (2003), p. viii.
[152] Gabor et al. (2003), p. viii.
[154] Ibid., p. E-4.
[156] Ibid., p. E-10.

[149] Ibid., p. E-7.
[151] Bartlett et al. (2004a), p. E-8.
[153] Bartlett et al. (2004a), p. E-4.
[155] Ibid., p. E-4.

Do the various office practices make a difference in food stamp participation decisions? In June 2000 (the month of the survey), more than 4 million potentially eligible households did not participate in food stamps, more than half as many as were enrolled.[157] Where there were a large number of outreach efforts, nonparticipating, apparently eligible households were more likely to be aware of their potential eligibility. However, perceived food stamp eligibility declined when outreach was combined with Medicaid or State Children's Health Insurance Program (SCHIP). The report speculates that the food stamp message was probably diluted. Awareness could be changed if people applying for Medicaid or SCHIP were appropriately referred to the food stamp office.[158] Households with earnings were less likely to complete the application if the office was only open 8 a.m. to 5 p.m., Monday through Friday. Pro-participation attitudes on the part of the supervisors increased completed applications. Fingerprinting or finger imaging decreased completed applications. The number of completed applications declined if the office requested that parents not come with their children. The report notes that there were probably other office practices, not picked up in this study, that affected the application process.[159] It appears (on more limited data) that eligible families are more likely to leave in a recertification month. Leavers who failed to complete the recertification process mentioned the difficulty with the documentation requirements, having to miss work, and confusion about requirements.[160]

A USDA report (based on 2003 data) on the effect of food stamp errors on household purchasing states that of the 9,148,146 households receiving food stamps, 88.2 percent received the correct amount, 6.3 percent received overpayments, 3.7 percent received underpayments, and 1.7 percent were not eligible. The average overpayment was $97 per month, and the average underpayment $78 per month. Underpayments lowered average household gross income from 80 percent to 74 percent of the poverty line, and overpayments raised average household gross income from 94 percent to 102 percent of the poverty line.[161]

Recently, H&R Block announced that its tax offices in twelve of the most populous states would provide clients, free of charge, with food stamp applications, local contact information, and brief "what to do next" instructions.[162] As a vice-president of H&R Block puts it, "Because we're in a

[157] Ibid., p. E-10.   [158] Ibid., p. E-8.
[159] Ibid., p. E-9.   [160] Ibid., p. E-9.
[161] Institute for the Study of Homelessness and Poverty (2005). "Research Notice: U.S. & California, Health Insurance Coverage: Estimates from the National Health Interview Survey" (Centers for Disease Control and Prevention's National Center for Health Statistics).
[162] "H&R Block Helps Put Food on the Table; Tax Offices in 12 States Provide Food Stamp Applications to Millions of Clients" (2005). *Business Wire*, January 27, 2005. The states are California, Texas, New York, New Jersey, Pennsylvania, Illinois, Georgia, Michigan, Massachusetts, Virginia, Missouri, and North Carolina.

unique position as tax professionals to assist our clients in assessing their financial situations, we think it only makes sense that we take the next step to help ensure that they're taking full advantage of programs that can improve their lives." According to the announcement, federal offices estimate that only 54 percent of those eligible are receiving benefits. The Food and Nutrition Service appreciates H&R Block's effort to improve food stamp participation.[163]

The National School Lunch Program, the second-largest federal food program, served almost 30 million children in fiscal year 2004 (42.7 million children are eligible), at a cost of more than $7.6 billion.[164] Free lunches are available for children in families at or below 125 percent of the poverty line and at a reduced price for families with incomes between 125 and 185 percent of the poverty line.[165] The program operates in about 95 percent of all schools. There is also a School Breakfast Program. School breakfasts are served to almost 9 million elementary and secondary school students, and lunch is served to 27 million, which has increased to 72 percent of those eligible. The combined cost is about $7.4 billion.[166] A recent study reported that nearly 1 in 4 eligible children were not enrolled in either the free or the reduced-price lunch program, and nearly 1 in 5 eligible children did not get a free school breakfast because the school did not offer the program.[167]

The Special Supplemental Nutrition Program for Women, Infants, and Children (WIC) provides vouchers for food, supplemental food, and nutritional information for all pregnant and lactating women and children up to five years old who are medically certified to be at risk nutritionally and whose income is less than 185 percent of the poverty line. The WIC serves about 8 million low-income pregnant and postpartum women, infants, and children under age 5 who are nutritionally at risk[168] and provides food packages, nutrition counseling, and access to health services. The value of the average WIC package in 1995 was $43.12 per month, and the average monthly infant package $73.74. A GAO analysis estimated that every $1 spent on WIC resulted in $2.89 savings in health care during the first year after birth and $3.50 in savings over eighteen years.[169]

Recently, the administration signed the Child Nutrition and WIC Reauthorization Act of 2004, which expands the availability of nutritious meals and

[163] Ibid.
[164] U.S. Department of Agriculture (n.d.). "National School Lunch Monthly Data." Retrieved from http://www.fns.usda.gov/pd/slmonthly.htm; U.S. Department of Agriculture (n.d.). "Annual Summary of Food and Nutrition Service Programs." Retrieved from http://www.fns.usda.gov/pd/annual.htm.
[165] A. Stormer & G. G. Harrison (2003). "Does Household Food Security Affect Cognitive and Social Development of Kindergartners?" (IRP Discussion Paper No. 1276–03, Institute for Research on Poverty, University of Wisconsin–Madison), pp. 3–4.
[166] Ibid., p. 4.   [167] Rosenbaum & Neuberger (2005), p. 7.
[168] Shapiro, Parrott, & Springer (2005), p. 2.   [169] Reported in Schapiro et al. (2005), p. 2.

snacks to more children in school, in outside school programs (e.g., the Summer Food Service Program), and in child care. The school meal application process is simplified, including direct certification of food stamp households; extending the eligibility period through the full school year for low-income families; providing migrant, homeless, and runaway children with automatic eligibility; as well as other measures to improve nutrition.[170]

Anne Gordon and her colleagues report that there are innovative practices at 20 state or local WIC agencies.[171] The breast-feeding support programs go beyond required services, which include staff training, offering clients prenatal breast-feeding education (classes or one-on-one, written materials, and/or videos), informing clients about food packages for breast-feeding mothers, and providing or referring support services after birth. In addition, there are peer counseling programs for mothers with premature or seriously ill infants and for teen mothers.[172] There are new health education and nutrition programs, including obesity prevention, preventive health care, and staff training and education. Some programs include home visits (funded by Medicaid); however, it is reported that collaborating with Medicaid care for coordination for high-risk pregnant women and infants is rare. Breast-feeding for current or former WIC participants is becoming more difficult because more low-income mothers are working. There also is some effort to make help available within twenty-four hours after a problem arises, ideally twenty-four-hour telephone availability, with follow-up calls. Finally, there is WIC Plus – interventions with substantial outside funding for services that go beyond WIC.[173]

Hunger and Food Insecurity

As late as the 1960s, severe hunger was a significant problem in America. Today, as a result of the food programs, hunger is relatively rare.[174] Lately, however, there has been an increase in food insecurity. Certain categories of low-income people are barred from food stamps – legal immigrants who are permanent residents cannot receive food stamps for the first five years they live in this country, no matter what their income; many unemployed people without children have to wait three months.[175]

Since 1996, the USDA has been collecting information on food insecurity. A family is considered "food insecure" if, at some time during the year, it was uncertain of having, or unable to acquire, enough food because of a lack of

---

[170] Food Research and Action Center (2004). "Current News & Analyses: Highlights of the Child Nutrition and WIC Reauthorization Act of 2004" (updated July 30).

[171] A. Gordon, H. Hartline-Grafton, & R. Nogales (2004). "Innovative WIC Practices: Profiles of 20 Programs" (Mathematica Policy Research, Economic Research Service, USDA, June).

[172] Ibid., p. x. [173] Ibid., pp. xii–xiii.

[174] Rosenbaum & Neuberger (2005), p. 1. [175] Ibid., pp. 6–7.

resources.[176] The Food Security Survey consists of an eighteen-item questionnaire that measures the severity of food insecurity, ranging from uncertainty
about food availability, to changing the types of food purchased, to reducing
adult intake, to reducing children's food. There are three classifications: food
secure, food insecure without hunger, and food insecure with hunger.[177] In
2002, 89 percent of all households were food secure; 7.6 percent (12.1 million) were food insecure without hunger; and 3.5 percent (3.5 million) were
food insecure with hunger. This is a slight increase from 2001.[178] The USDA
estimates that 45.5 percent of poor children experienced food insecurity in
2002.[179] Eleven percent of these children experience hunger.[180] Almost a third
of African Americans, Hispanics, and female-headed households worry about
having enough food. Ninety percent of recipients have incomes at or below
the poverty line. A recent study by Mathematica Policy Research found that
almost half (49.6%) of food stamp recipients experienced food insecurity; 28.1
percent were food insecure without hunger, 16.6 percent experienced moderate hunger, and 4.9 percent experienced severe hunger.[181] A study of hardship
families reported 29 percent of families below the official poverty line experienced "critical hardships," defined as not enough food to eat, missed meals,
lack of or postponed needed medical care, eviction, disconnected utilities, or
doubling up with families or friends.[182]

In Los Angeles County, almost a third (29.8%) of low-income adults (below
200% of poverty) – approximately 775,000 – are food insecure, and 8.2 percent (estimated 214,000) report periods of hunger.[183] A third (29.9%) of low-
income adults who are working are also food insecure, although unemployed
adults have higher rates of food insecurity and experiences of hunger (14.3%
vs. 7.2%). At least a third (36.2%) of African Americans and Hispanics (33.2%)
are food insecure as compared with 25.4 percent of Asians and 20.9 percent
of whites. Asians have the lowest proportion (3.2%) reporting hunger. Low-
income households with children have a higher rate of food insecurity than

[176] C. Gibson-Davis & M. Foster (2005). "A Cautionary Take: Using Propensity Scores to Estimate
the Effects of Food Stamps on Food Insecurity" (discussion paper, DP No. 1293-05, Institute for
Research on Poverty, University of Wisconsin–Madison, March), p. 5.

[177] Ibid., pp. 5–6. The examples they give, quoting from the USDA questionnaire, are these: "Worried
food would run out before I/we got money to buy more." "Couldn't afford to eat balanced meals."
"Adult(s) cut size of meals or skipped meals." "Children have not eaten for a whole day because
there wasn't enough money for food."

[178] Ibid., p. 6.

[179] M. Rank (2004). One Nation, Underprivileged: Why American Poverty Affects Us All. Oxford, New
York: Oxford University Press, p. 37.

[180] Gibson-Davis & Foster (2005), p. 6.   [181] Stormer & Harrison (2003), p. 3.

[182] J. Iceland (2003). Poverty in America: A Handbook. Berkeley: University of California Press, pp.
45–46.

[183] C. DiSogra et al. (2004). "Hunger In Los Angeles County Affects over 200,000 Low-Income
Adults, Another 560,000 at Risk" (Center for Health Policy Research, University of California Los
Angeles).

households without children, but there is no difference in rates of hunger. Those who lack English proficiency have higher rates of food insecurity. Only 1 out of 4 who report hunger say they are receiving food stamps.[184]

The demand on private food banks and soup kitchens has increased. There are approximately 33,000 food pantries and more than 5,000 emergency kitchens (often called soup kitchens). Mosely and Tiehen report that in 2000, pantries distributed an estimated 3.4 billion pounds of food, and kitchens distributed 173 million meals.[185] In the Kansas City metropolitan area, they found that 60 percent of people who used food pantries were also on food stamps. In other words, food stamps alone are insufficient for many families. Several studies report similar results – significant proportions of people who use food pantries and emergency kitchens are also on food stamps.[186] Private food assistance providers have reported a 16.5 percent increase between 1997 and 2000. America's Second Harvest reported that almost 60 percent of its providers report more clients in 2001 than in 1998.[187] According to an Urban Institute study, most families (46%) that use food pantries are working and have children.[188]

However, Winship and Jencks, relying on the CPS's Food Security Supplement, argue that although food-related problems declined among single-mother families between 1995 and 2000 and rose between 2000 and 2002, the rise was not as great as the previous decline. This was due to both welfare reform and "other social policy changes that encouraged single mothers to enter the labor force. As a result, single mothers' material standard of living probably improved more during this economic expansion than during earlier ones."[189] The authors point out that this is consistent with poverty trends; poverty rates for single-mother families did rise between 2000 and 2002, but the rise was small.[190] Others maintain that food insecurity is on the increase. After declining from 1995 to 1999, the prevalence of food insecurity among households with children rose from 14.8 percent in 1999 to 16.5 percent in 2002.[191]

---

[184] Ibid., pp. 2–3.

[185] J. Mosely & L. Tiehen (2004). "The Food Safety Net after Welfare Reform: Use of Private and Public Food Assistance in the Kansas City Metropolitan Area." Social Service Review (June): 268–83, p. 268.

[186] Ibid., pp. 270–71.   [187] Ibid. (2004), p. 274.

[188] Urban Institute. (n.d.). "Assessing the New Federalism. Fast Facts." Retreived from http://www.urban.org/center/anf/index.cfm.

[189] S. Winship & C. Jencks (2004). "How Did Social Policy Changes of the 1990s Affect Material Hardship among Single Mothers? Evidence from the CPS Food Security Supplement" (RWP04–027, John F. Kennedy School of Government, Harvard University, June), p. 2.

[190] Ibid., p. 20.

[191] K. Slack & J. Yoo (2004). "Food Hardships and Child Behavior Problems among Low-Income Children" (discussion paper, DP No. 1290-04, Institute for Research on Poverty, University of Wisconsin–Madison, November).

In looking at food insecurity and hunger, Kabbani and Yazbeck find that although there is considerable food insecurity, there is less hunger in households with children between ages 5 and 18 because of the National School Lunch Program.[192] Thus, despite the economic boom in the 1990s, Henry Freeman concludes there was little improvement in either homelessness or hunger. Freeman reports that there was no overall change in food insecurity between 1995 and 1998, again despite full employment and economic growth.[193]

Hunger and food insecurity have adverse effects on health, mental health, and the development of children. According to Stormer and Harrison, "in several U.S. subpopulations...hunger or risk of hunger is directly linked to poor physical, social, and mental well-being and to a decreased quality of life...[and] to be related to poorer disease management, poorer health status, and increased health care utilization for low-income persons with chronic illnesses....It is well established that chronic and acute malnutrition, even of mild degrees, adversely affects children's cognitive and social development [including] short-term memory, fatigue, irritability, dizziness, frequent headaches, frequent colds and infection and difficulty in concentrating, even controlling for poverty."[194] This is true even when levels of hunger are not severe enough to show up in clinical symptoms.[195] Stormer and Harrison report that hungry or at risk of being hungry children are more likely to be "socially dysfunctional, more likely to be receiving special education, more likely to have a history of mental health counseling, and more likely to have repeated a grade. They are more likely to be aggressive, irritable, and engage in fighting and stealing."[196] Food hardships are "correlated with parental stress, warmth, depression; thus, there is an indirect association between food hardship and behavior problems, which persist with older children."[197]

Child Care

Several child care programs are for low-income families to support work. Two programs were part of earlier welfare reforms – the Family Support Act (1988) and the AFDC Child Care and Transitional Child Care. In addition,

---

[192] N. Kabbani & M. Yazbeck (2004). "The Role of Food Assistance Programs and Employment Circumstances in Helping Households with Children Avoid Hunger" (Discussion Paper No. 1280-04, Institute for Research on Poverty, May).

[193] R. B. Freeman (2001). "The Rising Tide Lifts...?" In S. Danziger & R. H. Haveman (2001). *Understanding Poverty*. New York: Russell Sage Foundation; Cambridge, Mass.: Harvard University Press, p. 121.

[194] A. Stormer & G. Harrison (2003), pp. 4–5, citing Frongillo et al. (1999); Rose (2000); Nelson et al. (1998, 2001).

[195] Ibid., p. 5.   [196] Ibid., pp. 5–6.

[197] Slack & Yoo (2004), pp. 6–12.

there is the At-Risk Child Care and Child Care and Development Block Grant. Some of these programs were for AFDC families in job training or recently off welfare and at risk of going back on welfare. The programs were consolidated under PRWORA into the Child Care and Development Fund (CCDF). In 1998, expenditures for CCDF were $5.5 billion, which served 1.5 million children.[198]

When the TANF caseloads rapidly declined and the states had surpluses under the block grants, the "largest single redirection of TANF funds was to child care. Between 1997 and 2000, the amount of TANF funding used for child care grew from $249 million to $4 billion; the use of TANF funds was a major reason why the states were able to double the number of children receiving subsidies, raise provider payment rates, and expand child care quality initiatives during the late 1990s."[199] Since 2000, spending has remained relatively flat – about $3.5 billion in TANF funds. As TANF reserve funds decline, it is likely that spending on child care will decrease.[200]

Before the 1990s' recession, a significant amount of state money was spent on child care for the working poor. Most children of working parents (83%) regularly spend time in nonparental care, averaging thirty-five hours per week. Forty-five percent of children of nonworking parents are also regularly placed in child care but spend less hours per week.[201] Children of parents who are less educated and poorer are less likely to be placed in care. Thus, Hispanic children are less likely to be in care. Higher-income families, and also welfare leavers, are more likely to use structured care. Children of working single mothers spend the most time in care and are most likely to have multiple care arrangements, but these families tend to rely greatly on family care.[202]

Working families pay an average of $373 per month, out-of-pocket for child care, representing about 10 percent of family earnings. Poor families who pay for care spend, on average, 24 percent of earnings. About 28 percent of all working parents pay no out-of-pocket costs for child care.[203]

In California, most families at or below 75 percent of the state median income, which is the eligibility cutoff for child care subsidies (about $38,000), receive some assistance in paying for child care. Forty-six percent of poor families, one-third of former welfare recipients, and two-thirds of current recipients receive government or social services assistance in paying for care. However, current welfare recipients are less likely to receive free relative care, perhaps because the welfare system will reimburse relatives for providing care.[204]

[198] Levine & Scholz (2002), pp. 207–8.
[199] M. Greenberg & H. Rahmanou (2005). "TANF Spending in 2003." CLASP (January 18), p. 10.
[200] Ibid., p. 10.
[201] M. O'Brien-Strain, L. Moye, & F. L. Sonenstein (2003). "Arranging and Paying for Child Care" (Public Policy Institute of California), p. vi–vii.
[202] Ibid., p. vii.   [203] Ibid., p. vii.
[204] Ibid., pp. vii–viii.

In general, children in child care have more respiratory infections (allergies, ear infections, colds, pneumonia) and more gastroenteritis and other infections. Children in center-based care are at even greater risk. Depending on the child care center, there can be improvements (improved immunity and a reduction in asthma rates) or long-term consequences, for example, hearing loss due to chronic ear infections.[205] However, there are significant benefits for poor children in quality center-based child care.[206] A study reported by Kyunghee Lee used data from the Infant Health and Development Program (IHDP) that provided full-time quality center-based child care for predominately poor families for children from one to three years old. The children were premature and of low birth weight. Higher cognitive scores and lower behavioral problem scores were associated with maternal employment and hours spent in high-quality center-based child care.[207] However, the IHDP child care was expensive – $15,146 per child (personnel, operational, food, transportation, space); therefore, Lee argues that this kind of child care should be targeted for children where the benefits would be highest – working single parents.[208]

The health status of children in Head Start and Early Head Start differs. The education of parents about health issues has led to a reduced emergency room visits, increased immunization rates, improved dental care, and regular sources of medical care. Early Head Start children were more likely to visit a doctor for the treatment of chronic conditions or acute illnesses and receive dental care; immunization rates were somewhat higher (although they were high for the control group as well).[209] Full-year, full-day universal preschool could cost as much as $5 billion per year, although if eligibility were limited to families with the cutoff for the current subsidy programs, costs would fall to between $1.4 billion and $2.7 billion per year.[210]

A range of other federal and state programs purportedly address the issues of low-income young children and their families, but for most, their effect is insignificant. For example, the Child Abuse Prevention and Treatment Act, which addresses child abuse and prevention for at-risk families with children,

[205] K. Walker & A. Bowie (2004). *Linking the Child Care and Health Care Systems: A Consideration of Options.* Philadelphia: Public/Private Ventures, p. 3.

[206] K. Lee (2005). "Effects of Experimental Center-Based Child Care on Developmental Outcomes of Young Children Living in Poverty." *Social Service Review* (March). IHDP "was an eight-site randomized clinical trial designed to evaluate the efficacy of a comprehensive early intervention program for low birth weight, premature infants. . . . The staff-child ratio was 1:3 for children from 12 to 23 months and 1:4 for children from 24 to 36 months of age." There were licensing, staff training, supervision, special curricula for low-birth-weight children, and so on. In the sample, 80 percent of the mothers were black, 55 percent had less than a high school degree, 34 percent were younger than 18 at time of birth, and 74 percent were single (pp. 161–62).

[207] Lee (2005), p. 175.   [208] Lee (2005), p. 176.

[209] Walker & Bowie (2004), p. 5.

[210] O'Brien-Strain, Moye, & Sonenstein (2003), p. viii.

provides funding to states to support prevention, assessment, investigation, prosecution, and treatment activities and is a "rather minor piece of federal legislation" compared with the "epidemic proportions of the number of children who are reported as abused and neglected each year."[211]

In March 2005, the Senate Finance Committee passed a reauthorization for TANF that included $6 billion in new federal funds for child care assistance. Although this increase is crucial because funding for child support has remained flat for four years, it is still $1 billion less than what was approved by the Senate last year and would only cover the cost of inflation over the next five years.[212] Child care costs keep rising; consequently, the number of children receiving child care subsidies has fallen since 2003 and will continue to fall as funding remains flat. It is projected that there will be a 17 percent decline in subsidies over the next six years. Since 2001, about three-fifths of the states have lowered the eligibility as percentage of the poverty level for child care assistance. Twenty-four states have waiting lists. The new TANF work requirements will increase the need for more funds, but the states have been drawing on much of the unobligated TANF funds, which cannot continue unless services are cut. In fact, some states now have no carryover funds.[213] It has been suggested that state child care funds be restricted to welfare families and families transitioning off welfare, but this might mean that low-income families would have to go on welfare because they could not continue working without child care subsidies.[214]

Child Support

There has also been an increased effort to improve child support for custodial parents. The Child Support Enforcement and Paternity Establishment Program (CSE) provides services, not cash assistance, to all custodial parents. Services include aid in establishing paternity, obtaining court support awards, and collecting payments. The Personal Responsibility and Work Opportunity Reconciliation Act consolidated the various federal support funds into the TANF block grants; imposed more stringent requirements on the states; and established a nationwide, integrated, and automated network to improve the ability of states to locate noncustodial parents.

Child support is the second-largest income source for poor families, next to earnings. In 2003, 17.6 million children received child support for a total of $20.1 billion. In 2001, poor families received an average of $2,500 in support,

---

[211] Walker & Bowie (2004), p. 22.
[212] D. Ewen (2005). "The Senate's $6 Billion Child Care Provision: A Critical, but Modest, Investment." *CLASP* (April).
[213] M. Greenberg & H. Rahmanou (2005b). "Administration's TANF Proposal Would *Not* Free Up $2 Billion for Child Care." *CLASP* (April 13).
[214] Ewen (2005), pp. 2–3.

which amounted to almost a third (30%) of income. Families between 100 and 200 percent of poverty received almost $4,000, or 15 percent of income. Since 1996, when Congress modified the program as part of welfare reform, child support collection rates have more than doubled.[215] In Chapter 6, we discuss how much noncustodial parents can be expected to pay.

Child support is considered by policy makers to be a key income support for women who exit welfare.[216] One of the requirements of the CCDF is that the parent is required to apply to the state's child support enforcement (IV-D of the Social Security Act) program, if the parent is not receiving services from the program. The parent must cooperate to establish paternity (if unresolved) and pursue cash support. State services include location, paternity establishment, support order establishment, periodic notification if the order changes, and order enforcement. Some families may welcome state help in enforcement. The average child-support payment for families with an order is $358 per month. Low-income families receive somewhat less, but still the average payment is $250 per month. Others may have informal arrangements or worry about domestic violence.[217]

On the basis of a Survey of Income and Program Participation (SIPP) sample, child support payments were in fact received by more than a fifth (22%) of current and former recipients. However, the most disadvantaged also received the lowest rates of support. When child support is received, it amounts to about a quarter of family income. However, it is less than 10 percent of family income, on average, when all the eligible women are considered.[218] Welfare leavers are more likely to receive child support and higher amounts than those who stay on welfare. Leavers may be more proactive in seeking child support, and fathers may be more willing when they know the mothers will receive all of the payments. Or, the higher receipt may simply be because of the "mechanical" effect of receiving more of the collections paid on their behalf. Mothers on welfare receive only the pass-through, or in states that eliminated the pass-through, no child support.[219]

In a study of Wisconsin custodial mothers who obtained child-support orders, between 2001 and 2003, by Maria Cancian and Daniel Meyer, a substantial number did receive support and many received substantial amounts.[220] Child support payments reduced pre-child-support poverty rates by 16 percent

[215] V. Turetsky (2005). "The Child Support Program: An Investment That Works." CLASP (April).
[216] C. Miller et al. (2005). "The Interaction of Child Support and TANF: Evidence from Samples of Current and Former Welfare Recipients" (Report submitted to the Office of Assistant Secretary for Planning and Evaluation, U.S. Department of Health and Human Services, January), p. ES-1.
[217] P. Roberts (2004e). "Memorandum: Preliminary Analysis of Child Support Cooperation as a Condition of Eligibility for Subsidized Child Care." CLASP (November 19), pp. 1–2.
[218] Miller et al. (2005), pp. ES-3–4.   [219] Ibid., p. ES-5.
[220] M. Cancian & D. Meyer (2005). "Child Support in the United States: An Uncertain and Irregular Income Source?" (Discussion Paper No. 1298-05, Institute for Research on Poverty, University of Wisconsin–Madison, April).

and closed the poverty gap by an average of 44 percent (in 2001). However, there was a substantial amount of instability in the payments during the year and from year to year, and this was especially true for low-income pre-child-support families.[221]

Although the number of women receiving child-support payments has increased, more women are receiving higher payments, and child support is becoming a more important source of income, still, according to Miller and her colleagues, payments tend to be somewhat unreliable. They report that among women receiving child-support payments, between 35 percent and 39 percent did not receive payments for more than five consecutive months. The demographic characteristics of the mothers are associated with the likelihood of receiving child support. African American and Hispanic women and less-educated women are less likely to have child-support orders or to receive child support, and are more likely to receive lower amounts. However, African American women are more likely than whites to receive informal support. As women leave welfare, overall rates of child-support receipts remain relatively steady. Child-support receipt has little effect on employment status.[222]

Most welfare recipients lack awareness of the amount of support collected on their behalf and are likely to understate that amount. Most thought that the amount of child support was equal to or less than the pass-through amount even though the payments were higher. The fathers, too, generally did not know about the distribution rules. Women who left welfare because of the time limits were more likely to receive child support, possibly because caseworkers informed them at the time of exit.[223]

Miller and her colleagues believe that more generous pass-through and disregard policies can lead to an increase in both the number of fathers making payments and in the average payment amounts. Although child support can be an important contribution to income, probably because of the unreliability, child-support payments do not have a consistent effect on women's work and welfare.[224]

Education

Gaps in racial and ethnic school achievement are substantial. According to the 2002 National Assessment of Educational Progress, 16 percent of African American and 22 percent of Hispanic twelfth-grade students displayed "solid academic performance" in reading, compared with 42 percent of white children.

[221] Ibid., pp. 16–17.   [222] Miller et al. (2005), pp. ES-5–8.
[223] Ibid., pp. ES-9–13; see also M. Cancian, D. Meyer, & K. Nam (2005). "Knowledge of Child Support Policy Rules: How Little We Know" (Discussion Paper No. 1297-05, Institute for Research on Poverty, University of Wisconsin–Madison, April), which discusses the general lack of knowledge of child support rules of custodial parents under W-2. The authors note that the rules are complicated.
[224] Miller et al. (2005), pp. ES-11–14.

The same gaps existed in mathematics, science, and writing. Although most attention is paid to gaps in achievement among school-age children, there are sizeable racial and ethnic gaps by the time children enter kindergarten. According to one report, by Rouse and her colleagues, by the time children start school, about half of the school achievement test score gap already exists.[225] Moreover, they argue, there are long-lasting effects; "these children do less well in elementary and high school, are more likely to become teen parents, engage in criminal activities, be unemployed as adults, and suffer depression."[226] Emotional and social skills may be even more important – in fact, "a poll of kindergarten teachers found that they rate knowledge of letters and numbers as less important readiness skills than being physically healthy, able to communicate verbally, curious and enthusiastic, and able to take turns and share."[227] Early problems in self-regulation are often predictive of future problems.[228] In a national survey of 3,500 kindergarten teachers in the late 1990s, 46 percent of teachers reported that at least half of the children were having "problems following directions, some because of poor academic skills and others because of difficulties of working in a group."[229] African American and Hispanic children had more problems than whites.[230] Children of less-educated mothers or from lower-income families are less likely to attend preschool. Only 35 percent of Hispanic children aged 3–4 attend preschool compared with 45 percent of non-Hispanic children.[231] Children aged 4 in California are much less likely than those in the rest of the nation to attend preschool – 50 percent versus 63 percent. There is a similar gap for children age 5, although California's relatively early kindergarten enrollment age makes up for some of the gap for these children.[232] A recent RAND report states: "We at the RAND Corporation have found that the most important factors associated with educational achievement of children are not race, ethnicity, or immigrant states. Instead, the most critical factors appear to be socioeconomic ones."[233]

Although socioeconomic status explains a large part of the school readiness gap, socioeconomic status itself is a proxy for many underlying factors. Poor parents are less likely to talk to, read with, and teach children than higher status parents. However, it is not clear which aspects of socioeconomic status affect these parenting skills.[234] New research on brain development shows that

[225] C. Rouse, J. Brooks-Gunn, & S. McLanahan (2005). "Introducing the Issue. School Readiness: Closing Racial and Ethnic Gaps." *The Future of Children* 15(1, Spring): 5.

[226] Ibid., p. 6.   [227] Ibid., p. 6.

[228] Ibid., p. 6.   [229] Ibid., p. 6.

[230] Ibid., p. 7.

[231] O'Brien-Strain, Moye, & Sonenstein (2003), p. viii.

[232] Ibid., p. viii.

[233] S. Lara-Cinisomo et al. (2004). "A Matter of Class: Educational Achievement Reflects Family Background More than Ethnicity or Immigration." *RAND Review* (Fall).

[234] Rouse, Brooks-Gunn, & McLanahan (2005), pp. 8–9.

chronic stress or abuse can impair cognitive ability; however, the plasticity of the child's brain suggests the promise of targeted educational interventions.[235] It is estimated that both child and maternal poor health and behavior can account for as much as a quarter of the racial gap in school readiness.[236] Rouse and her colleagues say that African American and Hispanic mothers are less likely to talk to and read daily to their children than white mothers, and, it is argued, that this can account for half of the racial and ethnic differences in school readiness.[237] Center-based child care or preschool programs improve school readiness. African American children are more likely than white children to be enrolled in preschool programs, particularly Head Start; Hispanic children are less likely. However, African American children are more likely to attend lower-quality preschool programs than white children.[238] A recent summary says, "[T]aken together, family socioeconomic status, parenting, child health, maternal health and behaviors, and preschool attendance likely account for most of the racial and ethnic gaps in school readiness."[239]

As discussed in Chapter 6, preschool programs, as well as child care, have to address both the needs of at-risk children and their working mothers.[240] During the 1990s, states were expanding their child care funding; since 2001, there have been cuts in child care assistance in at least twenty-three states.[241]

Thus far, according to Rouse and her colleagues, there is no strong evidence that increasing parental income positively affects school readiness. A recent report of Brookings and Princeton (Rouse and her colleagues) concludes that high-quality center-based early childhood education is the most promising strategy for low-income three- and four-year-olds.[242] Thus far, few child care centers and Head Start programs (discussed shortly) meet the standards of high quality – small classes, a high teacher-pupil ratio, college-educated teachers with training in early childhood education, and a cognitively stimulating curriculum.[243] Teachers have to be able to identify and work with children with moderate and severe health and behavioral problems. Parental skills should be improved to reinforce what the children are learning, including dealing with behavioral problems and health care. The preschool programs should be integrated with the kindergartens to ease the transitions. Thus far, high-quality early childhood programs reach only a small proportion of low-income children.[244]

[235] Ibid., p. 9.   [236] Ibid., p. 9.
[237] Ibid., p. 10.   [238] Ibid., p. 10.
[239] Ibid., p. 11.
[240] R. Schumacher et al. (2005). "All Together Now: State Experience in Using Community-Based Care to Provide Pre-Kindergarten" (paper prepared for the Brookings Institution & University of North Carolina on Creating a National Plan for the Education of 4-Year Olds," CLASP, rev., February), pp. 4–5.
[241] Ibid., p. 6.
[242] Rouse, Brooks-Gunn, & McLanahan (2005), p. 12.
[243] Ibid., p. 12.   [244] Ibid., pp. 12–13.

Head Start provides preschool for about eight hundred and fifty thousand children. Through the 1990s, there was an increase of 136 percent, at an annual cost of $4.7 billion.[245] In 2003, 1,047,500 children and 9,548 pregnant women received Head Start services, which was a 4 percent increase from 2002 and a 9 percent increase from 2001. Early Head Start, which serves primarily infants, toddlers, and pregnant women, is relatively small, serving approximately 8 percent of the total Head Start enrollment.[246] Head Start primarily serves children from low-income families – nearly three-quarters were from families below the poverty line. More than half (56%) are in single-parent families, most (61%) of whom were working.[247] The Head Start children are racially diverse – 31 percent African American, 31 percent Hispanic, 28 percent white, 3 percent American Indian, 2 percent Asian, and 1 percent Hawaiian or other Pacific Islander. More than a quarter (27%) of Head Start children had a primary language other than English. In most families (77%), neither parent had more than a high school degree. A fifth (21%) of the families were on TANF; 72 percent of the families had one or both parents employed. Nearly half (45%) of Head Start children and 53 percent of Early Head Start Children needed full-day, full-year child care because of the schedules of their parents. About 19 percent of all Head Start children and 75 percent of Early Head Start Children are enrolled in eight-hour-a-day or more services.[248] Ten percent of Head Start children and 20 percent of Early Head Start children received child care subsidies.[249]

Hart and Schumacher note other benefits to Head Start – increasing access to continuous medical and dental care, disability screening, and special education, as well as a variety of other services (e.g., adult education, housing assistance, transportation assistance).[250] Most (87%) Head Start children received medical screening, a quarter (24%) were assessed as needing treatment, and most (89%) of those who needed treatment received follow-up medical treatment. Of those who received dental screening (78%), 28 percent were diagnosed as needing treatment, and 77 percent of that group did receive treatment.[251] Head Start children are significantly more likely to have health insurance (89%) than all poor children (79%), either Medicaid or Early and Periodic Screening, Diagnosis, and Treatment (EPSDT) program, or a combination of Medicaid and CHIP, or private insurance (14%).[252]

Early Head Start provides services to pregnant women. Of these women, almost a quarter are younger than 18, and about the same number are identified as medically at "high risk." Services include both prenatal and postpartum

[245] Levine & Scholz (2002), p. 206.
[246] K. Hart & R. Schumacher (2004). "Moving Forward: Head Start Children, Families, and Programs in 2003" (Policy Brief No. 5, Head Start Series, CLASP, June), pp. 1–2.
[247] Ibid., p. 5.   [248] Ibid., p. 4.
[249] Ibid., p. 5.   [250] Ibid., p. 2.
[251] Ibid., p. 2.   [252] Ibid., p. 3.

health and mental health care.[253] Ninety-four percent received prenatal and postpartum health care, and 92 percent received prenatal and breast-feeding education. Thirteen percent of Head Start children were diagnosed with a disability (2002), and 91 percent received special services. Head Start families received parent education (32%), health education (27%), and adult education, job training, and ESL (23%).[254] A random-assignment study found that there were improvements in parents suffering from depressive symptoms, although the symptoms themselves were not significantly reduced, nor was there an increase in mental health services. There were improvements in three-year-olds whose mothers were at risk of depression.[255] There is also a Migrant Head Start program for children from birth through age 5.[256]

In addition to Head Start, there has been a considerable growth in state pre-kindergarten programs as more attention is being paid to school readiness.[257] Rachel Schumacher and her colleagues at the Center for Law and Social Policy (CLASP) report that there are initiatives in at least thirty-eight states and the District of Columbia, compared with only ten in 1980. About 740,000 children are served, at a cost of more than $2.5 billion in state funds. Most programs are part day and part year and targeted to four-year-olds based on income or other risk factors. Six states (Georgia, New Jersey, New York, Oklahoma, West Virginia, and Wisconsin) have plans for universal access to prekindergarten. Some programs are offered exclusively in the schools, whereas others use both schools and community-based child care.[258] Most (71%) children are in public school programs, 15 percent are in child care centers, 7 percent are in Head Start, and less than 1 percent are in faith-based settings.[259]

Schumacher and her colleagues identified at least twenty-nine states that are currently operating formal mixed programs – both in the public schools and in community-based child care settings.[260] Most state funding provides for less than a full day – hours range from 2.5 to 6.5, although some states specifically address the needs of working families and require that a certain amount

[253] Ibid. (2004), p. 4.
[254] K. Irish, R. Schumacher, & J. Lombardi (2004). "Head Start Comprehensive Services: A Key Support for Early Learning for Poor Children" (Policy Brief No. 4, Head Start Series, CLASP, January), p. 2.
[255] The children were more engaged in play with their parents, sustained attention while at play, and exhibited less negativity toward their parents. S. Lawrence, M. Chau, & M. Lennon (2004). "Depression, Substance Abuse, and Domestic Violence" (National Center for Children in Poverty, Columbia University, Mailman School of Public Health, June), p. 6, citing Mathematica Policy Research, Inc. (2002). "Early Head Start Research and Evaluation Project: Making a Difference in the Lives of the Infants and Toddlers and Their Families." Vol. 1: "The Impact of Early Head Start" (final technical report, Princeton, N.J.).
[256] Irish, Schumacher, & Lombardi (2004).
[257] Schumacher et al. (2005), p. 1.
[258] Ibid., pp. 2–3.
[259] Ibid., pp. 3–4.
[260] Ibid., pp. 9–10.

of funds be available to provide full-day, full-year (both variously defined) care. Some programs are targeted, and some require copayments. The states set standards for teacher qualifications, child ratios, curriculum, and other service requirements. The standards usually exceed state child care licensing standards. However, according to Schumacher and her colleagues, this creates problems in retaining community-based teachers. Child care teachers are low wage, but the standards for the prekindergarten programs are higher. Thus, when the community-based prekindergarten teachers reach the higher-level standards, they leave for better pay in school-based settings. Some states provide funds for training and staff development, scholarships, and so forth for community-based teachers. Although forty-five states and the District of Columbia invest in prekindergarten programs, only about 10 percent of all three- and four-year-olds are served by the state-funded programs. Only one is "universal" for all four-year-olds.[261]

Public policy on the care and education of infants and toddlers is further behind. Most working families do not have access to affordable quality care for children younger than age 3. For example, Early Head Start serves less than 3 percent of eligible children.[262] Only a handful of states provide sufficient funding to support a quality program during the times that are needed.[263] Publicly funded preschool slots are in short supply. In California, a recent study found that 326,758 children, aged 3 to 5, who were eligible for subsidized preschool, were not being served. More than three-quarters (76%) of publicly funded programs reported waiting lists that "sometimes were years long."[264]

Between 7 million and 15 million children are "latchkey children." When school lets out at 3 p.m., they return to an empty house because their parents are still working and safe, affordable, after-school programs are insufficient.[265] In 2001, both parents in almost 70 percent of married couples, with children between ages 6 and 17, worked outside the home, and 79 percent of mother-only families did. Many of these parents work full time, evenings, nights, or irregular shifts. The Food Research and Action Center estimates that "the difference between the parents' work schedules and their children's school schedules often totals between 20 and 25 hours a week."[266] These children are at increased risk of crime (perpetrators or victims), substance abuse, and sexual

[261] Ibid., pp. 25–31.
[262] J. Lombardi et al. (2004). "Building Bridges from Prekindergarten to Infants and Toddlers: A Preliminary Look at Issues in Four States" (discussion paper, Zero to Three Policy Center, April), p. 1.
[263] Schumacher et al. (2005), pp. 50–51.
[264] C. Rivera (2004). "Many Children, Few Preschool Slots," Los Angeles Times, February 9, 2005.
[265] Food Research and Action Center (2004). Afterschool Guide: Nourish Their Bodies, Feed Their Minds. Washington, D.C.: Food Research and Action Center, p. 4.
[266] Ibid., p. 4.

activity. After-school programs have been shown to decrease these risks and improve academic performance and health (by providing snacks and meals). In addition to providing nutrition, food seems to be an important attraction for older students.[267] The National School Lunch Program reimburses school-sponsored after-school programs for snacks. The program can be on or off school grounds and also can be offered by another organization, as long as the school sponsors the program. The Child and Adult Care Food program, which is operated by schools, local government agencies, and nonprofits, will also reimburse for snacks and, in some cases, meals. The Summer Food Service Program will provide funds to feed children during summer vacation or, if attending school yeararound, during breaks in the summer. The after-school programs are required to provide educational and enrichment programs. Sports and recreational activities can be included as long as they are open to all; competitive sports teams are not included. All of the programs are either means tested (if the child qualifies for free or reduced-price school meals) or the families have to live in a low-income area (50% or more of the children in one of the schools are eligible for free or reduced-price school meals). Reimbursement is tied to the number of snacks or meals served and thus funding increases with increases in the program. There are mandatory nutritional guidelines as well as health and safety standards. The programs only operate on school days or in the summer if the school is in session; weekend or school holiday programs are not reimbursed.[268]

Some programs for adolescents seem successful. As reported by Kemple and Scott-Clayton, Career Academies serve high schools, especially those that struggle to keep students in school and prepare them for postsecondary education and employment opportunities.[269] Typically, serving between 150 and 200 students from grades 9 or 10 through 12, Career Academies offer "(1) small learning communities to create a more personalized, supportive leaning environment; (2) combine academic and career and technical curricula around a career to enrich teaching and learning; (3) establish partnerships with local employers to provide career awareness and work-based learning opportunities." There are more than 2,500 academies nationwide.[270]

MDRC conducted a rigorous evaluation of Career Academies in a diverse group of nine high schools in medium- and large-school districts, serving a

[267] Ibid., p. 6.
[268] Ibid., p. 7. An example given is an after-school program in a low-income area, which is serving snacks to fifty children. It could receive about $5,400 per year, and with each new child, an additional $108. Snacks must include two out of the following four components: milk; fruits and vegetables (including juice); grains; and proteins. E.g., a glass of milk and an apple would qualify. A supper has to include all four components, e.g., a turkey sandwich, an apple, carrot sticks, and milk (pp. 9, 12).
[269] J. Kemple, with J. Scott-Clayton (2004). "Career Academies: Impacts on Labor Market Outcomes and Educational Attainment" (MDRC, March).
[270] Ibid., p. ES-1.

cross section of student populations. The control groups were students who applied unsuccessfully; applicants were randomly selected. Previous reports showed that the Academies were effective in raising higher levels of interpersonal support from teachers and peers and that students at high risk of dropping out increasingly completed high school, improved attendance, obtained more credits toward graduation, and gained work-learning internships. However, some students may have substituted more career-related courses for academic core courses and "thereby mitigated the employment-related benefits of the programs."[271]

The current report examines the educational attainment and postsecondary labor market experiences four years after scheduled graduation. Earnings for young men increased an average of $212 per month over the four years, which is an 18 percent increase over average earnings of the non-Academy group. The effect on the earnings is substantially higher than other workers who have had one or two years of postsecondary education or a GED. The report says that these findings are particularly "noteworthy in light of the declining labor market prospects for young men in recent years, particularly among young men with limited post-secondary education."[272] The increase in total earnings was probably due to an increase in the hours worked and the hourly wages; that is, the Academies were likely to have helped the men get better jobs. However, there was no effect, either positive or negative, on the young women. The report speculates that the women in the sample were more focused on attending postsecondary education or taking care of their children, although the women with children did have a slight boost in earnings per month.[273]

Housing

Lack of affordable housing has become a major problem for the poor and working poor. Housing assistance now consists entirely of rent subsidies (Section 8). Currently, there are about 3.4 million rental units, with an annual cost of $22.4 billion (fiscal year 2004),[274] with long waiting lists.[275] A recent report by the Office of Policy Development and Research (U.S. Department of Housing and Urban Development [HUD]) documents the "worst-case housing needs" from 1978 to 1999, with an update in 2001.[276] "Worst-case" needs

---

[271] Ibid., p. ES-2.

[273] Ibid.

[275] National Low Income Housing Coalition (2004). "Out of Reach 2004." Washington, D.C.: NLIH. In the meantime, authorized vouchers are being reduced. Institute for the Study of Homelessness and Poverty (2005). "Local Effects of Voucher Funding Shortfalls Reports that Los Angeles City Housing Authority Will Cut an Estimated 1,995 Families in 2005."

[276] Office of Policy Development and Research (2003). "A Report to Congress on Worst Case Housing Needs. Plus Update on Worst Case Needs in 2001" (U.S. Department of Housing and Urban Development, December).

[272] Ibid., p. ES-3.

[274] http://www.hud.gov/offices/cfo/pafinal.pdf.

are defined as unassisted renters with very low incomes (below 50% of area median income) who pay more than half of their income for housing or live in severely substandard housing."[277] The most common problem is severe rent burdens. In 2001, there was an estimated 5.07 million households of very low income renters who had worst-case needs. Three-quarters of the worst-case needs had incomes below 30 percent of the area median income. In 1999, 4.6 million renter households without assistance had worst-case needs, including 3.6 million children, and HUD estimates that in 2001, there were only forty-two affordable units for every 100 renters with incomes below 30 percent of the area median. "Critical housing needs," defined as those with incomes below 120 percent of the area median, rose to 14.46 million between 1999 and 2001. The number of renters with incomes below 80 percent of the area median who paid more than half of their income for housing rose by 1 million.[278] Between 1997 and 1999, the number of worst-case renters dropped; this was due to a rise in incomes among very low income renters, not an increase in affordable housing. However, the share of renters experiencing "severe housing problems" increased.[279]

In a recent report of the California Budget Project, the incomes of the median low-income renters not only failed to keep up with inflation but actually registered its "largest decline between 1989 and 2002," adjusting for inflation. The household income of low-income renters – at the twentieth percentile – fell 10.3 percent, from $16,249 to $14,580. Many of these low-income renters are paying more than half of their income for housing. In Orange County (south of Los Angeles), 73.2 percent of households with incomes below $20,000 pay more than 50 percent of their income on housing.[280] In Los Angeles, the fair-market value for a two-bedroom apartment is $1,021, which is only affordable for families earning at least $40,840, or the equivalent of three minimum wage jobs.[281] "Many California renters live with substandard conditions, such as lack of electricity, a lack of complete kitchen and/or bathroom facilities, frequent breakdowns of heating systems, water leaks, or large areas of peeling paint or plaster."[282] Not surprisingly, there has been an increase in homeless families. The U.S. Conference of Mayors reported that in 2002, 13 percent of the homeless population of Los Angeles was families with children, an increase of 10 percent from the previous year. A report found that approximately two-thirds of the homeless families recently lost CalWORKS (California's TANF) benefits; many (42%) had some type of disability.[283] Federal housing assistance has either declined or has not kept pace with demand.

[277] Ibid., p. xix.   [278] Ibid., p. xx.
[279] Ibid., pp. 2–4, 9.
[280] California Budget Project (2004b). "Locked Out 2004: California's Affordable Housing Crisis" (January), p. 2.
[281] Ibid., p. 6.   [282] Ibid., p. 9.
[283] Ibid., p. 18.

The waiting list for public housing. or Section 8 housing assistance has grown by more than two thousand families per month in 2002. The city estimates that it is meeting only 8 percent of need.[284]

Compounding the lack of affordable housing is the continuing geographic concentration of poverty and residential segregation, which is still very high among African Americans, regardless of socioeconomic status; the spatial isolation of Hispanics and Asians has also increased, especially among recent immigrants. In short, "poverty concentration continues to plague American cities."[285]

Starting in the 1990s, new approaches were undertaken to transform the nation's public housing developments.[286] A prominent strategy was designed to broaden the income mix of public housing tenants through work. With some of the most severely distressed public housing, initiatives were undertaken to replace the old buildings with new housing that included a mix of subsidized and unsubsidized units for a broader range of incomes.[287] There is a report on the Rainer Vista housing development, which was to be rebuilt under a federal HOPE VI grant (Housing Opportunities for People Everywhere), with participation in Jobs-Plus Community Revitalization Initiative for Public Housing Families (Jobs-Plus), jointly developed by HUJD, the Rockefeller Foundation, and MDRC. This project was especially challenging not only because of the anxieties, disruption, and uncertainties of the loss of the homes but also because many of the residents were immigrants who, collectively, spoke twenty-two different languages.[288]

The program (1998) offered all nondisabled, working-age residents three types of services and supports: "(1) employment and training services, including job search, education and training, and services focused on career advancement; (2) financial incentives to subsidize earnings, particularly to offset higher rents based on increased earnings; (3) community support for work to strengthen social ties (meetings, workshops, etc. to exchange information, prepare resumes, etc.)."[289] During the demolition and reconstruction, some residents would be relocated, at least temporarily, to other public housing units or private housing (with rent subsidies) or shifted to other apartments, which would subsequently be demolished. Under the HOPE IV grant, community support services were offered. The services were offered both to tenants who planned to move back and those who planned to relocate permanently.[290]

[284] Ibid., pp. 18–23.
[285] M. Zonta (2005). "Review Essay. Housing Policies and the Concentration of Poverty in Urban American." *Social Service Review* (March): 181–85, p. 182.
[286] E. Liebow et al., with S. Blank (2004). "Resident Participation in Seattle's Jobs-Plus Program" (Environmental Health and Social Policy Center, MDRC, Seattle, Washington, October).
[287] Ibid., p. ES-1.   [288] Ibid., p. ES-1.
[289] Ibid., pp. ES 1–2.   [290] Ibid., p. ES-2.

Seattle was one of six cities selected to test the effectiveness of Jobs-Plus (the other cities were Baltimore, Dayton, Chattanooga, two sites in Los Angeles, and St. Paul). Despite the highly diverse tenant population, nearly two-thirds of the tenants participated in the employability services and financial incentives. However, even though there was an "energetic" and highly personalized employment program, a "considerable proportion" of residents remained skeptical that they would be helped, partly because of the sharp decline in the Seattle economy. Many residents saw highly qualified workers competing for entry-level and low-wage jobs.[291] A strong effort was made to address the diversity of the tenants (e.g., translating materials in multiple languages, diverse outreach workers, partnerships with social service agencies that specialized in immigrant and refugee populations). One unforeseen adverse consequence was that initially, some U.S.-born residents were of the impression that the program was mainly for immigrants.[292]

Considerable effort was made with community organizations to recruit and train residents for positions on the Leadership Team, a formal body that represented tenants on housing and community issues in the development. A Leadership Team did emerge that did reflect the broad diversity of the tenants and assumed responsibility for overseeing the operation of the Job Resources Center. A sense of resident ownership developed. Residents then used their community organizing and management skills to convince the housing authority to reserve some of the rebuilt units for residents in good standing who wanted to return and help establish relocating priorities. However, as the redevelopment proceeded, the Jobs-Plus staff tended to concentrate on the needs of the tenants who chose to remain, at the expense of those who elected to move elsewhere.[293]

Health Care

Social Security recipients qualify for Medicare and poor people for Medicaid. Both programs are very extensive and expensive. State Children's Health Insurance Program supplements Medicaid by providing health care for children in families with income somewhat above the Medicaid limits. Medicaid and State Children's Health Insurance Program (SCHIP) provide health insurance for 55 million people.[294] As described by Katz, there was a long struggle to provide health care, even for the elderly and the poor.[295] The American Medical Association and other health professional organizations vigorously opposed public health insurance. President Roosevelt would not include it in the 1935 Social Security Act, fearing it would jeopardize the pension

[291] Ibid., p. ES-4.
[293] Ibid., pp. ES-5–6.
[295] Katz (2001).

[292] Ibid., pp. ES-4–5.
[294] Shapiro, Parrott, & Springer (2005), p. 3.

proposals. Private prepaid health insurance (primarily Blue Cross and Blue Shield) started to grow primarily through employment.[296] Finally, in 1965, Congress approved Medicare and Medicaid. This was not national health insurance; rather, the basic distinction between the "deserving" and "undeserving" poor was maintained even in health insurance. Medicare was for those aged 65 and older. Part A covers hospital costs, and Part B doctor bills. Part A, financed primarily through the payroll tax, is compulsory. Part B is funded through general revenues and individual premiums. Neither covers the full costs of health care (a large exclusion is long-term care); those who can afford it purchase additional insurance, called "Medigap."[297] Medigap insurance is expensive, and since 1980, Medicaid pays Medicare deductibles and Part B premiums for poor people. Medicare reimburses hospitals and doctors for reasonable costs and prevailing fees; thus, argues Katz, "this open-ended funding arrangement... unleashed the inflation of medical costs."[298] Medicare was instantly popular. Millions of elderly saw doctors and entered hospitals. According to Katz, the proportion of elderly who had never seen a doctor declined from 20 percent to 8 percent; 100,000 elderly entered a hospital per week during the first three years.[299] Medicare has grown from $16.9 billion in 1967 to $252 billion in FY 2002.[300] More than half (52%) of the benefits go to poor families.[301]

Medicaid is the health insurance for the poor and is a joint federal-state matching grant program. Medicaid cost $244 billion in fiscal year 2002.[302] Like AFDC (and now TANF), states have considerable discretion concerning eligibility and benefits, with significant variation among the states. Hospitals and doctors are reimbursed at lower rates than Medicare.[303] Medicaid and SCHIP are usually the only health insurance available for the more than 55 million low-income people, including 40 million children and parents and 12 million people with chronic disabilities. Currently, Medicaid pays nearly 20 percent of all health expenditures and nearly half of all money spent on long-term care.[304] Most recipients (more than 70%) are poor. Low-income families (less than 200% of the poverty line), spend approximately 70 percent of their income on basic living expenses (housing, transportation, food) and 7 percent on health care.[305] Nevertheless, millions of nonaged Americans are

---

[296] Ibid., chap. 10.

[297] Ibid., p. 260.

[298] Ibid.

[299] Ibid., p. 261.

[300] U.S. Health and Human Services. 2003 CMS Statistics. Retrieved from http://www.cms.hhs.gov/home/rsds.asp.

[301] Levine & Scholz (2002), p. 199.

[302] U.S. Health and Human Services. 2003 CMS Statistics.

[303] Katz (2001), p. 260.

[304] Kaiser Commission on Medicaid and the Uninsured (2004). "Faces of Medicaid" (Kaiser Family Foundation, April), p. 2.

[305] C. Williams et al. (2004). "Challenges and Tradeoff in Low-Income Family Budgets: Implications for Health Coverage" (Kaiser Commission on Medicaid and the Uninsured, Kaiser Family Foundation, April), p. 1.

not covered by Medicaid. Most have employer-based health insurance, but, at present, almost 46 million Americans have no health insurance at all. This is an increase of 800,000 uninsured people since 2003.[306] Medicaid enrollment was expanded in the late 1980s and early 1990s; without this expansion, more than a million additional adults would be without health insurance.[307] More recently, a number of states have implemented new or increased cost sharing for Medicaid and SCHIP, which has resulted in a loss of enrollment in several states.[308]

Not surprisingly, there is a relationship between income and wealth and health.[309] Health insurance coverage fell for families with annual income of less than $75,000. Almost 16 percent of people did not have health insurance in 2003, an increase from 14.2 percent in 2000.[310] More than a third (nearly 37%) of low-income families (200% of poverty) – 3.4 million – had a least one parent who lacked health insurance. In many cases, their employers do not provide health insurance but their earnings make them ineligible for government insurance. Among poor working families, almost half had at least one parent without health insurance.[311]

Those in the top 5 percent of the income distribution can expect to live, on average, nine years longer than those in the bottom 10 percent. Medicaid and Medicare have helped, but the poor still have the lowest rates of health care services. In 2002, approximately a third of the poor had no insurance for the entire year.[312] When illness becomes serious enough, they use hospital emergency rooms for primary care.

In a study of low-income (less than 200% of the poverty line) families in three cities (Baltimore, Des Moines, Oakland), the Kaiser Family Foundation reported lower earnings as a result of the recession (2003). The families are working harder to try and make up for the lost income, live from paycheck to paycheck, and rotate paying bills (with rent coming first), and almost none

---

[306] Center on Budget and Policy Priorities (2005). "The Number of Uninsured Americans Continued to Rise in 2004" (August 30), p. 1.

[307] Shapiro, Parrott, & Springer (2005), p. 3.

[308] S. Artiga & M. O'Malley (2005). "Medicaid and the Uninsured: Increasing Premiums and Cost Sharing in Medicaid and SCHIP: Recent State Experiences" (Kaiser Family Foundation). The report gives several examples of states that have raised the costs for families with incomes up to 150 percent of poverty and experienced significant disenrollments. Disenrolled families were left uninsured.

[309] A. Wenzlow et al. (2004). "An Empirical Investigation of the Relationship between Wealth and Health Using the Survey of Consumer Finances" (Institute for Research on Poverty, University of Wisconsin, August). The study is based on the Survey of Consumer Finances (SCF), a nationally representative survey of families on income and assets. SCF is triennial of a cross section of approximately four thousand to five thousand families.

[310] D. Leonhardt (2004). "More Americans Were Uninsured and Poor in 2003, Census Finds." New York Times, August 27.

[311] T. Waldron, B. Roberts, & A. Reamer (2004). "Working Hard, Falling Short: America's Working Families and the Pursuit of Economic Security" (national report, Working Poor Families Project, Annie E. Casey Foundation, Washington, D.C.), p. 10.

[312] Rank (2004), pp. 39–40.

of these working families have employer-sponsored health insurance.[313] Even those who have employer health insurance, have trouble paying the premiums. Regular monthly spending on health care is usually not high, but many families have large, unpaid medical bills, mostly from accidents or other one-time, unexpected problems, or chronic conditions.[314] Those without health insurance are reluctant to seek health care because of the debt. Although most of the parents lack health insurance, most of the children are covered though Medicaid and SCHIP. The Kaiser report states that "opportunities to obtain coverage and protection from medical bills were largely outside their grasp." Many families are not offered employer insurance or do not qualify because of work hours, short tenure, or changing jobs. Nongroup insurance is too costly and has high deductibles. The Kaiser report states that private insurance now costs, on average, $3,400 per year for an individual and $9,068 for a family. Tax credits, ranging between $1,000 and $3,000 per year, would not be much help to low-income working families.[315] Although the children are covered, the income eligibility of the parents is much lower. Childless adults usually do not qualify for Medicaid. In the meantime, the states, facing increasing budgetary pressures, are imposing premiums and cost sharing, dropping benefits, and reducing eligibility.[316]

Although states have some discretion as to eligibility, they now have to cover former TANF recipients and pregnant women and children with incomes up to 133 percent of the poverty line; they can expand this to 185 percent of the poverty line. These changes led to a large expansion of the rolls, to 40.6 million people in 1998. Medicaid also covers the disabled and the elderly who are poor, and these groups absorb most of the costs. Medicaid expenditures doubled in the 1990s to $188.8 billion (1998).[317] When the rolls went down, especially post-1996, the Medicaid rolls also dropped significantly even though many former recipients were still eligible. Subsequently, states began efforts to re-enroll recipients, and the rolls have increased.

Pressure is now mounting in the states to reduce Medicaid spending as fiscal conditions have deteriorated over the past three years. Cuts in eligibility, limits on benefits, and increases in cost sharing will likely result in increases in the uninsured, unmet needs for people with disabilities, and a reduction in health for people with significant medical and long-term needs.[318] At the same time, the states are resisting pressures from the White House to reduce Medicaid funding.

Trying to Reform Health Insurance

By 1970, the problems with the U.S. health care system became manifest. As described by Katz, in an effort to try and control rising health care costs,

---

[313] Williams et al. (2004), pp. 1–2.
[315] Ibid., p. 11.
[317] Levine & Scholz (2002), pp. 201–3.

[314] Ibid., p. 8.
[316] Ibid., p. 2.
[318] Kaiser Commission (2004), p. 2.

the federal government, in the 1970s, began to promote health maintenance organizations (HMOs). The idea was that with a prepaid, fixed premium, the HMO would have an incentive to hold down utilization and costs. Health maintenance organizations grew slowly until the 1990s. Other attempts at regulating and planning also failed to contain costs.[319] In 1981, the Reagan Administration reduced Medicaid costs by reducing eligibility and allowing state programs more flexibility. The Reagan Administration also changed the reimbursement formula for hospitals – there would be a fixed amount per diagnosis on admission to encourage hospitals to cut costs – called "prospective payment." Both hospital admissions and average length of stay declined.[320] Other cost-cutting measures included a Medicare fee schedule for doctors and increasing cost sharing, deductibles, and premiums. According to Katz, these measures were effective in reducing the expected growth of Medicare by 20 percent.[321]

One of the most dramatic examples of the class politics in health care was the brief life of the Medicare Catastrophic Care Act (MCCA).[322] To help the elderly cope with the high costs of catastrophic illness or extended care, Medicare would pay deductibles and co-insurance for the very poor and reduce the costs for the rest of the low-income elderly. However, to pay for this, Medicare costs were raised for the middle-income elderly. The AARP supported the change, but other lobbying groups and the middle-income elderly opposed it. It was repealed the following year, except for some Medicaid benefits. As Katz states, "Even minimal changes [in Medicare] are expensive, and the elderly, when they are asked to pay for them directly, object, especially if benefits are slanted toward the poor and away from the middle class."[323]

In the meantime, the health care industry consolidated and eventually became dominated by huge business-like conglomerates. In Katz's terms, it was a "corporate makeover."[324] There was a rise in investor-owned hospitals and group practices by doctors with joint ownership in for-profit hospitals. Still, costs were not reduced. Employer plans became both more expensive and less comprehensive. Along with the changes in the labor market, the proportion of covered employees declined from 86 percent to 74 percent. Only about half the poor were covered by Medicaid. The spread of managed care, however, reduced the ability of hospitals to finance uncompensated care.[325] The elderly, even with Medicare, still spent more than a fifth of their income on health care.[326] President Clinton's attempt at health care reform collapsed in 1994. The public was more interested in controlling health care

[319] Katz (2001), pp. 263–64.   [320] Ibid., p. 264.
[321] Ibid., p. 264.   [322] Ibid., p. 265.
[323] Ibid., p. 265.   [324] Ibid., p. 266.
[325] Ibid., p. 275.   [326] Ibid., p. 266.

costs than extending coverage to the uninsured. Since then, national health insurance has dropped off the political agenda.[327]

The major changes in health care occurred in the private sector. With the spread of managed care and the "marketization" of health care, employers were able to both reduce costs and shift more of the costs onto employees.[328] By the mid-1990s, "health care had become a trillion-dollar-a-year industry, with its income divided as follows: hospitals, including the big and fast-growing chains ($410 billion); physicians ($200 billion); insurance companies ($65 billion); and others ('dentists, optometrists, physical therapists and pharmacies') (over $100 billion). Battles in health care revolved as much around profits as around the quality and extent of care."[329] Many public hospitals serving the indigent suffered losses and were forced to cut back staff, beds, and services as Medicaid patients were assigned to HMOs. The for-profit hospitals increased their costs and tried to avoid Medicaid patients.[330]

In the meantime, HMOs began to suffer losses. In addition to closing hospitals and medical centers and reducing staff, HMOs began to drop Medicaid programs because of the decline in government reimbursement rates (by 20% between the mid- and late-1990s); similarly, HMOs dropped more than 700,000 Medicare patients between 1998 and 1999. The federal government estimated that an additional 200,000 would be dropped by 2000.[331] The rise in health costs did begin to slow, starting in 1996, but this mostly benefited employers and providers as they continued to shift more of the cost to their employees; insurance companies continued to increase Medigap insurance; the premiums for Medicare Part B increased; and more public assistance recipients were removed from Medicaid.[332] But the pressures remained – the aging population, technology, pharmacology – and costs continued to rise, as did the number of uninsured.[333] As Katz points out, "those particularly vulnerable were the low- and middle-income families, young adults, the near aged, minorities, immigrants, employees in small businesses, the self-employed, those in temporary and part-time jobs, those who change jobs, new employees who have pre-existing conditions."[334] The most common reason California employers give for not offering health coverage is high premiums. About half of California employees who were eligible did not participate because the plan was too expensive. On average, the worker's share of the premium was 30 percent – average annual cost for family health coverage was $7,481 for an HMO, $10,020 for a prefered provider organization plan.[335]

---

[327] See Katz (2001), pp. 266–73, for a discussion of the failure of the Clinton health care reform.
[328] Ibid., p. 276.   [329] Ibid.
[330] Ibid.   [331] Ibid., pp. 280–81.
[332] Ibid., p. 281.   [333] Ibid.
[334] Ibid., p. 282.
[335] California Budget Project (2005). *Lasting Returns: Investing in Health Coverage for California's Children*. Sacramento, Calif.: CBP.

There was a move by the Clinton Administration and the Democrats to establish a patients' bill of rights, which, among other things, would allow suits against HMOs for the denial of treatment, but it was defeated. In reaction, various health care reforms were enacted in the states – patients' rights, price controls on prescription drugs, and nursing staff ratios.[336] At the same time, cost-cutting reforms continued. Sharp reductions were made in Medicare's home health care provisions. Congress put on a cap, limited the amount of payments, tightened eligibility, and restricted home visits to clients with short-term, acute care needs. By 1998, there was a considerable reduction in the number of home visit agencies and visits.[337]

Nursing home care consumed a fifth of Medicaid expenses in 1996. In 1997, Congress reduced the nursing home rates and allowed the states to reduce payments, as part of a $15 billion in reduction in the federal share of Medicaid. Congress also repealed federal and state quality-of-care standards for nursing homes. Subsequently, there were exposés of nursing home scandals.[338]

One of the most serious problems for Medicare patients at or below the poverty line was the cost of prescription drugs. A 1998 study reported that 2 million of the poor and near-poor elderly spent more than half of their income on health care costs that were not reimbursed by Medicare. Political battles were joined over the issue of controlling prescription drug costs, as well as other health care reforms. But partisan differences prevented any legislation from being enacted. As Katz summarizes, "Health care reform remained a complicated, politically explosive issue."[339]

Health Insurance for Low-Income Children

A significant change came with insurance for low-income children – the State Children's Health Insurance Program (SCHIP) enacted in 1997. The SCHIP specifically targeted the children of working families, where the family earnings were too high for Medicaid but private insurance was unaffordable. In 1997, approximately 11 million children, 16 percent of all children, were uninsured. The proportion of children covered by their parents' employer-based insurance had declined from 67 percent in 1987 to 59 percent in 1995.[340] In 1998, $24 billion was set aside over five years to cover the costs of insurance, administration, and outreach. A provision was made to target only uninsured children, not children who already had coverage. Matching funds of $4.3 billion were appropriated, with the federal government paying a larger share than it did for Medicaid.[341] The

[336] Katz (2001), p. 284.
[337] Ibid., pp. 286–87.
[338] Ibid., p. 287.
[339] Ibid., pp. 288–92.
[340] B. Wolfe & S. Scrivner with A. Snyder. (2003a). "The Devil May Be in the Details: How Characteristics of SCHIP Programs Affect Take-Up" (Discussion Papers No. 1272-03, Institute for Research on Poverty, University of Wisconsin), p. 2.
[341] Wolfe & Scrivner (2003a), p. 1.

money would go to the states to add to their existing programs. States were given broad flexibility to create or expand existing programs, to expand Medicaid, or to combine the two and to set eligibility criteria in terms of age, income, resources, and residency, within broad federal guidelines.[342]

States can change Medicaid eligibility, although once eligibility is established, then all families and their children below that threshold are entitled to enroll. SCHIP is different. These are separate programs and are not entitlements. States have a great deal of flexibility; they can establish presumptive eligibility, waiting periods during which the child is uninsured (to prevent "crowding out" of private insurance), and application procedures. Four states extended eligibility to parents under waivers.[343] Although eligibility thresholds are subject to state changes, enrollment can also be capped by the states in response to budget deficits.[344] During the economic expansion of the 1990s, the states engaged in rapid implementation and "unprecedented investment in both outreach and enrollment simplification."[345] Enrollment increased rapidly, from less than 2 million in 1999 to nearly 4 million by June 2003. The rates of the uninsured dropped from 12.6 percent to 10.1 percent between 1999 and 2001.[346]

Although states vary widely in terms of programs, Wolfe and her colleagues say that "an average level of coverage appears to be emerging" – an upper limit of 200 percent of the poverty line.[347] By 2000, forty-seven states (including the District of Columbia) no longer required a personal interview, and an increasing number dropped an asset test for Medicaid or SCHIP.[348] All states but two accept applications by mail or fax, thirty-six states have dedicated phone lines, others provide Web sites, and six states use community organizations.[349]

In the first five years of the program, the states made substantial progress because of the program's flexibility. On the basis of Current Population Studies (CPS) data for 1998, 1999, and 2000, Wolfe and her colleagues report that several factors increased the take-up rate, such as children in fair or poor health, a parent with more schooling or a work limitation, and a family with higher income. Take-up rates were lower with older parents, nonwhite or Hispanic, and recent residence. Somewhat surprisingly, take-up was lower when

---

[342] Ibid., p. 3.   [343] Ibid., p. 1.

[344] I. Hill, H. Stockdale, & B. Courtot (2004). "Squeezing SCHIP: States Use Flexibility to Respond to the Ongoing Budget Crisis" (Series A, No. A-65, Urban Institute, New Federalism, Issues and Options for States, State Children's Health Insurance Program Evaluation, June), p. 4.

[345] Ibid., p. 2.

[346] Ibid., p. 2. The report is part of multiyear evaluation of SCHIP by the Urban Institute. Thirteen SCHIP administrators and other officials were interviewed. The thirteen states include four SCHIP programs with the largest enrollment (California, New York, Florida, and Texas), which, together, account for nearly two-thirds of SCHIP enrollment.

[347] Wolfe & Scrivner (2003a), p. 4.   [348] Ibid., p. 6.

[349] Ibid., pp. 6–7.

the parent was a full-time worker. Children were more likely to be re-enrolled when SCHIP was part of Medicaid rather than a separate program. Presumptive eligibility was important in the early years of the program. Requiring personal interviews was not important, primarily because so few states had this requirement. Dedicated phone lines were the most important in increasing enrollment. Expanding coverage to families with children costs more but does reduce the proportion of uninsured.[350]

Wisconsin developed a program that substantially increased the enrollment of low-income mothers. Shortly after initiating its welfare reform, Wisconsin Works (W-2; discussed in Chapter 4) adopted its SCHIP program, called BadgerCare,[351] which began in 1999. Unlike most other SCHIP programs, adults were included. Medicaid was also expanded by providing insurance for both children and adults with incomes below 185 percent of the poverty line; those enrolled can remain on the program until their income exceeds 200 percent of the poverty line. There were two goals: to reduce the low-income uninsured population and to help welfare leavers who found jobs that did not provide insurance. According to Wolfe and her colleagues, BadgerCare did reduce the proportion of low-income people without health insurance.[352] Once enacted, enrollment in "family-based" public health insurance (families that include a minor child and are not covered by SSI) increased substantially, with a higher proportion of adults than children. Total enrollments increased from 218,000 in 1999 to 367,000 at the end of 2001, including 90,000 in BadgerCare.[353] Looking at three cohorts of low-income, single mothers who were on welfare and then left welfare in terms of whether they are covered by public health insurance, have any insurance, or are without coverage in 1995, 1997, and 1999, at the time of exiting welfare, all of the leavers were eligible for Medicaid, and about 80 percent enrolled. Over the next four years, until BadgerCare started, the percentage eligible fell to 63 percent and less than 20 percent were enrolled. The proportion who were eligible (over 90%) and enrolled increased substantially (nearly 30% of the leavers) after the introduction of BadgerCare. There were similar significant increases in the next cohort. In sum, BadgerCare substantially increased the public health insurance for low-skilled single mothers.[354]

By 2003, nearly every state had experienced three years of budget deficits, and SCHIP is starting to feel the pressure.[355] At first, states resorted to reserves, special "rainy day" funds, accounting maneuvers, and tobacco settlement

---

[350] Ibid., pp. 7–25.
[351] B. Wolfe et al. (2004). "Extending Health Care Coverage to the Low-Income Population: The Influence of the Wisconsin BadgerCare Program on Insurance Coverage" (Discussion Paper No. 1289-04, Institute for Research on Poverty, University of Wisconsin, October).
[352] Ibid., pp. 1–2.   [353] Ibid., p. 5.
[354] Ibid., p. 24.   [355] Hill, Stockdale, & Courtot (2004), p. 1.

funds. By 2003, real cuts had to be made. Most states made cuts in Medicaid, education (both K–12 and higher education), and public safety. At first, SCHIP was spared because it was relatively small, very popular (insuring low-income children), and had a high federal matching rate.[356] However, in a study of thirteen states, the Urban Institute reported that SCHIP was now feeling squeezed. Enrollment was frozen in three states; thousands of children were placed on waiting lists. Nearly a third of the states made it more difficult for families to apply. Half the states raised or imposed cost sharing. Nearly half the states froze or reduced reimbursement rates to providers. Outreach was discontinued in most states.[357] In 2003, four states (in the study) cut SCHIP eligibility. Texas reduced income thresholds; three other states instituted enrollment caps. Texas also imposed a ninety-day waiting period for new enrollees. Alabama's cap put 11,500 children on the waiting list; Florida's waiting list increased to more than 100,000 children; about a quarter were noncitizen children eligible only for a state-funded program.[358] Most states use various forms of cost sharing, premiums, enrollment fees, and co-payments, although, until recently, they have been modest. Now, most states are increasing the costs.[359] Previously, states had maintained reimbursement rates to providers but that has changed. Nearly half of the states have either frozen the reimbursement rates or cut the rates.[360] According to the Centers for Disease Control and Prevention, 14.7 percent of poor children and 15.1 percent of near-poor children (up to 200% of the poverty line) were uninsured in 2004.[361]

However, SCHIP still remains popular and has done better than other state programs. A majority of states have preserved or even expanded their benefits.[362] New efforts to simplify enrollment and renewal procedures were undertaken in two-thirds of the states. Innovative enrollment initiatives were undertaken in large states, such as California and New York.[363] Four states actually expanded the program. Some states (e.g., Michigan and Washington) extended the program to include pregnant women with incomes up to 185 percent of the poverty line; Massachusetts extended it to up to 200 percent and Minnesota to 275 percent of the poverty line.[364] A few states tightened the eligibility process, but most (two-thirds) simplified the process. For example, New York, "in an unprecedented move," implemented "presumptive eligibility" for SCHIP renewals.[365] California streamlined enrollment in Medi-Cal

[356] Ibid., p. 1. The report is part of multiyear evaluation of SCHIP by the Urban Institute. Thirteen SCHIP administrators and other officials were interviewed.
[357] Ibid., p. 2.   [358] Ibid., p. 3.
[359] Ibid., pp. 6–8.   [360] Ibid., p. 8.
[361] Institute for the Study of Homelessness and Poverty (2005).
[362] Hill, Stockdale, & Courtot (2004), p. 3.   [363] Ibid., p. 2.
[364] Ibid., p. 4.   [365] Ibid., p. 5.

and Healthy Families.[366] Although most states eliminated outreach programs, many outreach programs are continuing on the local level.[367]

In sum, the SCHIP picture is mixed. There have been reductions in many of the states and an increase in cost sharing. However, programs have expanded in other states; and the reductions, although certainly serious, have been quite modest in comparison to other state programs and to employer-based insurance. For example, all the states have a SCHIP program with eligibility, on average, of more than 200 percent of the poverty line. The applications in every state have been simplified, requiring a minimum of verification, and coverage lasts at least six months. Benefits are comprehensive. Combined with Medicaid, the rate of uninsurance among low-income children has been reduced from 23 percent to just more than 17 percent. States' budgets are starting to improve somewhat; however, states have used up their rainy-day funds and tobacco settlements, and the federal matching is becoming increasingly uncertain.[368]

California has a number of programs. Each has different eligibility requirements and offers different services. Ten counties have programs for health coverage for uninsured children who do not qualify for Medi-Cal or Healthy Families. The barriers to enrollment include complexity, the renewal processes, lack of knowledge, and the association of Medicaid with welfare. With immigrant families, there are language barriers, lack of understanding of program rules, or the fear of repercussions if they use public benefits.[369]

California used SCHIP funding to create the Healthy Families Program, which provided coverage for more than 640,000 children, in June 2004.[370] Medi-Cal provided coverage for about 3 million children in 2003. Still, many low-income children are not insured. In California, almost 1.7 million children, ages 0–17, were uninsured at least part of the year in 2002, and almost two-thirds of these children were eligible for one of the state's programs.[371] This was approximately 907,000 children. Children more likely to be uninsured were disproportionately racial/ethnic minorities or were very poor. Most of California's uninsured children are in working families, 69.6 percent were in families in which the head was working full time year-round, and 85.2 percent were in families where the head worked at least part time. Many lacked

[366] Ibid., p. 5. "The "express lane eligibility" uses information from the federal Free and Reduced Lunch Program application to complete the Medi-Cal applications, and the "CHDP Gateway" allows uninsured children who receive checkups through the state's Child Health and Disability Prevention (CHDP) program to be "pre-enrolled in two months of Medi-Cal/Healthy Families coverage while CHDP providers complete and submit a formal application on their behalf."
[367] Ibid., pp. 5–6.   [368] Ibid., pp. 9–10.
[369] California Budget Project (2005). *Lasting Returns: Investing in Health Coverage for California's Children*. Sacramento, Calif.: CBP.
[370] Ibid.
[371] C. A. Mendez-Luck et al. (2004). "Many Uninsured Children Qualify for Medi-Cal or Health Families" (policy brief, UCLA Center for Health Policy Research, June), p. 1.

access to employment-based insurance and reported affordability as the primary reason they were not insured. Uninsured children are twice as likely to report fair or poor health and four times more likely to lack a usual source of care, compared with insured children, which makes treating both chronic and acute diseases more difficult. Uninsured children are more likely to use emergency rooms as a regular source of care and more likely to have unmet needs for prescription drugs, dental care, and medical care.[372]

Various proposals to increase eligibility include expanding and improving express lane eligibility; implementing the Newborn Hospital Gateway; bridging children's transfer from Medi-Cal and Healthy Families to county coverage programs; allowing Medi-Cal applicants to self-certify income; simplifying the renewal process; making Healthy Families premiums easier to pay; maximizing federal funding for local outreach and enrollment assistance; restoring state support for certified application assistants (CAAs) who help applicants complete paperwork. Other state innovations include expanding eligibility; allowing higher income families to purchase health coverage through state "buy-in" programs; helping families cover the cost of employment-based health coverage through premium-assistance programs; and allowing employers and families to purchase coverage through state-subsidized programs.[373]

Another serious child health problem involves the more than 500,000 children in foster care.[374] According to the most current federal data, more than 19,000 young people, aged 18–21 "aged out" of foster care in fiscal year 2001. They often face multiple obstacles in the transition to adulthood but have little support and few resources. Many have already suffered from abuse, neglect, or abandonment. In the only nationally representative study (1992), half suffered from substance abuse, two-thirds had not completed high school or obtained a GED, 61 percent had no job experience, and 17 percent were pregnant. In a follow-up study two-and-a-half to four years later, only about half had completed high school, fewer than half held jobs, and a quarter experienced homelessness at least one night. Several state studies found comparable results. There are various state and federal programs. Under the Foster Care Independence Act of 1999 (renamed the Chafee Foster Care Independence Program), the states are required to contribute 20 percent matching. Many states have supplemented with their own funds; others did not provide the match. In fiscal year 2003, the federal government authorized $60 million in postsecondary and training vouchers. The HUD Family Unification Program (FUP) offers housing assistance in the form of time-limited vouchers to youth 18–21 who left foster care. Other services include education, counseling, job

[372] California Budget Project (2005); Mendez-Luck et al. (2004), pp. 1, 4.
[373] California Budget Project (2005).
[374] R. Sherman (2004). "Serving Youth Aging Out of Foster Care. Welfare Information Network." *The Finance Project*, Issue Note, 8(5, October).

training, and leadership training to the unemployed and out of school aged 16–24.[375]

Health of Children of Immigrants

Although immigrants are 11 percent of the U.S. population, children of immigrants now make up 22 percent of the 23.4 million children in America – the fastest-growing share of children.[376] Most of these children, 93 percent of those under age 6, are citizens. Most live with one or more noncitizen parents. Twenty-nine percent of children under age 6 live with at least one undocumented parent. Despite higher rates of hardship, children of immigrants, even though citizens, use public benefits less than other children, probably because their parents are unaware of or afraid to apply for benefits.[377] Children of immigrants under age 6 are more likely than other children to live in two-parent families (86% vs. 75%), but more likely to live in two-parent families with low incomes (less than 200% of the poverty line) (50% vs. 26%), and less likely to have both parents working (43% vs. 50%).[378] The parents have low education and limited English, which adversely affects school performance.[379] The children of immigrants are less likely to receive public benefits and more likely to experience food- and housing-related hardships.[380] Despite the substantial increase in Medicaid coverage, as well as other programs, between 1999 and 2002 (from 45% to 57%), young low-income children of immigrants were twice as likely to be uninsured as children of natives (22% vs. 11%). Young children of immigrants are twice as likely to be in fair or poor health compared with children of natives, and more than twice as many lack a usual source of health care.[381] Center-based child care can increase early development, socialization, and language skills, as well as the transition of home to school, but children of immigrant parents are far less likely to be in center-based child care, especially with parents of low education, than children of natives.[382]

Summary: Child Well-Being

The Child Well-Being Index (CWI) consists of seven domains of social indicators of well-being: family economic well-being, health, safety/behavioral concerns, educational attainments, community connectedness, social relationships, and emotional/spiritual well-being.[383] The financial status of

---

[375] Ibid.

[376] R. Capps et al. (2004). "The Health and Well-Being of Young Children of Immigrants" (report, Urban Institute, Washington, D.C.), p. ix.

[377] Ibid., p. ix.   [378] Ibid.

[379] Ibid.   [380] Ibid., p. x.

[381] Ibid.   [382] Ibid.

[383] K. Land (2005). "Project Coordinator 2005 Report" (A Composite Index of Trends in the Well-Being of Our Nation's Children, The Foundation for Child Development Index of Child Well-Being [CWI], 1975–2003, with Projections for 2004, March 30), p. 3. The CWI is computed and updated annually.

families with children, after improving in the 1990s, declined after 2000. In 2003, the poverty rate for families with children younger than 18 rose from 16.2 percent to 17.2 percent, although still below the levels of the mid-1990s. There have been significant improvements in infant mortality, children, and youth; however, obesity has grown steadily. Education has improved for both three- and four-year-olds who attend preschool and young adults aged 25–29 who receive college degrees. There has been an increase in the percentage of children living in single-parent families. From 2002 to 2003, there was a decline in the suicide rate. Teen birth rates, violent victimization rates, violent criminal activity rates, smoking, drinking, and drug use have improved.[384] The adolescent and teen birth rates (ages 10–17) have declined since the early 1990s, with the largest overall decrease among teens (ages 15–17). Since the late 1990s, there has been a decrease in cigarette smoking, alcohol use, and illicit drug consumption among adolescents and teens. The most significant improvements have been in crime victimization and offending since their peaks in the mid-1990s.[385] According to the CWI, part of the decline in criminal behavior has been the decline of the crack cocaine epidemic. Employment opportunities for young men and women grew, and the police increased their presence in communities. However, as the CWI report points out, the decreases in the safety/behavioral trends extended well beyond the decline in the crack cocaine epidemic and during periods when job opportunities were not robust and other behavioral characteristics (birth rates, cigarette and alcohol consumption) declined as well. Several factors may be involved, such as increased parental activity and changes in public policies (e.g., tougher criminal laws, targeted advertising).[386]

The state of poor children is particularly disturbing. During the 1990s, the rate of children living in low-income families (less than 200% of the federal poverty line – $37,700 for a family of four) declined; since 2000, the trend has increased. In 2002, 16 percent of American children – more than 11 million – lived in families at or below the poverty line; more than a third (37%) – more than 26 million – lived in low-income families.[387] Younger children are more likely to live in low-income families – 42 percent of infants and toddlers; 40 percent of preschoolers; 40 percent of kindergarteners; 38 percent of school-age children; and 32 percent of adolescents. Although most low-income children are white, black (58%) and Hispanic (62%) children are disproportionately in low-income families and account for the increase in the number of children in low-income families.[388] Most of these children (56%) live in families with at least one parent employed full time, year-round;

[384] Ibid., pp. 5–6.   [385] Ibid., pp. 6–9.
[386] Ibid., pp. 10–11.
[387] National Center for Children in Poverty (2004a). "Low-Income Children in the United States" (Mailman School of Public Health, Columbia University, May), p. 1.
[388] Ibid., p. 2.

28 percent have a parent who works at least part time; and only 16 percent do not have an employed parent.[389]

Almost a third (32%) of children do not live in a two-parent family.[390] Most (23%) live with their mothers. Until 1995, the proportion of children living in single-parent families increased but has stabilized since then. In 2002, 34 percent of all births were to unmarried women, an increase from 32 percent in 1995. Although the overall birth rate among unmarried women has not changed much, there have been changes in the ages of the mothers. The birth rate of unmarried women ages 15 to 19 has declined by more than a fifth since 1994; the birth rate for unmarried women ages 20 and older has continued to increase, but at a slower rate.[391] The decline in adolescent birth rates was the largest among African Americans, (non-Hispanics) – more than half between 1991 and 2002 (from 86 to 41 per 1,000 females ages 15 to 17). The declining adolescent birth rates are the result of declining adolescent pregnancy rates; there were decreases not only in live births but also in induced abortions and fetal losses.[392]

Between 1994 and 2003, there has been an increase in proportion of children with at least one foreign-born parent, from 15 percent to 20 percent. More than a third (34%) of native children with at least one foreign-born parent had a parent with less than a high school education; the percentage rises to 43 percent of foreign-born children with at least one foreign-born parent, compared with 10 percent of native children with native parents.[393]

The percentage of young adults, ages 18 to 24, who completed high school or a GED, increased only slightly to 87 percent (2001). Ninety-one percent of non-Hispanic whites completed high school, compared with 86 percent of African Americans (non-Hispanics) and 66 percent of Hispanics. In 2003, 34 percent of white (non-Hispanics) ages 25–29, completed a bachelor's or more advanced degree, compared with 18 percent of African Americans (non-Hispanics) and 10 percent of Hispanics. Hispanic adults not only have the lowest higher education rates but have not experienced the recent significant increases among white (non-Hispanics) and African Americans (non-Hispanics).[394]

However, there has been a significant decline in the level of violence affecting young people, both serious crime victimization and offending. Since 1993, victimization rates dropped 74 percent and offending rates dropped 78 percent.[395]

Lack of family income is only part of the problem. James Heckman and his colleagues argue that family environment and resources are far more

[389] Ibid.
[390] Forum on Child and Family Statistics (2004). "America's Children in Brief: Key National Indicators of Well-Being, 2004" (Federal Interagency Forum on Child and Family Statistics), p. 1.
[391] Ibid., p. 5.   [392] Ibid., p. 8.
[393] Ibid., p. 5.   [394] Ibid., p. 13.
[395] Ibid., p. 10.

important in promoting postsecondary education and social attachment than
family income during adolescence.[396] They say that the family environment in
early childhood "cumulate(s) in adolescence in the form of crystallized cognitive abilities, attitudes, and social skills that explain inequalities in later socioeconomic attainment."[397] They point out that a greater percentage of children
are living in adverse family environments than in the past. More are living
in very poor, often single-parent families, with parents of low-educational
attainment. Children in these families are less likely to complete high school,
graduate college, or be employed. Younger mothers with less schooling provide less cognitive and emotional stimulation than are necessary for forming
skills and abilities, and when these opportunities are missed, remediation is
prohibitively expensive. Differences in childhood ability, as measured by cognitive test scores, appear as early as age 6 and disparities often persist at later
ages (IQ at later ages is highly correlated with IQ at age 10) as well as childhood behaviors and attitudes ("noncognitive skills"). The gaps in behavioral
skills are significantly reduced when controlling for the mother's ability, family income, family structure, and location.[398] The emphasis today is almost
exclusively on achievement scores – the No Child Left Behind Act of 2001 –
but Heckman and his colleagues argue that these are only a few of the many
skills necessary for success. They say that "motivation, trustworthiness, perse-
verance, dependability, consistency are important predictors of educational
achievement." The noncognitive skills are usually ignored because of the difficulty of reliable measures.[399] Heckman and his colleagues compared GEDs
with high school dropouts, and GEDs are now about 15 percent of all young
adults with high school credentials. They are as smart as high school graduates
who do not go on to college, score higher on the Armed Forces Qualification Test (AFQT) than dropouts, and have higher earnings. However, they
tend to lack other skills. White male GEDs have the highest "participation in
illegal drug use and selling, fighting, vandalism, and petty theft." According
to Heckman and his colleagues, they are "wise guys," lacking in foresight,
persistence, and/or the ability to adapt to changing environments.[400] The policy prescriptions are early investment in children. They say that small-scale
studies of early childhood investments have shown "remarkable success," with
lasting effects on learning and motivation. In the High/Scope Perry Preschool
Program, an intensive two-year preschool program for highly disadvantaged
children, the children performed better in almost every area of schooling,
work, and social life, and the program was cost-effective over the long run. The
Perry Program was replicated in the Chicago Child-Parent Centers (CPC),

[396] "Inequality in America: What Role for Human Capital Policies?" *Focus.* 23(3, Spring 2005): 1–10.
     A report discussing the issues raised by James Heckman at an Institute for Research on Poverty
     seminar, University of Wisconsin–Madison, November.
[397] Ibid., p. 2.   [398] Ibid., pp. 3–4.
[399] Ibid., pp. 5–6.   [400] Ibid., p. 6.

which was early intervention in public schools in very low-income neighborhoods. The CPC started in 1967 and is one of the oldest federally funded
preschool programs. It has served more than 100,000 children at some twenty-
four sites. The children consistently performed better in schools, were less
likely to be involved in the juvenile justice system, and had higher earnings
as adults.[401] Heckman and his colleagues say that these early interventions
primarily improved noncognitive areas, such as motivation, attitudes, persistence, and social integration. Mentoring and motivation programs for juveniles also have a high payoff but not as high as early interventions. Training programs are inefficient policy investments for low-skilled adults (including Job
Corps).[402]

Mary Campbell and her colleagues come to the same general conclusion –
children in families with the least human capital start at an even greater relative disadvantage. Parents' schooling is positively and significantly associated
with their children's high school graduation and years of schooling. The percentage of people in the neighborhood who did not complete high school is
strongly and negatively associated with educational attainment. Once other
family characteristics are controlled, being a single parent does not affect educational attainment. Those at the bottom of the educational distribution fall
farther behind. Again, the policy implications are to provide greater preschool
opportunities for three- and four-year-olds to improve school readiness.[403]

According to Gale and Kotlikoff, the current fiscal policies, if allowed to
continue, will have serious, negative consequences for children's programs.[404]
They base their conclusions on estimating the fiscal deficits created by the
present tax cuts and the Medicare bill. These deficits will have to be paid for
eventually by tax increases and/or budget cuts. For example, in 2014, when
(if) the tax cuts and the Medicare expenditures become permanent, the government would be presented with the following options: "a 53 percent cut in
Social Security benefits; a 63 percent cut in Medicare benefits, a complete
elimination of the federal component of the Medicaid program, plus additional cuts; a 13 percent cut in all noninterest spending; a 58 percent cut in
all spending other than interest, defense, homeland security, Social Security,
Medicare, and Medicaid; a 38 percent increase in payroll taxes; or a 138 percent
increase in corporate tax revenues."[405] They point out that several of the key
programs for children are discretionary and "have a second-class citizenship
status in the budgetary process" (Head Start, WIC, education, and others).[406]

[401] Ibid., p. 7.   [402] Ibid., p. 7.
[403] M. Campbell et al. (2005). "Economic Inequality and Educational Attainment across a Gen-
     eration." *Focus* 23(3, Spring): 11–15. Institute for Research on Poverty, University of Wisconsin–
     Madison.
[404] W. Gale & L. Kotlikoff (2004). "Effects of Recent Fiscal Policies on Children." *Tax Notes*
     (June 7).
[405] Ibid., pp. 1288–89.   [406] Ibid., p. 1289.

Another problem with children's programs is that almost all recent social policy initiatives have been generated by tax credits or deductions, and "almost one half of all children live in households that do not pay any federal income tax after adjusting for existing credits."[407] These families are only helped if the credit is refundable, but lately Congress has resisted this approach. The authors note that cuts are already being made in education, Head Start, WIC, and low-income housing assistance in the 2005 budget.[408] Federal spending for the elderly is three times the amount spent for children and is projected to increase.[409] They argue that if all or most of the recent tax cuts (2002, 2003) are allowed to expire, this would be more than 2 percent of the gross domestic product (GDP) and would be more than enough to finance an "enormously ambitious and expansive program of investment in children," which would include a substantial child allowance, increased earnings supplements for low- and moderate-income families with children, increased parental leave, expanded after-school programs, marriage-promotion demonstration, improved health services such as universal prenatal/perinatal screening, insurance for all children under the age of 18, intensive intervention for severe behavioral and emotional issues, early childhood education, universal preschool for four-year-olds, and improved neighborhoods for poor children.[410] To minimize the vicissitudes of the annual budget process, they propose creating a trust fund or independent board to supervise spending on children's programs.[411]

A recent report of the Center on Budget and Policy Priorities estimates that according to the Bush administration's budget projections, overall funding for education and training programs, including K–12 programs, would be reduced to 14 percent below the 2005 level adjusted for inflation.[412] The center projects that by 2010, 670,000 fewer families would receive WIC services and 300,000 fewer children would receive child care subsidies. There would be 370,000 fewer rental assistance vouchers and 120,000 fewer children in Head Start.[413]

Who Uses the Welfare State?

Mark Rank, using Panel Study of Income Dynamic (PSID) data, gathered information on whether a household received any cash or in-kind public assistance at some point during a prior year. Cash or in-kind public assistance included food stamps, Medicaid, housing, AFDC/TANF, SSI, and General Assistance.[414] The "welfare state" here is defined as means-tested programs, the

---

[407] Ibid., p. 1289.   [408] Ibid., p. 1290.
[409] Ibid., p. 1290.
[410] Ibid., pp. 1290–91. The authors take these proposals from Sawhill (2003).
[411] Gale & Kotlikoff (2004), citing Gale & Sawhill (1999), p. 1291.
[412] S. Parrott et al. (2005). "Where Would Cuts Be Made under the President's Budget?" (Center on Budget and Policy Priorities, revised Feb. 28), p. 3.
[413] Ibid., p. 3.   [414] Rank (2004), p. 101.

Table 3–2. *The use of the welfare state*

Over a 20-year period (households)	
Cash assistance	8.3%
In-kind assistance	12.6%
By age 35	
Cash assistance	22.4%
In-kind assistance	38.1%
By age 50	
Cash assistance	30.1%
In-kind assistance	50%
By age 65	
Cash assistance	37.6%
In-kind assistance	64%

Source: Constructed from Rank (2004).

programs for poor people, not the universal programs such as Social Security and Medicare or unemployment and disability. Jacob Hacker points out that the relief of poverty is only a small part of the public welfare state. Only about a quarter of the total spending is targeted on the poor; most goes to universal programs, such as Social Security and Medicare (Table 3–2).[415]

Over a twenty-year period, 8.3 percent of households received cash assistance, 12.6 percent received in-kind assistance, and 14.2 percent received either one. By age 35, 22.4 percent received cash, 38.1 percent in-kind, and 38.7 percent either one. At age 50, 30.1 percent received cash, 50 percent in-kind, and 50.9 percent either one. By age 65, 37.6 percent received cash, 64.2 percent in-kind, and 65 percent either one.[416] Mark Rank points out that Americans are much more likely to use in-kind assistance than cash during their life course. Of the two-thirds who received either cash or in-kind assistance, 63 percent used Medicaid, 52 percent food stamps, 13 percent AFDC, 10 percent SSI, and 14 percent some other welfare program. The most used programs, by far, are Medicaid and food stamps.

Rank says that these are remarkable statistics. The common assumption is that welfare is used by the "other," a small minority who cannot make it. The opposite is the truth. As Rank points out, the fact that most Americans use a public assistance program at least once during their adult life is consistent with the likelihood of experiencing poverty and economic vulnerability during the life course.[417]

How much time is spent on public assistance (Table 3–3)?

Between ages 20 and 35, more than a third (38.7%) will have used public assistance at least one year (any point in time counts as one year), 23.3 percent two or more consecutive years, 16.8 percent three or more consecutive years,

[415] Hacker (2002), p. 10.   [416] Rank (2004), p. 103.
[417] Ibid., p. 103.

Table 3–3. *Time spent on public assistance*

Parameter	Percentage
Ages 20–35	
At least 1 year	38.7%[a]
2 or more consecutive years	23.3%
3 or more consecutive years	16.8%
4 or more consecutive years	11.3%
5 or more consecutive years	8.5%
By age 50	
1 or more consecutive years	50.9%
2 or more consecutive years	31.3%
3 or more consecutive years	23.2%
4 or more consecutive years	15.8%
5 or more consecutive years	12%
By age 65	
1 or more consecutive years	65%
2 or more consecutive years	41.4%
3 or more consecutive years	31.8%
4 or more consecutive years	21.1%
5 or more consecutive years	15.9%

[a] Any point in time counts as one year.
Source: Constructed from Rank (2004).

11.3 percent four or more consecutive years, and 8.5 percent five or more years. By age 50, the percentages rise to 50.9 percent (one year), 31.3 percent (two or more years), 23.2 percent (three or more years), 15.8 percent (four or more years), and 12 percent (five or more years). By age 65, the percentages are 65 percent (one or more years), 41.4 percent (two or more years), 31.8 percent (three or more years), 21.1 percent (four or more years), and 15.9 percent (five or more years). From these figures, Rank concludes that although the likelihood of using public assistance one or two consecutive years across an adult life is considerable, a higher use of public assistance is less likely.[418]

The total years of using public assistance across adulthood is considerably greater than the number of consecutive years. By age 65, 65 percent will have used public assistance at least one year, 58.7 percent at least two different years, and 40.3 percent in five or more different years. Thus, says Rank, spells of public assistance do reoccur during the life course. And once a person uses public assistance, he or she is quite likely to use it again. Ninety percent of those who have ever used public assistance at least once will do so again during adulthood.[419] Therefore, as with poverty, public assistance use is far more widespread than currently assumed. "In fact, two-thirds of all Americans between ages 20 and 65 at some point turn to a public assistance program,

[418] Ibid., pp. 104–5.   [419] Ibid., p. 105.

while 40% access a welfare program in five or more years during adulthood."[420] Although most use is made of Medicaid and food stamps, 38 percent receive some type of cash assistance as well.[421]

The Impact of the Welfare State on Poverty

What have been the antipoverty effects of these various programs? The Center on Budget and Policy Priorities, in a recent report, says that the "public benefit programs reduced the number of poor Americans by 27 million people, in 2003, from 58 million to 31 million."[422] This includes 14 million elderly and almost 5 million children. Almost half (11 million) of those lifted out of poverty were by means-tested benefits. For those who still remained poor, the severity of their poverty was considerably reduced. Most elderly Americans (35 million) were covered by either Medicare or Medicaid. Nearly one-third of all poor children were raised above the poverty line. However, as pointed out, most other western countries do a far better job of reducing poverty, especially among children.[423]

Nevertheless, the poverty gap has remained stable over time. Levine and Scholz calculate the poverty gap, as of 1997, as follows: With the standard deduction and personal and child exemptions, plus a $500 child credit, poor families with children do not pay any positive federal taxes. For low-income earners without children, whose incomes are near the poverty line, there is a small amount of federal tax. However, payroll taxes are significant. Whatever the income, all families pay the employee's share, which is 7.65 percent, and the self-employed pay 15.3 percent.[424] As to in-kind benefits, Levine and Scholz value food stamps at the cost to the government because the food stamps do not exceed the food needs of the typical family. They value Medicaid about the cost of a typical HMO policy. They increase the value to the elderly and disabled by 2.5 to reflect their greater medical needs. The value of Medicare is 2.5 times the average cost of a fee-for-service plan, adjusting for differences in regional costs. They use HUD's fair-market rent to estimate the value of in-kind housing benefits.[425]

In 1997, the pretax and pretransfer poverty gap was $19.6 billion. Almost 30 percent (29%) of all families and unrelated individuals were below the poverty line. The effects of taxes and all transfers totaled $59 billion, or $1,104 per recipient family. More than half (55.3%) of these benefits went to families with pretransfer incomes below the poverty line. Almost a quarter (24%) of

[420] Ibid., p. 105.   [421] Ibid., p. 106.

[422] Shapiro, Parrott, & Springer (2005), p. 1.

[423] Ibid., pp. 1–2. For a summary of the lack of mobility in the United States, see *The Economist* (2005). Special Report. "Meritocracy in America" (January 1): 22–24.

[424] Levine & Scholz (2002), p. 214.   [425] Ibid., p. 214.

total program costs filled 72.4 percent of the total poverty gap and a post-tax, post-transfer poverty rate of 10 percent.[426]

The major programs – Social Security, Disability Insurance (DI), Medicare, UI, workers' compensation – are universal rather than targeted. Approximately half of the recipients are poor; thus, only between 27 percent and 37 percent of benefits directly reduce the poverty gap. Nevertheless, because of the size of these programs – especially Social Security and Medicare – they have a significant impact on lowering the poverty rate.[427] Food stamps, AFDC (now TANF), and housing assistance are tightly targeted; most of the benefits (78%) reduce the poverty gap. Medicaid, SSI, and the EITC have large antipoverty effects.[428]

Levine and Scholz point out the remarkable stability of the poverty gap. It was roughly $19.7 billion in 1979, 1984, and 1997. Despite antipoverty effects of the tax and transfer system, almost 30 percent of the poverty gap remains. They attribute this stability to the stagnant trends in real income and stable antipoverty policies.[429] There are differences, however, among subgroups. The elderly receive $35.6 million in transfers per month (primarily Social Security), which fills just about the entire poverty gap (99%). The poverty gap for single-parent families is reduced by 79 percent, but this still leaves 17.5 percent of families poor. Two-parent, childless families are less well targeted, but their poverty rate is low (6.5%); other than food stamps and disability, there is little public aid.[430]

What have been the effects of transfers on behavior? As to labor markets, Levine and Scholz report in a 2001 study that with single mothers, the EITC accounted for a 61 percent increase in employment between 1984 and 1996. However, there were small effects from changes in state maximum welfare benefits, benefit reductions, Medicaid expansions, job training, child care subsidies, family formation policies, and assets changes. They say that there is a growing body of evidence that the most important factor is the growth in post-transfer wages.[431]

Thus, over the past thirty years, although there have been changes in the mix of antipoverty policies and the composition of the poor, with the exception of Medicaid and related health programs, there has been little change in aggregate antipoverty spending and little change in the reduction of poverty. They give three reasons. Although polls show that the public generally thinks that there is too little spending to help the poor, there is a lack of concern for the poverty problem among both the public and the politicians. There is also the perception of little confidence as to what works; thus, except for Head Start, there is little enthusiasm for TANF, as well as other antipoverty

[426] Ibid.
[428] Ibid.
[430] Ibid., pp. 215–17.

[427] Ibid., p. 215.
[429] Ibid.
[431] Ibid., pp. 218–20.

programs. And third, since the 1970s, the fiscal climate has not been favorable: the "stagflation" of the 1970s and the deficits in the 1980s and part of the 1990s. Major changes, argue the authors, will have to come about through increased spending, rather than reshuffling the amount spent on existing programs, which is 1.5 percent of GDP. If this amount were simply increased to 1.91 percent, which was the highest fraction in the past thirty years, there would be an additional $34 billion for new programs.[432]

In addition to these shortcomings, there is no national, universal health insurance. Access to health care, except for the elderly, remains dependent on employment, and now, less and less available at the low end of the labor market.[433] More than 45 million (almost 16%) Americans lack health insurance.[434] In the meantime, the risks are increasing for workers who are injured or become disabled or unemployed.[435] Social Security Disability Insurance is restrictive and benefits are low. Nevertheless, as part of the 1996 welfare reforms, drug and alcohol addiction were excluded from coverage.[436] Compared with other advanced countries, even counting private benefits, there is far less support for families, unmarried mothers, housing, and active labor market policies (e.g., job training, job creation).[437]

As the welfare rolls have declined sharply, those who are left would more likely face greater difficulties in trying to meet the demands of both work and family, especially if the work requirements increase. In Milwaukee County, where there has been a significant decline in the welfare rolls, it was found that the number of TANF applicants who were involved with the child welfare services increased considerably.[438] In a recent study, there was an increased level of substance abuse associated with TANF mothers leaving welfare more than once "for negative reasons," failing to find employment, and poor prospects for earned income.[439]

The Center for Law and Social Policy recently published a report based on the financial data of the Department of Health and Human Services (DHHS) for TANF and the state maintenance of effort (MOE) funds for fiscal year 2003.[440] The block grant system is funded annually. In 2003, $17.2

---

[432] Ibid., pp. 221–28.
[434] Leonhardt (2004).
[436] Ibid., pp. 209–16.
[438] M. Courtney et al. (2005). "Involvement of TANF Applicant Families with Child Welfare Services." *Social Service Review* (March). The increase was not due to the greater involvement of TANF caseworkers because few reports came from this source; most reports of suspected child maltreatment came from the traditional sources – teachers, counselors, and neighbors. Much anecdotal evidence came from the TANF caseworkers – the remaining applicants had less human capital and were more likely to have suffered from family violence, substance abuse, and mental illness (pp. 151–52).

[433] Katz (2001), pp. 14–15.
[435] Katz (2001), p. 195.
[437] Ibid., p. 16.

[439] D. Chandler et al. (2004). "Substance Abuse, Employment, and Welfare Tenure." *Social Service Review* (December): 628–51.
[440] Greenberg & Rahmanou (2005).

billion in new TANF funds were distributed to the states.[441] As noted, the states had surpluses that increased as the welfare rolls continued to drop during the 1990s. Under PRWORA, the states were required to use the TANF surplus to maintain their level of spending on welfare and related programs, termed MOE.[442] In addition, there were state budgetary increases throughout the 1990s. The states spent relatively large amounts of money, including the TANF surpluses, to help the working poor, especially child care, as well as other programs. The state budgetary situation changed with the 2000 recession. State programs have been cut, including MOE spending. Starting in 2001, the states began spending at levels higher than their annual block grants, drawing on unspent funds from prior years.[443] About 35 percent of TANF and MOE funds were spent on basic assistance and 18.1 percent on child care. The amount currently spent on basic assistance is 64 percent less than in the peak year of 1994. Child care spending has been flat for the past three years. The rest was spent on a variety of categories, for example, work-related activities, refundable tax credits, and pregnancy prevention.[444] CLASP reports, "For the third consecutive year, states spent and transferred more TANF funds than they received in their annual block grants."[445] In 2003, the states spent $16.3 billion and transferred $2.7 billion to other block grants, thus using $19 billion, even though they received $17.2 billion.[446] The states continued the practice of drawing on unspent funds from prior years, and overall, the carryover funds, in all the states, declined from $5.8 billion (2002) to $3.9 billion (2003). Only about a third (35%) of TANF and MOE funds are spent on basic assistance. The second-largest amount (18%) is spent on child care, but this has not increased for the past three years and remains below its peak in 2000. Less than 10 percent is spent on work-related activities (education and training, work subsidies, work expenses, etc.), and this too has either remained flat or declined since 2002. The Center for Law and Social Policy reports that relatively large amounts, nearly $4.5 billion, are spent on categories with limited information from federal reporting and suggests that much of this is for child welfare and juvenile justice.[447] A large share of TANF and MOE funds are not spent on families receiving cash assistance. Funds are "probably" spent on low-income working families (e.g., child care, refundable tax credits), the child welfare system, pregnancy prevention, family formation."[448] Because of deficiencies in reporting, it is

[441] Ibid., p. 2. This included basic family assistance grants, supplemental grants, and out-of-wedlock bonuses.
[442] Ibid., p. 3. States are required to spend at least 75 percent of their 1994 historic spending level. Unspent TANF block grant funds can be carried over to subsequent years but are considered spending obligations on the states – called "unliquidated obligations," or "unobligated balances."
[443] Ibid., p. 9.   [444] Ibid., pp. 4–6.
[445] Ibid., p. 1.   [446] Ibid., p. 2.
[447] Ibid., p. 1.
[448] Ibid., p. 11. "Probably" because of ambiguities in the reporting requirements.

hard to be precise as to what is going on in the states. Nevertheless, without any increase from Congress, "it is virtually inevitable" that the states will cut their spending. The Center for Law and Social Policy mentions in particular the child care spending that has already declined since 2000, as well as expenditures for low-income families who are not connected to TANF.[449] The level of unspent carryover funds has declined for three consecutive years and will be exhausted in most states within the next few years. Except for some additional funds for child care, the reauthorization bills do not provide for any increase in TANF funding. When the states had surpluses, they could avoid trade-offs. That is no longer the case. Between 1996 and 2004, only eight states raised cash assistance to keep pace with inflation; "in most states, the nominal benefit is the same or lower than in 1996."[450]

The Private Welfare State: Workers

Most workers are insured through their employment.[451] Employee benefits, called "fringe benefits," expanded during World War II when wages were frozen. Over the next four decades, the system continued to grow, eventually covering most workers with health care and most of retirement and life insurance. Many employers offer sick leave, family care leave, and child care services. According to Katz, employee benefits have increased from about 8 percent of total compensation in 1960 to 18 percent in 1993. In 1994, employers contributed $746.5 billion for benefits, with most going to retirement (47%) and health care (41%). Worker contributions totaled $306 billion.[452] Although considered part of the "private" welfare state, these benefits are both highly regulated and, to a large extent, publicly financed. Private pensions are regulated by the 1974 Employee Retirement Income Security Act (ERISA), which sets minimum standards for funding and coverage and requires that benefits be made available after a certain number of years of employment.[453] Much of the funding comes through tax policy – exclusions, deductions, and credits – which is the equivalent of direct government spending but which show up in the form of foregone revenue rather than direct government expenditures. The largest are federal exclusions of employer-sponsored health insurance and pension contributions. According to Hacker, together these two exclusions amount to nearly $200 billion of foregone revenue.[454]

The better-off workers, of course, are the main beneficiaries of the private welfare system not only because of the tax subsidies but also because of the more generous benefits. Hacker estimates that the distributional benefits of the tax breaks are $535 for those earning between $20,000 and $29,000; $1,684

[449] Ibid., p. 2.   [450] Ibid., pp. 9–10.
[451] Hacker (2002); Katz (2001), p. 171; Stone (2004).
[452] Katz (2001), p. 179.   [453] Hacker (2002), p. 10.
[454] Ibid., p. 11.

for those earning between $50,000 and $74,999; and $2,357 for those earning $100,000 or more.[455] The privatized systems not only favor the better off, but they serve to shape, if not foreclose, alternative social policy initiatives. Vested interests, notes Hacker, often of low visibility, closely monitor proposed changes. The prime example, of course, is health care.[456]

Reflecting the changes in the labor market, the private welfare system for workers is becoming less supportive; costs are rising, and benefits are shrinking. The differences in employee benefits between large and small firms, union and nonunionized workers, full-time and part-time workers, and men and women workers are growing. A larger share of the rising costs are being paid by workers, especially in health care.[457]

There are some federal and state mandates on employers – Social Security, disability, accidental death, workers' compensation, and UI – but as Katherine Stone points out, these are bare-minimum provisions. Most employees relied on employers for health insurance, long-term disability, and pensions. Now, there is increased risk, uncertainty, and vulnerability.[458] Older workers can no longer expect a secure job lasting until they retire. The low-skilled workers have neither the training nor the ability to retrain for the new labor market. And the risk averse would prefer to stay with the same employer. Almost all of these workers, says Stone, will have periods of unemployment. Changing jobs can mean gaps in health insurance or loss of coverage for preexisting conditions. It may be that workers who change jobs will qualify for benefits with their new employer, but employers are cutting back on benefits, and there are usually waiting periods for health insurance as well as exclusions for preexisting conditions.[459]

The new approach of employer insurance is changing from risk sharing to individual responsibility.[460] Although most Americans have health insurance through employment, the percentage of full-time employees in large and medium-size firms has declined from 97 percent in 1983 to 76 percent in 1997, and the percentage of all workers with no insurance increased from 13.9 percent in 1990 to 16.3 percent in 1998.[461] In addition to declining coverage, health insurance has become more expensive, has more exclusions, and has more limitations on coverage. The costs of health insurance have been rising – between 1980 and 1998, more than 300 percent – and an increasing share of this cost has been shifted to employees. Between 1983 and 1997, the average employee contribution increased from $10.13 per month to $39.14 per month – more than 400 percent. In addition, there has been an increase in co-payments and deductibles. According to the Kaiser Foundation, employees are paying 48 percent more in contributions than they were paying three years ago. The

[455] Ibid., p. 39.
[457] Katz (2001), pp. 183–86.
[459] Ibid., p. 245.
[461] Ibid., pp. 245–46.

[456] Ibid., pp. 25–26, 50–57.
[458] Stone (2004), p. 243.
[460] Ibid., p. 245.

result, says Stone, is that more and more workers are opting out of coverage because it is too expensive. An additional factor in the decline in coverage is that more contingent, part-time, temporary workers are ineligible. With waiting periods and exclusions for preexisting conditions, insurance becomes less valuable.[462]

Previously, health plans spread the risks and costs by covering large pools that combined the healthy with those more at risk. Now, the trend is the reverse – to divide the covered workers into distinct risk groups and increasing the price for the less healthy or denying coverage altogether. Employers are offering "cafeteria" plans, where employees select different levels of coverage and benefits. These plans are praised for increasing employee choice and limiting employer costs, but they also serve to divide the pool, leaving older, less healthy workers with rising costs. There are also now defined contribution plans for health insurance; again, employees can tailor their health plans. Employees can also use flexible spending accounts (FSAs) where they can set aside a certain portion of pretax income (up to $5,000) to pay for uninsured medical costs.[463]

Stone views these developments as troublesome. They will harm both employers and workers. Low-wage workers would be unlikely to purchase sufficient insurance, and employees who do not have adequate insurance often delay needed health care and thus have more frequent and longer absences from work.[464]

Stone argues that health insurance has to be both portable and affordable. Under a statute passed in 1986, employers have to offer employees who leave the opportunity to continue coverage for eighteen months, known as COBRA, but at the employee's expense.[465] Additional amendments require group plans to reduce the waiting periods for preexisting conditions.[466] However, while increasing coverage opportunities for employees who change jobs, there is still the problem of affordability for those in the middle or lower end of the income distribution. Increasingly, health insurance is becoming an unaffordable luxury for these groups.[467] At the same time, SSDI and workers' compensation, the public welfare safety nets for the ill and disabled, are now more stringent and pay lower benefits.

There have been significant changes in private sector retirement pensions.[468] Stone reports that between 1985 and 2000, the percentage of full-time employees of large establishments with retirement plans declined from 91 percent to 70 percent. And those who change jobs often lose valuable rights,

[462] Ibid., p. 247.   [463] Ibid., pp. 247–48.
[464] Ibid., p. 249.
[465] Consolidate Omnibus Budget Reconciliation Act (1986); Stone (2004), p. 249.
[466] Health Insurance Portability and Accountability Act (HIPAA); Stone (2004), p. 250.
[467] Stone (2004), p. 250.   [468] Ibid.

regardless of whether the job change was voluntary. In addition, there has been a dramatic shift that has moved risk and responsibility from the employer to the employee.[469] Previously, most pensions were "defined benefit" plans. The employee is guaranteed a specific benefit at the time of retirement based on years of employment and the final salary. It is a fixed schedule. Benefit schedules provided greater benefits to long-term employees to compensate for lower, earlier salaries, called "back-loading." Employers contribute to a fund sufficient to cover liabilities, which is monitored by the IRS and the U.S. Department of Labor and insured by the federal government.[470] Employees who change jobs lose either the higher amounts of the benefits or all of their benefits if they leave before the plans vest. Federal law requires that defined benefit plans either vest gradually over a three- to seven-year period or all at once within five years of employment. However, employees who leave after their plan vests but before retirement age lose a lot – the benefits remain frozen until retirement age and do not increase with inflation.[471]

Most pension funds are invested in stocks. The long bear market in the early 2000s has been "devastating," and, according to Stone, many plans now lack sufficient assets to cover their liabilities. Stone says that as of September 2003, Standard & Poor estimated that of its 500 companies that offered defined benefit plans, 322 were in debt. The federal regulatory agency estimates that as of May 2003, the total corporate pension deficit was $300 billion.[472]

Since the 1980s, many employers have changed the pensions from defined benefit plans to defined contribution plans.[473] As described by Stone, under the defined contribution plan, the employer contributions are based on the number of hours worked. Employees usually contribute as well, with some choice about investments, and benefits are based on the value of the account at the time of retirement. Thus, the risk of a market decline or bad investment decision is on the employee. Defined contribution plans now are more popular than defined benefit plans. In 1985, approximately 80 percent of full-time workers in large and medium firms were covered by defined benefit plans; by 2000, only 36 percent. At the present time, 90 percent of employer plans are defined contribution.[474] Employers favor defined contribution plans because the risk shifts to the employees. Stone says that employees who are mobile like them because benefits generally vest sooner and these plans usually pay a lump sum when they leave or accounts continue to grow if a lump sum is not taken.[475] Now, 401(k) plans are becoming increasingly popular, but also are riskier for employees. Under these plans, employees can purchase stock with

---

[469] Ibid., p. 251.

[470] The Pension Benefit Guaranty Corporation (PBGC); Stone (2004), p. 251.

[471] The statute is Employee Retirement and Security Act (ERISA); Stone (2004), pp. 251–52.

[472] Stone (2004), p. 252.   [473] Ibid.

[474] Ibid., p. 253.   [475] Ibid.

pretax dollars. Many of these plans require that the funds be heavily invested in the firm's stock. At the present time, 55 percent of all full-time employees in medium and large firms participate in such plans.[476] The contributions and the fund's earning are tax deferred. The 401(k) funds will grow with the stock market, and all taxes are deferred until retirement. However, the employee is betting on the continued solvency of the firm, thus risking not only the job but also the retirement. Other changes also risk retirement. Employees can take out loans on their funds, and most plans now provide a lump sum on retirement rather than a lifetime annuity.[477]

In the past decade, reports Stone, many corporations are adopting a new kind of pension plan that is a hybrid between a defined benefit and defined contribution plan called a "cash balance plan."[478] The employer contributes a percentage of income and interest to a hypothetical account for each employee at a predetermined rate. When the employee leaves, he or she can either take the accumulated account as a lump sum or leave the account to accumulate interest. The cash balance plan offers portability for younger and more mobile workers, but it has been argued that they discriminate against older workers because the annual rate of accrual declines as retirement approaches. Stone points out that the cash balance plans were introduced because when the defined benefit plans were converted, many companies underestimated the disastrous accrual effects on older workers.[479]

The "Third Sector"

The "third" or "independent" sector, too, is large and complicated. It encompasses both the huge Catholic Charities USA, with an annual budget of $2 billion, to the local food pantry and soup kitchen. The National Center for Charitable Statistics reports that in 2003 there were more than 1.3 million nonprofit organizations registered with the IRS with reported revenues totaling more than $200 billion.[480] In 1998, the sector employed about 11 million paid workers who represented 7 percent of the total U.S. employed workers. It also employed close to 6 million volunteers, and the value of their time was estimated to be $225 million.[481] The field is dominated by health, education more than, and human service nonprofit organizations. As such, it plays an increasingly central role in the provision of welfare state services and benefits.

[476] Ibid., p. 254.   [477] Ibid., p. 255.
[478] Ibid.   [479] Ibid.
[480] National Center for Charitable Statistics (n.d.). "Number of Nonprofit Organizations in the United States 1996–2004." Retrieved from http://nccsdataweb.urban.org/PubApps/profile1.php?state=US. (Sources: IRS Business Master File 12/2004 [with modifications by the National Center for Charitable Statistics at the Urban Institute to exclude foreign and governmental organizations].)
[481] Independent Sector (2001).

A majority of the nonprofit organizations are small. Most of the resources are concentrated in a small number of very large organizations. For example, in a study of nonprofit organizations in Los Angeles County, the researchers found that the largest organizations have a far greater share of total revenues than their share in clients. Almost half (46%) of organizations that spend less than $500,000 annually and serve more than a quarter (27%) of the clients receive only 1.7 percent of the total revenues. Organizations with expenditures of more than $5 million are much fewer (17% of the total), and though they do serve more clients (32%), they do that with a disproportionate amount of resources – 87 percent of the revenues.[482]

The nonprofit sector has changed significantly in recent decades. Starting in the 1960s, large amounts of federal money were appropriated for social services. State and local governments used much of this money to contract with private agencies. Private contractors began playing an increasing role in the delivery of services. Most human services are now delivered by either for-profit or not-for-profit agencies (about 60%), compared with government (about 40%).[483] A major part of this share comes from Medicare and Medicaid, with most of the money going to hospitals and other providers.[484] The use of private contractors also increased with the 1996 welfare reform by allowing states to contract for welfare-to-work programs. The privatization of homeless shelters has increased.[485] Indeed, as noted by Lester Salamon, "By the late 1970s, federal support to American nonprofit organizations outdistanced private charitable support by a factor of two to one."[486] However, during the Reagan Administration in the early 1980s, there was a significant decline in federal funding of about 25 percent to nonprofit organizations in such fields as social services, education, and community development.[487] (It was followed by another cut in the mid-1990s.) In addition, the Reagan Administration encouraged for-profit firms to enter the health field, especially in such areas as home health, child care, and psychiatric and rehabilitation hospitals, where they dominate.[488] Most recently, the Bush Administration has increased funding for faith-based nonprofits. There is a line item in the federal budget called the

---

[482] Y. Hasenfeld et al. (2003). "Serving a Dynamic and Diverse Metropolis: The Human Services Nonprofit Sector in Los Angeles" (summary report, UCLA Center for Civil Society, Los Angeles).

[483] N. Marwell (2004). "Privatizing the Welfare State: Nonprofit Community-Based Organizations as Political Actors." *American Sociological Review* 69(April): 265–91, p. 266.

[484] Katz (2001), p. 144.

[485] M. Diller (2000). "The Revolution in Welfare Administration: Rules, Discretion, and Entrepreneurial Government." 75 *N.Y.U. Law Review* 1121; Katz (2001), pp. 153–55.

[486] L. M. Salamon (2003). "The Resilient Sector." In L. M. Salamon (Ed.), *The State of Nonprofit America*. Washington, D.C.: Brookings Institution Press, p. 12.

[487] K. N. Gronbjerg & L. M. Salamon (2002). "Devolution, Marketization, and the Changing Shape of Government-Nonprofit Relations." In L. M. Salamon (Ed.), *The State of Nonprofit America*. Washington, D.C.: Brookings Institution Press, pp. 447–70.

[488] Salamon (2003), p. 15.

Compassion Capital Fund. The administration claims that religious organizations received $2 billion in fiscal 2004 from 169 different programs.[489]

Other changes in governmental policies have affected the nonprofit sector and its ability to sustain its traditional goals. Gronbjerg and Salamon point to the increase in consumer-side subsidies, such as the Medicaid voucher program and child care subsidies, greater reliance on managed care models, and insistence on performance-based contracts.[490] These changes resulted in a shift "away from mission-driven efforts to deliver effective services and toward cost-control, efficiency and minimum standards of care."[491]

The increasing competition for government funding, the entry of for-profit firms, and the search for new funding sources has transformed the nonprofit sector. As Salamon noted, "Nonprofit organizations are increasingly 'marketing' their 'products,' viewing their clients as 'customers,' segmenting the market, differentiating their outputs, identifying their 'market niche,' formulating 'business plans,' and generally incorporating the language, and the style of business management."[492] To obtain needed resources, nonprofit organizations have increasingly resorted to charging fees, undertaking business ventures, and entering into partnerships with for-profit firms. Not surprisingly, there is lobbying in efforts to influence the awarding of contracts.[493] Taken together, these transformations of the nonprofit sector raise serious concerns about their historic mission to serve the poor and the disadvantaged and to promote social justice.[494] We visit some of these issues when we explore the privatization of TANF.

As noted, the Bush Administration has been advocating Charitable Choice, in part as an antidote to the commercialization of the nonprofit sector and as a way to promote and strengthen community-based services in high-poverty areas. As noted by Chavez, "policy makers have recently discovered the role played by inner-city congregations in running soup kitchens, homeless shelters, and other social service projects."[495] Charitable Choice will make it easier for religious congregations to obtain federal funding for social services. However, according to Chavez, only a fraction of the congregations have the capability of providing social service programs. The most common social service activities are food (33% of the congregations) and housing (20% of the congregations) related. Moreover, most congregations are very small and lack the organizational capability to launch major social service programs.[496]

[489] J. DeParle (2005). "Hispanic Group Thrives on Faith and Federal Aid." New York Times, May 3.
[490] Gronbjerg & Salamon (2003), pp. 434–60.
[491] Ibid., p. 458.   [492] Salamon (2003), p. 38.
[493] Marwell (2004); DeParle (2005).
[494] P. Frumkin & A. Andre-Clark (1999). "The Rise of the Corporate Social Worker." Society 36 (6, September/October): 46–52.
[495] M. Chaves (2002). "Religious Congregations." In L. M. Salamon (Ed.), The State of Nonprofit America. Washington, D.C.: Brookings Institution Press, p. 287.
[496] Ibid., pp. 289–90.

A study by Cnaan and Brodie of congregations in Philadelphia, a majority African American, found that, on average, each congregation reported providing 2.4 different community-service programs.[497] According to Cnaan and Brodie, "almost half of the congregations offered food pantries, and more than a third summer day camps, recreational programs for teens, and clothing closets. About a quarter of the congregations offered music performances, soup kitchens, and educational tutoring."[498] On average, each congregation serves thirty-nine of its own members and sixty-three nonmembers living in its neighborhood.[499] The authors estimate that the replacement value of the services of their sample of 1,376 congregations is about $247 million. Cnaan and Boddie conclude that congregations do provide an important safety net to people in need in the neighborhoods. Although most congregations seem to welcome Charitable Choice, it is difficult to assess what might happen to them when they become service contractors, especially the degree to which they can maintain their original mission in the face of numerous contractual regulations. At the same time, although they provide highly needed services, one should not lose sight of their limited capability to respond to the more basic service needs of their communities.[500]

By the 1980s, public housing construction was over. Community development corporations (CDCs) were then started to help provide affordable housing.[501] The idea was that local citizens would be involved in economic development in low- and moderate-income communities. In 1994, it was estimated that there were about two thousand CDCs. Most were small, producing between 30,000 and 40,000 units of affordable housing per year (eligibility – incomes below 80 percent of the median in the neighborhood). Although the emphasis has been on housing, CDCs develope commercial and industrial space (23 million square feet), provide loans to businesses, and are credited with more than 60,000 jobs.[502] Despite these accomplishments – they have tripled the average level of public housing units – CDCs remain too small to reverse the spread of persistent poverty in the cities.[503]

Conclusions

The overview of the American welfare state – both public and private – shows very clearly the central importance of the work ethic. The better-off workers also have the better benefits – from the private, but heavily subsidized, welfare

---

[497] R. A. Cnaan & S. C. Boddie (2001). "Philadelphia Census of Congregations and Their Involvement in Social Service Delivery." *Social Service Review* 75(4): 559–80.
[498] Ibid., p. 569.   [499] Ibid., p. 570.
[500] Ibid.   [501] Katz (2001), p. 167.
[502] Ibid.
[503] Ibid., pp. 168–70. See S. Cummings (2001). "Community Economic Development as Progressive Politics: Towards a Grassroots Movement for Economic Justice." 54 *Stan. L. Rev.* 399; W. Simon (2001). *The Community Economic Development Movement.* Durham, N.C.: Duke University Press.

state. Those who are not working, but considered outside of the paid labor market, are clearly treated more favorably than those who are expected to support themselves through earnings. The comparison is between those aged 65 who have worked their adult life in covered employment and the able-bodied adults. For the latter, assistance is carefully tailored so as not to provide disincentives to work – benefits are very low, often for a short period; there are mandatory work requirements (sometimes public jobs that are for the relief benefit only); and administration is at the local level. Then, there are those in ambiguous situations, who are *involuntarily* unemployed. They can receive benefits, but, to preserve the work ethic, benefits are low and short term. There are those who claim to be disabled. They can receive aid, but only if they can show that they are not malingering. Proving disability is difficult, most claimants are rejected, and there are periodic re-evaluations.

There have been significant changes in the American welfare system, which is especially true when one considers the changes that have occurred in the risks that the welfare state is supposed to mitigate – the vast changes in work and families. Jacob Hacker makes the important point that retrenchment has largely occurred because of the failure of programs to respond to these changes and the increasing privatization of risk.[504] Perhaps the most notable example of the former is the UI system, which is now seriously inadequate in its response to low-wage, contingent, "flexible" employment. The primary example of the latter is the health insurance system. It relies primarily on employment-based insurance, which is increasingly less available to the new contingent, part-time, temporary workforce. Hacker would also include the privatization of pensions, which forecloses serious reconsideration of the Social Security system.[505] And, it is the less-privileged worker that bears the costs.

In the meantime, between June 2001 and September 2003, the national TANF caseload has remained flat. Changes have been relatively small. Twenty-six states and the District of Columbia reported increases in their welfare caseloads; twenty-four states reported decreases. In contrast, the number of families participating in food stamps increased by 2,064,112 between September 2001 and September 2003. It is unclear why the TANF caseloads have remained relatively flat or declined when unemployment and food stamp participation has increased.[506]

It is possible that efforts to reduce the deficit will take a "large and disproportionate bite" out of programs for low-income people.[507] Last year, there were deep reductions in Section 8 vouchers, the principal low-income housing

[504] Hacker (2004), pp. 256–57.   [505] Ibid., p. 257.
[506] CLASP Update (2004). "President's Budget Cuts Child Care for More Than 300,000 Children." *CLASP* 17(3, March): 2.
[507] I. Shapiro & R. Greenstein (2005). "Cuts to Low-Income Programs May Far Exceed the Contribution of These Programs to Deficit's Return" (revised, Center on Budget and Policy Priorities, February).

assistance program, with cuts expected to reach 30 percent by 2009. Newspapers also report plans to cut Medicaid, which will result in a significant reduction in health care insurance for low-income families. There were also proposals to reduce the EITC. Poverty has risen for three consecutive years. (The latest year for the data was 2003.) Nearly 36 million people are now below the poverty line. Similar numbers are either hungry or threatened by hunger – called "food insecure" – at some point during the year. The depth of poverty has increased – greater in 2002 (last data year) than in any year on record, going back to 1975 (the data include noncash benefits and EITC). Children are especially likely to be poor: 17.6 percent in 2003. There is little reason to believe that these figures have improved significantly since 2003. Employment is essentially the same in 2004 as in 2003 – in both years, an average of 62.3 percent of adults were employed. Wages at the bottom fell further behind inflation. With the expiration of the temporary federal unemployment benefits at the end of 2003, some 3.5 million workers exhausted their regular unemployment benefits in 2004 before finding a job, the largest number on record.

In sum, very large numbers of Americans are poor, near poor, or at risk of dropping below a standard, minimally adequate budget – food, shelter, clothing, no restaurant meals (even McDonald's), no movies. The low-wage labor market is spreading and becoming even more uncertain. There is less full-time work and more temporary work. More single mothers are trying to earn a living but face difficulty finding (often expensive) child care, which is often of poor quality. Many suffer from employment barriers, in addition to discrimination. Split and variable work schedules require multiple child care arrangements. Transportation is a major problem – dropping off and picking up children, getting to and from work. Health care for poor children increased for a time but is now threatened. Lack of affordable housing is probably at an all-time high. Low-quality child care, schools, housing, neighborhoods, and family environments are becoming more problematic, threatening the future of millions of children. Many children with immigrant parents face even greater difficulties. The response of the American welfare state to poverty and inequality, never adequate, is becoming even less so. The United States ranks near the bottom when compared with other developed countries.

4   Demonizing the Single-Mother Family
The Path to Welfare Reform

Single-mother families are in a unique position. General assistance (GA) – the cash aid programs for single adults and childless couples – is much more miserly than TANF (formerly AFDC): the benefits are much lower, the work requirements more onerous, the time limits shorter, and in some states, it has been abolished. General assistance recipients are sometimes pitied, more often stigmatized, but are of low visibility, more or less out of sight. Single-mother families, however, are highly visible – the most visible of all welfare recipients. They are the most controversial and the most stigmatized. The United States is unique among the industrialized countries in how it treats this group of the poor. The reason for this hated position is the explosive combination of racial discrimination and children.

The origins of Aid to Dependent Children (ADC) started in the latter nineteenth century. In the Colonial period, poor mothers were more likely to receive aid than poor men – except poor mothers who were African American or Indian.[1] Throughout most of the nineteenth century, Catholics, the Irish, Jews, and immigrants from southern Europe were objects of prejudice and discrimination.[2] They suffered all the ills of poverty and neglect in the large urban slums. There was little or no public support for these groups, however needy. Most African Americans were still in the rural South. Then, by the mid-twentieth century, after the great migrations to the North, prejudice was directed primarily at African Americans. In addition to racial and ethnic discrimination, single mothers had their own special baggage. Single mothers have always been suspect as sexually promiscuous, working in the paid labor market, and improper mothers. From the beginning, welfare for these families

[1] R. Herndon (2004). "'Who Died an Expense to This Town': Poor Relief in Eighteenth Century Rhode Island." In B. G. Smith (Ed.), *Down and Out in Early America*. University Park, Pa.: Pennsylvania State University Press.

[2] J. Higham (2002). *Strangers in the Land: Patterns of American Nativism, 1860–1920*. New Brunswick, N.J.: Rutgers University Press; R. Smith (1997). *Civic Ideals: Conflicting Visions of Citizenship in U.S. History*. New Haven, Conn.: Yale University Press.

was opposed because aid would provide disincentives to form and sustain two-parent families, reward out-of-wedlock births, encourage irresponsible fathers, threaten family life, and promote improper child rearing. But, unlike single adults or childless couples, single mothers could not be treated too harshly; otherwise children would suffer and homes would be broken up (which would be more costly for the state). Besides, children were innocent victims. The rest of the industrialized world has always recognized the importance of the children and has constructed welfare programs so that mothers, with reasonable support, could raise their children, but not in the United States. Its response has been to *demonize* the single mother. Unless welfare programs are harsh and stigmatizing, these women will be encouraged to have children, shun marriage, and perpetuate dependency. Who would choose welfare over a "normal" family life? Only those women who lack the proper values of majoritarian America. At first, it was those of disfavored religion and ethnic origins; then it was African Americans. Aid to Dependent Children represents the powerful combination of racial, gender, and sexual discrimination and is unique in its deliberate injury to innocent children. By industrial world standards, it is shameful. How did we get to this position?

The Colonial Period

Contrary to the American myth, as well as the stories told by many historians, from the earliest days of the colonies, there was significant poverty. In addition to slaves, many whites arrived as and remained indentured servants. There were large numbers of single-mother families. Husbands were often absent as sailors, were killed in the wars, were looking for work, or had left the family. There were accidents, disease, fires, and calamities that impoverished individuals and families.[3]

Initially, aid was outdoor relief in the community and was reserved for settled residents – strangers (including those looking for work) were "warned out," or expelled. At least as far as men were concerned, poverty was a moral fault; the individual was to blame rather than accidents, disease, wars, and depressions.[4] Local officials determined who was worthy, how much aid to extend, and the circumstances of aid. Men were expected to find work and support themselves and their families. Single mothers were viewed more favorably, but this too was a moral judgment. They were widows, deserted, or never married. The distinction reflected the patriarchal norms – women were not expected to take care of themselves when they were without a husband; they

---

[3] G. Nash (2004). "Poverty and Politics in Early American History." In B. G. Smith (Ed.), *Down and Out in Early America*. University Park, Pa.: Pennsylvania State University Press.

[4] Ibid. In the early part of the nineteenth century, several towns (including New York) required relief recipients to wear badges sewn on their clothes.

were inherently dependent. Most often children and mothers were bound out to families who would provide shelter and assistance (carefully specified by the town officials) in return for indenture. Aid was usually brief, to help a family over a bad patch.[5]

Although mothers in general were more likely to receive some form of relief, from the earliest days, single mothers of color (African American, Indian) and their children were treated differently. Ruth Herndon describes the disparate treatment of women and their children in eighteenth-century Rhode Island:

> Councilmen tended to keep a close eye on women of color who lived independently in Rhode Island towns, a scrutiny prompted in part by official responsibility to relieve poverty that always lurked outside the door of women struggling to support themselves and their children on the meager wages of a domestic servant or a farm laborer. But officials were also on the alert because Indian and black women often lived in households without male heads, raising the children in one place while their mates worked elsewhere as sailors, soldiers, and laborers. To town authorities, these women were out of their proper places, disconnected from the patriarchal households on which white New England was officially built. They were wives without husbands and daughters without fathers, but also, perhaps most important, people of color without masters. Women so completely out of place posed a threat to order, and this threat had a distinctly sexual overtone, as evidenced by the accusations of prostitution leveled at women of color and by the frequent, easy assumption of town officials that the children of these women were 'bastards' whom the town fathers would eventually have to bind out with indentures.[6]

Town officials closely monitored women of color but seldom gave them relief. More often, they were warned out – expelled from the town to fend for themselves and their children. More women were warned out than men in the towns of eighteenth-century Rhode Island, but these women were disproportionately of color. "Between 1750 and 1800, about one-fifth (22%) of those warned out were identified as 'Indian,' 'mustee,' 'mulatto,' 'Negro,' 'black' and 'of color.'" In Providence, in 1800, half of all those warned out were women of color even though "Negroes" were only 5 percent of the population.[7] When black or Indian women were mentioned on the relief rolls, they were usually very old.[8] Typically, they received a small amount for a final illness or burial. Hernandon found no records of a woman of color receiving aid for more than a few months.[9]

[5] K. Wulf (2004). "Gender and the Political Economy of Poor Relief in Colonial Philadephia." In B. G. Smith (Ed.), *Down and Out in Early America*. University Park: Pennsylvania State University Press.

[6] Herndon (2004), p. 146.   [7] Ibid.

[8] Ibid., p. 147.   [9] Ibid.

In the latter part of the eighteenth century, there were two wars, depressions, and changes in demography. Destitution and disorder increased. There was an increase in "needy strangers." Towns, already paying high taxes, first sought to cut relief expenses. Relief was seen as encouraging idleness, so the use of workhouses caught on, where all the poor in the town could be boarded together and engage in some useful occupation.[10] The basic idea was to get poor men back to work. Rehabilitating men and putting them back to work was viewed as the solution to women's poverty.[11] In Philadelphia, the Pennsylvania Hospital for the Sick Poor was opened in 1752, followed by the Bettering House in 1768. Although strongly opposed by the overseers of the poor, outdoor relief was abolished. Women, along with their children, were more likely to be sent to the Bettering House, but women were also sent to the almshouse, whereas men were sent to the workhouse. According to Karin Wulf, attitudes toward poverty did not change. What did change was the promotion of male independence as the major poverty policy.[12]

Between 1790 and 1820, county poorhouses replaced outdoor relief.[13] Several reasons were advanced: to control the costs of outdoor relief and to avoid the "pampering" by private households, a more careful division of "worthy" and "unworthy" was needed to effectively relieve the misery of the former and to reform the latter. There was to be rigid schedules of work, very little social intercourse (and no sexual intercourse), and teaching the "'habits of industry' necessary for success in an increasingly commercial economy."[14] Increasingly, the poor were blamed for their condition. Idleness and intemperance were particularly condemned. "Almshouse rules and regulations . . . strongly suggest a punitive intent on the part of legislators and relief officials, that is, an effort to make institutional life so unpleasant that most poor folk would take pains to avoid it."[15] Poorhouse inmates were criticized as lazy drunkards who used the poorhouse when the weather was too cold. Of course, there were those who had no choice but to enter the poorhouse – the old, the sick, the infirm. Thus, in Michael Katz's words, those who had to enter the poorhouse were held "hostage" to deter those who might think that welfare was preferable to work.[16] Monique Bourque, however, examining the records of poorhouses in the Philadelphia region, concludes that, in many cases, administration was less harsh. There often was a commercial and social relationship between the poorhouse and the local community, which administrators

---

[10] Ibid., p. 150.   [11] Wulf (2004), pp. 171–72.

[12] Ibid., pp. 180–81.

[13] M. Bourque (2004). "Poor Relief 'Without Violating the Rights of Humanity.'" In B. G. Smith (Ed.), *Down and Out in Early America*. University Park: Pennsylvania State University Press, p. 189.

[14] Ibid.   [15] Ibid., p. 198.

[16] M. Katz (1986). *In the Shadow of the Poor House: A Social History of Welfare in America*. New York: Basic Books.

regarded inmates as residents of the community sometimes referred to as "family."[17]

In most towns, poorhouses did not work, and the towns turned to "auctioning off" the poor; that is, interested households would bid for the opportunity to board "certain 'lots' of poor people." For a while, auctioning off, especially children, became the preferred method of relief – for those not warned out. Rates of warned out fluctuated (reached its peak in the mid-1780s), depending on economic conditions and increases in population. The Revolutionary War was particularly hard on the poor. Before the war, Herndon reports that poor relief was the most significant budget item for towns in Rhode Island. Then, the war taxes came, along with the severe dislocations of husbands leaving for the army, others looking for work, and large numbers of needy strangers. Poor relief was cut drastically.[18] Eventually, says Herndon, taxpayers grew weary of caring for the poor on an individual basis within the community. In early nineteenth century, the poor would be segregated in farms, orphanages, and other institutions.[19]

Throughout the colonial period, large numbers of orphans and "half" orphans (children who had lost one parent) were indentured to adults. The Charleston Orphan House, the first public orphanage, was created in 1790 out of concern for cost of caring for and educating children.[20] Only poor white orphans were admitted, not African Americans. The average population was about 100, but few were "full orphans."[21] Typically, children spent five or six years in the orphanages before being indentured (usually around age 12), although a minority returned to their families. Mortality was relatively high, especially for young children.[22] John Murray notes that "no poor orphan had it easy in eighteenth-century America, and many aspects of orphanage must have been difficult." But he says, the alternatives were not pleasant either. He quotes Barry Levy as characterizing the binding out of destitute or abandoned children in Massachusetts as "unsentimental, often abusive, [and] exploitative." Many children were a source of cheap labor. In New England, orphan care was outdoor relief. The Charlestown orphanage was expensive.[23]

During the Colonial period, several themes are noted that will endure throughout welfare history. Despite significant adverse structural conditions – wars, depression, accidents, disease, sickness – the poor were judged as morally blameworthy. This was universally true of men – outdoor relief was usually denied or they were sent to the workhouses. Single mothers were also

---

[17] Bourque (2004), pp. 193–96.   [18] Herndon (2004), pp. 155–56.

[19] Ibid., p. 157; Wulf (2004), pp. 181–82.

[20] J. Murray (2004). "Bound by Charity: The Abandoned Children of Late-Eighteenth-Century Charleston." In B. G. Smith (Ed.), *Down and Out in Early America*. University Park: Pennsylvania State University Press.

[21] Ibid., pp. 217–18.   [22] Ibid., pp. 221–22.

[23] Ibid., p. 228.

individually judged, but white mothers were viewed as "naturally" dependent. They constituted most of the outdoor relief rolls. The moral evaluation was different for women of color. They were not deserving of relief; it was denied or they were expelled from the community. Children (of white single mothers) were treated differently. Whereas relief for the mothers was usually brief and carefully itemized, children were more likely to be boarded out or indentured for long periods. They were supported in the indentured families, who were expected to provide them with education and work experience.

The creation, administration, and ultimate demise of the poorhouses illustrate several continuing themes. There was the disjuncture (at least in many cases) between legislation, rules, and regulations and actual administration. Public statements were harsh, full of blame, and called for severe conditions. Yet, on the ground, administration was different. Ground-level administrators exercised discretion and made their own moral judgments about recipients. The creation of the poorhouses was an exercise in symbolic politics, of myth and ceremony.[24] The legislature loudly proclaimed to majoritarian society that the poor were idle, shiftless, and abused the system and that confining them to the poorhouse would not only correct their behavior but also serve as an example to others similarly inclined. In fourteenth-century England, the first public assistance statutes provided for alms to the needy but prohibited giving alms to the able-bodied – the demon was the "sturdy beggar," the drunkard, the cheater, the malingerer. This is the ceremony that "validates" the myth that perpetuates the stereotype.

We shall find these themes as welfare history unfolds in the next two centuries – moral blame, race and gender discrimination, and symbolic politics. In the nineteenth century, immigrant single mothers and their children replaced women of color as unworthy. African American women then reassumed the role post–World War II.

The Origins of Aid to Dependent Children

As the welfare state developed, separate categories of the poor were extricated from the general mass of poor at the local level. For many reasons, these new categories of poor were considered "deserving" and were excused from the punitive policies directed at the paupers. Thus, the nineteenth century witnessed the rise of state asylums for the blind, the deaf, and the insane. State institutions were created for Civil War orphans, and an extensive pension system was established for Civil War veterans.[25]

---

[24] M. Edelman (1971). *Politics as Symbolic Action: Mass Arousal and Quiescence*. Chicago: Academic Press; J. Meyer & B. Rowan (1977). "Institutional Organizations: Formal Structure as Myth and Ceremony." *American Journal of Sociology* 83: 340–63.

[25] T. Skocpol (1992). *Protecting Soldiers and Mothers: The Political Origins of Social Policy in the United States*. Cambridge, Mass.: Belknap Press.

Initially, poor single-mother families were treated no differently than the general mass of poor at the local level. Except for a relatively few white widows, they were viewed with suspicion. The mothers received small amounts of aid, and the children were indentured. In the late nineteenth century, the Child Savers (elite, white Protestant, mostly women, mostly from the Northeast) sought to "save" children growing up in what they believed were dangerous conditions – poverty, urban slums, immigrant homes (primarily from southern and eastern Europe), Catholics, intemperance, and promiscuity. Children were to be "rescued," which included placing them in farm families in the Midwest.[26] The reformatory movement was started to send these at-risk children to live in cottages in the country under adult supervision. At the turn of the twentieth century, juvenile courts were established with jurisdictions over "delinquent, dependent, and neglected" children. "Dependent" (i.e., poor) and "neglected" were considered precursors to delinquency. The juvenile courts could send the child to a reformatory or place the family on probation.

The Child Savers began to believe that if a family was only poor, but the single mother was otherwise "fit and proper," perhaps the family could be supported in their own homes. The first statute reflecting this belief was the Illinois Fund to Parents Act in 1910; by the end of the decade, most states had similar statutes. This was the start of "welfare." The official term was Aid to Dependent Children (ADC), although the popular name at that time was "Mothers' Pensions."[27]

The origins of ADC demonstrate that it was as much about social control as income support. The program was limited to "deserving" mothers. Although most statutes were broad enough to include mothers who were divorced, separated, or deserted, in most states, with few exceptions, mothers who were not widows or were of color were excluded.[28] Moreover, in most states, jurisdiction was in the juvenile or county courts, rather than the county departments of welfare, which administered Aid to the Blind and Old Age Assistance (established shortly after ADC). The day-to-day administration of ADC was often controlled by the local charitable organization societies, who initially opposed the program and were determined not to allow aid to encourage family breakup, irresponsible fathers, sexual promiscuity, or other forms of misconduct. Finally, even though the programs were for "worthy widows," or, one would have thought, the "deserving" poor, there were work requirements. In several states, the juvenile court could require the mother to work. The vast majority of single-parent families, however, were considered

[26] L. Gordon (1999). *The Great American Orphan Abduction*. Cambridge, Mass.: Harvard University Press; Gordon (1988). *Heroes of Their Own Lives: The Politics and History of Family Violence, Boston 1880–1960*. New York: Viking.

[27] J. Handler (1995). *The Poverty of Welfare Reform*. New Haven, Conn.: Yale University Press.

[28] W. Bell (1965). *Aid to Dependent Children*. New York: Columbia University Press.; G. Mink (1998). *Welfare's End*. Ithaca, N.Y.: Cornell University Press.

undeserving; they were excluded from the program and thus forced to work in the paid labor market with the rest of the undeserving poor.

Aid to Dependent Children was not changed much by the New Deal. The Roosevelt administration was concerned primarily with unemployment and Social Security pensions, not welfare. The state programs – Old Age Assistance (OAA), Aid to the Blind, and ADC – were turned into grants-in-aid under the Social Security Act of 1935, which meant that the federal government would pay half the costs. There were a few federal requirements, but the states retained most control, especially financial eligibility. The ADC programs remained small and mostly composed of white widows through World War II.[29]

The "Suitable Home"

To qualify for state aid, mothers had to demonstrate that they were "proper and competent custodians of their children." The "suitable home" ideology of ADC reflected the domestic code of the mother as a homemaker responsible for maintaining a good home life and providing for the proper moral, physical, and mental development of her children.[30] Single mothers who did not conform to the moral code were viewed as immoral and dangerous to their children. To qualify for aid, the mother had to prove that she was morally "fit." How to distinguish between fit and unfit mothers became a major concern for both state legislators and local welfare officials. Some states such as Massachusetts and Michigan required that "no male boarder, other than the mother's brother or father could live in the home."[31] Local welfare departments were left to interpret "suitable home" according to prevailing community standards. Local offices and individual workers employed their own moral conceptions in defining suitable homes. As Winifred Bell puts it, "Emphasis was placed according to the importance attached to certain subjective standards by the community, the agency and the individual worker."[32] Lack of uniform standards meant that workers turned to widely accepted stereotypes. Typically, it meant that mothers with illegitimate children and women of color were excluded from aid. Not surprisingly, in many states coverage was limited to "gilt-edged widows"; that is, the most "fit and deserving" were white widows.[33]

There were also considerable local variations in the organization of welfare offices and the eligibility practices. Political appointees staffed local offices. Resources varied widely, reflecting both local attitudes and the availability of public funds. In 1939, the federal government required the selection of workers by a merit system, but still, most workers were not trained professionals.[34]

---

[29] Katz (2001), p. 4. Until 1950, OAA had more recipients than ADC.
[30] Bell (1965), p. 5.   [31] Ibid., p. 7.
[32] Ibid., p. 41.   [33] Ibid.
[34] Ibid., p. 134.

Offices were understaffed and workers overburdened by the complex processes of determining eligibility and their periodic review. Many applicants had to wait a considerable period to get their applications reviewed, and workers tended to "cool out" families they viewed as morally suspect.[35] A review by the federal Bureau of Public Assistance of records from several welfare offices showed repeatedly that welfare workers relied on their own personal moral beliefs to determine eligibility. According to Winifred Bell, welfare departments instituted processes that were highly biased and which placed considerable emphasis on surveillance and imposition of coercive standards of conduct.[36]

The "Welfare Queen" and the Welfare "Crisis"

Starting in the late 1950s and early 1960s, ADC emerged from the shadows of U.S. welfare policy to center stage, where it has remained. As noted, there were large migrations of African American families out of the South into northern urban centers. Instead of finding jobs and a better life, there was significant unemployment, poverty, and lack of decent, affordable housing. There were large increases in single families and unwed mothers. At first, the states held the line with welfare, but then, as a result of the civil rights and legal rights movements, welfare rights organizations, and Democratic politics, the state walls were breached, and the rolls expanded significantly. In 1960, there were 3.1 million ADC recipients, 4.3 million in 1965, 6.1 million in 1969, and 10.8 million by 1974.[37] In addition to the rise in rolls and costs, the program changed from largely white widows to mothers who were divorced, deserted, and unwed, many of whom were disproportionately African American. Welfare was now in "crisis." The term "welfare" took on a new meaning – a "despised program of last resort," for the "undeserving" who carried the stigmas of race and sex.[38]

The welfare crisis has re-ignited a number of myths – including the myth of crisis. The overriding myth continues to be that welfare persists because of the characteristics of the families, not because of larger, structural conditions of society. Such conditions as gender and race discrimination, lack of decent jobs especially for African American males, work-related benefits child care, housing, transportation, and all the other societal conditions that affect the lives of lower-income and poor people, especially people of color. The myths are invariably negative: families migrate to states that have higher welfare benefits; families choose welfare rather than work; families engage

---

[35] Bell (1965).   [36] Ibid., pp. 161–62.

[37] J. Patterson (1981). *America's Struggle against Poverty, 1900–1980*. Cambridge, Mass.: Harvard University Press.; F. Piven & R. Cloward (1977). *Poor People's Movements: Why They Succeed, How they Fail*. New York: Pantheon Books.

[38] Katz (2001), p. 4. Katz argues that the real reason that ADC became controversial was due to the Cold War; that is, it was "welfare state socialism," rather than the changing case rolls (p. 5).

in a number of fraudulent practices to establish and maintain eligibility. For example, fathers or other men secretly cohabit with the mothers and provide hidden assistance; fathers fail to either marry the mothers or support their children but live off the mother's welfare check; mothers have children out of wedlock to stay on welfare and increase their benefits; the welfare adults, in addition to promiscuity and welfare fraud, engage in other forms of deviant behavior such as substance abuse, drug dealing, and other crimes; teens raised in welfare homes fail at school and engage in all sorts of deviant behavior, including crime and delinquency and out-of-wedlock births, thus producing generational dependency.

Blaming the individual has a long history in the United States.[39] During the Colonial period, women of color were demonized. During the nineteenth century, first the Irish, and then the immigrants from eastern and southern Europe (Jews, Italians, Greeks, Slavs, etc.) were condemned for their lower-class, deviant behaviors. During the Depression, with poverty and hardship clearly caused by major economic dislocations, sympathy was primarily reserved for the "submerged middle class" – the hard-working people who lost their jobs through no fault of their own. For those at the bottom, the emphasis was primarily on individual behaviors.[40]

The current ideological myth behind all the other myths is the "welfare queen" (a term popularized by President Reagan) – the young African American unwed mother, having children to get on and stay on welfare, the failure to "properly" socialize the children, who grow up and repeat the same behaviors, as well as engage in crime, delinquency, and substance abuse. In short, welfare is breeding a criminal class. The "welfare queen" myth is the joining of the two stereotypes: race and the "undeserving poor." African Americans as the stereotypical *welfare* recipient only became prominent with the welfare "crisis." The term "undeserving" is as old as welfare itself and the belief that poverty is caused by individuals' lack of effort. Joining "welfare" and "undeserving," as Martin Gilens points out, comes from the historic view, stemming from slavery, that African Americans are inherently lazy. Thus, African American welfare recipients are primarily undeserving.[41]

The groundwork was laid for the "welfare queen" by several well-publicized studies, which purported to show that the poor or the lower classes had special, unique dysfunctional individual characteristics.[42] A prominent example

---

[39] A. O'Connor (2001). *Poverty Knowledge: Social Science, Social Policy, and the Poor in Twentieth-Century U.S. History.* Princeton, N.J.: Princeton University Press.

[40] Higham (2002); R. Smith (1997). *Civic Ideals: Conflicting Visions of Citizenship in U.S. History.* New Haven, Conn.: Yale University Press.

[41] M. Gilens (1999). *Why Americans Hate Welfare: Race, Media, and the Politics of Antipoverty Policy.* Chicago: University of Chicago Press. See also M. Abramovitz (2005). "Race and the Politics of Welfare Reform" (Book Review). *Social Service Review* 79: 382.

[42] The following section relies heavily on the excellent work of O'Connor (2001) and Patterson (1981).

was the work of W. Lloyd Warner, who studied communities in the 1930s (Newburyport, Mass.; Natchez, Miss.; and a Chicago's South Side African American neighborhood). He concluded that more important than income and wealth were "class-specific cultural practices [that] socialized and prepared individuals for their inherited stations in the social order – and that made upward mobility a difficult, potentially hazardous climb."[43] Among the poor, Warner distinguished between the "deserving" and "undeserving" poor. The "'upper-lower' groups were 'honest but poor,' and lived in orderly neighborhoods . . . and took pride in their ability to get by without relief. They cared about the education of their children. The 'lower-lowers' cared little about education and resisted outside attempts to improve their lot. They were marginally employed, disorderly and 'shiftless,' . . . lived on the 'wrong side of the tracks.' . . . [T]hey satisfied themselves with immediate gratifications, and lived by a quasi-criminal, sexually uninhibited moral code." The "lower-lowers" were "generally satisfied with their place on the status hierarchy."[44] Employers regarded their "shiftlessness, irresponsibility, lack of ambition, absenteeism, quitting . . . as 'innate' perversity of white and negro workers [as] in fact *normal responses* that the worker has learned from his physical and social environment."[45]

Alice O'Connor states that by the mid-1930s, significant psychological characteristics were ascribed to lower-class culture: "undisciplined, aggressive, unable to defer gratification because they were raised without sexual or impulse control . . . children without basic personality traits that motivated achievement."[46] Still, Warner believed that lower-class culture could be changed with economic opportunity. It was only later that the "'culture of poverty' began to assume the aura of psychological determinism."[47]

Influential studies in the late 1930s and early 1940s claimed a distinctive African American "pathological lower-class culture stemming from white prejudice in the large, unassimilated poor populations of the deep South and the northern cities."[48] Several African American scholars (e.g., DuBois, Fraser, and Johnson) agreed on some of the characteristics of African American life – matriarchy, male joblessness, and so on – but argued that this was an adaptation to racism and poverty, "a step towards a reorganization of life on a more intelligent basis" rather than a pathology. The matriarchal family was a way for the African American women to move toward independence.[49]

One of the most influential studies was Gunnar Myrdal's *An American Dilemma* (1944). Myrdal blamed the castelike racism in the United States for the plight of African Americans – "family instability, religious 'emotionalism,'

---

[43] O'Connor (2001), p. 62.
[45] Ibid., p. 64 (emphasis original).
[47] Ibid., p. 66.
[49] Ibid., p. 83.

[44] O'Connor (2001), pp. 62–63.
[46] Ibid., p. 65.
[48] Ibid., p. 76.

high crime rates, 'superstition,' 'provincialism,' 'personality difficulties,' and 'other characteristic traits.'"[50] He used the term "vicious circle" to describe the interaction of lack of skills, education, economic exploitation, low status, and racial discrimination, which are "'independent factors, mutually cumulative in their effects'; thus, poverty itself breeds poverty."[51] The "vicious circle" took on a life of its own and became the "reigning metaphor in liberal social analysis for the next three decades."[52]

The analysis of Mrydal, and others, took on a new salience during the post–World War II boom when the ADC rolls exploded; the perception was that the newcomers were disproportionately African American single, unwed mothers, even though, as Katz points out, the most significant growth was among white families.[53] With the rising prosperity and the resurgence of the nuclear, patriarchal family, poverty, that is, African American poverty, was a "paradox" – the poor were a culturally, self-contained, deprived group. Oscar Lewis's *Culture of Poverty* struck a responsive chord.[54] On the basis of his study of rural poverty in Mexico, he argued that poverty had universal cultural characteristics that were passed down from generation to generation and transcended rural and urban and regional and national boundaries. The characteristics, which Lewis identified, were "resignation, dependency, present-time orientation, lack of impulse control, weak ego structure, sexual confusion, and inability to defer gratification."[55] There was a growth and spread of behavioral sciences that emphasized individualized, psychological characteristics. In the African American lower-class matriarchal society, mothers alone could not properly nurture their children, which led to delinquency, personality disorders, and confused gender roles. The inability to defer gratification became a "certifiable personality disorder."[56] The culture of poverty, according to O'Connor, "captured an undercurrent of pessimism, foreboding."[57]

Michael Harrington's *The Other America* reinforced the ideology of the culture of poverty. "They are a different kind of people. They think and feel differently; they look upon a different America than the middle class looks upon."[58] Although Harrington called for large social change, the culture of poverty focused more on individual rehabilitation rather than societal redistribution.[59]

---

[50] Ibid., p. 95. [51] Ibid., p. 96.

[52] Ibid.

[53] M. Katz (2001). *The Price of Citizenship: Redefining the American Welfare State*. New York: Metropolitan Books, p. 362, n. 16.

[54] First developed in O. Lewis (1959). *Five Families: Mexican Case Studies in the Culture of Poverty*. New York: Basic Books.

[55] O'Connor (2001), pp. 117–18. [56] Ibid., pp. 109–10.

[57] Ibid., p. 121.

[58] M. Harrington (1981). *The Other America. Poverty in the United States*. New York: Penguin Books, first published in the 1962; O'Connor (2001), p. 122.

[59] O'Connor (2002), p. 122–23.

The Attacks on Welfare

As described by Ellen Reese, the intellectual and popular attacks on welfare, which began in the mid-1940s, started with complaints by journalists,
politicians, welfare officials, and business groups about fraud and the waste of
money, which undermined the family, sexual morality, and the work ethic.[60]
In several states, there were complaints about families with "several children"
receiving benefits higher than the average worker. There were welfare scan-
dals. As reported by Katz, a headline in the *New York Times* in 1947, read
"Woman in Mink with $60,000 Lived on Relief in a Hotel." She was an
unmarried mother. In 1949, a *Saturday Evening Post* article, "Detroit Cracks
Down on Relief Chiselers" used only single mothers with children as examples. The complaints accelerated in the 1950s. In 1951, a *Saturday Evening
Post* article, "The Relief Chiselers Are Stealing Us Blind," cited only ADC.[61]

At the same time, there was the glorification of the American patriarchal
family. Women were to return to their "proper" roles and not compete with
men for the anticipated shortage of jobs. Family experts, joined by the media,
extolled the traditional family. Marriage and fertility rates rose dramatically.[62]
African Americans were considered the opposite. There was the growth of
concentrated poverty, the rise of single-parent families, fears of crime, and
delinquency. Employment remained highly segregated along both racial and
gender lines, even though the 1950s were prosperous and the poverty rate
declined, the per capita earnings of African American families with children
was less than half of white families. Earnings were particularly low for African
American women. Unemployment was especially high in major cities – three
to four times higher for African American women than for white women in
Chicago, Cleveland, Detroit, New York, and Philadelphia.[63]

Out-of-wedlock births tripled between 1940 and 1958, with African American women having the highest rate.[64] The percentage of African American
out-of-wedlock children rose from 25 percent to 34 percent, compared with
10.9 percent for whites.[65] Between 1945 and 1950, the number of welfare recipients doubled to more than 2 million. There was a temporary decline between
1950 and 1953, but by 1960, the caseload had more than tripled. In part, the
expansion was due to required changes in the application procedures, which
made diversion by the states more difficult.[66] The composition of the rolls
changed as well – widowed families declined from 43 percent in 1937 to less
than 8 percent in 1961.[67] The percentage of African American families rose

[60] E. Reese (2005). *Backlash against Welfare Mothers: Past and Present.* Berkeley: University of
California Press.
[61] Katz (2001), p. 5.   [62] Reese (2005), p. 16.
[63] Ibid., p. 60.   [64] Ibid., p. 57.
[65] Katz (2001), p. 7.   [66] Reese (2005), p. 58.
[67] Ibid., p. 57. In part, the decline of white widows was due to the expansion of Old Age and Survivors
Insurance, in 1939, to survivors who previously were on ADC.

from 31 percent in 1950 to 48 percent in 1961. In some cities, the concentration of African American families on welfare was even higher – for example, over 90 percent in Chicago.[68]

During this period, there was an absence of advocacy for poor women. Some social workers were interested in reform but mainly through casework. Women's organizations were in decline. Civil rights had started but was mostly interested in desegregating public facilities.[69]

According to Reese, racial attacks become more prominent with the rise of the civil rights movement.[70] President Truman introduced a bill to establish a permanent Fair Employment Practices Commission. By executive order, racial discrimination was prohibited in the military and the federal civil service. In the South, more than 80 percent of the public opposed Truman's civil rights program.[71] *Brown vs. Board of Education* (1954) provoked violent opposition, especially in the South. African Americans began to mobilize and engage in political protest. There were rallies and racial violence. The "Dixiecrats" and white supremacists opposed not only Truman's civil rights programs but also the policies associated with the New Deal and Truman's Fair Deal – the "communistic welfare state."[72]

Puerto Rican and Mexican immigration also fueled hostility and opposition to welfare. Between 1940 and 1950, almost 900,000 Puerto Ricans immigrated, mostly to New York City, where they experienced discrimination, segregation, and other forms of hostility. In Los Angeles, San Diego, Chicago, Philadelphia, and Harlem, there were riots and other disturbances against Mexican immigrants. The "magnet" thesis provided another basis for the attacks on welfare. Although in New York City, Puerto Ricans make up 11 percent of the welfare population (African Americans were 10%), teachers, social workers, and politicians claimed that Puerto Ricans were incapable of assimilation and employment and thus lured to New York City to obtain welfare. The New York City welfare commissioner reported that most Puerto Ricans were self-supporting and not responsible for the increase in the welfare rolls. Other reports confirmed this for both African Americans and Puerto Ricans. Nevertheless, a residency law was enacted in 1960 to "close our borders to the chiseling free-loader."[73] By 1966, thirty-nine states had adopted a residency requirement.[74]

The "welfare queen" stereotype emerged – African American women having children to avoid work by receiving welfare. Again, the stereotype drew on the historical slavery image of African Americans as "lazy, hypersexed, reckless breeders." African American unwed mothers were the product of an

[68] Ibid., pp. 55–57.   [69] Ibid., pp. 60–62.
[70] Ibid., p. 92. Reese dates the start of racialized attacks from the 1940s and 1950s, although Quadagno and Gilens date these attacks to the 1960s (pp. 98–99); J. Quadagno (1994). *The Color of Welfare: How Racism Undermined the War on Poverty.* New York: Oxford University Press; Gilens (1999).
[71] Reese (2005), p. 92.   [72] Ibid., pp. 93–94.
[73] Ibid., p. 187.   [74] Ibid., pp. 95–98.

"'accepted way of life' in an inferior culture."[75] There were two views of the so-called fallen woman – one, that she should be punished, or, from social scientists, and psychologists, that she should be "reformed." The latter view was buttressed by arguments that absent fathers led to personality disorders in children, including the inability to defer gratification.[76]

During the 1950s, the states began to adopt restrictive practices. The most common were the "employable mother" and a stricter "suitable home" requirement. By 1960, almost half of the states restricted ADC through one or both of these policies.[77] There had been a long practice of states informally pushing welfare recipients into low-wage work when workers were scarce (e.g., harvest time) by cutting off aid, providing very low benefits, or diversion. In states with large caseloads and a large percentage of African American recipients, formal employment rules were adopted. Eighteen states required mothers to accept available employment if child care was available, but this requirement was often ignored.[78] However, there were no formal work requirements in more than half of the states.[79] In several states, including California and Illinois, the farm bureaus lobbied for work requirements to ensure that there was a supply of labor during harvests.[80]

Many local communities felt morally threatened by the rise of families of color (including those with illegitimate children) seeking aid and by the increasing costs of aid.[81] Several states reduced their financial support for the program, and fraud investigations became more prevalent. They reinforced the prevailing ideology that aid encourages African American mothers to have more illegitimate children and erodes their motivation to work.[82] Many communities seized on the ambiguity of the "suitable home" rule by instituting more punitive practices. Workers made sure that the mothers did not maintain contacts with any man ("man-in-the-house" rule) and made eligibility for aid contingent on establishing paternity. In some states, the applicants had to pledge "not to have any male caller coming to my home nor meeting elsewhere under improper conditions . . . and to not knowingly contribute or be a contributing factor to [my children] being shamed by my conduct. I understand that should I violate this agreement, the children will be taken from me."[83] Midnight raids in search of the elusive man were common. Fear of fraud resulted in extensive use of "collateral contacts" with relatives, neighbors,

---

[75] Ibid. See also Gilens (1999); K. Crenshaw (1989). Demarginalizing the Intersection of Race and Sex: A Black Feminist Critique of Antidiscrimination Doctrine, Feminist Theory and Antiracist Politics, University of Chicago Forum 139–67. Reprinted in *The Politics of Law: A Progressive Critique* (2nd ed. edited by D. Kairys, New York: Pantheon, 1990).
[76] Reese (2005), pp. 99–100.   [77] Ibid., p. 64.
[78] Ibid., pp. 64–65, 81.   [79] Ibid., p. 111.
[80] Ibid., p. 83. Mechanization did reduce the demand for cotton, but vegetables and fruits were not mechanized until the 1960s and 1970s (p. 89).
[81] Bell (1965), p. 67.   [82] Ibid., pp. 64–65.
[83] Quoted in Mink (1998), p. 37; Reese (2005), p. 66.

friends, landlords, merchants, employers, schools, police departments, health
agencies, public agencies administering unemployment compensation and
old-age and survivors' insurance, banks, and credit bureaus to uncover hidden family resources.[84] Welfare offices developed specialized investigation
and fraud detection units. Workers used their authority and considerable discretion to invade homes at will and to demand rules of conduct regarding
child rearing and child care, money management, and work. The relationship between the welfare workers and their clients was based on mistrust,
suspicion, and the presumption of client immorality. Welfare applicants and
recipients had little if any rights.[85]

In 1959, the Florida legislature included failure to provide a "stable moral
environment" as a legitimate reason to remove children from the home. Local
welfare departments seized the opportunity to classify more than half of their
caseload as failing to provide a suitable moral environment. The majority
of these cases were African American mothers. Fearing that they might lose
their children, many "voluntarily" withdrew from aid or avoided applying.[86]
A similar phenomenon occurred in Louisiana. In 1960, the state dropped
about 30 percent of the cases from the rolls, most of them African American,
because they were not deemed to have "suitable homes." The reason given
was that state law denies aid to mothers who give birth to out-of-wedlock
children after being on aid (foreshadowing the family cap under TANF).
The law was applied retroactively, affecting 22,501 children, 95 percent of
them African American (although African American children were 66 percent of the recipients). There was strong opposition from African American
churches and national and community advocacy groups. At first, the U.S.
Social Security Commissioner approved the policy. During hearings conducted by Social Security Administration, state officials "agreed that their law
was as frankly directed toward saving public funds as it was toward improving family morals."[87] Then, the Secretary of Health, Education and Welfare
(HEW) ruled that a welfare department could not declare a home unsuitable
for a child and allow the child to remain in the home. As a result, Louisiana
and four other states had to revise their policies.[88]

A final example is the notorious Newburgh, New York, crisis in 1961.[89]
Between 1950 and 1960, Newburgh experienced a major economic decline.
Factories closed, resulting in high unemployment and declining property
values. At the same time, the city experienced a 151 percent increase in its
African American population. The newly appointed city manager, Joseph
Mitchell, blamed the welfare migration of African Americans for its fiscal

[84] Bell (1965), p. 87.
[85] Ibid., p. 88.
[86] Ibid., pp. 124–36.
[87] Ibid., p. 145.
[88] Reese (2005), pp. 73–76.
[89] L. Levenstein (2000). "From Innocent Children to Unwanted Migrants and Unwed Moms: Two
Chapters in the Public Discourse on Welfare in the United States, 1960–1961." *Journal of Women's
History* 11(4): 10–33.

problems.[90] He then proposed new eligibility rules, which as we see, are remarkably similar to those enacted in PRWORA in 1996. They included "a curtailment of ADC for women who had additional illegitimate children, a three-month limit on all grants to able-bodied persons, and stringent work relief requirements."[91] Although Mitchell's claims could not be supported by data, nevertheless they resonated well not only in Newburgh but nationally by linking the rise in welfare costs and other urban ills with African Americans. Eventually, the federal government forced him to back down.

By 1962, twenty-four states had enacted "man in the house" or "substitute father" rules. In some states, aid would be terminated even for a casual affair. Maximum grants – a ceiling on the number of children per family that would be supported – were established in some states. In eight states and eighteen large cities, special fraud investigation units were established. In response to the charge that "deadbeat dads" were not supporting their families, Congress overrode the requirement that ADC cases be kept confidential and passed the Notice to Law Enforcement Officials (NOLEO), which required welfare agencies to notify local law enforcement agencies in cases of desertion so that child support enforcement proceedings could be initiated. Public inspection laws became widespread.[92] Nineteen states required applicants to take legal action against the father. Welfare agencies could deny aid to families who refused to cooperate with local law enforcement. Still, prosecutors rarely went after absent fathers for child support.[93]

The Child Support Act of 1974 created the office of Child Support Enforcement, with comparable offices established by the states. The federal government would pay three-fourths of state enforcement expenses. The act was strengthened in 1980 and 1984, with states fixing payment guidelines and withholding wages of delinquent parents. By 1985, as family demographics changed, the absence of fathers' support was viewed as a serious, widespread problem. Liberals and women's groups that had opposed strengthening child support enforcement changed their position. The amount of awards began to increase, although only about a third of single parents received payments. Because the payments were generally low, neither poverty nor welfare dependency were changed.[94]

The Liberal Response to Welfare: The War on Poverty

As Mimi Abramovitz points out, the post–World War II period also had a liberal side. Significant social legislation was enacted – school lunches (1946), mental health (1946), hospital construction (1946), employment (1946), housing (1949), school milk (1954), and vocational rehabilitation (1954). The

[90] Ibid., pp. 16–17.
[91] Ibid., p. 17.
[92] Reese (2005), pp. 66–71.
[93] Ibid., p. 66.
[94] Katz (2001), pp. 66–69.

1950 Social Security amendments expanded coverage, raised welfare benefits, and provided aid to medical care for welfare families. In 1956, disability was added to Social Security. Medicaid and Medicare were enacted in 1965, as well as federal aid to elementary and secondary schools, urban renewal, and support for low-income housing.[95] *Brown vs. Board of Education* (1954), while arousing racial hostility, also ushered in a period of civil rights law reform litigation. Federal courts outlawed racial discrimination in public accommodations, transportation, and other fields. At first, activists went to the South to challenge discrimination. Martin Luther King Jr. led marches, which various civil rights organizations joined. Attention turned to discrimination in the North. There were rallies, marches, and demonstrations. In some cities, welfare recipients organized and conducted sit-ins in welfare offices, demanding better treatment.[96] Through marches, sit-ins, and demonstrations, they put pressure on state and local governments to increase enrollments and welfare benefits.[97] During the 1960s, civil rights were established for the mentally ill, the disabled, women, learning-disabled children, and so forth. Coming off the Eisenhower years, John F. Kennedy was elected president in 1960 with the promise of a liberal, forward-looking America. During the 1960s, the Democratic Party began to court inner-city African Americans. Local political leaders pressured state and local welfare offices to let down barriers. In 1972, the Supreme Court declared that welfare was an "entitlement" and that recipients were entitled to due process hearings if claims were denied.[98] Thus, Katz argues that one reason for the dramatic increases in the welfare rolls was not the rise of single-mother families but rather the increase in the percentage of eligible families able to enter the rolls as a result of the civil rights and welfare rights movements.[99]

During this period, conflicting views about the nature and causes of poverty were advanced. Liberal economists argued that poverty was basically a problem of lack of income and that, as a result of the long period of economic growth, the country could afford to abolish the poverty gap. Other liberals, while agreeing on the need for more income support, argued that barriers inhibited the access of the poor to a growing economy.[100] Cloward and Ohlin published their influential book, *Delinquency and Opportunity*, in 1960, which emphasized the blocked opportunities for young people living under slum conditions.[101] Scholars and journalists "helped rediscover urban poverty."[102]

[95] M. Abramowitz (1988). *Regulating the Lives of Women: Social Welfare Policy from Colonial Times to the Present.* Boston: South End Press, p. 335.

[96] Piven & Cloward (1977).   [97] Abramovitz (1988), p. 336.

[98] *Goldberg v. Kelly*, 397 U.S. 254 (1970).   [99] Katz (2001), p. 7.

[100] Patterson, pp. 112–13.

[101] R. Cloward & L. E. Ohlin (1960). *Delinquency and Opportunity: A Theory of Delinquent Gangs.* Free Press: Glencoe, Ill.

[102] Patterson (1981), p. 101.

President Kennedy, although concerned about the issues of poverty, concentrated on expanding the economy and reducing unemployment.[103] His basic approach was to "help people help themselves" through training, education, and services. In 1961, he established a Committee on Juvenile Delinquency and Youth Crime, which, financed "comprehensive action" programs in several cities, including the Mobilization for Youth in New York City (MFY). This program included employment, training, education, antidiscrimination, and neighborhood service centers, and became a prominent model for the community action programs of the War on Poverty.[104] The Ford Foundation's Gray Areas project funded MFY, as well as many other community action programs, but would only deal with assimilation, not racism.[105] Another program was the Manpower Development and Training Act (MDTA), with a mission to help people help get off welfare. Although by 1973, MDTA had enrolled 2.2 million people in job training at a cost of $3.2 billion, at its height, MDTA enrolled only about 300,000 people per year, even though there were many more applicants than slots.[106]

As part of the liberal Kennedy period, the focus on welfare shifted from punishment to rehabilitation, fueled in part by the "rediscovery" of social problems, such as unemployment, family breakup, illegitimacy, delinquency, and mental illness.[107] For a considerable time, the social work profession had been arguing for prevention and rehabilitation rather than merely providing relief. There was also the growing perception of "multiproblem families" and chronic dependency. U.S. Health, Education, and Welfare Secretary Abraham Ribicoff, in advocating for social services, stated, "Too much emphasis has been placed on just getting an assistance check into the hands of an individual. If we are ever going to move constructively in this field, we must come to recognize that our efforts must involve a variety of helpful services, of which giving money payment is only one."[108]

The services approach appealed to conservatives because it promised to reduce dependency and welfare costs. Substituting services for cash would prevent "the ADC mother with a dozen illegitimate kids, the relief checks that buy liquor instead of food, the able-bodied man who spurns a decent job to stay on relief."[109] The key concept was "opportunity." Sergeant Shriver, who headed the task force on antipoverty, stated, "I'm not at all interested in running a hand-out program, or a 'something for nothing' program."[110]

Although the states continued to reduce ADC benefits, the federal government sought to strengthen family life (and reduce the welfare rolls) through

[103] Ibid., p. 127.
[104] Ibid.
[105] O'Connor (2001), p. 135.
[106] Patterson (1981), p. 127.
[107] Abramovitz (1988), p. 329.
[108] G. Steiner (1971). *The State of Welfare*. Washington, D.C.: Brookings Institution, p. 36.
[109] Patterson (1981), p. 132.
[110] Quoted in Patterson (1981), p. 135.

the Public Welfare Amendments of 1962, called the Social Service Amendments.[111] The federal government would reimburse the states for 75 percent of the cost of rehabilitation or preventive services.[112] Federal funding was provided for special training for social workers. Aid to Dependent Children was renamed Aid to Families with Dependent Children (AFDC). The name of the Bureau of Public Assistance was changed to the Bureau of Family Services. Aid to two-parent families (AFDC-UP), enacted as a temporary measure in 1961, was extended for five years.[113]

Leaders of the social work profession, such as Elizabeth Wickenden and Winifred Bell, were also critical of the current structure of public welfare. They pointed to restrictive and inconsistent eligibility and residency requirements, the use of moral judgments to restrict aid, lack of understanding of the importance of social services, the failure to integrate public and child welfare programs, and the organizational impediments arising from delegation of responsibility to administer aid to the local level. Although they recommended universalizing eligibility criteria, they saw the expansion of social services as a key to reforming welfare. They agreed that in many instances individuals just needed basic services – financial assistance, medical care, and improved housing. Yet, they argued that in other cases the problem of dependency was a consequence of "an interaction between personal responsibility, social expectations and environmental factors."[114] Cash assistance alone would not ameliorate the problem. Rather "the knowledgeable help and support of an understanding social worker may be a necessary catalyst in breaking a self-defeating pattern and hence a very good investment of public funds."[115] Bell in her testimony on the Public Welfare Amendments of 1962 described ten demonstration projects in several welfare departments around the country. These projects employed professionally trained social workers who specialized in ADC cases. With an emphasis on strengthening the family and reduced caseloads (thirty-five to fifty cases), the workers were able to make frequent home visits and "for the first time, the agency was not merely a watchdog, determining to ferret out abuses and irregularities. Now skilled counseling and trained concern were extended, and in this climate problems were more apt to be confided, and social workers and families had a chance to become partners in a mutual undertaking. It is little wonder that positive changes occurred."[116] According to Bell, these demonstration projects resulted in improved family functioning, increased employment, and reduction in the rolls.[117]

[111] Abramovitz (1988), p. 330.   [112] Patterson (1981), p. 131.

[113] Abramovitz (1988), p. 331.

[114] E. Wickenden & W. Bell (1961). *Public Welfare, Time for a Change* (The project on Public Services for Families and Children, sponsored by the New York School of Social Work of Columbia University), p. 21.

[115] Wickenden & Bell (1961), p. 21.   [116] Bell (1965), p. 373.

[117] Ibid., p. 373.

The new myth that social services could transform local welfare department failed to acknowledge the inherent contradictions in the approach itself as well as the realities at the local level. Indeed, it foreshadowed the implementation of TANF thirty-four years later. First, the goal of rehabilitation had to compete with the goal of eligibility determination and redetermination. The central task of the welfare department to determine eligibility and enforce compliance overwhelmed the counseling tasks. The two tasks are inherently incompatible. As Bell puts it, "The public assistance worker not only has the disadvantage of high caseloads. Unlike social workers in family agencies or community clinics, he has the demanding task in determining and redetermining eligibility."[118] Second, the idea of transforming welfare workers to professional social workers was highly unrealistic. Only about 4 percent of all welfare workers were professionally trained, and there were no signs that, even with added resources, schools of social work would be willing or capable of turning graduates to work in public welfare.[119] Third, both at the federal and state level, insufficient resources were allocated for rehabilitation. In states such as Massachusetts, caseworkers were overwhelmed by large caseloads, and most had no professional social work training. Moreover, there were no resources to forge effective interorganizational relations with other service organizations to provide needed services such as job training, day care, and rehabilitative services. For many of these organizations, serving welfare mothers would not be a high priority. Fourth, the service technology – social casework – was highly indeterminate. It was expressed in the professional rhetoric of "producing change in the lives of welfare recipients through the techniques of counseling, advice and guidance."[120] Or as Martha Derthick put it, "Casework, in short, is what the caseworker does."[121] Moreover, social casework generally assumes a voluntary relationship between the client and the worker, hardly the case in the welfare department. The new mandate, while not increasing the actual services welfare recipients obtained, greatly expanded the paperwork for the workers who had to document how each contact with the client constituted a "unit of service" so that the department would qualify for the federal match.

Again, it is important to recognize that considerable local variations existed in organizational practices. Bell reports that departments that had more restrictive eligibility requirements were less likely to provide social services (i.e., casework). Moreover, each state and county provided their own operative

[118] Ibid., p. 158–59.   [119] Steiner (1971), p. 39.
[120] J. F. Handler & E. J. Hollingsworth (1971). The "Deserving Poor": A Study of Welfare Administration. Chicago: Markham Publishing Co., p. 55.
[121] M. Derthick (1970). The Influence of Federal Grants: Public Assistance in Massachusetts. Cambridge, Mass.: Harvard University Press, p. 136.

definition for "social services."[122] Paradoxically, the concept of social services proved to be just as elusive as the idea of the "worthy" poor. In both instances, it gave local welfare departments and their workers considerable discretion in deciding what they meant. Still, welfare rolls and costs increased.[123]

Over time, the recognition that eligibility determination and social case-work expressed incompatible moral assumptions and service technologies resulted in the decoupling of the two functions. Indeed, the social work profession strongly advocated for the separation because it did not want to be associated with the morally problematic function of aid determination. In her famous editorial in *Social Work*, Gordon Hamilton strongly advocated for the separation, writing that "the money function disables or overwhelms the social services."[124] According to Mary Jo Bane and David Ellwood, "social workers argued that the dual role of counselor and investigator was impossible to achieve. Such perceptions of coercion, accurate or not, poisoned the 'therapeutic' value of the counselor/client relationship."[125] The separation was urged on welfare departments by the federal government in 1967 and mandated in 1972.[126]

The most noteworthy policy during this period was the War on Poverty, which fit within this rehabilitative tradition.[127] The Johnson Administration was restrained financially with the Vietnam war and a tax cut. This eliminated the possibility of jobs and income support for the poor.[128] The final bill, called the Economic Opportunity Act, contained a variety of "opportunity" programs, including community action; Jobs Corps; Neighborhood Youth Corps; Volunteers in Service to America (VISTA), a domestic peace corps; as well as loans for farmers and rural businesses. However, funding was small.[129] Although this view was supportive of the poor, it still ignored the structural conditions that produced poverty. As Patterson states, during this time, millions of poor were not in the labor force; they needed income more than opportunity. In the addition to the lack of decent jobs, there was extensive racial discrimination. But, the agreed-upon program was developing

---

[122] Bell (1965), p. 161.   [123] Patterson (1981), pp. 132–33.
[124] G. Hamilton (1962). "Editorial." *Social Work*, p. 128.
[125] M. J. Bane & D. T. Ellwood (1994). *Welfare Realities: From Rhetoric to Reform*. Cambridge, Mass.: Harvard University Press, p. 15.
[126] W. H. Simon (1983). "Legality, Bureaucracy, and Class in the Welfare System." *Yale Law Journal* 92: 1198–269.
[127] Patterson (1981), p. 134. There are differences of opinion about the reasons the Office of Economic Opportunity (OEO) and the War on Poverty were established. Patterson disagrees with Cloward and Piven that it was to reach and placate African American militancy. In 1963, black social movements were largely integrationists, nonviolent, and confined to the South. He also disagrees that it was a political strategy to bolster the faltering coalition within the Democrats. The civil rights bill proposed in 1963 was enough to develop black political support.
[128] Ibid., p. 141.   [129] Ibid.

opportunity – a hand up, not a handout. The War on Poverty "never seriously considered giving poor people what many of them needed most: jobs and income maintenance."[130]

In addition to being seriously underfunded, the War on Poverty suffered from administrative disorganization, bureaucratic infighting (principally with the Department of Labor), and conflicts between professional social workers and community activists. Liberals complained about the lack of funds; conservatives complained that too much money was spent for political activism (as well as the usual charges of bribery and corruption). State and local officials objected to community action and especially the "maximum feasible participation" requirements that challenged local governments.[131] At about this time, the civil rights movement and inner-city blacks became militantly active. The first urban riots broke out in 1964 in Harlem and spread to more than twenty cities throughout the country. There was a major reaction from state and local governments. The Office of Economic Opportunity (OEO) tried to cut back the number of poor on the community action boards to a third, which further aroused activists. There were other compromises but after 1965, Johnson turned from supporting OEO, and it began to lose its programs. Community action remained until the 1970s, when OEO was abolished.[132]

As O'Connor points out, although racism was a subtext, the analysis emphasized an individualized pathology – poverty breeding poverty. Liberals believed that the cycle could be broken by limited strategic interventions, which was the strategy of the War on Poverty. Subsequently, she argues, the conservatives used the same analysis to explain why the liberal antipoverty interventions were ineffective.[133]

It was during this period that a debate reopened between the structuralists and the culturalists about the causes of poverty.[134] The culturalists maintained that the poor were somehow "different" from mainstream society; that they were apathetic, present-minded, or mentally ill and could not "defer gratification"; that these cultural traits were both "familial and intergenerational."[135] The Council of Economic Advisers adopted this view in 1964. After noting that 40 percent of ADC parents had come from welfare families, the council said, "Poverty breeds poverty. A poor individual has a high probability of staying poor."[136]

The opposite view – the "structuralists" – agreed on a distinctive subculture but disagreed as to the causes and the policy responses. They argued that even though there was hard-core "'institutionalized pathology' that could

[130] Ibid., p. 136.   [131] Ibid., pp. 143–46.
[132] Ibid., pp. 147–48.   [133] O'Connor (2001), p. 97.
[134] Patterson (1981), p. 115.
[135] Patterson (1981), pp. 118–19, citing in particular Harrington's *Other America* and Oscar Lewis's *Culture of Poverty*, both of which were very influential during this period.
[136] Patterson (1981), p. 120.

become self-perpetuating, the vast majority of African American poor accepted mainstream values but were the victims of racism and the lack of opportunities. This group called for job creation, income guarantees, desegregation, targeting programs for men, and anti-discrimination measures for African American women."[137]

Then came the Moynihan report, *The Negro Family: The Case for National Action* (1965). The report coined the term "a tangle of pathology." According to Moynihan, the "startling increase in welfare dependency" was primarily caused by the rise in female-headed households.[138] The roots of the decline of the African American family were in slavery, then compounded by racism, segregation, urbanization, male unemployment, and persistent poverty. This, in turn, led to a culture of immediate gratification, delinquency, and crime that was then passed on from generation to generation. Moynihan pointed out that the ADC rate once correlated with African American male unemployment but that since 1962, it was rising even though unemployment was declining. The implication was that the conditions of the African American family were so pathological that expanded opportunities would be futile.[139] The report was issued just after the Watts riot in Los Angeles. By now, African American militancy was dividing the civil rights movement.[140]

The Moynihan report – that the plight of African Americans was caused by their long-standing culture – did not go unchallenged. There was a renewed interest in structural issues. For example, studies showed that although the white out-of-wedlock birth rate was still lower than the African American, it had actually increased faster in the 1950s; that the African American rate had in fact stabilized in 1958; and that out-of-wedlock birth rates were related to broad social changes that affected all races. The effect of slavery on the two-parent family was also challenged. The two-parent family had, in fact, survived slavery and was the norm. Single-parent families were the result of male mortality and were not necessarily dysfunctional. Poverty and racial discrimination caused family instability and its harmful consequences.[141] The "cultural" explanation of juvenile delinquency was also challenged. Studies showed that welfare poor youth had far lower delinquency rates than other juveniles, many poor youth were not delinquent, and the police were more likely to arrest poor African Americans. Finally, the relationship between southern migration and welfare, crime, and delinquency was also refuted.[142]

Between 1965 and 1970, the peak of OEO, the number of poor dropped from 33 to 25 million, and total federal spending on social welfare more than doubled – education, Social Security, health, and welfare. Some of the War on Poverty programs – Head Start, Neighborhood Youth Corps, and Legal

---

[137] O'Connor (2001), p. 202.

[138] Patterson (1981), pp. 101–2.

[139] O'Connor (2001), p. 202.

[140] O'Connor (2001), p. 196.

[141] Patterson (1981), pp. 102–3.

[142] Ibid., p. 104.

Services – reached millions of people. Community action varied. Some programs led to significant counterattacks by local politicians, others led to the start of local African American political organization. It was very difficult to get the poor to participate in community action programs.[143] Nevertheless, as Patterson points out, despite the promises of the Johnson administration, the War on Poverty was always poorly funded – an average of about $1.7 billion per year from 1965 to 1975. Poverty was not going to be abolished.[144]

According to Patterson, the failure of OEO to deliver during this period demonstrated, at least to some, that what the poor needed were jobs and income support, not just opportunities. Still, the War on Poverty, along with the civil rights movement, legal rights, and other social movements, heightened concern about poverty, which helped acceptance of other programs for the poor, such as aid to education and Medicaid in 1965.[145] Even during the Nixon administration, some reforms continued. In the meantime, the states and local officials developed effective lobbies for federal funds for a variety of state activities, such as drug abuse and mental illness.[146]

The Triumph of the "Welfare Queen"

Nevertheless, even though this was supposed to be a liberal period, most Americans continued to believe the worst about poverty.[147] Urban crime continued to rise, and several cities experienced riots. It seemed as if crime and racial disorder was spreading. A 1955 report on juvenile delinquency stated that it was a "national epidemic . . . unless this cancer is checked early enough, it can go on spreading and contaminate many good cells in our society."[148] In the early 1960s, as economic conditions deteriorated, there were significant increases in welfare, crime, delinquency, and substance abuse. It was believed that teenage boys, growing up in welfare families, became gang members and delinquents. The press began to run stories of welfare cheats, illegitimacy, and delinquency. According to Patterson, attitudes toward welfare hardened. Most believed that most welfare recipients were African American. Most Americans wanted no aid for additional out-of-wedlock children, the sterilization of mothers, strict work requirements, in-kind benefits instead of cash, and residency requirements.[149] Most people believe that poverty was due to a lack of effort and careful money management; 84 percent agreed that too many were receiving welfare who should be working; 71 percent felt that many on welfare were "not honest about their need." Politicians condemned the welfare system – it

[143] Ibid., p. 149.
[144] Ibid., pp. 151–52.
[145] Ibid., pp. 152–54.
[146] Patterson (1981), pp. 182–83.
[147] Ibid., pp. 123–24.
[148] 1,000 Delinquents, quoted in Patterson (1981), p. 100.
[149] Patterson (1981), pp. 109–10.

attracted lazy migrants to the more generous states (in the North), disrupted families and encouraged illegitimacy, and undercut the work ethic.[150] In 1967, 42 percent of the public blamed poverty on "lack of effort," compared with 19 percent who attributed poverty to "circumstances beyond control." In 1969, almost 60 percent said that poverty was due to "lack of thrift and proper money management," 84 percent said that welfare recipients should work, and more than 70 percent thought that many welfare recipients were dishonest about their need. In 1967, Ronald Reagan, in his inaugural speech as governor of California, declared, "We are not going to perpetuate poverty by substituting a permanent dole for a paycheck."[151] Senator Huey Long of Louisiana said that the welfare system was being "manipulated and abused by malingerers, cheaters, and out-right frauds." He coined the term "brood mares."[152]

According to Mimi Abramovitz, in 1966, the average grant for a family of four was $1,728 per year, which was barely half of the poverty line. Significant percentages lacked basic necessities (11% had no kitchen; 24% had no running water; 17% had children who sometimes missed school due to lack of clothing, etc.).[153]

Martin Gilens, in his book *Why Americans Hate Welfare*, says that "welfare" is considered a code word for "black," and most Americans believe that the problems of African Americans are caused by their own lack of effort.[154] It is this negative attitude about African Americans that is most powerful in shaping views about poverty and welfare. African Americans are viewed as inherently lazy, and the stereotype is continually reinforced by the media portrayals of the African American underclass, even though the underclass is only a small proportion (about 11%) of African Americans.

It is the media's distortions of African Americans that Gilens holds largely responsible for the misperceptions about the poor and the negative attitudes toward welfare. Before the 1960s, African Americans were generally ignored by the media. Before 1964, most pictures of the poor were white. Then, with the welfare "crisis," civil rights, and the urban riots, African Americans not only began to be extensively covered by the media, but the images were increasingly negative.[155] Between 1965 and 1967, when government antipoverty programs began to be criticized, news depictions of poverty became racialized. For example, when the Job Corps came under attack (e.g., poor screening, inadequate facilities, high dropout rates, hostility from local communities), the media showed more pictures of African Americans than whites. The same disproportionate number of pictures occurred when community action programs came

[150] Ibid., pp. 171–72.
[151] Quoted in Abramovitz (1988), p. 335.
[152] Quoted in Abramovitz (1988), p. 335.
[153] Abramovitz (1988), pp. 335–36.
[154] Gilens (1999); see also M. Fellowes & G. Rowe (2004). "Politics and the New American Welfare States." *American Journal of Political Science* 48(2, April): 362–73.
[155] Ibid., p. 9.

under criticism, and the focus turned to urban poverty.[156] The stories and pictures of African Americans increased with the rise of the welfare "crisis." In 1972–73, with stories on housing, urban problems, and unemployment, Gilens says that highest percentage of stories featured African Americans.[157] During the 1974–75 recession, stories on unemployment primarily showed whites, whereas stories on poverty and welfare primarily showed African Americans. For favorable stories of employment programs (e.g., the Comprehensive Employment and Training Act), the pictures were primarily of whites. The negative stories of welfare primarily showed African Americans.[158] With the Reagan recession (1982–83), there were sympathetic stories of whites trying to cope with the cutbacks in government programs.[159] Gilens claims that there was even more racial bias in the TV news coverage than in magazines and newspapers. The most powerful images were of the African American urban ghettos. Even though most news reporters were generally liberal, Gilens argues that it was subconscious racial stereotypes that influenced both the content of the news stories and, most importantly, the pictures.[160]

Gilens maintains that numerous studies have shown that media stories about specific instances (e.g., stories about a welfare family) have a powerful influence on public opinion – much more so than reports and statistics. "What matters more is the race of the person in the news stories, not the statistics on racial composition."[161] "The response of a picture of a poor white person is to create more jobs, improve the economy; of a poor African American, people should work harder and acquire skills." And in states with a higher percentage of African Americans, the public is much more hostile to welfare.[162]

As the attacks on the War on Poverty increased, so too did the negative coverage of African Americans. The tendency was to show pictures of African Americans when stories about the poor were critical; when stories more positive (e.g., during periods of economic hardships), pictures would more often be of whites.[163] Even though the perception that the beneficiaries of programs were primarily African Americans, there would still be support for programs that were designed to help the poor improve. The chief concern was undermining the work effort. Welfare was not a "right," and welfare recipients were not primarily victims of the economic system.[164] Government, a large majority said, should do more to fight poverty and homelessness, and to improve health and education, displaced workers, and the elderly, but the government should not do more for welfare. Public opinion matters, says Gilens. If public attitudes on a particular issue change by as much as 20 percent, then government policy follows in more than 90 percent of the time.[165]

---

[156] Ibid., pp. 111–19.
[158] Ibid., pp. 123–24.
[160] Ibid., pp. 129–33.
[162] Ibid., p. 174.
[164] Ibid., pp. 8–9.

[157] Ibid., pp. 122–23.
[159] Ibid., pp. 125–27.
[161] Ibid., pp. 134–35.
[163] Ibid., pp. 6–7.
[165] Ibid., pp. 12, 25.

According to Gilens, there are several reasons "welfare" is viewed differently than most other government programs. Generally, there is more support for welfare when the economy is weak, there is more support for welfare among those with lower incomes. Perceptions of waste or inefficiency do not seem to be that important in attitudes toward welfare spending. However, racial attitudes, by far, are the most important when combined with doubts about the true needs of welfare recipients.[166] There is the strong belief that many of the recipients are undeserving, that most are taking advantage of the system, and that they could find work if they tried hard enough. Most Americans believe this lack of effort because of their attitudes toward race. African American images dominate the perceptions of welfare and extreme poverty – the welfare queen, the homeless, gang members, drug addicts. "Discussions about 'urban policy' or 'how to help American cities' is taken to mean 'what should we do about poor black neighborhoods, crime, and poverty.'"[167] According to Gilens, beliefs that African Americans "lack a commitment to the work ethic is the most powerful predictor of attitudes towards welfare."[168] He argues that this stereotype stems from the days of slavery when African Americans were considered to be lazy. Today, the stereotype of the African American mother is that she will not look for a job but instead will have more children to stay on welfare.[169]

Thus, there is very strong support for work requirements as well as time limits. At the same time, there is also a willingness to make exceptions for significant physical or mental disability, for young children (most favor exemptions where the child is under one year old but favor work where the child is more than three years old), and if the unemployment rate of the area is high. There is a willingness to continue benefits for children even if parents are cut off. They favor exemptions for part-time work, for first-time welfare use after many years of working, and help with child care and transportation.[170] Gilens concludes that saving taxpayer money is less important than preserving the work ethic and reducing out-of-wedlock births.[171]

Thus, it was the combination of the long-standing attitudes that African Americans are lazy and can work if they want to that came together in the mid-1960s, reinforced by the negative media images in the subsequent decades. The media have been instrumental in reinforcing these negative stereotypes. "Deserving poor" programs are supported – education, training, job creation, welfare-to-work, the EITC, health care, child care, transportation – but not welfare.[172]

[166] Ibid., p. 60.
[168] Ibid., p. 76.
[170] Ibid., pp. 185–91.
[172] Ibid., pp. 204–13.

[167] Ibid., p. 68.
[169] Ibid., pp. 95–98.
[171] Ibid., p. 192.

The Transformation of Welfare Departments

In the meantime, the welfare rolls continued to grow – from 3.5 million in 1961 to almost 5.0 million in 1967 – the proportion of unwed participants grew (from 21.3% to 28.4%, or almost half of the increase in the rolls), and the proportion of nonwhites rose to almost 50 percent. During this period, costs rose from $994 million to $2.2 billion.

As described by William Simon, welfare departments acquired a new organizational form characterized by the formalization of entitlement, bureaucratization of administration, and proletarianization of the workforce.[173] The goals of the welfare department were to verify eligibility, write checks, and reduce errors.[174] Relations became limited to other public agencies that could provide documentary verification to claims of eligibility such as family status, income and assets, unemployment and work history, health, birth of children, school enrollment, and living arrangements. Rules and regulations attempted to govern every possible contingency, resulting in volumes of instructions updated and changed, often before workers had a chance even to absorb the instructions they replaced. If prior norms allowed workers to exempt a car from an applicant's assets when judged to be "needed," now the car could not be counted if its value was more than $1,500.[175] Eligibility determination became highly mechanistic and impersonal, focusing on the verification. "The Massachusetts welfare department gives applicants a list of thirty documents that they may be asked to supply.... Many of the documents must meet stringent technical requirements."[176]

The organization of work was divided into several discrete units. Applicants began at "intake," which consisted of staff specializing in eligibility determinations. Once eligibility was established, clients were typically assigned an "eligibility technician" responsible for periodic eligibility redetermination. These workers had large caseloads of about 200 cases. If the client was required to participate in a work program, she would be referred to a separate "human resources" unit.[177]

To ensure reduction in errors, quality control units were established. They used statistical methods to select a sample of cases to review for possible payment errors. The review was very detailed as states were subject to penalties if the error rates exceeded a certain acceptable level.[178] There were two characteristics to these reviews. First, they were concerned with overpayments rather than underpayments, reflecting the moral assumption that many welfare recipients were undeserving and prone to cheating. Second, most of the

---

[173] Simon (1983), p. 1199.   [174] Bane & Ellwood (1994), p. 16.
[175] Simon (1983), p. 1202.   [176] Ibid., p. 1205.
[177] Simon (1983). See also Bane & Ellwood (1994).
[178] No state was actually penalized despite error rates.

errors could be classified as "paper errors" unrelated to substantive eligibility determination.[179] Quality control intensified organizational hierarchy by adding bureaucratic layers to supervise, check, and monitor frontline work.[180]

The new organization of work also led to further "de-skilling" of the workers to lower-level, low-paid clerical positions. Indeed, in many welfare departments, the eligibility workers were not appreciably different from the applicants they processed and came to resent the recipients for getting an undeserving entitlement denied to them.

Putting Recipients to Work

In 1967, Congress repealed the social service amendments and instituted, for the first time, a federal work requirement the Work Incentive Program (WIN). This program was both the carrot and the stick. Before WIN, there was a 100 percent tax rate on AFDC – every dollar earned was deducted from the welfare grant.[181] The WIN incentives changed the 100 percent tax rate to earnings-related deductions of $30 per month, one-third of the earnings, and work-related expenses. Although this was an improvement, the tax rate was still 66 percent. The WIN program expanded welfare administration. There were job training and wage subsidization. All recipients, except those who were aged, ill, or living too far from a WIN project, were required to register for work, accept referrals for work or training, and take a bona fide offer of employment. Failure to comply would result in a denial of benefits for three months or a reduction in the grant. "Soft" social services were to be replaced by concrete, employment-related services; rehabilitation and prevention was to be replaced by job search, job placement, and on-the-job training.[182]

Ideologically, at the federal level, the WIN program changed the obligations of welfare mothers. Previously, they were expected to raise a family in return for benefits; now they were expected to become self-sufficient. The mandatory features reflected the view that welfare recipients were either unmotivated or unwilling to work, in other words, that many welfare mothers were "undeserving."[183] However, the changes were also favored by liberals who argued that the 100 percent tax rate was a disincentive.[184]

The WIN was a failure. Many states decided that mothers of preschoolers were "inappropriate" for training or work and thus exempt because of the lack of jobs, the high costs of day care, and the resistance of welfare departments. Only a small number found permanent jobs.[185] In practice, only fathers (under AFDC-UP), dropouts older than 16, and a few mothers of school-age

[179] E. Z. Brodkin & M. Lipsky (1983). "Quality Control in AFDC as an Administrative Strategy." *Social Service Review* 57: 1–34.

[180] Simon (1983), p. 1211.

[181] Abramovitz (1988), p. 333.

[182] Ibid., p. 339.

[183] Patterson (1981), pp. 174–75.

[184] Ibid., p. 174.

[185] Abramovitz (1988), pp. 339–41.

children were considered "appropriate" to register for either work or training. In 1971, the Talmadge amendments toughened the work requirements. The category of recipients required to register for work or training was expanded and included mothers of school-age children. Training was reduced and work emphasized. States were to be penalized if at least 15 percent of the caseload was not referred. Slightly more were referred and employed, but again, there were not enough job openings.[186]

Meanwhile the attacks continued. President Nixon, in his State of the Union message (1971), said, "The current welfare system has become a monstrous consuming outrage – an outrage against the community, against the taxpayer, and particularly against the children it is supposed to help." President Carter, at a news conference in 1977, picked up the same themes – welfare was "anti-work, anti-family, inequitable in its treatment of the poor and wasteful of taxpayers' dollars."[187]

The next major attempt to reform ADC was the Family Support Act (1988) (FSA). By this time, according to Senator Moynihan, there was a "new consensus" to "convert welfare from a permanent or even extended circumstance to transition to employment."[188] There should be mutual obligations. Again, as Katz points out, the reforms focused on reducing welfare dependency through increasing work requirements and reducing benefits rather than improving the low-wage labor market, addressing the lack of jobs in the inner cities, or poverty. On the other hand, there were also provisions to increase child care, education and job training, and child-support enforcement.[189]

The FSA was preceded by a Manpower Development Research Corporation (MDRC) study of work programs in eleven states. Help with job searches did lead to increased earnings. However, the earnings increase was modest (and did not deduct work-related expenses); the increase came from longer hours rather than higher wages; some got off welfare, but few escaped poverty, and many returned to welfare. Furthermore, the MDRC study did not include mothers with children between three and six years of age, who were to be included under the FSA. A GAO study arrived at the same conclusions – very modest results. Nevertheless, the results were hailed as a "success" by state governors and welfare reformers – that workfare "worked."[190] There were prior attempts at work programs. The Comprehensive Employment and Training Act was effective, but it was cut in 1980 by Republicans who believed that it interfered with labor markets. It was replaced by the Job Training Partnership Act (JTPA), which offered assistance to employers looking for low-wage labor. However, results were meager.[191] There was agreement on improving child-support enforcement. States were to offer education, job skills

[186] Patterson (1981), pp. 175–76.
[188] Quoted in Katz (2001), p. 62.
[190] Ibid., pp. 71–73.
[187] Quoted in Gilens (1999), pp. 1, 235.
[189] Katz (2001), p. 57.
[191] Ibid., pp. 62–66.

training, and job placement and training, called JOBS. There was to be active case management. Medicaid and child care would be extended for one year after employment. The most controversy centered on requiring mothers with children between ages 3 and 6 to participate.[192]

As with WIN, results were modest. Congress underfunded the program. Funds for education and training were insufficient. With high caseloads, there was very little personalized case management. State programs reached only a small fraction of clients, and wages were declining.[193]

State Waivers to Increase Work Requirements

Public assistance was sharply reduced in the 1991–92 recession. AFDC benefits were either cut or frozen in forty states; in thirty-eight states, GA was reserved for the able bodied, and benefits were cut for the disabled, the elderly, those with temporary disability, and the unemployed.[194] Public attitudes hardened. The response of the federal government was to grant waivers to the states to allow them to institute their own versions of welfare reform. By 1996, there were waivers in forty-three states. Some states cut benefits; others offered work incentives, including combining welfare with work, transitional child care and health care. Others relied on sanctions.[195]

One of the most famous of the state waiver programs was Wisconsin Works, or W-2, started in 1986. Under W-2, eventually, all recipients were subject to the work requirements, with the emphasis on quick job placement with minimal training. There were mandatory time limits. However, there was extensive child care support, health care, transportation assistance, and the full use of the EITC and food stamps. One-stop job centers provided intensive case management and job search and placement. Caseloads dropped significantly. However, state unemployment was below national levels, three-quarters of the caseload decline occurred before the reforms took effect, and many families were sanctioned (mostly in Milwaukee), with an increase in poverty and homelessness. Wisconsin Works was very costly – it was estimated that with all the incentives and work supports, the program spent about twice as much per family.[196] Other states as well instituted tough programs. The measure of success was the reduction in the caseloads.[197]

---

[192] Ibid., pp. 73–75.   [193] Ibid., pp. 75–76.
[194] Ibid., pp. 83–89.   [195] Ibid., pp. 90–93.
[196] Ibid., pp. 93–101. The cost estimates are from Haveman. For a positive view of W-2, see L. M. Mead (2004). *Government Matters: Welfare Reform in Wisconsin.* Princeton, N.J.: Princeton University Press. For a recent critical review of W-2, see J. DeParle (2004). *American Dream: Three Women, Ten Kids, and a Nation's Drive to End Welfare.* New York: Viking.
[197] Katz (2001), p. 102–3. In liberal Massachusetts, benefits were reduced, time limits were imposed, teen parents had to live at home and complete high school, and welfare for able-bodied recipients would last for sixty days only, after which they would have to either get a job or perform community service (p. 102).

Still, the rolls continued to grow – to a high of 11.3 million in 1976. Then, the rolls stabilized between 1976 and 1986. At the same time, the real value of AFDC benefits declined by 47 percent between 1970 and 1995.[198] Myths and false reports continued to blame welfare. The Heritage Foundation claimed that the War on Poverty cost $5.4 trillion between 1965 and 1994. In fact, the largest program for the poor was Medicaid, and only 16 percent of the cost was for AFDC. In 1993, AFDC cost $22 billion, which was less than 10 percent of the cost of Social Security. It did not matter. The country was alarmed by the rise of out-of-wedlock births. In 1994, 70 percent of African American births were out of wedlock, and at least half were poor. The conservatives claimed that welfare destroyed families. Dependency was the most important issue, not jobs or income. Welfare had to be reformed to enforce work, morals, and family values. It did not matter that the rolls increased even though benefits declined or that the fertility of African American women was declining, or that after the 1991–92 recession, welfare rolls began to decline, along with out-of-wedlock births and the number of children living in single-parent families. Welfare rolls remained high in several conservative, southern states, and in the older, inner cities. Everyone, it seemed, hated welfare.[199] By the 1990s, as Katz states, AFDC was "the most disliked public program in America."[200]

"Ending Welfare as We Know It"

The attacks on the welfare state were part of the conservative change in American politics: high taxes, bureaucracy, government, the ineffectiveness and corruption of local government, and so forth. Most now believed that the federal welfare state programs of the 1960s had failed. There was the call for less government and private markets. In Katz's term, there was a "cultural panic" about dependency. "Responsibility for economic security should rest on individuals, not with the state."[201]

Then, in 1996, both Republicans and Democrats, responding to President Clinton's campaign promise to "end welfare as we know it," united in passing a major change – the Personal Responsibility Work and Opportunity Reconciliation Act (PRWORA) – which, among other things, replaced AFDC with TANF.[202] Welfare is no longer an "entitlement" – "a term that is almost as negative as 'welfare.'"[203] There are stiff work requirements and, for the first time in welfare history, time limits. As discussed later, although time limits vary, in general, welfare is limited to a five-year cumulative lifetime limit.

---

[198] Ibid., p. 11.
[200] Ibid., p. 1.
[199] Ibid., pp. 319–23.
[201] Ibid., pp. 17–30.
[202] Katz (2001), p. 1. Eighty percent of Americans supported Clinton's campaign promise to "end welfare as we know it."
[203] Ibid., p. 325.

Federal grants-in-aid to the states were changed to block grants. The amount of the block grant is calculated on the basis of the state's AFDC caseload during the 1990s. In addition to increasing state discretion, the importance of this change was that under the grant-in-aid, the federal government would reimburse the states as the rolls expanded, or, conversely, the states would lose federal dollars when the rolls went down. Now, because the block grants are fixed, the states make money by cutting the rolls.

In Chapter 6, we discuss the work requirements in detail. Briefly, states are required to move an increasing percentage of welfare recipients into the workforce over the next six years, starting with 25 percent of the adults in 1997 and increasing to 50 percent by 2002. States could exempt up to 20 percent of the caseload; the criteria were not specified. States are required to reduce grant amounts for recipients who refuse to participate in "work or work activities." The work requirements are to be enforced by funding cuts in the block grants. Although the idea of work requirements, as we have seen, was not new, the difference was in the significant ideological and policy commitment to employment, enforced by the time limits.

In addition to the work requirements, there were a variety of provisions dealing with "family values," which are discussed in detail in Chapter 7. Funding was made available to states to encourage marriage. Federal funds could not be used to support minor parents under age 18 who were not in school or other specified educational activities, living with their parents, or in another adult-supervised setting. States are required to reduce a family's grant by 25 percent if they fail to cooperate (without good cause) with efforts to establish paternity. States may eliminate cash assistance to families altogether or provide any mix of cash or in-kind benefits they choose. They can deny aid to all teenage parents or other selected groups, deny aid to children born to parents receiving aid, deny aid to legal immigrants (since modified), or establish their own or lower time limits. States can provide new residents with benefits equal to the amount offered in their former states for up to one year (subsequently declared unconstitutional by the U.S. Supreme Court).[204] States may choose to deny cash assistance for life to persons convicted of a drug-related felony (which in many states can consist of possession of a small amount of marijuana).

What are the results thus far from these reforms? The biggest story has been the dramatic decline in the welfare rolls, although the decline started in 1994 rather than in 1996. By 1998, there was a 44 percent decline.[205] Whites left faster than African Americans and Hispanics; declines were slower in urban areas.[206] Total expenditures for AFDC/TANF peaked at $30.1 billion in

---

[204] *Saenz v. Roe*, 526 U.S. 489 (1999).   [205] Katz (2001), p. 334.
[206] Ibid., p. 334.

fiscal year 1995, and then fell 23 percent in the next three years as caseloads dropped 34 percent. Then, total spending increased, but in fiscal year 2001, it still was $5 billion below the 1995 peak. Reduced state spending accounted for almost $4.2 million of the decline and reduced federal spending for almost $1.4 billion. The share of federal spending was about 54 percent to 55 percent under AFDC, declined to 52 percent in fiscal year 1998–99, but since has risen to 60 percent in fiscal year 2001. In real value, federal expenditures declined almost 22 percent and state expenditures almost 40 percent from the peak levels of 1995. During the same period, average TANF caseloads fell 57 percent.[207] As discussed in Chapter 2, most welfare leavers are employed, but most are still in poverty.

Although the rolls are starting to rise somewhat now in some parts of the country, as the economy has slowed, practically all politicians are proclaiming the 1996 welfare reforms as a "success," that finally welfare has ended as we know it. In fact, "welfare reform" has dropped off the political radar screen. So far, contrary to predictions, there has been "no race to the bottom" among the states. As noted, during the boom time, significant state money was spent on work-related supports, much of it going to the working poor and not necessarily welfare recipients. Now, with the recession and the state fiscal crises, this aid has been sharply reduced.

Conclusions: A Return to Colonial Welfare

For the past half century, single mothers and their children have been demonized. Although they are not the worst off in terms of actual cash assistance, because they are families with children, they are very close to the bottom. As compared with all other aid recipients, they are the most prominent lightning rod for political attacks. They receive aid, but only reluctantly, and with all sorts of conditions designed to counter perceived incentives for immoral behavior. In a fundamental sense, welfare is eerily reminiscent of the Colonial period. There was outdoor relief but rarely given to men and certainly not the able-bodied. Mothers were more likely to get relief, but only if they were white, it was short term, there was supervision, and the children were indentured to be properly educated and learn work skills and habits. Their mothers were not to be trusted. Women of color (African Americans and Native Americans) were considered unworthy of aid and expelled from the community. For the past decades of "welfare reform," when the program was identified with African American single mothers, there were increasing work requirements, but most significantly, as is discussed in Chapter 5, women are expelled from welfare and have to survive as best they can.

[207] U.S. House of Representatives, The Green Book (2004). "Background Material and Data on Programs within the Jurisdiction of the Committee on Ways and Means," pp. 7–58.

The next chapter focuses on administering welfare. Repeatedly, we enact policies and programs for welfare without paying attention to administrative capacity. We assume that local welfare agencies can adjust and can handle complex social services, as well as employment services. Yet, administrative response – or lack of response – is crucial to the well-being of the mothers and their children. It is at the field level that discretion and power is exercised over the lives of these people. How do the agencies respond? What can we expect of them? What happens to the mothers and the children in the day-to-day encounters? Instead of seriously confronting these issues, programs and requirements are enacted, they are delegated to the field level, and we move on to the next policy issue. The myth is that something is accomplished; the ceremony is that occasionally something positive happens, but the reality is the opposite.

Throughout welfare history, there have been enduring myths about who welfare recipients are, why the rolls have expanded, and what to do "about" welfare. Since World War II, the economy has gone up and down, and the country has gone through liberal and conservative periods. Nevertheless, the myths endure and are now stronger than ever.

Chapter 6 addresses the work and the low-wage labor market, which are the central focus of the current welfare reform. Who are welfare recipients, and why do they need welfare? What is their employment record, their attitudes toward work? We examine the myths of the low-wage labor market and show how difficult it is for poor single mothers to stay employed and independent of welfare. In the context of work, we present the issues of the declining welfare rolls. Is it true that "welfare reform" – and what is meant by welfare reform – is significantly responsible for the decline in the rolls? In Chapter 7, we turn to family issues – the marriage initiatives, paternity and child support enforcement, teenage sexual behavior. We look at the fathers – what is their role in the family? How much can we expect from child support? We conclude with a discussion of whether welfare leavers are better off. How are they surviving? Are they escaping poverty? And what is happening to the children?

5   The Welfare Bureaucracy

As discussed in Chapter 4, following the post–World War II explosion of the welfare rolls, the welfare bureaucracies were transformed to manage strict eligibility and payment verification to control "waste, fraud, and abuse." Then, under the Social Service Amendments in 1962, they were to perform social services, and when the social service approach was abandoned, they then had to administer work programs. The result was a wide disjuncture between the intent or rhetoric of the policies and their actual implementation. The field-level agencies simply lacked the personnel, training, and incentives to do either social services or employment services as long as accurate eligibility and payment determinations remained the primary goal. This disjuncture continues to plague the welfare bureaucracies as they cope with the work requirements first implemented under the state demonstration projects and now under Temporary Aid to Needy Families (TANF).

There are several reasons for the gap between the intent of the policy and its actual implementation. First, a major purpose of welfare policies that target the "undeserving" poor is to affirm dominant moral beliefs about the work ethic, family structure, gender relations, and race and ethnicity.[1] As is discussed in Chapter 7, Personal Responsibility and Work Opportunity Reconciliation Act (PRWORA) affirms "family values." It contains such explicit moral tenets as "marriage is the foundation of a successful society. Marriage is an essential institution of a successful society that promotes the interests of children. Promotion of responsible fatherhood and motherhood is integral to successful child rearing and the well-being of children."

These moral pronouncements are seldom uncontroversial. Politicians, at the national level or state level, enact the broad moral statements. At the field level, they expect local welfare agencies to uphold these symbols but make distinctions by promulgating rules and regulations. The local welfare

---

[1] J. F. Handler & Y. Hasenfeld (1991). *The Moral Construction of Poverty*. Newbury Park, Calif.: Sage Publications.

departments are expected to adopt ceremonies that reflect these symbols and separate between the "deserving" and "undeserving" in how they categorize and process the poor, by enforcing eligibility requirements, by monitoring compliance, and by sanctioning failures to comply.[2] By delegating to local authorities the responsibility to do the actual administration, the upper-level politicians buffer themselves from the conflicts that inevitably arise from their implementation. It is at the local level that the conflicts about who is morally deserving are fought.[3]

The delegation suits the needs of the local level. Here is where the moral conflicts of welfare are most keenly felt. Neighbors are needy by misfortune; strangers are morally suspect. As discussed in Chapter 4, from the earliest days of welfare, the "settlement" rule ensured that only residents of the community were deserving of relief, while strangers were driven out.[4] As discussed in Chapter 3, in the public welfare state, the distinction between the "deserving" and "undeserving" describes the jurisdictional allocation of the various programs. The deserving poor programs are universal and administered at the federal level – Social Security and Medicare. The undeserving poor programs are administered at the state and local level – AFDC (now TANF) and general relief. The distinction was preserved in the Social Security Act of 1935. The state programs were funded through grants-in-aid. There are federal regulations, but there was still, and continues to be, a great deal of state and local autonomy. There has always been considerable room for local values and political and economic interests to play themselves out in the administration of the local welfare departments. There has always been a pervasive effort by state and local officials to interpret, bend, and even subvert federal regulations to suit their needs.[5] Dialectic tensions between policy making at the national level and actual administration at the local level continues.[6]

Second, the implementation of welfare policies at the community level is an expression of local culture and political economy. The enactment of policies is not only affected by the local economy and the number and characteristics of the poor but also by the political elite, local government bureaucracies and practices, and the existence of various interest groups that view welfare as an opportunity or threat. The generosity or stinginess of local welfare officials tends to reflect the ideologies of the political elites as well as the perceived threat of the poor. In their seminal book *Regulating the Poor*, Frances Fox

---

[2] Ibid., p. 30.   [3] Ibid., p. 30.

[4] J. C. Brown (1940). *Public Relief 1929–1939*. New York: Henry Holt and Co., p. 3; R. Herndon (2004). "'Who Died an Expense to This Town': Poor Relief in Eighteenth Century Rhode Island." In B. G. Smith (Ed.), *Down and Out in Early America*. University Park: Pennsylvania State University Press.

[5] See, e.g., B. Bernstein (1982). *The Politics of Welfare*. Cambridge, Mass.: ABT Books; M. Derthick (1975). *Uncontrollable Spending for Social Services Grants*. Washington, D.C.: Brookings Institution.

[6] See, e.g., M. Katz (1986). *In the Shadow of the Poor House: A Social History of Welfare in America*. New York: Basic Books.

Piven and Richard Cloward argue that political elites use public aid as a form of social control.[7] When local unemployment rises and is accompanied by civil disorders, officials tend to expand the welfare rolls. Although there is much debate about the validity of their thesis, Richard Fording has shown that although the rise in unemployment and urban riots expands welfare generosity, the expansion is contingent on state liberalism and the size of the state's African American population (the relationship is curvilinear).[8] Similarly, Joe Soss and colleagues show that states that enact tougher TANF sanction policies are more likely to have a larger number of African Americans in their caseload, higher unmarried birth rates, more conservative government, less vigorous party competition, and smaller welfare caseload per population, and the states had made earlier requests for AFDC waivers.[9]

When welfare is delegated to the local level, the commitment of resources will vary considerably by locale. Historically, spending on welfare or aid was always driven by the idea that it should be kept to a minimum.[10] This was pretty much the case before states and the federal government established categories of aid and specified minimal standards of cash and noncash assistance. Still, both local economies and political ideologies combine to influence the capability and willingness of states and counties to invest resources into their welfare programs. Even with federal matching grants, programs such as TANF and Medicaid vary widely from state to state. Indeed, from the enactment of ADC to the passage of PRWORA, states have had considerable discretion in setting their own eligibility requirements and levels of aid. For example, in 2003, a family of three (parent and two children) received a maximum monthly grant of $201 in Texas, $373 in Ohio, and $577 in New York City.[11] Moreover, communities are very sensitive to the costs of welfare, and when these costs rise, there are strong political and administrative pressures on the local welfare departments to curb them by tightening eligibility.

Third, welfare workers can exercise considerable discretion in the ways they administer the welfare rules.[12] Formally, welfare workers are subject

---

[7] F. F. Piven & R. Cloward (1971). *Regulating the Poor: The Functions of Public Welfare*. New York: Vintage Books.

[8] R. Fording (1997). "The Conditional Effect of Violence as a Political Tactic: Mass Insurgency, Welfare Generosity, and Electoral Context in the American States." *American Journal of Political Science* 41: 1–29. See also, e.g., A. Hicks & D. H. Swank (1983). "Civil Disorder, Relief Mobilization, and AFDC Caseloads: A Reexamination of the Piven and Cloward Thesis." *American Journal of Political Science* 27: 695–716; L. Isaac & W. R. Kelly (1981). "Racial Insurgency, the State, and Welfare Expansion: Local and National Level Evidence from the Postwar United States." *American Journal of Sociology* 86: 1348–86.

[9] J. Soss et al. (2001). "Setting the Terms of Relief: Explaining State Policy Choices in the Devolution Revolution." *American Journal of Political Science* 45: 78–395.

[10] Brown (1940), p. 16.

[11] Green Book (2004). "Background Material and Data on Programs Within the Jurisdiction of the Committee on Ways and Means."

[12] E. Z. Brodkin (1997). "Inside the Welfare Contract: Discretion and Accountability in State Welfare Administration." *Social Service Review* 71(1): 1–33.

to voluminous rules and regulations. Jody Sandfort, studying local welfare offices adapting to welfare reform, notes, "Extensive policy manuals sit on each worker's desk in binders.... Each quarter, new administrative rules issued from the central administrative office must be inserted into these manuals.... A mere list of all the forms available is thirty-three pages long."[13] Yet, she point out that the structure set by the rules does not guide frontline actions. "Front-line workers exert their own judgments and develop their own strategies for utilizing administrative rules, completing standard forms, and responding to clients."[14]

Because workers have considerable power advantage over their clients, workers, in fact, control the flow of information from the clients to the welfare department and vice versa. What they wish to acknowledge or ignore and how they interpret the information enables them, in effect, to enact policy at the street level.[15] They can always manipulate the information and find rules or organizationally sanctioned rationales to justify their actions. Welfare clients, who are relatively powerless, become dependent on the workers to construct their case in moral terms: Is the client telling the truth about a missed appointment, the failure of child care, and so on? They have little recourse to redress such constructions.[16] Workers can also selectively enforce the rules because much of their encounters with clients cannot be readily monitored. Paradoxically, the greater the volume of rules and regulations that welfare workers must abide by, the more discretion they have. Potential clients are much less likely to be aware of the complex rules, and the workers have more opportunities to select, choose, and ignore them.[17] Thus, the workers' own personal beliefs and experiences influence how they implement welfare policies. Welfare departments have rarely been professionalized. Most welfare workers are not professionally trained social workers. They lack the professional training, socialization, and values that are needed to institutionalize professional behavior. In other words, they lack the professional buffer between their personal values and their conduct toward their clients.

Taken together, these forces lead to considerable variations in how local welfare departments administer welfare. In effect, each county has its own version of welfare policy as it is expressed in the day-to-day practices of its welfare workers. The fortunes or misfortunes of welfare recipients are inextricably tied to where they live.

---

[13] J. R. Sandfort (2000). "Moving beyond Discretion and Outcomes: Examining Public Management from the Front Lines of the Welfare System." *Journal of Public Administration Research and Theory* 10: 729–56.

[14] Ibid., p. 742.

[15] M. Lipsky (1984). "Bureaucratic Disentitlement in Social Welfare Programs." *Social Service Review* 58: 3–27.

[16] J. F. Handler (1986). *The Conditions of Discretion: Autonomy, Community, Bureaucracy.* New York: Russell Sage Foundation.

[17] M. Lipsky (1980). *Street-Level Bureaucracy.* New York: Russell Sage Foundation.

Welfare Bureaucracy as an Enactment of Moral Symbols

The periodic changes in welfare policy bring with them transformations in the organization of welfare departments. As new symbols are emphasized, such as the virtue of working single mothers, and others are discarded, such as aid as an entitlement, welfare bureaucracies are restructured to express them. In Chapters 2 and 3, we described the historical changes in the moral conceptions of poor single mothers. Still, throughout this history, the core tasks of the welfare department have remained unchanged. First and foremost, they must determine who deserves aid. The burden falls on the applicant to demonstrate worthiness and to pass several financial and behavioral tests to attain eligibility. Closely related is the task of periodic redetermination of eligibility. Again the burden falls on the recipient to demonstrate continued deservingness. Failure by the recipient to complete required redetermination forms is taken as a sign of ineligibility. A third central task of the welfare department is to enforce compliance and root out fraud. Much of the organization of welfare departments is driven by these tasks. Periodically, a fourth task is added, the provision of needed social services. However, this task has always been marginal and an add-on to the main objectives of assessing deservingness.

No matter how welfare departments respond to new legislative mandates, they institutionalize a set of underlying moral assumptions that have remained fairly constant, regardless of the particular twists and changes they experienced in each era.[18] First, welfare mothers have always been viewed as "outsiders." Being poor is always an individual moral fault. Therefore, the question of deservingness pervades much of the administration of welfare. Second, giving public aid is always seen as a threat to the work ethic. Therefore, the conditions and amount of aid have forced recipients to work. Giving aid should never privilege the recipients over the lowest-wage workers. Third, dependence on aid is morally corrupting. It encourages cheating, fraud, and laziness. Fourth, welfare is always about upholding the dominant moral code regarding family relations, gender, and ethnicity. This is done through coercive intrusion into the lives of the recipients, whether through "home investigations," setting a "family cap," or imposing restrictions in how the grant can be used. Fifth, giving aid involves stereotyping and morally degrading recipients. Today, the stereotype focuses on young African Americans in the inner city or Latino immigrants. Over time, the recognition that eligibility determination and social case work expressed incompatible moral assumptions and service technologies resulted in the decoupling of these two functions. Indeed, the social work profession strongly advocated for this separation because it did not want to be associated with the morally problematic function of aid determination.

---

[18] J. Handler & Y. Hasenfeld (1997). *We the Poor People: Work, Poverty and Welfare*. New Haven, Conn.: Yale University Press.

In her famous editorial in *Social Work*, Gordon Hamilton strongly advocated for the separation, writing that "the money function disables or overwhelms the social services."[19] According to Mary Jo Bane and David Ellwood, "Social workers argued that the dual role of counselor and investigator was impossible to achieve. Such perceptions of coercion, accurate or not, poisoned the 'therapeutic' value of the counselor/client relationship."[20] The separation was urged on welfare departments by the federal government in 1967 and mandated in 1972.[21]

The effects of the new organizational practices on worker-client relations were quite apparent. The division of labor and high staff turnover prevented the formation of any continuous relationship. The relations became far less trusting and more adversarial. As Simon points out, "the worker's success depends on compliance with coercively enforced, intensively monitored rules that primarily require her to police the claimant's paper-pushing and bureaucratic hoop-jumping. She works with anxious awareness of pervasive but only partially predictable supervisory authority in circumstances that minimize her ability to respond to the claimant's particular needs."[22]

In such a bureaucratic system, clients with problems became problem clients because they require more paperwork, more time to process the case, and create a greater probability of error. Discretion was exercised through the workers' control over information and when and how to invoke various regulations. The onus of responsibility falls on the clients to prove and maintain their eligibility. Most case closures are due to administrative reasons – the failure of the clients to submit proper forms in a timely fashion. In short, paperwork replaces people work, resulting in what Michael Lipsky terms "bureaucratic disentitlement."[23] Although the bureaucratization of welfare had given recipients some legal protection in claiming benefits, it also increased the number of bureaucratic hurdles they had to jump and gave welfare workers more power in the ways they enforced a complex and ever-changing array of rules and regulations. Benefits to recipients were curtailed and terminated under the guise of obscure and hidden bureaucratic rules.

The "New" Welfare-to-Work Ideology

The ascendancy of conservatives to power signaled another shift in the moral assumptions about welfare recipients. It culminated in a liberal and conservative "consensus" expressed in the Family Support Act of 1988 and more

---

[19] G. Hamilton (1962). "Editorial." *Social Work*, p. 128.
[20] M. J. Bane & D. T. Ellwood (1994). *Welfare Realities: From Rhetoric to Reform*. Cambridge, Mass.: Harvard University Press, p. 15.
[21] W. H. Simon (1983). "Legality, Bureaucracy, and Class in the Welfare System." *Yale Law Journal*, 92: 1198–269.
[22] Lipsky (1984), pp. 1221–22.   [23] Ibid.

recently in the passage of PRWORA in 1996.[24] In several respects, the moral
and organizational assumptions that underlie PRWORA and its vision of the
welfare department hark back to some of the early days of the states' mothers'
aid programs and ADC.

Welfare is no longer an entitlement. By replacing AFDC with block grants,
responsibility for the care of poor families has shifted back to the states. As
noted by the State Policy Documentation Project, "Section 401(b) of the
PRWORA repeals [the entitlement], explicitly stating that Part A of the law
'shall not be interpreted to entitle any individual or family to assistance under
any State program funded under this part.' The legal implications of this
provision and its relationship to constitutionally protected rights to due process
and equal protection are uncertain. What is clear is that states, by statute or
constitution, are free to create an entitlement to assistance, or to establish
rules for the provision of assistance in the absence of an entitlement."[25] True,
the federal government sets strict time limits on the use of federal funds for
family assistance (lifetime assistance for five years), a work trigger rule that
requires recipients to engage in work activities after a maximum of twenty-four
months and that 50 percent of the recipients are required to participate in a
"creditable set of work related activities" for thirty hours per week. In addition,
states are required to spend at least 75 percent of their "historic" level (i.e.,
1994) for programs replaced by TANF.[26]

Still, the federal government has devolved much of its historic responsibility
for poor families to the states. The states, in turn, have made highly diverse and
complex policy choices regarding eligibility, level of benefits, work requirements, sanctions, duration of aid, and transition to self-support.[27] In particular,
states vary in the degree to which they have made restrictive or liberal policy
choices in such areas as work requirements, time limits, family cap, and sanctions.[28] For example, thirty-two states impose requirements that must be met
while application for aid is pending. These include "cooperating with child
support enforcement requirements, participating in an assessment, signing a
Personal Responsibility Contract, attending orientation, and participating in
work activities."[29]

States no longer have to guarantee a minimum or continued level of assistance. In bad economic times, when state revenues decline and the need for

[24] Handler & Hasenfeld (1997), pp. 209–30.
[25] State Policy Documentation Project (2000). "State Policy Documentation Project (SPDP)" (Center on Law and Poverty and the Center on Budget and Policy Priorities).
[26] U.S. Congress, Committee on Ways and Means (2004).
[27] G. Rowe (2000). "State TANF Policies as of July 1999: Welfare Rules Databook" (Assessing the
New Federalism, Washington, D.C., Urban Institute).
[28] R. C. Lieberman & G. M. Shaw (2000). "Looking Inward, Looking Outward: The Politics of State
Welfare Innovation under Devolution." *Political Research Quarterly* 53: 215–40; Soss et al. (2001).
[29] State Policy Documentation Project (2000).

assistance increases, states cannot count on the federal government for addi-tional funds once the block grant is exhausted.[30] Indeed, twenty-three states have explicit language making availability of aid contingent on state appropri-ation or funding.[31] In all, whatever limited protection welfare recipients had from the vagaries of the dominant ideologies and political economies of their states under the old AFDC program has been eroded under TANF. Indeed, in their study of variations in post-TANF state welfare policies, Matthew Fellowes and Gretchen Rowe find that states enacting strict eligibility requirements, more rigid work requirements, and less generous cash benefits have a higher proportion of African American recipients, are ideologically less liberal, have a higher-income representational bias, and are dominated by Republican leg-islators.[32] States are also influenced by the policies enacted by neighboring states, especially their welfare generosity.

Second, the work test is the cornerstone of TANF. Requiring recipients to work reinforces the long-standing moral assumption that cash assistance creates dependency and erodes the work ethic. Failing the work test signals lack of deservingness. Put differently, the social rights of welfare recipients are made contingent on meeting obligations to the state. As expressed by Lawrence Mead, accepting public aid signals a failure in citizenship that justifies the right of the state, in return to public assistance, to exercise paternal authority – requiring the recipients to work, demanding that they lead a moral life and raise their children to become law-abiding citizens.[33] Almost all states make receipt of aid contingent on participation in work activities. States have broad discretion in spelling out what constitutes work activities, as well as exemptions from them, and most of them delegate that discretion to the counties. There are considerable variations in what constitutes "authorized activities" that can be counted toward meeting the work requirements. Still, as we show, regardless of which "work test" each state and county implement, it has clearly become a major tool, coupled with sanctions, in denying aid and reducing the welfare rolls.[34]

Third, the concept of the "good" mother has changed and is incorporated in TANF. If in the past the model welfare recipient was the "gilt-edged widow," now it is the mother who works full-time while raising her children with proper care. If the majority of mothers are now in the labor force, why can't welfare mothers be? Consequently, about half of the states require recipients with

[30] TANF provides for very limited contingency funding ($1.9 billion) in the form of matching grants to states experiencing high and increasing unemployment.
[31] State Policy Documentation Project (2000).   [32] Fellowes & Rowe (2000).
[33] L. M. Mead (1986). *Beyond Entitlement: The Social Obligations of Citizenship.* New York: Free Press.
[34] A. J. Cherlin et al. (2002). "Operating within the Rules: Welfare Recipients' Experiences with Sanctions and Case Closings." *Social Service Review* 76: 387–405; R. E. Rector & S. E. Youssef (1999). *The Determinants of Welfare Caseload Decline.* Washington, D.C.: Heritage Foundation.

children older than one year to participate in work activities. Sixteen states require mothers with children younger than one but older than three months to participate in work activities. Six states give no exemption.[35]

Again, dependence on welfare is viewed as corroding proper parenting roles and harming children. As a result, as discussed in Chapter 7, twenty-one states have a family cap policy restricting benefits to children born to a recipient parent. Moreover, laying the specter of the "underclass" squarely at their doorsteps has reaffirmed the moral condemnation of never-married mothers. Marriage, paternity, and childsupport have to be strengthened. Many states require women applying for aid to cooperate with child-support enforcement agents and identify the father. In addition, most states require applicants to sign a "personal responsibility" contract that sets a variety of behavioral requirements: "participation in work activities, child and/or minor parent school attendance, cooperation with child support enforcement requirements, child immunization or preventive health measures, participation in life skills or parenting training, substance abuse provisions, and agreement to achieve self-sufficiency within a set time period."[36] Failure to meet these requirements can result in sanctions.

Fourth, TANF relies heavily on sanctioning recipients to attain their compliance. Noncompliance, without good cause, with either the work requirements or the personal responsibility contract, can trigger sanctions. Indeed, states are given considerable leeway to implement stringent sanctions. States are free to choose full-family sanctions that eliminate both the adult and child portions of the grant. States may also tinker with the sanction durations such that, for example, the first act of noncompliance could result in a six-month penalty. In addition, states may impose a lifetime ban on welfare receipt for repeated acts of noncompliance. Consequently, sanctions and threat of sanctions have become one of the hallmarks of TANF.[37] Indeed, TANF encourages states and counties to use sanctions as a means to achieve compliance because states that fail to achieve minimum rates of participation by adult recipients (40% for single-parent families and 90% for two-parent families) are themselves subject to penalty.

Organizationally, TANF devolves responsibility to the local level and encourages the privatization of public assistance through contracts with the private sector (both for profit and nonprofit) as well as with religious and charitable organizations (known as "charitable choice"). Local discretion is celebrated and viewed as the most effective way to respond to the problems of welfare dependency.

---

[35] Fellowes & Rowe (2000).   [36] State Policy Documentation Project (2000).
[37] H. Goldberg & L. Schott (2000). "A Compliance-Oriented Approach to Sanctions in State and County TANF Programs" (Center on Budget and Policy Priorities, Washington, D.C."); L. Pavetti, M. K. Derr, & H. Hesketh (2003). "Review of Sanction Policies and Research Studies" (Mathematica Policy Research, Inc., Washington, D.C.).

Once again, according to the 1996 welfare reform, welfare departments are being transformed to institutionalize these moral conceptions. Welfare departments have developed new organizational forms whose overall goal is to place recipients in the labor market and to encourage "family values." The new organizational myth is that welfare departments are no longer in the business of determining eligibility and providing cash assistance. Rather, they are employment agencies, assisting the recipients into the labor market.

The Welfare Department as an Employment Agency

Once again, welfare reform (TANF) imposes on welfare departments two inherently incompatible goals. The first, and the traditional goal, is the determination of and ongoing monitoring of deservingness for aid, which Bane and Ellwood characterize as an "eligibility compliance culture."[38] The second goal is rehabilitative, enabling recipients to become gainfully employed, encouraging marriage, and reducing out-of-wedlock pregnancies. The first goal calls for a people-processing technology or what Jerry Mashaw calls bureaucratic rationality.[39] It employs a technocratic perspective in which decisions are justified on the basis of available facts in relation to existing rules. As described by Bane and Ellwood, the interaction between recipients and workers is to determine eligibility.[40] Eligibility forms control the interaction and its content. Most of the worker's and the recipient's time is consumed by determination and maintenance of eligibility. Little time is spent on helping the recipient become self-sufficient.

In contrast, helping recipients become self-supporting calls for a people-changing technology in which the interpersonal relations between the worker and the client are the key determinant of the service outcomes. This is a professional model. Service decisions are based on assessment of the particular attributes and problems presented by each client and judgment of the most effective way to respond to them. Interaction with clients is continuous and extensive, and the worker is interested in many of the clients' attributes that might affect their well-being. The effectiveness of the worker is based on problem-solving skills learned through extensive training and is contingent on developing a sustained trusting relationship with the clients. Organizationally, such a technology requires a professional structure in which staff are given considerable autonomy.[41]

In choosing which organizational form to adopt, welfare departments face considerable pressures to retain the bureaucratic over the professional

---

[38] Bane & Ellwood (1994), p. 6.
[39] J. L. Mashaw (1983). *Bureaucratic Justice: Managing Social Security Disability Claims.* New Haven, Conn.: Yale University Press.
[40] Bane & Ellwood (1994), p. 6.   [41] Handler & Hasenfeld (1997).

structure. The same external and internal forces that produce the highly bureaucratic structure in the welfare department still exist and are even reinforced under TANF. First, the same client ideologies that pervade the welfare department have only been reinforced under TANF. These ideologies continue to define welfare recipients as morally deficient and untrustworthy. The punitive approach, setting time limits on receipt of aid, making aid contingent on mandatory work requirements, and using sanctions to enforce compliance, signal and justify treating recipients as pathologically dependent on welfare, lacking in work ethic, unmotivated, and shirking their responsibilities as mature adults and parents.

Second, welfare departments face strong pressures to reduce the welfare rolls, meet the federal quotas, curb costs, and comply with accountability measures based on quantity rather than quality. In response, the form-driven processing of applicants and recipients is, therefore, expanded to incorporate and meet these new demands. The deprofessionalized welfare workers, lacking any appreciable training in interpersonal skills, continue to process large numbers of cases and enforce more rules and requirements.

Third, and most important, the entrenched bureaucratic structure used to determine eligibility and to enforce compliance crowds out the professional structure needed to provide employment services. As long as welfare departments and their workers must process applicants for aid, certify the eligibility of those on aid, and enforce the work requirements, little room is left for any significant ongoing helping relationship. Indeed, in such an environment, one would expect that the response of welfare departments to the new TANF work requirements would be to incorporate them into their existing bureaucratic practices, put the onus on the recipients to comply with them, and enforce the new work requirements through coercive means. Choosing such a strategy has the advantage of minimizing organizational transformation costs, relying on existing practices and minimizing organizational risks.

Therefore, welfare departments, as institutionalized organizations, have adapted in two compatible ways. First, they have given expression to the new moral rules in their formal structure and standard operating procedures. In particular, they have adopted a "work first" model that is consonant with dominant cultural norms about the "deserving" poor. At the same time, as we see, the revamped formal structure has not changed much of the day-to-day work of their welfare workers. Second, many have decoupled the new employment services from their welfare work by creating separate organizational units or contracting them to other organizations.[42]

---

[42] T. L. Gais et al. (2001). "The Implementation of the Personal Responsibility Act of 1996." In R. Blank & R. Haskins (Eds.), *The New World of Welfare* (pp. 35–64). Washington, D.C.: Brookings Institution Press.

The "Welfare-to-Work" Approach

Welfare-to-work, which is at the heart of TANF, has generally based on the demonstration model at Riverside County, California.[43] This model, particularly its approach to processing clients into the labor market, has become the template for most welfare-to-work programs around the country. Several other states and counties also experimented with similar welfare-to-work approaches (e.g., Arkansas; Cook County, Ill.),[44] but Riverside came to epitomize the new approach to welfare. Implemented in the 1980s as part of California's Greater Avenues for Independence, Riverside emphasized a strong employment "message," inexpensive job search, and quick entry into the labor market pursuant to the philosophy that a low-paying entry-level job is better than no job and could lead to a better job. The message was addressed to the staff as well as the recipients. Case managers encouraged recipients even with limited education to try job search first. Similarly, recipients who had attendance problems in basic education classes were reassigned to job search. Typically, recipients were assigned to "job club." It consisted of a series of sessions on how to prepare a resume, search for a job, and how to appear for a job interview. It was followed by several weeks of supervised job search that included calling employers and lining up interviews.

Case managers were especially recruited for commitment to the mission of agency and were tightly organized and monitored. The staff engaged in close monitoring of attendance and recipient job performance and provided support services for employment or employment-related problems.

Unique to Riverside, the staff engaged in extensive job development; in fact, workers were specifically hired for this task. The county was able to promise local employers job applicants "that afternoon." Employers cooperated to save the costs of screening large numbers of job applicants responding to general employment-wanted ads. Staff performance was rated, in large part, on job development and placement. Thus, the staff, in practice, emphasized their ability to find the participants jobs and to offer them needed services to get and keep the job.

Although hailed as a "success," the results of Riverside were marginal. In year 3, the recipients who worked averaged $84 more per month in earnings than the controls, or less than $20 more per week.[45] Moreover, this average increase came about because more recipients began to work and for longer

---

[43] J. Riccio, D. Friedlander, & S. Freedman (1994). "GAIN: Benefits, Costs, and Three-Year Impacts on a Welfare-to-Work Program" (Manpower Demonstration Research Co., New York).

[44] J. M. Gueron & E. Pauly (1991). *From Welfare to Work.* New York: Russell Sage Foundation.

[45] Riccio, Friedlander, & Freedman (1994). In year 3, the experimentals earned $1,010 more than the controls (an increase of 40%). In year 1, the difference was $920 and in year 2, $1,183. All earnings are in late 1980s dollars and are based on averages for the entire sample, including those with zero income.

hours, rather than because of an improvement in wages. In fact, Riverside might have achieved the results by getting the recipients in the experimental group to switch from the informal to the formal economy. In the last quarter of year 3, recipients in the experimental group were $77 better off than recipients in the control group (or $26 per month). In year 3, only 19 percent of the participants in the experimental group, compared with 16 percent of the participants in the control group, had a total income above the poverty line.[46] In addition, only 31 percent of the participants in the experimental group were employed in the last quarter of year 3, and about a third never worked during the entire three-year period.[47] Thus, the benefits to the recipients of the Riverside program were very modest. However, most importantly, the researchers found that Riverside produced a positive best benefit-cost ratio – the government saved money. "This return was exceptionally large in Riverside – $2.84 per every net $1 invested."[48]

Moreover, the debate about the best strategy to increase earnings and reduce the welfare rolls – investing in human capital such as basic education versus getting welfare recipients to accept any job – was settled in favor of the latter with the results of the National Evaluation of Welfare-to-Work Strategies.[49] In particular, the evaluation of three sites in which recipients were randomly assigned to either an employment-focused program or a basic education program showed that the employment-focused programs had produced higher employment and earnings rates and resulted in faster exit from welfare. Equally important, the employment-focused approach was considerably cheaper.[50] Although there was some recognition that the quality of adult education may have had an effect on the results, little attention was given to this issue.

---

[46] Ibid., pp. 156–60.

[47] Among all the counties, whites and African Americans experienced the largest gains. The increases for Latinos and for Asian/others were small and not statistically significant. Alameda produced significant and relatively large earnings for African Americans – and its sample was almost entirely long term and resided in the inner city. Moreover, these gains applied to registrants who were in need of basic education. Three counties had large numbers of Latinos in the sample, but only in Riverside was there a significant earnings gain and welfare reductions for Latinos, as well as whites and African Americans. Finally, except for Riverside, the earnings effects were "weak" for the most disadvantaged recipients, defined as more than two years on AFDC, no employment in the year preceding Greater Avenues for Independence (GAIN), and a high-school dropout. See Daniel Friedlander, "The Impacts of California's GAIN Program on Different Ethnic Groups: Two-Year Findings on Earnings and AFDC Payments" (Manpower Demonstration Research Corporation, 1994).

[48] Riccio, Friedlander, & Freedman (1994), p. xlvii.

[49] G. Hamilton (2002). "Moving People from Welfare to Work: Lessons from the National Evaluation of Welfare-to-Work Strategies" (U.S. Department of Health and Human Services. Administration for Children and Families, Office of the Assistant Secretary for Planning and Evaluation; U.S. Department of Education, Office of the Under Secretary; Office of Vocational and Adult Education, Washington D.C.).

[50] Ibid., pp. 10–11.

One can readily see why the model of "work first" at Riverside would be institutionalized as the dominant welfare-to-work service technology. First, it readily embodies the main tenets of TANF. The organizational form of "work first" produces the required ceremonies to reinforce the dominant myths about welfare recipients. It affirms the myth that welfare recipients lack work ethic and prefer to depend on welfare. It employs ceremonies like sending recipients to job club/job search as confirmation that little preparation is needed to find a job. Second, it comports well with the eligibility culture of the welfare departments by providing a readily available "work test" of deservingness. Applicants or recipients failing to participate in job search become undeserving for cash aid. Third, the service technology can be easily routinized. Processing recipients into job searches does not require extensive individualized practices, nor does it entail implementing complex employment services. Indeed, despite state variations, there is a standard content and sequence of "work first." Recipients must attend an orientation, followed by a period in a job club, then proceeding to an individual job search. Recipients typically fall into two groups, those with a high school diploma or GED and those without. The latter group have the option to attend remedial education to obtain a GED before or concordant with the job search. Fourth, the "work first" service technology relies on sanctions and threat of sanctions to attain compliance. It precludes the need to invest in extensive worker-client relations. At the same time, it grants welfare workers considerable discretion. Finally, work first is relatively inexpensive, requires limited case management expertise, and has the virtue of deterring applications and hastening exit.[51]

Use of Sanctions

Although sanctions, formal (e.g., administrative case termination) and informal (e.g., refusal to consider extenuating circumstances), have always been a feature of welfare, they are a defining feature of TANF and frame much of the encounters between welfare workers and recipients. Temporary Assistance for Needy Families not only increases the range of behaviors that are sanctionable but also increases the significance of sanctions by allowing states to implement more severe penalties.[52] States can choose gradual or immediate full-family sanctions, and they may set the duration of the sanction from one to six months for the first infraction. States may impose a lifetime ban on

[51] For a description of the New York City's Employment Services and Placement System, see S. Youdelman, with P. Getsos (2005). "The Revolving Door: Research Findings on NYC's Employment Services and Placement System and Its Effectiveness in Moving People from Welfare to Work" (A Research Project by Community Voices Heard, July 2005).
[52] Y. Hasenfeld, T. Ghose, & K. Larson (2004). "The Logic of Sanctioning Welfare Recipients: An Empirical Assessment." *Social Service Review* 78: 304–19; Pavetti, Derr, & Hesketh (2003).

welfare receipts for repeated acts of noncompliance. Temporary Assistance for Needy Families encourages states to use sanctions because states that do not sanction recipients who fail to meet the stringent work requirements are themselves subject to penalty.

The TANF block grants change the state incentives to sanction. Under AFDC, if the state sanctioned a recipient, the state would lose the federal portion of the grant-in-aid for the recipient, which could be as high as 50 percent. Under the block grant system, the amount that the state receives is fixed; thus, the state saves the entire client grant.

The justification of sanctions is couched in both moral and utilitarian terms.[53] According to Mead, the state has the moral right to impose its paternal authority on citizens who depend on it (i.e., welfare recipients) by requiring them to meet their obligations such as work. Failing to do so justifies penalizing them.[54] From a utilitarian perspective, sanctions are seen as an effective mechanism to elicit compliance because they alter the cost and benefits of being on welfare. That is, recipients make a rational choice whether to comply with the work requirements or lose their benefits. Raising the costs of noncompliance makes the alternative option of participation in work activities more attractive. If, however, recipients opt to lose their benefits, it is an indication that they are not truly needy.[55] Threats and use of sanctions are also seen as an effective way to discourage entry and hasten exit from welfare because they increase the costs to applicants and recipients to be on welfare.

Sanctions can also be an attractive tool in the hands of case managers who face the difficult task of eliciting compliance by their clients. For case mangers, attaining compliance determines their ability to meet the mandatory requirements of work first. Threats of sanctions require far less investment in time and energy to attain compliance than through establishing and maintaining rapport and trusting relationships with the clients.[56] Moreover, use of threats leads to flight behavior, namely, leaving welfare. Whether workers actually impose sanctions will depend on the ease or difficulty in handling the paperwork and other bureaucratic requirements associated with sanctions. Still sanctions are widely used. The MDRC studies of welfare reform in Cleveland, Philadelphia, and Miami report, on the basis of surveys of recipients, a rate of sanctions that ranges from less than 30 percent in Cleveland and Philadelphia to 50 percent in Miami.[57] According to Pavetti, Derr, and Hesketh, studies that followed cohorts of recipients over time, thus providing

[53] Hasenfeld, Ghose, & Larson (2004).   [54] Mead (1986).

[55] Rector (1993).

[56] Y. Hasenfeld & D. Weaver (1996). "Enforcement, Compliance, and Disputes in Welfare-to-Work Programs." *Social Service Review* 70: 235–56.

[57] T. Brock et al. (2004). "Welfare Reform in Miami" (MDRC, New York), pp. 1–234. Keep in mind that in the MDRC surveys the samples were drawn from high-poverty neighborhoods and included mostly long-term recipients.

more accurate estimates, show rates ranging from 45 percent to 60 percent.[58] A study of sanctions in Wisconsin[59] found that in the first year of being on welfare 51 percent of the women were sanctioned; in the second year the rate increased to 60 percent, and by the fourth year, the rate was 64 percent. In other words, use of sanctions is quite pervasive and characterizes a key aspect of worker-recipient relations.

Although applicants and recipients are routinely told about sanction policies, it is far less clear that they actually understand them or are even aware of being sanctioned. A study of sanctioned families in Tennessee finds that 34 percent of the families did not understand the welfare requirements.[60] Twenty-five percent of sanctioned parents in Iowa did not understand the rules.[61] A report by the Office of the Inspector General (1999) for the U.S. Department of Health and Human Services indicates that welfare recipients are seldom informed of good cause exemptions from work program participation. In fact, they are often led to believe that the sanctions for nonparticipation are more severe than is the case. Evidence suggests that the most common reason for being sanctioned is missed appointments.[62] Hasenfeld, Ghose, and Larson, in their study of sanctions in four counties in California, found that although most recipients knew that failure to attend orientation will result in sanction, only 63 percent were aware that failure to attend a required activity without good cause would lead to a sanction.[63] More important, almost 50 percent of the sanctioned recipients were unaware that they had been sanctioned. Wilson, Stoker, and McGrath (1999) also found that a majority of the recipients in their study were unaware of sanctions against them.[64]

Studies on who is at risk of being sanctioned show convincingly that recipients who are more vulnerable and with greater barriers to employment are more likely to be sanctioned.[65] Several studies have shown that recipients with more children, who lack work experience, and with limited education are more likely to be sanctioned.[66] Similarly, recipients with health,

[58] Pavetti, Derr, & Hesketh (2003).
[59] C.-F. Wu et al. (2004). "How Do Welfare Sanctions Work?" (Discussion Paper No. 1282–04, Institute for Research on Poverty, Madison, Wis.).
[60] R. Overby (1998). "Summary of Surveys of Welfare Recipients Employed or Sanctioned for Noncompliance" (University of Memphis, Memphis, Tenn.).
[61] L. A. Nixon, K. F. Kauff, & J. L. Losby (1999). "Second Assignments to Iowa's Limited Benefit Plan" (Mathematica Policy Research, Inc., Washington, D.C.).
[62] Goldberg & Schott 2000; Cherlin et al. (2002).
[63] Hasenfeld, Ghose, & Larson (2004).
[64] L. A. Wilson, R. P. Stoker, & D. McGrath (1999). "Welfare Bureaus as Moral Tutors: What Do Clients Learn from Paternalistic Welfare Reforms?" *Social Science Quarterly* 80(3): 473–86.
[65] For a review, see Pavetti, Derr, & Hesketh (2003).
[66] Cherlin et al. (2002); A. Kalil, K. S. Seefeldt, & H.-C. Wang (2002). "Sanctions and Material Hardship under TANF." *Social Service Review* 76(4): 642–62; D. F. Polit, A. S. London, & J. M. Martinez (2001). *The Health of Poor Urban Women: Findings from the Project on Devolution and Urban Change.* New York: MDRC.

mental health, or substance abuse problems are far more likely to be sanctioned. These studies also show that recipients who experienced domestic violence are also at greater risk of being sanctioned. Lack of resources, such as access to child care, adequate transportation, or caring for disabled family members, also increases the risk of being sanctioned.[67] Finally, because different welfare offices develop their own sanction practices and may discriminate on the basis of ethnicity, the particular office to which recipients are assigned can also influence their chances of being sanctioned.[68]

What are the consequences of being sanctioned? Wu and colleagues, tracking administrative data on recipients in Wisconsin show that 71 percent of those who were sanctioned experienced it for a short time (one month) and returned to full benefit after a sanction.[69] One of the difficulties in relying on administrative records, especially monthly entries, is that they may reflect less a change in the behavior of the sanctioned recipient than a reconsideration by the case manager. That is, case managers may initiate a sanction, possibly to get the attention of their client, only to quickly reverse it, once they are satisfied with the client's explanation. Indeed, a longitudinal study by Lee, Slack, and Lewis[70] that relies on both survey and administrative data shows that sanctions have not produced the desired behavioral changes. Threat of sanctions did not have an effect on either work or welfare use, and actual sanctions reduced the likelihood of being employed and increased the likelihood of shifting to the informal labor market. Most important, sanctions increase hardship in paying for food, rent, and utilities.[71] Using data from the "Fragile Families and Child Wellbeing Study," Reichman and colleagues show that mothers receiving TANF who were sanctioned within twelve months of the third year after the birth of their child experienced considerably greater hardship than nonsanctioned mothers.[72] Although the two cohorts of mothers receiving TANF had similar sociodemographic characteristics and levels of hardship at year 1 (and controlling for other variables), the sanctioned mothers at year 3 "are 85 percent more likely to report any material hardship than nonsanctioned mothers. They are 63 percent more likely than nonsanctioned mothers to report maternal and child hunger, 76 percent more likely to report having their utilities

---

[67] Cherlin et al. (2002); D. J. Fein (1999). "The ABC Evaluation: Carrying and Using the Stick: Financial Sanctions in Delaware's A Better Chance Program" (report prepared for the U.S. Department of Health and Human Services, Division of Social Services, Abt Associates, Cambridge, Mass.); Hasenfeld, Ghose, & Larson (2004); Kalil, Seefeldt, & Wang (2002).

[68] Hasenfeld, Ghose, Larson (2004); Wu et al. (2004).

[69] Wu et al. (2004), p. 28.

[70] B. J. Lee, K. S. Slack, & D. A. Lewis (2004). "Are Welfare Sanctions Working as Intended? Welfare, Receipt, Work Activity and Material Hardship among TANF-Recipient Families. *Social Service Review* 78: 370–403.

[71] Lee, Slack, & Lewis (2004), p. 391.

[72] N. E. Reichman, et al. (2005). "TANF Sanctioning and Hardship." *Social Service Review* 79: 215–36.

shut off, and 79 percent more likely to report being unable to receive medical care (due to cost) for themselves or a child."[73] Their findings have been replicated in several other studies.[74]

Therefore, the insistence on using sanctions cannot rest on either its underlying moral or utilitarian assumptions. Rather, at the organizational level, sanctions represent a confirmation of the institutional rules that the welfare department is expected to embody. Use of sanctions strengthens the legitimacy of the department by demonstrating that its practices echo the intent and the moral assumptions that guide TANF. It is a ceremonial enactment and confirmation of the myths about welfare recipients. At the worker's level, use of sanctions gives the welfare workers a sense of control over fairly chaotic and difficult encounters with their clients. Welfare workers have to contend with recipients whose lives are wrought with instabilities and frequent crises that impinge on their ability to adhere to the work first requirements. To attempt to address these crises would require the workers to mobilize resources that are often beyond their capabilities. They lack access to needed services, do not have the professional expertise, and work under organizational rules and constraints that discourage individualized responses. Use of sanctions is a way to typify the clients' problems as failure to comply, justifies a fairly standard response, and puts the onus on the recipients.

Routinization and Discretion

The use of sanctions is indicative of the two key, yet somewhat contradictory, organizational practices in the administration of welfare-to-work programs – routinization and discretion. Sanctions can be triggered merely by a flag from the program's computerized data system that a recipient had failed to attend a required activity and did not respond to a computer-generated letter requesting that she schedule a "for cause" hearing. Yet, it is up to the individual case manger to decide whether to invoke the sanction. Thus, on the one hand, the welfare-to-work program is routinized through bureaucratic mechanisms such as a computerized client information system, detailed manuals of rules and regulations, and standard operating procedures that reduce the options available to case managers. On the other hand, despite these onerous systems, case managers have a great deal of discretion because of their ability to control the content and flow of the information from the clients to the system and because they can selectively ignore or pay attention to certain client attributes in assessing needs that could then justify their decisions. At the same time, to cope with the inherent ambiguities and conflicting expectations of the program, case managers respond by developing a set of

---

[73] Ibid., p. 226.

[74] Fein (1999); Kalil, Seefeldt, & Wang (2002).

routines that reflect both the constraints of resources, their assumptions about welfare recipients, and the conditions of their work.[75]

Evelyn Brodkin's study of work programs in Chicago (the precursor to TANF) recounts how, despite the ostensible emphasis on individualized case management, the workers responded mostly by trying to meet caseload quotas.[76] In trying to reduce costs while maximizing federal reimbursement, Illinois shifted the work program from emphasizing education and training to a mandatory program emphasizing job search. Other constraints added to the reduced social service approach to welfare recipients. Because the department had deprofessionalized its casework staff, it was unable to staff the work program with trained workers. Moreover, because of union rules, most workers were recruited from the income eligibility and grant determination units that emphasize highly bureaucratic routines. The pressure to meet caseload quotas further eroded giving attention to the specific service needs of the recipients. As a result, "caseworkers tended to define client needs to fit the available slots, avoid eliciting service claims, and pressure clients to accept the bureaucratic construction of welfare rights and obligations."[77] At orientation, workers conveyed a dual message of helper, assisting recipients in becoming employed, but also rule enforcer, using sanctions to attain compliance. Yet, it became clear that they could do little more than refer them to only a few job-related activities.[78] Moreover, assessment became more of a ritual because they had few resources to respond to individual client needs. At the same time, workers used their discretion to allocate scarce resources to favored clients. In the same fashion, although workers were expected to identify and to respond to client personal barriers such as drug use or mental illness, the preferred mode was not to elicit or to ignore such information, mostly because handling such cases required skills the workers did not have, and they distracted from meeting management performance expectations.

A similar pattern was observed in the relations between workers and recipients in the W-2 program.[79] Wisconsin Works is set up as a four-tier program in which

1. Applicants that are deemed "employable" are offered employment services but no cash.
2. Applicants that fail to locate work are offered "trial jobs" that are subsidized employment for which they are paid minimum wage for hours worked.

[75] J. R. Sandfort (1997). "The Structuring of Front-Line Work: Conditions within Local Welfare and Welfare-to-Work Organizations in Michigan" (paper presented at the annual conference of the Association for Public Policy Analysis and Management, Washington, D.C.).
[76] Brodkin (1997), p. 11.   [77] Ibid., p. 15.
[78] Ibid., p. 14.
[79] S. Gooden, F. Doolittle, & B. Glispie (2001). "Matching Applicants with Services: Initial Assessments in the Milwaukee County W-2 Program" (MDRC, New York).

3. Applicants that are deemed not job ready are placed in community service jobs (CSJ), are expected to work forty hours per week, and get a flat grant (not adjusted to family size) of $673 per month that is reduced for every hour missed of work.

4. Applicants that are not job ready because of substantial unemployability or incapacities of self or family members are placed in W-2 Transition (W-2T), must participate in various activities to address their barriers such as substance abuse, and receive a flat grant of $628 per month that can be reduced for failure to attend.

As recipients gain in work experience and skills they are expected to move to a higher rung.

In practice, the choices for the case managers were either CSJ or W-2T. Over time, as the workers perceived new applicants to have more problems, they were more likely to be placed in W-2T.[80] More important, the case managers based the assignment mostly on their informal impressions. As noted by the researchers,[81] "a key component that the [case managers] consider in deciding an applicant's initial tier placement is the overall 'feel' of the applicant, based on their assessment of such factors as previous job history, education, interests, attitudes, and personality." In W-2, the case managers are also responsible for determining eligibility. Therefore, much of the intake interview is controlled by a computerized client system, which includes up to 480 screens, depending on the nature of the case.[82] It structures both the content and sequence of the interview, adding to a high degree of routinization. The researchers also identify several practice principles that the case managers have developed.[83] They include the following:

1. Relying heavily on impressions of the applicant during the intake interview.
2. Using CSJ as a catchall tier because of its flexibility and less demanding documentation.
3. Focusing on activities, not the tier.
4. Following agency norms in assigning activities, some of which are intended to provide an opportunity for further assessment.

In other words, within the constraints of the program's real service options, the case managers rely on few client characteristics, their own personal impressions and experiences, and the prevailing norms of their agencies to typify the clients and fit them into one of these two options. It is a system that is driven both by a high degree of routinization of client processing and a high degree of staff discretion.[84]

[80] Ibid.
[81] Ibid., p. 12.
[82] Ibid., p. 66.
[83] Ibid., pp. 92–93.
[84] For a recent study of W-2, see J. DeParle (2004). *American Dream: Three Women, Ten Kids, and a Nation's Drive to End Welfare*. New York: Viking.

Table 5–1. *Percent changes in social services spending, state fiscal years 1995 to 1999*

State	Poverty relief	Child care	Employment & training	Poverty prevention	Mental health & other	Child protection	All social services
California	−29	115	52	32	39	64	4
Georgia	−51	76	56	34	4	31	−1
Missouri	−29	120	111	11	20	54	16
Wisconsin	−48	168	20	5	12	34	−8

Source: Ellwood and Boyd (2000).

Provision of Social Services

An important programmatic addition to "work first" is the provision and access to supportive services, both pre- and postemployment, particularly child care, health care, and transportation.[85] Other services may include access to mental health and domestic abuse and substance abuse programs. Funding for child care comes from the Child Care and Development Fund block grants. Similarly, states and counties were able to fund other services and benefits because the federal block grants and the required maintenance of effort (MOE), coupled with the rapid decline in caseload, provided them with unprecedented fiscal resources. Douglas Besharov (2002) estimates that spending by the states for child care from all sources increased by 60 percent from 1996 to 1999. In their study of changes in spending on social services since the implementation of TANF in four states, Debora Ellwood and Donald Boyd find that spending on cash aid declined by 29 percent to 51 percent, while spending for child care increased dramatically by 76 percent to 168 percent.[86] Expenditures for employment and training also increased by 52 percent to 111 percent. A similar pattern can be observed in California's CalWORKs. Although cash assistance declined by 25 percent from fiscal year 1996 to FY 1999 (which was faster than the 18% drop in the caseload; Table 5–1), the allocations for social services and child care almost quadrupled.[87] Still, with the exception of Missouri, overall spending on social services either remained the same or declined somewhat, suggesting that the effect of TANF has been in the reallocation of social services spending.

[85] J. Strawn, M. Greenberg, & S. Savner (2001). "Improving Employment Under TANF." In R. Blank & R. Haskins (Eds.), *The New World of Welfare* (pp. 223–24). Washington, D.C.: Brooking Institution Press.

[86] D. A. Ellwood & D. J. Boyd (2000). "Changes in State Spending on Social Services since the Implementation of Welfare Reform: A Preliminary Report" (Nelson A. Rockefeller Institute of Government, Albany, N.Y.), pp. 1–35.

[87] J. A. Klerman et al. (2000). *Welfare Reform in California: State and County Implementation of CalWORKs in the Second Year.* Santa Monica, Calif.: RAND Research, p. 79.

Table 5–2. *U.S. fiscal year 2002 use of TANF and MOE funds*

Annual TANF block grants (including supplemental grants and bonuses)			$17,004,190,260
Total federal TANF funds available (including unspent prior year funds)			$23,358,058,624
Unliquidated obligations at the end of fiscal year 2002			$3,133,163,514
Unobligated balance at the end of fiscal year 2002			$2,678,316,026
MOE obligations at 75%			$10,389,102,066
MOE obligation at 80%			$11,061,708,867

	Federal TANF funds	State (MOE) funds	Federal and state funds
Total funds spent	$14,587,709,021	$10,826,673,522	$25,414,382,543
Transferred to CCDF	$1,926,299,277	n/a	$1,926,299,277
Transferred to SSBG	$1,031,375,598	n/a	$1,031,375,598
Total funds used	$17,545,383,896	$10,826,673,522	$28,372,057,418
How funds were used			
Basic assistance	$4,554,262,318	$4,853,971,200	$9,408,233,518
Child care spent or transferred	$3,498,280,480	$1,932,277,175	$5,430,557,655
Spent directly	$1,571,981,203	$1,932,277,175	$3,504,258,378
Transferred to CCDF	$1,926,299,277		$1,926,299,277
Transferred to SSBG	$1,031,375,598		$1,031,375,598
Transportation and supportive services	$339,283,992	$244,726,293	$584,010,285
Authorized under prior law	$1,791,317,253		$1,791,317,253
Work subsidies	($4,960,092)	($27,123,513)	($32,083,605)
Education and training	$325,834,290	$135,671,806	$461,506,096
Other work activities/expenses	$1,799,818,704	$497,625,536	$2,297,444,240
Individual Development Account	$7,186,410	$501,806	$7,688,216
Refundable EITC or other refundable TC	$143,015,335	$622,485,931	$765,501,266
Nonrecurrent short-term benefits	$143,479,567	$94,270,522	$237,750,089
Pregnancy prevention	$323,900,131	$401,799,696	$725,699,827
Two-parent formation	$215,256,688	$68,848,978	$284,105,666
Administration and systems	$1,633,421,671	$983,454,540	$2,616,876,211
Other nonassistance	$1,743,911,551	$1,018,163,552	$2,762,075,103

Source: Greenberg and Richer (2003).

Indeed, in fiscal year 2002, of the total $28.4 billion in combined TANF and MOE expenditures, states spent only 33 percent of all TANF funds for "basic assistance" (Table 5–2). Nineteen percent of the funds were spent on child care. A broad category of other services, especially child welfare, constituted 16 percent of the funds. Only 2 percent of the funds were spent on education and training, and about 8 percent was spent on other work activities (not including education and training) and transportation. States spent less than 10 percent on "administration and systems."[88]

Now, as states are experiencing greater fiscal difficulties, there is considerable pressure to reduce such expenditures. In California, for example, funding for the counties was reduced by $47 million, required cost-of-living adjustments to cash aid were delayed, and funding for adult education and community college for recipients was cut by $74 million.[89] As Mark Greenberg points out, the recent economic downturn essentially stopped the decline in the welfare rolls and caused the state to face a serious financial squeeze.[90] Without compensatory help from the federal government, states have been forced to cut back their budget for social services, including reduction in cash aid and child care.

The reliance on block grants exposes the administration of TANF to two interrelated risks that can be quite detrimental to the recipients. First, there is no longer a certainty that services will be available, especially during economic hard times, just when recipients might need them most. Second, with the delegation of decisions on how to allocate such funds to state and local jurisdictions, there is no longer a debate about such policies at the national level, making it very difficult for advocates for the poor to influence such policies.

State Variations: Do They Matter?

Within the work first approach, states may adopt several variations. Thomas Gais and colleagues identify several variants in their multistate study.[91] States may pursue either a goal of work participation or a goal of caseload reduction, and they may adopt different strategies to achieve the goals. These may range from motivating recipients to work via various incentives, to providing supportive services to overcome personal barriers. These choices reflect the dominant political culture of each state, especially moral assumptions about welfare recipients, and are generally consonant with its historical approach to its poor people (Table 5–3). They also take place within the particular economic structure of the state, especially its labor market.

State choices in implementing TANF become institutionalized rules that are implemented in the local welfare offices. States that emphasize work participation as their goal may offer various financial incentives to "make work pay." Minnesota, for example, known for its progressive policies, has

---

[88] M. Greenberg & E. Richer (2003). "How States Used TANF and MOE funds in FY 2002: The Picture from Federal Reporting" (Center for Law and Social Policy, Washington, D.C.).

[89] California Budget Project (2004c). "Budget Backgrounders: Making Dollars Make Sense." Retrieved from http://www.cbp.org/2004/0402calworks.pdf.

[90] "Welfare Reform, Phase Two," *The American Prospect Online*, Aug. 13, 2004.

[91] Gais et al. (2001).

Table 5–3. *State variations in implementing work first*

Strategy	Goal: work participation	Goal: caseload reduction
Motivational	Minnesota, Missouri	Wisconsin
Restrictive		Texas
Employment services	Michigan, Tennessee	
Support services	Kansas, Utah	West Virginia, Washington

Source: Adapted from Gais et al. (2001).

"made a commitment to provide basic support for families to move toward self sufficiency, including development of a state-wide health insurance plan for low-income uninsured families,[92] child care assistance for low-income working families (Basis Sliding Fee Child Care Program) and the Working Family Credit (the state's Earned Income Tax Credit)."[93] Minnesota Family Investment Program (MFIP) also offers a generous income disregard up to 120 percent of the poverty line. Still, the key emphasis is on job search activities. There are prescribed set of activities recipients must follow including orientation, one week of job club, and several weeks of supervised job search. Individuals who fail to obtain a job are reassessed and may be recycled through the same process again. Relatively few are referred for further training.[94] Recipients who are non-English speakers may combine job search activities with English as a Second Language (ESL). In addition to the financial incentives, recipients may be sanctioned for noncompliance. In an evaluation study by Auspos and colleagues, about 29 percent were sanctioned.[95]

Local offices have considerable autonomy in implementing the program, but the emphasis on work first is dominant. The county welfare department processes applications that involve several steps, starting with a client access worker who gathers basic information that leads to an eligibility interview by financial workers. Applicants are also required to participate in an orientation session. During the eligibility interview, applicants are also given a list of employment providers. The provider offers orientation and develops an employment plan mostly focused on job search.[96] It is clear that most recipients are aware of both the job search requirements and the financial incentives the program offers.[97] In Hennepin County, many of the employment services

---

[92] Minnesota Care.

[93] K. Tout et al. (2001). "Recent Changes in Minnesota Welfare and Work, Child Care, and Child Welfare Systems" (Urban Institute, Washington, D.C.), p. 1.

[94] P. Auspos, J. A. Hunter, & C. Miller. (2000). "Final Report on the Implementation and Impacts of the Minnesota Family Investment Program in Ramsey County" (MDRC, New York).

[95] Ibid.

[96] Health Systems Research and Abt Associates (2003), chap. 8.

[97] Auspos, Hunter, & Miller (2000), pp. 22–23.

are contracted mostly to private nonprofit agencies.[98] The county also uses welfare-to-work funds to provide mental health and substance abuse treatment services that can be counted as work activity.[99]

Other states, such as Michigan, convey the work-first goal by emphasizing employment services and strengthening job skills. Michigan is characterized by a safety net that is relatively more comprehensive than the average for the nation.[100] Michigan Family Independence Program (FIP) is unique because it does not enact a time limit on benefits. The Family Independence Program also offers a "fairly generous earned income disregard whereby recipients can keep the first $200 of their earnings and 20 percent of the rest without affecting their grant,"[101] and it has a strong work-first message. Recipients are expected to participate in job search activities. However, since 1999, the state allows "clients to satisfy the work requirement either by combining 10 hours of employment with class and study time or by attending a full-time, short-term vocational training program."[102] Similar changes were made to enable postemployment training. Yet, even these changes still make it difficult for recipients to balance the work requirement, training, and family obligations.[103] The state has a fairly strong sanctions policy. Failure to comply can result in the termination of the entire family from FIP.

Local welfare offices are branches of the state agency and thus have limited discretion in implementing FIP. Much of their responsibility is centered on income eligibility. Work First – the employment and training services for welfare recipients – is the responsibility of the state Department of Career Development. Its local boards have considerable discretion in how to deliver the employment services and the selection of the private agencies that will provide them.[104] Hence, in Michigan, recipients must interact with two separate sets of organizations. Later, we discuss some of the consequences of such an arrangement. In addition to the various case managers clients may have in the various Work First agencies, in the local FIP offices, such as Detroit, they are handled by a family independence specialist who conducts "intake and eligibility work, and also works with the client to develop a plan for achieving self-sufficiency, identifies barriers to employment, and addresses those barriers through referrals to or provision of support services."[105] Because Detroit contracts with more than thirty different agencies to provide Work First services, the specialist must spend considerable time communicating with their counterparts in these agencies.[106]

[98] Tout et al. (2001), pp. 6–7.   [99] Ibid., p. 8.
[100] K. S. Seefeldt, J. Leos-Urbel, & P. McMahon (2001). "Recent Changes in Michigan Welfare and Work, Child Care, and Child Welfare Systems" (Urban Institute, Washington, D.C.).
[101] Ibid., p. 5.   [102] Ibid., p. 6.
[103] Ibid., p. 6.   [104] Ibid., p. 8.
[105] Ibid., p. 9.   [106] Ibid., p. 9.

States that push for caseload reduction may also pursue several different strategies. Wisconsin has attracted national attention through its "radical" approach to "minimize families' dependence on cash."[107] The underlying moral assumption driving the design of W-2 is that "families, not government, are responsible for providing for their needs."[108] From this basic assumption, W-2 is guided by norms stressing that there is no entitlement to aid; families and community agencies are the primary sources of aid; every person, with proper assistance, can work; only work should pay; and market mechanisms for delivering services are the most effective and efficient.[109] As a result, and as noted earlier, W-2 is set up as a four-tier employment ladder, beginning with the lowest rung of transitional placement for recipients with serious employment barriers. Then the second rung, which consists of community service jobs for those who lack basic skills and work habits, leading to the third rung of trial jobs, which are subsidized employment, and ending with unsubsidized employment. The tiers, or rungs, are designed so that recipients will move up the ladder as they move toward employment.

Wisconsin Works is administered through contracts with private agencies. In Milwaukee, for example, there are five such providers, each responsible for a specific region. The contracts are based on a "capitation model, whereby agencies receive a flat sum to operate W-2, including funds for administration, direct services and cash grants. If the agency can run the program for less than its grant from the state, it can keep up to 7 percent of the full grant amount in profit."[110] There is, therefore, an incentive to direct applicants away from cash grants when possible. Later, we discuss the issues involved in contracting out and their effect on workers and recipients.

Applicants are seen initially by a resource specialist who makes an initial assessment and tries to divert the applicant to other agencies in the community for assistance. If the applicant wishes to continue with W-2, she is then scheduled to meet with a financial and employment planner (FEP) for an assessment. She is also scheduled to meet with a county worker – the supportive services planner (SSP) – who determines eligibility for food stamps, Medicaid, and child care. The FEP determines which rung the applicant would be assigned to and has considerable discretion in making that decision. With the decline in welfare caseloads and the changing profile of applicants to those having more employment barriers, most applicants are referred to either CSJs or W-2T.[111] Many of the employment services are provided by job centers that are co-located at the W-2 agencies.

[107] Gais et al.(2001), p. 53.
[108] J. Ehrle et al. (2001). "Recent Changes in Wisconsin Welfare and Work, Child Care, and Child Welfare Systems" (Urban Institute, Washington, D.C.), p. 1.
[109] Gais et al. (2001), p. 53.   [110] Ehrle et al. (2001), p. 9.
[111] Gooden, Doolittle, & Glispie (2001).

Some states, notably Texas, rely on restrictive application and verification procedures to make it difficult to apply or to stay on welfare. The implementation of TANF in Texas reflects the state's dominant ideologies about the poor and the role of government. These are "(1) local control; (2) smaller, more efficient government; and (3) an emphasis on work and individual responsibility."[112] Much of it is manifested by the fact that Texas has a limited safety net for poor people and very low benefit levels. Indeed, the state's constitution limits welfare expenditures to no more than 1 percent of the state's budget.[113]

The state's TANF program provides a maximum $201 monthly grant for a family of three with no income. It requires a personal responsibility agreement and sets penalties for failure to meet any of its provisions. There are time limits from one to three years, depending on the recipient's level of education and work experience. There are sanctions on the adult portion of the grant. Families are eligible for twelve to eighteen months of transitional Medicaid and child care. They are also eligible for food stamps if their income is below 130 percent of the poverty line.[114]

The state operates a highly centralized and computerized eligibility determination system used in local intake offices. "DTHS [Texas Department of Human Services] automated systems have supported implementation of aggressive antifraud measures and have streamlined parts of the application and ongoing eligibility process. The focus on fraud reduction has also added barriers for people applying for benefits."[115] The processing of applications has become quite onerous because of the complexity of the forms, data entry requirements, and the need to verify much of the information. "During the interview, the Texas Works worker first must explain to the client all aspects of what the program requires the client to do, as laid out in the Personal Responsibility Agreement. Then the worker must enter all information into the state's eligibility database, and verify income and assets using a combination of other online databases."[116] There is little if any local discretion, and staff cutback has increased the burden on the eligibility workers. It is estimated that 25 percent to 40 percent of all applications received from April 1998 to June 1999 were diverted either by redirecting them from TANF before application or denying the application for nonfinancial reasons.[117] In addition, despite the automated integration of TANF, food stamps and Medicaid data sets, "once enrolled, as many as 40% of children have been dropped from Medicaid within a year. Moreover, use of food stamps in Texas fell by 44% between 1996 and 2000."[118]

[112] R. Capps et al. (2001). "Recent Changes in Texas Welfare and Work, Child Care, and Child Welfare Systems" (Urban Institute, Washington, D.C.), p. 1.
[113] Ibid., p. 2.   [114] Ibid., p. 1.
[115] Ibid., p. 1.   [116] Ibid., p. 8.
[117] D. Schexnayder et al. (2002). "Texas Families in Transition: Surviving without TANF" (Department of Human Services, Austin), p. xiii.
[118] Capps et al. (2001), p. 5.

The welfare-to-work component of the program, called Choices, is adminis-tered by the local one-stop centers. Applicants must attend a one-day workforce orientation before eligibility is approved.[119] There is a rigid sequence of work activities beginning with a planning session and proceeding to four to six weeks of job club and job search. If participants fail to get a job, they may be recycled through the process again or be referred to additional education and train-ing. The one-stop centers also provide a variety of support services including childcare and transportation. Sanctions for noncompliance are used quickly and frequently. "Sanctions can be initiated easily because of the automatic communication between the Texas Works eligibility and Choices program databases. But once imposed, the sanctions are difficult to lift if a sanctioned recipient comes back into compliance."[120] Because eligibility and welfare-to-work are administered by two different bureaucracies there are coordination and communication difficulties between them. This has resulted in inappro-priate processing of cases or denial of services.[121]

Utah represents a model in which the emphasis on work is coupled, at least in theory, with extensive supportive services.[122] The state imposes a thirty-six-month lifetime limit and requires participation in work activity as a condition for cash aid. However, the definition of "work activity" is very broad, giving welfare workers considerable discretion. The state provides a fairly generous earned income disregard of the first $100 and 50 percent of the remainder. Noncompliance results in a reduction of $100 in the monthly cash aid. There is no family cap. The state "places strong emphasis on educa-tion and training, and invests considerably in developing individualized self-sufficiency plans. It provides funding for virtually anything required for recipi-ents to be able to work – transportation, uniforms, tools, and other work-related activities."[123]

Administratively, the state has consolidated several state agencies, including those in charge of employment insurance, family support, job training, child care, and other employment and training programs into a new Department of Workforce Development.[124] Regional offices administer the work program and the workers can access the support services on site. At the core of the Fam-ily Employment Program is an intensive individualized case management approach. Once eligibility is determined, each recipient must work closely with the case manager to develop a self-sufficiency plan that is geared to her specific needs. The case managers operate under the assumption that recip-ients experience many employment barriers that can be removed through

[119] Ibid., p. 9.   [120] Ibid., p. 6.
[121] Ibid., p. 10.
[122] G. C. Bryner (2002). "Welfare Reform in Utah" (Nelson A. Rockefeller Institute of Government, Albany, N.Y.).
[123] Ibid., p. 7.   [124] Ibid., p. 9.

the provision of individually tailored services.[125] Therefore, participation is broadly defined. For example, participation may include education, training, part-time employment, mental health counseling, parenting education, and substance abuse treatment. Case managers are encouraged to develop strategies to engage recipients with multiple employment barriers. It is assumed that with appropriate help, families with multiple problems can eventually become self-sufficient. Therefore, there are no exemptions from participation. All recipients, even those with disabilities, are expected to engage in some activities. Case managers "carefully monitor progress. Enforcement is strict."[126]

To implement this model, specially trained workers have been hired and are assigned relatively small caseloads (thirty to thirty-five cases). Still, the staff feel that they are in "uncharted territory, often having to rely on trial and error to identify the best strategy for helping a family overcome their barriers to employment."[127] They provide home visits, one-on-one counseling, and conduct regular reviews. Still, the most common work activity is job search (62%), and only 13.5 percent are in job skill training. Other staff are working on child care issues, child enforcement, or treatment. On average, recipients spend twenty-two hours per week on their assigned activities.[128] Those assigned to job search/job readiness activity spend, on average, five months in it.[129] Moreover, over time the proportion of recipients not in any activity increases and can reach 40 percent. There are also no appreciable differences in activity assignments between short-term and long-term recipients.[130] This suggests that despite the individualized case management model, there are no appreciable differences in how these recipients are assigned to various activities.

The state has been quite successful in reducing the welfare rolls by enforcing the self-sufficiency plan. In any month, about 8 percent to 9 percent of the cases are terminated because of noncompliance.[131] In addition, the program benefited from a low unemployment rate. Nonetheless, a study of former long-term recipients concluded that "their average monthly income dropped by over $300" and that they were in a highly precarious situation.[132]

Finally, states may use supportive services to minimize the use of cash aid. West Virginia, one of the poorest states in the nation, has adopted this approach, in part because of the chronically depressed economy of the state. Local offices of the state WV WORKS administer the program. Applicants

[125] L. Pavetti (1995). "And Employment for All: Lessons from Utah's Single Parent Employment Demonstration Project" (paper presented at the Seventeenth Annual Research Conference of the Association for Public Policy and Management, Washington, D.C., November, 1995).
[126] Bryner (2002), p. 14.   [127] Pavetti (1995).
[128] Kauff, Derr, & Pavetti (2004).   [129] Ibid., p. 57.
[130] Ibid., p. 62.   [131] Bryner (2002), p. 14.
[132] Ibid., p. 21.

are required to sign a personal responsibility contract, attend an orientation session, agree to an employability plan, and document efforts to find
a job, while the application is pending. West Virginia offers work incentive by
disregarding 60 percent of earned income (raised from 40%). Failure to comply results in progressively harsher sanctions. The first sanction leads to a
third reduction in cash aid for three months, the second sanction to two-
thirds reduction for three months, and the third sanction terminates the case
for at least six months.

Historically, the state's approach to work first has been through Community Work Experience Program (CWEP) because of the high unemployment
rate.[133] Recipients had to work for their cash assistance in public and nonprofit organizations. An evaluation by MDRC has shown that CWEP did not
improve employability or improved income.[134] With the passage of TANF,
the state was very concerned about its ability to meet the block grant requirements, especially the MOE, and embarked on a very aggressive effort to close
cases. This strategy entailed tactics such as establishing a complicated process
for determining benefits, sending clear signals to current and potential welfare
clients that the state's program was 'work first,' and using short-term services
and benefits to divert recipients from long-term enrollment."[135] Reducing the
caseload also reduced the state's mandated work participation rate. According
to Plein, early in the implementation, the state even counted SSI as income in
determining eligibility until court challenges ended the practice.[136] Not surprisingly, in one year (1998–99), the caseload declined by almost 60 percent.
However, such a decline was clearly not matched by increased employment.[137]
There was also a high rate of return to the welfare rolls in subsequent years
due to the poor economy. For this reason, the state relies heavily on CWEP
and community service programs. Still, the majority of the new or reenrolled
recipients are not participating in work activities because the state has met its
mandated rate because of caseload reduction and because the state permits
a twenty-four-month exemption from work activities within the sixty-month
lifetime limit.[138]

District offices are expected to offer support services that "range from clothing vouchers, to small cash grants to assist clients in obtaining professional
licenses and equipment, to payments to cover incidental expenses associated with job interviews and employment, to relocation assistance, to vehicle
insurance payments."[139] Case managers are encouraged "to use diversion and

---

[133] L. C. Plein (2001). *Welfare Reform in a Hard Place: The West Virginia Experience*. Albany, N.Y.:
Nelson A. Rockefeller Institute of Government.
[134] J. Ball (1984). "Interim Findings on the West Virginia Community Work Experience Demonstrations" (MDRC, New York).
[135] Plein (2001), p. 15. [136] Ibid., p. 16.
[137] Ibid., p. 18. [138] Ibid., p. 23.
[139] Ibid., p. 25.

support services to prevent initial enrollment. Frontline staff may dissuade families from entering the rolls by offering alternative benefits such as food stamps, emergency assistance, help in getting child support, assistance from community service organizations, or formal diversion payment."[140] However, most of the support services were devoted to transportation.[141]

Understandably, regional offices have tried to conserve their supportive services resources and to urge their clients to use local community services instead. This has created tensions as community social service organizations face an increasing demand for their services while experiencing serious budget constraints.[142] There are also tensions between WV WORKS and the state's Bureau of Employment Programs, which administers the Work Investment Act (WIA), thus forcing the district offices to be responsible for CWEP.[143]

Given the state's precarious economy, the effect of VW WORKS on its recipients is discouraging. A survey of former recipients who have reached their time limits shows that only 27 percent of them were employed and almost all had income of $10,000 or less in 2002.[144] Many experience considerable hardship. Most continue to use programs such as food stamps, Medicaid, and school clothing vouchers and free or reduced-price school meals.[145] In general, a majority of the recipients expressed satisfaction with their encounters with the welfare workers. However, they had more mixed views about the helpfulness of the job training they had received, and a majority of those needing child care had difficulties finding it.

There are other state variations on these two goals. In part, the picture is more complex because of the different degree of autonomy counties have been granted in implementing TANF at the local level. Ohio, for example, "consolidated eight funding streams into a single block grant to counties with approved 'partnership agreements' for welfare reform giving counties considerable power and flexibility."[146] Other states attempt to maintain tight control through regional offices and complex computer systems that are supposed to track every decision made by welfare workers. In addition, several states and counties have relied heavily on private for-profit and nonprofit organizations to deliver services under welfare-to-work, and the activities of these organizations are more difficult to track.

Integrated vs. Specialized Case Management

To reconcile the two incompatible goals of eligibility determination and "work first," states and counties have adopted various organizational options. One

---

[140] Gais et al. (2001), p. 56.
[141] Plein (2001), p. 25.
[142] Ibid., p. 30.
[143] Ibid., p. 29.
[144] R. J. Dilger et al. (2004). "WV WORKS 2003: Perspectives of Former Recipients Who Have Exhausted Their 60 Months of Program Eligibility" (Interdisciplinary Research Taskforce on Welfare Reform, West Virginia University, Charleston).
[145] Ibid., p. iii.
[146] Gais et al. (2001), p. 57.

option is to create an integrated case management model, in which the function of income assistance and welfare-to-work are combined. An early experiment with such a model has shown that the integrated model achieved a higher level of attendance in orientation and participation in work activities, though the sanctioning rate was the same as the traditional model.[147] One possible explanation is the greater ability of the workers in the integrated model to track their clients even though the workers found that balancing the two functions was quite demanding. In addition, over a two-year period, the integrated model resulted in a reduction of $156 in cash assistance per participant. However, there were no differences in employment or earnings.

The integrated model was fully implemented in Ohio, wherein the state has given the counties considerable autonomy in implementing the welfare-to-work program.[148] Cleveland opted to decentralize the welfare offices to eleven local neighborhood offices with a mission to be both "user-friendly" and have a "relentless" focus on employment.[149] The message to applicants was conveyed by big banners in the waiting areas proclaiming, "Your clock is ticking. . . . Cash benefits are limited to a total of 36 months in your lifetime. It's the law. Talk to your caseworker about time limits."[150] The job titles of the welfare workers were changed to self-sufficiency coaches, although less than half received any additional training to do their work. The workers pushed their clients to engage in any work activity, some of which was contracted to nonprofit organizations. Recipients with less than a high school degree were routed to remedial education, whereas those with a high school degree were pushed to get a job right away.[151] Ohio has a strict thirty-six-month time limit, and the county succeeded in terminating almost all cases reaching the time limit, because most of these families were already working. Although the county offered special assistance to terminated recipients, few used them.[152]

The perspective of the recipients diverged significantly from those of the case managers. A majority of the surveyed recipients "felt that case managers pushed them to get jobs before they were even ready."[153] Most felt that the case managers "just wanted to enforce the rules."[154] Researchers report that "despite the county's commitment to creating a 'user-friendly' welfare agency, many of the women found their case managers to be condescending, rude, untruthful, unresponsive or vindictive."[155] Respondents also had mixed feelings about job club/job search. In other words, from the respondents' perspective, the case managers behaved not much differently from the traditional eligibility workers

---

[147] T. Brock & K. Harknett (1998), "A Comparison of Two Welfare-to-Work Case Management Models." *Social Service Review* 72: 492–520.
[148] T. Brock et al. (2002), "Welfare Reform in Cleveland: Implementation, Effects, and Experiences of Poor Families and Neighborhoods" (MDRC, New York), pp. 1–194.
[149] Brock et al. (2002), p. 29.   [150] Ibid.
[151] Ibid., p. 37.   [152] Ibid., pp. 41–42.
[153] Ibid., p. 47.   [154] Ibid., p. 47.
[155] Ibid., p. 48.

in a culture of bureaucratic rule enforcement. An integrated approach does not seem to soften the great pressure on the workers to push the recipients into work and enforce the strict time limits.

An alternative approach is to decouple eligibility and cash assistance from employment services by creating separate units for each function. Philadelphia represents an example of allocating the responsibility of income eligibility and welfare-to-work into two separate units within the welfare office.[156] Welfare reform in Pennsylvania requires newly enrolled recipients to complete an eight-week job search. During the first twenty-four months on aid, "participation" is defined very broadly, both in terms of permissible activities and hours. After twenty-four months, recipients must participate in a work activity that does not include training and education for at least twenty hours per week. Noncompliance results in termination of the adult portion for those within the twenty-four-month time limit and termination of aid for those who are on TANF beyond twenty-four months. The entire welfare system is administered by the state through local regional offices.

To implement TANF, the regional offices have created a new Career Development Unit (CDU) responsible for the welfare-to-work component. In Philadelphia this was done by reassigning eligibility workers to the new unit and providing them with additional training about the new policies and regulations.[157] In some CDUs, workers specialized in handling recipients who received aid beyond twenty-four months. The average caseload per worker was more than 190 clients.[158]

Newly enrolled recipients who fail to find a job after the initial eight-week job search are invited to an orientation in which representatives of various contracted vendors try to recruit them to their programs. These usually consist of job readiness training but may also offer specific job skill training. In general, for these recipients without a high school degree, the case managers stress the importance of getting a GED or for those with a high school degree, the push is to get a job. Even though education is allowable for recipients who have been on aid for less than twenty-four months, few actually enrolled.[159]

For recipients who crossed the twenty-four-month threshold, case managers have little discretion in assigning them to work activities. "The set sequence began with another month of job search and job club, followed by programs providing unsubsidized employment, and it ended with volunteer work."[160] Recipients who want to enroll in additional education or training have to do it on top of the twenty-four hours per week of the approved work activity.

The monitoring of the recipients is done mostly through a computerized tracking system and communication with recipients is facilitated by the use

[156] C. Michalopoulos et al. (2003). "Welfare Reform in Philadelphia: Implementation, Effects, and Experiences of Poor Families and Neighborhoods" (MDRC, New York).
[157] Ibid., pp. 29–30. [158] Ibid., p. 33.
[159] Ibid., p. 35. [160] Ibid., p. 36.

of voice mail. Still, because some vendors fail to update the system regularly, case managers remain in the dark about the level of participation of their clients.[161] The use of sanctions is highly discretionary, and the process is quite cumbersome. The number of sanctioned cases is increasing.[162]

Interviews with a sample of recipients reveal that most were quite aware of the rules, but few understood that they could return to welfare if they lost their job as long as they did not exhaust the sixty-month lifetime limit.[163] Recipients were very eager to trade welfare for work because they found welfare to be demeaning whereas they saw work as giving them respect.[164] Although recipients were generally aware of transitional benefits, they claimed that they did not get the information from their case managers and often were told they were not eligible for any. Recipients also pointed out that even when they qualified for such benefits, they experienced very burdensome administrative barriers, and some lost them as a result.[165]

A sample of current welfare recipients or those who have been on welfare within twelve months of the interview (presumably those who had most difficulty in getting a job) were asked to evaluate their relations with their case managers. They presented a very mixed picture. According to the researchers "only 24% of the ongoing recipients said that welfare staff took the time to get to know them and their situation, and 28% said that staff would help them deal with problems affecting their participation in welfare-to-work activities. By comparison, 62% said that case managers pushed them to get jobs even before they were ready, and 76% agreed with the statement that case managers 'just wanted to enforce the rules.'"[166]

In an ethnographic study of a group of recipients, the women voiced concern about lack of predictability of the new system and their perception that the workers exercised considerable discretion in making decisions about their benefits.[167] It was this sense of the hassle that motivated them to stay away from welfare altogether. These women also felt that job club was of little value.[168] Interviewed recipients also reported a much higher rate of sanctioning than the official records, possibly because they also included administrative case closure.[169]

Privatization of TANF: Who Benefits?

A third alternative in restructuring the welfare department is to contract out some or all its functions to private for-profit and nonprofit organizations.[170] It

[161] Ibid., p. 37.
[162] Ibid., p. 40.
[163] Ibid., p. 45.
[164] Ibid., p. 47.
[165] Ibid., p. 48.
[166] Ibid., p. 51.
[167] Ibid., p. 52.
[168] Ibid., p. 54.
[169] Ibid., p. 55.
[170] S. McConnell et al. (2003). "Privatization in Practice: Case Studies of Contracting for TANF Case Management" (final report, Mathematica Policy Research, Inc., Washington, D.C.).

may take several forms, ranging from contracting out all of TANF functions, including eligibility determination, to private organizations (e.g., Wisconsin) to a more common practice of purchasing employment-related case management (e.g., Delaware and San Diego). Temporary Aid for Needy Families has expanded considerably the option of contracting out by eliminating the requirement, under AFDC, that only government employees can determine program eligibility. The act permits contracting out the administration of TANF and its services, and under its charitable choice provision, it permits contracts with faith-based organizations on the same basis as any other private provider.[171] The GAO estimates that in 2001, more than $1.5 billion, or at least 13 percent of all federal TANF and state MOE expenditures, were spent on such contracts.[172] The bulk (80%) went to contracts with nonprofit organizations, 8 percent to faith-based organizations, and 13 percent to for-profit organizations. Most of the contracts are for employment (e.g., education and training) and supportive services.

The nonprofit providers include a mix of several large national organizations such as Goodwill Industries, Catholic Charities, AFL-CIO, and well-established local social service agencies, such as the YWCA, the Urban League, and the Opportunities Industrialization Centers.[173] Two national corporations, Maximus and Affiliated Computer Services, dominate the for-profit providers. Maximus, in existence for more than twenty-eight years and with 5,000 employees, provides a wide range of contract services, ranging from fleet management to child support services. A publicly traded corporation, Maximus reported revenues of more than $500 million in 2003 and net income of about $53 million. Affiliated Computer Services is a Fortune 500 company specializing mostly in information technology. Its government industry group provides contract services to federal, state, and local governments in such areas as child-support payment collection, Medicaid payments, and welfare-to-work. In 2004, the company reported revenues of $2.4 billion or 59 percent of total revenues from its government clients. It operates about ninety-nine one-stop centers across the country.

The rationale for privatization is well known.[174] By introducing market mechanisms, especially competition, private providers are motivated to deliver services as efficiently as possible. Consequently, contracting should result in cost savings to government. Competition also ensures that providers

[171] GAO (2002). "Welfare Reform: Federal Oversight of State and Local Contracting Can Be Strengthened" (U.S. General Accounting Office, Washington, D.C.) pp. 1–59.
[172] Ibid., p. 8.
[173] P. Winston et al. (2002). "Privatization of Welfare Services: A Review of the Literature" (Mathematica Policy Research, Inc., Washington, D.C.).
[174] J. D. Donahue (1989). *The Privatization Decision: Public Ends, Private Means.* New York: Basic Books; E. Sclar (2000). *You Don't Always Get What You Pay For: The Economics of Privatization.* Ithaca, N.Y.: Cornell University Press.

would optimize the quality of their services, therefore providing higher-quality services than a single monopolistic provider such as government. Accountability is enforced because government can select the best services at the lowest cost among the competitors. According to Winston and colleagues, available studies on cost savings or quality present a mixed picture.[175] Sclar also notes that comparative cost studies produce ambiguous results because these are dependent on a complex array of organizational, technical, and contractual factors.[176]

A second rationale for privatization is the flexibility it provides government by procuring specified services from a wide array of potential providers who can tailor their services to serve specific groups of consumers. Contracting also enables government to overcome bureaucratic inertia, inflexible civil service regulations, and other administrative barriers that slow and limit the ability of government to provide the services directly. Moreover, contracting provides an incentive to innovations because they enhance the competitive edge of the potential providers. Finally, contracting can also reduce or at least check the growth of government, often seen as a desirable political payoff.[177]

A key issue about privatization is what the economists term "contractual incompleteness," the inability to specify in advance all the future conditions and contingencies that the contract needs to address.[178] That is, government faces uncertainty about the type of services it may actually need as these may change over time, and it encounters asymmetry of information because of the difficulty in assessing the quality of the service. At the same time, the providers of the service often have a monopoly over knowledge and expertise and can potentially exploit their consumers.[179] Therefore, government monitoring of the contract and its ability to enforce accountability become a major concern and can be quite costly.

According to Sclar, contractual incompleteness leads to three major problems.[180] The first is principal-agent problems in which the contractor uses the information asymmetry to advance its own interests at the expense of government. The second is adverse selection, whereby the government selects the lowest-cost contractors, who are, in fact, least qualified to provide the service.[181] The third issue is moral hazard, whereby the contractor has insufficient incentives to fulfill the goals of government. To minimize these problems requires

---

[175] Winston et al. (2002).   [176] Sclar (2000), p. 68.
[177] Winston et al. (2002).
[178] K. Eggleston & R. Zeckhauser (2002). "Government Contracting for Health Care." In J. Donahue & J. S. Nye Jr. (Eds.), *Market-Based Governance* (pp. 29–65). Washington, D.C.: Brookings Institution Press; Sclar (2000).
[179] H. Hansmann (1987). "Economic Theories of Nonprofit Organizations." In W. W. Powell (Ed.), *The Nonprofit Sector: A Research Handbook*. New Haven, Conn.: Yale University Press.
[180] Sclar (2000), pp. 102–18.   [181] Ibid., p. 108.

an effective enforcement system of incentives and penalties that may raise considerably the administrative costs of the contract.

A related issue is the degree to which a competitive market of providers exists and the extent to which government can sustain and enhance the market's competitiveness. On the one hand, government incentives may create new opportunities for providers to enter the market.[182] On the other hand, once contracts are made, government has the incentive to reduce transaction costs by limiting the number of contracts and by relying on the same providers for renewal of contracts, thus driving potential bidders out of the market.

Another key issue in contracting social services is to determine the price of the service and an appropriate rate of return for the provider. There is a need to determine what a unit of service is, how many such units are necessary to attain the desired outcome, and how many such units each staff person can deliver over a specified period. For example, to provide mental health counseling to welfare recipients would require an estimation of the hours of contact per referred recipient to address or manage the problem. It also requires a decision about the level of expertise needed to provide the unit of service and the labor costs associated with it. In addition, the number and type of service units need to be adjusted to the nature of the problem and the attributes of the client. Clearly, there is no straightforward algorithm to calculate the costs of such services. Service providers rely on their experience and the prevailing patterns in their service sector. However, as providers bid for contracts, they are motivated to reduce the cost of service through various economizing measures such as lower staff expertise and costs, fewer units of service, and the like. Potentially, such measures can have deleterious effects on the quality of the service.

Payment structures also influence the degree of risk each party wishes to assume. McConnell and colleagues identify four types:[183]

1. Pay-for-performance – contractors are compensated only on the basis of meeting defined performance goals such as number of clients served, number of clients placed in jobs, or number of clients who remained employed for a specified period of time. Contractors may also earn bonuses if they exceed their targets. There is clearly an incentive for the contractors to meet such performance goals while facing a high risk of failure. One way to reduce risk is to negotiate performance goals that accord with the accepted norms in the industry. Another strategy known as "creaming" is to select, when possible, preferred clients with the potential of meeting such goals as was the case under the Job Training

[182] J. A. Baum & C. Oliver (1992). "Institutional Imbeddedness and the Dynamics of Organizational Populations." *American Sociological Review* 57(4): 540–59.

[183] McConnell et al. (2003).

Partnership Act.[184] Contractors also have an incentive to generate favorable information attesting to their high performance.

2. Cost reimbursement – these contracts compensate the contractors on the basis of the expenses they incur up to a designated limit. Such contracts may also include performance measures. They do not determine level of payment but may be used in the decision to renew the contract. The risk to contractors is that they may exceed the limit. Therefore, they have an incentive to reduce costs, especially because the difference between the reimbursement and the actual costs represents a "profit" for them. In addition, contractors have an incentive to reduce costs to remain competitive. The risk to government is that the expenses may not reflect the true cost of the services.

3. Fixed-price contracts – are based on a set fee per client, regardless of the actual cost. Again, performance measures may be included, but these do not affect the fee. Such contracts shift the risk from government to the contractor. Here too, contractors have an incentive to reduce costs below the fee in order to generate "profit."

4. Hybrid forms – which may combine features of pay-for-performance with reimbursement or fixed fees.

Each form of payment bears consequences on how the contractors will interact with their clients. While pay-for-performance provides incentives for case managers to work with their clients to achieve the desired measures, much depends on the essence of these measures. Typically, in welfare-to-work the performance measures are reductions in welfare rolls, job placements, job retention, and wages. Case managers have an incentive to move rapidly as many recipients as possible to the job market, irrespective to their level of readiness or the personal problems they may face. They also have an incentive to prevent their return to welfare so that recipients stay in the job market. In contrast, under cost reimbursement, case managers are less constrained from providing a broader array of services to meet the specific needs of their clients, if the costs of such services are reimbursable. At the same time, the agency may pressure them to provide unnecessary or low-quality services to boost profit. Under fixed-price contracts, case managers may be pushed to provide fewer, less-intensive, or lower-quality services to lower costs and increase the profit margin.

Much is being made of the differences between for-profit and nonprofit contractors.[185] It is assumed that because nonprofit organizations are not driven by a profit motive, they are more committed to meet the needs of their clients and to offer high-quality services. Nonprofit organizations are viewed as imbued

---

[184] Donahue (1989).

[185] B. A. Weisbrod (1988). *The Nonprofit Economy*. Cambridge, Mass.: Harvard University Press.

by a culture of altruism and voluntarism that are manifest in a service-delivery structure that attempts to promote trust between staff and clients.[186] In general, studies that compare the quality of services between nonprofit and for-profit organizations tend to conclude that the former provide higher-quality services.[187] Nonetheless, as the competitive pressure from for-profit organizations increases, these advantages begin to erode.[188] In addition, nonprofits are not immune from a motivation to generate high profit, which they can use to fund other ventures, expand, and grow or distribute internally as salary and benefit increases.[189]

To compete with for-profit organizations for government contracts, non-profit organizations face a serious disadvantage because they lack access to capital and managerial resources needed to bid, market, and operate the program. As a result, in service areas where the potential for profit are significant, such as child care, elder care, and welfare-to-work, nonprofits face stiff competition from for-profit providers.[190] Small nonprofit organizations are at a particular disadvantage because they face a greater risk of failure to meet their contractual obligations.

For privatization to deliver on its promises, several conditions must exist. According to John D. Donahue, the services to be delivered must be specified in advance; the performance of the providers, especially of service outcomes, must be readily measured; unsatisfactory contractors can be readily replaced; and competition is maintained.[191] Sclar adds the importance of proven knowledge and expertise to deliver the services.[192]

In the case of welfare, these conditions seldom prevail. The clients to be served have diverse characteristics and multiple needs, making it difficult to specify in advance the service they require. Even specific services such as job club or child care may need to be modified to accommodate the distinct circumstances of the clients. In addition, social services have intangible elements to them that are not readily visible, such as the quality of the relations between case managers and clients. Yet, these intangible elements are often the most critical in achieving the desired outcomes.

Measures of outcomes, let alone service quality, are particularly problematic. There are uncertainties about the desired outcomes themselves,

---

[186] Weisbrod (1997).

[187] H. Schid (2000). "For-Profit and Nonprofit Human Services: A Comparative Analysis." *Social Security* (Special English Edition) 6: 161–179.

[188] L. Clarke & C. L. Estes (1992). "Sociological and Economic Theories of Markets and Nonprofits: Evidence from Home Health Organizations." *American Journal of Sociology* 97: 945–69.

[189] Hansmann (1987).

[190] P. Frumkin (2002). "Service Contracting with Nonprofit and For-Profit Providers." In J. D. Donahue & J. S. Nye Jr. (Eds.), *Market-Based Governance* (pp. 66–87). Washington, D.C.: Brookings Institution Press.

[191] Donahue (1989).   [192] Sclar (2000).

especially because the service provider does not have much control over environmental factors that affect the desired outcomes. For example, to determine the performance of a provider of job club/job search services requires setting normative criteria of the expected proportion of clients who should get a job after completion of the program and the duration of the job, while taking into account the various attributes of the clients (e.g., their work history, level of education), the supply of low wage jobs at the local labor market, and the hiring patterns of employers.[193] It is a daunting task. Not surprisingly, contractors often settle on performance rather than outcome measures such as number of clients being served or on crude outcome measures, such as proportion placed in jobs with little regard to the consequences for the well-being of the clients. Even to measure performance, let alone outcomes, requires a complex system of recordkeeping and regular on-site monitoring and auditing. Mostly, the monitoring focuses on adherence to specific rules and procedures that do not guarantee quality.

Moreover, contractors have the advantage of information asymmetry by controlling much of the information they generate for government monitoring. Case managers control much of the content of the information they collect and record about their clients, the services they provide, and the impact of these services. Clients seldom have the capacity to challenge such information, and auditors will have to expend considerable energy, time, and resources to obtain such information independently of the contractors. Therefore, contractors are likely to overstate positive results.

The ability to replace failing service providers is also difficult because the supply of such providers is limited and the start-up costs for new providers are quite high. As Sclar points out, "Most public contracting takes place in markets that range from no competition (monopoly) to minimal competition among very few firms (oligopoly)."[194] Moreover, once government selects a set of contractors they tend to gain an advantage through their ongoing relations with officials and drive potential competitors from the market. Government also has a preference for few large contractors to reduce administrative and monitoring costs.[195] This also tends to drive smaller organizations from the market.

The ability to find contractors that have the knowledge and expertise to deliver the needed services is also problematic. In the case of welfare eligibility, for example, the knowledge and experience of the public welfare workers cannot be readily replicated, lest the contractors hire many of them, which is indeed the case.[196] Similarly, the ability to provide quality employment

---

[193] H. Holzer (1996). *What Employers Want: Job Prospects for Less-Educated Workers.* New York: Russell Sage Foundation.
[194] Sclar (2000), p. 69.   [195] McConnell et al. (2003).
[196] E.g., DeParle (2004).

services also depends on experience and knowledge that is only available to agencies that have had a long history in providing such services.

Most important, the underlying motivation to contract public services, including welfare-to-work, is primarily ideological and political rather than economic.[197] It is driven by an ideology that citizenship rights and liberties are best protected by markets rather than the state; a political desire to reduce the role of government; a disdain of the civil service system; and antipathy of public service unions. As a result, although the decision to contract public services, such as welfare, is justified on the basis of cost and efficiency, it is almost always driven by political considerations.

Having set such a political process in motion, it develops its own momentum. Contractors become a significant interest group that can mobilize political resources to exert influence over government, especially in shaping policies and regulations that would favor them. Individual contractors with access to political decision makers may curry favor to gain an advantage by being granted a privileged position. In turn, public officials committed to privatization have an incentive to justify the benefits of contracting out by highlighting assumed gains while ignoring or suppressing negative results. In this effort, they are joined by the contractors who wish to keep the officials in office.

Contracting can also produce significant changes in the interorganizational network of the service providers. In the case of welfare, large case management contractors, such as Maximus, typically subcontract or partner with various local service providers for needed services.[198] The large contractor gains not only access to important services but can use the network to bolster its legitimacy.[199] In turn, these service providers depend on the contractor, who controls access to public funding. As the same time, the dominance of the contractor may impose costly constraints on the subcontractor or partner, resulting in a precarious relationship. Moreover, complex interorganizational relations must be negotiated between the welfare department, the lead contractor, and the many subcontractors. These involve reconciling among different interests and ideologies, establishing communication and information sharing systems, tracking clients across several systems, and instituting multilevel systems of monitoring and accountability. The probability of coordination difficulties and failures increases dramatically, and most of the costs will be borne by the clients as they try to maneuver through this complex network.

The economic, political, and organizational context of contracting public services, such as welfare, to private organizations produces significant risks. First, contractors may use their advantageous position to engage in what Sclar terms opportunistic behavior, such as overcharging, diverting payments to

---

[197] Sclar (2000).   [198] McConnell et al. (2003).
[199] Ibid., p. 24.

nonrelated activities, or even paying off officials.[200] As Sclar notes, "The fine line between guile in negotiation and outright corruption is too often quite thin and permeable."[201] Second, contractors, especially for-profit organizations, can readily exit if they decide that the expected profits do not materialize, that the constraints and obligations of doing business with government are too costly, or that they have better opportunities elsewhere. This could place the entire program in jeopardy. Similarly, as the political context changes (e.g., elections, exposés of inefficiencies and corruption), officials may decide to terminate contracts because they no longer have legitimacy or serve their political interests.

Not surprisingly, many of the issues that plague privatization of social services manifest themselves in contracting out welfare case management. The argument that contracting out welfare case management is more efficient and effective cannot be sustained. An evaluation of the Arizona Works Pilot Program compared the performance of Maximus, the for-profit provider, with that of the public welfare department.[202] Maximus received the contract to administer a version of TANF, known as Arizona Works, in Eastern Maricopa County (which includes Phoenix), whereas the welfare department administered a somewhat different version of TANF, known as EMPOWER, in the rest of the county.[203] Although there were some differences between the two programs, such as the monthly grant amount, both placed a strong emphasis on job placement. Maximus was generally successful in implementing the program, though the local offices had to undergo numerous administrative changes as the contractor adjusted to such issues as staff turnover and reduced funding.[204] As a result of frequent changes in staffing and in management practices, case managers expressed confusion and attributed complaints by participants to being reassigned to different case managers.[205]

The contract with Maximus included a base payment plus incentives based on performance measures that included job placement rates, employment retention, and reduction in long-term caseload as compared to EMPOWER.[206] For the duration of the contract from 1999 to 2002, Maximus received more than $16 million including incentive payments. The incentive payments did not reflect better performance than EMPOWER, but rather the differences in the contexts in which the two programs operated (e.g., different neighborhoods, caseload characteristics) and the way records were kept.[207] Indeed, one interesting finding of the evaluation is the discrepancy between the data on performance measures produced by Maximus staff and

[200] Sclar (2000), p. 97.   [201] Sclar (2000), p. 106.
[202] B. Kornfeld, D. Porcari, & L. R. Peck (2003). "The Arizona Works Pilot Program: A Three-Year Assessment" (Arizona Department of Economic Security, Abt Associates Inc., Cambridge, Mass.).
[203] Kornfeld, Porcari, & Peck (2003), p. xix.   [204] Ibid., pp. 3–8.
[205] Ibid.   [206] Ibid., p. xviii.
[207] Ibid., p. xviii.

the employment and earning data as recorded by employers, suggesting that the staff tended to overreport measures of success.[208]

The more rigorous evaluation, which attempted to control for some of these variations, found little difference in the performance and outcomes of both providers. As noted by the researchers, "Arizona Works had no impact on the employment and average quarterly earnings."[209] Similarly, the program had no effect on welfare receipt.[210] In terms of costs and benefits, the total costs of Arizona Works "exceeded projected cost estimates by $5.8 to $9.2 million."[211] In other words, privatization of TANF may, in fact, be more costly, thus undermining its efficiency justification, let alone effectiveness.

The experience of Miami-Dade with privatization of TANF demonstrates the political volatility of the process, the issue of coordinating different service providers, and the problems with quality.[212] Florida opted to devolve the welfare-to-work component to local coalitions, typically the local board administering the Job Training Partnership Act (JTPA). These coalitions, in turn, contracted with local service providers to administer the welfare-to-work program.[213] Regional state offices of the Department of Children and Families (DCF) retained the responsibility for welfare eligibility and benefits. In Miami-Dade County, the mayor decided to form a coalition independent of JTPA. It issued a contract to Lockheed, which partnered with several local agencies, to deliver most of the welfare-to-work program. As noted by Thomas Brock and colleagues, "The coalition's plan fell victim to outside political maneuvering and internal management problems almost from the start."[214] There was considerable opposition to the contract with Lockheed, and a second round of contracts were issued, mostly to the Miami-Dade Community College District and the County public schools.[215] In addition, the coalition's board experienced internal management problems with escalating welfare-to-work expenditures, while failing to meet the anticipated participation rates. There were also newspaper exposés about favoritism and inappropriate hiring by the Miami-Date public schools.[216] Subsequent legislative changes reassigned the local responsibility for the welfare-to-work program to the local JTPA board, which, in turn, issued contracts with twenty-eight organizations to operate new one-stop centers.[217] Yet, about half of these one-stop centers failed to meet their performance standards and had to be terminated.[218]

Thus, in three years, there were major turnovers in the contractors. The changes in contractors did not alter the basic welfare-to-work service technology, which consisted of an orientation, assignment to job club, followed by a

[208] Ibid., p. xiii.
[210] Ibid., pp. 10–4.
[212] Brock et al. (2004).
[214] Ibid., p. 32.
[216] Ibid., pp. 32–33.
[218] Ibid., p. 34.

[209] Ibid., p. xxv.
[211] Ibid., pp. 11–8.
[213] Ibid., p. 31.
[215] Ibid.
[217] Ibid., p. 33.

period of individualized job search.[219] Nor did the changes improve the quality of the services. The research team found offices closed during business hours, variations in the information given to recipients, and poor job club instruction, including one in which "an instructor read aloud from Whoopi Goldberg's biography for more than an a half-hour and seemed unable to draw any clear lesson for the clients to take away."[220] Not surprisingly, the DCF and welfare-to-work staff had low opinions about the contractors, feeling that many were "only in it for the money."[221]

Despite the poor-quality case management, and maybe because of it, there was a high use of sanctions. The percentage of recipients who were referred to or who received sanctions in an average month reached 61 percent, "the highest observed in any MDRC study of a state or county welfare-to-work program."[222] Moreover, the researchers concluded that "the high rate of sanctioning was to some degree a reflection of administrative problems and inconsistent case management practice among Lockheed, the community colleges and public schools, and the One-Stop staff."[223]

It is probably not surprising that recipients had a low opinion of the program. A survey and ethnographic interviews with a sample of current or recent recipients showed considerable dissatisfaction with the program. Recipients "expressed resentment toward staff, whom they perceived as uncaring, rude, and poorly informed."[224] Because so many recipients were sanctioned, there was a decline in the number participating in work activities. Few of the respondents had positive remarks about the work activities, with most feeling that they were a waste of time.[225]

Finally, we return to Wisconsin, which has pioneered in privatizing welfare by aggressively contracting out all of its TANF functions, including eligibility determination and monitoring (except for food stamps and Medicaid) and W-2 case management to private for-profit and nonprofit organizations.[226] Wisconsin's new privatized approach has been hailed as a major innovation in public management and received the Innovation in American Government Award in 1999 by the Kennedy School of Government at Harvard. In reality, all the pitfalls Sclar warns about have plagued the privatization of Wisconsin's TANF.[227] Milwaukee County, where most welfare recipients reside, was divided into six regions, and in response to the state's request for proposal,

[219] Ibid., p. 41.
[220] Ibid., p. 43.
[221] Ibid., p. 42.
[222] Ibid., p. 44.
[223] Ibid.
[224] Ibid., p. 62. Because the interviewed recipients were a random sample of long-term recipients living in the poorest neighborhoods, it is possible that their experiences with the workers were more contentious (T. Brock, personal communication).
[225] Ibid., p. 63.
[226] B. M. Sanger (2003). *The Welfare Market Place: Privatization and Welfare Reform*. Washington, D.C.: Brookings Institution Press.
[227] DeParle (2004); Sanger (2003); Sclar (2000).

five organizations were selected, four of which (except for Maximus) had been providers of employment services.[228] The five contractors were

1. YW Works, a limited liability corporation founded in 1996 as a joint venture between the YWCA, which has had a long history of community and employment services, and NCR Health, Inc., which provides health care and employment assistance management services.
2. United Migrant Opportunity Services (UMOS), a nonprofit, community-based organization, founded in 1995 to serve migrant and farm labor workers in Wisconsin.
3. Opportunities Industrialization Center (OIC), a nonprofit organization founded in 1967 to provide employment services to inner-city poor residents.
4. Employment Solutions, a nonprofit subsidiary of Goodwill Industries, which in 1995 became a JOBS center.
5. Maximus.[229]

For the first year, the total contact amount exceeded $154 million, with contracts ranging from a high of $54 million to Employment Solutions to a low of $19.5 million to YW Works.[230] Payments were based on cost reimbursement plus performance-based bonuses. The contracts stipulated that any unexpended funds that were 7 percent or less of the total contract value were to be paid as unrestricted profits. If unexpended funds exceeded 7 percent, the contractor could keep 10 percent of the remaining fund as unrestricted profit (presumably an additional incentive to reduce the welfare rolls); 45 percent was to be invested by the contractor in the community, and 45 percent was retained by the state Department of Workforce Development.[231]

From the beginning, it was apparent that several of the contractors were failing to provide quality services. As noted by Jason DeParle, the agencies were performing poorly, in part, because the case mangers were hired with limited qualifications and were poorly trained or supervised. Maximus, for example, "encouraged hiring of family and friends, calling it an effective way to lure and keep talent."[232] Not surprising, the agency found itself with incompetent caseworkers.

Attending a class at OIC, DeParle reports that the job counselor simply read from an occupations almanac. As DeParle puts it, "It was social work as farce."[233] He also found that clients had a very difficult time contacting their

[228] Gooden, Doolittle, & Glispie (2001).   [229] Ibid., p. 20.
[230] Wisconsin Legislative Audit Bureau (1999). "Wisconsin Works (W-2) Expenditures" (No. 99-3, Joint Legislative Audit Committee, Madison).
[231] Wisconsin Legislative Audit Bureau (2001). "An Evaluation of Wisconsin Works (W-2) Expenditures" (Joint Legislative Audit Committee, Madison), p. 32.
[232] DeParle (2004), pp. 234, 239.   [233] Ibid., p. 197.

case managers. Although recipients were assigned to various work activities, mostly job search and motivational classes, it was evident to observers such as DeParle that most of them were not getting meaningful services.[234] Indeed, one contractor was repeatedly fined for mishandling cases.[235] According to Sanger, the state auditors confirmed that clients were not informed about the range of services available to them and that "few had adequate assessment of their needs, had been lifted out of poverty, or had been placed in more intensive education and training programs that might have led to self-supporting jobs. The auditors implied that contract agencies simply did not offer services if clients did not request them."[236] It was clearly a strategy to reduce costs and increase profit.

Even though the contractors had failed to provide adequate services to their clients, they were able to meet their performance standards because these standards "focused on process, not results."[237] To renew their contracts, the agencies only had to show that the case managers had a caseload of fifty-five clients, that 95 percent of the employability plans were up-to-date, and that 80 percent of the clients were assigned to activities.[238] It was easy for the agencies to meet these criteria because they spoke nothing about the substance or the quality of the service. Moreover, the performance data entry on the state client-tracking computerized system could be easily manipulated to show favorable results.[239]

Because of a much faster decline in the caseload (48% from 1997 to 2000) than anticipated by the state, the contractors were awash with excess funds. However, instead of using the excess funds to improve the quality of services or obtain additional services for their clients, the contractors tended to spend it on organizational maintenance such as public relations and staff and managerial benefits. This was made possible because fiscal and programmatic accountability were wholly inadequate. The county's Private Industry Council (PIC) was contracted to provide technical assistance and oversight, including financial, but state auditors found out that many of the responsibilities were not met.[240] In particular, the PIC failed to monitor whether agency expenditures were appropriate. Consequently, as noted by the state auditors, "We found that Maximus and Employment Solutions had inappropriately billed the State for numerous unallowable costs, including expenditures associated with pursuing out-of-state contracts, entertainment, unallowable staff benefits, and donations to other organizations."[241] DeParle reports that Maximus, for example, spent more then $1 million on billboard and TV adds, as well as "Maximus

[234] Ibid., pp. 230–50.   [235] Ibid., p. 332.
[236] Sanger (2003), p. 57.   [237] DeParle (2004), p. 246.
[238] Ibid., p. 247.   [239] Ibid., p. 248.
[240] Wisconsin Legislative Audit Bureau (2001).   [241] Ibid., p. 42.

water bottles and Maximus visors . . . Maximus golf balls, towels and tees."[242] In addition, it spent thousand of dollars on employee entertainment. It could not provide justification or relevance to W-2 of almost 73 percent of the transactions examined by state auditors.[243] The other contractors also used contract funds to spend large sums of money on public relations, and Employment Solutions used more than $270,000 to bid on a contract in Arizona.[244] There were also instances of corruption by officials in awarding at least one of the contracts.[245]

By 2003, only three agencies remained as contractors, belying the idea that privatization could enhance competition. Moreover, to ensure that clients are aware of benefits they are entitled to and services they can receive, county workers, under a contract from the state, took over the initial intake and assessment before referring them to the contract agencies.[246] This shift to the public sector was obviously designed to mitigate the tendency of the contractors to skimp on services to maximize profit.

Finally, a longitudinal study of applicants to W-2 in Milwaukee shows no improvement in employment or earning by applicants receiving W-2 services, compared with those who did not.[247] The applicants group did enjoy a much higher total annual income when cash assistance and food stamps were included ($8,583 vs. $3,379), clearly benefiting from the combination of cash assistance and participation in program activities. At the same time, both groups experienced the same level of hardship, with 52 percent of the applicants group experiencing food insecurity and 47 percent unable to pay their rent or mortgage.

As the case studies demonstrate, the privatization of TANF does not live up to its promises. Moreover, for the clients, it raises additional barriers to accessing services. First, because federal regulations prohibit the administration of food stamps and Medicaid eligibility by private organizations, private agencies cannot administer the programs as they do with TANF eligibility. Applicants and recipients have to transact with two different sets of organizations, where, in the past, both functions were merged in the welfare department. As a result, applicants who are denied TANF eligibility or welfare recipients, especially those who get off welfare, may not be aware that they are still eligible for food stamps and Medicaid, which explains the decline in the proportion of eligible recipients getting either food stamps or Medicaid. Even internally to the TANF program, recipients are likely to experience greater access difficulties because they still have to negotiate among several different service providers to obtain the services they need. They may be processed by the

---

[242] DeParle (2004), pp. 243–45.   [243] Ibid., p. 243.
[244] Ibid., p. 246.   [245] Ibid., p. 332.
[246] Sanger (2003), p. 57.
[247] A. Dworsky, M. Courtney, & I. Piliavin (2003). "What Happens to Families under W-2 in Milwaukee County, Wisconsin?" (executive summary, Chapin Hall, Chicago).

welfare department for eligibility or referred to a contractor to meet their work participation requirements, and the contractor typically refers them to other service providers for needed services such as remedial education, child care, and mental health services. To access each of these services requires that the recipients have the bureaucratic experience distinct to each provider. In addition, the costs of coordination among the providers escalate with each additional contact point. Hence, the probability of miscommunication and coordination failures rises further, adding to the burden on the recipients who have to negotiate through this complex system. Recipients experience delays and frustrations in getting needed services, and many fall between the cracks and simply give up.

To conclude, the variations in organizational forms in administering TANF do not seem to alter much the core relations between case managers and recipients for several reasons. First, no matter what the organizational structure in which these relations are embedded, their aim is to achieve high levels of case closure and exit to work. Second, the case managers have to place recipients in similar labor markets that are characterized by a limited supply of jobs, and the jobs themselves pay low wages, are often temporary and unstable, and have difficult work schedules. Third, the welfare workers work within a very similar service technology that centers on job club and job search. Work activities are similarly defined and leave few options for the workers. Fourth, the compliance of clients is based on coercive measures, namely, the threat or use of sanctions. These measures frame the nature of the encounter between the workers and their clients.

Changing the Culture of the Welfare Department

The myth that the welfare department has been transformed into an employment agency is enacted through symbols. The titles of the welfare workers are changed, as in Michigan from assistance payment worker to family independence specialist. In Texas, they are now works advisors. Other symbols are displayed. As described by Gais and colleagues, "a big banner in the lobby of one office proclaimed 'Welcome Job Seekers!' Posters in the waiting room said 'You Have a Choice, Choose a Job – Work First.' 'Work First so that your child is not the next generation on welfare.' 'Life works if you Work First.' The message was the same in another state's welfare office: 'Job Seekers Welcome!' and, in English and Spanish, 'Time is Running Out/Welcome Job Seekers, Your Independence is our success.'"[248]

Yet, at the front line, rather than seeing a major shift from a culture of eligibility and compliance to a culture of services toward self-sufficiency, most

---

[248] Gais et al., pp. 35–64.

welfare departments have incorporated the new work requirements into the
"old" culture. That is, the work requirements are translated into a set of rules
that the workers enforce in the same manner they enforce other eligibility
and compliance requirements.[249] In their study of TANF application process
in eighteen states, the researchers found that the process of determining eligibility has not radically changed; rather, it has become more complex.[250]
Applicants are required to provide more information about their work history;
welfare workers include in their routines information about the work requirements and emphasize the importance of compliance with various behavioral
requirements. In many offices, additional steps have been added to the application process, such as meeting with a career development officer, completing
a work orientation session, or going through job search. In addition, applicants may be referred to or offered various support services. The increased
complexity of the application process and making eligibility contingent on
demonstrating willingness to participate in work activities has clearly affected
rates of approval. As noted by the researchers, from 1996 to 2000, there was a
drop of 19 percent in the number of applications filed and a drop of 24 percent
in the number approved. Approval rates steadily declined from about 63 percent in 1992 to 51 percent in 2001.[251] The researchers caution that, in addition
to changes in rules and application processes, other external factors could
also contribute to the decline. There are, of course, considerable variations
not only among states but also among local welfare offices. In Providence,
Rhode Island, 61 percent of the applicants were certified for TANF whereas in
Cook County, Illinois, only 19 percent were certified.[252] Welfare workers may
use informal means to deter applications. In six different sites that were studied more intensively, the researcher found that the welfare offices normally
require at least two visits to complete the application process. Most offices also
include an orientation or screening interview that may discourage potential
applicants to file. In those offices requiring applicants to engage in job search
before approval (e.g., Cook County), many applicants decide to terminate
the process.[253] Thus, with the exception of those offices requiring job search
as part of the application process, little has changed from AFDC in terms of
the emphasis on eligibility determination, calculation of benefit levels, and
prevention and detection of fraud.

Indeed, there is a wide gap between the new organizational myth and the
behavior of the welfare workers on the ground. In their study of the implementation of TANF in eleven sites, Irene Lurie and Norma Riccucci found that
although the espoused goals emphasized employment and self-sufficiency,

---

[249] Ibid.
[250] Health Systems Research and Abt Associates (2003).
[251] Ibid., chap. 5.   [252] Ibid., chap. 13.
[253] Ibid.

the frontline staff continued to be driven by accuracy in determining eligibility and benefits and getting the work done on time.[254] The workers themselves saw little change in their own jobs "with the exception of an enormous amount of additional paperwork.[255] Although the job titles of the workers changed to reflect the emphasis on employment, the researchers found that much of their training focused on the new rules such as time limits, new rules about Medicaid and food stamps, and the Personal Responsibility Agreement. Yet, "workers received little training for conducting new job responsibilities that are unrelated to eligibility processing."[256] Consequently, the processing of applicants has not changed much. As Lurie and Riccucci write, "The eligibility interviews we observed usually mentioned the need to work and always referred applicants to the work agency. However, very little time was spent discussing work or coaching the clients about employment. Discussion of work generally was crowded out by the enormous amounts of information that the worker must collect to complete the application for assistance."[257]

Conclusions

Throughout its history, the welfare bureaucracy has been shaped by three powerful interacting forces: (1) Institutionally dominant moral rules that distinguish between the deserving and undeserving poor; (2) the local community in which the bureaucracy operates, reinforcing the values and interests of the local political elites, and the constraints of the local political economy; and (3) the welfare bureaucrats and workers who respond and adapt to the external demands, while advancing and protecting their own interests by institutionalizing street-level practices that structure and guide how they process and treat welfare recipients. Nonetheless, although welfare departments evolve and change in response to transformations in these interacting forces, they are characterized by strong bureaucratic inertia. No matter what other functions are tacked on, the welfare department is fundamentally structured around eligibility determination, verification of deservingness, and detection of fraud. Moreover, the entire reward structure of the welfare department centers on limiting entry and hastening exit from the welfare rolls. These core functions crowd out many of the others, including social services.

The best way to understand the welfare bureaucracy is to observe how it processes and treats those who seek its services.[258] First, applicants for aid always face a series of locally defined administrative hurdles that serve as a

---

[254] I. Lurie & N. M. Riccucci (2003). "Changing the 'Culture' of Welfare Offices: From Vision to the Front Lines." *Administration and Society* 34: 663–64.

[255] Ibid., pp. 653–77.   [256] Ibid., p. 671.

[257] Ibid., p. 672.

[258] Bane & Ellwood (1994); Brodkin (1997); Lipsky (1984).

test of their neediness and trustworthiness. The aim of these hurdles is to set
the costs of applying high to discourage entry. Welfare workers start with an
assumption that persons seeking aid are neither truly needy nor trustworthy
and put the onus on them to prove otherwise. Second, the voluminous rules
and regulations that define eligibility and other participation requirements
give the workers considerable discretion in how they are applied and interpreted. The discretion enables the workers to enact both their own personal
and the locally dominant moral conceptions about who is deserving. It also
gives the workers a great deal of power and control over the recipients. Third,
applicants and recipients have very limited access to knowledge about what
they are entitled to, knowledge that is mostly controlled by the workers. As a
result, they become highly dependent on the workers to get benefits and services. Fourth, welfare workers typify recipients into a simple set of categories.
These categories enable the workers to ignore the variations and idiosyncrasies
presented by the recipients, to gain control over the flow of work, and to justify
their actions. Most important, the use of such categories routinizes welfare
work. Fifth, becoming a recipient is always a tentative category subject to
threats of withdrawal of benefits. Continued monitoring and verification of
eligibility dominate welfare work. Administrative rules and worker discretion
are routinely invoked to terminate benefits and to hasten exit. Hence, the
majority of cases are terminated because recipients fail to follow administrative regulations. Sixth, there is always a locally defined work test in the
administration of welfare. It may take several forms, from setting the grant
level low enough to force recipients to work "off the book" or making receipt
of aid contingent on participation in work activities. Finally, compliance by
the recipients is mostly achieved through the use of coercive means such as
threats to terminate benefits, denial of services, and use of sanctions. Recipients
are generally powerless to counter these coercive measures whose application
hastens exit.

Despite the rhetoric of welfare reform, the "reformed" welfare bureaucracy
continues to uphold these features. At its core, the "new" welfare department, public or private, is still preoccupied with eligibility, verification, and
detection of fraud. It is organized to discourage entry by setting numerous
administrative barriers, including such requirements as evidence of job search,
paternity identification, and attending job orientation prior to eligibility determination. It hastens exit by setting a tough work test, requiring recipients to
engage in work activities as a condition of receipt of aid, coupled with liberal
use of sanctions for those who fail to meet it. The work test itself, participation
in work activities, is highly routinized, typically consisting of an orientation
followed by job club/job search. Recipients are generally classified into two
major categories, mostly on the basis of their level of education: those that
are job ready and those that require remedial education. Some social services
are offered, such as child care and transportation, but their availability is not

assured. Employment-enhancing services, such as education and training, are generally not available.

The distinctiveness of the "new" welfare department is in its aggressive enforcement of the work requirements, while allowing welfare recipients to keep a greater portion of their cash aid. It pushes recipients off the rolls by setting time limits and pushing them into the low-wage labor market. There is little evidence to suggest that it has transformed itself into a true employment and social service agency. This is not to deny that in some jurisdictions, local political forces have supported a greater transformation of their welfare departments toward the social service model. But, these are the exceptions rather than the norm.

6 Work and the Low-Wage Labor Market
Mothers and Children

The central feature of welfare reform is work in the paid labor market. Not only will paid work reduce the rolls, costs, fraud, and poverty but also will reform the poor. It is through paid labor that parents will provide the proper role models for the socialization of the children. The work ideology at the federal level was first adopted with the Work Incentive Program (WIN) program in 1967, and, at least nationally, represented a fundamental change in the conception of the family. Before 1967, it was believed that the proper role of the mother was to stay at home and raise the family. Now, the proper role is paid employment, which eventually culminated in the 1996 welfare reform.

There are a number of assumptions – or myths – that support the work strategy: that there are sufficient jobs, that employers will hire welfare recipients, that welfare recipients have to be required to work, that the children of welfare leavers will be adequately cared for, that the family will have adequate health support, and that working in these jobs will reduce poverty. The entire family will be better off when supported by earned income. In this chapter, we explore these myths.

The chapter is divided into two parts that are intimately connected with each other. First, we consider single mothers and the low-wage labor market. What kinds of jobs are available? How employable are single mothers, especially those who have left or are in the process of leaving welfare and have small children? What are the material conditions of these women when they are working? How much do they earn? What are the costs of working (including taxes)? Are they able to earn a basic, adequate standard of living? The second part of the chapter deals with the important issue of child care. What kind of child care is available for the children of these working mothers? How much does it cost? What is the quality of the child care? We are concerned with the well-being of the children, that they are healthy and develop both cognitively and socially. If the children do not do well, this not only harms the children but also limits the ability of the mothers to work in the paid labor force and care for the children. The family is a unit. The issues are inseparable.

What Kinds of Jobs Are Available? The Low-Wage Labor Market for Women

One of the great myths about the low-wage labor market is that it is a stepping stone to better and more stable employment. The reality is far more complex, and in fact, the majority of those employed in the low-wage labor market remain there, stuck with low-wage jobs, have few if any benefits, and experience considerable job instability and insecurity.

Estimates of the size of the low-wage labor market vary by the definition researchers use. Andersson, Holzer, and Lane, using the Longitudinal Employer-Household Dynamics (LEHD) program data, define persistent low earners as those with an annual earnings of $12,000 or less for each of a three-year base period of 1993–95 and limit the age of the workers to be between twenty-five and fifty-four. They find that about 8 percent of the workers were persistently low-wage earners by that definition.[1] About one-third of the workers were partially low-earners, earning less than $12,000 per year at least part of that time.[2] Eileen Appelbaum and her colleagues found that in 2001, almost a quarter of the labor force (23.9%) or 27.5 million Americans, working full-time, earned less than $8.70 per hour, for an annual income of $17,400, which is roughly the poverty line for a family of four.[3] They estimate that, depending on the area, a family of four – two parents with two children – requires an income between $27,000 and $52,000 to maintain a basic standard of living. The median income for these families is about $35,000. Their estimate for the range of income necessary for a single working parent with two children is between $22,000 and $48,000. In the late 1990s, despite the booming economy, 29 percent of working families with children under age 12 had incomes less than what was needed for basic family budgets in their communities.[4]

Schochet and Rangarajan,[5] using an hourly wage of full-time work that would generate annual earnings below the poverty line for a family of four, estimate that about a third of all workers are employed in the low-wage market. Mishler, Bernstein, and Allegretto[6] use a similar definition and show that 24.3 percent of all workers earned poverty wages in 2003. The percent

[1] F. Andersson, H. J. Holzer, & J. Lane (2005). *Moving Up or Moving On: Who Advances in the Low-Wage Labor Market?* New York: Russell Sage Foundation, p. 27.

[2] Ibid., p. 27.

[3] E. Appelbaum, A. Bernhardt, & R. J. Murnane (Eds.) (2003). *Low Wage America: How Employers Are Reshaping Opportunity in the Workplace.* New York: Russell Sage Foundation, p. 1.

[4] Appelbaum, Bernhardt, & Murnane (2003), p. 1.

[5] P. Schochet & A. Rangarajan (2004). "Characteristics of Low-Wage Workers and Their Labor Market Experiences: Evidence from the Mid- to Late 1990s" (Mathematica Policy Research, Inc., Princeton, N.J.), pp. 1–161.

[6] L. Mishel, J. Bernstein, & S. Allegretto (2005). *The State of Working America 2004/2005.* Ithaca, N.Y.: ILR Press.

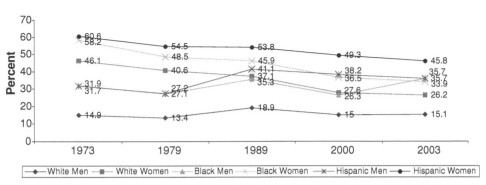

Figure 6–1. Poverty-Level Wage Earners by Ethnicity and Gender: 1973–2003. *Source:* Mishel, Bernstein, & Allegretto (2005), pp. 132–33.

of workers in the low-wage market varies by gender and ethnicity. As shown in Figure 6–1, women are more likely to earn poverty wages than men, and Hispanic and African American workers are more likely to earn poverty wages than white workers. About 46 percent of Hispanic women are low-wage workers compared with 34 percent of black women and 26 percent of white women. Among men, 36 percent of Hispanic men earn poverty wages, compared with 26 percent of African American and 15 percent of white males. Also, as can be seen also from Figure 6–1, there was a major increase in the size of the low-wage labor market between 1979 and 1989, and then it experienced a decline during the economic growth of the mid-1990s.

The rise and persistence of the low-wage labor market reflects the "new" economy, which is characterized by increasing wage inequality and the decline in return to high school education. Bernhardt and colleagues,[7] using National Longitudinal Survey of Youth (NLSY) data, followed two cohorts of young men and women entering the labor market, the first cohort from 1966 to 1981 and the second cohort from 1979 to 1994. They find that, in comparison to the first cohort, the second cohort experienced greater job instability, with high school dropouts experiencing the greatest job separation. Increase in job separation, including involuntary job loss, resulted in reduced job tenure.[8] The recent cohort experienced lower upward job mobility. Permanent wage growth has declined by 21 percent, compared with the earlier cohort.[9] There was also a greater increase in job inequality. Explaining the lower wage growth for those with less education to two major factors, the researchers note "about 60% derives from declining return to experience, which indicates that the new economy has brought with it a harsh process whereby disadvantage builds on itself and cumulates over time. About 40% derives from stronger penalties

---

[7] A. D. Bernhardt et al. (2001). *Divergent Paths: Economic Mobility in the New American Labor Market.* New York: Russell Sage Foundation.

[8] Ibid., pp. 69–86.   [9] Ibid., p. 148.

of job instability."[10] Indeed, the major earning gains were driven by college graduates working in a few privileged industries – finance, insurance and real estate, and professional services.

Bernhardt and colleagues define chronic low-wage workers as those who at age 34 had a permanent wage (computed on the basis of long-term wage trajectory) of less than $11 per hour (in 1999 dollars, which was about 1.4 of the poverty line).[11] They find that although 12 percent of the workers in the first cohort were low-wage workers, 27.6 percent in the second cohort were low-wage workers. The rise in low-wage workers in the second cohort was not confined to those with high school education or less. It rose for all educational levels, from 14.4 percent to 35.3 percent for high school or less, from 10.5 percent to 25.4 percent for some college, and from 10.4 percent to 14.1 percent for those with a college degree or higher. In part, this was due to the increase in low wage jobs throughout the entire economy. In industries such as manufacturing, there was a 130 percent increase in low-wage jobs between the first and second cohort. It rose by 132 percent in transportation and communication; 119 percent in wholesale and retail trade; 92.5 percent in construction, mining, and agriculture; and 91 percent in business and repair services, entertainment and recreation, and personal services.[12] Moreover, "the nature of the employer-employee contract has changed within industries, and one result has been a greater incidence of poor and working poor careers."[13] There has also been a greater concentration of working poor at the "bottom" of the service industries – retail trade, personal services, entertainment and recreation, and business and repair services – industries that provide little opportunities for wage improvement.

The increase in wage inequality, especially in the 1980s, is attributable to several factors, most prominently the decline in the real value of the minimum wage and the technological changes, especially computerization, which have increased the wage disparity between skilled and unskilled workers.[14] Computerization has increased the demand for highly educated workers, depressed the demand for "middle educated" workers, and has had little effect on unskilled workers concentrated mostly in the service industries noted previously (e.g., guards, cleaners, orderlies).[15] The effects of skill-biased technological changes on wage inequality are vividly shown in a case study of the retooling of a food processing plant.[16] When the plant shifted to a food processing technology

[10] Ibid., p. 149.   [11] Ibid., p. 153.
[12] Ibid., p. 159.   [13] Ibid., p.159.
[14] For a review, see D. H. Autor, L. F. Katz, & M. S. Kearney (2005). "Trends in the U.S. Wage Inequality: Re-Assessing the Revisionist" (unpublished manuscript). Downloaded from http://econ-www.mit.edu/faculty/download_pdf.php?id=967.
[15] Ibid., p. 28.
[16] R. M. Fernandez (2001). "Skill-Biased Technological Change and Wage Inequality: Evidence from a Plant Retooling." American Journal of Sociology 107(2): 273–320.

that relies heavily on computerization and other electronic devices, there was a significant increase in the complexity and the level of skills required to operate the equipment. This has resulted in increased wage disparities in the plant. Workers that had the needed skills received a wage premium whereas the wages of the other workers remained stagnant. Existing and newly hired high skilled workers, especially those with the skills to maintain the complex machinery, saw their wages rise rapidly, leading to a sharp rise in wage inequality. At the same time, the technological changes have also added to gender and racial inequality in the plant. The workers in the high-skills jobs, including the new hires, were mostly white males, while women and minorities became overrepresented in the low-skill jobs.[17] These inequalities would have been even more extreme had it not been for the presence of a labor union in the plant and the commitment of the management to not lay off workers because of the transition. A similar pattern was observed when a large bank computerized its check processing.[18] The computerization eliminated jobs that could be programmed and held by workers with high school education only. In contrast, it has created new jobs requiring complex skills to deal with exceptions processing. To fill these positions, the bank began to look for candidates who show initiative and strong problem-solving skills, thus favoring college graduates.[19]

Low-wage employment in the "new" economy also results in higher job instability, and "unstable employment thus appears to have played a much more prominent role in producing chronic low wage growth in recent years."[20] In addition, there has been an increase in the "stickiness" of employment in the low-wage market. In the first cohort, 58.6 percent started in a low-wage job and 49.4 percent ended in a low-wage job. In the more recent cohort, 65.7 percent started in a low-wage job and 59.8 percent ended in a low-wage job, which is a 21 percent increase.[21] The trap in low-wage jobs is also coupled with an increase in job instability, which further reinforces the "stickiness" in the low-wage job market.[22]

The reasons for the low-wage trap are multiple. In response to economic pressures, most employers reduced costs by reducing wages, especially for frontline workers with only a high school education. One strategy was to retain the same workers but freeze wages, reduce benefits, and increase workload. For example, in a study of several high-end hotels, housekeepers received no pay increases for six years; in other hotels, the yearly increases amounted to 10 to 20 cents per hour. At the same time, the workload (the number of rooms to be cleaned) increased steadily over past two decades. Hospitals, another

[17] Ibid., pp. 311–14.
[18] D. H. Autor, F. Levey, & R. J. Munane (2002). "Upstairs, Downstairs: Computers and Skills on Two Floors of a Large Bank." *Industrial and Labor Relations Review* 55(3): 432–47.
[19] Ibid., p. 445.   [20] Bernhardt et al. (2001), p. 162.
[21] Ibid., p. 165.   [22] Ibid., p. 166.

example, have reduced the wages of nursing assistants, food service workers, and housekeeping.[23]

In a variety of entry-level, labor-intensive jobs, immigrants have replaced native workers, allowing employers to reduce costs and benefits and increase workloads. Another strategy has been the increasing use of temporary workers through subcontracting or outsourcing, and relocating jobs to low-wage areas, either domestically or abroad. Workers who are relative well paid but nevertheless less skilled are especially vulnerable. In 1999, about a third of hospitals outsourced food services, 27 percent housekeeping, and 62 percent laundry. Outsourcing of restaurants by hotels to avoid unions and reduce labor costs is virtually industry-wide. In addition to lowering wages, internal labor markets no longer provide promotion opportunities for frontline workers.[24]

When jobs are routine, repetitive, and predictable – for example, information processing – then workers can be replaced through technology – for example, ATM machines, check imaging, and optical recognition. For the jobs that remain, either the skill requirements are raised or the jobs are divided into narrower tasks with lower pay.[25] The results are stagnant wages, the rapid growth of contingent or subcontracted jobs, and declining upward mobility.[26]

Andersson, Holzer, and Lane[27] also examine the extent to which low-wage workers are able to escape their predicament. They show that persistent low-wage earnings (defined as $12,000 or less for each year during a three-year base period of 1993–1995, in 1998 dollars) is a consequence of both personal attributes and firm characteristics. Women in all race-ethnic categories were more likely to be low-wage earners, and Hispanic women were particularly at greater risk.[28] Black males were more likely to experience greater job instability and lower frequency of employment.[29] Most low-wage jobs are concentrated in retail trade and service sectors (especially personal services, social services, and hotels) but also in apparel and textile products.[30] The characteristics of these low-wage industries include small size, high turnover, but most important, low-wage premia. The authors suggest that *"the presence of low earners in a firm seems strongly related to the firm wage premium,* instead of (or perhaps in addition to) being related to low earners' own characteristics."[31] Therefore, they conclude that the firm's pay policy is a major reason for the presence of low-wage workers.[32]

Following the trajectories of the low-wage earners over nine years, Andersson, Holzer, and Lane found considerable mobility. Over two-thirds of the

[23] Appelbaum, Bernhardt, & Murnane (2003), pp. 10–11.

[24] Ibid., pp. 11–13.   [25] Ibid., p. 14.

[26] Ibid.   [27] Andersson, Holzer, & Lane (2005).

[28] Ibid., p. 30.   [29] Ibid., p. 31.

[30] Ibid., p. 35.   [31] Ibid., p. 38.

[32] Ibid., p. 39.

low-wage earners improved their earnings. Mean annual earnings more than doubled over the entire period.[33] Still, most only partially escaped low earning status. Personal characteristics matter. Males were more likely to transition to higher earnings than females, and white males were more likely to transition upward than any other racial-ethnic group.[34] Type of industry or firm also matters a great deal. Those escaping low earnings were more heavily concentrated in construction, manufacturing, transportation and utilities, and wholesale trade.[35] They were also more likely to work for large firms with low rates of turnover. Most important, a majority of workers who remained in firms that have low-wage premia could not escape low earnings.[36] The researchers show that "access to high-wage firms, independently of the characteristics of the workers themselves, has important effects on the ability of low earners to improve their earnings status in subsequent periods."[37]

These findings are replicated in a study by Schochet and Rangarajan, using data from the longitudinal panel of the SIPP for the period 1995–2000.[38] Defining low-wage workers as those earning an hourly wage at which a full-time worker would have annual earnings below the poverty line for a family of four, each worker was followed for forty-eight months. Although most worked full-time, many still earned wages considerably below the low-wage cutoff value.[39] There was considerable movement in and out of low-wage jobs, but two-thirds of those who moved to better paying jobs returned to low-wage jobs. Women, in particular, tended to exit and return to low-wage jobs or unemployment.[40] Overall, about 50 percent of the low-wage workers were still in low-wage jobs three years later.[41]

There was also considerable mobility and instability in employment. The researchers note that "about one-half of the [job] spells ended within four months after the job started, about three-quarters ended within one year, and nearly 90 percent ended within two years."[42] About a third of the males and 22 percent of the females exited to a higher paying job within a year. The rest of the spells either ended in another low-wage job or unemployment.[43]

The fact that gender and race play a significant factor in the transition out of low earnings suggests that employers in the low-wage labor market make hiring decisions that are influenced by race, ethnicity, and gender. According to Holzer,[44] employers in the low-wage market emphasize two sets of skills.

[33] Ibid., p. 51.
[34] Ibid., p. 56.
[35] Ibid., p. 60.
[36] Ibid., p. 61.
[37] Ibid., p. 69.
[38] P. Schochet & A. Rangarajan (2004). "Characteristics of Low-Wage Workers and Their Labor Market Experiences: Evidence from the Mid- to Late 1990s" (Mathematica Policy Research, Inc., Princeton, N.J.), 1–161.
[39] Ibid., p. xvii.
[40] Ibid., p. xix.
[41] Ibid., p. 93.
[42] Ibid., p. 130.
[43] Ibid., p. 132.
[44] H. Holzer (1996). *What Employers Want: Job Prospects for Less-Educated Workers*. New York: Russell Sage Foundation.

The first are cognitive skills, especially reading and writing, arithmetic, and computers. The second set of skills are "soft," namely, physical appearance and neatness, and demonstration of politeness and motivation. Moreover, employers are reluctant to hire someone with limited work experience or suspected criminal record. And, the preferred modes of hiring are informal referral mechanisms (e.g., current employees, networks) and newspaper ads.[45] Such recruiting and selection practices invariable include latent ethnic and gender preferences. Holzer[46] notes that employers prefer Hispanic applicants over black applicants, especially in manufacturing and blue-collar jobs, even if the former have lesser skills. They also prefer black female over black male applicants. Finally, suburban employers tend to discriminate against black applicants.

The study by Moss and Tilly[47] confirms many of these findings. Employers of low-wage workers have raised the "hard" skills requirements (i.e., education, experience, and training) for many of the jobs because of the increase in use in computer technology and provision of new services. The increase in these requirements makes it more difficult for residents of central cities to qualify for the jobs. More important, employers emphasize the importance of "soft" skills such as interaction and motivation. The assessment of such soft skills is obviously very subjective and is influenced by the personal experiences and stereotypes employers hold. Not surprisingly, these requirements for low-skill jobs result in hiring patterns that are discriminatory. They state, "Within racial and ethnic groups, *virtually every task requirement and credential is associated with greater probability of hiring a woman.* . . . Within gender, *almost every task requirement and credential is correlated with reducing hiring of blacks and Latinos* relative to non-Latino whites."[48] Indeed, Moss and Tilly find that employers are sensitive to the geography of race, ethnicity, and class, and their perceptions of these spatial arrangements influence their hiring decisions. They note, "for a substantial minority of employers, these mental maps contain a negative image of the inner city that is tied to race, class, and a variety of perceived urban ills such as crime, family breakdown, welfare dependency, and inadequate education."[49]

Finally, a study by Waldinger[50] points to the dynamics of the emergence of ethnic enclaves in the low-wage labor market, which reinforce discriminatory hiring practices. In Los Angeles, employers prefer to hire immigrants (mostly Latino) over African Americans because they perceive them to be more productive workers. Once these immigrant groups form a niche in a particular industry, the employers see an advantage of using the immigrant networks to

[45] Ibid., p. 51.   [46] Ibid., p. 104–5.
[47] P. I. Moss & C. Tilly (2001). *Stories Employers Tell: Race, Skill, and Hiring in America.* New York: Russell Sage Foundation.
[48] Ibid., p. 79 (italics in original text).   [49] Ibid., p. 207.
[50] R. Waldinger (1997). "Black/Immigrant Competition Re-assessed: New Evidence from Los Angeles." *Sociological Perspectives* 40(3): 365–86.

recruit and replace workers, further closing off the industry from blacks. At the same time, African Americans tend to opt out of the low-wage labor market, in part because they expect discrimination, thus reinforcing the immigrant industrial niche.

The Rise of Nonstandard Work

Jobs have become increasingly contingent or short-term and without benefits. Very few of the poor work full time, at least at one job – in 1998, only 13 percent of the poor were fully employed.[51] Peck and Theodore say: "Not only are employers adding temporary workers well in advance of permanent employees (as has been the pattern over the past 30 years), flexible employment strategies now appear to be a central feature of an elongated process of workforce adjustment, as employers add workers employed in temporary contracts, while continuing to shed permanent employees."[52] The instability of employment is not confined to the low-wage labor market. A survey in California reports that four out of ten workers have been at their jobs for less than three years and that just one-third fit the conventional mode – working outside of the home at a single, full-time job year-round as a daytime employee.[53] Re-employed workers usually suffer a decline in wages. Employment instability continues to be a major problem for the less-skilled and disadvantaged workers. They experience frequent and long spells of unemployment.[54] Low wages and unemployment are most severe for young workers, minorities, single-parent families, and those who lack a high-school diploma.[55]

Less than a third of all workers (29.1%) work the standard shift – thirty-five to forty hours per week, five days (Monday through Friday), mostly in the daytime. Although the labor force is highly gendered, there is not a great deal of difference in work schedules. About a quarter of men (26.5%) and a third of women (32.8%) work standard shifts.[56] In 1997, a fifth of all workers did not work a fixed daytime schedule, and two-fifths did not work five day a week, Monday through Friday. Part-time work (less than thirty-five hours per week) was more likely to be nonstandard. Fewer than 8 percent of nonstandard workers had two jobs.[57]

---

[51] Osterman (2001), p. 2. See J. Peck & N. Theodore (2005). "Temporary Downturn? Temporary Staffing in the Recession and the Jobless Recovery." *Focus* 23 (3) (Institute for Research on Poverty, University of Wisconsin–Madison, Spring).

[52] Peck & Theodore (2005), p. 38.

[53] D. Lee (1999). "Nature of Work Has Changed," *Los Angeles Times*, p. A1, September 6.

[54] Katz & Allen (1999), p. 8.

[55] G. Burtless (1999). "Growing American Inequality: Sources and Remedies." *Brookings Review* (Winter): 31–35.

[56] H. Presser (2003). *Working in a 24/7 Economy: Challenges for American Families.* New York: Russell Sage Foundation, pp. 1, 15.

[57] Ibid., pp. 15–18.

The entry of women into the paid labor force, the growth of the two-earner family, the rise in family income, and the aging of the population all combined to increase the demand for services in nontraditional hours. Thus, most of the demand for nonstandard work is in low-paying jobs in local markets.[58] Most of the 24/7 employees say that the jobs are not one of choice. Pay differences are not common and rarely a motivating factor. Nonstandard jobs are most prevalent for the young, single, less educated, and African American. However, because a fifth of all workers work other than a fixed daytime schedule and a third work weekends, nonstandard hours are prevalent among all subgroups. The ratio of nonstandard work is higher for married couples. A quarter of two-earner married couples have at least one spouse working a nonstandard schedule. With children, the share rises to a third. Ratios are still higher the younger the couples, the lower the education, and the larger the number of children. Higher ratios of African Americans work nonstandard hours than whites. "Split-shift" couples are more likely to be the working poor.[59]

Most (62.6%) of nonstandard workers said that the reasons for their jobs were the constraints of the jobs – they could not get any other job, the employer set the hours, it was the nature of the job. Only 5.7 percent said that the nonstandard job was because of child care arrangements, and about the same percentage (5.1%) gave better pay as the reason.[60]

The top ten nonstandard jobs were cashiers, truck drivers, commodities sales workers in retail and personal services, waiters and waitresses, cooks, janitors and cleaners, sales supervisors and proprietors, registered nurses, food serving and lodging managers, and nursing aides, orderlies, and attendants. Except for truck drivers, all of these jobs are in local services. Thus, for the most part, nonstandard work is not due to globalization. Most of the jobs are low paying. The average hourly earning (1997) was $8 per hour as compared with $9.50 for those in standard shifts. Thus, even though nonstandard work is not desired by most workers, as a group they are not rewarded with higher earnings.[61]

Currently, in the United States, 40 percent of all workers work nonstandard times – evenings, nights, rotating shifts, on weekends. The pervasiveness of nonstandard work has significant implications for the health and well-being of families and for social policy. As Harriet Presser puts it, "Today, nonstandard work has produced a new 'home time' family structure, especially for the working poor." Spouses are often not at home at the same time in the evening and not at the same time as their children. She questions the implications of these arrangements on the quality and stability of family life and the care of the children.[62] She says that as society moves toward a 24/7 economy, there

[58] Ibid., p. 5.
[60] Ibid., pp. 18–25.
[62] Ibid., p. 2.

[59] Ibid., p. 6.
[61] Ibid., pp. 20–25.

is a growing diversity in the number of hours people work. Even though the average number of hours worked each week has remained fairly constant (a difference of 1.1 hours between 1976 and 2001), there is more flextime and more work during "fringe times" on the traditional nine to five workday.[63]

Nonstandard work takes its toll on families. The presence and number of preschool-age children increases the likelihood that women, but not men, will work nonstandard hours. The same is true for younger workers (under age 30), the less educated, and nonwhites.[64] Both unmarried men and women are more likely to work nonstandard hours.[65] Presser argues that lack of sleep and fatigue increases the risks of a lower quality of marriages and marital dissolution. Health also suffers. There are higher risks of gastrointestinal disorders, higher rates of cardiovascular disease, breast cancer, miscarriage, preterm births, and low birth weights.[66]

The Bureau of Labor Statistics predicts continued job growth in the ten job categories that produce the most nonstandard work. Thus, there will be more nonstandard workers who will be disproportionately women, and to a lesser extent, disproportionately African American and Hispanics.[67] The assumption is that now most women will be employed most of their working lives, including their child-bearing years.[68]

Single mothers are more likely to work nonstandard schedules than married mothers, especially with children younger than age 5, and they generally work more hours but are more likely to have lower incomes. Single mothers more than married mothers rely on grandmother care, even though a high proportion of the grandmothers are otherwise employed.[69] Nonmarried mothers are more likely to give job constraints as the reason for nonstandard work than married mothers. Nonmarried mothers who earned less than $400 or more per week are substantially more likely to work nonstandard hours than those who earn more. In fact, the largest percentage of nonmarried mothers working nonstandard hours were those who earned less than $400 per week and had children younger than age 5. One-quarter of nonmarried mothers with children younger than 5 worked nonstandard hours, and almost 40 percent worked weekends. Proportions were even higher for those with lower incomes (less than $400 per week).[70] Still, high numbers of dual-earner couples also worked nonstandard hours, with or without children. More than one-third of couples with children younger than 5 had at least one spouse working nonstandard hours. And the proportions are even higher for those will relatively lower incomes (less than $50,000 per year).[71]

[63] Ibid., pp. 2–3.
[65] Ibid., p. 42.
[67] Ibid., p. 43.
[69] Ibid., p. 68.
[71] Ibid., pp. 69–77.

[64] Ibid., pp. 34–35.
[66] Ibid., pp. 7–10.
[68] Ibid., pp. 59–60.
[70] Ibid., p. 78.

Studies have suggested that staying with an employer is likely to yield returns for low-skilled workers.[72] However, only those who leave their initial job, move to employers with higher wage premia, and stay there are likely to see significant wage improvement. For welfare recipients, both in pre- and post-PRWORA periods, there is a weak positive association between length of labor force participation and earnings.[73] As a result, policy makers and analysts concerned with the well-being of low-income families emphasized the benefits of sustained labor force participation and lengthened job tenure. They tended to locate employment instability within workers rather than workplaces, emphasizing the need for "work supports" that help lower-skilled workers meet job requirements by overcoming "barriers" to employment as having young children.[74] Lambert, Waxman, and Haley-Lock question this position. They argue that "work supports may not have their intended effect if, in fact, job tenure and earnings growth are driven as much by structural aspects of jobs and workplaces as by the personal qualities of workers."[75] The researchers studied low-wage jobs in four sectors of Chicago's urban economy – retail, hospitality, shipping/transportation, and financial services. They examined multiple sources of instability in low-skilled jobs, which are defined as jobs that require no higher than a high school education and are not considered seasonal or temporary.[76]

Job instability is measured by turnover rates, number of hours worked, and scheduling of work hours. Turnover rates vary both within and across employers and industries. Of the sixty jobs for which they have specific turnover data, annual turnover rates range from 0 percent to 500 percent. Half of the jobs had an annual turnover rate exceeding 50 percent and a third exceeding 80 percent.[77] There is substantial variation in turnover rates among lower-skilled jobs *within* employers. Thus, job retention for lower-wage earners is at least partially a function of the job. Workers entering lower-skilled jobs often have a low probability of remaining in a particular job for even a few months.[78]

The number of hours worked also varies a great deal. In all the industries studied, the employers practice "workloading" or "workload adjustments"

[72] T. Gladden & C. Taber (2000), "Wage Progression among Less Skilled Workers." In D. E. Card & R. M. Blank (Eds.), *Finding Jobs: Work and Welfare Reform* (pp. 160–92). New York: Russell Sage Foundation.

[73] M. Cancian et al. (2000). "Before and After TANF: The Economic Well-Being of Women Leaving Welfare" (special report, Institution for Research on Poverty, University of Wisconsin), p. 77.

[74] S. Danziger et al. (2000) "Work, Income and Material Hardship after Welfare Reform." *Journal of Consumer Affairs*, p. 34.

[75] S. Lambert, E. Waxman, & A. Haley-Lock (2001). "Against the Odds: A Study of Instability in Lower-Skilled Jobs" (School of Social Service Administration, University of Chicago), p. 1.

[76] Ibid., p. 3. The research combines multiple sources of data (administrative, interview, and observation) to develop an understanding of variations (across jobs, workplaces, and industries) in daily workplace practices.

[77] Ibid., p. 6.   [78] Ibid., p. 7.

during off-peak seasons. Workers are given few hours to work for weeks, even months at a time, during off-peak time. Most workers do not apply for unemployment during period of "workload adjustment" because of fear of losing health insurance and seniority.[79]

The temporal structure of work is another source of instability. For many lower-wage earners, work is scheduled along multiple dimensions: days of the week, time of the day or shift, and length of shift or time worked on a given day. Although an employee may hold a five-days-a-week job on paper, his or her life must actually accommodate seven days. In general, to work a job that varies from ten to fifteen hours a week, employees must structure their time so that they are available to work the highest end of the range, even though they are rarely guaranteed that number of hours week to week. When schedules change frequently or with little notice, employees must absorb the effect of these fluctuations. Conflicts with family arrangements, other jobs, or transportation can undermine an employee's ability to hold the job.[80] Also shifting schedules may upset other work arrangements on which the employee depends for sufficient income – many low-wage workers have multiple jobs – and scheduling shifts may undermine some workers' strategies for making ends meet.[81] When shifts shift, seniority often governs the bidding process. New employees, usually the least-established members of the workforce, generally fall to the back of the line in the process. "The new people always get the worst shifts."[82] In sum, although employers, caseworkers, and policy makers may view job loss as employee-initiated, the high annual turnover rates of many lower-skilled jobs suggest that workers' chances of remaining employed are often slim. Furthermore, in lower-skilled jobs, the chances of job loss are highest among those most recently hired.[83]

A prime example of the state of the low-wage labor market is Wal-Mart.[84] Wal-Mart employs more than 1 million workers, which makes it now the largest employer in the United States. It is the largest food retailer and the third largest pharmacy in the country (a 19% share), and it is expanding rapidly. Wal-Mart's wages and benefits are significantly below the standards in the retail market. As a result, other major grocery chains are trying to reduce their wages and benefits significantly. Further, Wal-Mart jobs are replacing existing higher-paying jobs, not adding jobs. In several studies, nearby communities lost up to 47 percent of their retail trade after Wal-Mart opened.[85] In a recent study, using 2001 data, of all active full-time and part-time workers with Wal-Mart for at least

---

[79] Ibid., p. 12.
[81] Ibid., p. 15.
[83] Ibid.
[80] Ibid., p. 13.
[82] Ibid., p. 16.

[84] A. Dube & K. Jacobs (2004). "Hidden Costs of Wal-Mart Jobs. Use of Safety Net Programs by Wal-Mart Workers in California" (Briefing Paper Series, University of California at Berkeley, Institute of Industrial Relations; Center for Labor Research and Education, August 2).
[85] Ibid., p. 3.

one year (about 65% of the workforce), more than half (54%) earned below $9 per hour; 21 percent earned between $9.00 and $9.99, and another 16 percent earned between $10 and $10.99 per hour.[86] These wages are significantly below the average wage of large retailers (with 1,000 or more employees). Wal-Mart workers earn on average 31 percent less than workers in other large retailers – $9.70 versus $14.01.[87] Many Wal-Mart workers lack health care benefits. Wal-Mart reports that only 48 percent of its employees enrolled in its health plan. As compared with other large retailers, 23 percent fewer Wal-Mart employees have employer-sponsored health care coverage. The study compared Wal-Mart wages and benefits of nonmanagerial workers in the San Francisco Bay area with unionized grocery workers. The average for Wal-Mart employees was $9.40 per hour, compared with $15.31 for the unionized grocery workers, and they are half as likely to have health benefits.[88] One result of Wal-Mart's wage and benefits policies is that a substantial number of Wal-Mart employees and their families have to rely on public safety-net benefits. The study estimates that in California, the total cost to the public for public assistance benefits for Wal-Mart employees is $86 million per year – $32 million in health care expenses and $54 million in other assistance. If other large retailers in California followed the Wal-Mart path, the total cost of public assistance in California would increase $410 million to $1.46 billion. Nationally, the estimates could be as much as an additional $2 billion a year.[89]

Stuck in Low-Wage Jobs

The "work first" philosophy of welfare reform emphasizes immediate employment over formal job preparation and assumes that workers will be able to use the skills and knowledge gained in initial jobs to qualify for better-paying jobs. However, employment mobility is also a myth. Regardless of whether it was true in the past, today low-wage workers are not moving up the economic ladder.[90] Only one-fifth of the jobs held by less-educated workers are in "starter" occupations, which require little training or experience and are associated with subsequent well-paying occupations. Most routes up the ladder are inaccessible to many less-educated workers.[91] According to a recent study, the 1990s' job expansion was mostly concentrated at the high end (20%) as well as the very low end (17%) of the job structure. Moreover, it was "a racially polarized job expansion," as most of these bottom-end employment opportunities were dominated by minorities, whereas the so-called good jobs were

---

[86] Ibid., p. 4.
[88] Ibid., p. 5.
[90] Mishel et al. (2000).
[91] L. Kusmin & R. Gibbs (2000). "Less-Educated Workers Face Limited Opportunities to Move Up to Good Jobs" *Rural America* 15(3): 33.

[87] Ibid.
[89] Ibid., p. 7.

filled by whites. The very slow rate of growth of jobs in the lower-middle range of job quality makes it increasingly difficult for employees in the bottom tier of the employment continuum to move up to higher quality jobs. In other words, even if welfare recipients and leavers gain work experience and receive on-the-job-training, there are few middle-range job opportunities to move up to.[92]

Schochet and Rangarajan in their study do find some wage growth. Over the three-year period, real wages increased by 25 percent. Still, about 50 percent of the male workers and 60 percent of the female workers continued to earn wages that put their earnings below the poverty line.[93] The researchers also find that job characteristics made a significant difference. Workers in jobs with higher initial wages, health benefits, and full-time work experienced greater job growth.[94]

Andersson and colleagues also find that low-wage workers who voluntarily changed jobs initially and then stayed with the same employer in 1999–2001 showed the greatest improvement in earnings.[95] About 42 percent of those who moved and then stayed with their new employers escaped low earnings completely by 1999–2001. In contrast, only 17 percent escaped completely while staying with their initial employers. Still, we should keep in mind that of the initial cohort of low earners, after six years, 29 percent remained low earners, 44 percent partially escaped, and only 28 percent fully escaped low earnings.[96] The key to escaping low wages is changing jobs to industries that have a higher wage scale, such as construction, manufacturing, transportation/communication/utilities, and wholesale trade.[97] The researchers find that temporary agencies are also more successful in placing many low-wage earners in high-wage industries.[98] However, Autor and Houseman present contradictory findings.[99] Using a quasi-experimental design, they track the employment experiences of participants in welfare-to-work programs and the Workforce Investment Act who were either placed in jobs via temporary agencies versus direct hires.[100] They find that after two years, the initial positive effects of temporary agencies disappears when compared with direct hires and that the "probability of earnings above welfare thresholds are negative."[101]

---

[92] A. Alstott (1999). "Work vs. Freedom: A Liberal Challenge to Employment Subsidies" *Yale Law Journal* 108: 967–1058; E. Wright & R. Dwyer (December 2000/January 2001), "The American Jobs Machine: Is The New Economy Creating Good Jobs?" *The Boston Review* 25(6): 21–26.

[93] Schochet & Rangarajan (2004), pp. 93–94.   [94] Ibid., pp. 103–104.

[95] Andersson et al. (2005), pp. 78–86.   [96] Ibid., p. 82.

[97] Ibid., p. 90.   [98] Ibid., pp. 91–92.

[99] D. Autor & S. Houseman (2005). "Temporary Agency Employment as a Way out of Poverty?" (Paper presented at the National Poverty Center Conference on "Working and Poor: How Economic and Policy Changes Are Affecting Low-Wage Workers," Washington, D.C.

[100] The quasi-experimental design ensured that for each type of placement the participants had the same personal characteristics.

[101] Autor & Housemen (2005), p. 29.

The Workforce Investment Act (WIA)

The Workforce Investment Act (WIA) (1998) was enacted to facilitate greater coordination of public-funded employment and training programs. The goal is to create local one-stop workforce development locations with access to "core" services that would provide intensive services and training. There are no income or program eligibility conditions. Several programs are to partner with the one-stop centers – Unemployment Insurance (UI), veterans and seniors employment programs, and Job Corps. Under WIA, most funds for adult, youth, and dislocated worker programs go to the local workforce investment boards (WIBs). Flexible vouchers are provided by the boards for training or career advancement services through individual training accounts (ITAs).[102]

Although WIBs have the potential to become a universal service delivery system, so far, this has not happened. Local boards must first serve welfare recipients and other low-income, low-wage individuals. At the same time, WIA funding is tied to specific performance measures, primarily new jobs and earnings gains. This creates incentives in favor of the unemployed or other groups (e.g., youth, dislocated workers) rather than those already working, because there are potentially larger earnings gains from an unemployed worker getting a job than moving a working client into a higher paying job. In addition, thus far, there are limited funds for WIA for training and other services that could benefit low-wage workers.[103]

There are also differing views as to the main purposes of the WIA – is it a "social service" agency or an employment service to bring together employers seeking workers with job seekers? There are higher rates of participation for TANF families or former TANF. Possibly, non-TANF people do not apply because of the stigma associated with the offices. In addition, most of the offices are not open after traditional work hours or on weekends. Finally, supportive services (e.g., subsidized child care, transportation) are not available for those who want to pursue training. Now, with the fiscal crises, there is a lower priority for services for low-income working families and states are postponing or cutting back on planned job retention and advancement services.[104]

There was an in-depth, eight-state study of the state and local WIA (Florida, Indiana, Maryland, Michigan, Missouri, Oregon, Texas, and Utah).[105] Sixteen local areas and more than thirty local one-stop career centers were studied. Leadership roles varied – in some states, the governor's office took the lead, whereas the local workforce area took the lead in others. Business engagement

[102] J. Miller, L. Grossman, F. Molina, & S. Golinka (2004). "Building Bridges to Self-Sufficiency. Improving Services for Low-Income Working Families" (MDRC, NGA Center for Best Practices, March), pp. 1–13.

[103] Ibid., p. 13. [104] Ibid., pp. 16–17.

[105] C. Barnow & C. King (2005). "The Workforce Investment Act in Eight States" (prepared for the U.S. Department of Labor, Employment and Training Administration; Nelson A. Rockefeller Institute of Government, State University of New York, February).

was strong at the local level in half the states. No matter what the administration, all agreed that funding was not adequate and that services had to be rationed, especially costly services such as training. Only a fraction of those eligible were served.[106] There was also great variation in the organization of the one-stop career centers. In some states, the WIA, the employment service, and TANF are integrated. The report found that the employment service is usually a key partner, but there was variation in the relationships with other public agencies. In some states, the WIA controls the state's TANF development funds; in other states, TANF is an optional partner. The UI system is a mandatory, but "minimal," partner.[107] There are also various relationships with community colleges, the vocational rehabilitation and veterans' employment, and training services. When the WIA was initially implemented, the emphasis was on work first; subsequently, the U.S. Department of Labor (USDOL) said that work first was not mandatory and that states could emphasize training. Again, there is variation among the states. In several states, local WIB officials were disappointed with the state labor market information systems and had to rely on private vendors.[108] States are required to maintain an eligible training provider (ETP) list so that customers can make informed choices, but the implementation of the ETPs, the voucher-like ITAs, varied. There was concern about the performance management system, notably the inability to adjust for the characteristics of the participants and local economic conditions.[109] "This study, consistent with previous studies of performance management for training programs, found evidence that local areas engaged in behavior to make their performance appear better than it actually was. This included 'creaming'... and strategic behavior regarding the timing of program entries and exits.... State and local officials and One-Stop Career Center staff were nearly unanimous in expressing displeasure with the performance measurement and management under WIA."[110] Most felt that the "arbitrary numeric goals" of the WIA distorted the performance of the program, and that there was a higher quality in the state and local programs before the WIA. State and local officials noted the decline in funding, which lessened flexibility to meet needs despite the increasing changes in the labor market.[111]

The Impact on Welfare Leavers
Although a majority of the leavers work full time, they still experience a high rate of poverty and are earning only half of the average household income.[112]

---

[106] Ibid., pp. vi–vii.   [107] Ibid., p. vii.
[108] Ibid., p. ix.   [109] Ibid., p. ix.
[110] Ibid., p. x.   [111] Ibid., pp. xi–xii.
[112] R. Moffitt & J. Roff (2000). "The Diversity of Welfare Leavers: Background Paper to Policy Brief 00-02, The Diversity of Welfare Leavers" (Working Paper 00-01, Welfare, Children, and Families: A Three-City Study).

The jobs most likely available for welfare recipients are nonstandard, low-paying service work. TANF is not designed to help smooth the week-to-week, season-to-season variations in income that accompany shifting schedules and rapid job loss. Strict time limits on welfare receipt fail to take into account not only fluctuations in the economy but also the chronic instability of lower-wage work. The crude performance measures commonly employed by public agencies can be very damaging when coupled with employment instability.[113] Turnover rates among new hires, scheduling practices that require child care almost "on call, and workload adjustment [. . .] may leave workers with a job but no pay."[114]

As discussed in Chapter 2, between half and two-thirds find jobs shortly after leaving welfare, mostly in sales, food preparation, clerical support, and other service jobs. The wage is between $5.67 to $8.42 per hour and most do not receive benefits. These are relatively high number of weekly hours of work, but still there are substantial periods of unemployment as well as job loss. Earnings range from $8,000 to $15,144, thus leaving many families in poverty. Earnings increase largely from longer hours, not wages.[115] Most do not receive child care subsidies.[116] Many families are worse off because wages do not make up for lost benefits, even counting the EITC.[117] Thus, despite the political claims for success, the gains for welfare-to-work recipients are very modest and often fail to account for the costs of working – transportation, reciprocity in child care, missed days, and so forth.[118]

At any one point in time, about 40 percent of leavers are not employed.[119] Some (14%) rely on the earnings of a spouse or partner. More than a quarter say that they are disabled or sick or otherwise unable to work. Others report lack of access or lack of work supports, family responsibilities, and transitions; 69 percent of those not disabled are looking for work. Most do not receive unemployment, food stamps, or Medicaid benefits. Former recipients report more economic struggles than low-income mothers – more food insecurity, lack of money to pay rent or utilities, and having to move in with others.[120] A

---

[113] Lambert, Waxman, & Haley-Lock (2001), p. 19.

[114] Ibid., p. 19.

[115] J. Strawn, M. Greenberg, & S. Savner (2001). "Improving Employment Outcomes under TANF" (Center for Law and Social Policy (CLASP), February), pp. 6–7.

[116] L. Pavetti (1995). "And Employment for All" (paper presented at the Seventeenth Annual Research Conference of the Association for Public Policy and Management, Washington, D.C.), p. 48.

[117] M. Greenberg & M. Laracy (2000). "Welfare Reform: Next Steps Offer New Opportunities." (Neighborhood Funders Group Policy Paper No. 4, Center for Law and Social Policy, Washington, D.C.).

[118] Pavetti (1995), pp. 48–49.

[119] R. Haskins (2000). "The Second Most Important Issue" (unpublished manuscript prepared for the conference "The New World of Welfare," Committee on Ways and Means), p. 11.

[120] P. Loprest (1999). "Families Who Left Welfare: Who Are They and How Are They Doing?" (discussion paper, Assessing the New Federalism, Urban Institute, Washington, D.C.).

rise in no-parent families was recently reported. Mostly, very poor inner-city mothers could no longer cope with the low-wage labor market and take care of the children. Rather than leave them with an abusive father or stepfather, the children were placed with a grandmother or other relative.[121]

Chapter 2 points out that most welfare recipients and leavers are in and out of the labor market and therefore unlikely to qualify for UI – either the minimum hours and earnings requirements, given the instability of their jobs, or the "nonmonetary" requirements."[122] Although most of those who leave welfare to work may potentially meet the UI minimum monetary eligibility, they are likely to lose it over time, and those who lose their job in the first year are unlikely to meet the UI monetary eligibility.[123] Even these estimates may be overly optimistic. From 1980 to 2003, there has been a significant decline in the percentage of unemployed high school dropouts receiving UI, from 30 percent to 21 percent, and they are even less likely to benefit from UI during economic recessions.[124] Moreover, many mothers have "involuntary" reasons for leaving a job, that is, quitting a job because of child care and other family responsibilities and transportation difficulties.[125] In other words, for these women, welfare is the equivalent of unemployment compensation. In the past, when jobs disappeared or child care broke down, former recipients would return to welfare. Now, with the time limits, this option will no longer be available.

The Dilemmas of Child Care for Low-Wage Workers

Given the characteristics of the low-wage labor market, especially its non-standard work, child care becomes a major issue for the low-wage working mothers, particularly its effects on the health and well-being of the children,

[121] N. Bernstein (2002). "Side Effect of Welfare Law: The No-Parent Family," New York Times, July 29, p. 1.
[122] C. Gustafson & P. Levine (1998). "Less-Skilled Workers, Welfare Reform, and the Unemployment Insurance System" (NBER Working Paper W6489, National Bureau of Economic Research, Cambridge, Mass., March 1998); D. Maranville (2002). "Workplace Mythologies and Unemployment Insurance: Exit, Voice, and Exhausting All Reasonable Alternatives to Quitting" (unpublished manuscript); G. Lester (2004). "In Defense of Paid Leave" (unpublished manuscript, UCLA Law School, September 17); G. Lester (2001). Unemployment Insurance and Wealth Redistribution. 49 UCLA L. Rev. 335; L. Williams (1999). "Unemployment Insurance and Low-Wage Work." In J. F. Handler & L. White (Eds.), Hard Labor: Women and Work in the Post-Welfare Era. Armonk, N.Y.: M. E. Sharpe, chap. 8.
[123] A. Rangarajan & C. Razafindrakoto (2004). "Unemployment Insurance as a Potential Safety Net for TANF Leavers: Evidence from Five States" (Mathematica Policy Research, Inc., Washington, D.C.), pp. 1–45.
[124] P. Levine (2005). "Unemployment Insurance over the Business Cycle: Does It Meet Workers' Needs?" (Department of Economics, Wellesley College, April).
[125] Gustafson & Levine (1998), p. 3. In 1995, an individual working half-time for twenty-six weeks at $6 per hour meets the eligibility requirements in forty-seven states, p. 6.

and the ability of the family support their children. In Chapter 3, in the discussion of the welfare state, we describe the use and costs of child care and the various programs for child care assistance. Here, we are concerned not only with the availability and cost of child care but also the quality and the effect on family health and well-being.

The crisis in child care – especially for low-wage workers – cannot be overemphasized. Millions of infants, children, and adolescents are at high risk of being compromised both developmentally and in health because of mediocre child care.[126] The proportion of women with infants in the paid labor force increased from 31 percent to 59 percent between 1976 and 1998. More than half (51%) the women have infants younger than 1 year, and 57 percent of women with children younger than 3 are now in the paid labor force.[127] Currently, 75 percent of all children younger than age 5 are in child care while their mothers are working.[128] The current welfare reform requires mothers of young children – in some cases, three-month-old infants – to enter the paid labor force.

First, we consider how the mothers are coping, and then we turn to the issues for the children. The story of the challenges that mothers face on a daily basis – balancing shifting job schedules; being on-call; working overtime, evenings, and weekends, often on short notice; and facing multiple child care arrangements that have to be made – is simply wrenching. We present the data on the toll that these schedules take on the families, the lack of available child care subsidies, and conclude with evidence on the impact that low-wage work and poor child care have on the well-being of the children.

The Use of Child Care

More than 70 percent of all children younger than age 5 of working mothers are cared for by someone other than the parents.[129] The higher the income, the more likely the children – particularly three- and four-year-olds – will be in center-based care. Relative care is more frequently used by low-income

[126] L. Dodson, T. Manuel, & E. Bravo (2002). "Keeping Jobs and Raising Families in Low-Income America: It Just Doesn't Work" (a report of the Across the Boundaries Project, Radcliffe Public Policy Center and 9to5 National Association of Working Women, Radcliffe Institute for Advanced Study, Harvard University), pp. 10–11.

[127] J. Bromer & J. Henly (2004). "Child Care as Family Support? Caregiving Practices across Child Care Provider Types." *Children and Youth Services Review*, 26, 941–964.

[128] J. R. Henly & S. Lambert (2005). "Nonstandard work and child care needs of low-income parents" in S. M. Bianchi, L. M. Casper, & R. B. King (Eds.), *Work, Family, Health, and Well-Being*. Lawrence Erlbaum Associates, Inc.: Mahwah, N.J., pp. 473–92.

[129] J. Capizzano & G. Adams (2003). "Children in Low-Income Families Are Less Likely to be in Center-Based Child Care: Snapshots of America's Families" (Urban Institute, Washington, D.C.), p. 1. "Low income" is defined as 200 percent of the federal poverty line; "high income" is above 200 percent of the federal poverty line.

mothers of infants and toddlers.[130] In Table 6–1, we show the primary child care arrangements of preschoolers of employed mothers. For all working mothers, the most common arrangement is informal care. Only 23 percent of working mothers rely on day care centers (which include nursery, preschool, and Head Start). Women in non–day shift are least likely to use formalized childcare. Poor working mothers rely heavily on relatives or siblings (27%) and grandparents (25%). Similarly, mothers that received TANF (mostly single) rely heavily on grandparents (50%). In other words, for most poor women, child care in formal, structured, and supervised settings such as day care centers is the exception. For working mothers with grade-school children, after-school arrangements also depend mostly on informal care (parent, grandparent, sibling) with an increasing number of children in self-care (19%).[131] The 2002 National Survey of American Families finds similar results. For low-income (i.e., below 200% of the poverty threshold) working mothers with children younger than 5, only 25 percent are in center-based care (compared with 31% for higher-income working mothers), 11 percent are in family child care, 3.5 percent are cared by a nanny/babysitter, 29.5 percent by a relative (compared with 24% for higher-income working mothers), and 31 percent by a parent/other.[132]

The Costs of Child Care

A study by the Children's Defense Fund found that "the average annual cost for a one year-old in a child care center exceeds $4,750 in almost two-thirds of the 47 cities surveyed."[133] For an infant, the annual cost of center care was even higher, exceeding $5,500 in most cities. The annual cost of family child care, while lower, was still more than $4,500 per year of a four-year-old in about half the cities. There were considerable variations among the states. It was $3,900 in Arkansas and $12,978 in Massachusetts. For low-income families, even devoting 10 percent of their income to child care would cover less than half the cost of center care in most cities.[134]

Based on the 1999 National Survey of America's Families (NSAF), Linda Giannarelli and James Barsimantov found that 60 percent of working families with children younger than age 5 paid for child care at an average of $325 per

---

[130] Ibid.
[131] http://www.census.gov/population/www/socdemo/child/ppl-168.html.
[132] Capizzano & Adams (2003).
[133] K. Schulman (2000). "The High Costs of Child Care Puts Quality Care Out of Reach for Many Families" (issue brief, Children's Defense Fund, Washington, D.C.), p. 6.
[134] Ibid. In Los Angeles County, poor families (earning less than $24,000 per year) paid an average of $3,705 a year for full-time child care. Institute for the Study of Homelessness and Poverty (July 28, 2005), commenting on a report by the RAND Corporation, "Patterns of Child Care Use for Preschoolers in Los Angeles County."

Table 6-1. *Primary child care arrangements for preschoolers of employed mothers: spring 1999*[a]

	Parent	Grandparent	Relative or sibling	Day care center[b]	Family day care	Other nonrelative	School	No regular arrangement
All	22.5	21.7	16.8	23.1	11.4	9.7	2.8	4.8
WORK STATUS								
Full time	17.4	22.3	17.6	26.4	13.6	10.2	2.6	3.3
Part time	32.4	20.4	15	16.4	7.1	8.8	3.1	7.8
MARITAL STATUS								
Married	26.2	18.1	14	22.9	12.2	9.9	2.7	5.5
Widowed, separated, divorced	13.7	25.7	19.8	24.6	13.1	7.8	3.9	3
Never married	12.1	34.1	26.8	22.4	7.3	10.2	2.5	2.9
SHIFT								
Day shift	16.7	21.1	16	28.3	14	9.9	2.8	3.3
Nonday shift	32.9	22.6	18.1	13.6	6.7	9.4	2.7	7.6
Below poverty line	19	24.8	26.8	19.7	7.3	12	2.8	4.9
Received TANF	4.7	50	19.2	23	9.5	8.5	3.3	0

[a] Because of multiple arrangements, percentages may exceed 100.
[b] Includes nursery, preschool, and Head Start.
Source: U.S. Census Bureau. Survey of Income and Program Participation, 1999 Panel, Wave 10.

month, which was 10 percent of their total earnings.[135] For low-earning families (below 200% of the poverty threshold), 51 percent paid for child care at an average monthly cost of $237, which was 17 percent of their total earnings. Single-parent families paid 19 percent of their earnings for child care. Among families with earnings below the poverty threshold, a majority of the families cannot afford paid child care. Only 34 percent paid for child care, at an average cost of $190 per month, which was 23 percent of their earnings.[136] Although low-earning families may qualify for child care subsidies, the federal Child Care and Development Fund covers only about 15 percent of all eligible children. Again, there are wide state variations. In New Jersey, former welfare recipients now working pay between $125 and $150 a week, which is at least 40 percent of their take-home pay.[137] In California, child care costs average $373 per month; for families with incomes below the state median, this averages about 24 percent of earnings.[138] In Los Angeles, where 45 percent of all children between the ages 0 to 5 live in families with annual incomes below $24,000, the percent of annual income required to pay average full-time child care would be 24 percent. Yet, only 22 percent of these families receive some assistance. Therefore, a majority of mothers in such families do not work, and those who do rely mainly on relative care.[139]

Availability of Child Care Resources

For poor families, the costs of child care could be quite prohibitive unless they receive financial assistance. Low-income mothers who receive child care assistance are more likely to work. What child care resources are available to these mothers? When we take into account all the public policies that provide child care assistance, only a small fraction of eligible families actually receive them. As discussed in Chapter 3, in 1996, with the passage of PRWORA, Congress increased federal child care subsidies and authorized the states to use both federal and state TANF funds for child care.[140] Under the Child Care and Development Fund (CCDF), funds are made available to the states to provide child care assistance to TANF families, families who have left welfare, and

---

[135] L. Giannarelli & J. Barsimantov (2000). "Child Care Expenses of America's Families" (Occasional Paper No. 40, Urban Institute, Washington, D.C.), p. 5.

[136] Ibid., p. 9.

[137] D. Terry (2000). "U.S. Child Poverty Rate Fell as Economy Grew, but Is above 1979 Level," New York Times, August 11, p. A10.

[138] M. O'Brien-Strain, L. Moyé, & F. Sonenstein (2003). "Arranging and Paying for Child Care" (Public Policy Institute of California), p. 32.

[139] L. Chyu, A. Pebley, & S. Lara-Cinisomo (2005). "Patterns of Child Care Use for Preschoolers in Los Angeles County" (RAND Corp., Santa Monica, Calif.), pp. 1–56.

[140] J. Mezey (2004). "Child Care Programs Help Parents Find and Keep Jobs: Funding Shortfalls Leave Many Families without Assistance" (Center for Law & Social Policy, Washington, D.C., Feb. 10), p. 2.

other low-income working families.[141] Child care subsidies were to be made available to non-TANF families as well. Indeed, in fiscal 2000, most families (about 80%) receiving child care subsidies were not on welfare.[142] Recipients of CCDF must have incomes below 85 percent of the state median income,[143] children must be younger than 13, and the parents must either be working or in training programs, or the families must be in need of child protection services. In general, funds cannot be used to construct new facilities.[144] In fiscal year 2000, CCDF federal funds amounted to $5.1 billion; there was an additional $1.9 billion in state matching MOE and transfer funds. According to HHS, states also provided direct child care services under TANF in the amount of $1 billion. Wolfe and Scrivner estimate that approximately 18 percent of all four-year-olds received child care supports.[145]

State funding also increased during this period, although three-quarters of the growth came from federal dollars.[146] With the increase in resources, more families received child care assistance and the states undertook various initiatives aimed at improving the quality of care – training and educating teachers, increasing compensation for teachers who undertook training and education and remained in the field, and increasing provider payments.[147] In 1998–99, practically all (forty-five) states had prekindergarten programs, serving nearly seven hundred twenty-five thousand children, at a cost of approximately $1.7 billion. Still, many eligible children are not served.[148]

In California, 46 percent of poor families received some assistance in paying for child care.[149] But child care assistance appears to augment child care expenditures rather than decrease them. That is, low-income working families pay about the same amount of child care with or without assistance – on average, $277 per month because families who receive assistance are more likely to use structured care settings. However, it could be that assistance is more closely tied to structured settings (e.g., Head Start).[150]

Even though the number of children receiving child care assistance increased from 1 million to more than 2 million, between 1996 and 2001, federal and state funds could not meet the demand – most federally eligible children did not receive assistance. The Children's Defense Fund estimates

[141] B. Wolfe & S. Scrivner (2003). "Providing Universal Preschool for Four-Year Olds." In I. V. Sawhill (Ed.), *One Percent for the Kids: New Policies, Brighter Futures for America's Children*. Washington, D.C.: Brookings Institution Press, p. 119.

[142] Ibid.

[143] Ibid. This would vary from $16,000, for a family of three in Wyoming, to $39,000 in Connecticut.

[144] Ibid.   [145] Ibid.

[146] Mezey (2004), p. 2.   [147] Ibid.

[148] Children's Defense Fund (2003). "Prekindergarten Initiatives: Efforts to Help Children Enter School Ready to Succeed. 2003 Key Facts," p. 164.

[149] O'Brien-Strain, Moyé, & Sonenstein (2003), pp. vii–viii.

[150] Ibid., pp. 35–36.

that approximately 16 million children younger than age 13 in low-income families may need child care assistance, but only 2.2 million receive help from the Child Care and Development Block Grant (CCDBG).[151]

Moreover, with the appropriations bill of 2004, child care funds were set at the same level of funding as of 2002, resulting in a projected decline of 200,000 children receiving child care subsidies.[152] In the meantime, with states facing budget deficits of between $70 billion and $85 billion, cuts are being made in child care, early education, and school-age programs. Programs and staff designed to monitor quality have also been reduced.[153] Programs for infants and toddlers, such as Early Head Start and First Start, have been cut back as well as prekindergarten programs and programs for school-age children. Lower proportions of children from low-income families participate in these programs.[154] "Two-fifths of low-income working parents have significant problems finding care beyond school hours (after school, summer, vacations, or other school closing days) for their school-age children."[155]

According to the Children's Defense Fund, a number of these cuts are large.[156] In Ohio, it was projected that 18,500 children will lose their child care assistance and 30,000 in Connecticut. In most states, the TANF "reserves" have been exhausted, including funds to be used for child care. As a consequence, it is expected that at least half the states would have to cut back child care funding.[157] There are waiting lists for child care in more than a third of the states; "many lists have tens of thousands of children," more than 200,000 in California, 48,000 in Florida, 22,000 in Georgia, 17,000 in Massachusetts, and 38,000 in New York City.[158] Moreover, waiting lists are likely to underestimate the need "because many families are denied assistance or discouraged out of the system by a lack of information or perceived application difficulties." In a study of low-income families in a South Bronx neighborhood in New York

---

[151] Children's Defense Fund (2005). "Child Care Basics." (Children's Defense Fund Issue Basics: April 2005, Washington, D.C.). See also Ewen & K. Hart (2003). "State Budget Cuts Create a Growing Child Care Crisis for Low-Income Working Families" (Children's Defense Fund, Washington, D.C., March), p. 10.

[152] Ibid., p. 1.   [153] Ibid., p. 7.

[154] Ibid., pp. 7–8. "Only 44 percent of children ages three to five and not yet in kindergarten who are in families with income below $15,000 a year are participating in prekindergarten programs, compared with 71% of children in families with incomes of $75,000 or more." "School-age children living in families below the poverty line are one-third as likely as children living in families at or above 200 percent of the poverty line to participate in at least one enrichment activity after school" (p. 8).

[155] Ibid., p. 8.

[156] Ibid., p. 2. For example, Michigan cut programs by $36.2 million, North Carolina by $27.3 million, and a number of states were not able to provide state matching funds to draw on the federal CCDBG funds.

[157] Ibid., p. 3.

[158] Ibid., p. 4; M. Meyers & S. Gatenio (2003). "Early Education and Care in New York City" (paper presented at a conference on New York City and the Welfare State, Russell Sage Foundation, New York), p. 11.

City, only a little more than a third (37%) of families who reported needing child care and appeared to be eligible had applied and been approved; 38 percent never applied because of lack of information, and 25 percent applied and were denied assistance or never heard back from the agency.[159] Several states have lowered income eligibility; others have restricted child care assistance only to families who are or have been on welfare.[160] Rates for child care providers have also been reduced despite the fact that "more than half of the states fail to set rates that reflect at least the 75th percentile of the current cost of child care . . ." and co-payments have been increased.[161]

Navigating the child care subsidy system can be quite complex and discourage families from applying or retaining subsidies.[162] Although some local welfare offices may facilitate the application and retention of child care subsidies, others can set complex administrative barriers. Parents who face other employment barriers (e.g., language, transportation) may experience greater difficulties in accessing and retaining child care subsidies.[163] Requiring working parents to make in-person visits to the appropriate offices, which are generally open only during working hours, also discourages application. Having to recertify eligibility periodically (usually every six months) may undermine the stability of child care.[164]

Under the Bush administration's proposed budget, child care funding will be frozen through 2009, thus preventing the states from maintaining their current levels. Currently, only about 15 percent of children eligible under the federal rules receive assistance. Families who are excluded often have to rely on poor quality care, pay a large proportion of their income for care, or both.[165] It is argued that the federal budget estimates of the number of children who will lose child care funds are too low because they fail to consider the declining state TANF funds. Both the OMB and the Congressional Budget Office project that state TANF spending will decrease over the next five years. At the current rate, most states will have spent down their TANF reserves within two years.[166] The Congressional Budget Office estimates that the number of children receiving funds will decline by 447,000 by fiscal year 2009.[167] The proposed increase in the work requirements will increase the demand for child care. The administration proposes to add an additional $1 billion for child care funding over the next five years, but this will not be sufficient to meet the demand.[168]

---

[159] Ibid., pp. 11–12.

[160] Ewen & Hart (2003), p. 5.

[161] Ibid., pp. 5–6.

[162] G. Adams, K. Snyder, & J. R. Sandfort (2002). "Getting and Retaining Child Care Assistance: How Policy and Practice Influence Families' Experiences" (Urban Institute, Washington D.C.), pp. 1–129.

[163] Ibid., p. 80.

[164] Ibid., p. 82.

[165] Mezey (2004), p. 1.

[166] Ibid., p. 2.

[167] Ibid., p. 2.

[168] Ibid., p. 3.

Head Start is currently the largest national program for low-income preschoolers.[169] It was started in 1965 and has now served millions of children. Most centers are part-day for the entire school year, although in a number of states, funds are used to extend services for the full day, full year. The rules require that 90 percent of the children be from TANF families or families with incomes below the poverty line. Thus, a large group of children is not served.[170] In fiscal year 2001, federal funding amounted to $6 billion, with the states adding an additional $200 million. Approximately 857,664 children were served (2000), or about 60 percent of the three- to four-year-olds who were eligible.[171] In fiscal year 2002, federal funding for Head Start was $6.5 billion, serving approximately 915,000 children.

Federal grants are also provided under the Individual with Disabilities Education Act (IDEA) for preschool children with disabilities and other special needs; in 2000–1, approximately 600,000 children were served, at a cost of approximately $390 million. Title I funds, in the amount of approximately $200 million (fiscal year 2001), were used for prekindergarten programs for high-priority school districts to help children succeed in school.[172] Under Title I of the Elementary and Secondary Education Act (ESEA), states can allocate a portion of federal funds to preschool programs. In 1999–2000, states spent approximately $407 million on preschool, which was less than 10 percent of their ESEA grants. Larger districts were more likely to spend ESEA money on preschoolers than smaller districts. Most districts (90%) set a minimum age of three to four years old. The GAO estimates that about 8 percent of preschoolers received some funds.[173] In sum, most federal and state policies and programs providing child care assistance to low-income families, while substantial, reach only a fraction of all eligible children, leaving a considerable gap in the ability of poor working families to reduce the relatively high costs of child care they incur.

Caring for Children with Health Problems

Children growing up in poor families are much more likely to experience various health problems, which, in turn, affect the ability of the parents to obtain or maintain adequate care for them.[174] In the fragile families study, 32 percent of the mothers reported disruption in work or school because of a

---

[169] Wolfe & Scrivner (2003), chap. 7, pp. 113–35.

[170] Ibid., p. 117.

[171] Ibid., pp. 118–19. The eligibility estimate is from the Children's Defense Fund.

[172] Children's Defense Fund (2003), p. 163, citing HHS, Head Start Bureau, 2002, U.S. Department of Education, 2001, 2002 data.

[173] Wolfe & Scrivner (2003), p. 120.

[174] J. Brooks-Gunn & G. Duncan (1997). "The Effects of Poverty on Children." *The Future of Children: Children and Poverty* 7(2): 55–71.

child's illness.[175] Children in poor families are also more likely to suffer from chronic illnesses and disabilities such as mental retardation, heart problems, poor hearing, and digestive disorders.[176] They too have adverse effects on the ability of single mothers to work (but less so for married mothers).[177] The National Survey of Children with Special Health Care Needs[178] estimates that 12.8 percent of all children have special health care needs, which are about the same across all income groups. Yet, the severity of the conditions is higher for poor children – 37 percent of children in poor families, compared with 16 percent of children in families with incomes of 400 percent of the poverty threshold or more.[179] Moreover, 40 percent of all children living in poverty need emotional, behavioral, or developmental services, compared with 23 percent of children in higher-income families.[180] Undoubtedly, it is much more difficult to arrange appropriate child care for such children. In fact, poor children with special health needs are less likely to obtain needed health and family support services. A study of welfare recipients found that 20 percent of the households had at least one child with chronic health conditions or disability, and about 9 percent of the households had a child with severe illness or disability.[181] The same study found that almost half the mothers indicated that care of the child reduced their ability to work[182] and that the families incurred considerable out-of-pocket costs, which increased the risk and depth of poverty.[183] Therefore, when these families qualify and receive SSI, it reduces the risk considerably.

Quality care and early education has been shown to help both the parents and children with disabilities or special needs. Nevertheless, according to a recent national study by the Research Council of the National Academy of Sciences, it is extremely difficult for families to find quality care for children with disabilities and other special needs. Child care centers are unwilling to accept such children. There are problems of transportation and coordination among services, and the general shortage of trained providers.[184] Care for

---

[175] M. L. Usdansky & D. A. Wolf (2005). "A Routine Juggling Act: Managing Child Care and Employment" (Working Paper No. 05–18-FF, Center for Research on Child Wellbeing, Princeton, N.J.), p. 6.

[176] J. Currie (2005). "Health Disparities and Gaps in School Readiness." *Future of Children* 15(1): 121.

[177] E. T. Powers (2003). "Children's Health and Maternal Work Activity." *Journal of Human Resources* 38 (3): 522–56.

[178] U.S. Department of Health and Human Services; Health Resources and Services Administration; Maternal and Child Health Bureau (2004). *The National Survey of Children with Special Health Care Needs Chartbook 2001.* Rockville, Md., U.S. Department of Health and Human Services.

[179] Ibid., p. 5.   [180] Ibid., p. 3.

[181] A. Lukemeyer, M. Meyers, & T. Smeeding (2000). "Expensive Children in Poor Families: Out-of-Pocket Expenditures for the Care of Disabled and Chronically Ill Children in Welfare Families." *Journal of Marriage and the Family* 62: 399–415.

[182] Ibid., p. 407.   [183] Ibid., p. 410.

[184] Children's Defense Fund (2003). "Children with Disabilities and Other Special Needs: Opportunities to Participate in Quality Programs Must Be Expanded: 2003 Key Facts," citing Shonkoff & Phillips (Eds.) (2000).

infants and toddlers with disabilities or other special needs are in "extremely short supply." Parents of children with emotional or behavioral problems are twenty times more likely to report that their caregivers had quit. In a national survey of families with children with disabilities, one-fifth reported that someone in the family either had to quit work or reduce hours to take care of the child. Many low-income workers lack sick leave, paid leave, or flexible work options.[185]

There are two early childhood federal programs under IDEA. The Preschool Grants Program (1981) provides grants to states for services for children with disabilities, ages 3–5. Since fiscal year 1992, all states participate. In 2000–2001, nearly 600,000 children received services. Services can be provided in child care settings. Infants and toddlers (birth through third birthday) can receive services under the Grants to Infants and Families (Early Intervention) Program (1986). Programs are in all states, and in 2000–2001, about 231,000 children were served, at a cost of $417 million (FY 2002). Services can be provided in the child's home or a child care setting if the parents work outside the home. In addition, Head Start programs are required to allocate 10 percent of their funding for children with special needs. In 2000–2001, 13 percent of Head Start children received services. In addition, several states provide services – for example, children with special needs will have priority for child care assistance. The CCDBG gives states the option of extending eligibility for child care assistance beyond the usual age limit of 13; in several states, eligibility can extend to ages 19 and 21. Four-fifths of states offer higher reimbursement rates for providers caring for children with special needs; several states exempt the parents from co-payments. And in many states, prekindergarten programs target children with special needs.[186]

"It's Just Not Working"

Caring for children while working in the low-wage market presents a daunting challenge to the parents, especially single mothers. In the Radcliffe–9to5 National Association of Working Women Study, interviews with parents, teachers, and employers described the difficulties of meeting child care needs when trying to work in the low-wage labor market.[187] "Parents described child

---

[185] Ibid., pp. 113–14.   [186] Ibid., pp. 114–15
[187] Dodson, Manuel, & Bravo (2002). This was a two-year study of work and family conflicts for low-income working parents, usually mothers, conducted in Milwaukee, Denver, and Boston. Qualitative data were from parents, teachers, and child care providers working in low-income neighborhoods and employers who hire and supervise entry-level employees. The study extended over eighteen months and involved nearly 350 people in interviews and focus groups, in homes, workplaces, schools, churches, and community centers. The parents had annual income of less than 200 percent of the poverty line.

care not so much as a routine but as an orchestra, a complicated ever-changing array of age-specific arrangements."[188] Many parents do not have arrangements that cover their entire working and commuting day. Above all else, the high cost leads many to create fragmented patchworks of less-expensive informal care – which often tend to break down, causing parents to miss more work and to be late more often. Difficulties of meeting care needs, especially those with special care needs such as asthma, attention deficit hyperactivity disorder (ADHD), and learning disabilities – were a major theme among all groups.

Many parents and teachers emphasized the importance of supervision for preteens and adolescents. Yet, among various arrangements, the oldest child (some cases, younger than ten) would watch younger children for two evenings per week. A child as young as seven might be alone for almost an hour each morning before walking alone to the corner to catch the school bus. Parents on nonstandard schedules are more likely to be present when children come home from school (although they may be asleep). If not at home, then most children are cared for by other children, but a number are left alone.[189]

In this study, half of the participating parents had left welfare three or more years earlier or had never received welfare. Thus, ninety-seven families had higher hourly wages than those who have left welfare. Also, the median education level was higher than the median education level for welfare recipients nationally. About 40 percent were earning more than $10 per hour. Still, despite a relatively high hourly wage, most incomes were well below 200 percent of poverty line. Most single mothers have low annual incomes because many (almost 40 percent) work less than full time (37.5 hours per week). And, there is a high incidence of "churning" or job changing.[190]

The jobs that the parents held were administrative assistant, data entry clerk, day care teacher, factory or light manufacturing, fast-food server, and home health aide. Most parents liked having a job; they liked the paycheck and being role models. However, most said that the jobs failed to provide either minimal economic security or any real chance to advance economically or socially. Several parents reduced their hours or changed jobs because the costs of working exceeded any improvement in earnings. Working the first twenty hours provides a greater economic gain than adding additional hours because of the increased costs of child care and sometimes the loss of eligibility for food stamps, Medicaid, and public housing.[191]

Family and child care needs were cited as the most frequent reason for changing jobs or working less than full time.[192] Job turnover rates (combined

---

[188] Ibid., p. 7.
[189] Presser (2003), pp. 194–96. Presser thinks that parents may be reluctant to admit that their children are left alone after school.
[190] Dodson, Manuel, & Bravo (2002), p. 12.   [191] Ibid., p. 14.
[192] Ibid., p. 16.

quitting, firings, layoffs, job disappearance) can be as high as 40 percent annually among low-wage workers and are particularly high for women and workers of color. Teachers reported that children were anxious about their parents changing jobs schedules. It was also frustrating to teachers and school administrators who had to keep track of parents.[193]

Although most mothers said that their child care arrangements were acceptable (which is consistent with other research), a different story emerged from the in-depth interviews. There was great concern about the degree of trust or lack of trust in providers, especially with public and nonrelative providers. There were stories about overcrowded or neglectful centers of "voucher" families. More than half (52%) of the parents had no regular access to a car. Thus, in addition to expense, a major concern was proximity to child care and work. There was concern about the difficulty in reaching a child in case of an emergency. Several were concerned about the quality of child care as a reason for seeking a different, more conveniently located job. Child care arrangements were most successful (extensive, flexible, and trustworthy) with a co-parent or several close-kin relatives (most often grandparents), although there were several stories about neglectful relatives who took care of children only out of a sense of obligation.[194]

With the instability of both work and child care arrangements, for many families, no two weekdays had exactly the same child care routines.[195] Most parents described ongoing child care problems as the most common cause of conflicts and anxiety at work and often resulted in some kind of work sanction. Everyone – parents, teachers, and employers – expressed frustration about the instability of child care arrangements. Teachers and employers spoke of "dysfunctional families" – kids not getting proper supervision at home. Teachers complained about the condition of the children in school – sleepy, missed homework, too tired and unprepared to succeed in school, often sick, and falling behind academically – as well as the difficulty of scheduling appointments with parents and the lack of participation of parents in school activities. Teachers would see parents only when a child is in trouble.[196] The parents agreed on the importance of participating in schools and various educational activities, but only a few could manage to do so. When parents had to rely on older siblings (usually a daughter), there would be conflicts when they want to participate in school activities or get jobs. The mothers were constantly anxious about just getting by every day (e.g., no diapers so they could not take the child to day care). There was the difficulty of communicating the value of work to their children when they remain so poor.[197] Child care

---

[193] Ibid., p. 14.   [194] Ibid., p. 8.

[195] Forty percent of California children in care have two or more different arrangements per week; this percentage increased to 60 percent for single mothers. "Low-income working families and families combining welfare and work are the most likely to rely on multiple arrangements for very young children (under age 3)" (O'Brien-Strain, Moyé, & Sonenstein [2003], p. 26).

[196] Dodson, Manuel, & Bravo (2002), p. 9.   [197] Ibid., p. 17.

workers – themselves low-wage workers – changed jobs frequently and could not afford child care; several admitted they would not put their child in their center. Many children were pulled out of centers and put into some sort of kin-care when parents could not make the payments. In the study, 58 percent paid $50 or less per week and 22 percent between $50 and $100 per week. Parents define "flexibility at work" as being able to bring the child to the workplace. Often the children help out, copying documents, delivering files, cleaning offices, or sitting in fast-food restaurants and outside retail stores in malls waiting for their mothers to finish their work.[198]

The responsiveness of employers to child care and other family issues varied. Some employers tried to treat the workplace as a source of support, and workers valued this when looking for a job. However, this was a controversial topic among employers.[199] Employers complained that the unreliability and complexity of entry-level employees' child care can be a significant impediment to conducting business. Parents would have to leave work abruptly, refuse to accept scheduling changes, or not show up on a given day when child care broke down. Frequent phone calls had to be made during working hours to check on child care, arrange for changes, and so forth. Employers complained about the way schools would change schedules without apparent regard for the parents' work schedules,[200] and the use of sanctions was common. Nearly half of the respondents suffered job losses or lost wages, were denied promotions, or received written or verbal warnings as a result of trying to meet family needs. They felt that there was prejudice in terms of race and single mothers.[201]

All agreed on the need for parents to spend more time monitoring their children's nonschool lives. Child development experts say that the quality of children's care and opportunity to spend time building attachments to their parents is critical to lifelong well-being. Yet, "some parents were unable to spend more than a few waking hours each day with their children and many others might make it home in the evenings but after long days and long bus rides home have 'just enough to make dinner and crawl into bed.'"[202]

Child care difficulties increased considerably when there were children with special needs.[203] In the Radcliff–9to5 study, of the 187 children under the direct responsibility of the mother, 27 percent were diagnosed as having asthma,[204] 11 percent ADHD, and 18 percent with a learning disability. Others

---

[198] Ibid., p. 18.
[199] Ibid., p. 15.
[200] Ibid., p. 10.
[201] Ibid., p. 15.
[202] Ibid., p. 15.
[203] Ibid., p. 10.
[204] Nationally, the prevalence of asthma has risen dramatically over the past twenty years, but some studies suggest that it is still underdiagnosed, especially in the inner city. Asthma usually takes more than one health care visit to diagnose; thus rates are higher for children who are insured. M. Inkelas et al. (2003). "The Health of Young Children in California" (UCLA Center for Health Policy Research), pp. 16–17. A recent study showed that 50 percent of children who entered shelters in New York City had asthma ("Study Shows 50% of Children Enter Shelters with Asthma," *New York Times*, March 2, 2004).

had ongoing health issues – lead paint poisoning (3%); emotional problems, such as depression (14%); conflicts at school (25%); emotionally withdrawn (7%).

The overall higher prevalence of illness can present major challenges for families with limited resources. The quality and quantity of attention received by these children will have lifelong effects.[205] Caring for children with special needs is especially time consuming. Many of these children need ongoing specialized medical and educational attention, which can be physically and emotionally demanding on a caretaker, particularly the mother. There can be long waits, transportation hurdles, and lost work days.[206] Each health problem has its own rhythm, demands, and complexity. Parents are expected to attend meetings and follow-up appointments. ADHD children are particularly in need of dependable routines to build more focus and self-control. With asthma, there are often frequent episodes that sometimes require emergency intervention. Teachers, child care providers, nurses, and after-school teachers sometimes risk a mother's job by calling repeatedly when she is a work.[207]

The conclusion of the Radcliffe–9to5 National Association study was "It's Just Not Working." It is just not possible to raise children and keep a job. Job schedules, the lack of benefits, and especially low wages undermine the nurturing of children and threaten family stability.[208] Overall, the study found a deep commitment on the part of the parents to being employed and encouraging children to pursue education and get ahead to get a better job. But this was far outweighed by concerns, frustrations, and intractable conflicts.[209]

A recent study of child care problems among low-wage working mothers came to similar conclusions. Almost half of the mothers reported that their work schedule was dictated more by the demands of the job than the needs of the child.[210] Formal centers – licensed day care, licensed family child care, and preschools – frequently do not accommodate fluctuating work schedules or schedules that start earlier or end later than conventional daytime working hours.[211] More than two-thirds of children are in various forms of home-based

---

[205] Research has shown that the primary caregivers are the ones with the greatest impact on determining outcomes, both at school and in medical institutions, and they have the major responsibility for marshalling the public resources that ill or disabled children depend on.

[206] Dodson, Manuel, & Bravo (2002), p. 11. Poor children are much more likely "almost always" or "sometimes" have their activity limited by asthma (41.3%) than children between 100 percent and 200 percent of the poverty line (21.7%) or 300 percent of the poverty line or more (22.5%); Inkelas et al. (2003), p. 19.

[207] Dodson, Manuel, & Bravo (2002), p. 12.   [208] Ibid., p. 18.

[209] Ibid., p. 19.

[210] J. Bromer & J. Henly (2004). "Child Care as Family Support? Caregiving Practices across Child Care Provider Types." *Children and Youth Services Review*, 26: 941–64; J. R. Henly & S. Lambert (2005). "Nonstandard Work and Child Care Needs of Low-Income Parents." In S. M. Bianchi, L. M. Casper, & R. B. King (Eds.), *Work, Family, Health, and Well-Being* (pp. 473–92). Mahway, N.J.: Erlbaum.

[211] Bromer & Henly (2004), pp. 946–47.

care (relatives, nonrelatives), many of which are informal and unregulated. Most infants (41%) are in home-based care, compared with 7 percent in center-based care. Many center-based care centers do not accept children younger than age 2. Centers usually would not offer additional hours, especially in the evening, and charged late fees if children were not picked up on time.[212]

On the basis of qualitative studies of retail, hospitality, shipping/transportation, and financial services in Chicago, Bromer and Henly describe the tasks of arranging child care when lower-skilled jobs are increasingly nonstandard.[213] When business was slack, the common practice was "'workload adjustments' or 'workloading,'" that is, reducing or eliminating hours instead of layoffs. Sometimes, the off time could be quite lengthy. Retailers, especially, resorted to just-in-time labor scheduling to adjust to expected consumer demand. Weekly schedules were given just two days in advance to sales associates. Some employees were on a call-in basis. The daily hours for clerks in one bank varied with the workload; shifts could be six hours or ten hours. In some jobs, workers would be hired for a specific number of days per week but the actual days would shift from week to week. These workers had to be available for seven days of the week. Employer practices included upward fluctuating hours, multiple shifts and days, fluctuating shift durations, and shifts that either began earlier or ended later than standard day time child care hours.[214]

In addition to not qualifying for various benefits (e.g., employers may require ninety days of employment for health insurance), job instability often makes child care scheduling difficult. Centers and preschool not only have fixed schedules but also require payment even when the parent is not working if she wants to keep the slot. Similar difficulties are encountered with eligibility requirements for subsidized child care as eligibility, in most states, depends on employment, and there is often a mismatch with temporary changes. Given the instability in scheduling, it is not surprising that "unpredictability and variability of parental work can translate into unstable and erratic family routines. Parents' whose jobs have unpredictable start and end times, variable hours, and evening and weekend hours may have difficulty providing consistent meals, bed times, child care arrangements, supervision, and recreational opportunities for their children." They may also lead to "burdens and conflicts that ultimately strain interpersonal relationships and threaten their stability."[215]

---

[212] Henly & Lambert (2005), p. 483.

[213] Bromer & Henly (2004); Henly & Lambert (2005).

[214] Henly & Lambert (2005), pp. 483–86. Instability also caused significant turnover. In a sample of sixty jobs, turnover rates varied from 0 percent to 500 percent; half the jobs had turnover rates higher than 50 percent. Employers consider many of the turnovers "voluntary," but many are not. Employers prefer job applicants with "open availability," that is, those who do not ask for shift preferences. Workers would sometimes feel that they had to turn down promotions to supervisory positions because of increased hours and less flexibility.

[215] J. R. Henly, H. L. Shaefer & E. Waxman (forthcoming). "Nonstandard Work Schedules: Employer-vs. Employee-Driven Flexibility in Retail Jobs." *Social Service Review.*

The instability of work required parents to "package" a "patchwork" of child care, both within and outside of the formal child care system. Limited lead time and being on-call presented the most difficulties; parents had to set up tentative, just-in-case arrangements; they relied on family, friends, and neighbors. Parents needed child care providers who were available "at the last minute," given that work schedules changed on short notice.[216] The practice was "hectic and stressful, and was not always successful."[217] Frequently, there had to be multiple caretakers for a given child. Workers used family, friends, and neighbors ("kith and kin" care), licensed and unlicensed family caregivers, centers, and preschool.[218]

> For example, a retail sales clerk was scheduled two shifts during the week: from 11 a.m. to 5 p.m., and on Friday from 4 p.m. to 9 p.m. She also worked Saturday daytime shift from 10 a.m. to 5 p.m. She needed care that started as early as 9 a.m. (to account for commuter time) and ended as late as 10 p.m. She reported that she relied on her mother – her primary caregiver – as well as her son's paternal grandmother, her sister, and her boyfriend to accommodate the week's shifts.[219]

Among several of the places studied, there were informal work supports. Supervisors would be accommodating (e.g., ignoring or excusing absences or tardiness, telephone access, days off, "cut employees slack") and coworkers would help.[220]

Informal caregivers (kith and kin) provide the most flexibility and provide more intimacy and family-like qualities to caregiving, compared with centers.[221] Many parents say they prefer the family atmosphere of home-based care.[222] However, the informal caregivers often are under constraints from their own employment.[223] A third of grandmothers who are caretakers are otherwise employed, and they are more likely to be employed when the mother is single.[224]

Multiple caregiving is especially vulnerable to breakdown. Single mothers are especially at risk because they are more likely to have lower earnings and fewer child care options.[225] For low-income families, the most frequently reported child care shortage was during nonscheduled work hours.[226] The general lack of availability of formal child care options constrains employment for low-educated, low-earning women. Between 10 and 20 percent of all nonemployed mothers with young children do not work because of lack of

---

[216] Henly & Lambert (2005), p. 484.
[218] Ibid., pp. 485–86.
[220] Ibid., p. 487.
[222] Ibid., p. 947.
[224] Presser (2003), p. 198.
[226] Ibid., p. 201.

[217] Ibid., p. 485.
[219] Ibid., p. 486.
[221] Bromer & Henly (2004).
[223] Ibid., p. 957.
[225] Ibid., p. 199.

child care (availability as well as affordability). About 20 percent to 25 percent say that they would work more if there were not child care constraints. The estimates are higher for low-educated mothers working nonschedule shifts.[227]

The Quality of Child Care

A four-state study of children care concluded "child care at most centers in the United States is poor to mediocre, with almost half of the infants and toddlers in rooms having less than minimal quality."[228] The care in at least 40 percent of the rooms for infants and toddlers was "less than minimal quality"; good quality care was in only 8 percent (12) of the rooms. Less than minimal quality included lack of basic sanitary conditions for diapering and feeding, exposure to safety problems, lack of a warm, supportive relationship with adults, and lack of learning opportunities.[229] The Children's Defense Fund cites a study by the National Institute of Child Health and Human Development (NICHD) of 1,300 children – "three quarters (75 percent) of infant caregivers were not at all or only moderately stimulating of the children's cognitive development, and 20 percent were moderately or highly detached." The NICHD recommends one adult caring for no more than four infants or five toddlers or six two-year-olds. Most states allow considerably higher ratios.[230]

Many children are spending increasing time home alone, and low-income children are more likely to be in poorer and more dangerous neighborhoods. In one study of 872 welfare leavers in Arizona, almost half of the mothers with children younger than five years and 65 percent with children between six and twelve years old had no child care arrangements, not even with relatives or neighbors.[231] Based on U.S. Census data, more than 7 million children aged 5 to 14 care for themselves on a regular basis. Almost 10 percent of children aged 5 to 11 went home to an empty house during some part of the week, and 42 percent of children aged 12 to 14 spent time unsupervised.[232] Children who are engaged in constructive after-school programs have positive outcomes; yet, a majority of these children are not involved in such activities when not in school. Children left to care for themselves are at increased risk of getting

---

[227] Ibid., pp. 211–14.
[228] S. Helburn et al. (1995). "Cost, Quality, and Child Outcomes in Child Care Centers" (executive summary, University of Colorado, Denver).
[229] Children's Defense Fund (2003). "Infants and Toddlers," p. 86.
[230] Children's Defense Fund (n.d.). "Infants and Toddlers." Seventeen states allowed one adult for more than four nine-month-old children; twenty-four states allowed one adult for more than five eighteen-month old children; thirty-one states allowed on adult for more than six two-year-olds (p. 87).
[231] Dodson, Manuel, & Bravo (2002), p. 6.
[232] Children's Defense Fund (2003). "School-Age Child Care: Keeping Children Safe and Helping Them Learn while Their Families Work," p. 99.

involved in crime or becoming crime victims.[233] Yet, before- and after-school programs are in short supply. And costs are high: "Even part-time care for school-age children can total $3,500 or more per year."[234]

According to several studies, at least on some measures, the quality of informal care may be lower than with regulated formal care. Most welfare recipients would prefer formal child care arrangements, if it were available, and if they could afford it.[235] Because of the prevalence of nonstandard work, most mothers have to rely on mostly informal, multiple caregivers. In a study of 1,478 licensed, center-based child care in New York City (1998), only one offered care on a twenty-four-hour schedule, only twenty offered care during some evening and night hours, and only three offered care on weekends.[236] Scheduling is particularly difficult for single mothers. For children younger than age 5, the most common arrangement for all employed mothers is a neighbor or babysitter (family day care; 38.5%), grandparent (27%), followed by center care (25.6%). Single mothers rely more on grandparents and other relatives.[237] There was very little use of center care when mothers worked evenings or nights (7.1%) and a great deal of use of relatives when mothers worked evenings, nights, and weekends.[238] Whatever the work schedule, there was a high use of multiple caregivers for young children, but this was especially true for mothers working nonstandard schedules.[239]

Child care centers are at capacity. The Children's Defense Fund reports, "More than 50,000 babies are born in Chicago each year. Yet in 2001, there were only 438 slots for infants in child care centers and only 4,431 slots for infants in licensed child care homes in the city and surrounding suburbs. In Alameda County, California, there were approximately 21,600 children under age two living in households where all parents work, but only 6,300 slots in licensed child care centers and family care home." Similar shortages exist throughout the country.[240] As of 1998, New York City lacked child care slots for 61 percent of the children whose mothers are supposed to participate in workfare. The state comptroller estimates that the New York state will need child care for 61,000 children by the year 2001, but only 27,500 slots

---

[233] Children's Defense Fund (2003). "School-Age Child Care," p. 99. "The rate of juvenile violence is highest in the after-school hours between 3:00 p.m. and 7:00 p.m." "Teens left unsupervised at least three days a week after school were two to four times more likely than other teens to say that they had committed crimes, used drugs, and had sex, according to a 2001 survey. They were also four times more likely to have been a victim of crime."

[234] For example, in California, an estimated 2.25 million slots are needed, but the total licensed supply (758,000) meets only about one-third of the need. Children's Defense Fund (2003). "School-Age Child Care," p. 101.

[235] K. Newman (2000). *No Shame in My Game*. New York: Vintage Books.

[236] Presser (2003), p. 201.   [237] Ibid., pp. 174–78.

[238] Ibid., pp. 180–83.   [239] Ibid., pp. 186–88.

[240] Children's Defense Fund (2003). "Infants and Toddlers," p. 89.

are in the budget. There are currently 20,000 children on waiting lists for child care.[241]

As noted earlier, part of the problem of finding adequate child care assistance is due, no doubt, to the often decentralized, complex, and poorly coordinated systems, especially in large cities. Meyers and Gatenio say this about New York City: "A low income parent transitioning from welfare to work . . . might need to make three separate applications, to three different agencies, with three different eligibility criteria, as she moves from welfare-based to transitional to low-income child care assistance. Since funds are limited, especially for working families, she is quite likely to be wait-listed for assistance. This helps explain why even among employed parents, one quarter of the poorest families in the City have no child care and only 40 percent receive government assistance."[242]

Thus, working-poor mothers have to rely on informal care, mostly grandparents, siblings, and friends, which are likely to be not only more flexible, but cost less than formal care.[243] In New York City, nearly two-thirds of families use informal care by friends or relatives on a regular basis. About 20 percent arrange for care in their homes, from a sitter or nanny. And about a third use some form of formal care.[244] As the MDRC report on Job-First GAIN notes, many mothers do not pay cash for informal child care. Yet, as Katherine Newman has documented, they are expected to reciprocate through various kinds of services – child care, transportation, and shopping, all of which take time.[245] There is also the problem of unreliability – which is a significant problem in sharing transportation – especially when children are younger and the mother has to take shift work.[246]

The Effects of Child Care

Does it make a difference what kind of child care is used? A growing body of research suggests that the quality of child care significantly affects child development.[247] Following a sample of children from birth to four-and-a-half years old, the NICHD Early Child Care Research Network found that the quality of care affected the cognitive development of the children.[248] The more the caregiver offered language stimulation, the greater was the child's cognitive development. In addition, caregivers who were better trained, more educated,

---

[241] Children's Defense Fund, CDF, *New Studies Look at Status of Former Welfare Recipients* (CDF, Welfare in the States, May 27, 1998), www.childrensdefense.org/fairstart_statu, pp. 2–3.

[242] Meyers & Gatenio (2003), pp. 33–34.   [243] Dodson, Manuel, & Bravo (2002), p. 6.

[244] Meyers & Gatenio (2003), p. 18.   [245] Newman (2000).

[246] White (1999), chap. 6.

[247] NICHD Early Child Care Research Network (2003). "Does Quality of Child Care Affect Child Outcomes at Age 4 1/4?" *Developmental Psychology* 39(3): 451–69.

[248] Ibid., p. 459.

and more child centered provided higher-quality child care and thus had a positive effect on the development of the children under their care.[249] Indeed, the effect of the quality of child care on preacademic skills was as much as the effect of the quality of parenting and family poverty.[250] At the same time, the quantity of care has some adverse consequences. The more hours children spend in child care, the greater the reports by caregivers of problem behaviors. The effect of quantity on behavioral problems is greater than the effect of quality of parenting and somewhat less than family poverty.[251] Finally, the type of child care has some effects on the children as well. As the researchers point out, "children who had spent a higher proportion of their care hours in centers were especially likely to receive high ratings on externalizing problems at kindergarten age." Also, spending more of the care in centers at infancy is associated with lower preacademic skills at age $4\frac{1}{2}$, whereas spending more of the care in centers on toddlers improves preacademic skills.[252]

Turning specifically to low-income single mothers, a recent study examined the effects of differences in child care for the children who have recently left welfare for work.[253] As distinguished from previous studies, this one concentrated on low-income single mothers. The sample of single mothers was selected in 1998 shortly after the mothers entered welfare reform programs. The study was designed to answer whether early cognitive and social development varied according to center-based child care, compared with home-based care, the quality of care, and the stability of care. The study lasted five years. It consisted of interviews with the mothers, assessments of the children, and observations and interviews at center care and home-based settings for 451 families in San Francisco, San Jose (Calif.), and Tampa. The mothers were 41 percent African American, 32 percent Latina, and 24 percent white. Approximately 83 percent of the mothers were employed, with an average monthly income (both earnings and welfare) of $1,008. There were two waves of interviews – wave 1, when the mean child was two-and-a-half years old, and wave 2, when the child was approximately four years old. During wave 1, the child's baseline cognitive, language, and social-development proficiencies were assessed, and observations were conducted at the child care settings. A wide battery of child-assessment measures as well as home visits were

[249] K. A. Clarke-Stewart et al. (2002). "Do Regulable Features of Child-Care Homes Affect Children's Development?" *Early Childhood Research Quarterly* 17: 52–86.

[250] NICHD Early Child Care Research Network (2002). "Early Child Care and Children's Development Prior to School Entry: Results from the NICHD Study of Early Child Care." *American Educational Research Journal* 39(1): 133–64.

[251] Ibid., p. 154.

[252] NICHD Early Child Care Research Network (2004). "Type of Child Care and Children's Development at 54 Months." *Early Childhood Research Quarterly* 19: 225.

[253] S. Loch et al. (2004). "Child Care in Poor Communities: Early Learning Effects of Type, Quality, and Stability." *Child Development* 75 (1): 47–65.

conducted during wave 2.[254] Compared with other four-year-olds (a national Head Start evaluation), the four-year-olds had a lower proficiency on basic school readiness (e.g., ability to write one's own first name and to count aloud to twenty), and more behavioral problems were reported by their mothers.[255]

As employment increased, so did the use of nonparental child care (at least ten hours per week). By wave 2, 83 percent used child care. Center care increased from 29 percent to 40 percent, due, in part, to the increase in the age of the child. Assessments were made of the mothers' cognitive proficiency and mental health. At both waves 1 and 2, more than 40 percent of the mothers displayed depressive symptoms.[256]

As to the quality of the child care, observations were made at 158 centers (out of 196) and 136 home-based settings (out of 228) – in addition to child-staff ratios, maximum group size (as expected, child care centers had higher ratios), the physical structure, availability of appropriate learning and play materials, and the arrangement of activities were evaluated. Center-based caregivers had higher levels of education than home-based settings. The study measured the nature of the caregiver interactions – attentiveness and responsiveness, the capacity to explain misbehavior and to reason, engaging the children in problem solving, and general affect.[257]

The results were significant. On almost all cognitive measures, there were was a "strong, significant, and positive effect of participation in center-based programs...relative to children who remained with individual kith or kin providers."[258] This was true not only for those who were in center-based care for both waves but also for those who moved from home-based care to center-based care between waves 1 and 2. School readiness showed the strongest positive differences. The positive center effects held after controlling for mother's education and cognitive proficiency, children's baseline cognitive measures, the differences in the sites, and the age of the children. However, the mother's depression was associated with a higher incidence of children's social problems, a finding consistent with other studies. "Given the high proportion of mothers exhibiting depressive symptoms...the link between depression and social development provides evidence that mother's poor mental health may significantly hinder the social development of many low income children."[259] The mother's monthly income (earnings and welfare) was not related to children outcomes, when other variables were controlled. However, there were

---

[254] Ibid., pp. 48–50.   [255] Ibid., pp. 53–54.

[256] Ibid., pp. 50–51. Mental assessments were based on the Center for Epidemiologic Studies Depression Inventory. Several other measures were also used, e.g., Home Observation for Measurement of the Environment; mother's reported reading behaviors and engagement with children's activities; mother's cognitive and language proficiency.

[257] Ibid., pp. 50–52. Among other measures, the study used the Arnett Scale of Caregiver Behavior.

[258] Ibid., p. 55.   [259] Ibid., pp. 54–57.

fewer social problems when the mothers were on welfare and not working for earned income at wave 2. With mothers who had not completed high school, African American children with early social problems (wave 1) were also more likely to have social problems at wave 2. "The stability of child care had a strong and consistent positive impact on child outcomes."[260]

The study concluded: "We found a consistent, positive, and strong relationship between rates of child development in the cognitive domain and participation in center-based programs. These development effects were strongest for measures of school readiness and for children who were in a center at both Waves 1 and 2." These effects remained "sizeable even after controlling for age, ethnicity, mother's education, mother's work, and welfare status and income."[261] The quality of the child care – whether center based or home based – affected the child's cognitive and language development. Positive effects were associated with the education of caregiver; when there was less than a high school graduation, the children showed more social problems. The study, which focused on low-income mothers moving from welfare to work, "provides new evidence on the benefits of care stability and the possible negative impact of family child care homes on children's social development."[262]

Impact of Working in the Low-Wage Market on Child Development

Poor working mothers must struggle with potentially highly stressful circumstances, including working at low-paying, nonstandard, and unstable jobs; securing stable child care for their children; and attending to the socialization needs of their children. What are the effects of these and other stresses on the development of their children? In general, maternal employment that results in increased income has been shown to improve the interaction between mothers and children, especially their social and cognitive stimulation.[263] Aurora Jackson and Richard Scheines, in their longitudinal study of African American current and former welfare recipients with preschool children, attempt to explain the dynamic relationship between employment and child development.[264] They show that the mothers' employment improves their sense of self-efficacy, which, in turn, reduces depressive symptoms. Depressive symptoms negatively affect mothers' parenting, and positive mothers' parenting skills increases the children's cognitive development and reduces behavioral problems.

---

[260] Ibid., pp. 58–59. [261] Ibid., pp. 61–62.
[262] Ibid., p. 63.
[263] J. Brooks-Gunn et al. (2001). "Effects of Combining Public Assistance and Employment on Mothers and Their Young Children." *Women and Health* 32(3): 179–210.
[264] A. Jackson & R. Scheines (2005). "Single Mothers' Self-Efficacy, Parenting in the Home Environment, and Children's Development in a Two-Wave Study." *Social Work Research* 29(1): 7–20.

Studies that have looked at the transition of welfare recipients into work show mixed results. A synthesis of the results of five large-scale national welfare experiments conducted by MDRC shows that only programs that included earning supplements had modest positive effects on elementary school-age children, particularly their school's achievement.[265] Still, the authors caution that the majority of the mothers and their children "were still at risk of psychological, physical, and cognitive problems after being in the programs."[266] A similar analysis of the effects of such welfare experiments on adolescents shows that there were no positive impacts on school performance. In fact, on several measures the experimental group did worse than the control group. For younger adolescents (ages 10 to 13), "the programs lowered average school performance and increased grade repetition and receipt of special educational services."[267] Older adolescents were more likely to drop out. Even programs with income supplements did not produce better results.[268] The adverse results were especially pronounced for adolescent with younger siblings, suggesting that adolescents might be called on to assume more responsibilities at home, while actually being less supervised by their parents. However, a longitudinal survey of low-income children and their mothers shows that for preschool children, maternal employment and transition from welfare had no particular effects, positive or negative, on preschool children, but it did improve adolescents' mental health.[269] The authors speculate that "increased income may explain why adolescents' mental health improved when mothers went to work."[270]

These studies, however, do not address directly the possible negative effects of the low-wage jobs themselves. For example, for single mothers, working in low-wage and low-complexity jobs has been shown to result in a less nurturing home environment.[271] Similarly, Wen-Jui Han has shown that "maternal nonstandard work schedules in the first 3 years were significantly and negatively associated with children's cognitive outcomes, and this negative association

[265] P. A. Morris et al. (2001). "How Welfare and Work Policies Affect Children: A Synthesis of Research" (MDRC, New York).

[266] Ibid., p. 33. See also P. Morris, L. Gennetian, & G. Duncan (2005). "Effects of Welfare and Employment Policies on Young Children: New Findings on Policy Experiments Conducted in the Early 1990s." *Social Policy Report* 19(11). Society for Research in Child Development: "Even with the potential benefits offered by these programs [increasing income and center-based child care], these children in low-income families continue to be at risk for academic failure" (p. 12).

[267] L. A. Gennetian et al. (2004). "How Welfare Policies Affect Adolescents' School Outcomes: A Synthesis of Evidence from Experimental Studies." *Journal of Research on Adolescence* 14(4): 411.

[268] Ibid., p. 412.

[269] P. L. Chase-Lansdale et al. (2003). "Mothers' Transition from Welfare to Work and the Well-Being of Preschoolers and Adolescents." *Science* 299: 1548–52.

[270] Ibid., p. 1550.

[271] E. G. Menaghan, L. Kowaleski-Jones, & F. L. Mott (1997). "The Intergenerational Costs of Parental Social Stressors: Academic and Social Difficulties in Early Adolescence for Children of Young Mothers." *Journal of Health and Social Behavior* 38(1): 72–86.

was stronger if mothers started working nonstandard hours in the 1st year of the child's life."[272] One mitigating factor seems to be centered-based child care.[273] Other researchers found that for former welfare recipients, lengthy commuting time from home to work is associated with children's behavioral problems.[274]

Giving voice to former welfare recipients, who struggle to balance between work and care of their children, Andrew London and colleagues in their ethnographic study document how the women see the benefits of work as increasing their self-esteem, feeling a sense of independence, being less socially isolated, and presenting positive role models to their children.[275] The women feel that by working they contribute to the psychological development of their children. At the same time, the women are quite cognizant of the cost of going to work. They mention the high costs of child care and the difficulties in arranging it, being tired and having less time to spend with their children, having to juggle a hectic schedule, and how these contribute to their children's problems and school performance.[276]

Conclusions

Poor working single mothers and their children are buffeted by the interacting forces of the low-wage and child care markets. These markets cannot be viewed separately, as policy makers tend to do. Working in low-wage jobs that are contingent, unstable, and nonstandard hampers the ability of the mothers to secure decent and stable child care arrangements for their children. The child care market itself is bifurcated by income. Only those with high-skilled jobs and good income can afford to pay for better-quality, center-based child care, although the demand for formal care outstrips the supply. In contrast, low-wage workers, for whom child care consumes a greater proportion of their income, must rely on informal care, mostly kin, that is generally of low quality. Only a small proportion of these workers receive child care assistance that enables them to obtain higher-quality child care. Moreover, because low-wage jobs are unstable, have nonstandard shifts, and are subject to "workload adjustments," the mothers must resort to the more flexible informal child care offered by kin and neighbors, mobilize multiple caregivers, and leave children

[272] W.-J. Han (2005). "Maternal Nonstandard Work Schedules and Child Cognitive Outcomes." *Child Development* 76(1): 148.

[273] Ibid., p. 150.

[274] R. Duniforn & A. Kalil (2005). "Maternal Working Conditions and Child Well-Being in Welfare-Leaving Families" (Working Paper Series No. 05-5, National Poverty Center Working Papers Series, Ann Arbor, Mich.), pp. 1–36.

[275] A. S. London et al. (2004). "Welfare Reform, Work-Family Tradeoffs, and Child Well-Being." *Family Relations* 53(2): 148–58.

[276] Ibid., pp. 153–55.

unattended for extended periods. Formal child care is not only unaffordable, but it cannot accommodate to the mothers' shifting work schedules.

Nor can the mothers expect to exit the trap of low wages and poor child care. Most of them will be stuck in low-wage jobs, which offer limited mobility. Indeed, these jobs are characterized by declining returns to experience and increasing instability. As a result, a majority of the low-wage workers, especially single mothers, will remain poor. Nor can these workers expect appreciable improvements in access to better child care arrangements. Their children will be exposed to unstable and poor quality child care.

The costs to the mothers and their children are major. Remaining poor while working is detrimental to the well-being of the mothers and their children. The poorly paid, low-skill, unstable, and nonstandard jobs increase the risk of maternal depression and reduce the ability of the mothers to provide a nurturing home environment. These, in turn, lower the children's school performance and increase their behavioral problems. The cognitive development of the children is further compromised by low-quality child care.

Thus, the myth that low-wage work will ultimately lift single mothers and their children out of poverty and improve the children's quality of life is not supported by the actual reality of the low-wage and child care markets. Temporary Assistance for Needy Families has failed conspicuously to acknowledge the conditions that welfare recipients face in the low-wage labor market. Although policy makers, at least for awhile, have increased child care subsidies, they have failed to allocate sufficient resources to accommodate the needs of a majority of poor working mothers and their children. Yet, successful employment is contingent on receiving child care support. Single mothers who have child care subsidies are more likely to find standard jobs that have the "potential for long-term economic self-sufficiency."[277] Nor has public policy addressed the pervasive poor quality of much of the child care available to poor families.

In Chapter 8, Conclusions, we return to these issues – improving the low-wage labor market, the income of these families, and child care.

---

[277] E. Tekin (2004). "Single Mothers Working at Night: Standard Work, Child Care Subsidies, and Implications for Welfare Reform" (Working Paper 10274, National Bureau of Economic Research, January), p. 26.

7 Welfare Reform and Moral Entrepreneurship
Promoting Marriage and Responsible Parenthood and Preventing Teenage Pregnancy

For most Americans, welfare reform meant "ending welfare as we know it" – abolishing Aid to Families with Dependent Children (AFDC), dramatically increasing the work requirements and sanctions, and imposing time limits. Welfare was no longer going to be "a way of life." Perhaps less noticed, but a central feature of the reform agenda, were "family values." In fact, three out of the four purposes of the new legislation dealt with "family values."[1] In addition to the first goal of providing assistance to needy families, the goals of Personal Responsibility and Work Opportunity Reconciliation Act (PRWORA) are to "(2) end the dependence of needy parents on government benefits by promoting job preparation, work, and marriage; (3) prevent and reduce the incidence of out-of-wedlock pregnancies and establish annual numerical goals for preventing and reducing the incidence of these pregnancies; (4) encourage the formation and maintenance of two-parent families."[2] The legislation stated a series of findings to justify these goals. Among them are the following:

1. Marriage is the foundation of a successful society.
2. Marriage is an essential institution of a successful society that promotes the interests of children.
3. The increase in the number of children receiving public assistance is closely related to the increase in births to unmarried women.
4. The increase of out-of-wedlock pregnancies and births is well documented.
5. An effective strategy to combat teenage pregnancy must address the issue of male responsibility, including statutory rape culpability and prevention.

---

[1] M. Parke (2004). "Marriage-Related Provisions in Welfare Reauthorization Proposals: A Summary" (*CLASP*, updated March 1). Retrieved from http://www.clasp.org/publications/marr_prov_upd.pdf.

[2] Ibid., pp. 1–2.

6. The negative consequences of an out-of-wedlock birth on the mother, the child, the family, and society are well documented.[3]

On the basis of these and similar findings, the legislation concluded that "in light of this demonstration of the crisis in our Nation, it is the sense of the Congress that prevention of out-of-wedlock pregnancy and reduction in out-of-wedlock birth are very important Government interests."[4]

Implicit in the findings and conclusion is the assumption that the causes of poverty and welfare dependency are moral failures, and the purpose of PRWORA is to counter these failures by forcing welfare recipients to alter their behavior through the provisions in the act. Among them are requiring recipients to cooperate in establishing paternity and enforcing child support; sanctioning recipients if their children are not vaccinated or are truant from school; denying aid to teen parents who do not attend school or live in an adult-supervised setting; and allowing states to enact family caps, that is, refusing to pay additional support for children born to welfare mothers. In addition, states are given incentives to develop programs to promote marriages, reduce out-of-wedlock pregnancies, and promote abstinence education. Some states have spent significant amounts of TANF funds on such programs.[5] There was no TANF money specifically set aside for family planning (and generally, TANF cannot be spent on medical services). However, "pre-pregnancy family planning" is allowable under TANF.[6]

In addition, the Maternal and Child Health Block Grant has made available $50 million each year for abstinence education, with required matching funds. The definition of abstinence education includes "as its exclusive purpose, teaching the social, psychological, and health gains to be realized by abstaining from sexual activity."[7] There is no child care provision specifically tailored toward teen parents. As with adults, there is no guarantee of child care for those who are required to participate in mandated activities. However, states have the option to exempt a mother with a child under age 1, and states may not reduce or terminate TANF assistance if the refusal to work is based on a demonstrated inability to secure child care.[8] As part of its Healthy Marriage Initiative, the U.S. Department of Health and Human Services (HHS) has funded several demonstration projects to design, to provide, and to evaluate marriage skills programs.

---

[3] U.S. Congress (1996). *Personal Responsibility and Work Opportunity Reconciliation Act of 1996*, Title I, section 101.

[4] Ibid., section 101.   [5] Parke (2004), p. 1.

[6] Center on Law and Social Policy (CLASP) (2001). *List of Key Provisions in PROWRA Related to Teens and to Family Formation*. Retrieved from http://www.clasp.org/publications/list of key provisions.pdf.

[7] CLASP (2001), p. 2.   [8] Ibid., p. 2.

The reauthorization of TANF, known as the Deficit Reduction Act of 2005, includes $150 million per year (2006 to 2010) to promote healthy marriage and responsible fatherhood.[9] The Department of Health and Human Services will award funds on a competitive basis for research and demonstration projects, which must be voluntary. These projects may include such activities as public advertisement, education in high school, programs targeting unmarried pregnant women and unmarried expectant fathers, programs targeting engaged and married couples, divorce reduction programs, marriage-mentoring programs, and programs to reduce disincentive to marriage in mean-tested aid programs.[10] Promoting responsible fatherhood may include such activities as counseling and mentoring, improving the economic status of the fathers, and national media campaigns.[11]

These programs have raised concerns – women may be coerced or bribed to marry or to stay in an abusive marriage; married parents would be privileged over single parents; not enough protections are provided against domestic violence and other abuses.[12] Some women's groups (e.g., NOW Legal Defense and Education Fund) oppose government programs to promote marriage because they invade privacy, may ignore the risk of domestic violence, and coerce women to marry. Wade Horn, assistant secretary for Children and Families (HHS), says, "We know that this is a sensitive area. We don't want to come in with a heavy hand. All services will be voluntary. . . . The last thing we'd want is to increase the rate of domestic violence against women."[13]

There is great diversity among state activities, ranging from initiatives, commissions, and campaigns, changes in marriage and divorce laws, program activities and services, and policy changes in TANF and child support programs. Several states have changed their marriage and divorce laws. Five states (Florida, Maryland, Minnesota, Oklahoma, and Tennessee) have reduced marriage license fees for engaged couples to participate in marriage preparation or counseling classes. Three states (Arizona, Arkansas, and Louisiana) require couples applying for a marriage license to choose either between the existing law or a new "covenant marriage contract," which usually requires marriage education or counseling before marriage or divorce. Grounds for divorce are tightened to include only adultery, abuse, or abandonment, or after long periods of separation (usually two years).[14]

---

[9] P. Roberts (2005). "The Marriage and Fatherhood Provisions of the Deficit Reduction Act of 2005" (Center for Law and Social Policy, Washington, D.C.), pp. 1–3.

[10] Ibid., p. 2.   [11] Ibid., p. 3.

[12] T. Ooms, S. Bouchet, & M. Parke (2004). "Beyond Marriage Licenses. Efforts in States to Strengthen Marriage and Two-Parent Families. A State-by-State Snapshot." (CLASP, April,), p. 7.

[13] R. Pear & D. Kirkpatrick (2004). "Bush Plans $1.5 Billion Drive for Promotion of Marriage." New York Times, January 14, p. A1.

[14] Ooms, Bouchet, & Parke (2004), p. 14.

Since the mid-1990s, every state has made at least one policy change or undertaken at least one activity to promote marriage, strengthen two-parent families, or reduce divorce. A few offer financial incentives to marry, and others have separate state-funding programs to avoid the financial penalties for failure to meet the higher federal work participation rates for two-parent families. A few states have modified their child support regulations that could discourage marriage.[15] As of 2002, twenty-two states have set up separate state programs, exclusively with state money, for two-parent families.[16] Eight states changed their marriage and divorce laws. Seven states have dedicated significant TANF funds to support marriage-related activities. Nine states and one tribal agency offer welfare recipients financial incentives to marry.[17] Several states have created marriage "incentives." One state (West Virginia) offers a monthly $100 "bonus" for recipients who marry or are already married to the father of their children. Three states disregard the spouse's earnings for a limited amount of time.[18] In a few states, developers of marriage and fatherhood programs are working with domestic violence organizations, which in many states have been vocal critics of marriage-promotion efforts.[19] There has also been a growing number of responsible fatherhood programs that provide low-income noncustodial fathers (including previously cohabiting fathers) with employment services (job training and placement), child support assistance, peer support groups, parenting classes, legal assistance, and individual counseling.[20] Mediation services and co-parenting classes are offered to never-married couples to help noncustodial fathers so that they can co-parent more effectively (including paying child support).

Progressives have countered with a "marriage plus" agenda. According to Theodora Ooms, "it acknowledges that married and unmarried parents, mothers and fathers, may need both economic resources and non-economic supports to increase the likelihood of stable, healthy marriages and better co-parenting relationships. In addition, a marriage-plus agenda focuses more on the front end – making marriage better to be in – rather than the back end – making marriage more difficult to get out of."[21]

Whether the provisions to reinforce marriage and family values espoused by the legislation achieve their aims is the topic of much debate.[22] More important, the logic in promoting healthy marriages and responsible fatherhood

---

[15] Ibid., p. 15.   [16] Ibid., p. 16.

[17] Ibid., pp. 10–11.

[18] Ibid., p. 16. One TANF tribal agency provides a one-time bonus of $2,000 to welfare recipients who marry and an additional $1,500 if they have a traditional Native American wedding ceremony.

[19] Ibid., p. 11.   [20] Ibid., p. 14.

[21] T. Ooms (2002). "Marriage-Plus" (Center for Law and Social Policy, Washington D.C.), pp. 5–6.

[22] See, for example, L. A. Gennetian & V. Knox (2003). "Staying Single: The Effects of Welfare Reform Policies on Marriage and Cohabitation" (New York, MDRC); S. Hays (2003). *Flat Broke with Children: Women in the Age of Welfare Reform*. Oxford; New York: Oxford University Press.

represents what Albert Hirschman terms "the rhetoric of perversity,"[23] which, as we have emphasized, is a characteristic of the 1996 welfare reform. The legislation asserts that public assistance (i.e., welfare dependency), not poverty, reinforces personal moral failures, which causes social pathologies. In other words, the consequence has become the cause. Moreover, there is a subtext underlying the "family values" agenda. It is the moral condemnation of alternative family structures and particularly the degradation of poor single mothers of color. "Family values" reinforce the racially motivated stereotypes of "poor ghettos," which are supposedly characterized by promiscuity, irresponsible parenthood, an "epidemic" of teen pregnancies and debilitating welfare dependency.

As we show in this chapter, poverty, unemployment, low wages, and lack of human and social capital are the major causes of single parenthood and marital instability, teen pregnancy, and stunted child development. Moreover, the rhetoric of perversity omits fathers from welfare reform.[24] With the exception of the small TANF-Unemployed Parent program (applying mostly to the father), there are few programs or services that would provide income assistance, education, employment opportunities, and training to the fathers so that they have the resources to support their children. Indeed, in most states TANF eligibility and benefits are determined by the entire family income and resources, resulting in a disincentive for two-parent families. Moreover, in most states TANF child support provisions do little to raise the mother's income.[25] Yet, financial hardship and uncertainty are the key reasons fathers are absent.

As we show, married couples are usually better off than single mothers; children raised in two-parent families are usually better off than in children raised in single-parent families; children born to mothers who are not teens are usually better off. Nevertheless, and this is the critical perspective, although marriage, delayed pregnancy, and all the other family values provisions are important, none by themselves are sufficient. Families, whether one or two-parent, need financial support, good jobs, good child care, health care, education, and so forth. In other words, although "marriage plus" is preferable to just marriage promotion, as we detail in the next chapter, we are more in favor of "income plus."

Marriage and Poverty

There is compelling evidence that married families are less poor than single-parent families, possibly because such families gain from economies of scale,

---

[23] A. O. Hirschman (1991). *The Rhetoric of Reaction: Perversity, Futility, Jeopardy*. Cambridge, Mass.: Belknap Press.

[24] Hays (2003), p. 63.

[25] M. Carlson et al. (2005). "The Effects of Welfare and Child Support Policies on Union Formation." *Population Research and Policy Review* 23: 516–17.

Table 7–1. *Percent of households with children in poverty by race and household status, 1998*

Type of household	Percent of household in poverty			
	All Races	White	Black	Hispanic
Married couples	8.2	6.3	9.4	17.9
Cohabiting couples	16.0	10.8	18.4	27.6
Single parents, other adult in household	24.2	14.7	31.4	36.1
Single parents, no other adult in household	38.1	27.4	52.4	49.3
All households	14.4	9.3	28.4	25.0

Source: R. I. Lerman (2002). "How Do Marriage, Cohabitation, and Single Parenthood Affect the Material Hardship of Families with Children?" (Urban Institute, Washington, D.C.), p. 24.

risk sharing, and division of labor.[26] Paula Roberts gives this example: a couple with one child needs $15,670 per year to reach the poverty level. If they separate into one two-person family and one single person, they would need an additional $6,130 to reach the poverty level (a two-person unit needs $12,490; a single person, $9,310). If both adults work at a minimum wage job, the combined income would be $21,424, or 136 percent of the poverty line; if one works full-time and the other works only half-time (at the minimum wage), they would earn $16,068 per year.

Using data from the Panel of the Survey of Income and Program Participation (SIPP), Robert Lerman[27] shows that in households with children, approximately 8 percent of married couples were in poverty compared to 16 percent of cohabiting couples; 24 percent of single parents living with another adult in the household; and 38 percent of single-parent families (see Table 7–1).

There are variations by race with greatest risk of poverty among black and Hispanic single parents (no other adult in household). Married couples are also less likely to experience material hardship. According to Lerman, "hardship is significantly less likely among married couple households than among cohabiting couple or single parent households with similar observed characteristics."[28] One reason is that married couples are more likely to receive help from family, friends, and the community than cohabiting couples or single parents living with another adult in a nonromantic relationship.

[26] P. Roberts (2004b). "I Can't Give You Anything but Love: Would Poor Couples with Children Be Better off Economically if They Married" (Couples and Marriage Series, Policy Brief No. 5, CLASP, August); R. I. Lerman (2002). "Marriage and the Economic Well-Being of Families with Children: A Review of the Literature" (Urban Institute, Washington, D.C.), pp. 1–36.
[27] Lerman (2002). "How Do Marriage, Cohabitation, and Single Parenthood Affect the Material Hardships of Families with Children?" (Urban Institute, Washington, D.C.), pp. 1–38.
[28] Ibid., p. 18.

To what extent are the economic benefits of marriage due to a selection factor? Roberts concludes that "about half of the economic boost that comes from marriage is, in fact, due to selections – that is, the measurable characteristics of those who choose to marry."[29] For example, although cohabitation does increase positive economic outcomes, it is not as strong as marriage. Cohabitation has twice the poverty rate of married couples because income sharing may be less and relationships and commitments tend to be shorter, which means that there will be less of an accumulation of both income and wealth. In addition, cohabiting couples are less likely to receive family contributions.[30] Roberts cites several studies showing that, compared with cohabiting couples, those who get married are more likely to be older and better educated; the fathers are more likely to be currently working, more likely to have worked full time in the past year, more likely to have graduated high school, and more likely to be older than 25. Husbands with children earn higher wages and work more hours than nonhusbands with similar characteristics.[31] Indeed, because the earning capacities of unmarried men and women are considerably lower than those of married men and women, they are far less likely to escape poverty, at their current earnings, if they marry.[32]

Would the marriage effect benefit even young, underemployed, poorly educated couples who choose to marry? Lerman, using census data, simulated marriages among low-income mothers and men of similar background, age, and education and found that the declines in poverty would be substantial.[33] A 2003 study using census data found similar results – marriage does have a significant antipoverty effect when both the husband and wife are poor, holding constant family background, race and ethnicity, age, and education. The current likelihood of living in poverty would be reduced by a third if the couple had ever been married and by two-thirds if the couple remained married.[34]

However, the effect of marriage is not strong enough to reduce the adverse economic consequences of nonmarital birth. Several studies show that nonmarital childbearing is highly related to long-term poverty for the mothers. This is especially true when the mothers are poor or near poor at the time of birth. They are less likely to marry, less likely to stay married, and more likely to marry a man with poor economic prospects. Thus, marriage does not produce the same economic benefits for those who give birth *before* marriage as for those who give birth *after* marriage.[35]

[29] Roberts (2004b), p. 4.   [30] Roberts (2004b), pp. 3–4.

[31] Roberts (2004b), p. 4.

[32] W. Sigle-Rushton & S. McLanahan (2002). "For Richer or Poorer? Marriage as an Anti-poverty Strategy in the United States." *Population* 57: 509–26.

[33] R. I. Lerman (1996). "The Impact of U.S. Family Structure on Child Poverty and Income Inequality." *Economica* 63 (250S): S119–39.

[34] A. Thomas & I. Sawhill (2002). "For Richer or for Poorer: Marriage as an Anti-poverty Strategy" (The Brookings Institution, Washington, D.C.).

[35] D. Lichter, D. R. Graefe, & J. B. Brown (2003). "Is Marriage a Panacea? Union Formation among Economically-Disadvantaged Unwed Mothers." *Social Problems* 50(1): 60–86.

In sum, marriage can have a positive effect even among mothers with high poverty rates and low educational attainment. However, Roberts notes that being married does not eliminate poverty. Even if all unmarried mothers were to marry similar, available partners, the child poverty rate would drop only four percentage points. Although this would be a 25 percent drop, substantial poverty would remain. Marriage helps, but "it is clearly not a panacea." Being poor to begin with, a premarital birth, low-educational attainment, limited work experience, and race all influence the effect of marriage on poverty. The positive effects of marriage affect all racial and ethnic groups but are smaller for African American and Hispanic families. Furthermore, says Roberts, the fact that marriage can contribute to the reduction of poverty does not tell us which policies or programs will increase the marriage rate, which policies will promote healthy marriages, or which policies will not, at the same time, disadvantage single-parent families. "In short, marriage can be part of an anti-poverty strategy; but it is no substitute for other efforts to reduce poverty."[36]

Married and Poor

Although marriage tends to reduce poverty, in 2003 5 percent of married women (2.5 million) were poor, and 17 percent (8 million) were below 200 percent of the poverty line.[37] Poor women marry younger and have shorter marriages. Latinos constitute a high proportion of low-income couples – 35 percent, compared with 47 percent of non-Hispanic whites and 10 percent of African Americans. Latinos are more likely to be poor, marry early, and stay married.[38] Low-income couples have low education and employment levels. Forty-one percent of poor husbands lack a high school diploma, compared with 2 percent of affluent husbands. The educational characteristics of wives are similar. Only about half (51%) of poor husbands and 14 percent of wives have full-time jobs versus 92 percent of husbands and 62 percent of wives in the top income category.

Women with lower levels of education and from more disadvantaged neighborhoods are more likely to marry early. Even after accounting for differences in employment, multiple-partner fertility, and other factors, African Americans have lower odds of marrying than non-Hispanic whites.[39]

With upper-middle-income couples, parenthood follows the first marriage; with the economically disadvantaged, births are far more likely to precede

[36] Roberts (2004b), p. 8.
[37] D. Fein (2004). "Married and Poor: Basic Characteristics of Economically Disadvantaged Married Couples in the U.S." (Working Paper SHM-01, Supporting Healthy Marriage Evaluation, Abt Associates, July).
[38] Ibid., p. 6.
[39] R. Mincy & C.-C. Huang (2002). "Just Get Me to the Church . . .": Assessing Policies to Promote Marriage among Fragile Families" (Working Paper No. 02-02-FF, Center for Research on Child Wellbeing, February), pp. 10, 28.

marriage.[40] Many of the premarital births occur more than three years before marriage, and the baby's father is likely not to be the spouse. In a recent survey in Florida, Fein reports that 49 percent of low-income (under 200% of the poverty line) married couples had at least one child from a prior relationship, compared with 31 percent of couples with incomes at least 400 percent of the poverty line.[41]

Couples who are economically disadvantaged are just as likely to marry as others, but their marriages are much more unstable and become more so with increases in economic disadvantage. The probability of the marriage dissolving is much greater for women with less education and living in poorer neighborhoods (bottom 25% of neighborhood income level). According to Fein, "the effect of neighborhood income level is especially large." African American women have the highest risk of marriage dissolution, whatever their education level.[42]

Cohabitation rather than marriage has increased rapidly in the past two decades and about 35 percent of never-married cohabitants have children.[43] It is increasingly prevalent among low-income couples. Smock quotes a study by Bumpass and Lu showing that "the percentage of 19- to 44-year-old women who have cohabited at some point is almost 60 percent among high school dropouts versus 37 percent among college graduates."[44] Cohabitation increases marital instability, and children born to cohabiting couples experience greater economic hardships and transitions in family structure. According to Garfinkel and McLanahan, these are "fragile families."[45] As we discuss later, the study of "fragile families" found that at time of the childbirth, 51 percent of the couples were cohabiting.[46] Yet, the likelihood that these couples will get married in the years following the birth of the child is quite low.

The Fragile Families Study

What factors lead to the formation of single-parent families? The "Fragile Families and Child Wellbeing" study attempts to provide some answers.[47]

---

[40] Fein (2004), p. 4.   [41] Ibid., p. 5.

[42] Ibid., pp. 3–4.

[43] P. J. Smock (2000). "Cohabitation in the United States: An Appraisal of Research Themes, Findings, and Implications." *Annual Review of Sociology* 26: 1–20.

[44] Ibid., p. 4.

[45] I. Garfinkel & S. McLanahan (2002). "Unwed Parents: Myths, Realities, and Policy Making." *Focus* 22: 93–97.

[46] Center for Research on Child Wellbeing (2003). "Union Formation and Dissolution in Fragile Families." *Fragile Families Research Brief* 14: 1–3.

[47] For a description of the study, see I. Garfinkel et al. (2001). "Fragile Families and Welfare Reform: An Introduction. *Children and Youth Services Review* 23(4–5): 277–301; N. E. Reichman et al. (2001). "Fragile Families: Sample and Design." *Children and Youth Services Review* 23(4–5): 303–26.

"Fragile families" refers to unmarried parents and their children who face higher risk of poverty and family dissolution than traditional families. The sample is representative of all nonmarital births in seventy-seven U.S. cities with populations of more than 200,000 in 1999.[48] The average unmarried mother is in her early twenties. More than half have more than one child. Fifty-one percent of the mothers are non-Hispanic black, almost one-third are Hispanic, and 17 percent are non-Hispanic white or some other ethnicity. Less than 20 percent are immigrants.[49] The fathers, on average, are three years older than the mothers.[50] More than a third of the mothers and fathers lack a high school diploma, and about one-third do not have any education beyond high school. About 30 percent of the fathers have been incarcerated.[51]

The study follows the families from the birth of the child through age 5. The new mothers, mostly unwed, were interviewed in person in the hospital within forty-eight hours of birth. The fathers were interviewed either at the hospital or elsewhere as soon as possible after the birth. (The number of fathers who declined to be interviewed was larger than the mothers.) There are three follow-up interviews – when the child is approximately twelve months, thirty-six months, and sixty months old. In-home assessments were made at thirty-six months and sixty months. A comparison group of married persons was also followed in each city.

The most important finding from the baseline data was that "the great majority of unwed parents are committed to each other and to their children at time of birth."[52] According to the researchers, about half of all mothers were living with the father of their child when the child was born, whereas 33 percent were romantically involved but not cohabiting. Similarly, both parents were optimistic about their future relationship and were strongly in favor of marriage, viewing it as important for the well-being of their children. Most also felt that successful marriage depended on the ability of the father to have a steady job.[53]

Again, contrary to the stereotype that the fathers are indifferent, almost all (92%) contributed financially or otherwise (e.g., transportation) during the pregnancy; 83 percent of the mothers and 94 percent of the fathers wanted the father's name on the birth certificate; and 78 percent of the mothers and 89 percent of the fathers reported that the child would take the father's surname. Although these respondents were only the unmarried fathers who agreed to be interviewed, the mothers did report a high amount of intended father involvement.[54]

[48] Garfinkel & McLanahan (2002).
[49] Ibid., p. 94.
[50] Ibid.
[51] Ibid.
[52] Ibid.
[53] Ibid., pp. 94–95.
[54] S. McLanahan et al. (2003). "The Fragile Families and Child Wellbeing Study: Baseline National Report" (Revised, March), p. 10.

Table 7–2. *Relationship status in fragile families (in percent)*

At time of birth		12 months after birth of child				
		Married	Cohabiting	Visiting	Friends	Not in relationship
Cohabiting	48.2	14.6	59.6	4.6	10.9	10.4
Visiting	34.7	5.3	32.2	14.0	25.6	23.0
Friends	7.9	1.2	9.2	3.5	44.1	42.2
Not in Relationship	9.2	1.7	6.3	4.3	22.9	64.8

Source: Center for Research on Child Wellbeing. Fragile Families Research Brief No. 14. January 2004.

Still, "most unmarried parents are poorly equipped to support themselves and their children."[55] Employment patterns were sporadic, earning capacity low, and poverty widespread. Still, despite the difficult economic conditions, "most unmarried mothers are healthy and bear healthy children."[56] In part, this may be because almost all the mothers received prenatal care.

Despite the "high hopes and good intentions," very few, in fact, married by the time the child was twelve to eighteen months old. As shown in Table 7–2, among those cohabiting at time of birth, only 14.6 percent got married, 59.6 percent remained cohabiting, 4.6 percent were romantically involved but living apart ("visiting"), 10.9 percent were with friends, and 10.4 percent had no relationship. Among those who were romantically involved but living apart at time of birth ("visiting"), 5.3 percent got married, 32.2 percent were cohabiting, and 14.0 percent continued to be romantically involved but living apart.[57]

In part, the low marriage rate is due to the numerous barriers facing the new parents. These include high unemployment, a history of incarceration, mental health problems, family violence, and substance abuse.[58] The Fragile Family study estimates that only 36 percent of the couples were romantically involved at time of the child's birth and *did not* have any of these barriers.[59] Three sets of factors influence union formation – economic conditions, attitudes toward marriage, and quality of relations.[60] The probability of marriage increases when mothers have a high school degree or higher, the men have higher earnings, both have positive attitudes toward marriage, and the emotional

[55] Garfinkel & McLanahan (2002), p. 95.   [56] Ibid., p. 96.

[57] Center for Research on Child Wellbeing (2003). "Union Formation and Dissolution in Fragile Families." *Fragile Families Research Brief* 14: 1–3.

[58] Center for Research on Child Wellbeing (2003). "Barriers to Marriage among Fragile Families." *Fragile Families Research Brief* 16: 1–3.

[59] Ibid., p. 2.

[60] M. Carlson, S. McLanahan, & P. England (2004). "Union Formation in Fragile Families." *Demography* 41: 237–61.

quality of their relationship is high.[61] There are important ethnic differences. White, Mexican American, and other Hispanic parents are about 2.5 times more likely than African Americans to marry in the year after the nonmarital birth of their child.[62] Higher incarceration and lower employment rates among African American men, compared with white, Mexican American, and other Hispanic men, results in a shortage of marriageable African American men. In addition, the lower earning capacity of African American men compared with white men explains the disparity in the marriage rate between these two groups (but not between Mexican American and African American men). The supply of marriageable men may also explain why African Americans have a more positive attitude toward single mothers. Still, African American parents place a high value on marriage.[63]

The negative effects of incarceration on marriage, especially for African American men, cannot be overstated. The proportion of incarcerated men in their late thirties who have children is not significantly different than for nonin-carcerated men.[64] A high rate of incarceration not only reduces the availability of marriageable men but also damages their economic desirability.[65] It erodes women's trust in the men's ability to be good husbands.[66] Clearly, men who are incarcerated are less likely to get married; yet, the lingering effects of past incarceration on discouraging marriage are also evident but mostly because of the higher level of joblessness among ex-inmates.[67] Incarceration also leads to a higher divorce rate, particularly for white and Hispanic men.[68] Using the Fragile Family survey, Western also shows that there is a higher rate of domestic violence among men who were incarcerated, except for couples with a high-quality relationship.[69] Western concludes, "In the era of mass imprisonment, the penal system has joined the labor market as a significant influence on the life chances of young low-educated black men. . . . Imprisonment has also inhibited the formation of stable two-parent families in the low-income urban communities from which most of the penal population is drawn."[70]

The Fragile Family study also sheds some light on the relationship among welfare, child support, and marriage. A different study using data from the

[61] Ibid., p. 255.
[62] K. Harknett & S. S. McLanahan (2004). "Racial and Ethnic Differences in Marriage after the Birth of a Child." *American Sociological Review* 69: 790–811.
[63] Ibid., p. 808.
[64] B. Western (2004). "Incarceration, Marriage, and Family Life" (Center for Research on Child Wellbeing, Princeton, N.J.).
[65] W. J. Wilson (1987). *The Truly Disadvantaged: The Inner City, the Underclass, and Public Policy.* Chicago: University of Chicago Press, pp. 83–92.
[66] K. Edin (2000). "Few Good Men: Why Poor Mothers Don't Marry or Remarry." *American Prospect* 11: 26–31.
[67] Western (2004), pp. 22–23.
[68] Ibid., p. 25. According to the author, data limitation on black men makes estimations of divorce about them unreliable.
[69] Ibid., pp. 39–40.   [70] Ibid., p. 46.

1990, 1992, 1993, and 1996 panels of SIPP on female heads of household (which included cohabiting) by Fitzgerald and Ribar indicates that being on welfare increases the length of time the mother will remain unmarried. Similarly, living in a higher benefit state increases the likelihood of unmarried mothers entering welfare and delaying exit.[71] Interestingly, generous EITC seems to maintain the mothers' existing living arrangements and is associated with longer welfare spells, possibly because of the ability to combine welfare with work.[72] As expected, African American and Hispanic women were more likely to remain unmarried and on welfare. Being older than age 18 and having higher levels of education reduce both. Using data from the Fragile Family study, Julien Teitler and colleagues report similar findings.[73] While the mother is on TANF, she is less likely to get married. However, having ever been on TANF does not affect the likelihood of marriage. In other words, being on TANF has a short-term effect on delaying marriage. However, because most couples begin with a cohabiting relationship, then being on TANF does not result in greater risk of a breakup in the relationship. In fact, welfare generosity increases the likelihood that the couple will maintain their romantic relationship.[74] In other words, "when unmarried couples have greater access to (real or potential) income from welfare, they are more likely to continue to live together."[75] At the same time, as will be discussed, strong child-support enforcement discourages marriage.

The wide discrepancy between the high hopes for marriage and the low rate of actual marriage may paradoxically arise because couples actually buy into the ideal of marriage and aspire to have stable, long-term relationships.[76] According to Gibson-Davis and colleagues, "most couples insist that getting married ought to be a serious and irrevocable decision and should not be treated like it is 'just a piece of paper.'"[77] They also reject divorce as an option. Not surprisingly, the couples view cohabitation, precipitated by the birth of the child, as a first step toward marriage. Yet, setting a high bar for marriage actually discourages it because of the harsh realities these couples encounter. Uppermost they mention financial barriers (e.g., financial instability, lack of financial responsibility, and few assets) as marriage deterrents, followed by worries about the quality of the relationship.[78]

[71] J. M. Fitzgerald & D. C. Ribar (2005). "Transitions in Welfare Participation and Female Headship." *Population Research and Policy Review* 23: 641–70.
[72] Ibid., p. 659.
[73] J. O. Teitler et al. (2005). "Welfare Participation and Marriage" (Working Paper No. 2005-24, Center for Research on Child Wellbeing, Princeton, N.J.).
[74] Carlson, McLanahan, & England (2005).   [75] Ibid., p. 534.
[76] K. Edin, M. J. Kefalas, & J. M. Reed (2004). "A Peek Inside the Black Box: What Marriage Means for Poor Unmarried Parents." *Journal of Marriage and Family* 66: 1007–14; C. M. Gibson-Davis, K. Edin, & S. McLanahan (2005). "High Hopes but Even Higher Expectations: The Retreat From Marriage among Low-Income Couples." *Journal of Marriage and Family* 67: 1301–12.
[77] Gibson-Davis, Edin, & McLanahan (2005), p. 1309.
[78] Ibid., pp. 1307–9.

Table 7–3. *Child support payments to all women and women below the poverty line: 1978–2001*

	1978	2001
All women		
Percent awarded	59.1	63.0
Percent received payment	34.6	41.1
Percent received full payment	23.6	25.0
Women below the poverty line		
Percent awarded	38.1	55.7
Percent received full payment	17.8	31.3

Source: Committee on Ways and Means. U.S. House of Representatives (2004). *Background Material and Data on Programs within the Jurisdiction of the Committee on Ways and Means.* Washington, D.C.: U.S. Government Printing Office, Table 8.7.

Paternity Establishment and Child-Support Enforcement

Federal legislation in the past two decades has greatly strengthened the administration of paternity establishment and child-support enforcement. In 1975, Congress established the Child Support Enforcement Program (CSE). It provides federal matching funds to be used for enforcing support obligations by locating non-cohabitant parents, establishing paternity, establishing child-support awards, and collecting child-support payments. Since 1981, child-support agencies have collected spousal support on behalf of custodial parents, and in 1984, they were required to petition for medical support as part of most child-support orders.[79] States have implemented numerical formula to determine awards and automatic withholding of child support from the earnings of the non-cohabitant parent. Under PRWORA, states are required to increase the percentage of paternity identification (including use of DNA testing and the opportunity for new parents to acknowledge paternity at the hospital), develop an integrated, automated network linking all states to data about the location and assets of parents, implement more enforcement techniques, and revise the rules governing the distribution of past due (arrearage) child-support payments to former recipients of public assistance.

As a result, there has been considerable improvement in the rates of paternity establishment, reaching 74 percent in 2002, compared with 23 percent in the early 1980s.[80] However, the corresponding increase in child-support enforcement has been more modest. As shown in Table 7–3, from 1978 to

[79] Committee on Ways and Means, U.S. House of Representatives (2004). *Background Material and Data on Programs within the Jurisdiction of the Committee on Ways and Means.* Washington, D.C.: U.S. Government Printing Office, pp. 8-2–8-3.

[80] I. Garfinkel et al. (2003). "The Role of Child Support Enforcement and Welfare in Non-marital Childbearing." *Journal of Population Economics* 16: 55–70, p. 57; Committee on Ways and Means (2004), pp. 8–15.

2001, the percentage of women receiving awards has improved, but the percentage of women receiving full payment has not. The greatest improvement in obtaining awards and collecting payment has been for women below the poverty line. Still, by 2001, only 31 percent received any payment. There is also some evidence that child-support payments have a modest antipoverty effect.[81]

Currently, about 42 percent of children in the families who have left welfare receive child support. Child support averages $2,562 per year, which is about 30 percent of income.[82] According to a study in Washington State, families receiving regular child support stayed off welfare longer, found work faster, and had a slower rate of job loss.[83] Most (78%) former TANF recipients say that child-support payments have made a "very big difference" in their family income; another 8 percent said it made a "pretty big difference."[84]

Still, if increased paternity establishment and stricter child-support enforcement are meant to improve the income of families on welfare, they fall wide of their mark. First, as the Fragile Family study shows, even though paternity establishment is very high (72%), only 8 percent of the fathers have a legal obligation to pay child support. The gap is mostly due to cohabitation and informal support. Only 11 percent of non-cohabitant fathers pay any formal child support one year after the birth of the child.[85] A study of child support among welfare recipients in Wisconsin, which passes through the entire child-support payment to the mothers, also shows wide gaps between establishment of paternity and receipt of child support.[86] Looking at the children (rather than the mothers) during the first three months on welfare, 54 percent had paternity established, 40 percent had support orders, but only 14 percent received payment. The picture improves somewhat after two years on welfare but not by much. Twenty-two percent received payments.

Second, for both parents, there are financial disincentives for assigning child support to the state.[87] States have various policies regarding the amount of child support forwarded to the family versus the amount kept to recoup welfare costs and the forwarded amount's effect on their welfare grant. Currently,

[81] Committee on Ways and Means (2004), pp. 8–69.
[82] CLASP (n.d.). "Child Support Substantially Increases Economic Well-Being of Low- and Moderate-Income Families" (Research Fact Sheet), p. 1, citing Sorensen & Zibman (2000a). Retrieved from http://www.clasp.org/publications/CS_Economic_FS.pdf.
[83] Ibid., p. 2, citing Washington State study.
[84] Ibid., citing J. Pearson & N. Thoennes (2000). "A Profile of Former TANF Clients in the IVD Caseload" (Center for Policy Research, Denver, Colo.).
[85] Center for Research on Child Wellbeing (2003). "Child Support Enforcement and Fragile Families." Fragile Families Research Brief 15: 1–3.
[86] J. Bartfeld (2003). "Falling through the Cracks: Gaps in Child Support among Welfare Recipients." Journal of Marriage and Family 65: 72–89.
[87] M. R. Waller & R. Plotnick (1999). "Effective Child Support Policy for Low-Income Families: Evidence from Street Level Research." Journal of Policy Analysis and Management 20: 89–110.

sixteen states pass through and disregard $50 or more of child support per month; three states pass through and disregard some or all child support for purposes of fill-the-gap budgeting; two states do not pass through child support to families, however, their TANF grants are increased; two states pass through $50 per month but do not disregard that amount for TANF eligibility and benefits; and twenty-seven states and the District of Columbia do not pass through or disregard any child-support for families receiving TANF.[88] Thus, in most instances, the mothers might be better off financially if they can work out an informal support arrangement with the fathers.[89] The fathers also prefer such an arrangement because they can avoid court orders and the penalties for failure to comply. Many states establish the amount of support on the basis of full-time employment, which may not be readily adjusted to changing earning status. Therefore, low-income fathers not only may be forced to pay a higher proportion of their income but also risk large arrearages.[90] Use of informal support arrangements also reduces the potential conflict between the parents. Indeed, some evidence indicates that non-cohabiting mothers with formal child-support orders face a greater risk of domestic violence.[91]

Third, the noncustodial fathers of these children have very limited income. Cancian and Meyer,[92] also using data from Wisconsin, show that the formal earnings of the fathers were less than $8,000 for 1998 and 1999. A third of the fathers had no formal source of income. These noncustodial fathers, as noted earlier by the Fragile Family study, have many barriers to employment, including low education, sporadic employment history, housing instability, and prior incarceration.[93]

The logic behind stringent paternity establishment and child-support enforcement is that they "increase the costs of a non-marital birth to men by forcing them to take more financial responsibility for their children."[94] Therefore, they should reduce nonmarital births. It is less clear what the effect would be on the incentive for low-income unmarried couples to get married because the women often depend on the informal support by the fathers. A

---

[88] National Center for Children in Poverty (2004). "State Policy Choices: Child Support" (National Center for Children in Poverty, New York).

[89] Waller & Plotnick (2001), pp. 97–99.

[90] S. S. McLanahan & M. J. Carlson (2002). "Welfare Reform, Fertility, and Father Involvement." *The Future of Children* 16: 147–64.

[91] Center for Research on Child Wellbeing (2002). "Child Support Enforcement and Domestic Violence among Non-cohabiting Couples." *Fragile Families Research Brief* 13: 1–3.

[92] M. Cancian & D. R. Meyer (2004). "Fathers of Children Receiving Welfare: Can They Provide More Child Support?" *Social Service Review* 78: 179–206.

[93] See R. B. Mincy & E. J. Sorensen (1998). "Deadbeats and Turnips in Child Support Reform." *Journal of Policy Analysis and Management* 17: 44–51; J. M. Martinez & C. Miller (2000). "Working and Earning: The Impact of Parents' Fair Share on Low Income Fathers' Employment" (MDRC, New York).

[94] Garfinkel et al. (2003), p. 57.

study by Garfinkel and colleagues finds "strong evidence that stricter enforcement of child support deters non-marital birth."[95] At the same time, the Fragile Families study indicates that stricter child enforcement does reduce the chances that the unmarried couples would marry.[96] There is also some evidence that stricter child enforcement leads men to be more selective in their "mating patterns," choosing more educated women and women with "higher propensity to invest in their children" (measured by early prenatal care). Stated in other terms, stricter child enforcement reduces the fertility of women who are less likely to invest in their children, regardless of actual child-support receipt. Thus, stricter child enforcement policies may not only increase the financial resources available to the child but also affect the birth selection process.[97]

It is also claimed that child support has noneconomic positive effects on the children.[98] There are improvements in cognitive development, controlling for family income and other background characteristics; moreover, the effects are strongest for African American children in separated or divorced homes and for white children whose parents are unmarried.[99]

Promoting Healthy Marriages

Most of the initiatives to promote healthy marriages among low-income parents rely on marriage education, parenting and couple relationship skills, and marital counseling.[100] Such an approach is justified by what Garfinkel and McLanahan describe as the "magic moment" at birth when most of both parents, even though not married, share a commitment to each other and the new child.[101] They propose a home visit by a trained social worker shortly after birth (within a week or two) that would be both an assessment and referral service. The visit would include both the mother and the father. It would focus on both human capital (education, employment, health) and social capital (family, friends, community). Information would be made available for

[95] Ibid., p. 67.   [96] Carlson, McLanahan, & England (2005).

[97] A. Aizer & S. McLanahan (2004). "The Impact of Child Support on Fertility, Parental Investments and Child Well-Being" (Working Paper No. 04–03-FF, Center for Research on Child Wellbeing), pp. 1, 22–23.

[98] CLASP (n.d.). "Child Support."

[99] Ibid., p. 1, citing L. Argys et al. (1998). "The Impact of Child Support on Cognitive Outcomes of Young Children." Demography 35(2): 159–73.

[100] T. Ooms & P. Wilson (2004). "The Challenge of Offering Relationship and Marriage Education to Low-Income Populations." Family Relations 53: 440–47.

[101] I. Garfinkel & S. McLanahan (2003). "Strengthening Fragile Families." In I. V. Sawhill (Ed.), One Percent for Kids (pp. 76–92). Washington, D.C.: Brookings Institution Press. Other studies also find that a majority of unmarried mothers value marriage as a personal goal. D. Lichter, C. Batson, & J. B. Brown (2004). "Welfare Reform and Marriage Promotion: The Marital Expectations and Desires of Single and Cohabiting Mothers." Social Service Review 78(1): 3–25.

benefits and services – for example, EITC, TANF, food stamps, health care, child care, substance abuse treatment, education programs, employment services and job training, child support, and parenting classes.[102]

Garfinkel and McLanahan also propose three models of relationship programs.[103] The first would focus on communication skills, the second would focus on increasing intimacy and help in resolving personal issues, and the third would be mentoring new parents. New parents would be matched with older, more experienced couples who have a strong, stable relationship.[104]

Ooms and Wilson describe several demonstration programs that echo the "magic moment" rationale but caution that curriculums used in many of them were originally developed for middle-income white couples. For example, Oklahoma's marriage initiative offers low-income couples the Prevention and Relationship Enhancement Program (PREP), which was originally developed and used for committed middle-income white couples.[105] Michigan has implemented a project offering TANF recipients with new babies a six-week curriculum titled "Caring for My Family" that includes parenting and couple relationship skills and an emphasis on the importance of parental involvement and financial management. Louisiana has also used $1.4 million of TANF funds to develop a curriculum, including several booklets and videos, to be distributed to all couples applying for a marriage license. The state has also developed a curriculum specifically aimed at fragile, African American families.[106] Currently, several federally funded demonstration projects evaluate the effectiveness of such intervention models.

Although marriage education and relationship programs are worthwhile, they are clearly not the panacea for solving the problems facing fragile families. Indeed, they may divert attention from the core problem facing such families – economic insecurity and the failure of welfare policy to address it. Reporting on the Fragile Family study, Mincy and Huang find that the employment status of the father is the most important factor on the future of the relationship. If the father is employed during the week before the birth, the odds a household unit will be formed increase by 41 percent and the odds of marriage increase by 48 percent. They note that the importance of the father's employment is confirmed by other studies as well.[107]

As we have seen, the major reason that "the magic moment" fades is because the fathers experience high unemployment and lack of a steady job. Both parents are reluctant to marry in the face of economic uncertainties, and the

[102] Garfinkel & McLanahan (2003), p. 77.

[103] An example is the PREP program. S. Stanley, S. L. Blumberg, & H. Markman (1999). "Helping Couples Fight for Their Marriages: The PREP Approach." In R. Berger & M. Hannah (Eds.), *Handbook of Preventive Approaches in Couple Therapy*. New York: Brunner/Mazel; Garfinkel & McLanahan (2003), p. 79.

[104] Garfinkel & McLanahan (2003), pp. 79–80.   [105] Ooms and Wilson (2004), p. 443.

[106] Ibid., p. 444.   [107] Mincy & Huang (2002), pp. 9, 25.

relationship problems they experience become more acute in such a context. Limited education, lack of job skills, and prior incarceration are formidable barriers to becoming a reliable and stable provider for the family. This is amply demonstrated in the evaluation of the Parent's Fair Share (PFS) experiment. Designed to increase the earning capacity of low-income noncustodial fathers, PFS provided these men with an array of employment and training services, including job search, skill training, remedial education, and on-the-job training.[108] After two years, there was little overall improvement in employment, but some improvement in earnings. Those without a high school degree or with little recent work experience did see a modest improvement in employment and earnings. However, for the more-employable fathers, there was no improvement in earnings and a slight decline in employment.[109]

In contrast, programs that increase the amount of income available to single-parent families seem to increase their rate of marriage. Project New Hope targeted two poor neighborhoods in Milwaukee, offering the experimental group generous work support benefits, including wage supplements to raise the participants' income to the poverty level, child care subsidies, low-cost health insurance, and community service jobs for those who were not able to find employment. The program had two important organizational features. It was voluntary and totally outside the welfare system.[110] After a five-year follow-up "the marriage rate among New Hope program group members was 9% higher than the marriage rate among control group members."[111]

The Minnesota Family Investment Program (MFIP) also provided financial incentives to work by increasing the basic grant by 20 percent when the recipient went to work and by disregarding 38 percent of the earnings in calculating the family's grant level. The evaluation, using a random assignment, found that MFIP reduced the divorce rate in two-parent recipient families who were already receiving welfare. However, it had no effect on two-parent families who applied for welfare at the start of the evaluation.[112] One reason might be that such families exited welfare quickly.[113] For single parents, MFIP also resulted in a dramatic decline in domestic abuse, and a modest increase in marriage rates.[114] The Canadian Self-Sufficiency Project, which also provided strong financial incentives to work, increased the marriage rate in one province but decreased it in another.[115] What seems to be working is a model

[108] Martinez & Miller (2000).   [109] Ibid., p. 41.
[110] A. Gassman-Pines & H. Yoshikawa (2006). "Five-Year Effects of an Anti-poverty Program on Marriage among Never-Married Mothers." *Journal of Policy Analysis and Management* 25: 11–30.
[111] Gassman-Pines & Yoshikawa (2006), p. 24.
[112] L. A. Gennetian & V. Knox (2005). "The Effects of a Minnesota Welfare Reform Program on Marital Stability Six Years Later." *Population Research and Policy Review* 23: 567–93.
[113] Ibid., p. 587.
[114] L. Gennetian, V. Knox, & C. Miller (2000). "Reforming Welfare and Rewarding Work: A Summary of the Final Report on the Minnesota Family Investment Program" (MDRC, New York).
[115] Gennetian & Knox (2003), p. 21.

of income support that enables such families to combine earnings and income assistance without fear of time limits.

Despite its rhetoric, PRWORA does not encourage couples to stay together and get married. The categorical restrictions on various public assistance programs (e.g., TANF, child care, housing subsidies), as well as means tests, create disincentives to live together. Garfinkel and McLanahan propose several remedies to make TANF and related programs more marriage friendly.[116] They suggest that the TANF benefit for the second parent be at least 50 percent of the single-parent benefit in a one-parent family. The benefit for the second parent would continue if they marry. If the parents are not married, then the benefit would depend on both parents working or engaged in "some other socially productive activity (besides caring for the new infant)," for example, education and training. For the first year, the hours of work or education or training would be substantially less than what is currently required for a two-parent TANF family. TANF services would be offered to the father as well as the mother, although for the father, the emphasis would be on employment, unless there was a potential for further education.[117] Although these are useful proposals, we have no confidence in the underlying logic of TANF or its revisions. In the next chapter, we propose a different approach that is based on a children's allowance and improved benefits and income assistance for workers in the low-wage labor market.

Family Cap

The idea that welfare benefits encourage nonmarital births was revived during the 1970s and 1980s. Charles Murray's popular *Losing Ground* argued for this theory. Even though the incentive effects of welfare are relatively small in nonmarital births, the supporters of this theory were successful in promoting a family cap to decrease childbearing among welfare recipients as well as the number of children with absent fathers.[118]

Twenty-three states have some kind of "family cap" or "child exclusion" policy. Seventeen states have had these provisions through AFDC waivers prior to the 1996 reform.[119] The cap provides no increment in TANF benefits for a baby born to a welfare mother. The rationale for the family cap is both economic and moral. The family cap should be a disincentive for having more children and an incentive to use contraception while on welfare. The moral justification is that women on welfare do not deserve to have more children

---

[116] Garfinkel & McLanahan (2003), p. 78.   [117] Ibid., pp. 77–78.

[118] McLanahan & Carlson (2002).

[119] W. T. Dyer & R. W. Fairlie. (2005). "Do Family Caps Reduce Out-of-Wedlock Births? Evidence from Arkansas, Georgia, Indiana, New Jersey and Virginia." *Population Research and Policy Review* 23: 441–73.

while on aid. Opponents worry that the family cap will increase abortions and can compromise the well-being of children.[120]

In 1992, New Jersey became the first state to adopt the family cap, under a waiver. An evaluation of the New Jersey program in 1998 showed that the nonmarital birth rate had declined by 8 percent among welfare recipients and the abortion rate increased by 12 percent. However, many methodological questions have been raised about the validity of the experiment.[121] In Arkansas, the only other state with a rigorous evaluation, there was no significant effect of the family cap on nonmarital births.[122]

Several recent studies on the effect of the family cap reach the same conclusion. There is no evidence that it has reduced birth rates or increased the rate of abortion. Dyer and Fairlie compared the first five states to implement a family cap to states that did not implement a family cap. Using Current Population Surveys (CPS) data from 1989 to 1999, they find no difference in birth rates between family cap and nonfamily cap states.[123] Comparing New Jersey to nonfamily cap states in the Northeast, they find a small negative effect, but it is not significant. They also do not find that the family cap affects marriage rates. Joyce and colleagues use a different approach, comparing low-educated unmarried women with and without previous births in eighteen states with family cap.[124] Data on the women were also derived from CPS from 1992 to 1999. They also find no independent effect of the family cap on either birth rates or abortion rates. Kearney uses monthly state-level birth rates for women aged 15 to 34 to compare between family cap states and nonfamily cap states from 1989 to 1998.[125] She shows that "at no point between 1989 and 1998 does the average monthly fertility decline more sharply (or increase less steeply) for states that implement family cap relative to states that do not."[126]

One of the consequences of the family cap is to create a category of undeserving children known as "cap children."[127] Both these children and their mothers experience undue hardship. The child does not count as deserving support and the mother may not be exempt from her work requirement to care for her child or get additional child care support. Recently, a number of states have either eliminated the family cap or are beginning to phase it out.[128] Kansas considered the family cap but then decided that the sixty-month time limit was a sufficient disincentive. Maryland and Illinois repealed the policy

[120] J. Levin-Epstein (2003b). "Lifting the Lid off the Family Cap" (CLASP Policy Brief No. 1, Child-bearing and Reproductive Health Series, December), p. 1.
[121] T. Joyce et al. (2005). "Family Cap Provisions and Changes in Births and Abortions." *Population Research and Policy Review* 23: 475–511.
[122] McLanahan & Carlson (2002), p. 155.   [123] Dyer & Fairlie (2005), p. 457.
[124] Joyce et al. (2005).
[125] M. S. Kearney (2004). "Is There an Effect of Incremental Welfare Benefits on Fertility Behavior?" *Journal of Human Resources* 39: 295–325.
[126] Ibid., p. 308.   [127] Hays (2003).
[128] Levin-Epstein (2003b), pp. 2–3.

in 2004.[129] In Arizona, child support payments to a "capped" child go directly to the child rather than the state agency that recoups welfare costs. There have been several proposals in Congress to eliminate the family cap option, but none has passed.[130]

Domestic Violence

Although domestic violence occurs in all social classes, "women living in economically distressed families and communities are more likely to experience domestic violence, and the violence is more severe."[131] Patel and Turetsky note that lack of financial resources is one of the principal reasons that women often stay in or return to a violent partner.[132] Domestic violence can be a significant barrier to work. Abuse can be triggered or escalate when women enroll in job search, start work, or bring child-enforcement proceedings.[133]

Although PRWORA exempts families from the five-year lifetime limit if a member has been battered or subjected to extreme cruelty, it is the Wellstone/Murray amendment, titled Family Violence Option (FVO), which specifically addresses domestic violence.[134] According to Patel and Turetsky, states can grant temporary "good cause" waivers from the time limits, the work participation requirements, child-support cooperation, and family cap requirements, if compliance would increase the risk of domestic violence. States are required to screen and identify recipients with a history of domestic violence (but maintain confidentiality) and refer those so identified to counseling and supportive services. At present, forty-four jurisdictions have adopted the FVO, and the remaining ten have special provisions for victims of domestic violence in the current TANF state plans.[135] Although states have broad discretion under FVO, only those states that have adopted the FVO will receive "special consideration" when seeking to avoid penalties for failing to meet the participation requirements. States have to have an individualized self-sufficiency plan that will "'lead to work' in a safe and fair way, which is developed by a person trained in domestic violence."[136]

---

[129] National Conference of State Legislators, *Family Cap Policies*; downloaded from http://www.ncsl.org/statefed/welfare/familycap05.htm.

[130] Levin-Epstein (2003b), p. 3.

[131] N. Patel & V. Turetsky (n.d.). "Safety in the Safety Net: TANF Reauthorization Provisions Relevant to Domestic Violence" (CLASP, Washington, D.C.), referring to Office of Justice Programs (2004). "When Violence Hits Home: How Economics and Neighborhood Play a Role" (Research in Brief, U.S. Department of Justice, September, Washington, D.C.), p. 1.

[132] Patel & Turetsky (n.d.), p. 1, citing M. Davis, "The Economics of Abuse: How Violence Perpetuates Women's Poverty." In R. Brandwein (Ed.) (1999). *Battered Women, Children, and Welfare Reform: The Ties that Bind* (Thousand Oaks, Calif.: Sage); E. Lyon (1997). "Poverty, Welfare and Battered Women: What Does the Research Tell Us?" (The National Resource Center on Domestic Violence, Harrisburg, Penn.).

[133] Patel & Turetsky (n.d.), p. 1.

[134] Ibid., p. 3; 42 U.S.C. 608(b)(1).

[135] Patel & Turetsky (n.d.), p. 3.

[136] Ibid.

Ample research indicates that welfare recipients experience a higher rate of domestic violence than women in the general population.[137] Estimates of the number of welfare recipients severely abused in a lifetime range from a low of 33 percent to a high of 61 percent. Tolman and Rosen, using data from the Women's Employment Study (WES), find that 51 percent of welfare recipients in the sample experienced severe abuse in their lifetime and 15 percent in the past twelve months. Sixty-three percent reported lifetime physical abuse and 23 percent reported physical abuse in the past twelve months.[138] The comparative rates for a national sample of all women are 22 percent and 8 percent, respectively.[139] The women experiencing domestic violence in WES also had a much higher rate of physical and mental health problems, drug dependence, and material deprivation. However, these women did not show significant difference in employment than recipients who did not experience abuse.

Still, domestic violence must be considered an important barrier to employment, particularly because it may interact with other barriers such as physical and mental health problems. Several studies suggest that domestic violence does interfere with the ability of the women to work.[140] Using a panel study of welfare recipients in Illinois over three years, Riger and colleagues do find an association between recent experience of abuse and work instability.[141] In addition, as noted in Chapter 5, recipients who experience domestic violence are more likely to be sanctioned for noncompliance with TANF work requirements. No doubt, the relationship between domestic violence and employment is complex. Local employment conditions, the women's human capital, relations with partners (e.g., threats to the women if they seek employment), employment of the partners, and ethnicity all influence the ability of the abused women to work.[142]

How does TANF respond to the needs of these women? Apparently, not well. Reviewing several studies, Saunders and colleagues note an extremely low rate of domestic violence disclosure or detection rates.[143] Nor do workers routinely inform women about the services and exemptions available in the event of domestic violence. Apparently, workers are reluctant to ask about domestic violence and prefer that the women volunteer the information. The women, however, may also be reluctant to reveal abuse because of fear

---

[137] For a review, see R. M. Tolman & J. Raphael (2000). "A Review of Research on Welfare and Domestic Violence." *Journal of Social Issues* 56: 655–82.

[138] R. M. Tolman & D. Rosen (2001). "Domestic Violence in the Lives of Women Receiving Welfare." *Violence against Women* 7: 141–58.

[139] Tolman & Rosen (2001), p. 148.

[140] S. Riger, S. L. Staggs, & P. Schewe (2004). "Intimate Partner Violence as an Obstacle to Employment among Mothers affected by Welfare Reform." *Journal of Social Issues* 60: 801–18.

[141] Ibid., p. 812.

[142] S. Riger & S. L. Staggs (2004). "Welfare Reform, Domestic Violence, and Employment." *Violence against Women* 10: 961–90.

[143] D. G. Saunders et al. (2005). "TANF Workers' Responses to Battered Women and the Impact of Brief Worker Training." *Violence against Women* 11: 227–54.

of official repercussions. Moreover, even when the women do report being abused, they are unlikely to get help. A survey of welfare recipients and workers confirms these findings.[144] An ethnographic study by Lindhorst and Padgett of ten battered welfare recipients who experienced very dangerous acts of violence find that none received services through the FVO.[145] The women were not informed about FVO and its exemption provision. The recipients could not remember whether the workers asked them about domestic abuse. The workers, in turn, felt that it was up to the women to report the abuse, but some of the women were afraid to reveal it because the workers who enforce child support could use the information and provoke the abuser. Lindhorst and Padgett suggest several organizational reasons for the apparent failure of FVO, including the focus of the workers on case closure, lack of organizational and personal resources to respond to the women's needs, and workers' general distrust of welfare recipients.[146]

PRWORA and Teens

When Congress debated PRWORA in 1996, the subject of teen parents was at the center of attention. At that time, teen mothers on welfare were the symbol of all that was wrong with welfare. They came to signify the terrible social costs of the breakdown in family values and discipline, of rampant and irresponsible sexual behavior, and of a life mired in dependence on public assistance.[147] By sounding the alarm of a national crisis, lawmakers could reinforce values such as abstinence from premarital sex, the sanctity of marriage, and the importance of hard work and self-reliance. A key assumption of welfare reform was that parents would set a different example for their children. The children would be less likely to engage in risky behavior, to become pregnant, and more likely to complete their education and seek paid employment.[148] Six years later, the subject of teen parents has rarely come up, in part because of the continued decline in teen pregnancies, which, from 1991 to 2003, had plummeted by one-third.[149] Teen nonmarital birth rates also declined. According to the National Center for Health Statistics, "the teenage birth rate fell 3 percent in 2003 to 41.6 births per 1,000 women aged 15–19 years, another record low for the Nation.... Declines in rates have been especially striking for black

[144] Ibid., pp. 238–44.
[145] T. Lindhorst & J. D. Padgett (2005). "Disjunctures of Women and Frontline Workers: Implementation of the Family Violence Option." *Social Service Review* 79: 405–29.
[146] Ibid., pp. 421–25.
[147] J. Handler & Y. Hasenfeld (1997). *We the Poor People: Work, Poverty and Welfare*. New Haven, Conn.: Yale University Press.
[148] D. Fein (2003). "Transition to Welfare Parenthood by Welfare Recipients' Daughters: Do Recent Trends Suggest a Culture Change?" (Paper presented at the 25th Annual Research Conference of the Association for Public Policy and Analysis, Abt Associates, Inc., Washington, D.C., November 6), p. 1.
[149] National Center for Health Statistics (2005). *National Vital Statistics Reports*, 54, p. 2

teenagers: their overall rate dropped 45 percent since 1991. . . . Rate declines for all teenagers were substantial enough to more than compensate for the increased number of female teenagers, so that the number of births to women under the age of 20 dropped to the fewest since 1946, the first year of the baby boom."[150] The decline may be due, in part, to an increase in the use of contraceptives, which has risen substantially from 67 percent in 1988 to 75 percent in 2002 for females and from 71 percent to 82 percent for males.[151] In addition, the number of teen parents on welfare has declined. From 1996 to 2001, the number of teen parents on welfare has declined by 50 percent, although their share among all recipients rose from 1.9 percent to 2.3 percent.[152] Despite these positive developments, teen pregnancies and childbirth in the United States remain considerably higher than in other postindustrial countries. For example, the teen childbirth rate is twice as high compared with the United Kingdom and Canada and seven times higher than in Sweden.[153]

Teen Single Mothers, Fathers, and Their Children

Research indicates that the risk of becoming a teen single parent is associated with sociodemographic factors, such as being African American or Hispanic, living in a high-poverty neighborhood, paternal poverty, having a single mother, and low maternal education. Individual conditions, such as early sexual activity, antisocial behavior, poor performance in school, and affiliation with peers with similar characteristics also increase the risk.[154] Similar risk factors exist for teen fathers. However, protective factors are high educational expectations, high basic skills, and high self-esteem.[155]

What do we know about the fathers of the children of single teen mothers? Lopoo, using data from the Fragile Family study, compared these fathers with fathers married to teen mothers and fathers married to nonteen mothers. He found that they are much younger, more likely to be African American, have low levels of education, poor employment, lower earnings, and a history of incarceration and domestic violence.[156] Therefore, marriage is quite risky for teen mothers. Women who marry in their early teens are more likely

---

[150] Ibid., p. 2.   [151] Child Trends (2005). "Facts at a Glance."
[152] Committee on Ways and Means (2004), p. 7-4.
[153] J. E. Darroch, S. Singh, & J. J. Frost (2000). "Differences in Teenage Pregnancy Rates among Five Developed Countries: The Role of Sexual Activity and Contraceptive Use." *Family Planning Perspectives* 33: 244–50, 281.
[154] R. Levine Coley & P. Lindsay Chase-Lansdale (1998). "Adolescent Pregnancy and Parenthood." *American Psychologist* 53: 152–66; H. Xie, B. D. Cairns, & R. B. Cairns (2001). "Predicting Teen Motherhood and Teen Fatherhood: Individual Characteristics and Peer Affiliation." *Social Development* 10: 488–511.
[155] A. Kalil & J. Kunz (1999). "First Birth among Unmarried Adolescent Girls: Risk and Protective Factors." *Social Work Research* 23: 197–208.
[156] L. Lopoo (2005). "A Profile of the Men Who Father Children with Unwed, Teenage Women" (Working Paper No. 05-21-FF, Center for Research on Child Wellbeing, Princeton, N.J.), pp. 1–32.

to experience severe and persistent poverty; they are unlikely to have completed high school, be in poor health, and have an increased risk of sexually transmitted disease. They are likely to have a second birth fairly soon and experience a high divorce rate.[157] At the same time, there is an argument in favor of establishing paternity for minor parents. According to Paula Roberts, even if the father has little income, he has a financial responsibility, and this might encourage an early pattern of meeting that responsibility. In time, it is likely that his income will increase, and the child will be more secure financially. Although paternity should be established quickly and accurately, there should be adult oversight, including blocking paternity establishment in cases of rape, incest, and domestic violence.[158]

The consequences for children of unwed teens are not good. There are more premature births and more low-weight births. There are greater risks of death, mental illness, and other disabilities. Moreover, children of teen mothers do less well in school than children of mothers who delay childbearing. Kane and Sawhill report that "half are more likely to repeat a grade, standardized test scores are lower, they are less likely to finish high school, more likely to experience neglect and abuse, and end up in child protection and foster care." As adults, they are more likely to be unemployed and give birth as a teen. The negative effects are reduced but not eliminated when controlling for the characteristics of the mother. Kane and Sawhill say that the cost to society is estimated at $3,000 per teen mother (2003), which are the costs per student of a high-quality after-school program.[159]

There are, therefore, very good reasons to reduce teen parenthood, a goal set by PRWORA. We first look at the effects of PRWORA on teens on welfare. Then we explore the degree to which it is achieving its objectives of reducing out-of-wedlock birth, increasing school attendance, and discouraging forming an independent household among teens.

Teen Mothers on Welfare

The 1996 welfare reform has had an effect on teen parents. Minor teen mothers (aged 15–17) are much less likely to be on TANF.[160] Although the focus of welfare reform is on teen parents, only 12 percent of teen recipients have children

[157] P. Roberts (2004a). "No Minor Matter: Developing a Coherent Policy on Paternity Establishment for Children Born to Underage Parents" (Center for Law and Social Policy, Washington D.C.), pp. 1–38.
[158] Ibid., p. 22.
[159] A. Kane & I. Sawhill (2003). "Preventing Early Childbearing." In I. V. Sawhill (Ed.), One Percent for the Kids: New Policies, Brighter Futures for America's Children. Washington, D.C.: Brookings Institution Press, p. 60.
[160] G. Acs & H. Koball (2003). "TANF and the Status of Teen Mothers under Age 18" (No. A-62, New Federalism: Issues and Options for States, Urban Institute, June, Washington, D.C.), p. 1.

of their own.[161] The percentage of teen mothers who received cash assistance dropped considerably – from 25 percent in 1997 to only 5 percent in late 1999/ early 2000. Acs and Koball speculate that this drop may be only temporary and that the teen mothers may go on welfare at a later date. Almost 80 percent did receive other forms of assistance (food stamps, WIC, housing), which was about the same before and after the reform.

Living Arrangements

To qualify for aid, TANF requires teen mothers to live with a parent, a legal guardian, or an adult relative. They can be excused if such a living arrangement is not possible, would harm the child, or expose them to domestic violence. In such circumstances, other placements are possible – for example, an adult-supervised living arrangement or an independent arrangement.[162]

Most teen parents continue to live with their mothers and are in school. The research evidence on the living arrangement is limited and mixed. In one study, before 1996, teen mothers who lived with their parents obtained more schooling. However, a small post-TANF study in Michigan showed the opposite – a decrease in school enrollment and graduation. In addition, there is evidence (not statistically significant) of an increase in depression among teens living in a three-generation household.[163]

Funding is needed for alternative living arrangements for teen mothers who cannot live in approved situations. In the Center for Law and Social Policy (CLASP) survey of twenty state administrators, thirteen had concerns about the lack of alternative housing options or the difficulties in assessing the safety to teen mothers in current living arrangements. The Bush Administration has proposed $33 million for "second change" homes.[164]

School Attendance

As soon as their infants are twelve weeks or old, teen mothers must participate in school or approved training. Most state TANF officials believe that the school completion and activities requirements have positive effects, but these programs lack necessary supportive services (e.g., learning disability, mental health, and substance abuse counseling). Evaluations of school attendance programs before TANF showed moderate, if any, effects. In Ohio's Learning, Earning, and Parenting (LEAP) program, school enrollments, attendance, and the likelihood of graduating or receiving a GED did increase for those who were *already in* school but did not affect those who had already *dropped*

[161] J. Levin-Epstein & J. Hutchins (2003). "Teens and TANF: How Adolescents Fare under the Nation's Welfare Program: An Update on Women's Health Policy" (Issue Brief, Kaiser Family Foundation, December).

[162] Ibid., p. 3.   [163] Ibid.

[164] Center for Law and Social Policy (CLASP) (2001). *The Minor Parent Living Arrangement Provision.* Retrieved from http://www.clasp.org/publications/minor_parent.pdf.

out. The in-school participants also had higher employment and earnings. However, the positive effects disappeared after about two years. In California, teen parent participants did graduate at a significantly higher rate than non-participants, but half failed to graduate. In contrast to Ohio, in California, the most significant effects were on the dropouts. In Wisconsin, Learnfare had no effect on improving school attendance.[165]

Teen mothers are more likely to engage in risky behavior. Among all teens aged 15–17, 43.8 percent drink alcohol, 45.3 percent smoke, and 20 percent use marijuana. Teen mothers engage in all three risk-taking behaviors to a greater extent – 60 percent drink alcohol, 57.4 percent smoke, and 30.6 percent use marijuana. Further, teen mothers who live with parents do not reduce their risk-taking behavior by much, except in the use of marijuana.[166] The authors conclude that there is no evidence that teen mothers have been affected by welfare reform policies in general or by the residency and activities requirements. They speculate that if teen mothers continue to use welfare at this low rate they may fail to take advantage of training and other support services.[167]

Sanctions

Under TANF, both sanctions and bonuses can be used to enforce school attendance. Teen parents are sanctioned at higher rates than adults under TANF. In a survey by CLASP, in a single month, almost 2,500 teen parents were sanctioned in five states that collect data on school participation, which was a much higher rate than adults in those states. This is consistent with other studies that show that younger recipients are more likely to be sanctioned than older recipients.[168] According to a GAO study, the sanction rate for the teen mothers was higher than the sanction rate for TANF families in general – for example, 5.6 percent of teen mothers were sanctioned in California, compared with 0.9 percent of the general caseload. In Illinois, 10.5 percent of teen mothers were sanctioned, compared with 5.3 percent of the caseload.[169] Quite often, it is the more vulnerable families that are sanctioned. In South Carolina, it was the teen mothers with the lowest educational levels; in Utah, 72 percent of those sanctioned had three or more employment barriers. In Milwaukee (under AFDC), 20 percent of the teen mothers who were sanctioned had suffered abuse and neglect; 21 percent had been in the Children's Court

[165] Levin-Epstein & Hutchins (2003), pp. 3–4. For similar conclusions, see D. Campbell & J. Wright (2005). "Rethinking Welfare School-Attendance Policies." *Social Service Review* (March), pp. 2–28.
[166] Acs & Koball (2003), p. 4.   [167] Ibid., p. 5.
[168] Levin-Epstein & Hutchins (2003), p. 4.
[169] J. Levin-Epstein, C. Grisham, & M. Batcher (2001). "Comments to the U.S. Department of Health and Human Services Regarding Teen Pregnancy Prevention and Teen Parents Provisions in the Temporary Assistance for Needy Families (TANF)" (Center for Law and Social Policy, Washington, D.C., November 30), p. 9.

system. In Tennessee, because of concern over sanctions, a "customer review" showed that approximately one-third of the cases scheduled for closure at the time of the assessment were not closed. A University of Memphis review found that a third of families sanctioned for not signing a personal responsibility plan did not understand the requirement. Espstein and her colleagues say that much more attention has to be paid to the sanction notice process, including more personal interviews with teen mothers.[170]

Teen Children of Welfare Recipients

Personal Responsibility and Work Opportunity Reconciliation Act implicitly assumes that its work requirements will also have a positive developmental effect on the adolescents of welfare recipients. That is, by becoming employed, the parents will serve as positive role models to their children, and the increase in their income will enable them to invest more in them. As a result, the adolescents should have better school outcomes. An analysis of results from eight experimental studies of welfare-to-work programs does not support this assumption.[171] Gennetian and colleagues found that adolescents in the experimental groups were more likely to have lower school performance, perform below the average in the school, and repeat a grade.[172] The effects were more pronounced in programs that required the mothers to work or participate in employment-related activities and when there were younger siblings in the household. The researchers speculate that the mothers' employment reduced time available for adult supervision while pushing the adolescents into added household chores.[173]

Does PRWORA Affect Rates of Teen Pregnancy, School Dropout, and Independent Living Arrangements?

Lacking studies using experimental design, it is a difficult question to answer. Researchers have relied on a strategy of following cohorts of high-risk teens before and after the passage of PRWORA and assuming that, other things being equal, changes in their behavior could be attributed to welfare reform. Clearly, however, there may be many other factors that could affect the differences found in behavioral outcomes between the two cohorts.[174]

[170] Ibid., p. 10
[171] L. A. Gennetian et al. (2004). "How Welfare Policies Affect Adolescents' School Outcomes: A Synthesis of Evidence from Experimental Studies." *Journal of Research on Adolescence* 14: 399–423.
[172] Ibid., p. 410.   [173] Ibid., pp. 413–14.
[174] For a review, see P. Offner (2003). "Teenagers and Welfare Reform." (Urban Institute, Washington, D.C.), pp. 1–41.

Using data from the National Longitudinal Surveys of Youth (NLSY), Kaestner and O'Neill compared a teen cohort from 1979 with a cohort from 1997 and found that welfare reform has reduced nonmarital birth, reduced school dropout rates, and increased the proportion of teen mothers living with their parents.[175] But, Offner points to several methodological problems, including the fact that the two cohorts are separated by eighteen years, casting doubt about the validity of the findings.[176] To correct for these problems, Offner uses cohorts from 1989–92, 1993–96, and 1997–2001. He finds welfare reform is associated with reduction in school dropout rates, mostly for teens without children, but it had no appreciable effect on living arrangements, except for teens having a child during TANF, and a slight reduction in having children.[177]

Hao and Cherlin, using NLSY97, followed teens born in 1980–84 with data on fertility and school enrollment over the years from 1994 to 2000. Two cohorts between the ages of 14 and 16 were compared, the first during the pre-reform era and the second during the reform era.[178] They find that PRWORA has not significantly reduced pregnancy, childbirth, or school dropout as intended. Teen girls living with their welfare parents were more likely to have birth in the reform era, but this finding was not replicated for other disadvantaged family backgrounds.[179] The authors also acknowledge the limitations of this study, including following the girls only from the age 14 through the age 16. Thus, we conclude, tentatively, that PRWORA has not yet achieved its aims with regard to teens, except possibly in reducing school dropout rates. This is not surprising given the greater importance of community, family, and personal attributes in shaping the life course of teens.

Can Abstinence-Only-until-Marriage Programs Reduce Teen Pregnancies?

The public discourse on ways to reduce teenage pregnancies has always been a highly morally charged issue.[180] Not surprisingly, conservative religious groups and the Bush Administration have pushed to promote and fund abstinence-only-until-marriage education. The start of federal support for abstinence-only education was the Adolescent Family Life Act (AFLA), enacted in 1981. The goal was to prevent premarital teen pregnancy by establishing "'family centered' programs to 'promote chastity and self discipline.'"[181] Adoption was

---

[175] Quoted by Offner (2003), p. 12.   [176] Ibid., p. 13.

[177] Ibid., pp. 23–32.

[178] L. Hao & A. J. Cherlin. (2003). "Welfare Reform and Teenage Pregnancy, Childbirth, and School Dropout" (Department of Sociology, John Hopkins University, Baltimore, Md.), pp. 1–35.

[179] Ibid., p. 28.

[180] See, for example, K. Luker (1996). *Dubious Conceptions: The Politics of Teenage Pregnancy*. Cambridge, Mass.: Harvard University Press.

[181] Kaiser Family Foundation. (2002). "Sex Education in the U.S.: Policy and Politics" (March), p. 2.

promoted as a preferred option for pregnant teens; there were also support services for pregnant and parenting teens. The first year $11 million was appropriated; thereafter, funding was renewed annually, reaching $12 million in 2001. Funding was increased substantially with the 1996 welfare reform. Under section 510 of the Social Security Act, $50 million per year were to be allocated to the states for a period of five years for abstinence-only programs for both teens and unmarried adults. The legislation specifically prohibits use of the funds to advocate the use of contraceptives or discussion of contraceptive methods except to emphasize their failure rate.[182] States are required to match $3 for every $4 of federal money. In 2000, Congress passed a new abstinence-only education initiative funded through the Maternal and Child Health Block Grant's Special Projects of Regional and National Significance (SPRANS). Its purpose is to provide grants directly to community-based (including religious) organizations. Targeted to teens between ages 12 and 18, programs funded under SPRANS must teach eight points: [183]

1. Have as its exclusive purpose teaching the social, psychological, and health gains to be realized by abstaining from sexual activity.
2. Teach abstinence from sexual activity outside marriage as the expected standard for all school-age children.
3. Teach that abstinence from sexual activity is the only certain way to avoid out-of-wedlock pregnancy, sexually transmitted diseases, and other associated health problems.
4. Teach that a mutually faithful, monogamous relationship in the context of marriage is the expected standard of sexual activity.
5. Teach that sexual activity outside the context of marriage is likely to have harmful psychological and physical effects.
6. Teach that bearing children out of wedlock is likely to have harmful consequences for the child, the child's parents, and society.
7. Teach young people how to reject sexual advances and how alcohol and drug use increases vulnerability to sexual advances.
8. Teach the importance of attaining self-sufficiency before engaging in sexual activity.

Total federal spending on abstinence-only programs for 2004 reached $138 million with projected spending for 2005 at $268 million.[184] Despite the federal efforts, sex education policy is mostly decentralized. States vary in terms of

[182] C. Dailard (2002). "Abstinence Promotion and Family Planning: The Misguided Drive for Equal Funding" (The Gottmucher Report on Public Policy, New York), pp. 1–2.
[183] From Levin-Epstein & Hutchins (2003), Fig. 5, p. 6, excerpted from Section 510(b), Title V of Social Security Act.
[184] The Sexuality Information and Education Council of the United States (SIECUS) (2003). *Federal Spending for Abstinence-Only-until-Marriage Programs (1982–2006)*. Retrieved from http://www.siecus.org/policy/states/2004/federalGraph.html.

curriculum. Some give instruction on HIV/AIDS and other sexually transmitted diseases (STDs). The Kaiser Family Foundation says that more states
require education on HIV/AIDS than general sex education.[185] Specific
requirements as to what should be taught also vary. Some states require that
abstinence be taught, others that it be stressed; thirteen states require sex
education to cover contraception, but no state requires that birth control be
emphasized. Then, there is usually considerable discretion at the local school
district level.[186]

There is considerable debate about the effectiveness of abstinence only-
until-marriage programs, compared with "comprehensive" programs that
include both abstinence and education about contraception. Those who favor
abstinence only argue that education or discussion about contraception and
safer sex sends a mixed message and encourages sexual activity.[187] In contrast,
proponents of a comprehensive program argue that although young people
should abstain from sex until they are emotionally and physically ready, for
those who are sexually active, information about birth control, safe sex, and
disease prevention is essential. Most Americans (81%) are in favor of a comprehensive approach; 18 percent support abstinence only until marriage. The vast
majority (95%) of public schools offer some form of sex education, and most
principals (58%) say that their programs are comprehensive. A third (34%) of
the principals say that their schools teach abstinence only.[188]

Currently, four abstinence-only programs funded under Title V, section
510, are being evaluated using an experimental design.[189] There are substantial variations in the delivery of the various educational components, and
only one program has delivered all the educational components. In two of
the programs, the youth in the experimental groups were less supportive of
teen sex. No behavioral outcomes are yet available.[190] According to Douglas Kirby, there are only three evaluation studies that use experimental or
quasi-experimental designs and measure outcomes on sexual or contraceptive
use, pregnancy, and childbirth,[191] and "none of the three evaluated programs
showed an overall positive effect on sexual behavior, nor did they affect contraceptive use among sexually active participants."[192] In contrast, programs that
offer sex and HIV education that include information about use of contraceptives tend to delay the onset of sex, reduce the frequency of sex, or reduce

[185] Twenty-one states require both sex education and instruction on HIV/STDs; seventeen require
instruction on HIV/STDs but not sex education. Kaiser Family Foundation (2002), p. 3.
[186] Ibid., p. 3. [187] Ibid., p. 1.
[188] Ibid., p. 1.
[189] R. A. Maynard et al. (2005). "First-Year Impact of Four Title V, Section 510 Abstinence Education
Programs" (Mathematica Policy Research, Inc., Princeton, N.J.).
[190] Ibid., p. xxxiv.
[191] D. Kirby (2001). "Emerging Answers: Research Findings on Programs to Reduce Teen Pregnancy
(Summary)" (National Campaign to Prevent Teen Pregnancy, Washington, D.C.), pp. 1–21.
[192] Ibid., p. 8.

the number of sexual partners.[193] Kirby also reports that more comprehensive programs, such as those offered by health or family planning clinics, which include one-to-one counseling, clear instructions about contraceptives, and access to them, result in greater use of contraceptives without increase in sexual activity. Community learning programs for teens, which involve voluntary service in the community and structured time for group meetings, also demonstrate effectiveness in reducing incidences of unprotected sex.[194] There is also evidence to suggest that programs that combine youth development and reproductive health components lead to delayed sex and reduced pregnancy. One such exemplar program is the Children's Aid Society Carrera Program. It is a long-term and intensive program that combines a range of services, such as family life and sex education, tutoring and help with homework, work-related activities (e.g., job club, employment), sports activities, and comprehensive physical and mental health care. The evaluation of the program, using experimental design, shows positive results in sexual and contraceptive behavior, pregnancy, and birth among teens for at least three years.[195] Among the girls, there was a significant reduction in sexual activity (but not among the boys), and the pregnancy rate was reduced by half (10% among the participants vs. 22% among the controls). There were higher high school graduation rates and college enrollment.[196]

There is also a religiously and adult-driven social movement for adolescents to make a public pledge to abstain from sex until marriage. Bearman and Bruckner find that adolescents who pledge delay first intercourse. However, it is effective for younger and middle, but not older, adolescents and only when the pledgers are in a distinct self-conscious minority community. That is, once the pledging becomes the norm in the school, it loses its effectiveness.[197] In a follow-up survey when the adolescents were between the ages 18 and 24, the researchers find that there are no significant differences in STD infection rates between pledgers and nonpledgers. In part, this may be because pledgers are less likely to use condoms at first intercourse or be tested for STDs.[198] This finding raises further questions about the wisdom of abstinence-only programs, which fail to provide information about contraceptives and safe sex.

Conclusions

There is a pernicious quality to the emphasis on family values and responsible teen behavior when it diverts attention from the need to invest in poor families

[193] Ibid.   [194] Ibid., pp. 13–14.
[195] Ibid., pp. 15–16.   [196] Kane & Sawhill (2003), pp. 63–64.
[197] P. Bearman & H. Brückner (2001). "Promising the Future: Virginity Pledges and First Intercourse." *American Journal of Sociology* 106(4, January): 859–912, p. 902.
[198] H. Brückner & P. Bearman (2005). "After the Promise: the STD Consequences of Adolescent Virginity Pledges." *Journal of Adolescent Health* 36: 271–78.

and their children. As we have seen throughout this chapter, advocates of family values engage in the rhetoric of perversity. They attribute the hardships and difficulties that poor families and their teen children experience to their moral deficiencies, while ignoring the economic deprivations they experience. Their logic rests on the notion that had these families adopted traditional middle-class values they would have avoided their predicament. Yet, the low marriage rate in fragile families is not a result of rejection of middle-class values or the institution of marriage. Quite the contrary, both parents have high aspirations for marriage and see the importance of raising their children in a two-parent family. However, they do not marry because they face formidable economic barriers and uncertainties while lacking access to a decent income safety net. In addition, they live in unsafe and segregated neighborhoods that are deprived of economic opportunities. In other words, if we are serious about promoting family values we need to make major investments in fragile families. Even the modest proposals by Garfinkel and McLanahan to make TANF more family friendly[199] would demonstrate a truer commitment to family values than the current policies that devalue such families, particularly the fathers.

The same is true for reducing teenage pregnancies and childbirth. Effective programs require not only economic assistance to their parents but also major investments in their education. For example, as discussed more fully in Chapter 8, for teens living in poor neighborhoods, Kane and Sawhill propose investment in intensive year-around after-school programs that contain a mix of academics, community service, stipends for community work, and social and enrichment activities.[200] Such programs have been shown to be quite effective in reducing teen pregnancies and childbirth. Yet, they are not cheap, costing up to $4,000 per year per student. Kane and Sawhill estimate that about $1,000 per year on average per student would be sufficient. The total cost would be $2.5 billion. The benefits, at a minimum, would be at least $3,000 for every teen birth that is avoided.[201] Still, the current federal approach is to invest in abstinence-only programs that are relatively cheap yet fail to demonstrate effectiveness.

---

[199] Garfinkel & McLanahan (2003), pp. 77–78.   [200] Kane & Sawhill (2003), pp. 65–67.
[201] Ibid., pp. 68–69.

8   Addressing Poverty and Inequality

The Starting Point

1. This book is primarily about single mothers and their children. Other categories of people are poor and are clearly in need of help – two-adult families, childless couples, nonaged single adults, and children without families. A principal theme of this book is how this country has substituted "welfare" for poverty and inequality, how we have demonized the single-mother family, and why the more pressing issues are poverty and inequality. There is no moral or logical reason why other categories of the poor should not be included, and, as is discussed shortly, most of our proposals would apply to other categories of the poor. But in one book (already too long) we cannot cover everyone.

2. Even within the category of poor single-mother families, we cannot explore all the relevant issues. We concentrate on income support (basically, a children's allowance), reforming the low-wage labor market, improving child care, and community-based employment/services for those who have barriers to the labor market. Other relevant issues such as health care, affordable housing, education, transportation, and neighborhoods are clearly important to improving the lives of these families. We touch on these issues, but, again, we only mention the importance of these issues and discuss some of the parameters, but cannot deal with them in detail.

3. There has to be adequate income support for these families. By adequate support, we mean a *minimum adequate standard budget*, which is discussed at length in Chapter 2. A minimum adequate budget is *not* the official poverty line. It is considerably above the poverty line. The official poverty threshold by which our country judges "success" is seriously out of date and inadequate. Families at or below the poverty threshold have major problems in coping with just the daily necessities of life. They live on the edge and often suffer from food insecurity, inadequate housing, utility cutoffs, and poor health.

Even families who are "near poor" – within 200 percent of the poverty line – are seriously threatened. One significant change in their lives – sickness, an accident, the loss of job, an eviction – and the family is in poverty. This accounts for why so many Americans experience spells of poverty during the life course. This is unacceptable. We have to do better.

4. Families can only obtain a minimum adequate budget if they *combine* cash assistance with earned income. Cash assistance alone, such as a basic income guarantee, would be far too expensive, require large tax increases, and would crowd out other valuable programs, such as health care, child care, and housing.

5. We present various proposals for a children's allowance. The children's allowance would allow all families with children and no other income to at least reach the poverty threshold. The allowance would be based on the number of children per family. It would not be means tested. The various proposals suggest how higher-income families would be treated (e.g., phase-out plans).

6. This means that we would abolish TANF. This program is miserly, discrim- inatory, degrading, and expensive to administer. Everyone hates "welfare" and for good reason. It is time to stop demonizing single mothers. It is time to elim- inate the state and local welfare bureaucracies that have been so distorted by the demands of a dysfunctional, contradictory program. The universal chil- dren's allowance, with no conditions and no sanctions, would provide more income support than TANF without all of the baggage of "welfare."

7. Basic income support in the form of a children's allowance is, in effect, a basic income guarantee for families. It is morally and logically indistinguish- able from a basic income guarantee for all people – childless adults, single adults, and so on. The only reason we restrict our proposal to families with children is that a universal basic income guarantee, at this point in time, seems totally unrealistic, whereas there seems to be more support for helping poor children.

8. Our second main recommendation is improving the low-wage labor market for families who want an income higher than that provided by the children's allowance. As discussed in Chapter 6, the great majority of mothers are in the low-wage labor market. We have a number of recommendations:

   a. There should be guaranteed jobs for all who want to work; if necessary, there should be public jobs to fill the gaps.
   b. The minimum wage should be raised.
   c. The EITC should be raised and improved.

d. There are several ways that government and NGOs can help employers improve the working conditions of low-wage work and remain competitive.

e. There has to be job-related benefits, especially some form of government-subsidized health care.

f. There should be subsidized opportunities to enhance human capital.

g. The unemployment insurance (UI) system has to be reformed to take into account temporary, flexible, part-time work; at present, low-wage workers experience considerable episodes of unemployment that are not covered by the present system.

h. The Social Security Disability Insurance should be liberalized; now it is much too difficult for people who have employment barriers to qualify.

i. Supplemental Security Income (SSI) should be reformed to cover more adults and children who are in poor health. It is encouraging that before the recent recession, when states had budget surpluses, considerable public funds were spent on helping the working poor.

9. There has to be major improvements in the child care system. As described in Chapter 6, low-wage working single mothers are in a constant scramble to manage both contingent, multischeduled work and child care. Very large numbers of infants and preschoolers are in inadequate child care. They suffer developmentally, socially, and in health. (a) There should be extended family leave for mothers of infants; (b) there should be significant increases in child care subsidies so that mothers can purchase better child care; (c) there should be an increase in public and nonprofit support for quality child care centers.

10. Although not discussed at length in this book, prenatal and child health care should be improved.

11. Along with improvements in the child care system, there are several proposals for universal prekindergarten education. Millions of low-income children enter kindergarten with cognitive and social deficits that last throughout adolescence and diminish their educational and career opportunities.

12. Even with improvements in the low-wage labor market and child care, there will be mothers who cannot enter the paid labor force because of a variety of barriers. Some may need modest levels of support – job search, skills training; others will need more extensive services. There will be health needs as well as human capital needs. We propose the establishment of independent community-based public or nonprofit social service/employment services. The agencies would be evaluated on how they deal with the more difficult cases, rather than the current practice, which encourages "creaming" or fitting clients into available slots.

13. The provision of income support through some form of children's allowance and the separate, independent social/employment services emphasize one of our major conclusions: that there should be no sanctions for mothers who are not in the paid labor market. There are two principal reasons for this position: (a) there are multiple reasons why mothers are not in the paid labor force. Some may think it more important to attend to their children or other family matters or want to improve their education and employment skills. And others may wish to pursue other activities (e.g., charitable, community, artistic). They should make these decisions, not agency caseworkers who are under a variety of pressures and incentives to process clients and make decisions that are more determined by bureaucratic demands than client needs. Some mothers may have subtle barriers (e.g., unrecognized depression). Some will shirk or "abuse" the system. However, the number of shirkers or abusers is small, and most adults will not choose this lifestyle even if financially supported. There are always people looking for work who cannot find it. Antipoverty and welfare policy has always been fixated on the shirkers or abusers rather than assisting the large majority who "play by the rules." As a result, the obsession with the abusers has distorted and deformed welfare programs. (b) The second reason relates to administrative (in)capacity, discussed in Chapter 5. This point cannot be overemphasized. Repeatedly, welfare policies have been enacted without sufficient appreciation of the difficulties of implementation. Policy makers always blithely assume that work requirements and other conditions can be implemented and that local offices can effectively administer these new programs. Frontline workers cannot manage discretionary, judgmental services that carry penalties. As demonstrated in the past decade of welfare reform, overworked, undertrained workers resort to sanctions and diversion. They simply lack the resources and the capacity to provide skilled, sensitive, and effective social and employment services. And this has *always* been the case when aid is conditioned on the moral judgment of the recipient. It is time that we recognized that implementation is a *major* stumbling block and that those mothers and children who cannot negotiate the barriers should not pay the price.

The Interconnectedness of Poverty Issues

In discussions about poverty, welfare reform, the low-wage labor market, and child care, one has to discuss each topic. What we want to emphasize, however, is the *interconnectedness* of each of the areas. A single mother is a low-wage worker; she periodically becomes un- or underemployed; she is a mother; she and her children have health problems; they lack affordable housing; they live in less-than-desirable neighborhoods; their children often have inadequate health care and go to inferior schools. Their lives are fluid, and their circumstances change. As we pointed out in Chapter 2, this is true of poverty.

In a very important sense, the term "poverty" is misleading. It not only is seriously inadequate, but it gives the impression that it is a bright line: below it is bad, above it "everything is OK." But families barely get by with incomes substantially above the "poverty" threshold. Yet, we are constantly told that after welfare reform, things are not so bad because the poverty percentages of single-mother families and their children have not increased substantially. However, we have to account for the near poor as well as those officially below the poverty line and those in "extreme poverty" (half of the official threshold). As we have argued, in this country, there are very serious problems of inequality and hardship for families who work hard, play by the rules, but live day by day, barely making it. People move in and out of "poverty," but they rarely move very far, and one bump sends them back below the poverty threshold.

Therefore, when we discuss the various conclusions and recommendations, we want to always keep in mind the interrelatedness of the lives of these people. Improving the low-wage labor market ought to improve income, but this depends on the costs and quality of child care, transportation, health care, housing, and education. As we discuss, raising the minimum wage and reforming the unemployment system are essential, but the mother also needs reliable, good child care, and she and her children have to get good health care. The families need income, but income alone is not enough without decent housing, child care, health care, better schools, and safe neighborhoods. All of the recommendations are *necessary*, but each one separately is *not sufficient*. The topics have to be discussed separately, but they are not separate.

Welfare leavers disproportionately work in low-wage, low-skilled, nonstandard jobs. Most of these families are "playing by the rules." It may seem odd that we would use that phrase, but just as we want to reject the use of "poverty" as a standard, we reject the labels of "undeserving poor," the "African-American welfare queen," and in a prior age, Catholics, Irish, Italians, Jews, and others from southern Europe, and today, undocumented immigrants. Ever since the beginning of our Colonial history, when the first poor people asked for help, they were *blamed* for their condition. It did not matter that jobs were not available, that many were indentured tenants at the mercy of their landlords, that many were sick, that husbands and fathers died during the wars or at sea.[1] Poverty was still *their* fault, and that aid, if given, would have to be carefully supervised lest deviant behavior be encouraged. America still adheres to these views. As discussed in Chapter 4, the single mother continues to be demonized. The nonaged childless adults are treated even worse. In many states, there is no aid at all; in others, it is miserly and short term. They are usually confined to single hotel rooms (SROs) and shelters. We try to avoid them as they beg on the streets. Workers who lose their jobs or claim that

---

[1] See B.G. Smith (Ed.) (2004). *Down and Out in Early America*. University Park: Pennsylvania State University Press.

they are disabled are suspect. Are they trying hard enough to find another job? Unemployment insurance is low and short term; it must not encourage idleness. Disability is strict; most claims are rejected.

We strongly object to these views. The vast majority of single mothers, the subject of this book, have small families and they try hard to support themselves and their children in the paid labor market. The extensive ethnographic literature shows that they love their children and want them to succeed, but many face great odds. The combination of the demands of the low-wage labor market and balancing child care (see Chapter 6) is truly daunting. None of the readers of this book could succeed in such a high-wire balancing act. This is not to deny that many of these families suffer individual deficits. They lack skills; there are barriers to employment. Poor mothers do not read to their children, and so forth. What we reject is *blame* and the exclusive concern with individual reformation. Many of these families do need individual services, such as human capital development, education skills, and improvements in daily living, but this must not be done by ignoring the structural conditions under which these people live. Even during our most generous, liberal period – the War on Poverty – the emphasis was on individual behavior, not structural conditions. Poor people do need a "hand up," but the societal conditions in which they live have to be more hospitable. This we consistently ignore.

There were substantial changes in the 1990s, when the economy boomed and the states had surpluses. President Clinton significantly raised the EITC (discussed in Chapter 3). The EITC increases the income of the working poor. The states, with TANF and other surpluses, significantly helped the working poor with child care subsidies and state income supplementation. The country congratulated itself. The percentage of single-mother families in poverty did not rise and many of the working poor were lifted above the poverty line. But this makes our point. The poverty line cannot be the standard. As discussed in Chapter 2, many families above the poverty line still endure significant hardship and are continually threatened with sinking below the poverty line – the loss of a job, a breakdown in child care, an illness, an eviction. Despite the increase in state support, vast numbers of mothers could not afford decent child care, and many, many children are suffering. And now, with the recent recession, state surpluses have vanished and support for the working poor has declined.

The central thrust of our conclusions and proposals, then, focuses on the vast majority of families who are working, trying to work, poor or near poor, or threatened with poverty. There are four sets of proposals – and again, they are all *interrelated*:

1. Providing basic income support for all families with minor children that would not be dependent on earnings in the paid labor market. This would be a children's allowance. It would not be sufficient for a family

to maintain a basic, minimum budget, which is considerably above the present poverty threshold, but it would at least sharply reduce, if not eliminate "official" poverty.

2. Improving the low-wage labor market, making sure that decent jobs are available for all those who want to work, increasing the minimum wage, increasing the EITC, and increasing work-related benefits, child care subsidies, health benefits, vacations, and retirement benefits.

3. Improving child care. This would include paid family leave; increasing subsidies so that families can purchase quality child care; and increasing the supply of quality child care centers and providing universal, quality preschool.

4. Increasing the human capital and employment skills of the working parents or where parents have barriers to employment through community-based, independent public and private social service agencies. Thus, the proposals are *both* individually oriented and structural.

But what about childless adults? The answer here should be a basic income guarantee available to all and, when we propose reforms of the low-wage labor market *and* the guarantee of a good job *and* services for those who have barriers without sanctions, then we are approaching a basic income guarantee. Strong arguments have been made for a basic income guarantee; however, it is also argued that anything other than a very modest basic income guarantee (one that would provide a basic, adequate budget rather than the poverty threshold) would involve high tax rates and threaten other valuable programs (e.g., universal, adequate health care, child care).[2] What we propose will accomplish many of its objectives indirectly.[3] Our approach is strictly tactical. We have to concentrate on a few basic objectives. The book starts off with welfare reform and single mothers and their families. We make the argument that the great majority of these mothers are part of the working poor and the critical tasks are improving the low-wage labor market and increasing the income of families with children.[4] At least as judged by the improvement in

[2] P. Van Parijs (2004). "Basic Income: A Simple and Powerful Idea for the Twenty-first Century." *Politics and Society* 32(1): 7–40; B. Bergmann (2004). "A Swedish-Style Welfare State or Basic Income: Which Should Have Priority?" *Politics and Society* 32(1): 107–18; I. Garfinkel, C.-C. Huang, & W. Naidich (2002). "The Effects of a Basic Income Guarantee on Poverty and Income Distribution" (USBIG Discussion Paper No. 014, February 2002); E. O. Wright (2000). "Reducing Income and Wealth Inequality: Real Utopian Proposals." *Contemporary Sociology* 29: 143–56; Guy Standing (2002). *Beyond the New Paternalism: Basic Security as Equality.* London: Verso.

[3] P. Harvey (2005). "The Right to Work and Basic Income Guarantees: Competing or Complementary Goals?" *Rutgers Journal of Law and Urban Policy*, 2(1): 8–59; G. Standing (n.d.). "Why Basic Income Is Needed for a Right to Work" (unpublished manuscript on file with the authors).

[4] G. Dahl & L. Lochner (2005). "The Impact of Family Income on Child Achievement. Institute for Research on Poverty" (Discussion Paper No.1305-05, University of Wisconsin–Madison, August). This paper found that an increase in the EITC is correlated with an increase in the math test

the EITC and the state expenditures to help the working poor and children during the flush days of the 1990s, our country is at least somewhat supportive of the idea of helping the working poor and children. The book is about how we can do more on these two fronts. Health care, affordable housing, and education, as well as other social programs, are also crucial, but (at least for this book) we cannot take on everything and have to treat these issues lightly.

Why There Has to Be Both Jobs and Income Support

An ideal program would be a basic income guarantee that would allow families freedom to choose their lives. We think that the overwhelming majority of single mothers would, even with a basic income, work in the paid labor market. Others would choose a variety of activities, including taking care of their families. The problem is that a basic income conflicts with our other fundamental recommendation – that the standard should be the *minimum adequate budget*, which is significantly higher than the official poverty threshold. A basic income at this level would not be affordable.

Irwin Garfinkel and his colleagues propose four different basic income guarantee (BIG) plans: the Standard Plan, the Children Plus Plan, Single-Parent Plus Plan, and the Adult Plus Plan.[5] In the Standard Plan, all children to age 18 would receive $2,175 per year; all adults between age 18 and 65 $4,000, and the elderly, $8,000 or their Social Security payment. In the Children Plus Plan, each child would receive $4,000, each adult $3,150, and each elderly person $8,000. In the Single-Parent Plus Plan, the first adult with children would receive $6,000, other adults $3,000, each child $2,700, and each elderly person $8,000. In the Adult Plus Plan, each adult $6,000, each child $2,000, and each elderly person $8,000.[6] In all plans, Old Age, Survivors and Disability Insurance Program (OASDI) beneficiaries would either receive the BIG or their OASDI payments, whichever was higher. The plans would be taxable. In addition to the OASDI offsets, they propose eliminating 115 programs, as well as personal exemptions. They calculate the costs of all the plans as follows: The Standard Plan would cost about $1 billion; making the BIG taxable and eliminating exemptions reduces the net costs to $745 billion. The Adult Plus Plan is the most generous and would require an additional 5.5 percentage points in income tax rates.[7]

Garfinkel and his colleagues readily acknowledge that all of their plans are modest. Their justification is that there are other desirable social programs

scores and reading test scores of children (National Longitudinal Survey of Youth). "The results are even stronger when looking at children from disadvantaged families who are affected most by the large changes in the EITC."

[5] Garfinkel, Huang, & Naidich (2002).   [6] Ibid., p. 4.

[7] Ibid., pp. 4–5.

(e.g., universal education, health care, child care). A universal child care program would cost about $120 billion. Other programs, such as UI, Head Start, and WIC, should be improved. They also think it unwise to rely too heavily on a single program. A much larger BIG would require high marginal tax rates and discourage work in the legitimate labor market. They justify their plans on the reduction of poverty. The Adult Plus Plan – the most expensive to finance – reduces the overall poverty rate from 10 percent to fewer than 6 percent, the poverty gap by more than half – from $42 billion to $17 billion. "These are very significant improvements." The Child Plus Plan would reduce child poverty to 8 percent. The Single-Parent Plus Plan reduces child poverty to 11 percent.[8]

Although we do not deny the significant benefits from the Garfinkel plan, it seems clear that a BIG cannot accomplish the objectives that we propose. The standard is still the poverty line, and even here, it is reduced, not eliminated. The conclusion – which Garfinkel and his colleagues readily endorse – is that there has to be improvements in the low-wage labor market as well as a basic income. Neither one is sufficient, although both are necessary.[9] Others have made calculations for a BIG but also using the current poverty threshold.[10] Barbara Bergmann takes the same position – there cannot be high levels of a basic income without high taxes and sacrificing other programs.[11] Bergmann favors a Swedish-style welfare state, which provides many expensive services but also targets those in special need. There are what she calls "merit goods." These are goods that everyone should have and that there are people who would not be able or willing to acquire them. Although there may be disagreement on some of the items, her list includes schooling, health and mental healthcare, child care, free or partially subsidized college, decent housing, public transportation, and social services. Only a well-developed welfare state can provide these goods, but a state cannot afford a basic income grant at least of any significant size and the provision of quality merit goods.[12]

---

[8] Ibid., pp. 15–16, 20–21.   [9] Ibid., p. 20; Bergmann (2004).

[10] A. Sheahen (2005). "A Proposal to Simplify the Tax Code and Provide Every American with a Basic Income Guarantee" (unpublished manuscript) proposes an annual full BIG at the poverty level of $10,000 per adult and $2,000 per child. He would eliminate "all of the tax breaks and over half of the welfare programs." As with the other proposals, people who wanted more income would work in the paid labor market. The total cost of the proposal would be $1.9 billion. He would fund the proposal, among other things, by eliminating tax loopholes, adding a surcharge to incomes greater than $1 million and eliminating about 100 federal programs, with a 35 percent flat tax.

[11] Bergmann (2004).

[12] Ibid. One example she uses is child care. A free, universal system could cost $120 billion per year; a program with copayments, $60 billion. Improving the salaries of child care workers would add an additional 20 percent (p. 111). For a discussion of the pros and cons of a basic income (as well as other proposals, e.g., the stakeholders grant), see Wright (2000). Karl Widerquest questions Bergman's calculations. He claims that Bergmann uses the BIG as an "add on" for programs that already exist, e.g., an unemployed person would receive $15,000 in UI plus a $15,000 BIG, etc. "But that's not what anybody is proposing" (e-mail, August 8, 2005).

Our proposals build on some of the demonstration welfare-to-work projects that combined employment with subsidies and services. On the basis of several randomized welfare-to-work

Improving the Paid Labor Market

At present, the great majority of poor single mothers will be low-wage workers. As discussed in Chapter 6, single mothers average about $22,000 per year – from a variety of sources: earnings, welfare, family, friends. Earnings are the most important source, but just relying on earnings would generate income of about $13,000, which is below the poverty line. Income at this level is shameful. It has to be at least a minimum adequate budget, which is well above the official poverty line. And this is covers the necessities, no frills, no entertainment, no restaurant meals (not even fast food). Moreover, families even at this level are on the edge – a job loss, an illness, or an accident and they are back in poverty. As Philip Harvey points out, "labor markets tend to reward success with more success and punish failure with more failure."[13] This has to be changed. Success should be rewarded, but those who struggle in the low-wage labor market should not be punished.

The first task, then, is to improve the low-wage labor market. Nearly a third (32%) of American workers earn less than $15,000 per year, with an additional 20 percent earning between $15,000 and $25,000.[14] We think that there is substantial evidence that the great majority of single mothers would prefer work if the jobs were relatively decent, there were supportive services, and

experiments, Robert Havemen draws three conclusions: (1) the largest impact on employment and annual earnings come from programs that either require participation in employment services or that supplement earnings; (2) almost all of the programs that produced increased employment and earnings offered direct, and often substantial, earnings subsidies to low-skilled workers; there were only a few programs that increased both work and family income without supplements; (3) there were substantial, positive effects on school-age children in which both an increase in employment and in total income occurred. The principal programs that provided earnings supplements were the Canadian Self-Sufficiency Program (SSP), the Minnesota Family Investment Program (MFIP), and Milwaukee's New Hope Project. Whereas SSP and MFIP were offered only to families applying for welfare, New Hope was available to all low-income families. Child care and health care subsidies were also offered in New Hope. The MFIP offered employment, training, and job services. The Canadian SSP did not offer any services. The programs used different approaches; SSP had an income guarantee (i.e., welfare) and a graduated earnings subsidy if there was full-time employment. The MFIP had an income guarantee, a work bonus, and a graduated earnings subsidy without the requirement of full-time work. The MFIP, a welfare-to-work demonstration program, allowed long-term recipients to keep more of their cash assistance when they worked. There were significant changes – increased marriages and marital stability, a dramatic decline in domestic violence, and improved child outcomes (e.g., school performance). New Hope guaranteed a job plus a graduated earnings subsidy but only for full-time work. However, despite the differences in approach, all of these programs increased both earnings and total income. R. Haveman (2003). "When Work Alone Is Not Enough." In I. V. Sawhill (Ed.), *One Percent for the Kids: New Policies, Brighter Futures for America's Children*. Washington, D.C.: Brookings Institution Press, pp. 40–55.

[13] P. Harvey (2002). "Human Rights and Economic Policy Discourse: Taking Economic and Social Rights Seriously." *Columbia Human Rights Law Review* 33(2, Spring): 363–471, p. 439.

[14] L. Litchfield, J. Swanberg, & C. Sigworth (2004). "Increasing the Visibility of the Invisible Workforce: Model Programs and Policies for Hourly and Lower Wage Employees" (Final Report, Boston College Center for Work and Family, Carroll School of Management, April), p. 2.

families wanted a higher income than provided by a children's allowance. Improving the low-wage labor market would also help the men. We saw in Chapter 7 how important employment was for marriage or stable unions.

These jobs can be improved. The minimum wage should be raised.[15] The minimum wage, currently at $5.15 per hour, has not changed since 1997, and since 1968, its real value has fallen 64 percent. An increase of $1 per hour would significantly help families in the bottom one-third of the income distribution and significantly decrease the poverty rates of families where the head of the household is a minimum wage worker. There would be no budgetary costs, and there would be only minimal adverse effects on business and employ-ment.[16] Thirteen states (including the District of Columbia) have increased the minimum wage above the federal level; three more states have it under serious consideration.[17] Eileen Appelbaum and her colleagues, in urging an increase in the minimum wage at least to its 1979 level, if not higher, argue that the most recent economic evidence for negative effects on employment are quite small.[18]

At the current minimum wage, a full-time worker earns only $10,712 per year.[19] A report by the Economic Policy Institute challenges the often-repeated argument against raising the minimum wage because it is poorly targeted and would benefit mostly better-off working families.[20] The report argues that "the minimum wage is an effective tool for targeting families and households that rely heavily on low-wage work to maintain a decent standard of living."[21] The Fair Minimum Wage Act of 2004 proposes raising the federal minimum wage to $7.00. According to the Economic Policy Institute, nearly 60 percent of the benefits would go to families whose wages and salaries were in the bottom 40 percent although they earn only 15.8 percent of earnings. A substantial por-tion of these workers (38%) had incomes below 200 percent of the poverty line. The report states 1.4 million families have incomes just above 200 percent of the poverty line, and they depend on low-wage workers.[22] Furthermore, says the Economic Policy Institute, the minimum wage "is a fundamental state-ment of principle about the value of work, opportunity, and the responsibilities of employers."[23] Current rates allow employers to exploit the lack of bargaining power of the low-wage worker.[24]

[15] E. Appelbaum et al. (2005). "Low-Wage Employment in America: Results from a Set of Recent Industry Case Studies." *Journal of Socio-Economic Review* 3(2, May): 293–310, p. 305.

[16] Haveman (2003), p. 49. Eileen Appelbaum and her colleagues (2005) state that the most recent economic evidence indicates that the negative effects on employment would not be significant.

[17] J. Chapman & M. Ettlinger (2004). "The Who and Why of the Minimum Wage: Raising the Wage Floor Is an Essential Part of a Strategy to Support Working Families" (Issue Brief No. 201, Economic Policy Institute, August 6), p. 1.

[18] Appelbaum et al. (2005).   [19] Chapman & Ettlinger (2004), p. 3.
[20] Ibid., p. 1.   [21] Ibid.
[22] Ibid., p. 2.   [23] Ibid.
[24] Ibid., p. 3.

The earnings of 38 percent of low-wage workers (below 200% of the poverty line) contributed 68 percent of their total family income, almost half (47%) were married or had children, and 87 percent were 20 years of age or older.[25] Almost half (45%) of low-wage workers who were above the low-income line were married or had children. Thirty percent of low-wage workers above the low-income line were single adults without children. Many lived at home and their income was important for the families; 42 percent were in college.[26]

Even $8 per hour is not generous; full-time work yields only $16,640. Twenty-five percent of workers earning more than $8.00 per hour but with incomes below 200 percent of the poverty line were married parents, and 20 percent were single parents; many of these do not work full time.[27]

In California, in 2003, only 16.9 percent of workers earning within $1 of the minimum wage were teens. Low-wage workers are disproportionately Latino (32.6% of all workers, but 54.1% of low-wage workers).[28] Between 1996 and 2001, the California minimum wage law was raised, in steps, from $4.25 per hour to its current level of $6.75 per hour.[29] During this period, the earnings of both the low-wage and the median worker increased; the opposite happened during the period 1990–1996 when the minimum wage was not raised.[30] There was little, if any, loss of employment – for example, during the period of the increase, the annual growth in employment in food service and retail trade was greater than the average increase in total employment.[31] Nonetheless, despite the increases, the inflation-adjusted minimum wage has declined – 28 percent lower than in 1968, and a 4.7 percent decline since 2002. The California Budget Project estimates that a single parent with two children would have to earn $23.54 for a "basic family budget."[32]

Raising the minimum wage would not only increase the incomes of the workers but also protect firms that want to invest in upgrading the skills of workers and quality of the products. It would reduce the competition from firms that want to lower the wages of their most vulnerable employees and reduce the incentives for outsourcing and subcontracting.[33]

---

[25] Ibid.

[26] Ibid., pp. 4–5.

[27] Ibid., p. 6. Sixteen percent of the low-income, higher-wage workers were unemployed an average of nineteen weeks in 2002.

[28] California Budget Project (2004a). "Minimum Wage Increases Boost Earnings of Low-Wage California Workers" (Budget Brief, June), p. 1.

[29] Ibid., p. 4, n. 1.

[30] Ibid., pp. 1–2. Between 1996 and 2003, the earnings of workers at the tenth percentile of the earnings distribution rose by 19.9 percent, those at the twentieth percentile rose by 15.9 percent, and those at the median rose by 9.9 percent. During 1990–96, the hourly wages of all workers fell, at the tenth percentile by 9.9 percent, at the twentieth percentile by 8.4 percent, and at the median by 4 percent.

[31] Ibid., pp. 2–3.

[32] Ibid., p. 3.

[33] Appelbaum et al. (2005), p. 305.

The EITC has had a significant effect on increasing the employment of single mothers, reducing reliance on cash assistance, and reducing poverty.[34] Currently, the EITC increases for families with two children but not for families with three or more children. More than half (54%) of poor children live in these families.[35]

Robert Haveman suggests various options for increasing earned income. He would supplement the EITC, citing the examples of New Hope and SSP. The increase would apply to full-time workers (at least thirty hours per week). There should always be an incentive to increase work hours and earn higher wages. He would phase out the EITC slowly so that there would be only a 30 percent increase in the phase out for every $1 increase in income.[36] For single mothers who work full-time at $8 per hour, the EITC is largely offset by federal and state taxes (mostly payroll). Haveman would exempt the poorest families from these taxes. Because welfare checks are not taxed but paychecks for low-income workers are, there are disincentives to work even with work-related credits. One proposal would be a second benefit tier to the EITC for families with at least one full-time worker – for example, $2,000 for earnings up to $20,000, and then phased down. Studies have shown that various other options would result in substantial income supplementation and reduction in the poverty gap: reducing the EITC marriage penalty, increase income supplements across the board, target supplements on families with children, and increase the size of the credit for those who work substantial hours.[37] However, Haveman points out that the costs increase as the number of families receiving subsidies increases as the expansions go up the income distribution. On the other hand, there are marginal work disincentives with phase-outs, and many low-income families already have high marginal tax rates.[38]

He would accelerate the phasing in of the Child Tax Credit (CTC) so that it is fully phased in within five years. This would encourage work and reduce the marriage penalty.[39] In 1997, the CTC was added to work-supported benefits of low-income families. In 2001, it was made partially refundable, and it is scheduled to increase to $1,000 per child by 2010. The annual budgetary cost is estimated to be about $90 billion. The package, including the EITC and the dependent exemption, would cost about $90 billion, provides substantial assistance to some families, and encourages low-wage workers to work

[34] R. Greenstein (2005). "The Earned Income Tax Credit: Boosting Employment, Aiding the Working Poor" (Center on Budget and Policy Priorities, July 19), quoting Rebecca Blank that "there is 'unanimous' agreement that the EITC expansions implemented in the 1980s and 1990s increased employment among single parents." The report discusses the conclusions of Bruce Meyer and Dan Rosenbaum, Stacy Dickert, Scott Houser and John Scholz, Jeffrey Grogger, and Ron Haskins. According to Greenstein, based on census data (2002), "the EITC lifted 4.9 million people out of poverty, including 2.7 million children. *Without the EITC, the poverty rate among children would have been nearly one-third higher*" (emphasis original); Greenstein (2005), p. 3.
[35] Greenstein (2005), pp. 4–5.   [36] Haveman (2003), p. 50.
[37] Citing Sawhill & Thomas (2001); Haveman (2003), pp. 44–45.
[38] Haveman (2003), pp. 45–46.   [39] Ibid., p. 50.

full time. However, the package favors the poor and the upper-income families over the near-poor and the middle-income families. According to Haveman, the combinations create large marginal disincentives for middle-income families.[40]

Haveman suggests a variety of options to deal with these disincentives, but they involve additional budgetary costs. One proposal is to unify the family credit into a single, expanded refundable credit for families with children. There would be a 50 percent supplementation rate, for a maximum credit of $3,500 for earnings up to $7,000. Between $7,000 and $16,000, the credit would remain constant, and then begin to phase out at a 10 percent rate between $16,000 and $36,000. For earnings greater than $36,000, there would be a credit of $1,500 (which is equal to the approximate value of the CTC and the dependent exemptions). It is claimed that this integration and simplification would yield more work-related income for the poorest working families, substantially reduce the very high earnings disincentives, increase the support for middle-income families, and reduce the sizeable marriage penalty, especially for single parents. This would also simplify the federal tax code. There would be a single table instead of three separate tables for the separate tax subsidies. It is estimated that the costs of this proposal would be about $7 billion.[41]

Another proposal is to provide a full refund of the employee portion of the payroll tax on the first $10,000 of earnings of one parent with children earning less than $15,000 per year, with a phase-out above $15,000. This would provide nearly $800 per year in income supplements and would encourage full-time work, with a modest budgetary cost.[42]

Another proposal discussed by Haveman is the adoption of a marginal employer-based employment subsidy. An example would be a tax credit, or other financial subsidy, equal to 50 percent of the first $10,000 of wages paid to as many as fifty employees in the firm. This would stimulate jobs. He cites the New Jobs Tax Credit in the late 1970s, which was a "potent and cost-effective" means of increasing the employment of low-wage workers.[43] Others have proposed compensating mothers for child and family care.[44]

How much would this cost? In view of the supports already in place, Haveman estimates earnings could be supplemented substantially at a relatively small budgetary cost. For example, the simplified family credit proposal in

---

[40] Ibid., p. 46.

[41] Citing Sawicky, Cherry, & Denk (2002); Haveman (2003), p. 46.

[42] Haveman (2003), p. 47.

[43] Ibid., p. 48, n. 26. However, some have expressed doubts about employment subsidies. See, e.g., S. Hamersma (2005). "The Effects of Employer Subsidy on Employment Outcomes: A Study of the Work Opportunity and Welfare-to-Work Tax Credits" (Discussion Papers, DP No. 1303-05, Institute for Research on Poverty, University of Wisconsin–Madison, July).

[44] N. Zatz (2005). "Beyond Employment: Work Requirements, Caretaking, and Liberal Justice" (unpublished manuscript).

2003 would cost about $10 billion. For $15 to $20 billion, earnings could be supplemented even more, which would significantly support low-skilled workers in their efforts to hold full-time jobs. Accelerating the CTC would not affect budgetary projections. Supplementing the EITC for full-time workers to bring them up to the poverty line (three million poor families with at least one full-time worker) would cost about $15 billion. With two full-time workers, the costs would be about $10 billion. Along with a modest increase in the minimum wage, there would be a sizeable reduction in poverty for working poor families.[45]

Still, even with a full-employment economy, people are looking for jobs, or, discouraged, have dropped out of the labor market. People looking for jobs should have regular, direct-hire jobs and not be placed in temporary agency jobs. It has been shown that the practice of using temporary agencies as a stepping stone is not effective over the long term in either reducing poverty or increasing employment.[46]

We support guaranteed jobs for all those who want to work; this would include direct job creation if necessary.[47] Philip Harvey has long argued for this position. Macroeconomic policies can only go so far in reducing unemployment before inflation picks up. Other measures can reduce unemployment, for example, targeted educational and job training. Harvey thinks that shortening the normal working hours would not be effective because of the lack of targeting.[48] Direct job creation can be done through public works or services contracting with private firms, special employment programs, or expanding regular public sector jobs.[49] He argues that direct job creation could be "fiscally neutral" in that transfer payments would be reduced, tax receipts increased, and fees could be charged for some part of the output.[50] Direct job creation can be narrowly targeted to areas and populations with higher unemployment, which would reduce inflationary pressures. Employees moving into the regular market would also have anti-inflationary effects. Harvey does not suggest that direct job creation would be inflation-free but

[45] Haveman (2003), pp. 50–52.

[46] D. Autor & S. Houseman (2005). "Temporary Agency Employment as a Way out of Poverty?" (MIT Department of Economics and NBER, Cambridge, Mass.; W. E. Upjohn Institute for Employment Research, Kalamazoo, Mich.). "Although increasing job placements through temporary help agencies does raise the probability that Work First participants will earn above welfare and poverty thresholds over very short time horizons, these positive effects quickly dissipate. Over horizons of one to two years, placements in temporary agency jobs (relative to no job placement) do not increase the chances that participants will earn enough to leave welfare and escape poverty. . . . [O]ur results suggest that raising direct-hire placements is likely to be a much more effective means for job assistance programs to reduce welfare dependency among their clientele over both the short- and long-term" (p. 30).

[47] Harvey (2002). See also W. Quigley (2003). *Ending Poverty as We Know It: Guaranteeing a Right to a Job at a Living Wage.* Philadelphia: Temple University Press.

[48] Harvey (2002), pp. 449–57.   [49] Ibid., p. 457.

[50] Ibid., p. 457.

thinks the risks of unmanageable inflation are low.[51] In Harvey's view, a more serious problem is "displacement." For example, under CETA, almost all the positions that were created were used by local governments to replace regular employees, but then the program was redesigned to reduce the displacement effects. There are also "indirect displacement" effects, but Harvey argues that these too can be minimized.[52] He cites the New Hope Project in Milwaukee as an example where jobs were created for families below 150 percent of the poverty. The evaluations were favorable, although this was a small program (only about 100 jobs at any one time). Well-targeted direct job creation would not only reduce joblessness but also increase public goods and services, contribute to national wealth, and stabilize the business cycle. Examples would be programs for rehabilitation of abandoned or substandard housing, recreational activities for children, and home-care assistance for the elderly poor.[53]

There is a concern that creating a "right" to work, with a guaranteed decent job, would evolve into a "duty" to work.[54] After all, if a decent job is available, why isn't that person working? This is a concern, but society has always had a "duty" to work whether, in fact, there were jobs or not. What we have tried to argue in this book is that a duty to work invariably turns out to be practically impossible to administer fairly. We think that with the great majority of able-bodied adults taking earned employment, we should not fall into the moralistic trap of requiring work.

In addition to increasing earnings, the jobs themselves can be improved. Reviewing a series of case studies sponsored by the Russell Sage Foundation and the Rockefeller Foundation, Eileen Appelbaum and her colleagues describe a number of regional labor market institutions that set industry standards and disseminate best practices, reduce training costs, encourage cross-firm mobility, and explore "how multiemployer bargaining and high union density can establish strong job quality and productivity norms." In other words, it has been shown that many firms can successfully take the "high road." Examples include reducing turnover by reorganizing work to make jobs more interesting and rewarding (several hospitals), increasing productivity by using worker input (a major bank, a department store), as well as other examples. They cite other research showing how temporary agencies can provide workers with greater skills and government can support intermediary labor market institutions that increase skills and coordination of public training.[55] The Boston College Center for Work and Family issued a report describing fifteen case studies of business and organizations that improved working conditions for low-wage workers. Examples were taken from retail,

[51] Ibid., pp. 458–59.   [52] Ibid., p. 460–64.
[53] Ibid., p. 468.   [54] Standing (n.d.).
[55] Appelbaum et al. (2005), p. 305.

financial, manufacturing, child care, education, hospitality, and info-imaging. Programs ranged from dependent care, employment development, financial assistance, financial incentives, and scheduling/leaves. Benefits varied – a more stable workforce, less absenteeism, improved training, a more stable entry-level workforce, increased productivity, the message that the company cares, increased income, increased employee loyalty, motivation, and recruitment, and a sense of community.[56] Paul Osterman describes the organization and training of the Industrial Areas Foundation and several of its projects, which combined job development, long-term training, community organizing, and political activity to improve the wages and working conditions of low-wage workers.[57] Dresser and Rogers also describe cooperative efforts between employers and low-wage workers to improve training and working conditions. Examples include home health care, hotels, and other service industries.[58]

Existing and proposed policies and programs, including our own, to improve the economic well-being of the working poor require the development of an organizational capability that enables the working poor to benefit from them. Current employment support services such as one-stop centers, Employment Retention and Advancement (ERA), and subsidized child care are beset by too many bureaucratic barriers that result in disincentives for poor people to access them. Among them are complex application, eligibility, and recertification procedures; lack of knowledge about available programs; limited access points; and stigma.[59] Indeed, if a single mother with two children in Maryland, working full time at $6.00, would also get EITC, state EITC, food stamps, and child care subsidies, her total income would rise from $12,480 to $30,000. In addition, she would also be eligible for subsidized health care.[60]

The reasons many women fail to obtain these benefits are obvious. Typically, the benefits are administered by different bureaucracies, each with its own particular eligibility requirements and onerous application procedures. In many instances, there is little coordination among the bureaucracies, which means that applicants must go through the application process, eligibility determination, and recertification repeatedly for every program or service they wish to obtain. The resources available for the various benefits, such as subsidized child care or transportation assistance, often outstrip the demand

[56] Litchfield et al. (2004), pp. 8–14.
[57] P. Osterman (2003). "Organizing the U.S. Labor Market: National Problems, Community Strategies." In J. Zeitlin & D. Trubek (Eds.). *Governing Work and Welfare in a New Economy: European and American Experiments.* Oxford: Oxford University Press, chap. 9.
[58] L. Dresser & J. Rogers (2003). "Part of the Solution: Emerging Workforce Intermediaries in the United States." In Zeitlin & Trubek (Eds.), chap. 10.
[59] J. Miller et al. (2004). "Building Bridges to Self-Sufficiency: Improving Services for Low-Income Working Families" (New York, MDRA and the National Governors Association Center for Best Practices), pp. 1–95.
[60] Ibid., p. 8.

for them, requiring a high degree of rationing. The bureaucracies themselves operate at hours that make it difficult for working poor to access them. They are short of competent staff that are overworked and have few incentives to invest in their clients. Indeed, as we have noted in Chapter 5, staff attitudes toward poor people, in general, and welfare recipients, in particular, are generally negative and stigmatizing.

Even agencies such as the one-stop centers, mandated to provide integrated services to the unemployed, are not expected to offer TANF services, food stamps, Medicaid, or child care subsidies. The centers are only required to provide information about them.[61] In a study of thirty one-stop centers, only six provided easy access to at least four of seven work supports – EITC, subsidized childcare, food stamps, publicly funded health care, cash assistance, child support, and transportation assistance. Easy access meant that the staff was active either by providing on-site application or in making the appropriate referral.[62] Fifteen of the one-stop centers were judged to provide medium level of access by having information on all the programs and offering active referral to only one or two of the seven work support programs. Nine were judged as having low access to work supports. Most important, only one center made active referrals to get assistance with the EITC.[63] Several centers also had a negative attitude toward serving TANF clients.[64]

What is needed is an organizational form, which is dedicated to the following objectives:

1. Make an explicit commitment to serve low-income working families by making them part of the organization's core mission.
2. Adopt the goals of helping families raise their household income in order to achieve long-term well-being and economic stability.
3. Create service delivery structures that are readily accessible to working families and that provide services in a nonstigmatizing, user-friendly fashion.
4. Develop collaborative relationships with other organizations, and identify ways to coordinate services and share information across multiple public and private partners.[65]

A prototype of such an organization is exemplified in project New Hope.[66] Targeted for low-wage families, the demonstration project consolidated a series of benefits to encourage employment and reduce poverty – earning supplement, subsidized health insurance, subsidized child care, and for those who cannot find a job, referral to community service jobs. Operated by a nonprofit

[61] E. Richer et al. (2003). "All in One Stop? The Accessibility of Work Support Programs at One-Stop Centers" (Center for Law and Social Policy, Washington, D.C.), pp. 1–45.
[62] Ibid., p. 8.   [63] Ibid., p. 9.
[64] Ibid., pp. 26–27.   [65] Miller et al. (2004), p. 65.
[66] T. Brock et al. (1997). "Creating New Hope" (MDRC, New York).

agency with a long history of advocacy work and direct services to residents in high-poverty neighborhoods, the project successfully implemented these objectives. Several elements in the design of the program were crucial to its effectiveness. The program was voluntary and nonstigmatizing, it consolidated and administered its four key components in one site, and it was adequately funded to serve its target population. There were several key organizational factors that had contributed to its success. First, the governing board represented all the key constituents – "program participants, business leaders, government officials, and representatives from nonprofit and community organizations."[67] Second, the executive leadership was highly experienced in running community-based organizations and was fully committed to the aims of the project. Third, the service technology – the processing and provision of the benefits – consisted of operating procedures that were fairly straightforward, based on a review of wage stubs or proof of unemployment. Although the program was concerned about the issue of fraud, the use of UI records provided an effective check of unreported earnings.[68] For each benefit, operating procedures were developed to encourage rather than discourage access to it. Thus, the service technology was designed to motivate community residents to apply and to use the benefits available through the program. Fourth, and equally important, the line staff developed a strong commitment to the program and their roles were defined to facilitate positive interaction with clients.[69]

The project reps, as they were called, were the focal point through which clients could access all the needed services. The reps were knowledgeable about each service component and how to process requests for them. They melded four roles – gatekeepers to services, benefit processors, job coaches, and counselors/advisors. They easily moved from one role to another depending on the needs and circumstances of their clients. Not surprisingly, the clients had very high praise for their project reps.

It should not come as a surprise that the representatives were motivated and committed to serving their clients. They worked in an organization that had broad acceptance in the community, reinforced a client-oriented culture, provided access to necessary resources to respond to the needs of their clients, and had given the staff an active voice in organizational decision making. Having access to valued resources they could offer their clients in a voluntary and nonpunitive context contributed to positive and rewarding relationship between the staff and the clients.

This does not imply that the program did not experience numerous organizational challenges, particularly in fine-tuning its service technology. Nonetheless, the evaluation of New Hope shows that the program was well used, increased employment and earnings, increased stable employment and

[67] Ibid., p. 17.   [68] Ibid., p. 147.
[69] Ibid., pp. 128–39.

average wages, reduced poverty, substantially increased the use of formal child care, and ultimately improved children's school performance and positive social behavior.[70]

In addition, there are a number of related labor market laws and programs that should be reformed. In Chapter 3, we pointed out that UI was designed for a labor market that is vastly different then the labor market today – from the steady, full-time worker who temporarily loses his or her job to the intermittent, flexible, temporary, changing jobs with frequent spells of unemployment. The benefits are low, about a half of the average wage, and last only twenty-six weeks, but whether an employee can receive benefits for the maximum period depends on his or her work history.[71] The earnings requirements exclude the low-wage, part-time, temporary workers. Unemployment must be involuntary, and the claimant must be actively seeking reemployment.[72] In addition to earnings requirements, claimants are not eligible if they quit work, are discharged for "cause," or are unemployed because of a labor dispute, and they have to be available for "suitable" work. Workers are often disqualified if they have to leave for family reasons because they are not considered "able and available" for work.[73] Because UI assumes steady work and is based on earnings rather than time worked, it disadvantages women, African Americans, and other part-time, low-wage workers.[74] Only about one-third of the less-skilled men and 16 percent of less-skilled women qualified for UI, and only about a third of the unemployed actually received UI. That percentage has been declining steadily from a high of 75 percent in 1975.[75] Unemployment insurance should be reformed to take account of the realities of the present labor market by reducing the amount of qualifying time, making part-time workers eligible, extending the maximum benefit duration, increasing the amount of benefits, and other changes.[76]

Disability insurance (DI) remains strict, and benefits are low. The 1996 welfare reforms excluded drug and alcohol addition.[77] At present, not even half the claimants are successful. There are approximately 4.5 awards per thousand

---

[70] A. C. Huston et al. (2003). "New Hope for Families and Children: Five-Year Results of a Program to Reduce Poverty and Reform Welfare" (MDRC, New York), pp. 1–218.

[71] G. Lester (2004). "In Defense of Paid Leave" (unpublished manuscript, UCLA Law School), p. 59.

[72] Ibid., p. 60; J. Peck & N. Theodore (2005). "Temporary Downturn? Temporary Staffing in the Recession and the Jobless Recovery." Focus 23(3), 31–34.

[73] Lester (2004), p. 60; D. Maranville (2002). "Workplace Mythologies and Unemployment Insurance: Exit, Voice, and Exhausting All Reasonable Alternatives to Quitting" (unpublished manuscript).

[74] Lester (2004), p. 60; M. B. Katz (2001). The Price of Citizenship: Redefining America's Welfare State (1st ed.). New York: Metropolitan Books, pp. 222–32; Maranville (2002).

[75] Lester (2004), p. 60; Katz (2001), pp. 222–32; Maranville (2002).

[76] See P. Levine (2005). "Unemployment Insurance over the Business Cycle: Does It Meet Workers' Needs?" (Department of Economics, Wellesley College, discussing, as well, the proposals of the Advisory Council on Unemployment Compensation, 1994, 1996).

[77] Katz (2001), pp. 209–16.

covered workers. About 7.9 million people receive DI; most are poor.[78] Disability insurance should be made less restrictive, and benefits should be raised.

The National Labor Relations Act and the NLRB have to be changed. At present, the process is so cumbersome that victims of unfair labor practices – discrimination, union organization, unpaid overtime compensation – think that the remedies are useless. Unions are important in raising wages and protecting workers. Yet, U.S. labor law is now sadly lacking in protecting workers who want to organize and bargain collectively.[79] There has to be protection of undocumented workers. Particularly egregious is the refusal to grant overtime pay awards to undocumented immigrants, even though they are considered to be covered by the law.[80]

There are also proposals to provide a variety of work-related services – for example, child care, transportation assistance, skills training, and expanding public service employment.[81]

For those who have significant barriers to employment, SSI should be available. Benefits levels should be increased. It is estimated that only about half (9.2 million) of the 17.8 million people with employment-related disabilities receive either SSI or SSDI.[82] At the present levels, most beneficiaries are significantly below the poverty level. The limits on savings and assets are too low. Before 1996, legal immigrants who were permanent residents generally qualified for SSI on the same basis as U.S. citizens. Now, unless they entered the United States before August 22, 1996, they are ineligible even if they have become impoverished or severely disabled since coming to the United States. These restrictions are much more severe than food stamps, Medicaid, and TANF and cause considerable hardship.[83]

Increasing the Income of Families: A Children's Allowance

There are a number of proposals for a children's allowance. Greg Duncan and Katherine Magnuson propose a modest allowance. For families with incomes

[78] K. Levine & J. K. Scholz (2002). "The Evolution of Income Support Policy in Recent Decades." In S. Danziger & R. H. Haveman (Eds.), *Understanding Poverty* (pp. 199–200). New York: Russell Sage Foundation; Cambridge, Mass.: Harvard University Press.

[79] Appelbaum et al. (2005); K. V. W. Stone (2004). *From Widgets to Digits: Employment Regulation for the Changing Workplace*. Cambridge, New York: Cambridge University Press.

[80] M. Weiner (2005). "Can the NLRB Deter Unfair Labor Practices? Reassessing the Punitive-Remedial Distinction in Labor Law Enforcement." 52 *UCLA Law Review* 1579.

[81] Haveman (2003), p. 48.

[82] W. Wilen & R. Nayek (2004). "Relocated Public Housing Residents Face Little Hope of Return: Work Requirements for Mixed-Income Public Housing Developments." *Clearinghouse REVIEW, Journal of Poverty Law and Policy* (61, November–December), p. 526.

[83] E. Sweeney & S. Fremstad (2005). "Supplemental Security Income: Supporting People with Disabilities and the Elderly Poor" (Center on Budget and Policy Priorities, July 19), pp. 4–6.

below $60,000, the allowance would be $300 per month for the child between birth and one year; thereafter, $200 per month until the child is age 5. The same allowance would be available for a second child. They acknowledge that although there are economies of scale, there are the expenses of two formal child care arrangements. On the other hand, they would not have the child allowance available for more than two children.[84] The monthly child allowance would help stabilize and enhance the economic conditions of the family during a crucial period. The higher amount ($300) reflects the fact that infant care is more expensive. For those families earning more than $60,000, there is the new child tax credit, which would avoid the stigma of a means-tested program and help generate support for the child allowance. They argue that the monthly payment to the parent would be a more visible recognition of the importance of parenting than tax credits or deductions and less subject to manipulation by tax preparers.[85]

Duncan and Magnuson estimate there would be approximately 4.6 million children under age 1, 3 million of which would be eligible for the child allowance. There are 18.3 million children between ages 1 and 5, and 11 million would be eligible. The total cost would be $39.4 billion annually, but the net cost would be considerably less. The total cost would be reduced by taxable income and the elimination of the child tax credit and the child care tax deduction. States would also be allowed to consider half of the child allowance as allowable income for TANF eligibility and food stamps. This would produce a net cost of $29.1 billion (but under our proposal, TANF would no longer exist). Taxable income reduces costs by $4.6 billion; elimination of the child tax credit for children under age 5, but not for older children, would reduce net costs by $16 billion, when fully phased in by 2010, and the child care tax credit would save $1.7 billion.[86]

They say that the benefits would be significant for low-income families. Almost $20 billion would go to low-income families. They calculate that there would be a benefit-cost ratio of 1.5 or higher, which would eliminate any net long-term costs. The authors point out that some of the benefit-cost ratios of some early intervention programs are much higher than 1.5. "Simulating calculations, a single mother with two children earning $10,000, would have an increase in income by about $2,000 to $3,000; for those with incomes of $20,000, the gain could be as large as $3,200, although this would depend on the state child care subsidy. And low-income married couples would also gain."[87]

[84] G. Duncan & K. Magnuson (2003). "Promoting the Healthy Development of Children." In I. V. Sawhill (Ed.), *One Percent for the Kids: New Policies, Brighter Futures for America's Children.* Washington, D.C.: Brookings Institution Press, p. 26. They say that there is some evidence that the welfare family cap may have discouraged additional childbearing.
[85] Duncan & Magnuson (2003), pp. 26–27.　　[86] Ibid., pp. 26–29.
[87] Ibid., pp. 29–30.

Improving Child Care

In Chapter 6, we discussed the dire consequences for children in poor quality care. Mothers have to be able to afford better care. According to Duncan and Magnuson, early education that is center-based and intensive improves short-term cognitive development and long-term academic achievement, reduces special education placements, and increases grade promotion. Their proposed child care allowances would enable parents to purchase better child care.[88] Parental leave should be extended until the child is six months old. With a child allowance, the leave would be partially publicly financed.[89]

Child Care: The Very Early Period

Prenatal care and perinatal screening is one of the most cost-effective ways to promote the development of children.[90] It is also important with regard to the mental health needs of low-income women. According to Duncan and Magnuson, in 1998, 83 percent of mothers received prenatal care during the first trimester. However, for high-risk mothers (e.g., adolescents, low-income), only 63 percent received prenatal during the first trimester. Only 4 percent received either no care or very late care (third trimester). Of those who did not receive care, a third did not have insurance or other financial means. Therefore, they propose that the costs of at least one and perhaps two prenatal visits, as well as education and outreach, be provided for this relatively small group of mothers.[91] To reduce the risks on cognitive and social development, all mothers of infants younger than six months of age should not be required to work. Parental leave should be extended to six months, partially funded by a children's allowance.[92]

Support for services for children with various behavior, emotional, cognitive, and motor impairments is poor. There is both a lack of funding and trained professionals. Comprehensive screening and interventions are lacking.

---

[88] Ibid., pp. 21–22. The authors say that nonexperimental studies of Head Start, which is a less intensive and less expensive program, show important long-term behavioral and academic benefits. They favor more intensive programs, rather than a more universal standard. With few exceptions, programs to teach parents to be better parents do not result in better academic outcomes.

[89] Ibid., pp. 23–24.   [90] Ibid., p. 18.

[91] Ibid., pp. 18–19.

[92] Ibid., pp. 23–24. Although most children whose mothers work during the first year develop normally, there is research that shows that child care during this period can have negative effects on cognitive development that can be lasting, at least into early childhood. Duncan and Magnuson say that the risks increase significantly higher when low-income mothers work more than twenty hours per week. Therefore, they argue that all mothers be exempt from the TANF work requirements as long as their children are younger than six months old and then from full-time work requirements (thirty hours per week) when the child is between six months and one year.

Waiting lists are long. There is a lack of coordination between services. The problem, at this point, say Duncan and Magnuson, is the lack of solid evidence as to what works. Therefore, there should be more funding for basic research.[93]

Children: Preschool

It is by now quite clear that the preschool years are a "time of great risk – and opportunity – for long-term development."[94] Healthy development requires "prenatal and perinatal health care, adequate economic resources, responsive caregivers, and when called for, intensive early education and mental health interventions."[95] And, according to Duncan and Magnuson, there is "clear evidence of the dangers of prenatal exposure to poor nutrition, infections, and environmental neurotoxins (e.g., alcohol, lead)."[96] Quality child care is crucial. Early maternal employment affects the quality of care and the subsequent development at least for some groups of infants in low-income families. They argue that the preschool years should be viewed as a distinct period of needs. In addition to prenatal care, perinatal screening, and health and mental health services, there should be a stable and adequate standard of living for preschool children. For high-risk children, there should be intensive, center-based early education programs, starting at age 3. This would be in addition to the universal pre-K programs for four-year-olds.[97]

Barbara Wolfe and Scott Scrivner propose a universal preschool for all four-year-olds. They say that there is general agreement that four-year-olds benefit from a stimulating environment with other children, and this is true for all children, regardless of income, family composition, or prior child care.[98] Most jobs for adults are year round and there are considerable advantages for consistent child care. The full day would be part education, taught by early education specialists, and the rest would be child care, under the supervision of lead teachers. The cost would be lower than full-day school.[99] Although the benefits to low-income children from low-income families would be greater, they argue that all of society benefits when children starting kindergarten are better prepared and have improved developmental outcomes.[100] They note that between birth and five years important linguistic, cognitive, social,

---

[93] Ibid., p. 22.

[94] Duncan & Magnuson (2003).

[95] Ibid., p. 16.

[96] Ibid.

[97] Ibid., p. 17. For a discussion of the impact of Head Start on children with disabilities (more than 134,000 were enrolled), see D. Ewen & K. B. Neas (2005). "Preparing for Success: How Head Start Helps Children with Disabilities and Their Families" (CLASP, updated May 6).

[98] B. Wolfe & S. Scrivner (2003). "Providing Universal Preschool for Four-Year Olds." In I. V. Sawhill (Ed.), *One Percent for the Kids: New Policies, Brighter Futures for America's Children*. Washington, D.C.: Brookings Institution Press, pp. 113–35.

[99] Ibid., pp. 115–16.

[100] Ibid., pp. 113–14.

emotional, and regulatory skill development occurs. They cite as the most convincing study the Chicago Child-Parent Center (CPC), an intervention program in a low-income area. Participation in pre-K ages 3 to 5 was associated with lower special education placements and grade retention, significantly higher rates of school completion by age 20, and lower rates of juvenile arrest. The average cost per recipient was $7,000 and the benefits to society, $47,759. They point out that evidence from other studies is strongly consistent, although there are selection biases. Head Start has better results in terms of high school graduation, and at least for whites, college and earnings. African American males are less likely to be convicted of crime, and there is some evidence of improved high school completion.[101]

Wolfe and Scrivner suggest as a model the universal preschool for four-year-olds in Georgia.[102] The program – Georgia Voluntary Pre-K (GPK) – is open to all children; there are no income eligibility requirements. The program is offered a minimum of 6.5 hours per day, five days a week during the school year (180 days). The program is financed by the state lottery. When the program started in 1992, it served only 750 low-income families, but within two years, it was serving 15,500 low-income families. The average cost per child cost was $5,032. As a result of the growth in the lottery, the program was expanded and local matching requirements were dropped. By 1995, all four-year-olds were included regardless of income. By 1999–2000, 63,000 children were enrolled using approximately $225 million in lottery proceeds. Approximately 70 percent of all four-year-olds were either in GPK or Head Start. The staff-to-child ratio was 1:10, and there was a maximum of twenty children per class. The curriculum was set by the state, although localities could choose from state-approved models, which were adopted from national proposals. There are state regulations for the education and training of the staff, including degree or certificate requirements in early childhood education or a related field. Statewide, the average cost per child is $3,580 (2000). In addition to the lottery funds, the state uses federal funds, including CCDF and Head Start. State funds are used for extended day care in Head Start.[103]

In presenting their own plan for financing a universal preschool, Wolfe and Scrivner say there has to be a balance between generating large amounts of money and not overburdening lower-income families.[104] One option, they suggest, would be to expand elementary school to four-year-olds and add an extended child care component. The advantages of this alternative is its simplicity, small additional administrative costs, and a quick start-up. However,

[101] Ibid., pp. 115–16.   [102] Ibid., p. 123.

[103] Ibid. See also R. Schumacher et al. (2005). "All Together Now: State Experiences in Using Community-Based Child Care to Provide Pre-Kindergarten" (Brief No. 5, Child Care and Early Education Series, CLASP, May).

[104] Ibid., p. 124.

in addition to limitations on using the schools for the full year, there are potentially higher costs because of restrictions on the use of aides, lower salaries for aides, and having parents cost share.[105]

Instead, they would use the existing public sector subsidies for early childhood care and require parent contributions based on ability to pay and collected over time to prevent unnecessary hardship. They propose that most of the costs of the program would come from the parents, but according to ability to pay, which would be measured by their average federal tax rate over a ten-year period. For lowest-income parents, the revenue would be raised by reducing the rate of the EITC, but this would be capped. This proposal would increase family's average tax by 1 percent. It would reduce EITC subsidy by 2.5 percent (from 40.2% to 37.7%), which would lower maximum benefit from $3,816 to $3,579. The effective phase-out rate decreases to 19.5 percent. The family's payment would be recalculated annually. Enrolled parents would not be eligible for the CCDF and the dependent care tax credit. To encourage enrollment, child care costs would be deductible only if they were more than the average costs of the program under the dependent care tax credit or any other tax subsidy for child care or preschool. Payments would be made over ten years, with an annual maximum payment of $800. In addition, there would be a one-time annual fee of $150 for parents whose income is less than $35,000; if more than $35,000 then the one-time fee would be $300.[106]

The authors estimate that, based on the 2000 income distribution, the plan would raise $4,624 per child. If 85 percent were enrolled and enrollment was uniform across all income groups, the total raised would be $15.43 billion. The annual amounts per family would range from $125 to the $800 maximum. They would also add the funds currently available under the existing programs for four-year-olds – Head Start, CCDF, TANF, the value of the various tax credits – which they estimate to be about $6.4 billion. This amount, and the amount spent per child, would cover the average cost of a quality program. And revenues could be raised by increasing the fees for higher-income families. Either HHS or the IRS could collect the fees and distribute the payments.[107]

The authors concluded by noting the comparisons with other developed countries. Universal programs for three- to five-year-olds are increasing, and they are often full day, full year. In Belgium, France, and Italy, almost all (95%–99%) of three- to six-year-olds are enrolled, at no cost to the parents, with extended day services for extra fees, which are scaled according to income. In Denmark, Finland, and Sweden, early childhood care is geared more for the working mother. It is for the full workday, year-round, and because of the high labor force participation, between 73–83 percent of the preschool children participate. According to an OECD survey, most European countries are

[105] Ibid., p. 125.   [106] Ibid., p. 126.
[107] Ibid., pp. 129–31.

committed to universal child care.[108] In the meantime, the Bush Administration's budget proposals would provide for 300,000 fewer low-income children
receiving child care assistance by 2010.[109]

Improving the Neighborhood Effect

Helping children grow in a health environment also requires that we pay attention to the quality of the place in which they grow up. In 1990, approximately
8 million people were living in high poverty neighborhoods, which is almost
twice the amount in 1970.[110] As stated by Jens Ludwig, at least for some families, there is a variety of evidence that "place matters." William Julius Wilson
has argued for the importance of neighborhood effects – the interactions with
neighborhoods, the lack of role models, and the distance from jobs. In the
Gautreaux Program, thousands of African American families relocated from
one of the worst public housing projects in Chicago to more economically
and racially diverse neighborhoods. In time, there were substantial differences
in educational outcomes between the families who remained and those who
moved (5% vs. 20% dropouts, and 21% vs. 54% attending college, respectively).

Although there were some questions about the randomness of the
Gautreaux experiment, HUD was persuaded to sponsor a randomized
housing-voucher experiment called the Moving to Opportunity (MTO).[111]
The experiment started in 1994 in five U.S. cities (Baltimore, Boston, Chicago,
Los Angeles, and New York). As described by Jens Ludwig, very low income
families with children living in high-poverty census tracts in public housing or with Section 8 project-based housing (publicly financed but privately
operated) were randomly assigned to one of three treatment groups. The
experimental group could relocate to private market apartment using housing vouchers. This group was offered assistance in finding housing as well
as other services from a local nonprofit organization. They were restricted
to housing only in low-poverty neighborhoods. The comparison group was
offered vouchers but not constrained as to neighborhoods, and this group was
not offered counseling beyond what was available under the usual housing
voucher program. The control group was not given any additional assistance.

Ludwig reports that the short-term findings (two to four years) indicated
a substantial improvement in the mental and physical health of the parents

[108] Ibid., p. 131.
[109] H. Matthews & D. Ewen (2005). "President's Budget Projects 300,000 Low-Income Children to
Lose Child Care by 2010" (CLASP, February), p. 1. The budget would freeze child care funding
for 2006 and projects would remain frozen for the next five years.
[110] J. Ludwig (2003). "Improving Neighborhoods for Poor Children." In I. V. Sawhill (Ed.), *One
Percent for the Kids: New Policies, Brighter Futures for America's Children*. Washington, D.C.:
Brookings Institution Press, pp. 136–55.
[111] Ibid., pp. 137–41.

(self-reports) and the children, a reduction in the antisocial behavior of the children, and an increase in academic achievement. However, at least in the short term, better reported health did not result in improved employment or much change in welfare. There was an improvement in the quality of parenting (getting angry with children, criticizing or making fun of children, and children obeying night curfews). There were about half as many asthma attacks and injuries that required medical attention among the children, about half as many criminal victimizations, and 20 percent less depression and anxiety. There were greater improvements in reading, standardized tests, and math courses.[112]

Although there are limits to the MTO study (short-term effects, the difficulty of comparing across sites), Ludwig says that there are strong indications that strategies for mobility would be beneficial. These would include housing vouchers, subsidized housing developments in the suburbs or at least in economically mixed neighborhoods, and requirements on builders to set aside housing for low-income families. However, much depends on whether families are willing to relocate, and the negative consequences may increase for the families that remain.[113]

The Hard-to-Employ

Even with full employment and guaranteed public jobs, there will always be poor families, especially single mothers, who do not participate in the paid labor market. The lack of human capital makes individuals vulnerable to poverty. As we have argued throughout the book, lack of human capital should not be attributed to personal moral failures. Rather, it derives, in large part, from the structural failings of society – the shortage of good jobs, economic deprivation in inner cities and rural communities, the lack of decent and affordable child care, the holes in the safety net, barriers to needed services, the lack of affordable housing, and so forth. And those who have diminished human capital cannot compete.[114]

Therefore, it is important to keep in mind that a significant minority of the working-age poor would not benefit from a full-employment economy because they experience major barriers to employment – in addition to low human capital, health and mental health problems, disability, family care responsibilities, and discrimination.[115] Several studies of current and former welfare

[112] Ibid., pp. 143–47.　　　　[113] Ludwig (2003), pp. 147–50.

[114] M. R. Rank (2004). *One Nation, Underprivileged: Why American Poverty Affects Us All.* Oxford; New York: Oxford University Press, pp. 75–76.

[115] R. B. Freeman (2001). "The Rising Tide Lifts…?" In S. Danziger & R. H. Haveman (2001). *Understanding Poverty.* New York: Russell Sage Foundation; Cambridge, Mass.: Harvard University Press, p. 99.

recipients show a high prevalence of barriers to employment.[116] Depending on the study, between 30 percent and 45 percent have low education, anywhere from 15 percent to 51 percent lack work experience, between 20 percent and 36 percent have physical health problems, 11 percent to 35 percent have mental health problems, 7 percent to 15 percent experienced domestic violence, and 5 percent have substance abuse problems. Still, the majority of the women did enter the labor market. However, they experienced a high rate of job instability and exit. In one study, three out of four employed recipients experienced a job loss at one point.[117]

The rapid decline of the welfare rolls probably means that those still remaining on the rolls have the most serious barriers to employment.[118] Not all of these problems prevent work, but most would require special services and supports if these recipients are to obtain and retain employment. Supplemental Security Income is available, but only for the permanently disabled. Many of these recipients would not meet the strict SSI definition but still may find it difficult to hold a job.[119]

Most states just continue their "work first" strategies,[120] despite the fact that those with multiple barriers to employment need access to a system of coordinated social services to cope with and possibly overcome their barriers. The structure of the current social services system available to such persons is likely to fail them for several reasons. First, as noted earlier, access to needed services is often difficult, cumbersome, distant, and, most important, in short supply. Second, the system tends to compartmentalize the client's barriers, treating each problem discretely rather than viewing them holistically. For example, depressive symptoms that reduce the ability of a single mother to work may relate to financial stresses aggravated by abusive relations with a partner, thus contributing to the children's behavioral problems and failure in school. The children's problems, in turn, reinforce the depression and diminish the ability of the mother to earn an income.[121] Unless there is recognition that these multiple problems reinforce each other and must be addressed simultaneously, the success in resolving any one of them would be diminished. Yet, the service system is seldom structured to provide such coordinated services. Third, because the various services are financed through different

---

[116] K. Seefeldt (2004). "After PRWORA: Barriers to Employment, Work, and Well-Being among Current and Former Welfare Recipients" (National Poverty Center, Ann Arbor, Mich.), pp. 1–12.

[117] Ibid., p. 4.

[118] Y. Nam (2005). "The Role of Employment Barriers in Welfare Exits and Reentries after Welfare Reform: Event History Analysis." *Social Service Review* (June): 268–93.

[119] S. Zedlewski & P. Loprest (2000). "How Well Does TANF Fit the Needs of the Most Disadvantaged Families?" (Brookings Conference, revised draft December 29), p. 4.

[120] Ibid., pp. 18–22.

[121] A. Jackson & R. Scheines (2005). "Single Mothers' Self-Efficacy, Parenting in the Home Environment, and Children's Development in a Two-Wave Study." *Social Work Research* 29(1): 7–20.

funding streams, they are subject to different and conflicting eligibility and accountability requirements. This is particularly the case when the system is composed of public, nonprofit, and for-profit service providers, each of which has a different mission, organizational culture, and service technologies.[122] Fourth, and related, there are too many organizational barriers for sharing information, and the burden of service coordination often falls on the clients themselves.

To serve the hard-to-employ effectively would require a differently structured social service network operating in conjunction with the work support programs discussed earlier. In particular, and in contrast to the existing welfare-to-work approach to these families, such a network of services allows the clients to exercise an *exit* option because they still can count on the children's allowance. That is, the access to services will not be conditional on a mandatory work requirement. With the children's allowances, clients will seek services only if they feel that the services are worthwhile. Similarly, the service agencies will only enroll clients if they have something of value to offer. This means, of course, that there are no sanctions. This is a hard recommendation to swallow. Sanctions are so engrained in welfare history. But one of our most important points (see Chapter 5) is being realistic and honest about the great difficulties of discretionary issues of implementation. With few exceptions, sanctions result in arbitrariness, discrimination, and unfairness. They penalize the most vulnerable. They serve to make majoritarian society feel superior. True, there will be some who "abuse" the system, but they should not hold the rest of those in need hostage.

The network or consortium of services for the hard-to-employ should be based on the following principles:

1. Located in high-poverty neighborhoods, so that all the services needed by the hard-to-employ are within easy reach (e.g., the neighborhood served by the local elementary school).
2. Organized as a consortium or collaborative of all the relevant local public and private agencies with a community-based lead agency responsible for the coordination of the services.
3. During the period of participation, there would be income disregards in calculating subsidized rents and other benefits.
4. Financial incentives will also be available to the community-based agencies for participating in the consortium.
5. The governance of the consortium should provide for genuine participation of local residents.

[122] E.g., E. Bardach (1998). *Getting Agencies to Work Together: The Practice and Theory of Managerial Craftsmanship*. Washington, D.C.: Brookings Institution Press.

6. The services should be co-located in one setting allowing for a single point of entry.

7. All services should be provided on a voluntary basis, with clients exercising choice and active participation in the service decisions.

8. The array of services needed by each client would be coordinated through a case manager in the lead agency.

9. All participating agencies would be made accountable to serve the hard-to-employ through performance-based evaluation and frequent and independent feedback from the clients.

Again, there are several promising organizational prototypes of such a model.[123] The Jobs-Plus demonstration project is a consortium of agencies formed to serve the hard-to-employ in clusters of public housing projects. When implemented effectively, it has been reasonably successful in raising the average income of the residents.[124] At each of the selected sites, a consortium or collaborative was formed that included a partnership of the housing authority, the welfare department, the workforce development agency, resident representatives, employers, and other local service agencies.[125] The lead agency in the consortium – Job-Plus – provides (1) outreach and recruitment, often using local residents as outreach workers; (2) intake, enrollment, and assessment; (3) education, employment, and supportive service, several of which are available on site and others through referrals. The on-site services typically include basic education, job search, training, and job placement. Off-site services may include work experience and training opportunities. Supportive services include child care, transportation, and referrals to agencies that address such issues as substance abuse and domestic violence. Some of these services are offered by agencies whose workers are co-located on site.[126]

The key to the success of Job-Plus was the ability to develop a collaborative system of services provided by different public and private agencies. To do so, several strategies were used including a representative yet efficient governance

[123] E.g., H. S. Bloom, J. A. Riccio, & N. Verma (2005). "Promoting Work in Public Housing: The Effectiveness of Jobs-Plus" (MDRC, New York), pp. 1–262; F. Molina & C. Howard (2003). "Final Report on the Neighborhood Jobs Initiative: Lessons and Implications for Future Employment Initiatives" (MDRC, New York), pp. 1–39; B. Giloth (2005). "Good Jobs and Careers: What Communities Need to Do to Train and Move Low-Income, Low-Skilled People into Good Jobs and Careers" (Annie E. Casey Foundation, Baltimore, Md.); D. Fischer (2005). "The Road to Good Employment Retention: Three Successful Programs from the Jobs Initiative" (Annie E. Casey Foundation, Baltimore, Md.).

[124] Bloom, Riccio, & Verma (2005).

[125] L. Y. Kato & J. A. Riccio (2001). "Building New Partnerships for Employment: Collaboration among Agencies and Public Housing Residents in the Jobs-Plus Demonstration" (MDRC, New York).

[126] Ibid., p. 19.

structure to give voice to all the members of the consortium, cultivating close working relations among the frontline staff of the partner agencies, providing as many of the services on site, and developing an efficient client tracking system.[127] It also requires an active engagement of the local residents as partners in the design, development, and monitoring of the program.[128] The Neighborhood Jobs Initiative (NJI), similar to Job-Plus, targeted specific high-poverty neighborhoods by organizing a consortium of agencies to address the high unemployment in the neighborhood.[129] Here too the effectiveness of NJI depended on the ability of the lead community-based agency to forge a working partnership with all the relevant agencies in the neighborhood and to offer intensive case management to ensure that clients received the services they needed.[130] It also required that the lead agency develop close ties with local residents through intensive outreach efforts, listen to their needs, and tailor the services accordingly.[131].

We are mindful that to form and manage such a consortium or collaborative is a difficult organizational challenge. It is a time-consuming effort, requiring strong leadership, a clear sense of mission, considerable amount of community organization, and extensive efforts to forge linkages and partnerships among the local agencies. Most important, the formation and survival of such a consortium depends on a stable source of funding that provides sufficient incentives to each participating partner to offset the costs of collaboration.[132] In other words, each participating agency must realize additional benefits not available to it before that will make it worthwhile to modify agency policies and practices to increase collaboration. Each agency needs to see in the consortium a long-lasting opportunity to enhance its own survival and legitimacy in the community.

Of course, there is always the danger that participating agencies will "coolout" difficult clients or divert the additional resources to side benefits and other purposes. Therefore, it is imperative that a system of accountability be put into place. In addition to formal contracts, performance-based standards, and regular auditing, it must be built on the mutual relations among

---

[127] Kato & Riccio (2001). See also M. Greenberg & J. Noyes (2005). "Increasing State and Local Capacity for Cross-Systems Innovation: Assessing Flexibility and Opportunities under Current Law: Implications for Policy and Practice" (A Collaborative Project of the National Governors Association's Center for Best Practices, Hudson Institute and Center for Law and Social Policy, CLASP, Hudson Institute, January).

[128] Ibid., pp. 79–91.   [129] Molina & Howard (2003).

[130] Ibid., p. 6.

[131] Ibid., p. 23. Another example of adapting training programs to both the needs of the clients and the employers is the QUEST model described in Osterman (2003), p. 263.

[132] R. J. Chaskin (2000). "Lessons Learned from the Implementation of the Neighborhood Family Initiative: A Summary of Findings" (Chapin Hall Center for Children at the University of Chicago, Chicago), pp. 1–68.

the partners, the trust they develop among themselves, the monitoring role of the governing structure, and particularly the regular evaluation and feedback by the local residents.[133] Still, with all these challenges, the experiences of locality-based network of services for the hard-to-employ suggests that it can be a viable and effective approach requiring modest but sustainable investment of resources.

[133] Kato & Riccio (2000), p. 51.

References

Abramovitz, M. (1988). *Regulating the lives of women, social welfare policy from colonial times to the present*. Boston, Mass.: South End Press.

Abramovitz, M. (2005). Race and the politics of welfare reform (book review). *Social Service Review* 79: 382.

Acs, G., & Koball, H. (2003). TANF and the status of teen mothers under age 18. No. A-62, New Federalism: Issues and Options for States, Urban Institute, Washington, D.C., June.

Acs, G., Loprest, P., & Roberts T. (2003). Final synthesis report from ASPE "Leaver" grants. Report to the Office of the Assistant Secretary for Planning and Evaluation, Health Human Services, from the Urban Institute, Washington, D.C., November 2001.

Adams, G., Snyder, K., & Sandfort, J. R. (2002). Getting and retaining child care assistance: How policy and practice influence families' experiences. Urban Institute, Washington D.C.

Aizer, A., & McLanahan, S. (2004). The impact of child support on fertility, parental investments and child well-being. Working paper no. 04-03-FF, Center for Research on Child Wellbeing, Princeton, N.J.

Alstott, A. (1999). Work vs. freedom: A liberal challenge to employment subsidies. *Yale Law Journal* 108: 967–1058.

Altman, L. (2004). Study finds that teenage virginity pledges are rarely kept. *New York Times*. March 10.

Andersson, F., Holzer, H. J., & Lane, J. (2005). *Moving up or moving on: Who advances in the low-wage labor market?* New York: Russell Sage Foundation.

Appelbaum, E., Bernhardt, A., Murnane, R. J. (Eds.) (2003). *Low wage America: How employers are reshaping opportunity in the workplace*. New York: Russell Sage Foundation.

Appelbaum, E., Bernhardt, A., Murnane, R., & Weinberg, J. (2005). Low-wage employment in America: Results from a set of recent industry case studies. *Journal of Socio-Economic Review* 3, no. 2 (May): 293–310.

Argys, L., Peters, E., Brooks-Gunn, J., & Smith, J. (1998). The impact of child support on cognitive outcomes of young children. *Demography* 35(2): 159–73.

Artiga, S., & O'Malley, M. (2005). Medicaid and the uninsured. Increasing premiums and cost sharing in Medicaid and SCHIP. Recent State Experiences. Kaiser Family Foundation, Princeton, N.J.

Auspos, P., Hunter, J. A., & Miller, C. (2000). Final report on the implementation and impacts of the Minnesota Family Investment Program in Ramsey County. Manpower Demonstration Research Corporation, New York.

Autor, D., & Houseman, S. (2005). Temporary agency employment as a way out of poverty? Paper presented at the National Poverty Center Conference on Working and Poor: How economic and policy changes are affecting low-wage workers, Washington, D.C.; MIT Department of Economics and NBER, Cambridge, Mass.; W. E. Upjohn Institute for Employment Research, Kalamazoo, Mich.

Autor, D. H., Katz, L. F., & Kearney, M. S. (2005). Trends in the U.S. wage inequality: Re-assessing the revisionists. Unpublished manuscript. Retrieved from http://econ-www.mit.edu/faculty/download_pdf.php?id=967.

Autor, D. H., Levey, F., & Munane, R. J. (2002). Upstairs, downstairs: Computers and skills on two floors of a large bank. *Industrial and Labor Relations Review* 55(3): 432–447.

Ball, J. (1984). Interim findings on the West Virginia Community Work Experience Demonstrations. Manpower Demonstration Research Corporation, New York.

Bane, M. J., & Ellwood, D. T. (1994). *Welfare realities: From rhetoric to reform*. Cambridge, Mass.: Harvard University Press.

Bardach, E. (1998). *Getting agencies to work together: The practice and theory of managerial craftsmanship*. Washington, D.C.: Brookings Institution Press.

Barnow, C., & King, C. (2005). The Workforce Investment Act in eight states. Prepared for the U.S. Department of Labor, Employment and Training Administration; Nelson A. Rockefeller Institute of Government, State University of New York, February.

Bartfeld, J. (2000). Child support and the post-divorce economic well-being of mothers, fathers and children. *Demography* 37(2): 203–13.

Bartfeld, J. (2003). Falling through the cracks: Gaps in child support among welfare recipients. *Journal of Marriage and Family* 65: 72–89.

Bartlett, S., & Burstein, N. (2004). Food Stamp Program access study: Eligible nonparticipants. Abt Associates, Cambridge, Mass., May.

Bartlett, S., Burstein, N., Hamilton, W., & King, R. (2004). Food Stamp Program access study. Final report. Abt Associates, Cambridge, Mass, November.

Baum, J. A., & Oliver, C. (1992). Institutional imbeddedness and the dynamics of organizational populations. *American Sociological Review* 57(4): 540–59.

Bean, F. D., & Stevens, G. (2003). *America's newcomers and the dynamics of diversity*. New York: Russell Sage Foundation.

Bearman, P., & Brückner, H. (2001). Promising the future: Virginity pledges and first intercourse. *American Journal of Sociology* 106, no. 4 (January): 859–912.

Bearman, P., & Brückner, H. (2004). The relationship between virginity pledges in adolescence and STD acquisition in young adulthood. After the promise: The long-term consequence of adolescent virginity pledges. Paper presented at the National STD Conference, Philadelphia, March 9.

Bell, D. (1962). *The end of ideology*. New York: Collier.

Bell, W. (1965). *Aid to dependent children*. New York: Columbia University Press.

Bergmann, B. (2004). A Swedish-style welfare state or basic income: Which should have priority? *Politics and Society* 32(1): 107–18.

Bernhardt, A. D., Morris, M., Handcock, M. S., & Scott, M. A. (2001). *Divergent paths: Economic mobility in the new American labor market*. New York: Russell Sage Foundation.

Bernstein, B. (1982). *The politics of welfare*. Cambridge, Mass.: ABT Books.

Bernstein, N. (2002). Side effect of welfare law: The no-parent family. *New York Times*. July 29.

Bernstein, N. (2004). Young love, new cautions: Second of two articles: For a promising but poor girl, a struggle over sex and goals. *New York Times*. March 8.

Bernstein, J., Brocht, C., & Spade-Aguilar, M. (2000). How much is enough? Basic family budgets for working families. Economic Policy Institute, Washington, D.C.

Blank, R., & Shierholz, H. (2005). Explaining employment and wage trends among less-skilled women (May). Gerald R. Ford School of Public Policy, University of Michigan, Ann Arbor.

Blank, R. M., & Schmidt, L. (2000). Work and wages. Paper presented at the New World of Welfare: Shaping a Post-TANF agenda for policy. Washington, D.C., December.

Bloom, H. S., Riccio, J. A., & Verma, N. (2005). Promoting work in public housing: The effectiveness of Jobs-Plus. Manpower Demonstration Research Corporation, New York.

Bourque, M. (2004). Poor relief "without violating the rights of humanity." In B. G. Smith (Ed.), *Down and out in early America*. University Park, Pa.: Pennsylvania State University Press.

Boushey, H., Brocht, C., Gundersen, B., & Bernstein, J. (2001). Hardship in America: The real story of working families. Economic Policy Institute, Washington, D.C.

Brauner, S., & Loprest, P. J. (1999). Where are they now? What states' studies of people who left welfare tell us. Urban Institute, Washington, D.C.

Brock, T., Coulton, C., London, A., Polit, D., Richburg-Hays, L., Scott, E., & Verma, N. (2002). Welfare reform in Cleveland: Implementation, effects, and experiences of poor families and neighborhoods. Manpower Demonstration Research Corporation, New York.

Brock, T., Doolittle, F., Fellerbath, V., & Wiseman, M. (1997). Creating New Hope. Manpower Demonstration Research Corporation, New York.

Brock, T., & Harknett, K. (1998). A comparison of two welfare-to-work case management models. *Social Service Review* 72: 492–520.

Brock, T., Kwakye, I., Plyne, J. C., Richburg-Hays, L., Seith, D., Stepick, A., et al. (2004). Welfare reform in Miami. Manpower Demonstration Research Corporation, New York.

Brodkin, E. Z. (1997, March). Inside the welfare contract: Discretion and accountability in state welfare administration. *Social Service Review* 71(1).

Brodkin, E. Z., & Lipsky, M. (1983). Quality control in AFDC as an administrative strategy. *Social Service Review* 57: 1–34.

Bromer, J., & Henly, J. R. (2004). Child care as family support? Caregiving practices across child care provider types. *Children and Youth Services Review* 26(10): 941–64.

Bronfenbrenner, U. (1977). The fracturing of the American family. *Washington University Daily*. October 5.

Bronfenbrenner, U. (1977). Nobody home: The erosion of the American family. *Psychology Today* 10: 40–47.

Brooks-Gunn, J., & Duncan, G. (1997). The effects of poverty on children. *Future of Children: Children and Poverty* 7(2): 55–71.

Brooks-Gunn, J., Klebanov, P., Smith, J. R., & Lee, K. (2001). Effects of combining public assistance and employment on mothers and their young children. *Women and Health* 32(3): 179–210.

Brown, J. C. (1940). *Public relief 1929–1939*. New York: Henry Holt & Co.

Brown, P., Cook, S., & Wimer, L. (2005). Voluntary paternity acknowledgment. Discussion paper no. 1302-05, Institute for Research on Poverty, University of Wisconsin–Madison.

Brückner, H., & Bearman, P. (2005). After the promise: The STD consequences of adolescent virginity pledges. *Journal of Adolescent Health* 36: 271–78.

Bryner, G. C. (2002). Welfare reform in Utah. Nelson A. Rockefeller Institute of Government, Albany, N.Y.

Budig, M. J., & England, P. (2001). The wage penalty for motherhood. *American Sociological Review* 66(2): 204–25.

Burtless, G. (1999). Growing American inequality: Sources and remedies. *Brookings Review* (Winter): 31–35.

Caiazza, A., Shaw, A., & Werschkul, M. (2004). Women's economic status in the states: Wide disparities by race, ethnicity, and region. Institute for Women's Policy Research, Washington, D.C.

California Budget Project. (2004a). Minimum wage increases boost earnings of low-wage California workers. Budget brief. June.

California Budget Project. (2004b). Locked out 2004: California's affordable housing crisis. January.

California Budget Project. (2004c). Budget backgrounders: Making dollars make sense. February. Retrieved from http://www.cbp.org/2004/0402calworks.pdf.

California Budget Project. (2005). Lasting returns: Investing in health coverage for California's children. February.

California Budget Project. (2005a). Governor proposes to suspend state COLA and withhold federal COLA for SSI/SSP grants. Budget brief.

Campbell, M., Haveman, R., Sandefur, G., & Wolfe, B. (2005). Economic inequality and educational attainment across a generation. *Focus* 23, no. 3 (Spring).

Cancian, M., Haveman, R. H., Meyer, D. R., & Wolfe, B. (2000). Before and after TANF: The economic well-being of women leaving welfare. Special report, Institution for Research on Poverty, University of Wisconsin.

Cancian, M., & Meyer, D. R. (2004). Fathers of children receiving welfare: Can they provide more child support? *Social Service Review* 78: 179–206.

Cancian, M., & Meyer, D. (2005). Child support and the economy. Institute for Research on Poverty, School of Social Work, University of Wisconsin–Madison. May 12.

Cancian, M., & Meyer, D. (2005). Child support in the United States: An uncertain and irregular income source? Discussion paper no. 1298-05, Institute for Research on Poverty, University of Wisconsin–Madison. April.

Cancian, M., Meyer, D., & Nam, K. (2005). Knowledge of child support policy rules: How little we know. Discussion paper no. 1297-05, Institute for Research on Poverty, University of Wisconsin–Madison, April.

Cancian, M., & Reed, D. (2001). Changes in family structure: Implications for poverty and related policy. In S. Danziger & R. H. Haveman (Eds.), *Understanding poverty*. New York: Russell Sage Foundation; Cambridge, Mass.: Harvard University Press.

Capizzano, J., & Adams, G. (2003). Children in low-income families are less likely to be in center-based child care: Snapshots of America's families. Urban Institute, Washington, D.C.

Capps, R., Fix, M., Ost, J., Reardon-Anderson, J., & Passel, J. (2004). The health and well-being of young children of immigrants, Urban Institute, Washington, D.C.

Capps, R., Pindus, N., Snyder, K., & Leos-Urbel, J. (2001). Recent changes in Texas welfare and work, child care, and child welfare systems. Urban Institute, Washington, D.C.

Carlson, M., Garfinkel, I., McLanahan, S., Micy, R., & Primus, W. (2005). The effects of welfare and child support policies on union formation. *Population Research and Policy Review* 23: 513–42.

Carlson, M., McLanahan, S., & England, P. (2004). Union formation in fragile families. *Demography* 41: 237–61.

Casper, L. M., McLanahan, S. S., & Garfinkel, I. (1994). The gender-poverty gap: What we can learn from other countries. *American Sociological Review* 59(4): 594–605.

Cauthen, N., & Lu, H.-H. (2003). Employment alone is not enough for America's low-income children and families, living at the edge. Research brief no. 1, National Center for Children in Poverty, Columbia University, Mailman School of Public Health, New York.

Center for Law and Social Policy. (1998). "Abstinence unless married" education. November 16.

Center for Law and Social Policy. (n.d.). Child support substantially increases economic well-being of low- and moderate-income families. Research fact sheet. Retrieved from http://www.clasp.org/publications/CS_Economic_FS.pdf.

Center for Law and Social Policy. (n.d.). Child support payments benefit children in non-economic as well as economic ways. Research fact sheet.

Center for Law and Social Policy Update. (2004). President's budget cuts child care for more than 300,000 children. *Center for Law and Social Policy* 17, no. 3 (March).

Center for Research on Child Wellbeing. (2002). Child support enforcement and domestic violence among non-cohabiting couples. *Fragile Families Research Brief* 13: 1–3.

Center for Research on Child Wellbeing. (2003). Barriers to marriage among fragile families. *Fragile Families Research Brief* 16: 1–3.

Center for Research on Child Wellbeing. (2003). Child support enforcement and fragile families. *Fragile Families Research Brief* 15: 1–3.

Center for Research on Child Wellbeing. (2003). Union formation and dissolution in fragile families. *Fragile Families Research Brief* 14: 1–3.

Center on Budget and Policy Priorities. (Washington D.C.). (2005). Economic recovery failed to benefit much of the population in 2004. The Center, Washington, D.C. August 30.

Center on Budget and Policy Priorities. (2005). Local effects of voucher funding shortfalls: Local effects of cuts in housing voucher assistance in 2005 – California. Retrieved from http://www.cbpp.org/states/2-18-05hous-ca2.pdf.

Center on Budget and Policy Priorities. (Washington D.C.). (2005). The number of uninsured Americans continued to rise in 2004. The Center, Washington, D.C. August 30.

Chandler, D., Meisel, J., Jordan, P., Rienzi, B., & Goodwin, S. (2004). Substance abuse, employment, and welfare tenure. *Social Service Review* (December).

Chapman, J., & Ettlinger, M. (2004). The who and why of the minimum wage: Raising the wage floor is an essential part of a strategy to support working families. Issue brief no. 201, Economic Policy Institute, Washington, D.C.

Chase-Lansdale, P. L., Moffit, R. A., Lohman, B. J., Cherlin, A. J., Coley, R. L., Pittman, L. D., et al. (2003). Mothers' transition from welfare to work and the well-being of preschoolers and adolescents. *Science* 299: 1548–52.

Chaskin, R. J. (2000). Lessons learned from the implementation of the Neighborhood Family Initiative: A summary of findings. Chapin Hall Center for Children at the University of Chicago, Chicago.

Chaves, M. (2002). Religious congregations. In L. M. Salamon (Ed.), *The state of nonprofit America*. Washington, D.C.: Brookings Institution Press.

Cherlin, A. J., Bogen, K., Quane, J. M., & Burton, L. (2002). Operating within the rules: Welfare recipients' experiences with sanctions and case closings. *Social Service Review* 76(3): 387–405.

Child Trends. (2005). Facts at a Glance. retrieved from http://www.childtrends.org/files/facts_2005.pdf

Children's Defense Fund. (1998). New studies look at status of former welfare recipients. Retrieved from www.childrensdefense.org/fairstart_status.html.

Children's Defense Fund. (2003). Children with disabilities and other special needs: Opportunities to participate in quality programs must be expanded. 2003 key facts.

Retrieved from http://www.childrensdefense.org/earlychildhood/childcare/keyfacts2003_childcare.pdf.

Children's Defense Fund. (2003). Infants and toddlers are particularly vulnerable: Good child care and early education can play a vital role in their development. 2003 key facts. Retrieved from http://www.childrensdefense.org/earlychildhood/infant/keyfacts2003_infant.pdf.

Children's Defense Fund. (2003). Prekindergarten initiatives: Efforts to help children enter school ready to succeed. 2003 key facts. Retrieved from http://www.childrensdefense.org/earlychildhood/prekindergarten/keyfacts2003_prekindergarten.pdf.

Children's Defense Fund. (2003). School-age child care: Keeping children safe and helping them learn while their families work. 2003 key facts. Retrieved from http://www.childrensdefense.org/earlychildhood/schoolagecare/keyfacts2003_schoolagecare.pdf.

Children's Defense Fund. (n.d.). Census 2000: Child poverty data for states, counties, and large cities. Retrieved from http://www.childrensdefense.org/familyincome/childpoverty/census2000/childpovertydata.aspx.

Chyu, L., Pebley, A., & Lara-Cinisomo, S. (2005). Patterns of child care use for preschoolers in Los Angeles County. RAND Corp., Santa Monica, Calif.

Citro, C. F., & Michael, R. T. (Eds.). (1995). *Measuring poverty: A new approach.* Washington, D.C.: National Academy Press.

Clark, W. (2001). The geography of immigrant poverty: Selective evidence of an immigrant underclass. In R. Waldinger (Ed.), *Strangers at the gates: New immigrants in urban America.* Berkeley: University of California Press.

Clarke, L., & Estes, C. L. (1992). Sociological and economic theories of markets and nonprofits: Evidence from home health organizations. *American Journal of Sociology* 97: 945–69.

Clarke-Stewart, K. A., Vandell, D. L., Burchinal, M., O'Brien, M., & McCartney, K. (2002). Do regulable features of child-care homes affect children's development? *Early Childhood Research Quarterly* 17: 52–86.

Clemetson, L. (2003,). Poor workers finding modest housing unaffordable, study says. *New York Times.* September 9, p. 18.

Cloward, R. A., & Ohlin, L. E. (1960). *Delinquency and opportunity: A theory of delinquent gangs.* Glencoe, Ill.: Free Press.

Cnaan, R. A., & Boddie, S. C. (2001). Philadelphia census of congregations and their involvement in social service delivery. *Social Service Review* 75(4): 559–80.

Cody, S., Gleason, P., Schechter, B., Satake, M., & Sykes, J. (2005). Food stamp program entry and exit: An analysis of participation trends in the 1990s. Final report. Mathematica Policy Research, Inc. February.

Coley, R. L., & Chase-Lansdale, P. L. (1998). Adolescent pregnancy and parenthood. *American Psychologist* 53: 152–66.

Corcoran, M. (1995). Rags to rags: Poverty and mobility in the United States. *Annual Review of Sociology* 21: 237–67.

Corcoran, M. (2001). Mobility, persistence, and the consequences of poverty for children: Child and adult outcomes. In S. Danziger & R. H. Haveman (Eds.), *Understanding poverty*. New York: Russell Sage Foundation; Cambridge, Mass.: Harvard University Press.

Courtney, M., Dworsky, A., Piliavin, I., & Zinn, A. (2005). Involvement of TANF applicant families with child welfare services. *Social Service Review* (March).

Crenshaw, K. (1989). Demarginalizing the intersection of race and sex: A black feminist critique of antidiscrimination doctrine, feminist theory and antiracist politics, 1989

University of Chicago Legal Forum 139-67. Reprinted in *The politics of law: A progressive critique* 195–217 (2nd ed., edited by D. Kairys, New York: Pantheon, 1990).

Cummings, S. (2001). Community economic development as progressive politics: Towards a grassroots movement for economic justice. 54 *Stan. L. Rev.* 399.

Cunnyngham, K. (2005). Food stamp program participation rates: 2003. Mathematica Policy Research, Inc. May.

Currie, J. (2004). The take up of social benefits. National Bureau of Economic Research working paper series no. 10488, National Bureau of Economic Research. May.

Currie, J. (2005). Health disparities and gaps in school readiness. *Future of Children* 15(1): 117–38.

Dahl, G., & Lochner, L. (2005). Impact of family income on child achievement. Discussion paper no. 1305-05, Institute for Research on Poverty, University of Wisconsin–Madison. August.

Dailard, C. (2002). Abstinence promotion and family planning: The misguided drive for equal funding. The Gottmucher Report on Public Policy, New York.

Danielson, C., & Klerman, J. A. (2006). Why did the food stamp caseload decline (and rise)? Effects of policies and the economy. Institute for Research on Poverty discussion paper no. 1316-06. March. Available at http://www.irp.wisc.edu.

Danziger, S. K., Corcoran, M., Danziger, S., & Heflin, C. M. (2000). Work, income and material hardship after welfare reform. *Journal of Consumer Affairs* 34.

Danziger, S., & Gottschalk, P. (1995). *America unequal.* New York: Russell Sage Foundation; Cambridge, Mass.: Harvard University Press.

Danziger, S., & Gottschalk, P. (2004). *Diverging fortunes: Trends in poverty and inequality.* New York: Russell Sage Foundation.

Danziger, S., & Haveman, R. H. (2001). *Understanding poverty.* New York: Russell Sage Foundation; Cambridge, Mass.: Harvard University Press.

Danziger, S. K., Kalil, A., & Anderson, N. J. (2000). Human capital, physical health, and mental health of welfare recipients: Co-occurrences and correlates. *Journal of Social Issues* 56(4): 635–54.

Darroch, J. E., Singh, S., & Frost, J. J. (2000). Differences in teenage pregnancy rates among five developed countries: The role of sexual activity and contraceptive use. *Family Planning Perspectives* 33(5): 244–50, 281.

Davis, M. (1999). The economics of abuse: How violence perpetuates women's poverty. In R. Brandwein (Ed.), *Battered women, children, and welfare reform: The ties that bind.* Thousand Oaks, Calif.: Sage.

DeNavas-Walt, C., Proctor, B. D., & Mills, R. J. (2004). *Income, poverty, and health insurance coverage in the United States: 2003: Current population reports P60–226.* Washington, D.C.: U.S. Census Bureau.

DeParle, J. (2004). *American dream: Three women, ten kids, and a nation's drive to end welfare.* New York: Viking.

DeParle, J. (2005). Hispanic group thrives on faith and federal aid. *New York Times.* May 3.

Derthick, M. (1970). *The influence of federal grants: Public assistance in Massachusetts.* Cambridge, Mass.: Harvard University Press.

Derthick, M. (1975). *Uncontrollable spending for social services grants.* Washington, D.C.: The Brookings Institution.

Dilger, R. J., Blakely, E., Latimer, M., Locke, B., Plein, L. C., Potter, L. A., & Williams, D. (2004). WV WORKS 2003: Perspectives of former recipients who have exhausted their 60-months of program eligibility. Interdisciplinary Research Taskforce on Welfare Reform, West Virginia University, Charleston.

Diller, M. (2000). The revolution in welfare administration: Rules, discretion, and entrepreneurial government. 75 *N.Y.U. Law Review* 1121.

DiSogra, C., Yen, W., Flood, M., & Ramirez, A. (2004). Hunger in Los Angeles county affects over 200,000 low-income adults, another 560,000 at risk. Center for Health Policy Research, University of California, Los Angeles.

Dodson, L., Manuel, T., & Bravo, E. (2002). Keeping jobs and raising families in low-income America: It just doesn't work. A report of the Across the Boundaries Project, Radcliffe Public Policy Center and 9to5 National Association of Working Women, Radcliffe Institute for Advanced Study, Harvard University.

Donahue, J. D. (1989). *The privatization decision: Public ends, private means.* New York: Basic Books.

Donahue, J. D., Nye, J. S., & Visions of Governance in the 21st Century (Program). (2002). *Market-based governance: Supply side, demand side, upside, and downside.* Cambridge, Mass.; Washington, D.C.: Brookings Institution Press.

Dresser, L., & Rogers, J. (2003). Part of the solution: Emerging workforce intermediaries in the United States. In J. Zeitlin & D. Trubek (Eds.), *Governing work and welfare in a new economy: European and American experiments.* Oxford: Oxford University Press.

Dube, A., & Jacobs, K. (2004). Hidden costs of Wal-Mart jobs: Use of safety net programs by Wal-Mart workers in California. Briefing paper series, University of California at Berkeley, Institute of Industrial Relations; Center for Labor Research and Education. August 2.

Duncan, G., & Magnuson, K. (2003). Promoting the healthy development of children. In I. V. Sawhill (Ed.), *One percent for the kids: New policies, brighter futures for America's children.* Washington, D.C.: Brookings Institution Press.

Duniforn, R., & Kalil, A. (2005). Maternal working conditions and child well-being in welfare-leaving families. Working paper series no. 05-5. National Poverty Center Working Papers Series, Ann Arbor, Mich.

Dworsky, A., Courtney, M., & Piliavin, I. (2003). What happens to families under W-2 in Milwaukee County, Wisconsin? Executive summary, Chapin Hall, University of Chicago.

Dyer, W. T., & Fairlie, R. W. (2005). Do family caps reduce out-of-wedlock births? Evidence from Arkansas, Georgia, Indiana, New Jersey and Virginia. *Population Research and Policy Review* 23: 441–73.

Dyke, A., Heinrich, C. J., Mueser, P. R., & Troske, K. R. (2005). The effects of welfare-to-work program activities on labor market outcomes. Discussion paper no. 1295-05, Institute on Research on Poverty, Madison, Wis.

Economic Policy Institute. (2005). Social Security facts at a glance: Facts about Social Security benefits. Retrieved from http://www.epinet.org/content.cfm/issueguide_socialsecurityfacts. May 2005.

Edelman, M. J. (1971). *Politics as symbolic action: Mass arousal and quiescence.* Chicago: Markham Publishing.

Edin, K. (2000). Few good men: Why poor mothers don't marry or remarry. *American Prospect* 11: 26–31.

Edin, K., Kefalas, M. J., & Reed, J. M. (2004). A peek inside the black box: What marriage means for poor unmarried parents. *Journal of Marriage and Family* 66: 1007–14.

Edin, K., & Lein, L. (1997). *Making ends meet: How single mothers survive welfare and low-wage work.* New York: Russell Sage Foundation.

Eggleston, K., & Zeckhauser, R. (2002). Government contracting for health care. In J. Donahue & J. S. Nye Jr. (Eds.), *Market-based governance* (pp. 29–65). Washington, D.C.: Brookings Institution Press.

Ehrle, J., Seefeldt, K. S., Snyder, K., & McMahon, P. (2001). Recent changes in Wisconsin welfare and work, child care, and child welfare systems. Urban Institute, Washington, D.C.

Ellwood, D. A., & Boyd, D. J. (2000). Changes in state spending on social services since the implementation of welfare reform: A preliminary report. Nelson A. Rockefeller Institute of Government, Albany, N.Y.

England, P., Budig, M., & Folbre, N. (2002). Wages of virtue: The relative pay of care work. *Social Problems* 49(4): 455–73.

Esping-Andersen, G. (1999). *Social foundations of postindustrial economies.* Oxford; New York: Oxford University Press.

Esping-Andersen, G. (2002). *Why we need a new welfare state.* New York: Oxford University Press.

Ewen, D. (2005). The Senate's $6 billion child care provision: A critical, but modest, investment. Center for Law and Social Policy. April.

Ewen, D., & Hart, K. (2003). State budget cuts create a growing child care crisis for low-income working families. Children's Defense Fund, Washington, D.C. March.

Ewen, D., & Neas, K. B. (2005). Preparing for success: How Head Start helps children with disabilities and their families. Center for Law and Social Policy, updated May 6.

Federal Interagency Forum on Child and Family Statistics. (2004). *America's children in brief: Key national indicators of well-being.*

Fein, D. J. (1999). The ABC evaluation: Carrying and using the stick: Financial sanctions in Delaware's A Better Chance program. Report prepared for the U.S. Department of Health and Human Services. Division of Social Services, Abt Associates, Cambridge, Mass.

Fein, D. (2003). Transition to welfare parenthood by welfare recipients' daughters: Do recent trends suggest a culture change? Paper presented at the 25th Annual Research Conference of the Association for Public Policy and Analysis, Washington, D.C. November 6.

Fein, D. (2004). Married and poor: Basic characteristics of economically disadvantaged married couples in the U.S. Working paper SHM-01, Supporting Healthy Marriage Evaluation, Abt Associates, Cambridge, Mass. July.

Fellowes, M. C., & Rowe, G. (2004). Politics and the new American welfare states. *American Journal of Political Science* 48: 362–73.

Fernandez, R. M. (2001). Skill-biased technological change and wage inequality: Evidence from a plant retooling. *American Journal of Sociology* 107(2): 273–320.

Fischer, D. (2005). The road to good employment retention: Three successful programs from the Jobs Initiative. Annie E. Casey Foundation, Baltimore, Md.

Fisher, G. (1992). The development and history of the poverty thresholds. *Social Security Bulletin* 55(4): 3–14.

Fitzgerald, J. M., & Ribar, D. C. (2005). Transitions in welfare participation and female headship. *Population Research and Policy Review* 23: 641–70.

Focus. (2005). Inequality in America: What role for human capital policies? *Focus* 23, no. 3 (Spring): 1–10.

Food Research and Action Center. (2004). Afterschool guide: Nourish their bodies, feed their minds. Food Research and Action Center, Washington, D.C.

Food Research and Action Center. (2004). Current news & analyses: Highlights of the Child Nutrition and WIC Reauthorization Act of 2004. Updated July 30.

Fording, R. C. (1997). The conditional effect of violence as a political tactic: Mass insurgency, welfare generosity, and electoral context in the American states. *American Journal of Political Science* 41: 1–29.

Forum on Child and Family Statistics. (2004). America's children in brief: Key national indicators of well-being, 2004. Federal Interagency Forum on Child and Family Statistics.

Fragile Families Research Brief. (2003b). The effects of welfare and child support policies on union formation. No. 20. December.

Freeman, R. B. (2001). The rising tide lifts . . . ? In S. Danziger & R. H. Haveman (Eds)., *Understanding poverty*. New York: Russell Sage Foundation; Cambridge, Mass.: Harvard University Press.

Frumkin, P. (2002). Service contracting with nonprofit and for-profit providers. In J. D. Donahue & J. S. Nye Jr. (Eds.), *Market-based governance* (pp. 66–87). Washington, D.C.: Brookings Institution Press.

Frumkin, P., & Andre-Clark, A. (1999). The rise of the corporate social worker. *Society* 36, no. 6 (September/October): 46–52.

Gabor, V., Hardison, B. L., Botsko, C., & Bartlett, S. (2003). Food stamp program access study: Local office policies and practices. Abt Associates. December.

Gais, T. L., Nathan, R. P., Lurie, I., & Kaplan, T. (2001). The implementation of the personal responsibility act of 1996. In R. Blank & R. Haskins (Eds.), *The new world of welfare* (pp. 35–64). Washington, D.C.: Brookings Institution Press.

Gale, W., & Kotlikoff, L. (2004). Effects of recent fiscal policies on children. *Tax Notes* (June 7).

GAO. (2002). *Welfare reform: Federal oversight of state and local contracting can be strengthened*. U.S. General Accounting Office, Washington, D.C.

GAO. (2004). *TANF and SSI. Opportunities exist to help people with impairments become more self-sufficient*. No. GAO-04-878. September. Report to the Chairman, Subcommittee on Human Resources, Committee on Ways and Means, House of Representatives.

Garfinkel, I., Huang, C.-C., McLanahan, S. S., & Gaylin, D. S. (2003). The role of child support enforcement and welfare in non-marital childbearing. *Journal of Population Economics* 16: 55–70.

Garfinkel, I., Huang, C.-C., & Naidich, W. (2002). The effects of a basic income guarantee on poverty and income distribution. USBIG discussion paper no. 014. February 2002.

Garfinkel, I., & McLanahan, S. (2002). Unwed parents: Myths, realities, and policy making. *Focus* 22: 93–97.

Garfinkel, I., & McLanahan, S. (2003). Strengthening Fragile Families. In I. V. Sawhill (Ed.), *One percent for the kids: New policies, brighter futures for America's children*. Washington, D.C.: Brookings Institution Press.

Garfinkel, I., McLanahan, S., Tienda, M., & Brooks-Gunn, J. (2001). Fragile families and welfare reform: An introduction. *Children and Youth Services Review* 23(4–5): 277–301.

Garfinkel, I., Rainwater, L., & Smeeding, T. (2005). Equal opportunities for children: Social welfare expenditures in the English-speaking countries and western Europe. *Focus* 23(3): 16–23.

Gassman-Pines, A., & Yoshikawa, H. (2006). Five-year effects of an anti-poverty program on marriage among never-married mothers. *Journal of Policy Analysis and Management* 25: 11–30.

Gennetian, L. A., Duncan, G., Knox, V., Vargas, W., Clark-Kauffman, E., & London, A. S. (2004). How welfare policies affect adolescents' school outcomes: A synthesis of evidence from experimental studies. *Journal of Research on Adolescence* 14(4): 399–423.

Gennetian, L. A., & Knox, V. (2003). Staying single: The effects of welfare reform policies on marriage and cohabitation. Manpower Demonstration Research Corporation, New York.

Gennetian, L. A., & Knox, V. (2005). The effects of a Minnesota Welfare Reform Program on marital stability six years later. *Population Research and Policy Review* 23: 567–93.

Gennetian, L., Knox, V., & Miller, C. (2000). Reforming welfare and rewarding work: A summary of the final report on the Minnesota family investment program. Manpower Demonstration Research Corporation, New York.

Gershoff, E. (2003). *Low income and hardship among America's kindergartners*. National Center for Children in Poverty, New York.

Giannarelli, L., & Barsimantov, J. (2000). Child care expenses of America's families. Occasional paper no. 40, Urban Institute, Washington, D.C.

Gibson, C. (2002). *Understanding the stick (or is it the carrot?): The effect of welfare beliefs on family formation decisions*. Working paper no. 02-19-FF, Center for Research on Child Wellbeing. November.

Gibson-Davis, C. M., Edin, K., & McLanahan, S. (2005). High hopes but even higher expectations: The retreat from marriage among low-income couples. *Journal of Marriage and Family* 67: 1301–12.

Gibson-Davis, C., & Foster, M. (2005). A cautionary take: Using propensity scores to estimate the effects of food stamps on food insecurity. Discussion paper no. DP 1293-05, Institute for Research on Poverty, University of Wisconsin–Madison. March.

Gilens, M. (1999). *Why Americans hate welfare: Race, media, and the politics of antipoverty policy*. Chicago: University of Chicago Press.

Giloth, B. (2005). Good jobs and careers: What communities need to do to train and move low-income, low-skilled people into good jobs and careers. Annie E. Casey Foundation, Baltimore, Md.

Gladden, T., & Taber, C. (2000). Wage progression among less skilled workers. In D. E. Card & R. M. Blank (Eds.), *Finding jobs: Work and welfare reform* (pp. 160–192). New York: Russell Sage Foundation.

Glennerster, H. (2002). United States poverty studies and poverty measurement: The past twenty-five years. *Social Service Review* 79: 83–107.

Goldberg, H., & Schott, L. (2000). A compliance-oriented approach to sanctions in state and county TANF programs. Center on Budget and Policy Priorities, Washington, D.C.

Gooden, S., Doolittle, F., & Glispie, B. (2001). Matching applicants with services: Initial assessments in the Milwaukee County W-2 program. Manpower Development and Research Corporation, New York.

Gordon, A., Hartline-Grafton, H., & Nogales, R. (2004). Innovative WIC practices: Profiles of 20 programs. Mathematica Policy Research, Economic Research Service, USDA. June.

Gordon, L. (1988). *Heroes of their own lives: The politics and history of family violence: Boston, 1880–1960*. New York: Viking.

Gordon, L. (1999). *The great Arizona orphan abduction*. Cambridge, Mass.: Harvard University Press.

Gottschalck, A. O. (2003). *Dynamics of economic well-being: Spells of unemployment, 1996–1999.Current population reports*, P70–93. Washington, D.C.: U.S. Census Bureau.

Greenberg, M. (2004). Welfare reform, phase two. *The American prospect online edition*. September 1.

Greenberg, M., & Laracy, M. (2000). Welfare reform: Next steps offer new opportunities. Neighborhood Funders Group policy paper no. 4, Center for Law and Social Policy, Washington, D.C.

Greenberg, M., & Noyes, J. (2005). Increasing state and local capacity for cross-systems innovation: Assessing flexibility and opportunities under current law: Implications for policy and practice. A collaborative project of the National Governors Association's

Center for Best Practices, Hudson Institute and Center for Law and Social Policy; Center for Law and Social Policy, Hudson Institute. January.

Greenberg, M., & Rahmanou, H. (2005). TANF spending in 2003. Center for Law and Social Policy. January 18.

Greenberg, M., & Rahmanou, H. (2005b). Administration's TANF proposal would not free up $2 billion for child care. Center for Law and Social Policy. April 13.

Greenberg, M., & Richer, E. (2003). How states used TANF and MOE funds in FY 2002: The picture from federal reporting. Center for Law and Social Policy, Washington, D.C.

Greenstein, R. (2005). The Earned Income Tax Credit: Boosting employment, aiding the working poor. Center on Budget and Policy Priorities. July 19.

Gronbjerg, K. N., & Salamon, L. M. (2002). Devolution, marketization, and the changing shape of government-nonprofit relations. In L. M. Salamon (Ed.), *The state of nonprofit America*. Washington, D.C.: Brookings Institution Press.

Gueron, J. M., & Pauly, E. (1991). *From welfare to work*. New York: Russell Sage Foundation.

Gustafson, C. K., & Levine, P. B. (1998). Less-skilled workers, welfare reform, and the unemployment insurance system. NBER working paper no. W6489, National Bureau of Economic Research, Cambridge, Mass. March 1998.

H&R Block helps put food on the table; tax offices in 12 states provide food stamp applications to millions of clients. *Business Wire*. January 27, 2005.

Hacker, J. S. (2002). *The divided welfare state: The battle over public and private social benefits in the United States*. New York: Cambridge University Press.

Hacker, J. S. (2004). Privatizing risk without privatizing the welfare state: The hidden politics of social policy retrenchment in the United States. *American Political Science Review* 98: 243–60.

Hamersma, S. (2005). The effects of employer subsidy on employment outcomes: A study of the work opportunity and welfare-to-work tax credits. Discussion papers, DP no. 1303–05, Institute for Research on Poverty, University of Wisconsin–Madison. July.

Hamilton, G. (1962). Editorial. *Social Work*, p. 128.

Hamilton, G. (2002). *Moving people from welfare to work: Lessons from the national evaluation of welfare-to-work strategies*. U.S. Department of Health and Human Services. Administration for Children and Families. Office of the Assistant Secretary for Planning and Evaluation. U.S. Department of Education. Office of the Under Secretary. Office of Vocational and Adult Education, Washington, D.C.

Hamilton, G., Freedman, S., Gennetian, L., Michalopoulos, C., Walter, J., Adams-Ciardullo, D., et al. (2001). *National evaluation of welfare-to-work strategies: How effective are different welfare-to-work approaches? Five-year adult and child impacts for eleven programs*. Washington D.C.: U.S. Department of Health and Human Services. Administration for Children and Families. Office of the Assistant Secretary for Planning and Evaluation. U.S. Department of Education. Office of the Under Secretary. Office of Vocational and Adult Education, Washington, D.C.

Han, W.-J. (2005). Maternal nonstandard work schedules and child cognitive outcomes. *Child Development* 76(1): 137–54.

Handler, J. F. (1986). *The conditions of discretion: Autonomy, community, bureaucracy*. New York: Russell Sage Foundation.

Handler, J. F. (1995). *The poverty of welfare reform*. New Haven, Conn.: Yale University Press.

Handler, J. F., & Hasenfeld, Y. (1991). *The moral construction of poverty*. Newbury Park, Calif.: Sage Publications.

Handler, J. F., & Hasenfeld, Y. (1997). *We the poor people: Work, poverty and welfare*. New Haven, Conn.: Yale University Press.

Handler, J. F., & Hollingsworth, E. J. (1971). *The "deserving poor": A study of welfare administration*. Chicago: Markham Publishing Co.

Handler, J. F., & White, L. (1999). *Hard labor: Women and work in the post-welfare era*. Armonk, N.Y.: M.E. Sharpe.

Hansmann, H. (1987). Economic theories of nonprofit organizations. In W. W. Powell (Ed.), *The nonprofit sector: A research handbook*. New Haven, Conn.: Yale University Press.

Hao, L., & Cherlin, A. J. (2003). Welfare reform and teenage pregnancy, childbirth, and school dropout. Department of Sociology, John Hopkins University, Baltimore, Md.

Harknett, K., & McLanahan, S. (2004). Racial and ethnic differences in marriage after the birth of a child. *American Sociological Review* 69: 790–811.

Harrington, M. (1981). *The other America: Poverty in the United States*. New York: Penguin Books.

Harris, K. M. (1993). Work and welfare among single mothers in poverty. *American Journal of Sociology* 99(2): 317–52.

Harris, K. M., Guilkey, D., Cheng, M., & Veliz, E. (2003). Welfare reform and nonmarital childbearing in the transition to adulthood. Paper presented at the Annual APPAM Conference, Washington, D.C. November 6–8.

Hart, B., & Risley, T. R. (1995). *Meaningful differences in the everyday experience of young American children*. Baltimore: Paul H. Brookes Publishing Company, Inc.

Hart, K., & Schumacher, R. (2004). Moving forward: Head Start children, families, and programs in 2003. Head Start series, policy brief no. 5, Center for Law and Social Policy. June.

Harvey, P. (2002). Human rights and economic policy discourse: Taking economic and social rights seriously. *Columbia Human Rights Law Review* 33, no. 2 (Spring): 363–471.

Harvey, P. (2005). The right to work and basic income guarantees: Competing or complementary goals? *Rutgers Journal of Law and Urban Policy* 2(1): 8–59.

Hasenfeld, Y., Ghose, T., & Larson, K. (2004). The logic of sanctioning welfare recipients: An empirical assessment. *Social Service Review* 78(2): 304–19.

Hasenfeld, Y., Mosley, J., Katz, H., & Anheier, H. (2003). Serving a dynamic and diverse metropolis: The human services nonprofit sector in Los Angeles. UCLA Center for Civil Society, Los Angeles.

Hasenfeld, Y., & Weaver, D. (1996). Enforcement, compliance, and disputes in welfare-to-work programs. *Social Service Review* 70: 235–56.

Haskins, R. (2000). The second most important issue: Effects of welfare reform on family income and poverty. Unpublished manuscript prepared for the New World of Welfare conference, Committee on Ways and Means.

Haveman, R. (2002–03). When work alone is not enough. *La Follette Policy Report* 13(2).

Haveman, R. (2003). When work alone is not enough. In I. V. Sawhill (Ed.), *One percent for the kids: New policies, brighter futures for America's children*. Washington, D.C.: Brookings Institution Press.

Hays, S. (2003). *Flat broke with children: Women in the age of welfare reform*. Oxford; New York: Oxford University Press.

Health Systems Research Inc., & Abt Associates Inc. (2003). *Study of TANF application process*, Vol. 1. Washington, D.C.: U.S. Department of Health and Human Services; Administration for Children and Families.

Heclo, H. (1994). Poverty politics. In S. H. Danziger, G. D. Sandefur, & D. H. Wineberg (Eds.), *Confronting poverty* (pp. 396–437). New York: Russell Sage Foundation.

Helburn, S. W., Culkin, M. L., Howes, C., Bryant, D., Clifford, R., Cryer, D., Peisner-Feinberg, E., Kagan, S., & Economics Department. (1995). Cost, quality, and child outcomes in child care centers. Center for Research in Economic Social Policy; Economics Department, University of Colorado at Denver.

Henly, J. R., & Lambert, S. (2005). Nonstandard work and child care needs of low-income parents. In Bianchi, S. M., Casper, L. M., & King, R. B. (Eds.), *Work, family, health, & well-being* (pp. 473–92). Lawrence Erlbaum Associates, Inc.

Henly, J. R., Luke Shaefer, H., & Waxman, E. (forthcoming). Nonstandard work schedules: Employer- vs. employee-driven flexibility in retail jobs. *Social Service Review*.

Herndon, R. (2004). Who died an expense to this town: Poor relief in eighteenth century Rhode Island. In B. G. Smith (Ed.), *Down and out in early America*. University Park, Pa.: Pennsylvania State University Press.

Hicks, A., & Swank, D. H. (1983). Civil disorder, relief mobilization, and AFDC caseloads: A reexamination of the Piven and Cloward thesis. *American Journal of Political Science* 27: 695–716.

Higham, J. (2002). *Strangers in the land: Patterns of American nativism, 1860–1925*. New Brunswick, N.J.: Rutgers University Press.

Hill, I., Stockdale, H., & Courtot, B. (2004). Squeezing SCHIP: States use flexibility to respond to the ongoing budget crisis. Series A, No. A-65, Urban Institute, New Federalism, Issues and Options for States, State Children's Health Insurance Program Evaluation. June.

Hirschman, A. O. (1991). *The rhetoric of reaction: Perversity, futility, jeopardy*. Cambridge, Mass.: Belknap Press.

Hoff, T., Green, L., McIntosh, M., Rawlings, N., & D'Amico, J. (2000). Sex education in America: A series of national surveys of students, parents, teachers, and principals. Summary of findings, Kaiser Family Foundation. September.

Holzer, H. J. (1996). What employers want: Job prospects for less-educated workers. Russell Sage Foundation, New York.

Holzer, H. J., Offner, P., & Sorensen, E. J. (2004). Declining employment among young black men: The role of incarceration and child support. Institute for Research on Poverty, University of Wisconsin–Madison.

Hotz, V. J., Mullin, C., & Scholz, J. K. (2004). The effects of the Earned Income Tax Credit on the employment of low-wage populations: Are the apparent effects for real? Paper presented at the Tax Policy and Public Finance Workshop. April 15.

Hotz, V. J., & Scholz, J. K. (2003). The Earned Income Tax Credit. In R. Moffit (Ed.), *Means-tested transfer programs in the United States*. Chicago: University of Chicago Press; NEBR.

Huston, A. C., Miller, C., Richburg-Hayes, L., Duncan, G. J., Eldred, C. A., Weisner, T. S., Lowe, E., McLoyd, V. C., Crosby, D. A., Ripke, M. N., & Redcross, C. (2003). New hope for families and children: Five-year results of a program to reduce poverty and reform welfare. Manpower Demonstration Research Corporation, New York.

Iceland, J. (2003a). *Dynamics of economic well-being: Poverty 1996–1999*. No. P70–91. Washington, D.C.: U.S. Census Bureau.

Iceland, J. (2003b). *Poverty in America: A handbook*. Berkeley, Calif.: University of California Press.

Iceland, J. (2003c). Why poverty remains high: The role of income growth, economic inequality, and changes in family structure, 1949–1999. *Demography* 40(3): 499–519.

Iceland, J., & Baum, K. (2004). *Income poverty and material hardship: How strong is the association*. No. 04-17, National Poverty Center Working Paper Series, Ann Arbor, Mich.

Iceland, J., & Kim, J. (2001). Poverty among working families: New insights from an improved poverty measure. *Social Science Quarterly* 82(2): 253–67.

Iceland, J., Short, K., Garner, T. I., & Johnson, D. (2001). Are children worse off? Evaluating well-being using a new (and improved) measure of poverty. *Journal of Human Resources* 36(2): 398–412.

Independent Sector. (2001). The nonprofit almanac in brief. Washington, D.C.

Inkelas, M., Halfon, N., Uyeda, K., Stevens, G., Wright, J., Holtby, S., & Brown, R. E. (2003). The health of young children in California: Findings from the 2001 California Health Interview Survey. Los Angeles, CA: UCLA Center for Health Policy Research and First 5 California.

Institute for the Study of Homelessness and Poverty. (2005). *Research notice: U.S. and California, health insurance coverage: Estimates from the National Health Interview Survey.* Centers for Disease Control and Prevention, National Center for Health Statistics.

Irish, K., Schumacher, R., & Lombardi, J. (2004). Head Start comprehensive services: A key support for early learning for poor children. Policy brief no. 4, Head Start Series, Center for Law and Social Policy. January.

Isaac, L., & Kelly, W. R. (1981). Racial insurgency, the state and welfare expansion: Local and national level evidence from the postwar United States. *American Journal of Sociology* 86(6): 1348–86.

Jackson, A., & Scheines, R. (2005). Single mothers' self-efficacy, parenting in the home environment, and children's development in a two-wave study. *Social Work Research* 29(1): 7–20.

Jackson, T., Tienda, M., & Huang, C. (2001). Capabilities and employability of unwed mothers. *Children and Youth Services Review*, 23: 327–51.

Jencks, C. (2002). Does inequality matter? *Daedalus* (Winter): 49–65.

Jencks, C. (2004). The low-wage puzzle: Why is America generating so many bad jobs – and how can we create more good jobs? *The American Prospect* (January).

Joyce, T., Kaestner, R., Korenman, S., & Henshaw, S. (2005). Family cap provisions and changes in births and abortions. *Population Research and Policy Review* 23: 475–511.

Kabbani, N., & Yazbeck, M. (2004). The role of food assistance programs and employment circumstances in helping households with children avoid hunger. Discussion paper no. 1280-04, Institute for Research on Poverty, University of Wisconsin–Madison. May.

Kaestner, R., & O'Neill, J. (2002). Welfare reform changed teenage behaviors? Working paper no. 8932, National Bureau of Economic Research. May.

Kaiser Commission on Medicaid and the Uninsured. (2004). Faces of Medicaid. Kaiser Family Foundation. April.

Kaiser Family Foundation. (2002). Sex education in the U.S.: Policy and politics. Kaiser Family Foundation. March.

Kalil, A., & Kunz, J. (1999). First birth among unmarried adolescent girls: Risk and protective factors. *Social Work Research* 23: 197–208.

Kalil, A., Seefeldt, K. S., & Wang, H.-C. (2002). Sanctions and material hardship under TANF. *Social Service Review* 76(4): 642–62.

Kane, A., & Sawhill, I. V. (2003). Preventing early childbearing. In I. V. Sawhill (Ed.), *One percent for the kids: New policies, brighter futures for America's children.* Washington, D.C.: Brookings Institution Press.

Kangas, O. (2000). Distributive justice and social policy: Some reflections on Rawls and income distribution. *Social Policy and Administration* 34(5): 510–28.

Kato, L. Y., & Riccio, J. A. (2001). Building new partnerships for employment: Collaboration among agencies and public housing residents in the Jobs-Plus demonstration. Manpower Demonstration Research Corporation, New York.

Katz, B., & Allen, K. (1999). The state of welfare caseloads in America's cities: 1999. Center on Urban and Metropolitan Policy, Brookings Institution, Washington D.C.

Katz, M. B. (1986). *In the shadow of the poorhouse: A social history of welfare in America.* New York: Basic Books.

Katz, M. B. (2001). *The price of citizenship: Redefining America's welfare state.* 1st ed. New York: Metropolitan Books.

Kauff, J., Derr, M. K., & Pavetti, L. (2004). A study of work participation and full engagement strategies. Mathematica Policy Research, Inc., Washington, D.C.

Kaufman, L. (2004). It's a trend: Births out of wedlock are falling in New York. *New York Times.* October 2.

Kearney, M. S. (2004). Is there an effect of incremental welfare benefits on fertility behavior? *Journal of Human Resources* 39: 295–325.

Kemple, J., & Scott-Clayton, J. (2004). Career academies: Impacts on labor market outcomes and educational attainment. Manpower Demonstration Research Corporation. March.

Kirby, D. (2001). Answers: Research findings on programs to reduce teen pregnancy. Summary, National Campaign to Prevent Teen Pregnancy, Washington, D.C.

Klerman, J. A., Zellman, G. L., Chun, T., Humphrey, N., Reardon, E., Farley, D. O., Ebener, P. A., & Steinberg, P. (2000). Welfare reform in California: State and county implementation of CalWORKS in the second year. RAND Research, Santa Monica, Calif.

Knox, V., Miller, C., & Gennetian, L. (2000). Reforming welfare and rewarding work: A summary of the final report on the Minnesota Family Investment Program. Manpower Demonstration Research Corporation, New York.

Kornfeld, B., Porcari, D., & Peck, L. R. (2003). The Arizona Works Pilot Program: A three-year assessment. Abt Associates Inc., Cambridge, Mass.

Kusmin, L., & Gibbs, R. (2000). Less-educated workers face limited opportunities to move up to good jobs. *Rural America* 15(3): 33.

Lambert, S., Waxman, E., & Haley-Lock, A. (2001). Against the odds: A study of instability in lower-skilled jobs. School of Social Service Administration, University of Chicago.

Land, K. (2005). Project coordinator 2005 report. The Foundation for Child Development Index of Child Well-Being (CWI), 1975–2003, with projections for 2004.

Lara-Cinisomo, S., Pebley, A., Vaiana, M., Maddio, E., Berends, M., & Lucas, S. (2004). A matter of class: Educational achievement reflects family background more than ethnicity or immigration. *RAND Review* (Fall).

Lawrence, M., Bernstein, J., & Schmitt, J. (2000). *The state of working America 1999–2000.* Ithaca, N.Y.: Cornell University Press.

Lawrence, S., Chau, M., & Lennon, M. (2004). Depression, substance abuse, and domestic violence. National Center for Children in Poverty. Columbia University, Mailman School of Public Health. June.

Lee, B. J., Slack, K. S., & Lewis, D. A. (2004). Are welfare sanctions working as intended? Welfare, receipt, work activity and material hardship among TANF-recipient families. *Social Service Review* 78: 370–403.

Lee, D. (1999). Nature of work has changed. *Los Angeles Times.* September 6, p. A1.

Lee, K. (2005). Effects of experimental center-based child care on developmental outcomes of young children living in poverty. *Social Service Review* (March).

Leonhardt, D. (2004, August 27). More Americans were uninsured and poor in 2003, census finds. *New York Times.* August 27.

Lerman, R. I. (1996). The impact of U.S. family structure on child poverty and income inequality. *Economica* 63(250 Suppl.): S119–39.

Lerman, R. I. (2002). How do marriage, cohabitation, and single parenthood affect the material hardships of families with children? Urban Institute, Washington, D.C., pp. 1–38.

Lerman, R. I. (2002). Marriage and the economic well-being of families with children: A review of the literature. Washington, D.C., Urban Institute.

Lester, G. (2001). Unemployment insurance and wealth redistribution. 49 *UCLA L. Rev.* 335.

Lester, G. (2005). A defense of paid leave. 28 *Harv. J. L. & Gender* 1.

Levenstein, L. (2000). From innocent children to unwanted migrants and unwed moms: Two chapters in the public discourse on welfare in the United States, 1960–1961. *Journal of Women's History* 11(4): 10–33.

Levine, K., & Scholz, J. K. (2002). The evolution of income support policy in recent decades. In S. Danziger & R. H. Haveman (Eds.), *Understanding poverty*. New York: Russell Sage Foundation; Cambridge, Mass.: Harvard University Press.

Levine, P. (2005). Unemployment insurance over the business cycle: Does it meet workers' needs? Department of Economics, Wellesley College.

Levin-Epstein, J. (2005). To have and to hold: Congressional vows on marriage and sex. Center for Law and Social Policy. March.

Levin-Epstein, J. (2003b). Lifting the lid off the family cap. Center for Law and Social Policy, policy brief no.1, Childbearing and Reproductive Health Series. December.

Levin-Epstein, J., Grisham, C., & Batchelder, M. (2001). Comments to the U.S. Department of Health and Human Services regarding teen pregnancy prevention and teens parents provisions in the Temporary Assistance for Needy Families (TANF) block grant. Center for Law and Social Policy. November 30.

Levin-Epstein, J., & Hutchins, J. (2003). Teens and TANF: How adolescents fare under the nation's welfare program: An update on women's health policy. Issue brief, Kaiser Family Foundation. December.

Levin-Epstein, J., Ooms, T., Parke, M., Roberts, P., & Turetsky, V. (2002). Spending too much, accomplishing too little: An analysis of the family formation provisions of H.R. 4737 and recommendations for change. Center for Law and Social Policy. June 11.

Levy, F. (1998). *The new dollars and dreams: American incomes and economic change.* New York: Russell Sage Foundation.

Lewis, O. (1959). *Five families: Mexican case studies in the culture of poverty.* New York: Basic Books.

Lichter, D., Batson, C., & Brown, J. B. (2004). Welfare reform and marriage promotion: The marital expectations and desires of single and cohabiting mothers. *Social Service Review* 78(1): 3–25.

Lichter, D., Graefe, D. R., & Brown, J. B. (2003). Is marriage a panacea? Union formation among economically-disadvantaged unwed mothers. *Social Problems* 50(1): 60–86.

Lieberman, R. C., & Shaw, G. M. (2000). Looking inward, looking outward: The politics of state welfare innovation under devolution. *Political Research Quarterly* 53(2): 215–40.

Liebow, E., Reid, C., O'Malley, G., Marsh, S., & Blank, S. (2004). Resident participation in Seattle's Jobs-Plus program. Environmental Health and Social Policy Center, Manpower Demonstration Research Corporation, Seattle, Wash. October.

Lindhorst, T., & Padgett, J. D. (2005). Disjuncture of women and frontline workers: Implementation of the family violence option. *Social Service Review* 79: 405–29.

Lipsky, M. (1984). Bureaucratic disentitlement in social welfare programs. *Social Service Review* 58: 3–27.

Lipsky, M. (1980). *Street-level bureaucracy*. New York: Russell Sage Foundation.

Litchfield, L., Swanberg, J., & Sigworth, C. (2004). Increasing the visibility of the invisible workforce: Model programs and policies for hourly and lower wage employees. Final report, Boston College Center for Work & Family, Carroll School of Management. April.

Loch, S., Fuller, B., Kagan, S., & Carrol, B. (2004). Child care in poor communities: Early learning effects of type, quality, and stability. *Child Development* 75(1): 47–65.

Loeb, S., & Corcoran, M. (2001). Welfare, work experience and economic self-sufficiency. *Journal of Policy Analysis and Management* 20(1): 1–20.

Loeb, S., Fuller, B., Kagan, S., & Carrol, B. (2004). Child care in poor communities: Early learning effects of type, quality, and stability. *Child Development* 75(1): 47–65.

Lombardi, J., Cohen, J., Stebbins, H., Lurie-Hurvitz, E., Chernoff, J. J., Denton, K., Abbey, R., & Ewen, D. (2004). Building bridges from prekindergarten to infants and toddlers: A preliminary look at issues in four states. A discussion paper, Zero to Three Policy Center. April.

London, A. S., Scott, E. K., Edin, K., & Hunter, V. (2004). Welfare reform, work-family tradeoffs, and child well-being. *Family Relations* 53(2): 148–58.

London, R., & Fairlie, R. (2005). Economic conditions and children's living arrangements. Center for Justice, Tolerance, and Community, Department of Economics, University of California, Santa Cruz, and National Poverty Center.

Lopoo, L. (2002). *Maternal employment and teenage childbearing: Evidence from the PSID*. Working paper no. 02-21, Center for Research on Child Wellbeing. December.

Lopoo, L. (2005). A profile of the men who father children with unwed, teenage women. Working paper no. 05-21-FF, Center for Research on Child Wellbeing, Princeton, N.J.

Loprest, P. (1999). Families who left welfare: Who are they and how are they doing? Assessing the New Federalism, discussion paper, Urban Institute, Washington, D.C.

Ludwig, J. (2003). Improving neighborhoods for poor children. In I. V. Sawhill (Ed.), *One percent for the kids: New policies, brighter futures for America's children*. Washington, D.C.: Brookings Institution Press.

Lukemeyer, A., Meyers, M., & Smeeding, T. (2000). Expensive children in poor families: Out-of-pocket expenditures for the care of disabled and chronically ill children in welfare families. *Journal of Marriage and the Family* 62: 399–415.

Luker, K. (1996). *Dubious conceptions: The politics of teenage pregnancy*. Cambridge, Mass.: Harvard University Press.

Lurie, I., & Riccucci, N. M. (2003). Changing the "culture" of welfare offices: From vision to the front lines. *Administration and Society* 34: 653–77.

Lyon, E. (1997). Poverty, welfare and battered women: What does the research tell us? National Resource Center on Domestic Violence, Harrisburg, Penn.

Maag, E. (2005). Disparities in knowledge of the EITC. Tax notes, Tax Policy Center. Urban Institute and Brookings Institution, Washington, D.C.

Manpower Demonstration Research Corporation. (2005). Fast fact: Marriages are less stable for economically disadvantaged adults.

Maranville, D. (2003). Workplace mythologies and unemployment insurance: Exit, voice, and exhausting all reasonable alternatives to quitting. *31 Hofstra L. Rev. 456*.

Marcy, H. (2003). For success? Supporting pregnant and parenting teens in Chicago schools. Center for Impact Research. July.

Martinez, J. M., & Miller, C. (2000). Working and earning: The impact of parents' fair share on low income fathers' employment. Manpower Demonstration Research Corporation, New York.

Marwell, N. (2004). Privatizing the welfare state: Nonprofit community-based organizations as political actors. *American Sociological Review* 69(April): 265–91.

Mashaw, J. L. (1983). *Bureaucratic justice: Managing social security disability claims*. New Haven, Conn.: Yale University Press.

Mathematica Policy Research, Inc. (2002). Early Head Start research and evaluation project: Making a difference in the lives of the infants and toddlers and their families, Vol. 1: The impact of Early Head Start. Final technical report, Princeton, N.J.

Matthews, H., & Ewen, D. (2005). President's budget projects 300,000 low-income children to lose child care by 2010. Center for Law and Social Policy. February.

Maynard, R. A., Trenholm, C., Devaney, B., Johnson, A., Clark, M. A., Homrighausen, J., & Kalaly, E. (2005). First-year impact of four Title V, Section 510 abstinence education programs. Mathematica Policy Research, Inc., Princeton, N.J.

McConnell, S., Burwick, A., Perez-Johnson, I., & Winston, P. (2003). Privatization in practice: Case studies of contracting for TANF case management. Mathematica Policy Research, Inc., Washington, D.C.

McKernan, S.-M., & Ratcliffe, C. (2002). Transition events in the dynamics of poverty. Urban Institute, Washington, D.C.

McLanahan, S., & Carlson, M. (2002). Welfare reform, fertility, and father involvement: Children and welfare reform; www.futureofchildren.org.

McLanahan, S., & Carlson, M. J. (2002). Welfare reform, fertility, and father involvement. *The Future of Children* 16: 147–64.

McLanahan, S., & Garfinkel, I. (2002). Unwed parents: Myths, realities, and policymaking. Working paper no. 02-15-FF, Center for Research on Child Wellbeing. July.

McLanahan, S., Garfinkel, I., Reichman, N., Teitler, J., Carlson, M., & Audigier, C. (2003). The Fragile Families and Child Wellbeing Study: Baseline national report. Revised, March.

McMurrer, D., & Sawhill, I. V. (1998). *Getting ahead: Economic and social mobility in America*. Washington, D.C.: Urban Institute Press.

Mead, L. M. (1986). *Beyond entitlement: The social obligations of citizenship*. New York: Free Press.

Mead, L. M. (2004). *Government matters: Welfare reform in Wisconsin*. Princeton, N.J.: Princeton University Press.

Menaghan, E. G., Kowaleski-Jones, L., & Mott, F. L. (1997). The intergenerational costs of parental social stressors: Academic and social difficulties in early adolescence for children of young mothers. *Journal of Health and Social Behavior* 38(1): 72–86.

Mendez-Luck, C. A., Yu, H., Meng, Y., Chia, J., Newman, B. L., Sripipatana, A., & Wallace, S. P. (2004). Many uninsured children qualify for Medi-Cal or Healthy Families. UCLA Center for Health Policy Research. Policy brief. June.

Meyer, D., Cancian, M., & Cook, S. (2005). Multiple-partner fertility: Incidence and implications for child support policy. Discussion paper no. 1300-05, Institute for Research on Poverty, University of Wisconsin–Madison.

Meyer, J., & Rowan, B. (1977). Institutional organizations: Formal structure as myth and ceremony. *American Journal of Sociology* 83: 340–63.

Meyers, M., & Gatenio, S. (2003). Early education and care in New York City. Paper presented at a conference on New York City and the Welfare State. Russell Sage Foundation, New York.

Mezey, J. (2004). Child care programs help parents find and keep jobs: Funding shortfalls leave many families without assistance. Center for Law and Social Policy, Washington, D.C. February 10.

Michalopoulos, C., Edin, K., Fink, B., Landriscina, M., Polit, D., Polyne, J., Richburg-Hayes, L., Seith, D., & Verma, N. (2003). Welfare reform in Philadelphia: Implementation, effects, and experiences of poor families and neighborhoods. Manpower Demonstration Research Corporation, New York.

Michalopoulos, C., Schwartz, C., & Adams-Ciardullo, D. (2000). *National evaluation of welfare-to-work strategies: What works best for whom impacts of 20 welfare-to-work programs by subgroup.* Washington D.C.: U.S. Department of Health and Human Services. Administration for Children and Families. Office of the Assistant Secretary for Planning and Evaluation. U.S. Department of Education. Office of the Under Secretary. Office of Vocational and Adult Education.

Miller, C., Farrell, M., Cancian, M., & Meyer, D. (2005). *The interaction of child support and TANF: Evidence from samples of current and former welfare recipients.* Report submitted to the Office of Assistant Secretary for Planning and Evaluation, U.S. Department of Health and Human Services. January.

Miller, J., Molina, F., Grossman, L., & Golonka, S. (2004). Building bridges to self-sufficiency: Improving services for low-income working families. Manpower Demonstration Research Corporation and the National Governors Association Center for Best Practices, New York.

Mincy, R., & Huang, C.-C. (2002). Just get me to the church . . . : Assessing policies to promote marriage among fragile families. Working paper no. 02-02-FF, Center for Research on Child Wellbeing. February.

Mincy, R. B., & Sorensen, E. J. (1998). Deadbeats and turnips in child support reform. *Journal of Policy Analysis and Management* 17: 44–51.

Mink, G. (1998). *Welfare's end.* Ithaca, N.Y.; London: Cornell University Press.

Minnesota Family Investment Program Longitudinal Study. (2003). Special report on teen mothers. Program Assessment and Integrity Division, Minnesota Department of Human Services. January.

Mishel, L. R., Bernstein, J., & Allegretto, S. (2005). *The state of working America, 2004/2005.* Ithaca, N.Y.: ILR.

Moffitt, R., & Roff, J. (2000). The diversity of welfare leavers: Background paper to policy brief 00-02. Working paper 00-01.

Molina, F., & Howard, C. (2003). Final report on the Neighborhood Jobs Initiative: Lessons and implications for future employment initiatives. Manpower Demonstration Research Corporation, New York.

Morris, P., Gennetian, L., & Duncan, G. (2005). Effects of welfare and employment policies on young children: New findings on policy experiments conducted in the early 1990s. *Social Policy Report* 14(11).

Morris, P. A., Huston, A. C., Duncan, G. J., Crosby, D. A., & Bos, J. M. (2001). How welfare and work policies affect children: A synthesis of research. Manpower Demonstration Research Corporation, New York.

Mosely, J. L. T. (2004). The food safety net after welfare reform: Use of private and public food assistance in the Kansas City metropolitan area. *Social Service Review* (June): 268–83.

Moss, P. I., & Tilly, C. (2001). *Stories employers tell: Race, skill, and hiring in America.* New York: Russell Sage Foundation.

Murphy, K. M., & Welch, F. (2000). Industrial change and the demand for skill. In F. Welch (Ed.), *The causes and consequences of increasing inequality* (pp. 263–84). Chicago: University of Chicago Press.

Murray, J. (2004). Bound by charity: The abandoned children of late-eighteenth-century Charleston. In B. G. Smith (Ed.), *Down and out in early America.* University Park, Pa.: Pennsylvania State University Press.

Nam, Y. (2005). The role of employment barriers in welfare exits and reentries after welfare reform: Event history analysis. *Social Service Review* (June): 268–93.

Nash, G. (2004). Poverty and politics in early American history. In B. G. Smith (Ed.), *Down and out in early America*. University Park, Pa.: Pennsylvania State University Press.

National Center for Charitable Statistics (n.d.). Number of nonprofit organizations in the United States 1996–2004. Retrieved from http://nccsdataweb.urban.org/PubApps/profile1.php?state=US. (Sources: IRS Business Master File 12/2004 [with modifications by the National Center for Charitable Statistics at the Urban Institute to exclude foreign and governmental organizations]).

National Center for Children in Poverty. (2004). State policy choices: Child support. National Center for Children in Poverty, New York.

National Center for Children in Poverty. (2004a). Low-income children in the United States. Mailman School of Public Health, Columbia University. May.

National Center for Children in Poverty. (2005). Basic facts on low-income children in the United States. National Center for Children in Poverty, New York.

National Center for Health Statistics. (2005). *National vital statistics reports.*

National Conference of State Legislatures. (n.d.). Family cap policies. Retrieved from http://www.ncsl.org/statefed/welfare/familycap05.htm.

National Low Income Housing Coalition. (2004). Out of reach 2004. Retrieved from http://www.nlihc.org/oor2005/.

National Public Radio/ Kaiser Family Foundation/ Kennedy School of Government. (2004). Sex education in America. Principals Survey, Toplines. January.

Newman, K. (2000). *No shame in my game*. New York: Vintage Books.

NICHD Early Child Care Research Network. (2002). Early child care and children's development prior to school entry: Results from the NICHD study of early child care. *American Educational Research Journal* 39(1): 133–64.

NICHD Early Child Care Research Network. (2003). Does quality of child care affect child outcomes at age 4 1/4? *Developmental Psychology* 39(3): 451–69.

NICHD Early Child Care Research Network. (2004). Type of child care and children's development at 54 months. *Early Childhood Research Quarterly* 19: 203–30.

Nixon, L. A., Kauff, K. F., & Losby, J. L. (1999). Second assignments to Iowa's limited benefit plan. Mathematica Policy Research, Inc., Washington, D.C.

Nord, M., Andrews, M., & Carlson, S. (2002). *Household food security in the United States, 2002*. Food assistance and nutrition research report no. 35. Washington, D.C.: Food and Rural Economics Division, Economic Research Service, U.S. Department of Agriculture.

O'Brien-Strain, M., Moyé, L., & Sonenstein, F. L. (2003). Arranging and paying for child care. Public Policy Institute of California.

O'Connor, A. (2001). *Poverty knowledge: Social science, social policy, and the poor in twentieth-century U.S. history*. Princeton, N.J.: Princeton University Press.

Ouellette, T., Burstein, N., Long, D., & Beecroft, E. (2004). *Measures of material hardship: Final report*. Washington, D.C.: U.S. Department of Health and Human Services. Office of the Assistant Secretary for Planning and Evaluation.

Office of Justice Programs. (2004). *When violence hits home: How economics and neighborhood play a role*. Research in brief. U.S. Department of Justice, Washington, D.C. September.

Offner, P. (2003). Teenagers and welfare reform. Urban Institute, Washington, D.C.

Ong, P. M., & Miller, D. (2002). *Economic needs of Asian Americans and Pacific Islanders in distressed areas: Establishing baseline information*. Lewis Center for Regional Policy Studies, University of California Los Angeles.

Ooms, T. (2002). Marriage-Plus. Center for Law and Social Policy, Washington, D.C.

Ooms, T., Bouchet, S., & Parke, M. (2004). Beyond marriage licenses: Efforts in states to strengthen marriage and two-parent families. A state-by-state snapshot. Center for Law and Social Policy. April.

Ooms, T., & Wilson, P. (2004). The challenge of offering relationship and marriage education to low-income populations. *Family Relations* 53: 440–47.

Osberg, L. (2003). Time, money and inequality in international perspective. Dalhousie University, Halifax, Nova Scotia.

Osborne, C., McLanahan, S., & Brooks-Gunn, J. (2003). Is there an advantage to being born to married versus cohabiting parents? Differences in child behavior. Working paper no. 03-09-FF, Center for Research on Child Wellbeing. July.

Osterman, P. (2001). Employers in the low-wage/low-skill labor market. In R. Kazis & M. S. Miller (Eds.), *Low-wage workers in the new economy* (pp. 67–87). Washington, D.C.: Urban Institute Press.

Osterman, P. (2003). Organizing the U.S. labor market: National problems, community strategies. In J. Zeitlin & D. Trubek (Eds.), *Governing work and welfare in a new economy: European and American experiments*. Oxford: Oxford University Press.

Ouellette, T., Burstein, N., Long, D., & Beecroft, E. (2004). *Measures of material hardship: Final report*. Washington, D.C.: U.S. Department of Health and Human Services. Office of the Assistant Secretary for Planning and Evaluation.

Overby, R. (1998). Summary of surveys of welfare recipients employed or sanctioned for noncompliance. University of Memphis, Memphis, Tenn.

Pallas, A., & Nonoyama, Y. (2003). K-12 education in New York City. Paper presented at a conference on New York City and the Welfare State. Russell Sage Foundation, New York

Parke, M. (2004). Marriage-related provisions in welfare reauthorization proposals: A summary. Center for Law and Social Policy, updated March 1. Retrieved from http://www.clasp.org/publications/marr_prov_upd.pdf.

Parke, M. (2004). Who are "fragile families" and what do we know about them? Couples and Marriage Series, policy brief no. 4, Center for Law and Social Policy. January.

Parrott, S., Horney, J., Shapiro, I., Carlitz, R., Hardy, B., & Kamin, D. (2005). Where would cuts be made under the president's budget? Center on Budget and Policy Priorities. Revised February 28.

Patel, N., & Turetsky, V. (n.d.). Safety in the safety net: TANF reauthorization provisions relevant to domestic violence. Center for Law and Social Policy, Washington, D.C.

Patterson, J. T. (1981). *America's struggle against poverty, 1900–1980*. Cambridge, Mass.: Harvard University Press.

Pavetti, L. (1995). And employment for all: Lessons from Utah's Single Parent Employment Demonstration Project. Paper presented at the seventeenth annual research conference of the Association for Public Policy and Management, Washington, D.C.

Pavetti, L., Derr, M. K., & Hesketh, H. (2003). Review of sanction policies and research studies. Mathematica Policy Research, Inc., Washington, D.C.

Pear, R., & Hernandez, R. (2004). Campaign politics seen as slowing welfare law. *New York Times*. July 6.

Pear, R., & Kirkpatrick, D. (2004). Bush plans $1.5 billion drive for promotion of marriage. *New York Times*. January 14.

Pearson, J., & Thoennes, N. (2000). A profile of former TANF clients in the IVD caseload. Center for Policy Research, Denver, Colo.

Peck, J., & Theodore, N. (2005). Temporary downturn? Temporary staffing in the recession and the jobless recovery. *Focus* 23(3).

Piven, F. F., & Cloward, R. A. (1977). *Poor people's movements: Why they succeed, how they fail*. 1st ed. New York: Pantheon Books.

Piven, F. F., & Cloward, R. (1971). *Regulating the poor: The functions of public welfare*. New York: Vintage Books.

Plein, L. C. (2001). Welfare reform in a hard place: The West Virginia experience. Nelson A. Rockefeller Institute of Government, Albany, N.Y.

Polit, D. F., London, A. S., & Martinez, J. M. (2001). The health of poor urban women: Findings from the project on devolution and urban change. New York: Manpower Demonstration Research Corporation.

Powell, W. W. (1987). *The nonprofit sector: A research handbook*. New Haven, Conn.: Yale University Press.

Powers, E. T. (2003). Children's health and maternal work activity. *Journal of Human Resources* 38(3): 522–56.

Presser, H. B. (2003). *Working in a 24/7 economy: Challenges for American families*. New York: Russell Sage Foundation.

Quadagno, J. S. (1994). *The color of welfare: How racism undermined the war on poverty*. New York: Oxford University Press.

Quigley, W. P. (2003). *Ending poverty as we know it: Guaranteeing a right to a job at a living wage*. Philadelphia, Penn.: Temple University Press.

Rainwater, L., & Smeeding, T. M. (2003). *Poor kids in a rich country: America's children in comparative perspective*. New York: Russell Sage Foundation.

Rangarajan, A., & Razafindrakoto, C. (2004). Unemployment Insurance as a potential safety net for TANF Leavers: Evidence from five states. Mathematica Policy Research, Inc., Washington, D.C.

Rank, M. R. (2004). *One nation, underprivileged: Why American poverty affects us all*. New York: Oxford University Press.

Rank, M. R., & Hirschl, T. A. (2003). Estimating the probabilities and patterns of food stamp use across the life course. Report prepared for the Food Assistance and Nutrition Research Small Grants Program, United States Department of Agriculture, Economic Research Service, Washington, D.C., and the Joint Center for Poverty Research, University of Chicago and Northwestern University.

Rector, R. E. (1993). Welfare reform, dependency reduction, and labor market entry. *Journal of Labor Research* 14(3).

Rector, R. E., & Youssef, S. E. (1999). The determinants of welfare caseload decline. Heritage Foundation, Washington, D.C.

Reese, E. (2005). *Backlash against welfare mothers: Past and present*. Berkeley: University of California Press.

Reese, V. (2005). Maximizing your retention and productivity with on-boarding. *Employment Relations Today* 31(4): 23–29.

Reichman, N. E., Teitler, J. O., & Curtis, M. A. (2005). TANF sanctioning and hardship. *Social Service Review* 79: 215–36.

Reichman, N. E., Teitler, J. O., Garfinkel, I., & McLanahan, S. (2001). Fragile families: Sample and design. *Children and Youth Services Review* 23(4–5): 303–26.

Riccio, J., Friedlander, D., & Freedman, S. (1994). GAIN: Benefits, costs, and three-year impacts on a welfare-to-work program. Manpower Demonstration Research Co., New York.

Rich, L. (2001). Regular and irregular earnings of unwed fathers: Implications for child support practices. *Children and Youth Services Review* 23: 353–76.

Richer, E., Frank, A., Greenberg, M., Savner, S., & Turetsky, V. (2003). Boom times a bust: Declining employment among less-educated young men. Center for Law and Social Policy, Washington, D.C. July.

Richer, E., Kubo, H., & Frank, A. (2003). *All in one stop? The accessibility of work support programs at one-stop centers*. Center for Law and Social Policy, Washington, D.C.

Riger, S., & Staggs, S. L. (2004). Welfare reform, domestic violence, and employment. *Violence against Women* 10: 961–90.

Riger, S., Staggs, L. S., & Schewe, P. (2004). Intimate partner violence as an obstacle to employment among mothers affected by welfare reform. *Journal of Social Issues* 60: 801–18.

Rivera, C. (2004). Many children, few preschool slots. *Los Angeles Times*. February 9.

Roberts, P. (2004a). No minor matter: Developing a coherent policy on paternity establishment for children born to underage parents. Center for Law and Social Policy, March 11.

Roberts, P. (2004b). I can't give you anything but love: Would poor couples with children be better off economically if they married? Couples and Marriage Series, policy brief no. 5, Center for Law and Social Policy. August.

Roberts, P. (2005). Update on the Uniform Parentage Act: Memorandum. Center for Law and Social Policy.

Rosenbaum, D., & Neuberger, Z. (2005). Food and nutrition programs: Reducing hunger, bolstering nutrition. Center on Budget and Policy Priorities.

Rouse, C., Brooks-Gunn, J., & McLanahan, S. (2005). Introducing the issue: School readiness: Closing racial and ethnic caps. *The Future of Children* 15, no. 1 (Spring).

Rowe, G. (2000). State TANF policies as of July 1999: Welfare rules databook. Assessing the New Federalism, Urban Institute, Washington, D.C.

Salamon, L. (2002). *The state of nonprofit America*. Washington, D.C.: Brookings Institution Press.

Salamon, L. (2003). The resilient sector. In L. Salamon (Ed.), *The state of nonprofit America*. Washington, D.C.: Brookings Institution Press.

Sandefur, G. D., & Cook, S. T. (1998). Permanent exit from public assistance: The impact of duration, family, and work. *Social Forces* 77(2): 763–87.

Sandfort, J. R. (1997). The structuring of front-line work: Conditions within local welfare and welfare-to-work organizations in Michigan. Paper presented at the annual conference of the Association for Public Policy Analysis and Management, Washington, D.C.

Sandfort, J. R. (2000). Moving beyond discretion and outcomes: Examining public management from the front lines of the welfare system. *Journal of Public Administration Research and Theory* 10: 729–56.

Sanger, B. M. (2003). *The welfare market place: Privatization and welfare reform*. Washington, D.C.: Brookings Institution Press.

Saunders, D. G., Houlter, M. C., Pahl, L. C., Tolman, R. M., & Kenna, C. E. (2005). TANF workers' responses to battered women and the impact of brief worker training. *Violence against Women* 11: 227–54.

Saunders, E., Landsman, M., Graf, N., & Richardson, B. (2003). Evaluation of abstinence only education in Iowa. Five year report. University of Iowa School of Social Work, National Resource Center for Family Centered Practice. October.

Sawhill, I. V. (Ed.) (2003). *One percent for the kids: New policies, brighter futures for America's children*. Washington, D.C.: Brookings Institution Press.

Sawhill, I. V., & Thomas, A. (2001). *A hand up for the bottom third: Toward a new agenda for low-income working families*. Washington D.C.: Brookings Institution.

Sawhill, I. V., & Thomas, A. (2001). *A tax proposal for working families with children*. Washington D.C.: Welfare Reform & Beyond Initiatives, Brookings Institution.

Sawicky, M. B., Cherry, R., & Denk, R. (2002). The next tax reform: Advancing tax benefits for children. Working paper, Economic Policy Institute, Washington, D.C.

Schexnayder, D., Schroeder, D., Lein, L., & Dominguez, D. (2002). Texas families in transition: Surviving without TANF. Texas Department of Human Services, Austin.

Schmid, H. (2000). For-profit and nonprofit human services: A comparative analysis. *Social Security* (special English edition) 6: 161–79.

Schochet, P., & Rangarajan, A. (2004). Characteristics of low-wage workers and their labor market experiences: Evidence from the mid-to late 1990s. No. 8915–600, Mathematica Policy Research, Inc., Princeton, N.J.

Scholz, J., & Levine, K. (2001). The evolution of income support policy in recent decades. In S. Danziger & R. H. Haveman (Eds.), *Understanding poverty*. New York: Russell Sage Foundation; Cambridge, Mass.: Harvard University Press.

Schulman, K. (2000). The high costs of child care puts quality care out of reach for many families. Issue brief, Children's Defense Fund, Washington, D.C.

Schumacher, R., Ewen, D., Hart, K., & Lombardi, J. (2005). All together now: State experience in using community-based care to provide pre-kindergarten. Paper prepared for the Brookings Institution and University of North Carolina on "Creating a National Plan for the Education of 4-Year Olds." Center for Law and Social Policy. Revised February.

Schumacher, R., Ewen, D., Hart, K., & Lombardi, J. (2005). All together now: State experiences in using community-based child care to provide pre-kindergarten. Brief no. 5, Child Care and Early Education Series, Center for Law and Social Policy. May.

Sclar, E. (2000). *You don't always get what you pay for: The economics of privatization.* Ithaca, N.Y.: Cornell University Press.

Seefeldt, K. S. (2004). After PRWORA: Barriers to employment, work, and well-being among current and former welfare recipients. National Poverty Center, Ann Arbor, Mich.

Seefeldt, K. S., Leos-Urbel, J., & McMahon, P. (2001). Recent changes in Michigan welfare and work, child care, and child welfare systems. Urban Institute, Washington, D.C.

Sen, A. (1999). *Development as freedom.* New York: Alfred A. Knopf.

Sexuality Information and Education Council of the United States (SIECUS). (2003). *Federal spending for abstinence-only-until-marriage programs (1982–2006).* Retrieved from http://www.siecus.org/policy/states/2004/federalGraph.html.

Shapiro I., & Greenstein, R. (2005). Cuts to low-income programs may far exceed the contribution of these programs to deficit's return. Center on Budget and Policy Priorities. Revised February.

Shapiro, I., Parrott, S., & Springer, J. (2005). Selected research findings on accomplishments of the safety net. Center on Budget and Policy Priorities.

Sherman, A. (1997). *Poverty matters: The cost of child poverty in America.* Washington, D.C.: Children's Defense Fund.

Sherman, R. (2004). Serving youth aging out of foster care: Welfare information network. Issue note. *The Finance Project* 18, no. 5 (October).

Shonokoff, J., & Phillips, D. (2000). Committee on integrating the science of early childhood development, *From neurons to neighborhoods: The science of early childhood development*. Washington, D.C.: National Research Council.

Short, K., & Iceland, J. (2000). *Who is better off than we thought?* Paper presented at the annual meeting of the American Economic Association, Boston, Mass.

Sigle-Rushton, W., & McLanahan, S. (2002). For richer or poorer? Marriage as an anti-poverty strategy in the United States. *Population* 57: 509–26.

Simon, W. (2001). *The community economic development movement: Law, business and the new social policy.* Durham, N.C.: Duke University Press.

Simon, W. H. (1983). Legality, bureaucracy, and class in the welfare system. *Yale Law Journal* 92: 1198–269.

Skocpol, T. (1992). *Protecting soldiers and mothers: The political origins of social policy in the United States*. Cambridge, Mass.: Harvard University Press.

Skocpol, T. (2000). *The missing middle: Working families and the future of American social policy*. 1st ed. New York: W. W. Norton.

Slack, K., & Yoo, J. (2004). Food hardships and child behavior problems among low-income children. Discussion paper DP no. 1290-04, Institute for Research on Poverty, University of Wisconsin–Madison. November.

Smeeding, T. M., Rainwater, L., & Burtless, G. (2001). U.S. poverty in a cross-national comparison. In S. H. Danziger & R. H. Haveman (Eds.), *Understanding poverty* (pp. 162–85). New York: Russell Sage Foundation.

Smith, B. G. (Ed.) (2004). *Down and out in early America*. University Park, Pa.: Pennsylvania State University Press.

Smith, R. M. (1997). *Civic ideals: Conflicting visions of citizenship in U.S. history*. New Haven, Conn.: Yale University Press.

Smock, P. J. (2000). Cohabitation in the United States: An appraisal of research themes, findings, and implications. *Annual Review of Sociology* 26: 1–20.

Social Security Administration. (2004). *Fast facts & figures about Social Security, 2004*. SSA publication no. 13-11785, August. Office of Policy, Office of Research, Evaluation, and Statistics.

Somers, M. R., & Block, F. (2005). From poverty to perversity: Ideas, markets, and institutions over 200 years of welfare debate. *American Sociological Review* 70: 260–87.

Sorensen, E., & Zibman, C. (2000a). To what extent do children benefit from child support? Discussion paper no. 99-11. Urban Institute, Washington, D.C.

Sorensen, E., & Zibman, C. (2000b). *Child support offers some protection against poverty*. Series B, no. B-10, Urban Institute, Washington, D.C.

Soss, J., Schram, S. F., Vartanian, T. P., & O'Brien, E. (2001). Setting the terms of relief: Explaining state policy choices in the devolution revolution. *American Journal of Political Science* 45(2): 378–95.

Standing, G. (2002). *Beyond the new paternalism: Basic security as equality*. London: Verso.

Standing, G. (n.d.). Why basic income is needed for a right to work? Unpublished manuscript.

Stanley, S. M., Blumberg, S. L., & Markman, H. J. (1999). Helping couples fight for their marriages: The PREP approach. In R. Berger & M. Hannah (Eds.), *Handbook of preventive approaches in couple therapy*. New York: Brunner/Mazel.

State Policy Documentation Project. (2000). State policy documentation project (SPDP). Center on Law and Poverty and the Center on Budget and Policy Priorities.

Steiner, G. (1971). *The state of welfare*. Washington, D.C.: Brookings Institution.

Stone, K. V. W. (2004). *From widgets to digits: Employment regulation for the changing workplace*. Cambridge, New York: Cambridge University Press.

Stormer, A., & Harrison, G. G. (2003). Does household food security affect cognitive and social development of kindergartners? IRP discussion paper no. 1276-03, Institute for Research on Poverty, University of Wisconsin–Madison.

Strawn, J., Greenberg, M., & Savner, S. (2001). Improving employment under TANF. In R. Blank & R. Haskins (Eds.), *The new world of welfare* (pp. 223–224). Washington, D.C.: Brooking Institution Press.

Surgeon General's call to action to promote sexual health and responsible sexual behavior. (2001, July 9). <www.surgeongeneral.gov/library/sexualhealth/call.htm>

Sweeney, E., & Fremstad, S. (2005). Supplemental Security Income: Supporting people with disabilities and the elderly poor. Center on Budget and Policy Priorities.

Teitler, J. O., Reichman, N. E., Nepomnyaschy, L., & Garfinkel, I. (2005). Welfare participation and marriage. Working paper no. 2005-24, Center for Research on Child Wellbeing, Princeton, N.J.

Tekin, E. (2004). Single mothers working at night: Standard work, child care subsidies, and implications for welfare reform. Working paper no. 10274, National Bureau of Economic Research. January.

Temporary Assistance for Needy Families Program (TANF). (2002). *2002 TANF annual report to Congress.* Retrieved from http://www.acf.hhs.gov/programs/ofa/annualreport5/index.htm.

Terry, D. (2000). U.S. child poverty rate fell as economy grew, but is above 1979 level. *New York Times.* August 11, p. A10.

Thomas, A., & Sawhill, I. V. (2002). For richer or for poorer: Marriage as an anti-poverty strategy. Brookings Institution, Washington, D.C.

Tolman, R. M., & Raphael, J. (2000). A review of research on welfare and domestic violence. *Journal of Social Issues* 56: 655–82.

Tolman, R. M., & Rosen, D. (2001). Domestic violence in the lives of women receiving welfare. *Violence against Women* 7: 141–58.

Tout, K., Martinson, K., Koralek, R., & Ehrle, J. (2001). Recent changes in Minnesota welfare and work, child care, and child welfare systems. Urban Institute, Washington, D.C.

Trends in worst case needs for housing 1978–1999. (2003). *A report to Congress on worst case housing needs: Plus update on worst case needs in 2001.* Office of Policy Development and Research, U.S. Department of Housing and Urban Development. December.

Turetsky, V. (2005). The child support program: An investment that works. Center for Law and Social Policy. April.

Urban Institute. (n.d.). *Assessing the new federalism. Fast facts.* Retrieved from http://www.urban.org/center/anf/index.cfm.

U.S. Census Bureau. (1999). *Who's minding the kids? Child care arrangements: Spring 1999 detailed tables (PPL-168).* Retrieved from http://www.census.gov/population/www/socdemo/child/ppl-168.html.

U.S. Census Bureau. (1999). *Survey of income and program participation, 1999 panel, wave 10.* Retrieved from http://www.sipp.census.gov/sipp/.

U.S. Census Bureau. (2002). *Poverty in the United States.* Retrieved from http://www.census.gov/prod/2003pubs/p60-222.pdf.

U.S. Census Bureau. (2002). *Statistical abstract.* Retrieved from http://www.census.gov/prod/www/statistical-abstract-2001_2005.html.

U.S. Census Bureau. (2003). *Custodial mothers and fathers and their child support, 2001.* Washington, D.C.: U.S. Department of Commerce.

U.S. Census Bureau. (2004). *Current population survey, 2004 annual social and economic supplement.* Retrieved from http://www.census.gov/apsd/techdoc/cps/cpsmar04.pdf.

U.S. Census Bureau. (2004). *Income, poverty, and health insurance coverage in the United States: 2003.* U.S. Department of Commerce. Retrieved from http://www.census.gov/prod/2004pubs/p60-226.pdf.

U.S. Congress. (1996). *Personal Responsibility and Work Opportunity Reconciliation Act of 1996,* Title I, Section 101.

U.S. Department of Agriculture (n.d.). *National school lunch monthly data.* Retrieved from http://www.fns.usda.gov/pd/slmonthly.htm.

U.S. Department of Agriculture (n.d.). *Annual summary of food and nutrition service programs.* Retrieved from http://www.fns.usda.gov/pd/annual.htm.

U.S. Department of Health and Human Services. (2004). The 2004 HHS poverty guidelines: One version of the [U.S.] Federal poverty measure. Retrieved from http://aspe.hhs.gov/poverty/04poverty.shtml.

U.S. Department of Health and Human Services. (2004). *Indicators of welfare dependence: Annual report to Congress 2004.* Washington, D.C.: U.S. Department of Health and Human Services.

U.S. Department of Health and Human Services; Health Resources and Services Administration; Maternal and Child Health Bureau. (2004). *The national survey of children with special health care needs chartbook 2001.* Rockville, Md: U.S. Department of Health and Human Services.

U.S. Department of Health and Human Services. 2003 *CMS statistics.* Retrieved from http://www.cms.hhs.gov/CapMarketUpdates/Downloads/03CMSstats.pdf.

U.S. Department of Housing and Urban Development. *Performance and accountability report FY 2004.* Retrieved from http://www.hud.gov/offices/cfo/pafinal.pdf.

U.S General Accounting Office. (2002). *Earned Income Tax Credit eligibility and participation.* GAO-02-290R. Washington, D.C.

U.S. Goverment Accountability Office. (2004). *TANF and SSI: Opprtunities exist to help people with impairments become more self sufficient.* GAO-04-878. Washington, D.C.

U.S. House of Representatives, Committee on Ways and Means. The Green Book (2004). *Background material and data on programs within the Jurisdiction of the Committee on Ways and Means.* Washington, D.C.: U.S. Government Printing Office.

Usdansky, M. L., & Wolf, D. A. (2005). A routine juggling act: Managing child care and employment. Working paper no. 05-18-FF. Center for Research on Child Wellbeing, Princeton, N.J.

Van Parijs, P. (2004). Basic income: A simple and powerful idea for the twenty-first century. *Politics and Society* 32(1): 7–40.

Waldinger, R. (1997). Black/immigrant competition re-assessed: New evidence from Los Angeles. *Sociological Perspectives* 40(3): 365–86.

Waldinger, R. (Ed.). (2001a). *Strangers at the gates: New immigrants in urban America.* Berkeley: University of California Press.

Waldinger, R. (2001b). Up from poverty? "Race," immigrations, and the fate of low-skilled workers. In R. Waldinger (Ed.), *Strangers at the gates: New immigrants in urban America.* Berkeley: University of California Press, chap 3.

Waldron, T., Roberts, B., & Reamer, A. (2004). Working hard, falling short: America's working families and the pursuit of economic security. National Report from Working Poor Families Project, Annie E. Casey Foundation, Washington, D.C.

Walker, W., & Bowie, A. (2004). *Linking the child care and health care systems: A consideration of options.* Philadelphia: Public/Private Ventures.

Waller, M. R., & Plotnick, R. (2001). Effective child support policy for low-income families: Evidence from street level research. *Journal of Policy Analysis and Management* 20(1): 89–110.

Weiner, M. (2005). Can the NLRB deter unfair labor practices? Reassessing the punitive-remedial distinction in labor law enforcement. 52 *UCLA Law Review* 1579.

Weisbrod, B. A. (1988). *The nonprofit economy.* Cambridge, Mass.: Harvard University Press.

Welfare Information Network. (2004). Addressing linguistic and cultural barriers to access for welfare services. *Resources for Welfare Decisions* 18(5).

Wenzlow, A., Mullahy, J., Robert, S., & Wolfe, B. (2004). An empirical investigation of the relationship between wealth and health using the survey of consumer finances. Institute for Research on Poverty, University of Wisconsin. August.

Western, B. (2004). Incarceration, marriage, and family life. Center for Research on Child Wellbeing, Princeton, N.J.

White, L. (1999). Quality child care for low-income families: Despair, impasse, improvisation. In J. F. Handler & L. White (Eds.), *Hard labor: Women and work in the post-welfare era*. Armonk, N.Y.: M. E. Sharpe.

Wickenden, E., & Bell, W. (1961). Public welfare, time for a change: The project on public services for families and children. Sponsored by the New York School of Social Work of Columbia University.

Wider Opportunities for Women (WOW). (2004). Coming up short: A comparison of wages and work supports in 10 American communities. Retrieved from http://wowonline.org/docs/dynamic-CTTA-43.pdf. (Summer/Fall)

Wilen, W., & Nayak, R. (2004). Relocated public housing residents face little hope to return: Work requirements for mixed-income public housing developments. *Clearinghouse REVIEW, Journal of Poverty Law and Policy* no. 61 (November–December).

Williams, C., Rosen, J., Hudman, J., & O'Malley, M. (2004). Challenges and tradeoff in low-income family budgets: Implications for health coverage. Kaiser Commission on Medicaid and the Uninsured, Kaiser Family Foundation. April.

Williams, L. (1999). Unemployment insurance and low-wage work. In J. F. Handler & L. White (Eds.), *Hard labor: Women and work in the post-welfare era*. Armonk, N.Y.: M. E. Sharpe.

Wilson, L. A., Stoker, R. P., & McGrath, D. (1999). Welfare bureaus as moral tutors: What do clients learn from paternalistic welfare reforms? *Social Science Quarterly* 80(3): 473–86.

Wilson, W. J. (1987). *The truly disadvantaged: The inner city, the underclass, and public policy*. Chicago: University of Chicago Press.

Winship, S., & Jencks, C. (2004). How did social policy changes of the 1990s affect material hardship among single mothers? Evidence from the CPS food security supplement. No. RWP04-027, John F. Kennedy School of Government, Harvard University. June.

Winston, P., Burwick, A., McConnell, S., & Roper, R. (2002). Privatization of welfare services: A review of the literature. Mathematica Policy Research, Inc., Washington, D.C.

Wisconsin Legislative Audit Bureau. (1999). Wisconsin Works (W-2) expenditures. No. 99-3, Joint Legislative Audit Committee, Madison, Wisc.

Wisconsin Legislative Audit Bureau. (2001). An evaluation of Wisconsin Works (W-2) expenditures. Joint Legislative Audit Committee, Madison, Wisc.

Wolfe, B., Scrivner, S., with Snyder, A. (2003a). The devil may be in the details: How characteristics of SCHIP programs affect take-up. Discussion paper no. 1272-03, Institute for Research on Poverty, University of Wisconsin.

Wolfe, B., Kaplan, T., Haveman, R., & Cho, Y. (2004). Extending health care coverage to the low-income population: The influence of the Wisconsin BadgerCare Program on insurance coverage. Discussion paper no. 1289-04, Institute for Research on Poverty, University of Wisconsin. October.

Wolfe, B., & Scrivner, S. (2003). Providing universal preschool for four-year olds. In I. V. Sawhill (Ed.), *One percent for the kids: New policies, brighter futures for America's children*. Washington, D.C.: Brookings Institution Press.

Wood, R., & Burghardt, J. (1997). Implementing welfare reform requirements for teenage parents: Lessons from experience in four states. Report for the Office of Assistant Secretary for Planning and Evaluation. Mathematica Policy Research, Inc. October 31.

Wright, E. O. (2000). Reducing income and wealth inequality: Real utopian proposals. *Contemporary Sociology* 29: 143–56.

Wright, E., & Dwyer, R. (December 2000/January 2001). The American jobs machine: Is the new economy creating good jobs? *Boston Review* 25(6): 21–26.

Wu, C.-F., Cancian, M., Meyer, D. R., & Wallace, G. (2004). How do welfare sanctions work? Discussion paper no. 1282-04, Institute for Research on Poverty, Madison, Wisc.

Wulf, K. (2004). Gender and the political economy of poor relief in Colonial Philadelphia. In B. G. Smith (Ed.), *Down and out in early America*. University Park: Pennsylvania State University Press.

Xie, H., Cairns, B. D., & Cairns, R. B. (2001). Predicting teen motherhood and teen fatherhood: Individual characteristics and peer affiliation. *Social Development* 10: 488–511.

Youdelman, S., & Getsos, P. (2005). The revolving door: Research findings on NYC's employment services and placement system and its effectiveness in moving people from welfare to work. A research project by community Voices Heard. July 2005.

Zatz, N. (2005). Beyond employment: Work requirements, caretaking, and liberal justice. Unpublished manuscript.

Zedlewski, S. (1999). Work-related activities and limitations of current welfare recipients. Discussion papers, no. 99–06. Urban Institute, Washington, D.C.

Zedlewski, S., & Loprest, P. (2000). How well does TANF fit the needs of the most disadvantaged families? Brookings conference, December 29, p. 4.

Zelenak, L. A. (2004). Redesigning the Earned Income Tax Credit as a family-size adjustment to the minimum wage. *Tax Law Review* 57: 301–53.

Zonta, M. (2005). Review essay. Housing policies and the concentration of poverty in urban American. *Social Service Review* (March): 181–85.

Author Index

Subject Index

AARP. *See* American Association of Retired People (AARP)

abstinence programs. *See also* Adolescent Family Life Act
  block grant funding for, 283
  defined, 283
  effectiveness/ineffectiveness of, 15, 311, 314
  federal funding (2004/2005) for, 312
  religious/adult driven, 314
  sexually transmitted diseases and, 314
  Social Security Act funding of, 312

ADC. *See* Aid to Dependent Children (ADC)

ADHD. *See* attention deficit hyperactivity disorder (ADHD)

adjusted gross income (ARI) rules, 86

Adolescent Family Life Act (AFLA), 311

adolescents
  Career Academies for, 112
  declining birth/pregnancy rates for, 130
  successful programs for, 112

Adult Plus Plan, 323

AFDC. *See* Aid to Families with Dependent Children (AFDC)

AFDC-UP. *See* Aid to Two-Parent Families (AFDC-UP)

Affiliated Computer Services, 220

AFLA. *See* Adolescent Family Life Act (AFLA)

AFL-CIO, 220

AFQT. *See* Armed Forces Qualification Test (AFQT)

African American men
  incarceration of, 36, 293
  job instability of, 243

African American women
  educational progress of, 40
  eighteenth-century treatment of, 152
  Louisiana and, 165
  "man-in-the-house" rule against, 164, 166

marriage dissolution of, 290
midnight raids against, 164
myths regarding, 164
out-of-wedlock births of, 162, 165, 182
poverty rates for, 40

African Americans
  Democratic Party courting of, 167
  dire poverty of, 26
  education gaps for, 106, 107
  education's influence for, 35
  food insecurity of, 24, 25, 99
  lower-class matriarchal society of, 161
  male college graduates, 35
  male incarceration rates, 36
  median unemployment for, 35
  media's distortions of, 175, 176
  mid-twentieth century prejudice against, 150
  nonstandard work and, 247
  pathological lower-class culture of, 160
  perceived lack of commitment of, 177
  poverty as paradox, 161
  poverty rates for, 26, 33, 50
  stereotyping of, 9
  unemployment insurance disadvantage to, 77
  "welfare queen" mothers, 2, 9
  World War II/post–World War II migration of, 9

AGI rules. *See* adjusted gross income (ARI) rules

aid levels
  in New York City, 188
  in Ohio, 188
  in Texas, 188

Aid to Dependent Children (ADC), 1, 9
  as Aid to Families with Dependent Children, 169
  Charitable Organization Charities administration of, 156

Low Cost Food Plan (Agriculture Department), 22
lower-class culture
 African American pathological, 160
 physiological characteristics ascribed to, 160
low-wage earners
 business/organizations improving working conditions for, 331
 computerization's influence on, 241, 242, 245
 defined, 239, 241, 244
 employers hiring practices for, 244, 245
 escape possibilities for, 243, 244, 252
 Latinos as, 327
 limited opportunities for, 251
 minority dominance, 251
 outsourcing's influence on, 243
 "stickiness" of employment for, 242, 244, 251, 256
 technology replacement of, 243
 women as, 243

maintenance of effort (MOE) funds, 138
males, poverty rates for, 26
malnutrition, children influenced by, 101
Management and Budget Office, 20
"man-in-the-house" rules, 164, 166
Manpower Development and Training Act (MDTA), 168
Manpower Development Research Corporation (MDRC), 64
 career academies evaluated by, 112
 work programs studied by, 180
market, self-regulation of, 2, 3
marriage. See also Healthy Marriage Initiative; Oklahoma Marriage initiative
 African American women and dissolution of, 290
 causes contributing to instability of, 286
 cohabitation v., 288, 294
 as cure for poverty, 3, 4
 economic benefits of, 288
 economic uncertainty's influence on, 299, 300
 EITC's influence on, 85
 ethnic differences regarding, 293
 factors influencing probability of, 292, 293
 as foundation of successful society, 186
 incarceration's influence on, 293
 initiatives, 14
 nonstandard work and, 247
 poor people and, 289, 290
 poverty and, 286, 289
 promotion of healthy, 298, 301
 welfare's relation to, 294
 women and early, 289

"marriage plus" agenda, 285
marriage rates, factors affecting, 292
married couples. See also unmarried couples
 advantages of, 287
 qualities of, 288
 upper-middle-income, 289
married couples, low-income
 African Americans, 289
 education/employment levels of, 289
 Latinos, 289
 whites (non-Hispanic), 289
Maternal and Child Health Block Grant, 283, 312
Mathematica Policy Research, 99
Maximus Corporation, 220, 226
 Arizona Works Pilot Program evaluation of, 227, 228
 billing inappropriations by, 231
MCCA. See Medical Catastrophic Care Act (MCCA)
MDRC. See Manpower Development Research Corporation (MDRC)
MDTA. See Manpower Development and Training Act (MDTA)
media
 African American's distorted by, 175
 victory claimed by, 5
 whites v. African Americans in, 176
Medicaid, 6, 7, 25, 72
 American Association of Retired People and, 120
 anti-poverty effects of, 137
 cash/in-kind assistance and, 133
 children covered by, 119
 as component of welfare state, 8
 declining enrollments for, 11
 disabled people covered by, 119
 elderly Americans covered by, 136
 eligible children receiving, 63
 enactment (1965) of, 167
 as health insurance for poor, 117
 HMOs and, 121
 home visit funding by, 98
 nursing home care coverage by, 122
 for poor people, 116
 prescription drug problems involving, 122
 Reagan's influence on, 120
 SCHIP supplementation of, 116, 124
 state control of, 123, 125
 tax cuts potential influence on, 132, 133
Medi-Cal, streamlined enrollment for, 125, 126
Medical Catastrophic Care Act (MCCA), 120
Medicare, 25, 72
 as component of welfare state, 8
 components of, 117

women's groups, government programs
    opposition by, 284
Women's Policy Research Institute, 40, 46
work. *See also* welfare-to-work programs
    changing nature of, 75
    creation of right to, 331
    as exit from welfare, 4
    myths regarding, 238
    welfare recipient's requirement to, 179, 181,
        193
work, nonstandard
    African Americans and, 247
    Bureau of Labor Statistics predictions for, 248
    child care difficulties and, 271
    job types, 247
    married couples and, 247
    rise of, 246, 250
    single mothers and, 248
    women's influence on, 247
    worker percentage (40%) working, 247
    workload adjustments/workloading and,
        271
work bonus, Russell's idea for, 82
work ethic
    importance of, 147
    objective/moral components of, 70
work-first strategy, 3
    eligibility determination vs., 216
    Riverside, Calif., model program, 10, 11
    supportive services, 206
    welfare reform and, 251
Work Incentive Program (WIN), 179, 238
work programs, 204
    of Chicago, 204
    mandatory, 10
    MDRC study of, 180
workers
    employment longevity benefits to, 249
    poverty rates for full-time, 31

re-employment of, 246
temporary v. permanent, 246
UI's disadvantage to, 77
workers, part-time, 246, 250
    poverty rates of, 31
    UI's disadvantage to, 77
workers' compensation, 75, 137
work-first programs, 64
    of Michigan, 210
    state variations of, 208, 216
Workforce Development Department (Utah),
    213
Workforce Investment Act (WIA), 253, 254
    eight-state study of, 253
    funding for, 253
    individual training accounts (ITAs) of,
        253
    purposes of, 253
    TANF integration with, 254
    unanimous displeasure with, 254
    WIBs of, 253
workforce investment boards (WIBs), 253
Working Family Credit (Minnesota), 209
working poor, 30, 39
    economic hardships of, 32
    health insurance and, 118
    housing problems of, 113
    myths of, 251
    nonstandards work's influence on, 247
    service industries and, 241
    "split-shift" couples as, 247
workplace, bringing children to, 269
World War II (WWII)
    ADC enrollment after, 161, 186
    African American migration during/after, 9
    liberal programs after, 166
WV Works., 214

YMCA, 220

29245941R00234

Made in the USA
Lexington, KY
18 January 2014